Paris Metro

Paris: Metro

• The stations Liège and Rennes are closed after 8pm and on Sundays and holidays.

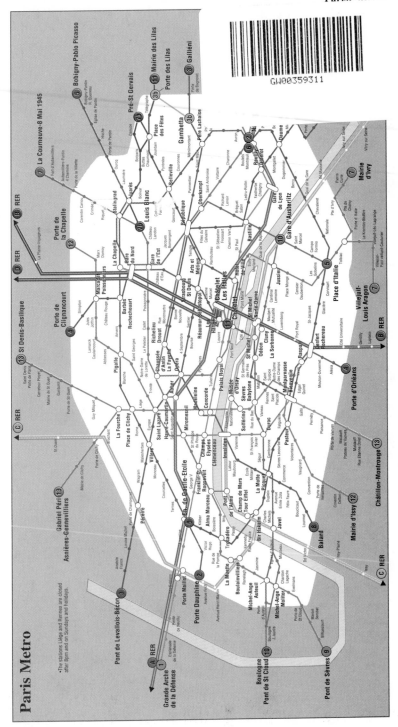

Paris: Overview and Arrondissements

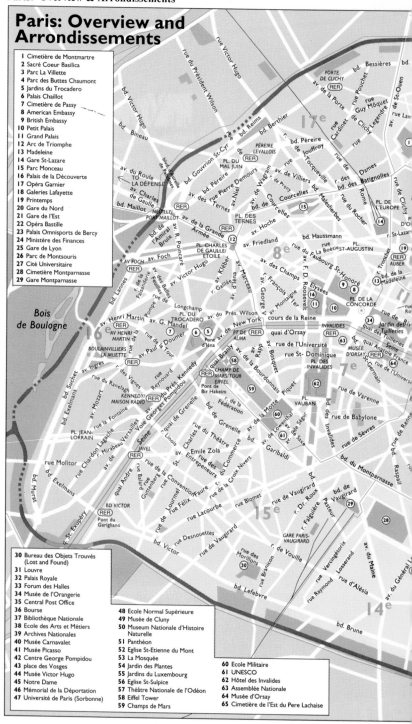

1 Cimetière de Montmartre
2 Sacré Coeur Basilica
3 Parc La Villette
4 Parc des Buttes Chaumont
5 Jardins du Trocadéro
6 Palais Chaillot
7 Cimetière de Passy
8 American Embassy
9 British Embassy
10 Petit Palais
11 Grand Palais
12 Arc de Triomphe
13 Madeleine
14 Gare St-Lazare
15 Parc Monceau
16 Palais de la Découverte
17 Opéra Garnier
18 Galeries Lafayette
19 Printemps
20 Gare du Nord
21 Gare de l'Est
22 Opéra Bastille
23 Palais Omnisports de Bercy
24 Ministère des Finances
25 Gare de Lyon
26 Parc de Montsouris
27 Cité Universitaire
28 Cimetière Montparnasse
29 Gare Montparnasse

Bois
de Boulogne

30 Bureau des Objets Trouvés
   (Lost and Found)
31 Louvre
32 Palais Royale
33 Forum des Halles
34 Musée de l'Orangerie
35 Central Post Office
36 Bourse
37 Bibliothèque Nationale
38 Ecole des Arts et Métiers
39 Archives Nationales
40 Musée Carnavalet
41 Musée Picasso
42 Centre George Pompidou
43 place des Vosges
44 Musée Victor Hugo
45 Notre Dame
46 Mémorial de la Déportation
47 Université de Paris (Sorbonne)

48 Ecole Normal Supérieure
49 Musée de Cluny
50 Museum Nationale d'Histoire
   Naturelle
51 Panthéon
52 Eglise St-Etienne du Mont
53 La Mosquée
54 Jardin des Plantes
55 Jardins du Luxembourg
56 Eglise St-Sulpice
57 Théâtre Nationale de l'Odéon
58 Eiffel Tower
59 Champs de Mars

60 Ecole Militaire
61 UNESCO
62 Hôtel des Invalides
63 Assemblée Nationale
64 Musée d'Orsay
65 Cimetière de l'Est du Pere Lachaise

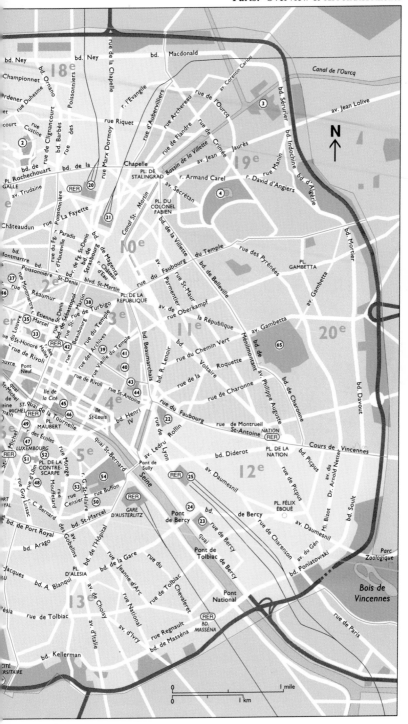

Paris: 1er and 2e

Gare
St-Lazare

R. d'Amsterdam

Rue de St-Lazare

Rue de la Chaussée d'Antin

9e

Rue de St-Lazare

Rue du Havre

Richelieu
Drouot M

St Lazare

Havre-
Caumartin

Chaussée
d'Antin

Boulevard Haussmann

La
Fayette

Rue Favart

Bd. Haussmann

Rue Auber

Rue

Opéra

Boulevard des Italiens

R.

Rue Pasquier

Rue Tronchet

Auber RER

Scribe

Bd. des
Capucines

Opéra
RER

Rue du Quatre

Septemb

Quatre
Septembre

R. Chabanais

Rue Daunou

Rue des
Capucines

Rue de la Paix

Rue D. Casanova

Rue des Petits Ch

Madeleine

Bd. de la
Madeleine

La Colonne

PLACE
VENDÔME

Pyramides M

Rue Thérèse

Avenue de l'Opéra

Madeleine

Rue Boissy d'Anglas

Rue Royale

8e

Rue St-Honoré

Rue de la Sourdière

Rue St-Roch

Rue St-Honoré

Rue des Pyramides

1er

R. de
Mondovi

Rue du Mont Thabor

Rue Castiglione

PLACE
ANDRÉ
MALRAUX

Concorde

Rue de Rivoli

Tuileries

Palais Re
Musée
Louvr

Jeu de Paume

PLACE DE
LA CONCORDE

JARDIN DES
TUILERIES

PLACE
CARRO

L'Orangerie

Quai des Tuileries

Pt. de la
Concorde

Seine

Pont
Solférino

Pont
Royal

Pont du
Carrousel

Quai Anatole France

Quai Voltaire

Assemblée
Nationale

Assemblée
Nationale

Musée
d'Orsay
RER

Musée
d'Orsay

Bd. St-Germain

Rue de Lille

7e

Ecole Nati
Superieur
Beau

Solférino

Rue de l'Université

0   1/8 mile

0   125 meters

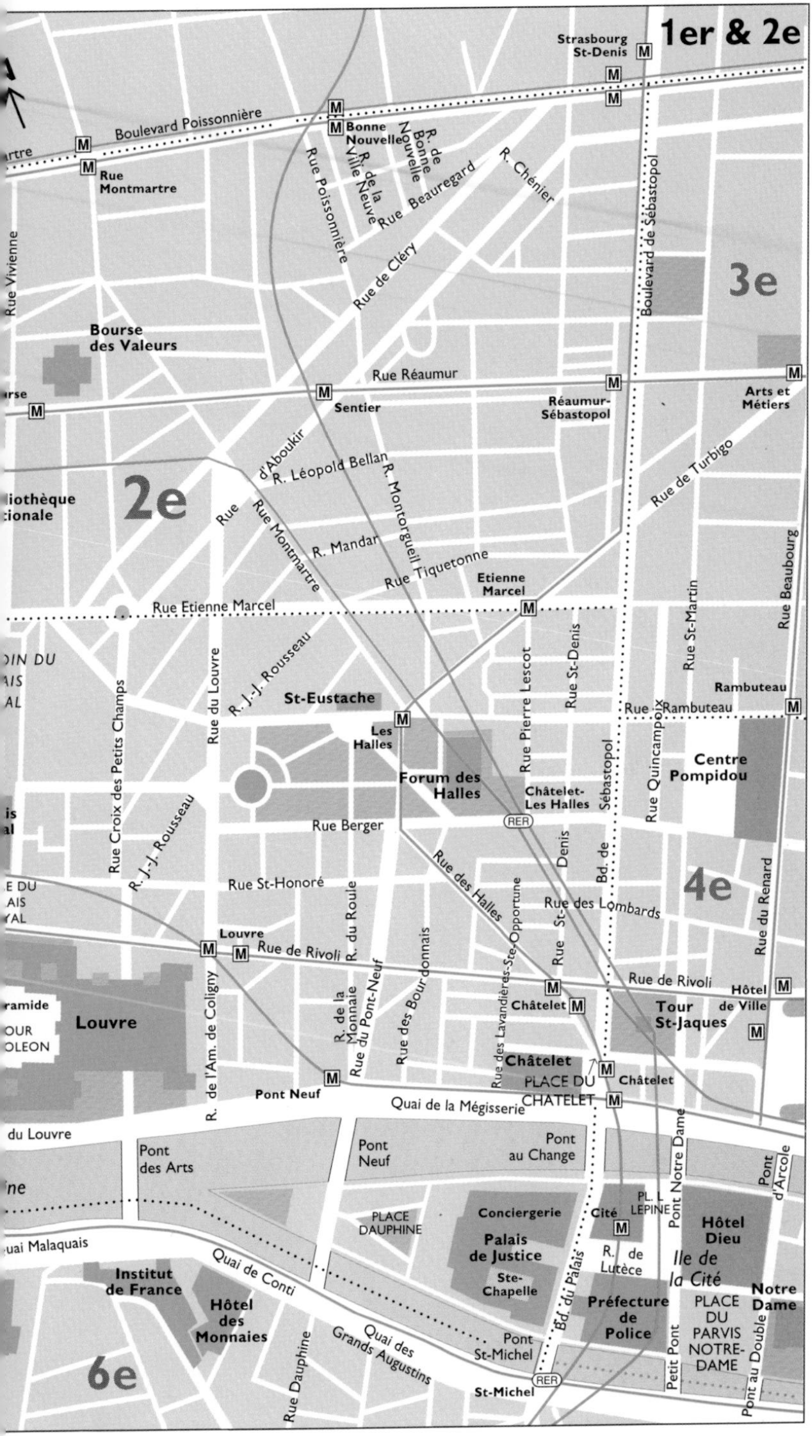

1er & 2e

Strasbourg
St-Denis
Ⓜ
Ⓜ

Boulevard Poissonnière

Ⓜ
Ⓜ
Ⓜ
Bonne
Nouvelle

artre

Ⓜ

Rue
Montmartre

R. de Bonne Nouvelle

Rue de la Ville Neuve

Rue Beauregard

R. Chénier

Rue Poissonnière

Boulevard de Sébastopol

Rue de Cléry

Rue Vivienne

3e

**Bourse
des Valeurs**

Rue Réaumur

Réaumur-
Sébastopol

Ⓜ

Arts et
Métiers
Ⓜ

rse

Ⓜ

Ⓜ
Sentier

Ⓜ

d'Aboukir

R. Léopold Bellan

R. Montorgueil

Rue de Turbigo

iothèque
ionale

2e

Rue

Rue Montmartre

Rue Mandar

Rue Tiquetonne

Étienne
Marcel

Rue Beaubourg

Rue Étienne Marcel

Ⓜ

DIN DU
AIS
AL

R. J.-J. Rousseau

Rue du Louvre

St-Eustache

Rue Pierre Lescot

Rue St-Denis

Rue St-Martin

Rambuteau
Ⓜ

Rue Croix des Petits Champs

Les
Halles
Ⓜ

Rue Rambuteau

**Centre
Pompidou**

Rue Quincampoix

is
al

**Forum des
Halles**

Châtelet-
Les Halles
(RER)

Sébastopol

E DU
AIS
YAL

R. J.-J. Rousseau

Rue Berger

Rue St-Honoré

R. du Roule

Rue des Halles

Rue des Lombards

Denis

Bd. de

St-

Rue

4e

Rue du Renard

ramide
OUR
OLEON

Louvre

Ⓜ
Ⓜ
Louvre
Rue de Rivoli

R. de la Monnaie

Rue du Pont-Neuf

Rue des Bourdonnais

Rue des Lavandières-Ste-Opportune

Rue St-Denis

Rue de Rivoli

Hôtel
de Ville
Ⓜ

Ⓜ
Châtelet
Ⓜ

**Tour
St-Jaques**
Ⓜ

du Louvre

R. de l'Am. de Coligny

Ⓜ
Pont Neuf

Châtelet
PLACE DU
CHATELET

Châtelet
Ⓜ

ne

Pont
des Arts

Quai de la Mégisserie

Pont
Neuf

Pont
au Change

Cité

Pont Notre Dame

Pont
d'Arcole

uai Malaquais

**Institut
de France**

Quai de Conti

PLACE
DAUPHINE

Conciergerie

PL. L.
LEPINE

**Hôtel
Dieu**

**Palais
de Justice**

R. de
Lutèce

**Ile de
la Cité**

**Hôtel
des
Monnaies**

Ste-
Chapelle

Bd. du Palais

**Préfecture
de
Police**

**Notre
Dame**

6e

Quai des Grands Augustins

Rue Dauphine

Pont
St-Michel

Petit Pont

PLACE
DU
PARVIS
NOTRE-
DAME

Pont au Double

(RER)
St-Michel

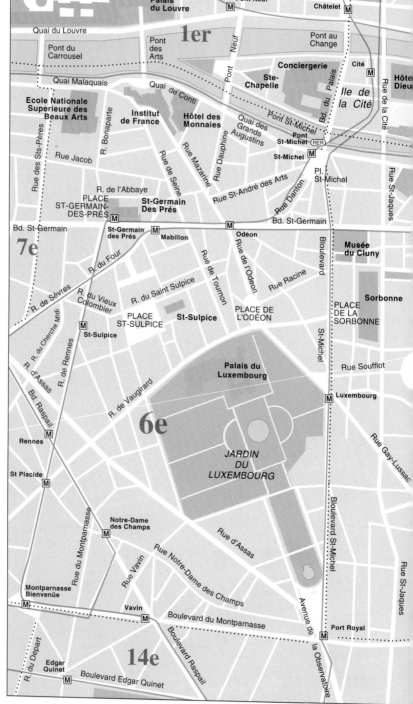

Palais
du Louvre

Pont Neuf

Châtelet

Quai du Louvre

1er

Pont au
Change

Pont du
Carrousel

Pont
des
Arts

Concergerie

Cité

Quai Malaquais

Quai de Conti

Ste-
Chapelle

Palais

Hôtel
Dieu

Ecole Nationale
Superieure des
Beaux Arts

Institut
de France

Hôtel des
Monnaies

Quai des
Grands
Augustins

Île de
la Cité

Rue de la Cité

Rue des Sts-Pères

Rue Jacob

R. Bonaparte

Rue de Seine

Rue Mazarine

Rue Dauphine

Pont St-Michel

Bd. du Palais

Pont
St-Michel

RER

St-Michel

Rue St-Jaques

R. de l'Abbaye

PLACE
ST-GERMAIN-
DES-PRÉS

St-Germain
Des Prés

Rue St-André des Arts

Rue Danton

Pl.
St-Michel

Bd. St-Germain

St-Germain
des Prés

Mabillon

Odéon

Bd. St-Germain

Musée
du Cluny

7e

Bd. St-Germain

R. du Four

Rue de l'Odéon

Boulevard

Sorbonne

R. de Sèvres

R. du Vieux
Colombier

R. du Saint Sulpice

Rue de Tournon

Rue Racine

PLACE DE
L'ODÉON

St-Michel

PLACE
DE LA
SORBONNE

R. du Cherche Midi

PLACE
ST-SULPICE

St-Sulpice

St-Sulpice

R. d'Assas

R. de Rennes

Rue Soufflot

Bd. Raspail

R. de Vaugirard

Palais du
Luxembourg

Luxembourg

Rennes

6e

Rue Gay-Lussac

St Placide

JARDIN
DU
LUXEMBOURG

Rue du Montparnasse

Notre-Dame
des Champs

Rue d'Assas

Boulevard St-Michel

Rue Vavin

Rue Notre-Dame des Champs

Rue St-Jaques

Montparnasse
Bienvenüe

Vavin

Boulevard du Montparnasse

Avenue de la Observatoire

Port Royal

R. du Depart

Edgar
Quinet

Boulevard Edgar Quinet

14e

Boulevard Raspail

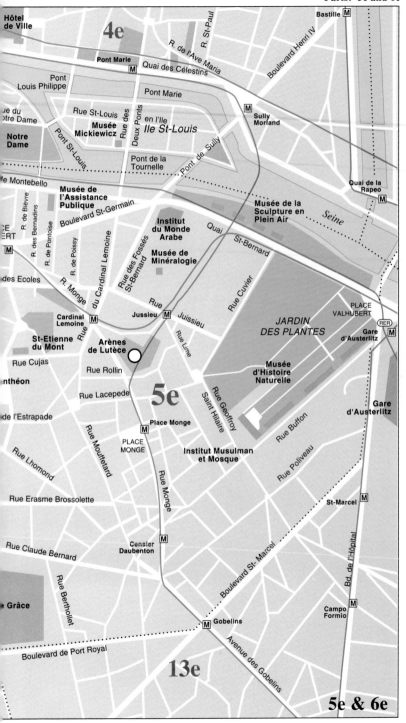

Paris: 5e and 6e

4e

Hôtel
de Ville

R. St-Paul

R. de l'Ave Maria

Bastille M

Boulevard Henri IV

Pont Marie
M

Quai des Célestins

Pont
Louis Philippe

Pont Marie

ue du
otre Dame

Rue St-Louis

Musée
Mickiewicz

Rue des Deux Ponts

en l'Île
Île St-Louis

M

Sully
Morland

Notre
Dame

Pont St-Louis

Pont de la
Tournelle

Pont de Sully

Quai de la
Rapeo
M

e Montebello

Musée de
l'Assistance
Publique

R. de Bièvre

R. des Bernadins

R. de Pontoise

Boulevard St-Germain

Institut
du Monde
Arabe

Quai

Musée de la
Sculpture en
Plein Air

Seine

St-Bernard

CE
ERT
M

R. de Poissy

Rue des Fossés
St-Bernard

Rue du Cardinal Lemoine

Musée de
Minéralogie

des Ecoles

R. Monge

Rue
Jussieu

Rue
Juissieu

Rue Cuvier

JARDIN
DES PLANTES

PLACE
VALHUBERT

Gare
d'Austerlitz
RER M

Cardinal
Lemoine M

Rue

Rue Lime

St-Etienne
du Mont

Arènes
de Lutèce

Rue Cujas

Rue Rollin

nthéon

Rue Lacepede

5e

Rue Geoffroy
Saint Hilaire

Musée
d'Histoire
Naturelle

Gare
d'Austerlitz

de l'Estrapade

Rue Mouffetard

Place Monge

PLACE
MONGE
M

Rue Buffon

Rue Lhomond

Rue Monge

Institut Musulman
et Mosque

Rue Poliveau

Rue Erasme Brossolette

St-Marcel M

Rue Claude Bernard

Rue Berthollet

Censier
Daubenton M

Bd. de l'Hôpital

Grâce

Boulevard St-Marcel

Campo
Formio M

Gobelins M

Boulevard de Port Royal

13e

Avenue des Gobelins

5e & 6e

Paris: RER

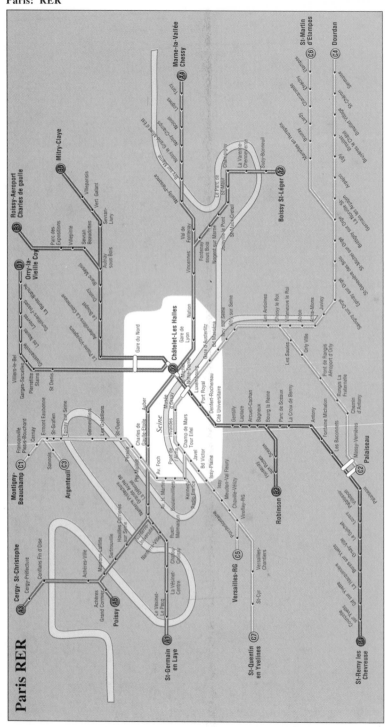

Paris RER

LET'S GO
Paris

■ Let's Go writers travel on your budget.

"Guides that penetrate the veneer of the holiday brochures and mine the grit of real life."
—*The Economist*

"The writers seem to have experienced every rooster-packed bus and lunar-surfaced mattress about which they write."
—*The New York Times*

"All the dirt, dirt cheap."
—*People*

■ Great for independent travelers.

"The guides are aimed not only at young budget travelers but at the independent traveler, a sort of streetwise cookbook for traveling alone."
—*The New York Times*

"Flush with candor and irreverence, chock full of budget travel advice."
—*The Des Moines Register*

"An indispensable resource. *Let's Go*'s practical information can be used by every traveler."
—*The Chattanooga Free Press*

■ Let's Go is completely revised each year.

"Only *Let's Go* has the zeal to annually update every title on its list."
—*The Boston Globe*

"Unbeatable: good sight-seeing advice; up-to-date info on restaurants, hotels, and inns; a commitment to money-saving travel; and a wry style that brightens nearly every page."
—*The Washington Post*

■ All the important information you need.

"*Let's Go* authors provide a comedic element while still providing concise information and thorough coverage of the country. Anything you need to know about budget traveling is detailed in this book."
—*The Chicago Sun-Times*

"Value-packed, unbeatable, accurate, and comprehensive."
—*Los Angeles Times*

Let's Go Publications

- Let's Go: Alaska & the Pacific Northwest 1999
- Let's Go: Australia 1999
- Let's Go: Austria & Switzerland 1999
- Let's Go: Britain & Ireland 1999
- Let's Go: California 1999
- Let's Go: Central America 1999
- Let's Go: Eastern Europe 1999
- Let's Go: Ecuador & the Galápagos Islands 1999
- Let's Go: Europe 1999
- Let's Go: France 1999
- Let's Go: Germany 1999
- Let's Go: Greece 1999 **New title!**
- Let's Go: India & Nepal 1999
- Let's Go: Ireland 1999
- Let's Go: Israel & Egypt 1999
- Let's Go: Italy 1999
- Let's Go: London 1999
- Let's Go: Mexico 1999
- Let's Go: New York City 1999
- Let's Go: New Zealand 1999
- Let's Go: Paris 1999
- Let's Go: Rome 1999
- Let's Go: South Africa 1999 **New title!**
- Let's Go: Southeast Asia 1999
- Let's Go: Spain & Portugal 1999
- Let's Go: Turkey 1999 **New title!**
- Let's Go: USA 1999
- Let's Go: Washington, D.C. 1999

Let's Go Map Guides

Amsterdam	Madrid
Berlin	New Orleans
Boston	New York City
Chicago	Paris
Florence	Rome
London	San Francisco
Los Angeles	Washington, D.C.

Coming Soon: Prague, Seattle

**Let's Go
Publications**

Let's Go
Paris
1999

Brian Martin
Editor

Researcher-Writers:
**Laura Beth Deason
Mercedes S. Hinton
Bulbul Tiwari**

Macmillan

HELPING LET'S GO

If you want to share your discoveries, suggestions, or corrections, please drop us a line. We read every piece of correspondence, whether a postcard, a 10-page email, or a coconut. Please note that mail received after May 1999 may be too late for the 2000 book, but will be kept for future editions. **Address mail to:**

> **Let's Go: Paris**
> **67 Mount Auburn Street**
> **Cambridge, MA 02138**
> **USA**

Visit Let's Go at **http://www.letsgo.com**, or send email to:

> **feedback@letsgo.com**
> **Subject: "Let's Go: Paris"**

In addition to the invaluable travel advice our readers share with us, many are kind enough to offer their services as researchers or editors. Unfortunately, our charter enables us to employ only currently enrolled Harvard-Radcliffe students.

❧

Published in Great Britain 1999 by Macmillan, an imprint of Macmillan General Books, 25 Eccleston Place, London, SW1W9NF and Basingstoke.

Maps by David Lindroth copyright © 1999, 1998, 1997, 1996, 1995, 1994, 1993, 1992, 1991, 1990, 1989, 1988 by St. Martin's Press, Inc.

Published in the United States of America by St. Martin's Press, Inc.

ISBN: 0 333 74753 4

First edition
10 9 8 7 6 5 4 3 2 1

Let's Go: Paris is written by Let's Go Publications, 67 Mount Auburn Street, Cambridge, MA 02138, USA.

Let's Go® and the thumb logo are trademarks of Let's Go, Inc. Printed in the USA on recycled paper with biodegradable soy ink.

About Let's Go

THIRTY-NINE YEARS OF WISDOM

Back in 1960, a few students at Harvard University banded together to produce a 20-page pamphlet offering a collection of tips on budget travel in Europe. This modest, mimeographed packet, offered as an extra to passengers on student charter flights to Europe, met with instant popularity. The following year, students traveling to Europe researched the first, full-fledged edition of *Let's Go: Europe,* a pocket-sized book featuring honest, irreverent writing and a decidedly youthful outlook on the world. Throughout the 60s, our guides reflected the times; the 1969 guide to America led off by inviting travelers to "dig the scene" at San Francisco's Haight-Ashbury. During the 70s and 80s, we gradually added regional guides and expanded coverage into the Middle East and Central America. With the addition of our in-depth city guides, handy map guides, and extensive coverage of Asia and Australia, the 90s are also proving to be a time of explosive growth for Let's Go, and there's certainly no end in sight. The maiden edition of *Let's Go: South Africa,* our pioneer guide to sub-Saharan Africa, hits the shelves this year, along with the first editions of *Let's Go: Greece* and *Let's Go: Turkey.*

We've seen a lot in 39 years. *Let's Go: Europe* is now the world's bestselling international guide, translated into seven languages. And our new guides bring Let's Go's total number of titles, with their spirit of adventure and their reputation for honesty, accuracy, and editorial integrity, to 44. But some things never change: our guides are still researched, written, and produced entirely by students who know first-hand how to see the world on the cheap.

HOW WE DO IT

Each guide is completely revised and thoroughly updated every year by a well-traveled set of over 200 students. Every winter, we recruit over 160 researchers and 70 editors to write the books anew. After several months of training, researcher-writers hit the road for seven weeks of exploration, from Anchorage to Adelaide, Estonia to El Salvador, Iceland to Indonesia. Hired for their rare combination of budget travel sense, writing ability, stamina, and courage, these adventurous travelers know that train strikes, stolen luggage, food poisoning, and marriage proposals are all part of a day's work. Back at our offices, editors work from spring to fall, massaging copy written on Himalayan bus rides into witty yet informative prose. A student staff of typesetters, cartographers, publicists, and managers keeps our lively team together. In September, the collected efforts of the summer are delivered to our printer, who turns them into books in record time, so that you have the most up-to-date information available for your vacation. Even as you read this, work on next year's editions is well underway.

WHY WE DO IT

We don't think of budget travel as the last recourse of the destitute; we believe that it's the only way to travel. Living cheaply and simply brings you closer to the people and places you've been saving up to visit. Our books will ease your anxieties and answer your questions about the basics—so you can get off the beaten track and explore. Once you learn the ropes, we encourage you to put *Let's Go* down now and then to strike out on your own. You know as well as we that the best discoveries are often those you make yourself. When you find something worth sharing, please drop us a line. We're Let's Go Publications, 67 Mount Auburn St., Cambridge, MA 02138, USA (email: feedback@letsgo.com). For more info, visit our website, http://www.letsgo.com.

HAPPY TRAVELS!

BULLFROG BIKES

GUIDED ENGLISH BIKE TOURS

- See many famous sites in Paris
- Everyday 10:30a.m. and 2:30p.m. and Sunday through Thursday nights 9p.m.
- Rain or Shine, no reservations needed
- Energetic, informative tour guides

- New Mountain Bikes / NewTandem Bikes included
- Price: 120 FF (About $20 US)
- Duration: $3\frac{1}{2}$ – 4 Hours
- Season: May 25th thru August 31st
- Meet other travelers, have great fun.

Hop, Skip and Jump through Paris with Bullfrog Bikes

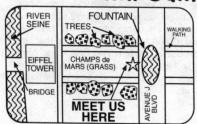

C'mon, meet us by the fountain

Table of Contents

Maps

Color Maps

How to Use This Book

As the cover of *Let's Go: Paris 1999* suggests, Paris is, as always, the City of Lights. In the Millennial blur, Paris is flashing across the Internet and the World in anticipation of the year 2000. From the Dark Ages to the Enlightenment, from the flicker of Nôtre-Dame candles to the flash of your camera, from the floodlights of the Eiffel Tower to the blast of New Year's fireworks, the city is glowing with the past and the future. But you'll have to move fast. Like Madonna's "Ray of Light," Paris is moving at lightspeed toward the Millennium with hundreds of festivals, exhibitions, and celebrations.

The Paris **Introduction** provides a completely new overview of Paris's history, architecture, fine arts, film, music, and literature, with special insights into Gallo-Roman, Medieval, Renaissance, Classical, Revolutionary, Empire, Belle Époque, WWI, WWII, Post-Colonial, Contemporary, and Millennial politics, culture, and style. Paris **Essentials** offers practical information on everything from passports and plane tickets to customs, money, health, safety, employment, study, consulates, publications, communications, and the Internet. We also offer information for women travelers, older travelers, bisexual, gay, and lesbian travelers, minority travelers, vegetarian and kosher travelers, those traveling with children, and those traveling alone.

The **Accommodations** chapter lists hundreds of hostels, hotels, and *foyers* in Paris's 20 arrondissements. Organized by individual arrondissement, each listing provides info on prices, location, and comfort, including wheelchair accessibility and special discounts for students, older travelers, and *Let's Go* readers. Similarly, the **Food and Drink** chapter offers listings of Paris's best budget restaurants, organized by arrondissement and selected to satisfy a variety of tastes and dietary concerns, including vegetarian and kosher menus, classic French, Thai, Italian, Algerian, Japanese, West African, Greek, Chinese, and Moroccan cuisine. In addition, we provide listings of groceries, food markets, classic, hip, and cyber cafés, *salons de thé*, wine bars, pubs, and sweets. The **Sights** chapter provides detailed info on Parisian monuments, museums, neighborhoods, streets, squares, cemeteries, and parks—all conveniently divided by arrondissement. The **Museums** chapter offers in-depth coverage of Paris's largest museums, including the Louvre, the Musée d'Orsay, the Rodin Museum, the Pompidou, the Invalides, the Musée de Cluny, the Picasso Museum, and La Villette, as well as over 50 smaller museums. In addition to the **Entertainment** chapter's fully revised sections on theater, cinema, music, jazz, dance clubs, bisexual, gay, and lesbian nightlife, sports, and festivals, *Let's Go: Paris 1999* features a special **Paris 2000: Millennium** section with information on the hundreds of events being organized for 1999 and 2000. The all-new **Shopping** chapter offers dozens of new listings of Paris's trendiest and most affordable department stores, flea markets, and shops for clothing, books, music, housewares, and services. Finally, **Trips from Paris** offers two sections on excursions from the city: **Daytrips** provides info on Versailles, Chartres, Disneyland Paris, and other nearby escapes, while the expanded **Weekend Trips** offers info on longer ventures to Normandy, Brittany, and the Loire Valley châteaux.

A NOTE TO OUR READERS

The information for this book was gathered by *Let's Go*'s researchers from May through August. Each listing is derived from the assigned researcher's opinion based upon his or her visit at a particular time. The opinions are expressed in a candid and forthright manner. Other travelers might disagree. Those traveling at a different time may have different experiences since prices, dates, hours, and conditions are always subject to change. You are urged to check beforehand to avoid inconvenience and surprises. Travel always involves a certain degree of risk, especially in low-cost areas. When traveling, especially on a budget, always take particular care to ensure your safety.

Let's Go Picks

Let's face it. This whole city is fabulous and you know it. Whether you are visiting for a few days or staying the whole year, part of the pleasure of your visit will be in discovering your own favorite cafés, bars, restaurants, shops, and museums. Despite cynical views to the contrary, Paris is always new and changing. As Honoré de Balzac wrote in 1834, "Paris is an ocean. Sound it: you will never touch bottom." To get you jump-started on your own Parisian adventure, *Let's Go: Paris 1999* offers a few favorites where you can feel *tendance* (trendy) and *très branché* (very hip).

Most Fabulous Restaurants Shaped like a large horseshoe, the neighborhood Marais bar **Au Petit Fer à Cheval** is a monument to all that is chic, hip, and unpretentious in the Marais. Invisible from the front, the few tables that huddle behind the bar are an oasis of *kir, chèvre, mousse au chocolat,* and *Gauloises* (see **Restaurants,** p. 112). Since 1947, Leroy Haynes's 9ème hangout **Haynes Bar** has been a center for African American expatriates, including Louis Armstrong, James Baldwin, and Richard Wright. Today, you can still order fresh-baked cornbread and bask in the glow of the Parisian Harlem Renaissance (see **Restaurants,** p. 118). Owned by a handsome couple, **Le Loup Blanc** in the 2ème offers French specialties, contemporary art exhibits, and all the charm of Gay Paree (see **Restaurants,** p. 110).

Most Innovative Museum The **Institut du Monde Arabe's** boat-shaped riverside façade represents Arab migration to France and the way Algerian, Moroccan, and Tunisian Parisians have changed the face of French identity itself. Like camera lenses, the Institute's circular windows celebrate the meeting point of Arabic art and technology. In addition to the Institute's exhibitions, films, and cultural events, the rooftop terrace has a fabulous view of Montmartre, the Sacré Coeur, the Seine, and the Île de la Cité (see **Museums,** p. 231).

Most Soothing Café and Hammam The **Mosquée de Paris's** soothing café, with decorative tiles, white-marble floors, and tropical shade trees, offers mint tea and *Maghrebin* pastries such as *kadaif*. The exquisitely tiled and ornately carved *hammam* provides afternoons of hot steam baths, cool-water pools, rigorous massage, and relaxing cushions (see **Cafés,** p. 130).

Best Visions of the Future Paris is speeding toward the Millennium, but architecturally, the future is already here. The industrial post-modernism of the **Centre Pompidou** (see **Museums,** p. 219), the geodesic domes and red neo-Cubism of **La Villette** (see **Museums,** p. 223), the stargate symmetry of the **Louvre Pyramid** (see **Museums,** p. 211), and the gleaming futurism of **La Défense** (see **Sights,** p. 208) seem to come right out of the 21st century. It's as if no one would be shocked if the Pyramid lifted off the Cour du Louvre, or if the Grande Arche de la Défense was a gateway to another dimension.

Trendiest Shop Though few of us can afford to buy anything here, the hottest spot this season seems to be **Colette,** an ultra-minimalist "anti-department store" with an eclectic selection of *couture,* accessories, and mineral water. Their Scandinavianesque water-bar offers over 50 different kinds of sparkling aqua from French *Evian* to Swedish *Ramlösa*. Colette's sense of Calvin Klein classicism, oh-so-bored minimalism, and California clean living projects a late-90s aesthetic where less is more, attitude is everything, and where the ultimate in *blasé* chic is to buy nothing at all (see **Shopping,** p. 257).

Best Party of the Millennium As the cover of *Let's Go: Paris 1999* suggests, Paris is, as always, the City of Lights. In the Millennial blur, Paris is flashing across the Internet and the World in anticipation of the year 2000 (see **Paris 2000,** p. 252). To signal the beginning of the next Millennium (or the end of the world as we know it), Paris will take centerstage with a year-long program of celebrations, events, exhibitions, and festivals all centered around the theme *Paris, City of Lights.* Think big, bright, and glamorous. With monuments cleaned, the Seine scented, and the streets draped in flowers, Paris will be decked out like a drag queen. Like Madonna's "Ray of Light," Paris will shine in 1999.

Paris: An Introduction

One winter day in 1932, I got the urge to climb to the top of Nôtre Dame at night...It was more beautiful than I had imagined! The dark, indefinable shapes were black as night, the fog over Paris was milk white! Scarcely discernible, the Hôtel-Dieu, the Tour Saint-Jacques, the Quartier Latin, the Sorbonne, were luminous and somber shapes...Paris was ageless, bodiless...Present and past, history and legend, intermingled.

—Georges Brassaï

TIMELINE

300 BC	The Parisii, a Celtic Tribe in Gaul, settle by the Seine on the Île de la Cité.
52 BC	Caesar invades Gaul. The Romans occupy the Île de la Cité and call it *Lutetia* and then Paris.
476	King Clovis and the Franks defeat the Romans and make Paris their capital.
768	Charlemagne takes power in Paris.
987	Hugh Capet ascends the throne and tries to unite France's kingdoms.
1163	Construction begins on Nôtre Dame.
1253	The Sorbonne is founded.
1348-49	The Black Death ravages Paris.
1429	During the Hundred Years War, Jeanne d'Arc tries to liberate Paris.
1572	During the Wars of Religion, Catherine de Medici orders the St. Bartholomew Massacre, killing 2000 Protestants.
1643	The Sun King, Louis XIV, takes the throne for 72 years and Versailles becomes the center of the court.
1789	The French Revolution begins with the storming of the Bastille. During the Terror, thousands lose their heads on Place de la Concorde.
1793	Napoleon Bonaparte crowns himself Emperor in Nôtre Dame.
1804	Revolution and the Second Republic.
1848	Baron Haussman redesigns Paris's boulevards, parks, and arrondissements.
1870	During the Franco-Prussian War, Paris is occupied and defeated.
1889	World Expo builds the Eiffel Tower.
1914-18	WWI ends with Treaty of Versailles.
1918-39	Roaring 20s and Depression 30s.
1940	During WWII, Paris is occupied as the Nazis parade down the Champs-Élysées; Parisian Jews deported to the Death Camps.
1944	Following D-Day, Paris is liberated.
1945	WWII ends; Charles de Gaulle returns.
1954	France's defeat at Dien Bien Phu.
1958	De Gaulle declares the 5th Republic and champions a new constitution.
1962	Algerian War ends France's Colonial Empire in North and West Africa.
1968	May Students' and Workers' Revolt.
1981	François Mitterand is elected to the presidency and begins his *Grands Projets* construction program in Paris.
1992	France narrowly ratifies the Maastricht Treaty and joins the European Union.
1995	Winter Strikes cripple Paris.
1998	Air France, Train Workers, and Disneyland Paris Strikes as France hosts and then wins the World Cup.
2000	Paris celebrates the Millennium.

▇ Ancient Paris

GAULS, FRANKS, AND ROMANS

First settled by the Gallic **Parisii** clan around 300 BC, the **Île de la Cité** offered protection from invaders while the Seine provided fresh water and an easy means of transportation and trade. The conquest of Gaul in 59 BC and of the Parisii island in 52 BC by Julius Caesar's troops intitiated 300 years of Roman rule. The Romans, who named the new colonial outpost **Lutetia Parisiorum** (Latin for "the Midwater-Dwelling of the Parisii"), expanded the city to the Left bank, building new roads (rue St. Jacques), public baths (Musée de Cluny), and gladiatorial arenas (Arènes de Lutèce), all of which can be seen in remarkably well-preserved ruins in the present-day 6ème arrondissement. By AD 360, the Romans had shortened the name of the now-resplendent outpost to Paris. Despite Roman prosperity, the advance of **Christianity** and barbarians threatened Roman-pagan rule and provided new heroes, including Paris' first bishop **St. Denis** (Dionysius) whose martyrdom by beheading in Paris's northern hilltop, Mount Mercury, in AD 270 gave the area its present-day name **Montmartre** (Mount of the Martyr). After the Romans beheaded St. Denis for his attempts to Christianize the city, he allegedly picked up his head and walked north; he collapsed on the site of the current Basilique de St-Denis, the traditional burial-place of France's kings and queens (see **Daytrips**, p. 284). When **Attila** and his marauding **Huns** tried to take the city in AD 450, the prayers of **St. Geneviève** reportedly diverted the invaders at Orléans and saved the city, thus making the devout nun Paris's patron saint and giving rise to the belief that Huns don't mess with Nuns (see **Goths**: Chartres, p. 287).

CLOVIS, CHRISTIANS, AND CHARLEMAGNE

In 476, **King Clovis** of the **Franks** defeated the Gallo-Romans and took control of Paris, founding France's first royal house (the Merovingians), naming Paris as its capital, and converting the entire city and its invading Franks to Christianity. The **Merovingian Dynasty** (400-751), named for one of Clovis' predecessors, Merovich, enjoyed almost 300 years of rule before Pepin the Short's son, **Charlemagne,** took power in 768 and established the **Carolingian Dynasty** (751-987). On Christmas Day, 800, Charlemagne was crowned Holy Roman Emperor by Pope Leo III. Charlemagne expanded his territorial claims and, although he was illiterate, renewed interest in the art and literature of the ancients, initiating what is known as the **Carolingian Renaissance.** Despite Charlemagne's conquest of most of the Western world, Paris suffered when Charlemagne moved his capital to Aix-la-Chapelle (Aachen, in northwestern Germany). When a wave of invaders consisting of **Viking Normans** and **Muslim Saracens** menaced Europe in the 9th and 10th centuries, Charlemagne's empire fell and France crumbled into fragments.

■ Medieval Paris

CAPETIANS, CONSTRUCTION, AND PROSPERITY

As the first **Millennium** approached, France consisted of scores of independent kingdoms, like **Bourgogne** (Burgundy), **Bretagne** (Brittany), **Normandie,** each with its own independent customs, languages, and traditions. The kingdom of France consisted only of the region surrounding Paris, known as the Île-de-France (and so named because it resembled an island surrounded by the region's many rivers). These medieval kingdoms were organized around the **feudal system,** which bonded peasant-worker vassals to their land-owner lords, who in turn swore allegiance to their kings.

Paris would not return to prominence until the election in 987 of the Count of Paris, **Hugh Capet,** to the throne. Under the rule of the **Capetian Dynasty** (987-1328), Paris flourished as a center of trade, education, and power. Capet's 12th-century descendants attempted to unite the various kingdoms into one centralized country. In 1163, construction began on Nôtre Dame Cathedral, which would take over 170 years to complete. The Capetians' most famous king, **Philip II** (1179-1223), expanded Paris's territory, refortified its walls, and paved the city's streets. With the establishment of the University of Paris in 1215 and the Sorbonne later in 1253, Paris reorganized into two distinct parts: the merchant Rive Droite (Right Bank) and the academic Rive Gauche (Left Bank). One of the last Capetians, the holy **Louis IX** (St. Louis), began construction of the **Sainte Chapelle** in 1245, just opposite the rising cathedral of Nôtre Dame on Île de la Cité. While new cathedrals inspired **pilgrimages** within France, the **Crusades** (1095-1291) encouraged long-distance travel. Both trade and papal power transferred to France in the 14th century when Pope Clement V moved to Avignon in 1309.

BUBONIC PLAGUE, 100 YEARS' WAR, & JOAN OF ARC

Like most of France's cities, 14th-century Paris suffered the ravages of both the **Black Death** (1348-49) and the **Hundred Years' War** (1337-1453), in which the Burgundians allied with the English against the French and Paris was stuck in the middle.

When the last Capetian, **Charles IV,** died in 1328, **Edward III** of England claimed his right to the French throne, based partly on land in Bordeaux that **Eleanor of Aquitaine** had ceded to England and partly on his relation to the **Duke of Normandy,** whose origins stemmed back to **William the Conqueror** and the **Battle of Hastings** in 1066. Were it not for the now mythical Joan of Arc, who allied with the Valois King **Charles VII** against **Henry V** of England, Paris might have become an English colony. Instead, Joan of Arc, a French peasant girl from Orléans who heard angelic voices telling her to save France, revitalized the Valois troops, crowned Charles VII king in 1429, and led the Valois to a string of victories. Attempting to win Paris back from the Burgundians in 1429, she was wounded in what is now the 1er arrondissement (see **Sights,** p. 140). Despite her successes, she was captured two years later by the English and burned at the stake in Rouen for heresy. Charles VII recaptured Paris in 1437 and drove the English back to Calais. The **Valois Dynasty** took over where the Capetians left off and moved toward a more unified France.

■ The Renaissance

RELIGIOUS WARS AND A UNIFIED FRANCE

The influence of the **Italian Renaissance** sparked a great interest in literture, art, and architecture in 16th century Paris. In 1527, Charles VII's descendent **François I** commissioned Pierre Lescot to rebuild the **Louvre** in the open style of the Renaissance and to begin work on the **Cour Carrée** (Square Courtyard). François I moved the official royal residence to the new Louvre and invited Leonardo da Vinci to his court, where the Italian painter presented La Jaconde (Mona Lisa) as a gift to the French king. During the reign of François's successor, **Henri II,** new mansions were added to the **Place des Vosges,** a masterpiece of French Renaissance architecture. However, when Henri II died in the square's Palais des Tournelles in 1563 following a jousting accident, his wife, **Catherine de Médicis,** ordered the Tournelles destroyed and began work on the **Tuileries Palace,** the **Pont-Neuf,** and the **Jardins des Tuileries.**

Joan of Arc heard angelic voices telling her to save France

Despite Paris's architectural renaissance and the literary influence of **Humanism,** religious conflict between French Protestant **Huguenots** (Calvinists) and **Catholics** initiated the **Wars of Religion** between 1562 and 1598. After the death of her husband Henri II, Catherine de Medicis effectively became France's ruler, controlling her three sons **François II, Charles IX,** and **Henri III** (all of whom died in succession before their mother). A fervent Italian Catholic, she was notoriously ruthless in the savage wars against the French Protestants of the southwest kingdom of Navarre, bordering the Pyrénées. Influenced by the progressive Humanism of his grandmother **Marguerite de Navarre** (and her Renaissance masterpiece, *The Heptameron*), **Henri de Navarre** agreed to marry Catherine de Medicis's daughter **Marguerite de Valois (Queen Margot)** in an effort to create peace between the two warring kingdoms. But the wedding was a trap. When all of the leading Protestants in France had assembled in Paris for the royal union in 1572, Catherine signaled the start of the St-Bartholomew's Day Massacre. A wild Parisian mob slaughtered some 2000 Huguenots. Henri's life was saved only by a temporary, not-exactly-voluntary conversion. Her plan did not work as she had expected. In 1589, Henri de Navarre acceded to the throne as **Henri IV de Bourbon,** ensuring peace, uniting France, and establishing the last of France's royal houses, the **Bourbons.** Upon his ascension to the throne at **St-Denis** (see **Trips from Paris,** p. 284), Henri IV converted to Catholicism, waving off the magnitude of his decision with the remark, *"Paris vaut bien une Messe"* (Paris is well worth a mass). His heart still lay with the Huguenots, though: in 1598, he issued the **Edict of Nantes,** which granted tolerance for French Protestants and quelled the religious wars for almost a century.

Jacques Cartier's discovery of Nouvelle France (Québec) on the North American banks of the St. Lawrence river in 1534, and Samuel de Champlain's establishment of a permanent settlement there in 1608, opened France's chapter on colonial history. This discovery would not only inspire the optimism that characterizes the spirit of the Renaissance but would also ensure France's place with England and Spain in the race for colonial expansion in the centuries to come.

■ Classicism and Absolute Monarchy

ABSOLUTE POWER: LOUIS XIII AND RICHELIEU

The French monarchy reached its height of power and extravagant opulence in the 17th century. When Henri IV died in 1610, his son **Louis XIII** was too young to rule alone. His first minister, the **Cardinal de Richelieu,** effectively ruled France with the boy king, consolidating the greatest centralized state Europe had ever seen, where sovereignty rested entirely with the monarch. He expanded Paris and built the **Palais du Luxembourg** (see **Sights,** p. 157) for the Queen mother, **Marie de Médicis,** and the Palais Cardinal (today the **Palais Royal**) for himself. This absolutist state, however, strained the already taut social fabric of France as Richelieu manipulated nobles into submission and teased the bourgeoisie with promises of social advancement.

THE SUN KING AND VERSAILLES

The power of the **Ancien Régime** (Old Regime) and the French monarchy reached its height during the reign of Louis XIV, the self-proclaimed Roi Soleil (Sun King), who took the throne in 1643, commissioned and took up permanent residence at the opulent Château de Versailles (see **Daytrips,** p. 269), and reigned for 72 years. Louis made Versailles into a magnificent showcase for regal opulence and noble privilege. The king himself was on display: favored subjects could come to observe the king and queen rise in the morning, wash, groom, and dine. Royal births were also public events. Louis XIV strove to put down any form of dissent in France. Operating on the principle of *"un roi, une loi, une foi"* ("one king, one law, one faith"), he revoked the Edict of Nantes in 1685 and outlawed duals at the court of Versailles. Despite his escape from Paris, Louis XIV commissioned the landscape architect André Le Nôtre to build a wide, tree-lined boulevard called the Grand Cours, today known as the **Champs-Élysées.** The Sun King also built the **Place Vendôme,** and his daughter, the Duchesse de Bourbon, commissioned the **Palais Bourbon,** which today houses the **Assemblée Nationale** (see **Sights: 6ème,** p. 160).

The light emanating from the French throne, however, could not eclipse serious domestic problems. The lavish expenditures of Louis XIV and his successors left France with an enormous debt (the improvements to Versailles consumed over half of his annual revenues for many years), and Louis's manipulation of the nobility led to simmering resentment. Part of Louis XIV's decision to move his royal residence to Versailles was his fear of uprising in Paris. As an eleven-year-old boy-king in 1648, Louis had witnessed the uprising of a coalition of dissatisfied and power-hungry nobles in a revolt known as the **Fronde.** The people tossed up barricades in the streets and chased the pre-teen king from the city. Although the Fronde was quenched, it illustrated the tensions between the French monarchy's absolutism and the increasing dissatisfaction of Parisian nobles and the bourgeois. The middle-class demanded political rights more in keeping with their share of the tax burden. While a strong king could deter these clamoring factions, a weak one could do little to hold back the rising tide. The Sun King's grandson and successor, **Louis XV,** continued to live in lavish style at Versailles into the late 18th century. Indifferent to government, Louis XV left the task to his ministers and advisors. As a result, his mistresses Madame de Pompadour and Madame du Barry wielded considerable social and political power. When reviewed though the lens of Louis XIV's and Louis XV's extravagance, the Fronde seems to have foreshadowed the setting of the French monarchical sun.

THE FRENCH REVOLUTION TO EMPIRE ■ 5

▓ From Revolution to Empire

THE FRENCH REVOLUTION

Popular discontent with the monarchy, its policies, and its excesses exploded into the French Revolution. By 1787, a financial crisis beset Versailles and Louis XVI called an **Assembly of Notables** to seek solutions. They suggested that an **Estates General,** an archaic French parliament including the three estates of nobility, clergy, and bourgeoisie, be called for the first time since Louis XIII had dismissed it in 1614. Debate ensued over the proper balance of power among the estates. In frustration, the bourgeoisie broke away and declared itself to be a **National Assembly.** When locked out of their chamber, the delegates moved to the Versailles tennis courts where they swore the **Oath of the Tennis Court** on June 20, 1789, promising to draft a new constitution. The Paris mob soon joined in the rebellion, angered by high prices for bread and worried by the disarray of the government.

On July 14, 1789, an impatient mob stormed the old fortress of the Bastille looking for arms and for political prisoners to liberate (they found only petty debtors). The French now celebrate July 14 *(le quatorze juillet)* as the **Fête Nationale, Bastille Day** (see **Festivals,** p. 246). Later that summer, with the enactment of the **Declaration of the Rights of Man,** which embodied the principles of *liberté, égalité,* and *fraternité,* the revolutionaries began to build society anew on the ashes of both feudalism and the Ancien Régime. Major reforms, like the abolition of guilds and the dismantling of the Church, transformed the nation but could not bring lasting peace to Paris. Cathedrals like Nôtre Dame and châteaux like Versailles were ransacked and vandalized by angry mobs. In 1793, the radical **Jacobin** faction, led by **Maximilien Robespierre** and his Committee of Public Safety, took over the Convention and began a period of suppression and mass execution known as the **Terror.** The Jacobins **guillotined** the king and queen (the much-maligned and misunderstood Austrian, **Marie-Antoinette**), as well as their enemies, and eventually one another. The ironically named **Place de la Concorde** (Harmony Square) was the site of more than 1300 beheadings (see **Sights: 8ème,** p. 166). The leading Jacobins were arrested in August, 1793, and the Terror came to an end.

> On July 14, 1789, an impatient mob stormed the Bastille looking for arms and for political prisoners to liberate

NAPOLEON AND EMPIRE

An exhausted French people yearned for stability and welcomed the rise of a man whom they felt could achieve it: **Napoleon Bonaparte.** This famed military commander took power in a coup in 1799 and by 1804 had declared himself **Emperor.** Napoleon established a strong central bureaucracy and the **Napoleonic Code,** a system of law that formed the basis of France's current legal system. He was not satisfied with ruling only France and soon initiated a series of military campaigns that nearly yielded him control of the entire European continent. Napoleon's Paris benefitted from his conquests and booty. With his interest in the ancient Egyptian and Roman worlds, Napoleon brought back countless sculptures from Alexandria and Italy, including the Louvre's *Dying Gladiator* and *Discus Thrower.* He ordered the constructions of the two triumphal Roman arches, the **Arc de Triomphe** and the **Arc du Carrousel,** topping the latter with a gladiatorial sculpture stolen from St. Mark's Cathedral in Venice. Napoleon's many new Parisian bridges, like the **Pont d'Austerlitz, the Pont Iéna,** and the **Pont des Arts,** spanned the Seine in elegant style. He ordered the constructionof a neo-Greco-Roman style temple, the **Madeleine,** and he finished the **Cour Carrée** of the Louvre, originally ordered by Louis XIV. But the monument that perhaps best exemplifies Napoleon's Empire style is the **Château de Malmaison** (see **Daytrips,** p. 282). Napoleon and Empress Josephine set the tone for the Empire style, replete with Egyptian motifs and high-waist dresses. Their coronation ceremony in Nôtre Dame, painted by the revolutionary painter **Jacques-Louis David** (and now on display in the Louvre) attests to their sense of grandeur, romance, and style. When Josephine failed to produce an heir, she and Napoleon amicably annulled their marriage, and Josephine moved permanently to Malmaison. The Emperor married **Marie Louise d'Autriche** and his armies pushed east to Moscow.

But the harsh Russian winter of 1812 prevented French domination. At the post-war conference in Vienna, European leaders reset the French borders to those of 1792 and installed **Louis XVIII,** the late king's brother, on the throne. Napoleon brought a temporary end to the short reign of Louis XVIII when he returned to Paris from his exile on the island of **Elba** in 1815. His ultimate defeat in Belgium at **Waterloo** came later that same year and he was once again banished from France, this time to **St. Helena.** The **Restoration** of the monarchy followed, and Louis XVIII resumed the throne, reinstating the Bourbon dynasty.

■ Republics, Restorations, & Revolutions

The 19th century saw the often confusing turn-over of restored monarchies, new republics, empires, and the three new revolutions that instigated them. Caught in this circle of revolution and reaction, France's quest for a stable regime continued. Louis XVIII's repressive successor, his brother **Charles X,** was France's last Bourbon king. In the **1830 Revolution,** the French revolted against the conservative king in violent armed protests. Power passed in July of 1830 to **Louis-Philippe,** whose more modest bourgeois lifestyle garnered him the name "the citizen king." In a symbolic gesture, he kept the Revolutionary tricolor as his flag and his monarchy was constitutional, not absolute. But his reign, known as the **July Monarchy,** lasted only until 1848 when rebellious Parisians once again took to the streets.

The **1848 Revolution** began when veterans of the 1830 revolt joined students in a march on the Chambre des Députés, demanding a Republic. Louis-Philippe abdicated peacefully, and the **Second Republic** was declared. In 1851 the Second Republic elected to the presidency an ambitious man named Louis-Napoleon Bonaparte, nephew to the great Napoleon. Aided by his popular slogan *"l'Empire c'est la paix"* (the Empire means peace), he successfully proclaimed himself **Emperor Napoleon III.** Napoleon III's reign saw the rapid industrialization of Paris, which brought the dangers of a swelling urban population, pollution, and poverty-stricken living conditions that Balzac's and Hugo's novels describe (see **Literature, p. 20**). Napoleon III ordered **Baron Georges Haussmann** to redesign Paris, razing old neighborhoods, eradicating bad living conditions, and replacing them with wide-boulevards, open parks, and new sewers (see **Museums, p. 228**). The grandeur of Haussmanization reflected the elegance of Second Empire style, embodied by the mythic Empress Eugénie. Haussmann redesigned the Bois de Boulogne (see Sights, p. 203) and the Bois de Vincennes (see **Sights, p. 207**), as well as the **Parc des Buttes de Chaumont** (see **Sights: 19ème, p. 198**). Napoleon III also commissioned **Charles Garnier** to design and build the **Opéra,** whose eclectic style stands as the Emperor's finest architectural achievement. Despite Napoleon III's extraordinary reconstruction of Paris, his downfall came in July 1870 with the defeat of the French in the **Franco-Prussian War.**

Paris responded by declaring the **Third Republic.** Unfortunately, the Prussian army, still at war with France, advanced to Paris and lay siege to the city for months, leaving its residents so desperate for food that they eventually slaughtered most of the animals in the zoo (see **Sights, p. 207**). At the end of January 1871, the leaders of the Third Republic capitulated, and the conservative regime of **Adolphe Thiers** began to make heavy restitutions to the Prussians. Parisians rebelled again in 1871 by establishing the Paris **Commune.** For four months, a committee of leftist politicians (many based in the workers' suburb of Montmartre) assumed power and rejected the Thiers government, which had fled to Versailles. The radical Parisians threw up barricades and declared the city a free Commune. When the city was invaded by vast numbers of French troops in an effort to recapture the city, the communards burnt the Hôtel de Ville, the Palais Royal, and Catherine de Medicis's Tuileries Palace before retreating ultimately to their last stand in the cemetery of Père Lachaise (see **Sights,** p. 199). The last of the *communards* were shot against the cemetery's **mur des fédérés** on the morning of May 21, 1871. The crushing of the Commune was quick and bloody. Many estimate that over 20,000 Parisians died, slaughtered by their compatriots in about a week. The defeat broke both the power of Paris over the provinces and of the Parisian proletariat over the city.

■ Belle Époque Paris

After over eighty years of revolutions, violence, and political instability, it is easy to understand why the period of peace, prosperity, and culture that followed between roughly 1890 and 1914 is called the **Belle Époque** (the Beautiful Period). The colors of the **Impressionists,** the novels of **Proust,** and the **World Expositions** of 1889 and 1900, which gave Paris the **Eiffel Tower, the Pont Alexandre III,** the **Grand** and **Petit Palais,** and the first **Métro** line, all reflected the optimism and energy of the Belle Époque. At the same time, however, industrialization and urbanization introduced many new social problems that challenged the Third Republic. Although the government's reforms laid the foundation for the contemporary social welfare state, social tensions continued to grow. The hypocrisy of French society was laid bare in 1894 with the **Dreyfus Affair,** in which Captain Alfred Dreyfus, a Jewish army officer, was found guilty of treason and sent to Devil's Island. While evidence pointing to his innocence piled up, the army refused to re-open the case. In a dramatic diatribe *J'accuse,* **Émile Zola** condemned the army, the government, and French society for anti-Semitism and corruption. Dreyfus was finally vindicated in 1906 but returned to France broken by his long penal servitude. The ethnic tensions Zola identified foreshadowed the 20th century conflicts that France would later have to confront in its colonial territories in the Carribean, the Antilles, Indochina, Maghrebian North Africa, and Sub-Saharan West Africa.

■ Twentieth Century

WORLD WAR I

World War I put an abrupt end to Paris's Belle Époque. Tensions between two European alliances, the **Triple Entente** (England, France, and Russia) and the **Triple Alliance** (Germany, Italy, and Austria-Hungary) exploded in 1914 when a Serbian nationalist assassinated the Habsburg heir to the Austrian throne, **Archduke Franz-Ferdinand,** in Sarajevo. Germany could have persuaded Austria to exercise restraint but did not. Austria marched on Serbia. Russia, playing the champion of its brother Slavs, responded, and suddenly virtually all of Europe was at war.

After advancing within 50km of Paris, the German offensive stalled at the **Battle of the Marne.** Four years of agonizing trench warfare ensued. The slaughter was staggering, magnified by such new weapons as machine-guns, tanks, planes, flame-throwers, and poison gas: all the ironic products of Europe's 19th-century industrialization and modernization. Germany's policy of unrestricted submarine warfare on all ships entering European waters provoked the United States into entering on the side of the Triple Entente. The entrance of the Americans in 1917 tipped the balance of power in favor of the British and the French (Russia had withdrawn in 1917 in the midst of its own violent revolution), and on Novemeber 11, 1918, the fighting stopped. The Germans were forced to sign the humiliating Treaty of Versailles in the Hall of Mirrors, where the the Prussian King Wilhelm I had ironically been crowned Kaiser of the German Reich in 1870 at the end of the Germany's victory over France in the Franco-Prussian War. The treaty, which imposed staggering reparations payments and a clause ascribing the blame for the war to Germany, lay the foundation for the great resentment that would result in World War II.

THE ROARING 1920S AND THE DEPRESSION 1930S

Parisians poured into the streets and danced with British, Canadian, and American soldiers to celebrate the end of the war. Despite the devastation of an entire generation of young men lost in the mustard-gas trenches of Europe, the party would continue well into the **roaring 20s**, when artists like **Cocteau, Picasso, Chagall,** and **Man Ray,** intellectuals like **André Gide** and **Colette,** performers like **Josephine Baker** and **Kiki de Montparnasse,** and expatriates like **Gertrude Stein, Ernest Hemingway, Ezra Pound,** and **F. Scott Fitzgerald** flooded Paris's cafés, dance-halls, and salons.

The party ended with the onset of the **Great Depression** in the 1930s and was exacerbated by the violent right-wing **Fascist demonstrations** of 1934 in which thousands of Parisians marched on Place de la Concorde and stormed the Assemblée Nationale. To combat the Fascists, Socialists and Communists united under **Léon Blum's** left-wing **Front Populaire,** seeking better wages, unionization, and vacation benefits. The Popular Front further split over Blum's decision not to aid the Spanish Republicans against the fascist Franco in the Spanish Civil War. The internal tensions betwen the right and the left, fascists and socialists, bourgeois and workers left France ill-equipped to deal with the dangers of Hitler's rapid rise to power and his impending mobilization on the opposite shores of the Rhine.

WORLD WAR II

After invading Austria, Czechoslovakia, Poland, Norway, and Denmark, Hitler's armies swept through the Ardennes in Luxembourg and blitzkrieged across Belgium and the Netherlands before entering Paris on June 13, 1940. Luckily, curators at the Louvre, sensing the inevitable **Nazi Occupation,** had removed many of its priceless works of art, including the Mona Lisa, and placed them safely into hiding. Photographic images of Nazi footsoldiers and SS troops goosestepping through the Arc de Triomphe are as haunting as the images of shocked and tearful Parisians lined up along the Champs-Élysées watching this chilling spectacle of Nazi power. The French signed a truce with the Germans ceding the northern third of the country to the Nazis and designating the lower two-thirds to a collaborating French government set up in Vichy. The puppet **Vichy** government under **Maréchal Pétain** cooperated with Nazi policy, including the **deportation** of over 120,000 French and foreign Jews to **Nazi concentration camps** between 1942 and 1944.

Soldiers broke down doors on the streets surrounding the rue des Rosiers in the largely Jewish neighborhood of the Marais in the 4ème arrondissement and hauled Jewish families to the Vélodrome d'Hiver (or Vél d'Hiv), an indoor winter cycling stadium, where Jews awaited transportation to French concentration camps like Drancy, in the northeast industrial suburb of Paris near St. Denis, or to camps farther east in Poland and Germany (the **Mémorial de la Déportation** on the Île de la Cité honors those who perished in the Holocaust; see **Sights,** p. 138). Unlike Denmark, where Danes worked together to smuggle their Jewish neighbors to safety in Sweden, WWII France was plagued by many profiteering and anti-Semitic **collaborators** (called *collabos*) who aided the **Gestapo.** Recently the French government and the Roman Catholic Church in France have acknowledged some responsibility for the deportations and for their moral apathy, but the issue remains controversial.

Despite hardships, Paris's theaters, cinemas, music-halls, and cafés continued to operate, largely for the Nazi soldiers and officers who now flocked to the French capital for R&R. Many of those restaurants and entertainers who continued to serve and sing for Nazi clients, like the **Moulin Rouge, Maxim's** (see **Sights,** p. 166), **Yves Montand, Maurice Chevalier,** and **Edith Piaf,** would later be criticized as collaborators at the end of the war. French women who took German lovers would, following liberation, have their heads shaved (as the Marguerite Duras and Alain Resnais film *Hiroshima Mon Amour* illustrates) and be forced to walk in the streets amid the spitting and taunting jeers of their neighbors.

The French are more proud of the women and men of the **Resistance,** who fought in secret against the Nazis throughout the occupation. In Paris, the Resistance fight-

Paris Is(n't) Burning

It almost was not. As the Allied troops made their way to Paris after their successful embarkment on the beaches of Normandy (see **Daytrips**, p. 313), **Hitler** and the occupying Nazi forces in Paris prepared for a scorched-earth retreat. By August 23, 1944, in obedience to direct orders from Adolf Hitler, *Wehrmacht* engineers had placed mines at the base of every bridge in Paris. Despite Hitler's admiration of Napoleon's monumental tomb in the Invalides (see **Sights**, p. 164) during his smug visit in 1940, more **explosives** were crammed into the basement of the **Invalides**, the **Assemblé Nationale**, and **Nôtre Dame**. The **Opéra** and **Madeleine** were on the list, and the **Eiffel Tower** was rigged so that it would topple and prevent the approaching Allies from crossing the Seine. A brief order from German commander **Dietrich von Choltitz** would reduce every major monument in Paris—ten centuries of history—to heaps of rubble and twisted iron. Although a loyal Nazi, the cultured general could not bring himself to destroy one of the most beautiful cities in the world. Pestered by Hitler's incessant question, "Is Paris burning?" von Cholitz stalled until the Allies had entered the city and relieved him of his burden. His courage saved Paris. In 1968, he was awarded the French *Légion d'Honneur* for his bravery in the face of a screaming Hitler.

ers (or *maquis*) set up headquarters far below the boulevards, in Haussman's **sewers** (see **Museums**, p. 228) and the ancient **catacombs** of the city (see **Sights**, p. 185). In London, **General Charles de Gaulle** established the **Forces Françaises Libres** (Free French Forces), declared his **Comité National Français** to be the government-in-exile, and broadcast inspirational messages to his countryman on the BBC (the first of which is now engraved above the **Tomb of the Unknown Soldier** under the Arc de Triomphe). On June 6, 1944, British, American, Canadian, and Québecois troops launched the successful D-Day invasion on the Normandy coast (see **Weekend Trips**, p. 313) and by the end of August, after four years of occupation, Paris was free. Again, Parisian civilians and Resistance fighters danced and drank with the American, Canadian, and British soldiers who had all worked together to liberate the city. General de Gaulle avoided residual sniper fire to attend mass at Nôtre Dame and give thanks for the **Liberation** of Paris. His procession down the Champs-Élysées was met with the cheers of thousands of elated and screaming Parisians.

After the war, as monuments to French bravery were established in the Musée de l'Armée and the Musée de l'Ordre de la Libération (see **Museums**, p. 221), and as thousands of French Jewish survivors began to arrive at the main Repatriation Center in the **Gare d'Orsay** (see **Museums**, p. 215), there was a great move to initiate change and avoid returning to the social and political stagnation of the pre-war years. General de Gaulle promised new elections once the war's deportees and exiled citizens had been repatriated, and the country sought a new constitution. In 1946, French women finally gained the right to vote, decades after their fellow English, American, Cuban, South African, Brazilian, Turkish, and Thai suffragists. But as constitutional reform lagged in bureaucratic gridlock later that year, De Gaulle resigned.

POST-COLONIAL PARIS

The end of the war also signalled great change in France's residual 19th-century **colonial empire**, especially in North Africa, West Africa, and Southeast Asia. While France proudly lauded its own liberation from Nazi occupiers, it expected to continue its colonial occupation of **Algeria** and **French Indochina** (now known as Vietnam). France's defeat in 1954 at the Vietnamese liberation of **Dien Bien Phu** inspired the colonized peoples of France's other protectorates and colonies, which all gained their **independence** in rapid succession: Morocco and Tunisia in 1956, Mali, Senegal, and the Ivory Coast in 1960. But in Algeria, France drew the line in the sand when Algerian nationalists, backed by the resistance efforts of the **FLN** (Front Libération National), moved for independence. With a population of over one million French

INTRODUCTION

colons or **pied-noirs** (literally "black feet" French) who were either born in or had immigrated to Algeria, France was reluctant to give up a colony that it had come to regard as an extension of the French *Hexagone*. The result was the Algerian War in 1962, where Algerian women, desperate for freedom, hid grenades under their tchadors to fight French soldiers in the casbah of Algiers.

The Fourth Republic came to an end in the midst of this chaos overseas. **De Gaulle** was called out of retirement to deal with the crisis and was voted into power by the National Assembly in 1958. Later that year, with a new **constitution** in hand, the nation declared itself the **Fifth Republic.** But the Algerian conflcit was growing worse. Terrorist attacks in Paris by desperate members of the FLN were met by curfews for North African immigrants. At a peaceful demonstration against such restrictions in 1961, police opened fire on the largely North African crowd, killing hundreds and dumping their bodies into the Seine. Amid the violence in Paris and the war in Algeria, a 1962 referendum reluctantly granted Algeria independence. Almost one hundred years of French colonial rule in Algeria since 1870 abruptly came to an end, and the French colonial empire crumbled in its wake. When President de Gaulle travelled to Québec in 1967 and gave courage to Québecois Nationalists with his famous declaration "Vive le Québec libre!" he seemed not only to be supporting the liberation of a Francophone people (as he had in the Resistance during WWII) but also to be admitting, post-Algeria, the importance of decolonization. But the repercussions of French colonial exploitation continue to haunt Paris, where racial tensions today run high between middle-class French, Arab North Africans, Black West Africans, and Caribbeans, many of whom are second and third generation French citizens.

REBELLION OF 1968

In the spirit of decolonization, revolt, and social change, univeristy students took to the streets in **May 1968,** demading educational and social reform. Frustrated by racism, sexism, capitalism, an outdated curriculum, and the threat of a reduction in the number of students allowed to matriculate, university students seized the Sorbonne. **Barricades** were erected in the **Latin Quarter,** and an all-out student revolt had begun. Students dislodged cobblestones from the streets to hurl at riot police, and their slogan "Sous les pierres, la plage" (under the stones lies the beach) not only

Sous les pierres, la plage" referred to the sandy soil that lay underneath, but also symbolized the freedom of the beach that lay beneath the rock-hard bureaucracy of French institutions. The situation escalated for several weeks. Police used tear gas and clubs to storm the barricades, while students fought back by throwing Molotov cocktails and lighting cars on fire. When 10 million state workers went on strike, paralyzing the country in support of the students, the government deployed tank and commando units into the city.

The Paris revolt—settled, in part, by concessions over university textbooks and curriculum committees—became a model for radical student uprisings in Mexico, Argentina, Québec, and the United States throughout the late 60s and 70s. Less surprising, the Parisian university system was almost immediately decentralized, with various campuses being scattered throughout the city and the nation so that student power could never again come together so explosively as it had in 1968.

THE 80S & 90S: EUROPEAN UNION & URBAN RACISM

Three political parties have dominated the French political scene since de Gaulle's exit in 1969. On the (moderate) right are two parties that formed when de Gaulle's old allies split in 1974: the **Union pour la Démocracie Française (UDF),** led by **Valery Giscard d'Estaing,** and the **Rassemblement pour la République (RPR),** led by **Jacques Chirac.** On the left is the **Socialist Party,** in power throughout the 1980s under **François Mittérrand,** and the **Communist Party,** which, though influential, holds few seats or political power.

De Gaulle's Prime Minister **Georges Pompidou** won the presidency in 1969 and was succeeded in 1974 by the UDF's Giscard d'Estaing. In 1981, Mittérand took over the presidency and the Socialists gained a majority in the Assemblée Nationale. Within weeks they had raised the minimum wage and added a fifth week to the French worker's annual vacation. But in the wake of the **1983 recession,** the Socialists met with serious losses in the **1986 parliamentary elections** and Mittérrand was forced to appoint Chirac as Prime Minister. The Socialists recovered in the 1988 elections, giving Mittérrand another term. He proceeded to run through a series of unpopular Socialist governments, one led briefly by **Edith Cresson,** who became France's first woman Prime Minister in 1992 but who was controversial due, in part, to her claim that all Anglo-Saxon men are homosexuals.

One of the most important challenges in the 80s and 90s has been the question of European integration. Despite France's support of the creation of the **European Economic Community (EEC)** in 1957, the idea of a unified Europe has met considerable resistance. Since the inception of the 1992 **Maastricht Treaty,** which expanded the 13-nation EEC to the more ambitious **Eureopan Union (EU),** the French have manifested profound unease about further integration, as many fear a loss of French national character and autonomy. Mittérrand led the campaign for a "Oui" vote in France's 1992 referendum on the treaty, which won by only the slimmest of margins.

France's isolationist tendencies showed themselves most shockingly in the **1986 parliamentary elections,** which saw the emergence of an ugly new force in French politics—the ultra-conservative, ideologically racist **Front National,** led by **Jean-Marie Le Pen,** which picked up 10% of the vote by blaming France's woes (unemployment in particular) on immigrants and foreigners. Le Pen's popularity reflects the difficulty France has had in adjusting to the influx of **immigrants** since the dissolution of its colonial empire since the 1950s. With high unemployment and cuts in health care and social programs, many blame immigrants for their social problems.

Today, almost half of France's predominantly North and West African immigrants live in or around Paris—particularly in the **13ème**, **19ème**, and **20ème** and in degrading suburban **HLMs** (*Habitations à Loyer Modéré* or public housing projects)—making up 13% of the city's population. Le Pen's slogan *"La France pour les français"* ("France for the French") reflects the kind of racist ideology that fuels France's xenophobia. In 1996, the Loi Pasqua (Pasqua Law, named for Chirac's Minister of the Interior) challenged the French citizenship of immigrants' children, even those who were born in France, and gave the police greater freedom in pursuing immigration violations. Police descended on North and West African neighborhoods in Paris, asking for identity papers and rounding up foreigners. Despite Le Pen's waining popularity, the Front Nationale won its first major mayorship in Toulon in 1995, enjoys great support in southern France, and continues to haunt the racially volatile nation's political and social landscape.

TOWARD THE MILLENNIUM: PARIS 2000

Despite controversies over his vast expenditures, Mittérand's **Grands Projets** plan transformed the architectural landscape of Paris, commissioning multiple projects with modern and grand millennial style. Inspired by Giscard d'Estaing's daring and controversial **Centre Pompidou** (see **Museums,** p. 219), Mittérand was responsible for the **Musée d'Orsay, la Villette,** the **Institut du Monde Arabe,** the **Louvre Pyramid,** the **Opéra de la Bastille,** the **Grande Arche de la Defénse,** and the new **Bibliothèque de France.** Although expensive and at times as controversial as the Eiffel Tower was in 1889, Mittérand's vision for a 21st century Paris has created some of the city's most breathtaking and experimental new architecture. Despite his extraordinary attention to the capital, Mitterand's other great legacy was his Socialist project to decentralize financial and political power away from Paris and into the hands of local governments outside the Île-de-France. The result was that smaller French cities like Lille and Montpelier became the beneficiaries of new architectural, cultural, and social projects. Mittérand ensured that Paris would remain the jewel of France, if not its absolute center.

In 1995 Mittérand chose not to run again because of his failing health, and Jacques Chirac was elected to the French presidency. With unemployment at 12.2% at the time of the election, Chirac faced a difficult year. The crisis ended in a massive and prolonged **Winter Strike** (*grève*) by students, bus drivers, subway operators, electricians, and postmen, who protested against budget and benefit cuts proposed by Chirac and his unpopular Prime Minister, **Alain Juppé.** For weeks, Paris was paralyzed and Parisians were forced to walk, bike, and rollerblade to work and to market. Stores kept reduced hours, mail delivery came to a halt, and occasional blackouts and ubiquitous traffic jams plagued the city. Despite hardships, many Parisians were glad to see the spirit of 1968 still alive and to rediscover their neighbors, local cafés, and corner markets while grounded in their neighborhoods by the transport strikes.

France moved slowly into 1996, recovering from the strike and mourning François Mittérrand, who died in early January. Later that year, President Chirac was denounced around the globe for conducting underground **nuclear weapons tests** in the **South Pacific.** He and Juppé were also criticized for spending cuts in national health care and for their proposal to eliminate mandatory male conscription in the French military.

Chirac now has to contend with a new Socialist Prime Minister, **Lionel Jospin,** who as the head of the Socialist majority in the Assemblée Nationale was appointed in 1998. With all of the world watching France as host of the 1998 World Cup, Air France, SNCF train workers, and Disneyland Paris employees went on strike in June, threatening to cripple the international sporting event. While the **strikes** were settled quickly, they illustrate continued dissatisfaction with employment benefits, labor, and social programs. France's victory in the final World Cup match against Brazil on July 12 renewed patriotic sentiment for a few glorious days in the streets of Paris. More than one million people celebrated the victory on the Champs-Élysées in the largest public celebration Paris has seen since the Liberation in 1944. As the Millennium approaches and the Eiffel Tower continues to count down the days on its digital display, Paris looks ahead to the year 2000 with plans that will celebrate the City of Light's relationship to the ancient and the future, the old and the new, its monuments and their moments in history: the Place de la Concorde and its obelisk will become an enormous sundial while the Place Charles de Gaulle Étoile will transform into a giant clock, with bright spotlights that will tick away the minutes to the Millennium around the twelve grand avenues that span out from the Arc de Triomphe.

■ Architecture

ROMAN BATHS AND MEDIEVAL CATHEDRALS

The **Romans** rebuilt Paris in their own image, with vineyards, baths, arenas, and the north-south rue St-Jacques/St-Martin, a road that led to Rome and that was a prototype for the major Parisian axes of today. The remnants of Roman Paris can be found in the partially reconstructed **Arènes de Lutèce,** the **baths** of the **Hôtel de Cluny,** and the residential **excavations** in the square in front of Nôtre-Dame. An early type of architecture modeled after Roman basilicas blossomed into the massive **Romanesque cathedrals** of the 11th century. The oldest parts of **St-Germain-des-Prés** show the immense walls and semicircular arches characteristic of this style. Prosperity in the 12th century allowed the invention of a new, far more ornate architectural style—the **Gothic.** From this period, Paris gained the **Basilique de St-Denis,** Europe's first Gothic cathedral (see **Daytrips,** p. 284), as well as the cathedral of **Nôtre-Dame** (see **Sights,** p. 136) and the jewel-like **Ste-Chapelle** (see **Sights,** p. 138).

King Philippe Auguste made Paris into a defensive capital, responding to regular raids by beginning work on the fortress of the **Louvre** and building the first walls around the city. The 12th century also saw the basic segregation that still characterizes the city's geography: Philippe Auguste's construction established political and ecclesiastical institutions on the **Île de la Cité,** academic ones on the **Left Bank,** and commercial ones on the **Right Bank.** By the 14th century, Paris's 80,000 inhabitants made it one of the great cities of Europe; at the same time, the 100 Years' War with the English and Burgundians threatened the city's lifeblood. To cope with the danger,

Charles V replaced the earlier wall with a larger wall on the Right Bank, guarded by the new **Bastille** fortress. Although destroyed in the 17th century, the wall's path can be followed down boulevard St-Martin and boulevard Beaumarchais (the northern and eastern edges of the 3ème arrondissement).

RENAISSANCE CHÂTEAUX

The most impressive legacies of the Renaissance are the luxurious **châteaux** built by royalty; the strife of the late Middle Ages kept these exquisite residences out of Paris and many were constructed along the valley of the Loire. François I had his nest at **Fontainebleau,** Catherine de Médici had hers at **Blois** and **Chenonceau** (see **Dayrips,** p. 301). Although both repeatedly promised to renovate the Louvre and move back into the city, nothing came of it except Catherine's **Tuileries palace** which was destroyed by Revolutionaries in the 19th century anyway. Henri IV had different plans; after fighting for almost four years to get into Paris, he was not about to leave. He changed the face of Paris, building the **Pont Neuf** and the **Place des Vosges.** He widened the roads and banned merchant overflow into the streets to accommodate carriages. His efforts were not quite enough; obstacles blocking the street slowed his carriage and enabled François Ravaillac to leap in and assassinate him in 1610. Merchants constructed the first lavish **Hôtel de Ville** (see **Sights,** p. 151).

Under Louis XIII's reign, Marie de Médici built the **Palais du Luxembourg** to remind herself of Italy, and Cardinal Richelieu built the **Palais Royal** to demonstrate his own power. The 17th century reign of the Sun King ushered in the **Baroque** age. Louis XIV banned Gothic architecture; in its place, Italianate domes popped up across the city's skyline. **Le Nôtre, Le Brun,** and **Le Vau** reigned as the triumvirate of French architecture, designing, landscaping, and decorating **Versailles** (see **Dayrips,** p. 269) and **Vaux-le-Vicomte** (see **Dayrips,** p. 278).

REVOLUTIONARY VANDALS & NAPOLEONIC MONUMENTS

Not too surprisingly, destruction outweighed construction during the French Revolution. Most of its impressive architectural achievements were temporary: an artificial mountain on the Champ de Mars, a cardboard Neoclassical interior for Notre-Dame, and sundry plaster statues of Liberty. More lasting were the various defacements, especially of churches and kings' statues. Like Louis

Today's city is the Paris remade under the direction of Baron Georges Haussmann

XIV and Marie Antoinette, the biblical kings of Nôtre Dame's grand **portals** all lost their heads, which were rediscovered only in 1977 and are now on display at the Musée de Cluny (see **Museums,** p. 222). Versailles was ransacked and **vandalized.** However, the Jacobins developed parts of the city previously owned by the Church and the nobility. Napoleon made further improvements in the early 19th century; he planned cemeteries, dug sewers, numbered houses, widened the streets, and carried the artistic riches of a continent to the Louvre. In addition to his château for Josephine at **Malmaison** (see **Dayrips,** p. 282), Napoleon's most triumphant contributions to Paris's monuments were the **Arc de Triomphe,** the **Arc du Carrousel,** and the **Madeleine,** all constructed in the neo-classical style of the Romans whom he admired.

NINETEENTH CENTURY: HAUSSMANIZATION

Despite revolution and political instability, the 19th century was a prosperous time for Parisian architecture. The government's decision that France's major railroads should all terminate in Paris guaranteed that the city would thrive as the center of manufacturing, a magnet attracting thousands of migrants from the provinces. Industrialization made many living quarters more pleasant, as glass became cheap and windows proliferated. But unchecked growth continued to swamp improvements, and many of Paris's one million people lived in congested slums.

Although traces of the past abound, parts of pre-19th-century Paris would be virtually unrecognizable to a modern visitor. Today's city is the Paris remade under the direction of Baron Georges Haussmann. From 1852 to 1870, Haussmann transformed Paris from an intimate medieval city to a centralized modern metropolis. Commissioned by Napoleon III to modernize the city, Haussmann tore long, straight boulevards through the tangled clutter and narrow alleys of old Paris, creating a unified network of **grands boulevards.** These avenues were designed not only to increase circulation of goods and people but also to make Paris a work of art, a splendid capital worthy of France. Not incidentally, the wide avenues also impeded insurrection, limiting once and for all the effectiveness of street barricades.

The changes during this period were momentous. The city doubled its area and Haussmann shifted the boundaries of the 20 existing *quartiers*, establishing Paris's present organization into 20 **arrondissements.** Five of Paris's seven hills were leveled; only **Montmartre** and the **Montagne Ste-Geneviève** remain. Twelve thousand structures were destroyed to create 136km of straight avenues. Wide sidewalks encouraged strollers, *flâneurs,* sidewalk cafés, and kiosks, but intimate neighborhoods were demolished to make room for boulevards, the new **Opéra Garnier,** and luxury apartments. The transformation of Paris continued into the early 20th century. Traffic circles, ubiquitous **pissoirs** (public urinals), and electrical lamps symbolized the city's modernity. The World Expositions of 1889 and 1900 inspired the Métropolitain subway system, the Grand and Petit Palais (see Sights, p. 170), and of course, the Eiffel Tower, an elegant celebration of modernity and steel (see **Sights,** p. 160).

TWENTIETH-CENTURY MODERNISM & SUBURBAN MISERY

Paris survived both World Wars fundamentally unscathed. In the interwar period, a few radical architects began to focus on new building materials. **Le Corbusier,** a Swiss citizen who lived and built in Paris, was a pioneer in the new material of reinforced concrete. During the postwar years, architects began to make buildings that would stand out rather than blend in. Most of the changes were made in the outer arrondissements, like the 13ème and the 17ème, leaving the historic core intact. The old marketplace of **Les Halles,** now a subterranean shopping mall, was torn down, and the *quais* of the Left Bank, like those of the Right, were almost converted into expressways—acts that inspired popular calls for conservation.

The city's history of expansion into the surrounding territory dates back to the emergence of working-class districts (*faubourgs*) in the late 18th century. In the 19th century, rail lines and trolleys made the suburbs more inviting. During the 50s and 60s, the government sponsored housing developments and a plan for a ring of "new towns" surrounding Paris, including **Marne-la-Vallée,** where **Disneyland Paris** is located. The 50s also initiated the construction of large housing projects or **HLMs** (*Habitations à Loyer Modéré*), concrete monstrosities originally intended as affordable housing, but which have become synonymous with suburban misery, racism, and the exploitation of the immigrant poor.

TWENTIETH-CENTURY FUTURISM

The 80s and 90s produced some of Paris's newest, most controversial, and experimental masterpieces. Inspired by President Giscard d'Estaing's daring **Centre Pompidou** in the late 70s, President Mittérrand initiated his famous 15-billion-franc Grands Projets program to provide a series of modern monuments at the dawn of the twenty-first century: from **La Défense** and its stunning **Grande Arche,** to **La Villette,** the **Institut du Monde Arabe,** the **Opéra Bastille,** I.M. Pei's modernist glass **Louvre Pyramid,** and the most-recently completed **Bibliothèque de France.** As Paris rounds the Millenium and enters the 21st century, new projects such as the renovation of the **Centre Pompidou** will continue to transform the capital. The **ZAC** project (Zone d'Aménagement Concerte) plans to build a new university, sports complex, public garden, and metro in the 13ème, Paris's most-rapidly redevelopping arrondissement.

■ Fine Arts

FROM ROMAN COINS TO MEDIEVAL MASTERPIECES

Gallo-Roman artifacts, coins, torques, and sculptures that have survived the centuries now rest in the Musée Carnavelet (see **Museums,** p. 227). Much of Paris's surviving **Medieval** art reflects religious and spiritual virtues. Stunning stained glass and intricate stone façades at **Chartres** (see **Daytrips,** p. 286), **Ste-Chapelle,** and **Nôtre-Dame,** among other churches, retold biblical stories for the benefit of the (usually illiterate) medieval churchgoer. Replicas of Parisian and provincial ecclesiastical masonry can be seen at close range in the Musée National des Monuments Français (see **Museums,** p. 221), while brilliant stained glass and intricate tapestries, like the **Lady with the Unicorn,** are displayed in the **Musée de Cluny** (see **Museums,** p. 222). The rise of monasteries brought the art of illumination to its height, as monks added ornate illustrations to the manuscripts they recopied. The Cluny, the Musée Marmottan (see **Museums,** p. 230), and the Chantilly Museum (see **Daytrips,** p. 280) display detailed manuscripts in gold-leaf and brilliant blues, including the Chantilly's **Très Riches Heures du Duc de Berry,** an illuminated prayer book whose portrayal of country peasants ushered in the naturalism of the **Northern Renaissance.**

FROM RENAISSANCE TO REVOLUTION

Inspired by the painting, sculpture, and architecture of the **Italian Renaissance,** 16th-century France imported its styles from Italy. François I brought the best Italian artists up north to decorate his palace at Fontainebleau. **Leonardo da Vinci** came and brought the **Mona Lisa (la Jaconde)** as a royal gift to the French monarch at the Louvre, where she still resides today. Later, under Louis XIV, French art flourished. **Nicolas Poussin** elaborated the theory of the "grand manner," with its huge canvases and panoramic subjects taken from mythology and history. The French **Académie Royale,** founded in 1648, came to value this style above all others, and all subsequent French painters had to contend with these weighty "academic" precepts. Claude Lorraine's idyllic landscapes defined the Académie's landscape tradition. In 1725, the Académie inaugurated annual **Salons,** held in the vacant halls of the Louvre. Sober scenes of everyday life by Chardin and Greuze stood in contrast to the flamboyant pastel Roccoco colors of Boucher and Fraggonard, whose work covered the gold-embossed salons and bedrooms of the aristocracy with flying cherubs and mischievous escapades. **Watteau** painted the *fêtes* and secret *rendez-vous* of the aristocracy, and **Elisabeth Vigée-Lebrun** painted the French nobility, like Marie-Antoinette, with a charm that years later earned her great success with the court of Russia.

Jacques-Louis David

Unlike many artists, Jacques-Louis David bridged the gap between the Ancien Régime, the French Revolution, and Napoleon's Empire without losing his head. David managed to survive and prosper by ingeniously painting with the times. From his pre-revolutionary paintings **(The Tennis Court Oath),** to his neo-classical revolutionary paintings **(The Oath of the Horatii, The Defeat at Thermopylae, The Rape of the Sabine Women, The Death of Socrates,** and **The Death of Marat)** that praise the Republican virtues of the Revolution using Greek and Roman themes (see the **Musée du Louvre,** p. 211), David honored the mob and the monarch of the moment. When the **Louvre** opened the royal collection to the public in 1793, David used mirrors to amplify the sight angles of his work and to increase his favor with the new leaders of the Revolution. In the early days of the First Empire, David changed allegiance, moved to the camp of Napoleon, and painted **The Coronation of Napoleon.** Napoleon's love of Egyptian, Roman, and Greek motifs reflected his admiration for Roman emperors. David was one of the first to exploit this new iconography, which, along with the Empress Josephine's high-waist dresses, came to be known as the **Empire style.**

NINETEENTH-CENTURY CLASSICISM & ROMANTICISM

The Restoration and July Monarchy marked the division that would define the rest of the century: the **Classical School** led by **Jean-Auguste Dominique Ingres,** a student of David, and the Romantic school led by **Eugène Delacroix.** Ingres's sinuous lines and sensual surfaces, in paintings like his *Odalisque,* contrasted with Delacroix's emphasis on brilliant colors, dramatic movement, and emotional excess in works like the orientalist *Death of Sardanopolous* (see the **Musée du Louvre,** p. 211 and **Musée d'Orsay,** p. 215). **Théodore Géricault** exploited the dramatic effects of Romanticism with darker and ominous overtones in his famous painting *The Raft of the Medusa* (also in the Louvre). Meanwhile the invention of **photography** by Parisians **Nièce** and **Daguerre** provided a new artistic medium, sparking an intense debate over the relative merits of painting and photography.

Disillusioned with Napoleon III and the Second Empire, artists and writers like Nadar and Baudelaire gathered in the cafés of the *quartier latin* and starved proudly in the garrets of Paris. Like the itinerant gypsies after which they were named (and the Puccini opera that depicted them *La Bohème*), the **Bohemians** proclaimed for themselves a life free from normal conventions. While urban Bohemians starved in the attics of Paris, artists like **Jean-François Millet** and **Henri Rousseau** followed the **Romantic** urge to escape to nature, retreating to **Barbizon** to paint the Fontainebleau forest and the French peasantry (see **Musée d'Orsay,** p. 215). Influenced by the social-Utopian theories of Charles Fourier, **Gustave Courbet** rejected Academic historical painting in favor of a "living art" that would portray what he saw around him. With France's growing 19th-century colonial empire in North and West Africa, Indochina, and the Antilles, orientalism and the exotic became inspirations for fashion, painting, and the decorative arts. Painters like **Jean-Léon Gérôme** and later **Paul Gauguin** created lush scenes of Turkish baths, snake-charmers, and Tahitian villagers. Responding to this new obsession with orientalism, Japanese *ukiyoe* prints, Chinese lacquered furniture, and East Asian silks, kimonos, and vases decorated Parisian homes from 1853 on, inspiring the nascent Impressionist movement.

Impressionism was once considered shocking art

NINETEENTH-CENTURY IMPRESSIONISM

Claude Monet, Pierre-Auguste Renoir, and **Frédéric Bazille** met during the 1860s in Paris and began to develop their now-famous technique. Accustomed to the smooth surfaces and clear-cut lines of Academic painting, critics objected to the rough brushwork and the blurry quality of the Impressionists. **Edouard Manet's** *Déjeuner sur l'Herbe* was refused by the Salon of 1863 but was later shown at the **Salon des Refusés,** along with 7000 other rejected salon works.

Many modern viewers are surprised to learn that Impressionism was once considered shocking art. In 1874, a group of young radicals lead by Monet and **Pissarro** established an independent exhibition, which included Monet's *Impression: Soleil Levant.* A snide critic labeled its creator an "Impressionist." Monet and his colleagues adopted this name, and the show became an annual event. Urban Impressionist paintings, like **Dégas's** *Le verre d'absinthe* and **Caillebotte's** *Rue de Paris, temps de pluie,* focused on cafés, boulevards, cabarets, and ballets. At the same time, the Impressionists' credo of *plein air* painting inspired Monet's *Water Lilies.*

The **Post-Impressionists** pushed painting further toward abstraction. **Cézanne's** overlapping planes of color evoked sculpture and geometry while **Van Gogh's** thick brush strokes and bold colors left the viewers of his own time cold. **Paul Gauguin,** to whom Van Gogh mailed his severed ear, left a family and a highly successful career as a stockbroker to paint Breton peasants and the natives of Tahiti. Meanwhile, **Pointillists** like **Seurat** explored a highly scientific type of dot-matrix painting, with works made up of tiny dots in primary colors. In sculpture, **Auguste Rodin** and **Camille Claudel** focused on a highly energetic, muscular shaping of bronze and stone.

During the last decades of the 19th century, Bohemia had moved outside Hauss-mann's city to the cabarets and cafés of **Montmartre**—an oasis for artists and bour-geois alike from the sterility of the modern city below. **Toulouse-Lautrec** captured the spirit of the Belle Époque in the vibrant silkscreen posters that covered Paris as well as in his paintings of brothels, circuses, and can-can cabarets. **Art Nouveau** transformed architecture, furniture, lamps, jewelry, fashion, book illustrations, and even the entrances to the Paris Métro (see the **Museée d'Orsay,** p. 218).

TWENTIETH CENTURY: FAUVISM, CUBISM, DADAISM

At the turn of the 20th century, a young group of artists led by **Henri Matisse** painted with increasingly brilliant colors and decorative surfaces. Critics labeled them the **fauves** (wild beasts), yet their wildness barely hinted at the extreme to which **Pablo Picasso** and **George Braque** would carry art with their **Cubist** experiments of 1907 to 1914. Cubist painting sought to represent the idea of an object rather than the object itself. In order to represent a three-dimensional "idea" on a flat canvas, Picasso presented his subjects from several angles at once. **Marcel Duchamp** added an ele-ment of dynamic movement to Cubism with his *Nude Descending a Staircase.* **Utrillo** and **Man Ray** formed part of the same set, while **Eugène Atget,** a photogra-pher who documented the streets and store-fronts of Paris, provided Picasso and his friends with photographic "sketches" to use as a basis for their art. **Marc Chagall's** Cubist fairy-tale pictures of his native Russian villages anticipated Surrealism.

During WWI, the Cubists and their circle dispersed. Horrified by the slaughter of the war, Duchamp switched from painting futurist machine-worshiping images to leading the **Dadaists,** a group of artists who focused on nonsense and non-art—draw-ing a mustache on a picture of the Mona Lisa to mock the institutions that led to the deaths of an entire generation of young men during the war, and exhibiting a urinal titled *La Fontaine* to graphically illustrate the relationship of art to mass-produced industrial objects and the ready-made iconography of the 20th century.

TWENTIETH-CENTURY SURREALISM, ABSTRACTION, AND FILM

The devastation of WWI profoundly affected post-war art. In 1924, **André Breton** published his *Surrealist Manifesto,* the beginning of the **Surrealist movement.** The Surrealists created an art of the subconscious in the wake of the tremendous slaugh-ter of the Great War. **René Magritte, Salvador Dalí,** and **Max Ernst** produced disturb-ing images of fallen angels, disfigured bodies, and melting clocks. During the 30s, photographers like **Brassaï** and **Kertész,** both emigrants from Hungary, recorded the streets and *quartiers* of Paris, especially Montmartre, in black and white. In 1937, Pic-asso exhibited *Guernica* in the Spanish pavilion of the Paris International Exposition. Depicting the bombing of a Basque town during the Spanish Civil War, *Guernica* provided one of the century's most moving condemnations of the horrors of war.

As the Germans advanced on Paris, the masterpieces of the Louvre were evacuated to basements and gardens in Paris and the provinces. Within days of the German entry into Paris, the invaders filled the Opéra and the theaters, which staged uncon-troversial farces to avoid offense. Braque and Picasso just kept painting, and musi-cians pulled out their Wagner and Beethoven scores. On May 27, 1943, hundreds of "degenerate" paintings by **Miró, Picasso, Ernst, Klee,** and **Léger** were destroyed in a bonfire in the garden of the Jeu de Paume. Tens of thousands of masterpieces belong-ing to Jewish collectors were appropriated and shipped to Germany. Only recently have serious inquiries into **stolen Nazi art** been addressed, as investigations into annulled Jewish bank accounts in Switzerland become a focus of public attention. Later 20th-century experiments in photography, installation art, video, and sculpture, such as Pierre et Gilles's exploitation of kitsch and camp in their iconographic and homoerotic photography, can be seen in the permanent collections and temporary exhibitions of the **Centre Pompidou** and the **Fondation Cartier pour l'Art Contem-porain** (see **Museums,** p. 227). Much of late 20th-century France's most exciting visual production can be found in the work of its prolific **film** industry.

■ Film

Ever since the **Lumière brothers** showed the world's first paid film screening in a Paris café in 1895, French filmmakers have continued to thrill and challenge their audiences. **Georges Méliès's** comic and melodramatic films and **Max Linder's** physical comedies spoke volumes through the silent medium, both in France and abroad. After WWI, French producers struggled with American distributors for cinema screenings, to show such films as **René Clair's** slapstick *Entr'acte* (1924), starring that grand-Dada of Dadaism, Marcel Duchamp, and **Luis Buñuel's** *Un Chien Andalou* (1928), featuring the Surrealist Salvador Dalí. The 1930s saw the arrival of sound and new films such as **Jean Vigo's** dark boarding-school drama *Zero for Conduct* (1933) and **Jean Renoir's** critique of *fin de siècle* bourgeoisie in *Rules of the Game* (1939). During WWII, Nazi censorship led to a move from political films to nostalgia and escapist cinema, such as **Marcel Carné's** *Children of Paradise* (1943-45).

After the war, a group of young intellectuals gathered by critic **André Bazin** for his film journal, **Cahiers du Cinéma,** took issue with Hollywood films–especially movie-musicals–which they believed favored the power of Hollywood producers over the vision of the director. By the late 1950s, the *Cahiers* began to support the **auteur theory,** by which they hoped to give directors more creative freedom over their screenplays, actors, and film productions. Encouraged by French government subsidies and by such Hollywood B-movies as Hitchcock gangster films and Fritz Lang westerns, these film critics swapped the pen for the camera and began in 1959 to make a whole new wave of French films. The new movement was appropriately called the Nouvelle Vague (New Wave) and included such films as François Truffaut's 400 Coups and Jules et Jim (1961), Jean-Luc Godard's À bout de souffle, **Jacques Rivette's** *Paris nous appartient* (1960), **Louis Malle's** *Zazie dans le métro* (1960), and **Alain Resnais's** *Hiroshima, Mon Amour* (written by **Marguerite Duras**). Godard's 1960s collaborations with actors **Jean-Paul Belmondo** and **Anna Karina** included *Vivre sa Vie* (1962), *Pierrot le Fou* (1965), and the car-crazy *Weekend* (1967). The success of the Nouvelle Vague not only revitalized French film. With mass-distribution in France and abroad it also introduced French actors and directors to the world at large.

This internationalization of French cinema in the 60s brought wider recognition of French film stars in the 70s and 80s, such as the stunning **Catherine Deneuve** (*Indonchine, Belle de jour, Les parapluies de Cherbourg*), the gothic priestess **Isabelle Adjani** (*La Reine Margot* and the American version of *Les Diaboliques* with Sharon Stone), the omnipresent **Gérard Depardieu** (*The Return of Martin Guerre, Cyrano de Bergerac, Danton, 1492, Germinal, Camille Claudel,* and most recently *The Man in the Iron Mask*), as well as **Juliette Binoche** (*Blue, The English Patient*) and **Julie Delpy** (*Europe, Europa* and the Eurail love story *Before Sunrise*).

An extraordinary range of new French films have found wide release abroad, are now available on video, and can serve as a wonderful introduction to French culture before you depart for your stay in Paris. Comedies like Édouard's Molinaro's campy **La Cage aux Folles** (1975), Colline Serraud's **Trois hommes et un couffin** (*Three Men and a Baby,* 1985), and Luc Besson's action thriller **Nikita** (1990) have all inspired American remakes, while more recent comedies like Jean-Marie Poiré's **Les Visiteurs** (1992) and François Ozon's **Sitcom** (1998) imitate and poke fun at American B-comedies and television sitcoms. Jean-Jacques Beineix's **Betty Blue** (1985), Claude Berri's **Manon des Sources** (1986) and **Jean de Florette** (1986), Louis Malle's WWII drama **Au Revoir les Enfants** (1987), Marc Caro and Jean-Pierre Jeunet's dystopic **Delicatessen** (1991), and Krzysztof Kieślowski's three colors trilogy, **Blue** (1993), **White** (1994), and **Red** (1994), have all become instant classics of 80s and 90s French cinema.

France's powerful influence on other Francophone cinema has produced such important post-colonial films as Gillo Pontecorvo's The Battle of Algiers (Algeria, 1966), Sembène Ousmane's **Xala** (Senegal, 1974), and Québecois films such as Denys Arcand's **Declin de l'empire américain** (1986) and **Jésus de Montréal** (1990),

Jean-Claude Lauzon's **Léolo** (1992), Pierre Falardeau's **Octobre** (1994), and most recently Michel-Marc Bouchard's **Les Feluettes** (*Lilies*, 1997).

Several recent French films have begun to explore the issue of gay identity and sexual orientation, including André Téchiné's Algerian War coming-of-age film **Les rose-aux sauvages** (*Wild Reeds*, 1994), Josiane Balasko's hilarious lesbian comedy **Gazon Maudit** (1995), Belgian Alain Berliner's transgender tragicomedy **Ma vie en rose** (1997), Cyril Collard's haunting HIV drama **Les nuits fauves** (*Savage Nights*, 1991), and Patrice Chéreau's most recent **Ceux qui m'aiment prendront le train** (*Those Who Love Me Will Take the Train*, 1998). Cédric Klapisch's hilarious **Chacun cherche son chat** (1996) painted gay and straight life in the hip *quartier* of the Bastille.

Some of the most explosive recent French films are the production of *cinéma beur*, the work of second- and third-generation North Africans coming to terms with life in the HLMs (housing projects) of suburban Paris. Rich with graffiti art and rap music, fraught with post-colonial politics and the horrors of urban racism, films like Mehdi Charef's Le Thé au harem d'Archi Ahmed (1986) and Mathieu Kassovitz's La Haine (1995) expose the xenophobia of a France not yet willing to accept the role of immigrant culture in the Parisian landscape of the 21st century.

■ Music

From the Gregorian chant of 12th-century monks in Nôtre-Dame, the 13th century ballads of Medieval troubadours, and the Renaissance masses of **Josquin des Prez** (c.1440-1521) to the Versailles court opera of **Jean-Baptiste Lully** (1632-87), the organ fugues of **Jean-Philippe Rameau** (1683-1764), and the virtuoso piano sonatas of expatriate Parisians **Frédéric Chopin** (1810-49) and **Franz Liszt** (1811-86), Paris has forever been alive with the sound of music and performance. Paris's 19th century musical tradition includes Impressionist composers **Claude Debussy** (1862-1918) and **Maurice Ravel** (1895-1937) and operatic works such as **Gounod's** *Faust* (1859), **Saint-Saëns's** *Samson et Dalila* (1877), **Bizet's** *Carmen* (1875), and **Berlioz's** *Les Troyens* (1858).

As one of the world's **jazz** capitals, Paris and its nightclubs have at one time played host to **Ella Fitzgerald, Louis Armstrong, Thelonius Monk,** and **Sidney Bechet,** and the capital still pulses with contemporary jazz, funk, acid jazz, and blues. Inspired by Paris's love for jazz and the city's reputation (since **Josephine Baker's** popularity in the 1920s) as safe haven for black performers escaping a more racist America, many African-American jazz musicians, including **Bud Powell, Kenny Clark,** and **Dexter Gordon,** came to play in the City of Light. After WWII, American jazz players like **Duke Ellington** played clubs like the Left Bank hotspot, **Le Caveau de la Huchette** (see **Sights,** p. 241), and jazz classics like **Miles Davis's** *April in Paris* helped the city's rain-slicked streets take on their saxophonic gloss.

Paris's cabaret and music theater tradition dates from 19th-century shows at venues like the *Théâtre des Variétés* where, as Balzac's *Cousine Bette* and Zola's *Nana* describe, audiences thrilled to musical dramas with naughty chorus girls and saucy stars. From Josephine Baker's **Bal Nègre** in the 1920s to Michel Berger and Luc Plamondon's 1979 musical-comedy, **Starmania,** Paris's theaters, *café-théâtres,* and *chansonniers* (see **Entertainment,** p. 236) have mixed music with dance and applause.

Similarly, **Jacques Brel's** and Juliette Greco's popular *chansons* charmed smoky cabarets in the 1960s. Some of Paris's most famous song divas, **Edith Piaf,** the Egyptian-born **Dalida,** and the Québecoise **Fabienne Thibeault** have now made way for such new *chanteuses* as **Patricia Kaas, Isabelle Boulay,** and the seductive **Mylène Farmer.** Recent pop hits have come from groups like **Les Négresses Vertes, Autour de Lucie, Dolly,** and **Louise Attaque** and soloists like **Axel Renoir, Étienne Daho,** and the Québecois **Jean LeLoup.** French R&B stars Native and Teri Moïse top the charts along with rap stars like MC Solaar, Alliance Ethnik, the controvesial NTM (Nique Ta Mère), and the more recent KDD (Kartel Double Dentente), whose lyrics speak out against urban crime, racism, and anti-immigrant prejudice in France.

■ Language and Literature

ORIGINS OF THE FRENCH LANGUAGE

The period between the Roman conquest of Gaul in 59 BC to the 9th century AD saw the slow development of the French language from **Gallic Latin** into many regional dialects, such as **Francien** in the north of France and **Provençal** in the south. By the mid-9th century, an intermediary language between Latin and Old French, called **Roman,** provided a common tongue with which the oldest French text, the **Serment de Strasbourg** (a treaty between Charlemagne's sons Louis I and Charles the Bald) was written in 842. The continued development of **Old French** in the 9th through 11th centuries produced simple texts on the lives of saints, such as the **Passion du Christ** and **La Vie de Saint Alexis.**

MEDIEVAL AND RENAISSANCE LITERATURE

Medieval France, however, produced an extraordinary number of literary texts, starting at the beginning of the 12th century with popular **chansons de gestes,** stories written in verse that recount tales of 8th-century crusades and conquests. The most famous of these, the **Chanson de Roland** (1170), dramatizes the heroism of Roland, one of Charlemagne's soldiers, killed in battle in the Pyrenées in 778. While *chansons de geste* entertained 12th century masses, the aristocracy preferred more refined literature extolling knightly honor and courtly love, such as the *Lais* (narrative songs) of **Marie de France,** the *romans* (stories) of **Chrétien de Troyes,** and Béroul's adaptation of the Irish legend of **Tristan et Iseult.**

During the 13th century, popular satirical stories called **fabliaux** celebrated the bawdy and scatological with tales of cuckolded husbands, saucy wives, and shrewd peasants. **Villehardouin's** and **Froissart's** historical chronicles stand in contrast to the mythical **Queste du Saint Graal** *(Quest for the Holy Grail),* **La Mort d'Artu** *(Death of King Arthur),* and Guillaume de Lorris and Jean de Meung's tract on courtly love, the **Roman de la Rose.** The 14th and 15th centuries produced the feminist writings of **Christine de Pisan,** the ballads of **François Villon,** and comic theater like the hilarious **Farce de Maître Pathelin.**

The Renaissance in France produced literary texts that challenged Medieval notions of courtly love and Christian thought. Insired by Boccaccio's *Decameron* and the Italian Renaissance, Marguerite de Navarre's Héptaméron employed pilgrim stories to explore the innovative ideas of Humanism. **Calvin's** humanist treaties criticised the Catholic Church and opened the road to the ill-fated Protestant Reformation in France. With Jacques Cartier's founding of Nouvelle France (Québec) in North America in 1534, French writers began to expand their perspectives on themselves and the world. **Rabelais's** fantastical *Gargantua* and *Pantagruel* imaginatively explored the world from giants' point of view, and **Montaigne's** *Essais* pushed the boundaries of individual intellectual thought. While the poetry of **Ronsard** and **Du Bellay,** the memoirs of **Marguerite de Valois,** and the works of **Louise Labé** contributed to the Renaissance's spirit of optimism and change, they also expressed anxiety over the atrocities of the 16th-century Wars of Religion.

SEVENTEENTH-CENTURY CLASSICISM

The founding of the **Académie Française** in 1635 gathered 40 men to regulate and codify French literature, language, and rhetoric. The rules and standards they set loosely at this time would soon solidify into rigid regulations, launching the "Classical" age of French literature. The Académie has ever since acted as the church of classical French letters (for more on the *Académie,* see **Sights,** p. 160).

Seventeenth-century French literature was not as rigid as the Académie, however. In the realm of philosophy, French thinkers reacted to the skepticism that had arisen in the wake of Humanism by establishing the foundations of **Rationalism,** which championed logic and order. *Cogito ergo sum* (I think, therefore I am) is the motto with which **René Descartes's** *Discours de la méthode* pushed Western thought in the Age of Reason. Mathemetician, scientist, and philosopher, **Pascal** wrote out his *Pensées*, in which he pondered man's rational place in the infinite universe, while **La Rochefoucauld's** *Maximes* painted a more pessimistic view of man's relationship to the world. **La Fontaine's** *Fables* and **Charles Perrault's** *Contes de ma mère l'oye (Fairy Tales of Mother Goose)* explored right and wrong in more didactic and deceivingly childish ways with such tales as La Fontaine's *Le Corbeau et le Renard (The Fox and the Crow)* and Perrault's *Cendrillon (Cinderella)*.

But the 17th century is perhaps most fmous for its theater. While **Corneille's** *Le Cid* and **Racine's** *Phèdre* take tragic looks at the lives of vengeful Spanish nobles and incestuous Greeks, both are thinly veiled critiques of the French nobility. Molière's comedies, such as L'École des femmes, Le Misanthrope, L'Avare, Le Malade imaginaire, and Tartuffe, use back-talking servants, comic dialogue, farce, and caricature to poke even more fun at French society. Even at the court of Versailles, where many of his plays were first performed to the accompaniment of music by Lully, Molière used comedy to express his own hilarious version of social criticism.

Published in 1678, **Madame de Lafayette's** *La Pincesse de Clèves* bridged the gap between the 17th and 18th centuries by creating a complex psychological study of one woman's love for two men, her husband and her lover. Lafayette questioned the simplicity of both Medieval courtly love and 17th-century classical love, and later inspired Laclos's *Les Liaisons Dangereuses* and Flaubert's *Madame Bovary*.

EIGHTEENTH CENTURY AND THE ENLIGHTENMENT

The Enlightenment championed *la Raison* (Reason) in its attemps to uncover a set of laws to explain human nature, knowledge, and society. **Diderot's** *Encyclopédie* audaciously sought to catalogue, systemize, and rationalize the whole of human knowledge. **Jean-Jacques Rousseau's** philosophical treatises, such as *The Social Contract* and *The Discourse on Inequality,* sought new ways of thinking about government, human nature, and the individual.

The Enlightenment's search for an ideal society inspired stories of fantastic journeys. While **Voltaire's** *Candide* went searching for "the best of all possible worlds," **Prévost's** *Manon Lescaut* found hers in the streets of 18th-century colonial New Orleans; similarly, **Montesquieu's** *Lettres Persanes* described French culture from the orientalist point of view of two Persian visitors. While **Bernardin de St-Pierre's** *Paul et Virginie* depicted love as an idyllic Roccoco painting, the **Marquis de Sade's** *Philosophy in the Boudoir* and **Laclos's** *Les Liaisons Dangereuses* explored darker sides of the erotic. **Beaumarchais's** plays *The Marriage of Figaro* and the *The Barber of Séville* foreshadowed the Revolution and the end of aristocratic and monarchical excess.

NINETEENTH CENTURY: ROMANTICISM, REALISM, NATURALISM, AND SYMBOLISM

Madame de Staël's essays *On Literature* carried on the analytical tradition of Diderot, Rousseau, and the Enlightenment. But, like **Chateaubriand's** novels *René* and *Atala,* they also ushered in 19th-century **Romanticism,** with its sometimes melancholy, sometimes idyllic focus on nationalism and modernity. Coinciding with the Industrial Revolution in France—the rise of factories, the growth of cities and the middle-class—Romanticism soon gave way to more cynical views of modern life, especially in Paris.

Written on the edge of Revolution at the end of 1830, **Stendhal's** *Le Rouge et le noir* mixes the passion of Romanticism with the more chilling details of **Realism.** **Honoré de Balzac** focused on the harsh realities of bourgeois society and industrial Paris in the novels of his *Comédie Humaine,* where penniless poets and *nouveaux riche* nobles foolishly fall in love with demanding courtesans. In Cousine Bette, Père Goriot, and Splendeurs et Misères des Courtisanes, Balzac paints grey-yellow pictures of Paris gutters, rooming houses, naughty theaters and bourgeois salons.

Similarly, **Victor Hugo's** novels, such as his epic tale of the 1848 Revolution *Les Misérables,* looked critically at French society. Confronting his readers with the harsh realities of Realism, **Flaubert's** novel *Madame Bovary* hinted at widespread unhappiness among bourgeois women. Inspired by Balzac and by Darwin's *Theory of Evolution,* **Émile Zola's** sordid and saucy novels, *Nana* and *Thérèse Racquin,* explored the dark **Naturalist** theme of survival-of-the-fittest in industrial Paris.

Other novels, like Rachilde's cross-gendered Monsieur Vénus, George Sand's cross-dressing Indiana, and Huysmans' decadent A Rebours (Oscar Wilde's inspiration for The Portrait of Dorian Gray) explored ideas of sexuality, identity, and decadence. **Charles Baudelaire** led the way to modernism with his perverse and beautiful prose poems in *Paris Spleen* and his images of a sordid modern Paris, seen through the eyes of the elderly, the poor, prostitutes, and lesbians in *Les Fleurs du Mal (Flowers of Evil).* Inspired by Baudelaire, a circle of younger poets—**Verlaine, Rimbaud,** and **Mallarmé**—tried to create a more musical poetry, founded in orientalist sounds, vivid images, and strong emotions. Rimbaud's and Verlaine's tempestuous love affair fueled the passionate verse that **Symbolism** hoped to express.

TWENTIETH CENTURY: BELLE ÉPOQUE TO WWII

In 1898, Belle Époque Paris's literary and artistic circles were split over the controversy of the **Dreyfus Affair** into two camps, the pro-Dreyfus supporters or *dreyfusard*s (Manet, Pissaro, Mary Cassatt) and the *anti-dreyfusards* (Cézanne, Renoir, Rodin). Works that confronted the affair's anti-Semitism, like Zola's *J'accuse* and Proust's *À la recherche du temps perdu (Remembrance of Things Past),* lay the foundation for a whole new literature in France that would explore issues of individual identity—including sexuality, gender, and ethnicity—in 20th century France.

Like Proust, Gide and Colette wrote frankly about homosexuality. Proust's portraits of Belle Époque Parisians in *Sodom and Gomorrah,* Gide's homerotic novels like *l'Immoraliste,* and Colette's sensual descriptions of 20s opium dens and 30s cabarets in *Le pur et l'impur* and *La Vagabonde* inspired later 20th-century feminist and homoerotic writing, like **Jean Genet's** *Querelle* (1947), **Monique Wittig's** *Les Guerillères* (1967), and **Hervé Guibert's** *Fou de Vincent (Crazy about Vincent).*

As in art, film, dance, and music, 20th-century French literature moved toward abstraction. Inspired by Marcel Duchamp and the nonsensical movement in art called Dadaism, the theatrical collaborations of choreographer Diaghelev, set-designer Picasso, composer Satie, and writer **Jean Cocteau** during WWI laid the foundation for even further abstraction following the war. In 1924, devastated by the overwhelming destruction of WWI, **André Breton** lead a group of writers and artists to pen the *Surrealist Manifesto,* which promised art that relied not on reason or control but on spontanaity, meaninglessness, and the absurd. **Surrealism** exercised a great influence on later absurdist French theater, such as **Eugène Ionesco's** *Rhinocéros,* expatriate **Samuel Beckett's** *Waiting for Godot,* and **Sartre's** *No Exit.*

TWENTIETH CENTURY: EXISTENTIALISM & FEMINISM

In the years before World War II, Jean-Paul Sartre extended Surrealist ideas of the absurd into **Existentialism,** a philosophical movement that would dominate the literary, political, and artistic scene in Paris in the 1950s and early 60s. Sartre's *Being and Nothingness,* written at the Café Flore (see **Classic Cafés,** p. 128) during the Nazi occupation, became a kind of manifesto of Existentialism, which declared that God is dead and that it is the absurd that governs our lives. Similarly, **Albert Camus** explored in his colonial Algerian novels, *L'Étranger* and *La Peste,* themes of indifference and meaninglessness that were central to Existentialist thought. During the 50s, the Existentialists met at the cafés of Montparnasse to discuss the absurd world around them. Sartre published *Huis Clos* in 1945, with its Existentialist premise that *"L'Enfer, c'est les autres"* ("Hell is other people").

Simone de Beauvoir, Sartre's lifetime companion, also wrote Existentialist novels like The Mandarins but is better known for her revolutionary feminist work The Second Sex, whose famous statement, "One is not born, but becomes a woman" inspired a whole generation of second-wave **Feminism** in the 50s, 60s and 70s. With their exploration of feminine and gender identity, writers like **Marguerite Duras** (*L'Amant*), **Nathalie Sarraute** (*Tropismes*), **Marie Cardinal** (*Les mots pour le dire*), **Christine Rochefort** (*Les stances à Sophie*), **Hélène Cixous** (*Le Rire de la Méduse*), **Luce Irrigaray** (*Ce sexe qui n'en est pas un*), and **Marguerite Yourcenar** (*Le Coup de Grace*), the first woman member of the Académie Française, sparked feminist movements in France and abroad. The founding of the publishing house *Des Femmes* (see **Books,** p. 263) in the 70s ensured that French women writers would continue to have a means of expressing themselves in print.

TWENTIETH CENTURY: NOUVEAU ROMAN & CRITICISM

Experimentation with narrative and perspective in the 50s and 60s led to the creation of the **nouveau roman** (the new novel), which abandoned conventional narrative techniques and created new ones, such as *sous conversation* (what people think as they converse). Among its best known exponents were Sarraute, Duras, and **Alain Robbe-Grillet** (*Projet pour une révolution à New York*).

From the 70s to the 90s, criticism, theory, and philosophy have exerted a great influence over literary, political, and intellectual life in France. French scholars and philosophers such as **Lacan, Foucault, Saussure, Barthes, Deleuze, Kristeva, Baudrillard,** and **Derrida** have been at the center of such intellectual movements as Cultural Criticism, Semiology, Structuralism, Deconstructionism, Post-Structuralism, and Post-Modernism. The 80s and 90s have also seen the emergence of new writers in France such as **Annie Ernaux** and **Hervé Guibert,** as well as a growing number of works by authors of North African origin, such as **Mehdi Charef's** *Le thé au harem d'Archi Ahmed* (1983). Late 20th-century political conflicts over immigrants, racism, and xenophobia have renewed interest in post-colonial Francophone literatures.

POSTCOLONIAL FRANCOPHONE LITERATURE

In the 20th century, many voices have emerged from France's former colonies and protectorates in the **Antilles** (Martinique and Guadeloupe), the **Carribean** (Haiti), **North America** (Québec), **North Africa** (the **Maghreb:** Algeria, Tunisia, Morocco), and **West Africa** (Senegal, Mali, Ivory Coast, Congo, and Cameroon). Although written in French, these novels, poems, and plays speak out against France's colonial exploitation, from the conquest of the Antilles and Carribean in the 16th-18th centuries and the occupation of North and West Africa in the 19th century to decolonization in the 1960s and the emergence of independent states (see **History,** p. 9).

Beginning in Paris in the 1920s with the foundation of the Négritude movement by African and Antilles intellectuals Aimé Césaire (Martinique) and Léopold Sédar Senghor (Senegal), Francophone literature began to flourish. Césaire's *Cahiers d'un retour au pays natale* and Senghor's *Anthologie de la poésie nègre et malgache* attempted to define a shared history and identity among black peoples in Africa, the Caribbean, the Antilles, and North America. Their work and the subsequent founding of the press **Présence Africaine** (see **Books,** p. 263) inspired generations of Francophone intellectuals on both sides of the Atlantic, including **Édouard Glissant** (Le sel noir), **Franz Fanon** (*Les damnées de la terre*), **Simone Schwarz-Bart** (*Pluie et vent sur Telumée Miracle*) and **Maryse Condé** (*Moi Tituba Sorcière*) from the Antilles; **Ousmane Sembène** (*Xala*), **Mariama Bâ** (*Une si longue lettre*), and **Birago Diop** (*Contes d'Amadou Koumba*) from Senegal; **Ferdinand Oyono** (*Une vie de boy*) and **Mongo Beti** (*Le Pauvre Christ de Bomba*) from Cameroun; **Yambo Ouologuem** (*Le Devoir de violence*) from Mali; **Saïdou Bokoum** (*Chaîne*) from the Ivory Coast; and **Sony Labou Tansi** (*La vie et demie*) from Congo.

While France relinquished its protectorates Morocco and Tunisia with relatively little resistance in the 1950s, its refusal to part with Algeria, where over one million French *pied noirs* resided, erupted into the Algerian War in 1960s (see **History,** p. 9). Since gaining its independence in 1962, Algeria has continued to suffer the scars of

France's colonial exploitation and since 1992 has been struggling to overcome the violence of a gruesome and bloody civil war. As a result, much *Maghrebin* writing is marked by a search for cultural identity, a conflict between colonial and post-colonial history, and a desire to create new and independent states. Some of the most prolific of these writers are **Kateb Yacine** *(Nedjma),* **Mohammed Dib** *(Qui se solvent de la mer),* **Rachid Boudjedra** *(La Répudiation),* and **Assia Djébar** *(Les femmes d'Alger dans leur appartement)* from Algeria; **Abdelkébir Khatibi** *(L'amour bilingue),* **Driss Charibi** *(La civilisation...ma mère!),* **Tahar Ben Jelloun** *(L'enfant du sable),* and **Ali Ghânem** *(Le serpent à sept têtes)* from Morocco; and **Albert Memmi** *(La statue de sel)* from Tunisia. North African immigration to France in the 70s, 80s, and 90s has had a profound impact on French language, culture, and politics. Many second- and third-generation *Maghrebin* writers in France, such as **Mehdi Charef** *(Le thé au harem d'Archi Ahmed)* have written about *beur* (slang for an Arab resident of France) culture, racism, and the difficulties of cultural assimilation.

The Indochinese victory against the French at Dien Bien Phu in 1954 offered a brief period of colonial liberation before the Vietnam War again brought occupation, exploitation, and violence. While many Vietnamese writers have abandoned the linguistic weight of their colonial past, some like **Linda Lê** *(Calomnies)* continue to write in French about issues of cultural identity and contemporary politics.

From the British conquest of New France in 1763 to the humiliating invasion of Québec by Canadian troops in October 1970, Québecois writers have struggled to maintain their linguistic and cultural identity. Since the *Révolution Tranquille* (Quiet Revolution) in the 1960s, the combined work of the *FLQ* (Front du Libération du Québec), the *Parti Quebecois,* the *Loi 101* (a law promoting the French language in Québec), and the Québecois people to gain independence from Anglophone Canada has inspired generations of Québecois writers, such as **Jacques Godbout** *(Salut Galarneau!),* **Michel Tremblay** *(Les Belles Soeurs),* **Anne Hébert** *(Kamouraska),* **Michèle Lalonde** *(Speak White),* and **Gaston Miron** *(L'Homme Rapaillé).* With an impending referendum on sovereignty likely by 2000, Québec may well ring in the Millennium as an independent country.

BOOKS ON PARIS

After WWI, a "lost generation" of literati moved to Paris from Ireland, England, and America—**James Joyce, Ernest Hemingway, Ford Maddox Ford, Ezra Pound, Gertrude Stein,** and **F. Scott Fitzgerald** among them. Above all, the expatriates sought a freedom in Paris they could not find at home, a sentiment best summed up by Gertrude Stein's famous statement, "America is my country, but Paris is my hometown."

This spirit has governed much of Paris's 19th- and 20th- century expatriate writers. For those of you who want to read about Paris through their eyes, or through those of some famous native Parisians, the following list may be helpful: **Charles Dickens's** *Tale of Two Cities,* **Victor Hugo's** *Les Misérables,* **Émile Zola's** *Nana* and *Thérèse Racquin,* **Honoré de Balzac's** *Old Goriot* and *Cousin Bette,* **Eugène Sue's** *Les Mystères de Paris,* **Henry James's** *The Ambassadors* and *The American,* **Marcel Proust's** *Remembrance of Things Past,* **Colette's** *The Pure and the Impure* and *The Vagabonde,* **Ernest Hemingway's** *A Moveable Feast,* **James Baldwin's** *Giovanni's Room,* **Henry Miller's** *Tropic of Cancer,* **Anaïs Nin's** *Journals,* **Gertrude Stein's** *Autobiography of Alice B. Toklas,* **Simone de Beauvoir's** *Mandarins,* **Somerset Maugham's** *The Moon and Sixpence,* **George Orwell's** *Down and Out in Paris and London,* and **Ned Rorem's** *Paris Diary.* **Art Buchwald's** recent memoirs, *I'll Always Have Paris* and *Leaving Home* recount his stories of post-WWII Paris after the Liberation. One of the most recent and elegant expatriate portraits of Paris is **Edmund White** and **Hubert Sorin's** *Our Paris: Sketches from Memory.*

Essentials

PLANNING YOUR TRIP

■ When to Visit

Some love Paris in the springtime, some love Paris in the fall, but if you have a choice, there are a few things to keep in mind. In August, tourists move in and Parisians move out on vacation. Smaller hotels, shops, and services may close during August while tourists flood those that remain open. If you avoid the Champs-Elysées, Versailles, and the Eiffel Tower, though, August can be pleasingly calm. Early and late summer are often quite cool. June is notoriously rainy and hot days don't hit Paris until July. Traveling during the off season is a great way to minimize your expenses. Airfares and hotel rates drop, travel is less congested, and museum lines are short. In the fall, the tourist-madness begins to calm down. Despite winter temperatures and rain, there is little snow. Regardless of the weather, New Year's Eve 1999 will glow with the Millennial excitement. For temperature and rainfall info, see **Appendix,** p. 318.

■ Useful Information

FRENCH GOVERNMENT INFORMATION OFFICES

Tourism is France's largest industry, and the French government gladly provides prospective visitors with free and sundry brochures from their official tourist offices in most anglophone countries (see also **French Consulates,** p. 27).

French Government Tourist Office: Call for free info packets including the helpful *France Discovery Guide* and the tourist paper *France Insider's News.* **U.S.:** 444 Madison Ave., 16th floor, New York, NY 10022 (tel. (212) 838-7800); 676 N. Michigan Ave., #3360, Chicago, IL 60611 (tel. (312) 751-7800); 9454 Wilshire Bd., #715, Beverly Hills, CA 90212 (tel. (310) 271-6665); **Québec (Canada):** 1981 Ave. McGill College, #490, Montréal, Québec H3A 2W9 (tel. (514) 288 4264); **U.K.:** 178 Piccadilly, London W1V OAL (tel. (0171) 629 1272). **Ireland:** 10 Suffolk St., Dublin 2 (tel. (01) 679 0813). **Australia:** 6 Perth Ave., Yarralumla, Canberra (tel. (02) 6216 0100); 25 Bligh St., Sydney, NSW 2000 (tel. (02) 9231 5244). **New Zealand:** contact the Australian branch or the Consular Section of the French Embassy at 1 Willeston St., Wellington (tel. (64) 4 4720 200).

Cultural Services of the French Embassy: U.S., 972 Fifth Ave., New York, NY 10021 (tel. (212) 439-1400). **U.K.,** 23 Cromwell Rd., London SW7 2EL (tel. (0171) 838 20 55). General information about France including culture, student employment, au pair jobs, and educational possibilities.

USEFUL PUBLICATIONS AND ORGANIZATIONS

Press and Information Division of the French Embassy, 4101 Reservoir Rd. NW, Washington, D.C. 20007 (tel. (202) 944-6060; fax (202) 944-6040; http://www.info-france-usa.org). Write for info about political, social, and economic aspects of France. Publishes a biweekly newsletter, *News from France,* as well as *France Magazine,* an informational quarterly.

Council on International Educational Exchange (CIEE), 205 East 42nd St., New York, NY 10017-5706 (tel. (888)-COUNCIL (268-6245); fax (212) 822-2699; http://www.ciee.org). A private, not-for-profit organization, Council administers work, volunteer, academic, internship, and professional programs around the world. They also offer identity cards (including the **ISIC** and the **GO25**) and a range of publications, including *Student Travels* (free).

Federation of International Youth Travel Organizations (FIYTO), Bredgade 25H, DK-1260 Copenhagen, Denmark (tel. (45) 33 33 96 00; fax 33 93 96 76; email mailbox@fiyto.org; http://www.fiyto.org), promotes educational, cultural, and social travel for young people. Member organizations include language schools, travel companies, national tourist boards, and other youth travel services. FIYTO sponsors the **GO25 Card** (http://www.go25.org).

International Student Travel Confederation, Herengracht 479, 1017 BS Amsterdam, The Netherlands (tel. (31) 20 421 2800; fax 20 421 2810; email istcinfo@istc.org; http://www.istc.org). A nonprofit confederation of student travel organizations. Members include International Student Surface Travel Association (ISSA), Student Air Travel Association (SATA), IASIS Travel Insurance, and the International Student Identity Card Association (ISIC).

The College Connection, Inc., 1295 Prospect St. Suite B, La Jolla, CA 92037, USA (tel. (619) 551-9770; fax 551-9987; email eurailnow@aol.com; http://www.eurailpass.com). Publishes *The Passport,* a booklet listing hints about every aspect of traveling and studying abroad. Free for *Let's Go* readers; send your request by email or fax only. Also sells railpasses with student discounts.

Michelin Travel Publications, Michelin North America, P.O. Box 19008, Greenville, SC 29602-9008 (tel. (800) 223-0987; fax 378-7471; http://www.michelintravel.com). Publishes 4 major lines of travel-related material: *Green Guides,* for sight-seeing, maps, and driving itineraries; *Red Guides,* which rate hotels and restaurants; *In-Your-Pocket Guides;* and detailed, reliable *Road Maps and Atlases.*

■ Internet Resources

Today, you can make your own airline, hotel, hostel, or car rental reservations on the Internet and connect personally with others abroad. **NetTravel: How Travelers Use the Internet,** by Michael Shapiro, is a very thorough and informative guide to all aspects of travel planning through the Internet (US$25).

THE WORLD WIDE WEB

The forms of the Internet most useful to budget travelers are the World Wide Web and Usenet newsgroups. **Search engines** (services that search for web pages under specific subjects) can significantly aid the search process. **Lycos** (http://a2z.lycos.com), **Alta Vista** (http://www.altavista.digital.com), and **Excite** (http://www.excite.com) are among the most popular. **Yahoo!** is a slightly more organized search engine; check out its travel links at http://www.yahoo.com/Recreation/Travel. Check out **Let's Go's web site** (www.letsgo.com) and find our newsletter, information about our books, an always-current list of links, and more. Let's Go lists specific websites throughout the Essentials chapter. One warning: some sites pose as sources of information but are actually newsgroups or advertising engines. The list below should help you get started, and will provide **links** to other reliable webpages.

Microsoft Expedia (http://www.expedia.msn.com) has everything you'd ever need to make travel plans on the web—compare flight fares, look at maps, make reservations. FareTracker, a free service within Expedia, sends you monthly mails about the cheapest fares to any destination.

Cybercafé Guide (http://www.cyberiacafe.net/cyberia/guide/ccafe.htm) can help you find cybercafés worldwide.

Foreign Language for Travelers (http://www.travlang.com) can help you brush up on your French language skills or learn a few words before you go.

The Paris Pages (http://www.paris.org) offer an impressive amount of information on sights, entertainment, nightlife, and current events as well as an interactive map of monuments and museums and a huge page of links to other Paris web pages.

City of Paris (http://www.paris-france.org) is the official website of the City of Lights. It offers information on visiting, studying, and living in Paris.

Paris Free Voice (http://www.parisvoice.com) is the magazine for English-speaking Parisians, offering up-to-date info on current events, movies, concerts, theater, and the latest expositions, cafés, and hotspots.

Pariscope (http://www.pariscope.fr) is the website of the weekly magazine sold in all Paris kiosks, listing movies, clubs, plays, concerts, and restaurants. Similar to the Paris Free Voice but in French.

The Virtual Paris Guide (http://smartweb.fr/paris) is, as it promises, the virtual trip through the city, with excellent photographs, graphics, and info to match.

Paris also boasts a number of hip and well-equipped **cybercafés** where you can communicate with your friends at home without paying the cost of an expensive phone call (see **Cyber Cafés,** p. 130). If you already have an email account, you may be able to access it in Paris via **telnet.** To get an email account before you leave home, contact **Hotmail** (http://www.hotmail.com) or **Compuserve** (http://www.compuserve.com) both of which are easily accessible in Paris.

■ Documents & Formalities

All applications should be filed several months in advance of your planned departure date. Remember that you are relying on government agencies to complete these transactions. Demand for passports is highest between January and August, so try to apply as early as possible. A backlog in processing can spoil your plans. When you travel, always carry on your person two or more forms of identification, including at least one photo ID. A passport combined with a driver's license or birth certificate usually serves as adequate proof of your identity and citizenship. Many establishments, especially banks, require several IDs before cashing traveler's checks. Never carry all your forms of ID together, however; you risk being left entirely without ID or funds in case of theft or loss. Leave photocopies of all your travel documents (including plane tickets, passport, credit cards, traveler's checks, and medical prescriptions) at home with a trusted family member or friend who can fax them to you in case of theft. Also carry several passport-size photos that you can attach to the sundry IDs or railpasses you will eventually acquire. If you plan an extended stay, register your passport with the nearest embassy or consulate.

FRENCH CONSULATES

The French consulate in your home country can provide info for your trip, arrange for visas, and direct you to info about tourism, education, and working in France.

Australia: Lvl 26, St. Martin's Tower, 31 Market St., 26th fl., Sydney, NSW 2000 (tel. (02) 9261 5779; fax 9283 1210).

Canada: 1, pl. Ville Marie, 02601 Montréal, Québec 83B4S3 (tel. (514) 878-4385; fax 878-3981). The French Embassy is in Ottawa.

Ireland: Contact the Consular Section within the French Embassy at 36 Ailesbury Rd., Ballsbridge, Dublin 4 (tel. (01) 260 1666; fax 283 0178).

New Zealand: Contact the Australia office or the Consular Section within the French Embassy (see **Embassies and Consulates,** p. 69).

South Africa: P.O. Box 11278, Johannesburg 2000 (tel. (27)(11) 331-3460 or 331-3468; fax 331-3497).

U.K.: 21 Cromwell Rd., London SW7 2DQ (tel. (0171) 838 2000; fax 838 2001). **Visa Section,** 6A Cromwell Pl., London SW7 2EW (tel. (0891) 887 733).

U.S.: Consulate General, 31 St. James Ave., Park Square Building, Suite 750, Boston, MA 02116 (tel. (617) 542-7374; fax 542-8054). **Visa Section,** open M-F 8am-noon. 12 branch offices in the U.S.; call to locate the closest branch.

ENTRANCE REQUIREMENTS

Citizens of Australia, Canada, Ireland, New Zealand, South Africa, the U.K., and the U.S. all need valid **passports** to enter France and to re-enter their own country. Some countries do not allow entrance if the holder's passport expires in under six months; returning home with an expired passport is illegal and may result in a fine. When you enter France, dress neatly and carry **proof of your financial independence,** such as a visa to the next country on your itinerary, an airplane ticket to depart, enough money to cover the cost of your living expenses, etc. Admission as a visitor does not include the right to work, which is authorized only by a work permit. Entering France to study requires a special visa, and immigration officers may also ask to see proof of acceptance from a school, proof that the course of study will take up most of your time in the country, and proof that you can support yourself. (For specific visa information, see **Visas**, p. 29; for customs info see **Customs: Arriving in France**, p. 31.)

PASSPORTS

Before you leave, photocopy the page of your passport that contains your photograph, passport number, and other identifying information. Carry one photocopy in a safe place apart from your passport, and leave another at home. These measures will help prove your citizenship and facilitate the issuing of a new passport if you lose the original. Consulates also recommend that you carry an official copy of your birth certificate separate from other documents.

If you do lose your passport, immediately notify the local police and the nearest embassy or consulate of your home government. To expedite its replacement, you will need to know all information previously recorded and show identification and proof of citizenship. A replacement may take weeks to process, and it may be valid only for a limited time. Some consulates can issue new passports within 24 hours if you give them proof of citizenship. Any visas stamped in your old passport will be irretrievably lost. In an emergency, ask for immediate temporary traveling papers that will permit you to reenter your home country. Your passport is a public document belonging to your nation's government. You may have to surrender it to a foreign government official, but if you don't get it back in a reasonable amount of time, inform the nearest mission of your home country.

Australia Citizens must apply for a passport in person at a post office, a passport office, or an Australian diplomatic mission overseas. An appointment may be necessary. Passport offices are located in Adelaide, Brisbane, Canberra City, Darwin, Hobart, Melbourne, Newcastle, Perth, and Sydney. A parent may file an application for a child who is under 18. Adult passports cost AUS$120 (for a 32 page passport) or AUS$180 (64 page), and a child's is AUS$60 (32 page) or AUS$90 (64 page). For more info, call toll-free (in Australia) 13 12 32, or visit http://www.austemb.org.

Canada Application forms in English and French are available at all passport offices, Canadian missions, many travel agencies, and Northern Stores in northern communities. Citizens may apply in person at any 1 of 28 regional Passport Offices across Canada. Canadian citizens residing abroad should contact the nearest Canadian embassy or consulate. Children under 16 may be included on a parent's passport. Passports cost CDN$60, plus a CDN$25 consular fee, are valid for 5 years, and are not renewable. Processing takes approximately 5 business days for applications in person; allow 3 weeks for mail delivery. Contact the Canadian Passport Office, Dept. of Foreign Affairs and International Trade, Ottawa, ON K1A 0G3 (tel. (613) 994-3500; http://www.dfait-maeci.gc.ca/passport/). Travelers may also call (800) 567-6868 (24hr.); in Toronto (416) 973-3251; in Vancouver (604) 775-6250; in Montréal (514) 283-2152. Refer to the booklet *Bon Voyage, But...*, free at any passport office or by calling InfoCentre at (800) 267-8376 (within Canada) or (613) 944-4000 for further help and a list of Canadian embassies and consulates abroad. For more, contact the Consular Affairs Bureau in Ottawa (tel. (800) 267-6788 (24hr.) or (613) 944-6788).

Ireland Citizens can apply for a passport by mail to either the Dept. of Foreign Affairs, Passport Office, Setanta Centre, Molesworth St., Dublin 2 (tel. (01) 671 1633; fax (01) 671 1092), or the Passport Office, Irish Life Building, 1A South Mall, Cork (tel. (021) 272 525; fax (021) 275 770). Obtain an application at a local Garda station or request one from a passport office. The new Passport Express Service, available through post offices, allows citizens to get a passport in 2 weeks for an extra IR£3. Passports cost IR£45 and are valid for 5 years. Citizens under 18 or over 65 can request a 3-year passport that costs IR£10.

New Zealand Application forms for passports are available in New Zealand from travel agents and Dept. of Internal Affairs Link Centres in the main cities and towns. Overseas, forms and passport services are provided by New Zealand embassies, high commissions, and consulates. Applications may also be forwarded to the Passport Office, P.O. Box 10526, Wellington, New Zealand. Standard processing time in New Zealand is 10 working days for correct applications. The fees are adult US$90, child US$46. An urgent passport service is also available for an extra US$90. Nine overseas posts, including London, Sydney, and Los Angeles, offer both standard and urgent services (adult US$130, child US$65, plus US$130 if urgent). The fee at other posts is adult US$260, child US$195; passports are issued within 3 working days. Children can no longer travel on a parent's passport—they must apply for their own, which are valid for up to 5 years. An adult's passport is valid for up to 10 years. For more information check out http://www.emb.com/nzemb or http://www.undp.org/missions/newzealand.

South Africa Citizens can apply for a passport at any **Home Affairs Office** or **South African Mission.** Tourist passports, valid for 10 years, cost SAR80. Children under 16 must be issued their own passports, valid for 5 years, which cost SAR60. If a passport is needed in a hurry, an **emergency passport** may be issued for SAR50. An application for a permanent passport must accompany the emergency passport application. Time for the completion of an application is normally 3 months or more from the time of submission. Current passports less than 10 years old may be **renewed** until December 31, 1999; every citizen whose passport's validity does not extend far beyond this date is urged to renew it as soon as possible to avoid the expected glut of applications as 2000 approaches. Renewal is free, and turnaround takes 2 weeks. For more info, contact the nearest Dept. of Home Affairs Office.

United Kingdom British citizens may apply for a **full passport,** valid for 10 years (5 years if under 16). Application forms are available at passport offices, main post offices, many travel agents, and branches of Lloyds Bank and Artac World Choice. Apply by mail or in person (for an additional UK£10) to one of the passport offices, located in London, Liverpool, Newport, Peterborough, Glasgow, Belfast. The fee is UK£21, UK£11 for children under 16. Children under 16 may be included on a parent's passport. The London office offers same-day, walk-in rush service; arrive early. The **British Visitor's Passport** has been abolished; every traveler now needs a standard passport. Call the U.K. Passport Agency (tel. (0990) 21 04 10).

United States Citizens may apply for a passport at any federal or state **courthouse** or **post office** authorized to accept passport applications, or at a **U.S. Passport Agency,** located in Boston, Chicago, Honolulu, Houston, Los Angeles, Miami, New Orleans, New York, Philadelphia, San Francisco, Seattle, Stamford, or Washington, D.C. Refer to the "U.S. Government, State Department" section of the telephone directory or the local post office for addresses. Parents must apply in person for children under age 13. You must apply in person if this passport is your first, if you're under age 18, or if your current passport is more than 12 years old or was issued before your 18th birthday. Passports are valid for 10 years (5 years if under 18) and cost US$65 (under 18 US$40). Passports may be **renewed** by mail or in person for US$55. Processing takes 3-4 weeks. **Rush service** is available for a surcharge of US$30. Given proof of citizenship, a U.S. embassy or consulate abroad can usually issue a new passport. Report a passport lost or stolen in the U.S. in writing to Passport Services, 1425 K St., NW, U.S. Dept. of State, Washington D.C., 20524 or to the nearest passport agency. For more info, contact the U.S. Passport Information's **24-hour recorded message** (tel. (202) 647-0518). For travel info, contact the Overseas Citizens Services, Room 4811, Dept. of State, Washington, D.C. 20520-4818 (tel. (202) 647-5225; fax 647-3000) or the Bureau of Consular Affairs homepage at http://www.travel.state.gov, or through the State Department site at http://www.state.gov.

VISAS

A visa is an endorsement that a foreign government stamps into a passport; it allows the bearer to stay in that country for a specified purpose and period of time. Most visas cost US$10-70 and allow you to spend within six months to a year from the date of issue. Visas are currently *not* required of visitors to France from EU member countries, New Zealand, Canada, and the United States, provided the stay does not exceed 3 months. Note that Australia is absent from this list. British citizens who have retained their Commonwealth passports may require a visa. A visa is required for *anyone* planning to stay more than three months (see below). It must be obtained from

the French consulate *in your home country.* For more information, send for *Foreign Entry Requirements* (US$0.50) from the **Consumer Information Center,** Dept. 363D, Pueblo, CO 81009 (tel. (719) 948-3334); http://www.pueblo.gsa.gov), or contact the **Center for International Business and Travel (CIBT),** 25 W. 43rd St. #1420, New York, NY 10036 (tel. (800) 925-2428 or (212) 575-2811 from NYC), which secures visas for travel to and from all countries for a variable service charge.

Requirements for a long-stay visa vary with the nature of the stay: work, study, or au pair. Apply to the nearest French consulate at least three months in advance. For a **student visa,** you must present a passport valid until at least 60 days after the date you plan to leave France, an application with references, a passport photo, a letter of admission from a French university or a study abroad program, a notarized guarantee of financial support for at least $600 per month, and a fee that fluctuates according to the exchange rate (about US$60).

To obtain a **work visa,** you must first obtain a work permit. After you have secured a job and a work contract, your French employer will obtain this permit for you and will forward it with a copy of your work contract to the consulate nearest you. After a medical checkup and completion of the application, the visa will be issued on your valid passport. Note, however, that it is illegal for foreign students to work during the school year, although they can receive permission from a *Direction départementale du travail et de la main-d'oeuvre étrangère* to work in summer. (For more info on working in France, see **Work,** p. 46.)

For an au pair stay of more than three months, an **au pair's visa** is required and can be obtained by submission of a valid passport, two completed application forms, two passport photos, a fee (between US$15-25), a medical certificate completed by a consulate-approved doctor, two copies of the au pair's work contract signed by the au pair, and proof of admission to a language school or university.

If you are staying longer than 90 days in France for any reason, you must obtain a **carte de séjour** (residency permit) once in France. Report to the local *préfecture* of the *département* in which you are residing. You must present a valid passport stamped with a long-stay visa, a medical certificate, six application forms completed in French, six passport photos, a letter of financial guarantee, and, if you're under 18, proof of parental authorization. Be prepared to jump through hoops, bark like a dog, and stand in line, perhaps repeatedly. Bring your Proust.

CUSTOMS: ARRIVING IN FRANCE

Unless you plan to import a BMW or a barnyard beast, you will probably pass right over the customs barrier with minimal ado. Visitors have an allowance of what they can bring into France. Anything exceeding the allowance is charged a duty. All travelers must declare articles acquired abroad, but only the truly profligate budget traveler will have to pay duties. Before leaving you should record the serial numbers of expensive (especially foreign-made) items that will accompany you abroad. Have this list stamped by a customs office before you leave to prevent being taxed on items you already own. To avoid problems transporting prescription drugs, carry them in the original containers and bring a copy of the prescription to show the customs officer.

CUSTOMS: GOING HOME

Upon returning home, you must declare all articles you acquired abroad and pay a **duty** on the value of those articles that exceed the allowance established by your country's customs service. Goods purchased at **duty-free** shops abroad are not exempt from duty or sales tax at your point of return; you must declare these items as well. "Duty-free" means that you need not pay a tax in the country of purchase.

Australia Citizens may import AUS$400 (under 18 AUS$200) of goods duty-free, in addition to 1.125L alcohol and 250 cigarettes or 250g tobacco. You must be over 18 to import alcohol or tobacco. There is no limit to the amount of Australian or foreign cash that may be brought into or taken out of the country, but amounts of AUS$10,000 or more, or the equivalent in foreign currency, must be reported. All foodstuffs and animal products must be declared on arrival. For information, contact the Regional Director, Australian Customs Service, GPO Box 8, Sydney NSW 2001 (tel. (02) 9213 2000; fax 9213 4000), or visit http://www.customs.gove.au.

Canada Citizens who remain abroad for at least 1 week may bring back up to CDN$500 worth of goods duty-free any time. Citizens or residents who travel for a period between 48 hours and 6 days can bring back up to CDN$200. Both exemptions may include tobacco and alcohol. You are permitted to ship goods except tobacco and alcohol home under the CDN$500 exemption as long as you declare them when you arrive. Goods under the CDN$200 exemption, as well as all alcohol and tobacco, must be in your hand or checked luggage. Citizens of legal age (which varies by province) may import up to 200 cigarettes, 50 cigars or cigarillos, 200g loose tobacco, 1.14L wine or alcohol, and 24 355mL cans/bottles of beer. For more information, contact Canadian Customs, 2265 St. Laurent Bd., Ottawa, Ontario K1G 4K3 (tel. (613) 993-0534); phone the Automated Customs Information Service at (800) 461-9999; or visit Revenue Canada at http://www.revcan.ca.

Ireland Citizens must declare everything in excess of IR£142 (IR£73 per traveler under 15 years of age) obtained outside the EU or duty- and tax-free in the EU above the following allowances: 200 cigarettes, 100 cigarillos, 50 cigars, or 250g tobacco; 1L liquor or 2L wine; 2L still wine; 50g perfume; and 250mL toilet water. Goods obtained duty and tax paid in another EU country up to a value of IR£460 (IR£115 per traveler under 15) will not be subject to additional customs duties. Travelers under 17 may not import tobacco or alcohol. For more information, contact The Revenue Commissioners, Dublin Castle (tel. (01) 679 27 77; fax 671 20 21; email taxes@iol.ie; http://www.revenue.ie).

New Zealand Citizens may import up to NZ$700 worth of goods duty-free if they are intended for personal use or as gifts. The concession is 200 cigarettes (1 carton), 250g tobacco, 50 cigars, or a combination of all 3 not to exceed 250g. You may also bring in 4.5L of beer or wine and 1.125L of liquor. Only travelers over 17 may import tobacco or alcohol. For more information, contact New Zealand Customs, 50 Anzac Ave., Box 29, Auckland (tel. (09) 377 35 20; fax 309 29 78).

South Africa Citizens may import duty-free: 400 cigarettes, 50 cigars, 250g tobacco, 2L wine, 1L of spirits, 250mL toilet water, 50mL perfume, and other consumable items up to a value of SAR500. Goods up to a value of SAR10,000 above this duty-free allowance are dutiable at 20%. Items sent to the Republic as unaccompanied baggage do not qualify for any allowances. You may not export or import South African bank notes in excess of SAR25,000. Consult the pamphlet *South African Customs Information,* available from the Commissioner for Customs and Excise, Private Bag X47, Pretoria 0001 (tel. (12) 314 99 11; fax 328 64 78).

United Kingdom Citizens or visitors arriving in the U.K. must declare goods in excess of the following allowances: 200 cigarettes, 100 cigarillos, 50 cigars, or 250g tobacco; 2L table wine; 1L strong liqueurs over 22% volume or 2L sparkling wine or other liqueurs; 60 cc/mL perfume; 250 cc/mL *eau de toilette;* and UK£145 worth of all other goods including souvenirs. You must be over 17 to import liquor or tobacco. Goods obtained for personal use (with duty and tax paid) within the EU do not require any further customs duty. Contact Her Majesty's Customs and Excise, Custom House, Nettleton Road, Heathrow Airport, Hounslow, Middlesex TW6 2LA (tel. (0181) 910-3602; fax 910-3765; http://www.open.gov.uk).

United States Citizens may import US$400 worth of goods duty-free and must pay a 10% tax on the next US$1000. You must declare all purchases, so have sales slips ready. The US$400 personal exemption covers goods purchased for personal or household use (including gifts) and cannot include more than 100 cigars, 200 cigarettes (1 carton), and 1L of wine or liquor. You must be over 21 to bring alcohol into the U.S. If you mail home personal goods of U.S. origin, you can avoid duty charges by marking the package "American goods returned." For more information, consult the brochure *Know Before You Go,* available from the U.S. Customs Service, Box 7407, Washington D.C. 20044 (tel. (202) 927-6724); http://www.customs.ustreas.gov.

YOUTH, STUDENT, & TEACHER IDENTIFICATION

The **International Student Identity Card (ISIC)** is the most widely accepted form of student identification. Flashing this card can procure you discounts on sights, theaters, museums, accommodations, meals, train, ferry, bus, airplane transportation, and other services. It also provides insurance benefits, including US$100 per day of in-hospital sickness for a maximum of 60 days and US$3000 accident-related medical reimbursement for each accident (see **Insurance,** p. 43). Cardholders have access to a toll-free 24hr. ISIC helpline whose multilingual staff can provide assistance in medical, legal, and financial emergencies overseas (tel. (800) 626-2427 in the U.S. and Canada; 181 666 9025 in the U.K; elsewhere call collect (44) 181 666 9025).

Many student travel agencies around the world issue ISICs, including STA Travel in Australia and New Zealand; Travel CUTS and via the web (http://www.isic-canada.org) in Canada; USIT in Ireland and Northern Ireland; SASTS in South Africa; Campus Travel and STA Travel in the U.K.; Council Travel, Let's Go Travel, STA Travel, and via the web (http://www.ciee.org/idcards/index.htm) in the U.S. When you apply for the card, request a copy of the *International Student Identity Card Handbook,* which lists by country some of the available discounts. You can also write to Council for a copy. The card is valid from September to December of the following year and costs US$20, CDN$15 or AUS$15. Applicants must be at least 12 years old and degree-seeking students of a secondary or post-secondary school. Because of the proliferation of phony ISICs, many airlines and some other services require other proof of student identity, such as your school ID card or a signed letter from the registrar attesting to your student status and stamped with the school seal. The **International Teacher Identity Card (ITIC)** offers the same insurance coverage and similar but limited discounts. The fee is US$20, UK£5, or AUS$13. For more information, consult http://www.istc.org; email isicinfo@istc.org.

The **GO25 Card** (http://www.ciee.org) is issued to non-student travelers who are under 26 by the Federation of International Youth Travel Organizations (FIYTO). This one-year card (US$20) offers many of the same benefits as the ISIC, and most organizations that sell the ISIC also sell the GO25 Card. A brochure that lists discounts is free when you purchase the card. To apply, you need a passport, valid driver's license, or copy of a birth certificate; and a passport-sized photo with your name printed on the back. Contact Travel CUTS in Canada, STA Travel in the U.K., or Council Travel in the U.S. (see **Useful Organizations,** p. 25).

DRIVING PERMITS AND CAR INSURANCE

If you plan to drive a car while abroad, you must have an **International Driving Permit (IDP),** though certain countries allow travelers to drive with a valid American or Canadian license for a limited number of months. Most car rental agencies don't require the permit. Valid for one year, the IDP must be issued in your own country. You must be at least 18 years old, and a valid driver's license from your home country must always accompany the IDP. Applications require one or two photos, a current local license, an additional form of identification, and a fee. In Australia, contact the **Royal Automobile Club (RAC)** or the **National Royal Motorist Association (NRMA),** surf http://www.rac.com.au, tel. (08) 9421-4271, or fax (08) 9221-1887. Canadians can obtain an IDP (CDN$10) through any office of the **Canadian Automobile Association (CAA),** 1145 Hunt Club Rd., Suite 200, K1V 0Y3 Canada (tel. (613) 247-0117, ext. 2025; fax (613) 247-0118; http://www.caa.ca). Irish citizens should contact the **Automobile Association** (tel. (1) 283-3555; fax (1) 283-3660; IR£4). In New Zealand, call the **Automobile Association (AA),** PO Box 5, Auckland (tel. (9) 377-4660; fax (9) 302-2037; http://www.nzaa.co.nz; NZ$8). In South Africa contact the **Automobile Association of South Africa,** P.O. Box 596, 2000 Johannesburg (tel. (11) 799 1000; fax (11) 799-1010; SAR28.50). In the U.K., IDPs are UK£4 at the local **AA Shop,** 5 Star Post Link, Freepost, Copenhagen Ct., 8 New St., Basingstroke RG21 7BA (tel. (1256) 49 39 32; fax (1256) 460 750; http://www.theaa.co.uk/travel). U.S. license holders can obtain an IDP (US$10) at any **American Automobile Association (AAA),** Travel Agency Services Dept., 1000 AAA Dr. (mail stop 28), Heathrow, FL 32746 (tel. (407) 444-4245; fax 444-4247).

Most credit cards cover standard **insurance.** If you rent, lease, or borrow a car, you will need a **green card,** or **International Insurance Certificate,** to prove

AU ROYAL CARDINAL HOTEL

1 RUE DES ECOLES, 75005 PARIS
METRO: JUSSIEU CARDINAL-LEMOINE

The ambiance at **AU ROYAL CARDINAL HOTEL** is indubitably lively, and this 2-star hotel maintains its rich tradition.

Situated in the Latin Quarter, you will find yourself in the heart of Paris, in close proximity to such attractions as the Cathedral of Notre-Dame, the I'lle Saint Louis, the Sorbonne, Saint-Germain-des-Prés, and Place Saint Michel.

Eric and his team will warmly welcome you and inform you about all of the tours, restaurants, monuments, and museums in order to help you better discover our beautiful city of Paris.

Come morning, our personnel will be happy to serve you a continental breakfast in the comfort of your room.

Each of these are fully equipped with all the modern comforts of home: private bathrooms, telephone, satellite television, blow dryers, chest, and doubled windows for a peaceful sleep.

Our Prices:	Room and breakfast included	
	Off-Peak	Peak
Single	390	475
Double	410	510
Twin	450	575
Triple	610	700
Quadruple	650	750

Please contact us, we are happy to povide you with additional information.
TEL: 33 1 43 26 83 64 –OR – 33 1 46 33 93 62   FAX: 1 44 07 22 32

that you have liability insurance. Obtain it through the car rental agency. If you lease a car, obtain a green card from the dealer. Some travel agents offer the card. Verify whether your auto insurance applies abroad; even if it does, you will still need a green card to certify this fact to foreign officials. Rental agencies may require you to purchase theft insurance. Ask for full details and requirements.

■ Money

Money may be the root of all evil, but in Paris it's a necessary one. Even a modest daily budget will probably fall between US$50-60. With some creativity and a little foot-work, however, you can get the most francs for your dollar, pound, or rand in the City of Light.

CURRENCY AND EXCHANGE

US$1 = 5.74F	1F = US$0.17
CDN$1 = 4.10F	1F = CDN$0.24
UK£1 = 9.73F	1F = UK£0.10
IR£1 = 8.44F	1F = IR£0.12
AUS$1 = 3.78F	1F = AUS$0.26
NZ$1 = 3.19F	1F = NZ$0.31
SAR1 = 1.03F	1F = SAR0.97

A Note on Prices and Exchange Rates

The information in this book was researched in the summer of 1998. Since then, inflation will have raised most prices at least 10%. Confirm the bulk trading rate in the finance section of major newspapers. This rate is better than the one you will find at banks and exchange offices but is the rate you will receive at ATMs.

The basic unit of currency in France is the **franc,** divided into 100 centimes and issued in both coins (5, 10, 20, and 50 centimes; 1, 2, 5, 10, and 20F) and paper notes (20, 50, 100, 200, 500F). It is more expensive to buy francs at home than in France, but converting some money before you go will allow you to zip through the airport while others languish in exchange lines. It's a good idea to bring enough French currency to last for the first 24-72 hours of a trip, depending on the day of the week you will be arriving (and allowing for unexpected French holidays). Travelers living in the U.S. can get foreign currency on the East Coast at **Capital Foreign Exchange** (tel. (888) 842-0880; fax (202) 842-8008) or on the West Coast at **International Currency Express** (tel. (888) 278-6628; fax (310) 278-6410). They will deliver foreign currency or traveler's checks overnight (US$12) or second-day (US$10).

In Paris, beware of *bureaux de change* at airports, train stations, and touristy areas such as the Champs Élysées, which generally have less favorable rates. Going off the beaten path may stretch your dollar further. Keep in mind, though, that running around Paris to get better rates will cause stress and reduce your sightseeing time. Many, but not all, banks will exchange money from 9am-noon and 2-4:30pm. For better rates, use your ATM card to withdraw funds (see **Cash Cards,** p. 37). Whenever changing money, exchange large sums at one time (though never more than is safe to carry around) to minimize losses on commission and ATM withdrawal fees.

American Express: 11, rue Scribe, 9^{ème}(tel. 01 47 77 77 07; fax 01 47 77 74 57). M: Opéra or Auber. Across from the back of the Opéra. Tolerable exchange rates and long lines in summer, especially M and F-Sa. No commission. Cardholders can cash US$1000 in personal checks from a U.S. bank every 21 days; bring your passport. The office receives moneygrams and holds mail for cardholders or for those with AmEx Traveler's Checks. English spoken. Open M-F 9am-6pm, Sa 9am-6:30pm.

Thomas Cook: 73, Champs Elysées, 8ème (tel. 01 45 62 89 55; fax 01 45 62 89 54). M: Franklin D. Roosevelt. If you do not have an AmEx card, you can receive money-grams at over 30 Thomas Cook locations in Paris. Contact the Champs Élysées branch for more info. English spoken. Open daily 8:30am-10:30pm.

At Train Stations: Less favorable rates for impatient travelers. **Gare d'Austerlitz,** 13ème (tel. 01 53 60 12 97). Open daily 7:30am-9pm. **Gare de Lyon,** 12ème (tel. 01 43 41 52 70). Open daily 6:30am-11pm. **Gare de l'Est,** 10ème (tel. 01 46 07 66 84; fax 01 46 07 11 79). Open M-F 9am-6:30pm, Sa 9:30am-5pm. **Gare du Nord,** 10ème (tel. 01 42 80 11 50). Open daily 6:15am-10:30pm. **Gare St-Lazare,** 8ème (tel. 01 43 87 72 51; fax 01 42 94 91 26). Open M-Sa 8am-7pm, Su 9am-5pm.

At Airports: Lousy rates. Exchange enough to get to Paris and change the rest in the city. **Orly-Sud:** located at Gate H (tel. 01 49 75 89 25; fax 01 49 75 89 34). Open daily 6:30am-11:30pm. **Roissy-Charles de Gaulle:** 2 locations: Terminal 1 (tel. 01 48 64 37 15) and Terminal 2 (tel. 01 48 64 54 03). Open daily 6am-11:30pm.

TRAVELER'S CHECKS

Traveler's checks are one of the safest and least troublesome means of carrying funds, as they can be refunded if stolen. Several agencies and many banks sell them, usually for face value plus a small percentage commission. Members of the American Automobile Association and some banks and credit unions can get American Express checks commission-free. **American Express** and **Visa** are the most widely recognized, though other major checks are sold, exchanged, cashed, and refunded almost as easily. Each agency provides refunds **if your checks are lost or stolen,** and many provide additional services. For a speedy refund, keep your check receipts separate from your checks. Leave a list of check numbers with someone at home, and ask for a list of refund centers when you buy your checks. Keep a separate supply of cash or traveler's checks for emergencies. Never countersign your checks until you are ready to cash them, and always bring your passport with you.

Depending on fluctuations in currency, you may gain or lose by converting your currency beforehand. While British and U.S. citizens can easily exchange their currencies for francs in France, New Zealanders and Australians may have difficulty. Buying **French franc traveler's checks** eliminates expensive multiple transactions. Most banks will cash French franc traveler's checks commission-free. Ask first.

American Express: Call (800) 25 19 02 in Australia; in New Zealand (0800) 44 10 68; in the U.K. (0800) 52 13 13; in the U.S. and Canada (800) 221-7282. Elsewhere, call U.S. collect (801) 964-6665. Available in Australian, British, Canadian, French, U.S., and (soon) South African currencies, American Express traveler's checks are the most widely recognized worldwide and the easiest to replace if lost or stolen. Checks can be purchased for a small fee (1-4%) at AmEx Travel Service Offices, banks, and American Automobile Association offices (AAA members can buy the checks commission-free). Cardmembers can order them by phone (tel. (800) ORDER-TC (673-3782)). AmEx offices cash their checks commission-free, although they often offer slightly worse rates than banks. You can also buy *Cheques for Two* that can be signed by either of two people traveling together. Request the AmEx booklet *Traveler's Companion,* which lists travel offices and stolen check hotlines. Visit their online travel office at http://www.aexp.com.

Citicorp: Call (800) 645-6556 in the U.S. and Canada; in Europe or Africa (44) 171 508 7007; elsewhere call U.S. collect (813) 623-1709. Sells Citicorp and Citicorp Visa traveler's checks in Australian, British, Canadian, U.S. currencies. 1-2% commission. Citicorp's World Courier Service home-delivers traveler's checks.

Thomas Cook MasterCard: For 24hr. cashing or refund assistance: from the U.S., Canada, or Caribbean call (800) 223-7373; from the U.K. call (0800) 622 101 free or (1733) 318 950 collect; from anywhere else call (44) 1733 318 950 collect. Checks in Australian, Canadian, U.S., British, French, South African, and EU currencies. 2% commission. Thomas Cook offices will cash checks commission-free.

Visa: Call (800) 227-6811 in the U.S.; in the U.K. (0800) 895 078; from anywhere else call (44) 1733 318 949 collect. Visa Traveler's Checks and credit card services.

CREDIT CARDS

In addition to extending credit, some cards offer services for travelers, from auto insurance to emergency legal aid. The easiest way to reserve a hotel room before you leave is to send a confirming fax with your card number after requesting a room by phone. Cards also extract **cash advances** in francs from associated banks and ATMs at wholesale exchange rates about 5% better than banks and exchange offices.

MasterCard (tel. (800) 999-0454) and **Visa** (tel. (800) 336-8472) are the most welcomed in shops and hotels; heavy surcharges keep small businesses and hotels out of the **American Express** (tel. (800) 843-2273) loop. AmEx cards work in ATMs at Crédit Lyonnais banks, AmEx offices, and airports. AmEx cardholders can sign up through AmEx's Express Cash service to access cash from their home account at any ATM with the AmEx trademark (see **Getting Money From Home,** below). Mastercard and Visa can access most ATMs in Paris; look for stickers saying EC or CB/VISA. Keep in mind that MasterCard and Visa have aliases here, **Eurocard** and **Carte Bleue.**

American Express (tel. (800) 843-2273) has a US$55 annual fee but offers a number of services. AmEx cardholders can cash personal checks at AmEx offices outside the U.S. and use Global Assist, a 24-hour hotline with medical and legal assistance (tel. (800) 554-2639 in U.S. and Canada; from abroad call U.S. collect (202) 554-2639). Cardholder benefits include airline, hotel, and car reservations, baggage loss and flight insurance, and mailgrams and cables. Amex can also hold your mail at one of the more than 1700 AmEx offices around the world.

ATM Alert!

All automatic teller machines require a four-digit **Personal Identification Number (PIN),** which credit cards in the United States do not always carry. You must ask your credit card company to assign you one before you leave. Without this PIN, you will be unable to withdraw cash with your credit card abroad. There are no letters on the keypads of most European bank machines, but the correspondence is the same as on telephones: ABC correspond to 2; DEF to 3; GHI to 4; JKL to 5; MNO to 6; PRS to 7; TUV to 8; and WXY to 9. If you mistakenly punch the wrong code into a Parisian ATM three times, the ATM will, for security reasons, eat your card. If you **lose your card** in Paris, call for help at the following numbers, all of which have English-speaking operators: **Mastercard** (tel. 08 00 90 13 87); **Visa** (tel. 08 00 90 20 33); **American Express** (tel. 01 47 77 72 00).

CASH CARDS

Automatic Teller Machines (ATMs) are everywhere in Paris. Depending on your home bank, you will probably be able to access your home account abroad. ATMs get the wholesale exchange rate, which is 5% better than the retail rate at banks and *bureaux de change.* Withdraw large amounts: for each withdrawal you make, your bank will charge a stiff fee (US$5). Keep your receipts—if an ATM gives you no cash, it may register a withdrawal on your next statement. As with credit cards in France, ATM's require a four-digit **Personal Identification Number (PIN).** A word of caution: there are no letters on the Parisian ATM keypads and if you punch the wrong code, the ATM will eat your card (see **ATM Alert!**).

In the U.S., call the **Cirrus** network (tel. (800) 4-CIRRUS (424-7787)) for a list of their international ATMs. In Paris, **Crédit Mutuel's Minibanque/24** and **Crédit Agricole** teller machines are on Cirrus. Consult Crédit Agricole's brochure *Rencontrez un specialiste* for an extensive list of ATM locations or look for one of the following:

ATMs: The following are on the **Cirrus** network: 5, rue de la Feuillade, 1er (M: Bastille); 8, rue St-Antoine, 4ème (M: Bastille); corner of rue Monge and rue des Bernardins, 5ème (M: Maubert-Mutualité); 22, rue de Sèvres at Le Bon Marché, 7ème (M: Sèvres-Babylone, open during store hours); 7, bd. Malesherbes, 8ème (M: Madeleine); 26, rue de Naples, 8ème (M: Europe); 35bis, rue de Provence, 9ème (M: Le Peletier); 94-96 bd. Magenta, 10ème (M: Gare du Nord); rue Montreuil, 11ème; 82, bd. Soult, 12ème (M: Porte Dorée); 53, av. des Gobelins, 13ème (M: Gobelins); 58, rue St-Charles, 15ème (M: Dupleix); 2, rue de l'Arrivée, 15ème (M: Montparnasse-Bienvenue); 28, rue d'Auteuil, 16ème (M: Église d'Auteuil); 30, av. Niel, 17ème (M: Pereire-Levallois); 13, rue des Abbesses, 18ème (M: Abbesses); 7, pl. des Fêtes, 19ème (M: pl. des Fêtes); 167-171, av. Gambetta, 20ème (M: Porte des Lilas).

ESSENTIALS

The **PLUS** system (U.S. tel. (800) 843-7587) works in most Visa ATMs. Institutions supporting PLUS are: **Crédit Commercial de France, Banque Populaire, Union de Banque à Paris, Point Argent, Banque Nationale de Paris, Crédit du Nord, Gie Osiris,** and ATMs in many **post offices.**

Visa Travel Money is a system by which you pay a bank a sum of money and receive in return a cash card with that amount pre-coded onto it. You choose a PIN code when you buy the card and can call a 24-hour assistance line if it is lost or stolen. You'll pay roughly a 2% commission, but your card works in Visa ATMs with no fee. In the U.S. call (800) 847-2399; elsewhere call U.S. collect (410) 581-9091.

GETTING MONEY FROM HOME

One of the easiest ways to get money from home is to bring an **American Express** card. AmEx allows its cardholders to draw cash from their checking accounts at any of its offices or affiliates, up to US$1000 every 21 days. AmEx also offers Express Cash, with over 100,000 ATMs in airports, hotels, banks, office complexes, and shopping areas worldwide. Express Cash withdrawals are automatically debited from the cardmember's checking account or line of credit. Green card holders may withdraw up to US$1000 in a seven day period. 2% transaction fee applies for cash withdrawals, with a US$2.50 minimum/$20 maximum. To enroll in Express Cash, Cardmembers may call (800) CASH NOW (227-4669). Outside the U.S. call collect (336) 668 5041.

Money can also be wired abroad through **Western Union** (tel. (800) 325-6000). In the U.S., call (800) CALL-CASH (225-5227) to cable money with your Visa, Discover, or MasterCard. The rates for sending cash are generally US$10-11 cheaper than with a credit card, and the money is usually available within an hour.

In emergencies, U.S. citizens can have money sent via the State Deptartment's **Overseas American Citizens Services,** Consular Affairs, Room 4811, U.S. Dept. of State, Washington, D.C. 20520 (tel. (202) 647-5225; nights, Sundays, and holidays (202) 647-4000; fax (202) 647-3000; email ca@his.com; http://travel.state.gov). For a fee of US$15, the State Department will forward money within hours to the nearest consular office. The office serves only Americans in the direst of straits; non-Americans should contact their embassies for information on wiring cash. Check with the State Department or the nearest U.S. embassy or consulate.

OPENING A BANK ACCOUNT

If you are planning a long-term stay in Paris and have a permanent address, you can open an account at any convenient financial institution and obtain an ATM card drawn on your French account. Most foreign banks can wire money to French accounts (for US$30-40 per transfer). Required minimum balances vary but are usually not steep for residents. Non-resident bank accounts require a hefty opening deposit and a high minimum balance (30,000F). Banks' main offices (often located near the Opéra) have foreign affairs departments that deal with such issues.

VALUE-ADDED TAX

The **VAT** (TVA in France) is a varying sales tax levied in the European Union. The French rate is 18.6% on all goods except books, food, and medicine. Luxury items such as video cassettes, watches, jewelry, and cameras are taxed at 33%. If you spend more than 2000F (4200F for EU members) in a particular store, you can participate in a complex, over-the-counter export program for foreign shoppers that exempts you from paying TVA. Ask the store for a *formulaire de détaxe pour l'exportation* (detax invoice) and a stamped envelope. At the border, show the invoices and your purchases to the French customs officials, who will stamp the invoices. If you're at an airport, look for the window labeled *douane de détaxe,* and be sure to budget at least an hour for your encounter with the French bureaucracy. On a train, find an official or get off at a station close to the border. Then send a copy back to the vendor. With this official TVA-exempt proof, they will refund the agreed amount. The refunds are sent to your bank account, a process that may take as long as six months.

TIPPING AND GRATUITY

Service is almost always included at meals in restaurants and cafés; look for the phrase *service compris* on the menu or just ask. If service is not included, tip 15-20%. Even when service is included, it is polite to leave extra *monnaie* (change) at a café, bistro, restaurant, or bar—one franc for a glass of wine, several francs for a meal. Similarly, you should tip hairdressers and cabbies 15%; theater ushers 2F; museum and tour guides 5-10F; bellhops 15F; chambermaids 20F per day.

■ Safety and Security

PERSONAL SAFETY

Self-preservation, as Jean-Jacques Rousseau once argued, is essential to life. Personal safety should be every traveler's first priority. Protecting your belongings should always comes second. While Paris is a relatively safe city, tourists are vulnerable to crime because they carry large amounts of cash and are not as street savvy as locals. To prevent theft, don't keep all of your valuables in one place. Try to avoid unwanted attention. The gawking tourist is a more obvious target than the low-profile traveler. Familiarize yourself with your surroundings before setting out and carry yourself with confidence. If you must check a map on the streets, duck into a café or shop.

As in many large cities, certain areas of Paris can be rough at night, including *Les Halles* and the *Bastille* area. Travelers should not walk around Pigalle, Barbès-Rochechouart, Montmartre, or Belleville alone at night. In general, the northern and eastern arrondissements are less safe than the southern and western ones. Find out about other unsafe areas from the tourist office or the manager of your hotel or hostel. Memorize Paris's emergency numbers (see **Emergency Help,** p. 42). If you are travelling alone, be sure that someone at home knows your itinerary and **never admit that you're traveling alone.** When walking at night, stick to busy, well-lit streets and avoid dark alleyways, parks, parking lots, and deserted areas. Whenever possible, *Let's Go* warns of unsafe neighborhoods, but you should exercise your own judgment.

If you are using a **car,** learn local driving signals, wear a seatbelt, drive slower and more cautiously than you would at home, and park your vehicle in a garage or well-lit area. Children under 40lb. should ride only in carseats, available from most car rental agencies. **Sleeping in your car** is illegal and dangerous. If your car breaks down, wait for the police to assist you. **Let's Go does not recommend hitchhiking** under any circumstances (see **Getting There,** below). There is no sure-fire set of precautions that will protect you from all of the situations you might encounter when you travel. A good self-defense course will give you more concrete ways to react to different types of aggression. **Impact, Prepare,** and **Model Mugging** can refer you to local women's and men's self-defense courses in the U.S. (tel. (800) 345-KICK) and in Canada (tel. (604) 878-3838). Workshop and course prices range from US$50-500.

The **Australian Department of Foreign Affairs and Trade** (tel. (2) 6261 9111) offers travel safety advisories at their website (http://www.dfat.gov.au). The **Canadian Department of Foreign Affairs and International Trade** (DFAIT; tel. (613) 944-6788 or (800) 267-8376) provides advisories and travel warnings at its website (http://www.dfait-maeci.gc.ca). Official warnings from the **United Kingdom Foreign and Commonwealth Office** (tel. (0171) 238-4503) are on-line at http://www.fco.gov.uk. For official travel advisories from the **United States Department of State** (tel. (202) 647-5225), check their website (http://travel.state.gov).

FINANCIAL SECURITY

Beware **con artists** and hustlers: they work in groups and use a wide range of predatory techniques: sob stories that require money, schemes too good to be true, diversions that distract you from pickpockets. **Don't put a wallet with money in your back pocket.** Never count your money in public. If you carry a purse, buy a sturdy one with a secure clasp, and carry it crosswise on the side. Secure packs with small combination locks. A **money belt** or **neck pouch** is the best way to carry cash; you can buy one at camping supply stores or budget travel offices. Even if worn on your stomach, fanny-packs will make your valuables highly visible and easy to steal.

In crowds, on buses, and on the metro, beware **pick-pockets,** especially during crowded rush hours. In public telephone booths, avoid saying your calling-card number out loud and when you punch it in, make sure no one can look over your shoulder. **Photocopies** of important documents allow you to recover them in case they are lost or filched. Carry one copy separate from the documents and leave another copy at home. Keep some money separate from the rest to use in an emergency. Label your luggage inside and out. Never leave your belongings unattended.

Travel Assistance International by Worldwide Assistance Services, Inc., 1133 15th St. NW, Suite 400, Washington, D.C. 20005-2710 (tel. (202) 828-5894; email wassist@aol.com); http://www.worldwide-assistance.com) provides a 24-hour hotline for travel emergencies (tel. (800) 821-2828). The **American Society of Travel Agents** (http://www.astanet.com) publishes *Travel Safety.* Send a self-addressed, stamped envelope to 1101 King St., Suite 200, Alexandria, VA 22314.

DRUGS

Two words: *Midnight Express.* Possession of drugs in France can end your vacation abruptly; convicted offenders can expect a jail sentence and fines. Never bring any illegal drugs across a border. Prescription drugs, particularly insulin, syringes, or narcotics, should be accompanied by a statement from a doctor and left in original labeled containers. Bring a copy of your prescription with you. In France, police may stop and search anyone on the street. It is not unknown for a pusher to increase profits by selling drugs to a tourist and then turning that person in for a reward. If you are arrested, your country's consulate can visit you, provide a list of attorneys, and inform family and friends, but they cannot get you out of jail. If you become involved in illegal drug trafficking, you're on your own. Write the Bureau of Consular Affairs, Public Affairs #6831, Dept. of State, Washington, D.C. 20520 (tel. (202) 647-1488) for more information and the pamphlet *Travel Warning on Drugs Abroad.*

■ Health

> For emergency health information, see **Emergency Health and Help,** below.

All food, including seafood, dairy, produce, and water, is normally safe in Paris. Although no immunizations are necessary for travel to France, be sure that your **inoculations** are up-to-date. Typhoid shots are good for three years, tetanus for 10. Always travel with any **medication** you may need on the road, and be sure to keep it in your carry-on luggage. Allergy sufferers should bring supplies of their preferred medications. Carry up-to-date prescriptions and/or a statement (with a translated version) from your doctor, especially if you use insulin, syringes, or narcotic drugs. If you wear glasses or contact lenses, carry an extra prescription and pair of glasses or arrange to have your doctor or a family member send a replacement pair in an emergency. In your passport, write the names of any people you wish to be contacted in case of a medical emergency, and also list any allergies or medical conditions of which you would want doctors to be aware.

Those with medical conditions (e.g. diabetes, allergies to antibiotics, epilepsy, heart conditions) may want to obtain a stainless steel **Medic Alert** identification tag (US$35 the first year, and $15 annually thereafter), which identifies the disease and gives a 24-hour collect-call information number. Contact Medic Alert, 2323 Colorado Ave., Turlock, CA 95382 (tel. (800) 825-3785). Diabetics can contact the **American Diabetes Association,** 1660 Duke St., Alexandria, VA 22314 (tel. (800) 232-3472) to receive *Travel and Diabetes* and a diabetic ID card, which carries messages in 18 languages explaining the carrier's diabetic status. **Global Emergency Medical Services (GEMS),** 2001 Westside Dr., #120, Alpharetta, GA 30201 USA (tel. (800) 860-1111, fax (770) 475-0058) provides 24-hour international medical assistance. The **International Association for Medical Assistance to Travelers (IAMAT)** offers a directory of English-speaking doctors worldwide. Contact chapters in **Canada,** 1287 St. Clair Ave. W, Toronto, M6E 1B8 (tel. (416) 652-0137), **New Zealand,** P.O. Box 5049, Christchurch 5, and the **U.S.,** 417 Center St., Lewiston, NY 14092 (tel. (716) 754-4883; email iamat@sentex.net; http://www.sentex.net/iamat).

AIDS, HIV, STDS

The World Health Organization estimates that there are around 13 million people worldwide infected with HIV, the virus that causes **AIDS (Acquired Immune Deficiency Syndrome).** While gay men, IV drug users, and hemophiliacs have been particularly hard-hit by AIDS, well over 90% of HIV-positive adults were infected through heterosexual sex, and women now represent 50% of all new HIV infections. Since 1993, AIDS (**le sida** in French) has been the second-largest killer (after car accidents) of Parisian men 24-44 years old.

The HIV virus is transmitted through direct blood-to-blood contact with an HIV+ person or HIV-infected blood products and through unprotected vaginal and anal intercourse. The risks of oral sex are a point of much controversy, but oral contact seems to nevertheless pose some risk of infection. Health professionals recommend the use of latex condoms with a water-based spermicidal lubricant. Never share intravenous drug, tattooing, or other needles. For more information on HIV, AIDS, and Safer Sex, call the **U.S. Center for Disease Control's** 24-hour Hotline at (800) 342-2437 or write the **Bureau of Consular Affairs,** #6831, Dept. of State, Washington, D.C. 20520, for their brochure, *Travel Safe: AIDS and International Travel.* In Europe, contact the **World Health Organization's** Global Program on AIDS, 20 Avenue Appia, 1211 Geneva 27, Switzerland (tel. (22) 791-2111) for more information. **Sexually transmitted diseases (STDs)** such as gonorrhea, chlamydia, genital warts, syphilis, and herpes are a lot easier to catch and are far more common than HIV. Swelling, sores, bumps, or blisters on the sex organs, rectum, or mouth are typical warning signs. Condoms may protect you from certain STDs, but oral or even tactile contact can lead to transmission.

BIRTH CONTROL AND ABORTION

Contraception is readily available in most pharmacies. To obtain **condoms** in France, visit a pharmacy and tell the clerk, *"Je voudrais une boîte de préservatifs"* (zhuh-voo-DRAY oon BWAHT duh PREY-zehr-va-TEEF). The French branch of the International Planned Parenthood Federation, the **Mouvement Français pour le Planning Familiale** (MFPF; tel. 01 42 60 93 20), can provide more information.

Abortion is legal in France, where the abortion pill, RU-486, was pioneered. For referrals on international reproductive health and abortion services, call the **Women's Health Coalition** (tel. (212) 979-8500) in New York or the **International Planned Parenthood Federation,** European Regional Office, Regent's College Inner Circle, Regent's Park, London NW1 4NS (tel. (0171) 487 7900; fax 487 7950).

No Préservatifs Added

Having invented the French kiss and the French tickler, the speakers of the language of love have long had *savoir faire* in all things sexual—safety included. In the age of responsibility, French pharmacies (you know, those flashing green crosses) provide 24-hour condom dispensers. In typical French style, they unabashedly adorn public streets on the sides of buildings. But when dining out, don't ask for foods without *préservatifs* or mistake your raspberry compote for a *capote.* Funny looks will greet you as listeners wonder what condoms would be doing in a baguette or on your morning croissant.

■ Emergency Health and Help

Ambulance (SAMU): tel. 15. Outside of Paris, call 01 45 67 50 50.

Fire: tel. 18. Firefighters are called *les Pompiers* in French. A fire is *un feu*.

Police: tel. 17. For emergencies only. Each arrondissement also has its own *gendarmerie* (police force) to which you should take your non-emergency concerns.

Poison: tel. 01 40 37 04 04. In French, but some English assistance is available.

Rape: SOS Viol (tel. 0 800 05 95 95). Call from anywhere in France for counseling, medical and legal advice, emotional support, and referrals. Open M-F 10am-6pm.

Hospitals: Hospitals in Paris are numerous and efficient. They will generally treat you whether or not you can pay in advance. Settle with them afterward and don't let financial concerns interfere with your health care. Unless your French is exceptionally good, you'll have the best luck at one of the anglophone hospitals. **Hôpital Franco-Britannique de Paris,** 3, rue Barbès, in the Parisian suburb of Levallois-Perret (tel. 01 46 39 22 22). M: Anatole-France. Considered a French hospital. Has some English-speakers and a good reputation. **Hôpital Américain de Paris,** 63, bd. Victor Hugo, Neuilly (tel. 01 46 41 25 25). M: Port Maillot, then bus #82 to the end of the line. In a suburb of Paris. Employs English-speaking personnel, but much more expensive than French hospitals. You can change U.S. dollars at the in-hospital *bureau de change*. If you have Blue Cross, your hospitalization is covered as long as you fill out the appropriate forms first, though every case is unique and depends on your type of coverage. They also can direct you to the nearest English-speaking doctor and provide dental services.

Pharmacies: Pharmacie des Halles, 10, bd. de Sébastopol, 1er (tel. 01 42 72 03 23). M: Châtelet. Open M-Sa 9am-midnight, Su noon-midnight. **Pharmacie Dhéry,** in the Galerie des Champs, 84, av. des Champs-Elysées, 8ème (tel. 01 45 62 02 41). M: George V. Open 24hr. **Grande Pharmacie Daumesnil,** 6, pl. Félix-Eboué, 12ème (tel. 01 43 43 19 03). M: Daumesnil. Visible as you exit the metro. Open 24hr. **Pharmacie Européenne,** 6, pl. de Clichy, 9ème (tel. 01 48 74 65 18). M: Place de Clichy. Open 24hr. **Pharmacie Opéra Capucines,** 6, bd. des Capucines, 9ème (tel. 01 42 65 88 29). M: Opéra. Open M-Sa 8am-12:30am, Su 10pm-12:30am. AmEx, MC, V. Every arrondissement should have a **pharmacie de garde** (pharmacy on call), which will open in case of emergencies. The locations change, but the name of the nearest one is posted on each pharmacy's door.

AIDS: AIDES, 247, rue de Belleville, 19ème (tel. 01 44 52 00 00). One of the oldest and most prolific AIDS public service organizations in France, AIDES runs a 24hr. hotline with info in French and English (tel. 0 800 840 800). The **Free Anglo-American Counseling Treatment and Support (FAACTS)** hotline (tel. 01 44 93 16 69) at the American Church also provides HIV support M, W, and F 6-10pm.

HIV: 43, rue de Valois, 1er (tel. 01 42 61 30 04). M: Palais-Royal or Bourse. Testing and treatment for STDs. Free consultations. Syphilis tests (free), plasma and chlamydia tests (300F), and free and anonymous HIV testing includes mandatory counseling. Call for appointments. English-speaking doctors available. Open M-F 9am-7pm. HIV testing also available at 218, rue de Belleville, 20ème (tel. 01 47 97 40 49). M: Télégraphe. Also at 3-5, rue de Ridder, 14ème (tel. 01 45 43 83 78; M: Plaisance; open M-F noon-6:30pm, Sa 9:30am-noon). Mandatory counseling, some English spoken. Results in 1 week. Free and anonymous.

Alcoholics Anonymous: 3, rue Frédéric Sauton, 5ème (tel. 01 46 34 59 65). M: Maubert-Mutualité. A recorded message in English will refer you to several numbers you can call to talk to telephone counselors. Daily meetings. Open 24hr.

Birth Control: Mouvement Français pour le Planning Familial, 10, rue Vivienne, 2ème (tel. 01 42 60 93 20). M: Bourse. Open M-F 9:30am-5:30pm. Call-in hours; walk-in services available too; call for info. Resources for info on birth control, pregnancy, abortion, STD prevention, domestic violence, and incest.

Drug Problems: Hôpital Marmottan, 17-19, rue d'Armaillé, 17ème (tel. 01 45 74 00 04). M: Charles de Gaulle Étoile. Not an emergency service. For consultation or treatment, open Sept.-July M, W-Th, and Sa noon-7pm, F 10am-7pm; Aug. M-F only.

Emotional Health: Services and aid are provided by a number of organizations. Try calling **SOS Crisis Help Line: Friendship** (tel. 01 47 23 80 80). English-speaking. Support and information for the depressed and lonely. Open daily 3-11pm. For personalized crisis-control and counseling (for anything from pregnancy to homesickness), the American Church (see **English-Language Religious Services,** p. 74) offers the **International Counseling Service (ICS)** (tel. 01 45 50 26 49), which provides access to psychologists, psychiatrists, social workers, and a clerical counselor. First consultation is free; payment thereafter is negotiable. Open M-Sa 9:30am-5pm. The office is staffed irregularly July-Aug. but will respond if you leave a message on its answering machine. Call for an appointment.

Insurance

Travel insurance covers four basic areas: medical problems, property loss, trip cancellation, and emergency evacuation. Beware of buying unnecessary coverage—your regular insurance policies may extend to travel-related medical problems and property loss. **Medical insurance** often covers costs incurred abroad; check with your provider. Your (family's) **homeowners' insurance** often covers theft during travel. Homeowners are generally covered against loss of travel documents (passport, plane ticket, railpass, etc.) up to US$500, but contact your provider for more information.

ISIC and **ITIC** provide basic insurance benefits, including US$100 per day of in-hospital sickness for a maximum of 60 days, and US$3000 of accident-related medical reimbursement (see **Youth, Student, and Teacher Identification,** p. 32). Cardholders have access to a toll-free 24-hour helpline whose multilingual staff can provide assistance in medical, legal, and financial emergencies overseas (tel. (800) 626-2427 in the U.S. and Canada; elsewhere call the U.S. collect (713) 267-2525). Most **American Express** (tel. (800) 528-4800) cardholders receive automatic car rental insurance (collision and theft, but not liability) and ground travel accident coverage of US$100,000 on flight purchases made with the card. **Council** offers the inexpensive Trip-Safe plan with options covering medical treatment, hospitalization, accidents, and baggage loss; **STA** offers a more expensive but comprehensive plan. Insurance companies usually require a copy of the police report for thefts, or evidence of having paid medical expenses (doctor's statements, receipts) before they will honor a claim. Always carry policy numbers and proof of insurance. Check with each insurance carrier for specific restrictions and policies.

Avi International, 90, Rue de la Victoire, 75009 Paris, France (tel. 01 44 63 51 07; fax 01 40 82 90 35). Caters primarily to the international youth traveler, covering emergency expenses, medical/accident, dental, and baggage loss. 24hr. hotline.

Travel Guard International, 1145 Clark St., Stevens Point, WI 54481 (tel. (800) 826-1300 or (715) 345-0505; fax (715) 345-0525). Comprehensive insurance programs starting at US$44. Programs cover cancellation, lost luggage, medical coverage, emergency assistance, and accidental death. 24hr. hotline.

Campus Travel, 105/106 St. Aldates, Oxford OXI IDD (tel. (01865) 258 000; fax 792-378). Available to travelers under 35 or with ISIC cards only. Offers packages that cover medical, property, cancellation, and liability costs. 24hr. hotline.

Globalcare Travel Insurance, 220 Broadway, Lynnfield, MA 01940 (tel. (800) 821-2488; fax (617) 592-7720; email global@nebc.mv.com; http://www.nebc.mv.com/globalcare. Complete medical, legal, emergency, trip cancellation, and travel-related services. GTI waives pre-existing medical conditions, and provides coverage for the bankruptcy of cruise lines, airlines, or tour operators.

Alternatives to Tourism

STUDY

If you choose your program well, study in Paris can be one of the most exciting experiences you'll ever have. Research your options carefully, as programs vary in expense, quality, living conditions, and exposure to French culture and language. French educational terminology and equivalencies are radically different from almost anywhere else. For pamphlets on various fields of study in France, contact the **Cultural Services of the French Embassy** (see **French Government Information**

Offices, p. 25). Many American undergraduates enroll in programs sponsored by U.S. universities, and most colleges offer info on study abroad. **Council** sponsors over 40 programs around the world (see **Student and Budget Travel Agencies,** p. 55). See **French Universities,** p. 45, for info on enrolling yourself in the Université de Paris. ·

General Programs and Resources

American Field Service (AFS), 310 SW 4th Avenue, Suite 630, Portland, OR 97204-2608 (tel. (800) 237-4636; fax (503) 241-1653; email afsinfo@afs.org; http://www.afs.org/usa). Offers summer, semester, and year-long homestay exchange programs for high school students. Financial aid available.

American Institute for Foreign Study (AIFS), College Division, 102 Greenwich Ave., Greenwich, CT 06830 (tel. (800) 727-2437 ext. 6084; http://www.aifs.com). Organizes semester and year-long programs for high school and college study in French universities. Scholarships available. Contact http://www.ygarcia@aifs.com.

College Semester Abroad, School for International Training, Admissions, Kipling Rd., P.O. Box 676, Brattleboro, VT 05302 (tel. (800) 336-1616 or 258-3267; fax 258-3500). Runs semester and year-long programs (US$8200-10,300). Financial aid.

Institute of International Education (IIE), 809 United Nations Plaza, New York, NY 10017-3580 (tel. (212) 984-5413; fax 984-5358; email iie-boks@iie.org). Nonprofit international and cultural exchange agency. Publishes *Academic Year Abroad* (US$43) and *Vacation Study Abroad* (US$37). Write for a list of publications.

International Schools Services, Educational Staffing Program, P.O. Box 5910, Princeton, NJ 08543 (tel. (609) 452-0990; fax 452-2690; email edustaffing@iss.edu; http://www.iss.edu). Recruits teachers with bachelor's degree and two years experience for instruction in English abroad. Nonrefundable US$100 application fee. Publishes *The ISS Directory of Overseas Schools* (US$35).

Language Schools

French universities, international organizations, and local schools all offer programs and cater to everyone from the barely conversant to the expert speaker. The tourist office in Paris has a list of nearly 15 schools approved by them. Speaking with former participants (a good school will gladly give you names) may help you find a good fit.

Alliance Française, École Internationale de Langue et de Civilisation Françaises, 101, bd. Raspail, 6ème, Paris or 75270 Paris Cedex 06 (tel. 01 45 44 38 28; fax 01 45 44 89 42; email afparis_ecole@compuserve; http://www.paris.alliancefrancaise.fr). M: Nôtre-Dame-des-Champs. French language courses (US $225). MC, V.

Cours de Civilisation Française de la Sorbonne, 47, rue des Écoles, 75005 Paris (tel. 01 40 46 22 11; fax 01 40 46 32 29). M: Odéon or St-Michel. Since 1919, this program has offered semester, year-long, and summer programs with lectures and language classes at all levels. **AIFS** (see above) arranges housing and meals.

Eurocentres, 13, passage Dauphine, 75006 (tel. 01 40 46 72 00; fax 01 40 46 72 06; email par-info@eurocentres.com; http://www.eurocentres.com). M: Odéon. Language and teacher refresher courses (US$500-5000). Open M-F 8:30am-6pm.

Institut de Langue Française, 3, ave. Bertie Albrecht, 8ème (tel. 01 45 63 24 00; fax 01 45 63 07 09; http://www.instlanguefr.com). M: Charles de Gaulle Étoile. Language, civilization, and literature courses (from US$210). Cash only.

Institut Parisien de Langue et de Civilisation Française, 87, bd. de Grenelle, 15ème (tel. 01 40 56 09 53; fax 01 43 06 46 30; email institut.parisien@dial.oleane.com). M: LaMotte-Picquet-Grenelle. French language, fashion, culinary arts, and cinema courses (from US$630).

French Universities

If your French is already fluent, direct enrollment in a French university can be more rewarding than a class filled with Americans. It can also be up to four times cheaper, although you may not receive academic credit at home. After 1968, the **Université de Paris** split into 10 independent universities, each at a different site and offering a different programs. The Sorbonne, now the Université de Paris IV, devotes itself to the humanities. French universities requires at least a *baccalauréat* degree or its equivalent (British A-levels or 2 years of college in the U.S.) for admission. Contact the cultural services office at the nearest French consulate. As a student at a French university, you will receive a student card *(carte d'étudiant)* upon presentation of your residency permit and a receipt for your university fees. In addition to standard student benefits, many additional benefits are administered by the **Centre Régional des Oeuvres Universitaires et Scolaires** (**CROUS**; see **Budget Travel Offices,** p. 71). Founded in 1955 to improve the living and working conditions of students, CROUS welcomes foreign students and can help answer your questions. The brochure *Le CROUS et Moi* lists addresses and info on student life. Pick up their guidebook *Je vais en France* (free), in French or English, from any French embassy.

WORK

To work in France, you need both a **work permit** and a **work visa.** With the exception of au pair jobs, it is illegal for foreign students to hold full-time jobs during the school year. Citizens of the European Union can work in any EU country. Students can check with their university's French language department, which may have connections to jobs abroad. Call the consulate for information about work permits. Students registered at a French university may get work permits for the summer with a valid visa, a *carte étudiant,* and proof of a job. After an academic year in France, Americans with a student *carte de séjour* can find part-time work if they will be enrolled at a French university in the fall. Check the French embassy's *Employment in France for Students* (see **French Government Information Offices,** p. 25). If you are a **U.S. citizen** or permanent resident and a full-time student at a U.S. university, **Council Travel** (see **Student and Budget Travel Agencies,** p. 55) can procure 3- to 6-month work permits for France (US$225).

Finding a Job

The internet is an excellent place to look for job listings before and after you arrive in Paris (see **Internet Resources,** p. 74). Once in Paris, start your job search at the **American Church** (see **English Language Religious Services,** p. 74), which posts a bulletin board full of job and housing opportunities targeting Americans and anglophiles (open M-Sa 9am-10pm). The jobs listed here tend to be of the babysitting and housekeeping variety. Those with ambition and an up-to-date resumé in both French and English should stop by the **American Chamber of Commerce in France,** 21, av. George V, 1st floor, 8*ème* (tel. 01 40 73 89 90; fax 01 47 20 18 62; M: George V) an association of American businesses in France. Your resumé will be kept on file for two months and placed at the disposal of French and American companies. Browse or purchase their excellent membership directory (100F, students 50F) for contacts. (Open M-F 9am-5pm. Admission 50F). The **Agence Nationale Pour l'Emploi (ANPE),** 4, impasse d'Antin, 8*ème* (tel. 01 43 59 62 63; fax 01 49 53 91 46; http://www.enpe.fr); M: Franklin D. Roosevelt has specific info on employment. Remember to bring your work permit and, if you have one, your *carte de séjour.* (Open M-W and F 9am-5pm, Th 9am-noon.) The **Chambre de Commerce et d'Industrie de Paris,** 27, ave. de Friedland, 8*ème* (tel. 01 55 65 55 65; fax 01 55 65 77 68; M: George V), provides the pamphlet *Foreigners: Starting Up Your Company in France* (48F). Their library at 16, rue Chateaubriand, is also a good resource. (Open M-F 9am-6pm. Admission 30F.) The **Centre d'Information et de Documentation Jeunesse (CIDJ),** 101, quai Branly, 15*ème* (tel. 01 44 49 12 00; fax 01 40 65 02 61; RER: Champ de Mars/Tour Eiffel), an invaluable state-run youth center provides info on education, resumés, employment, and careers. English spoken. Jobs are posted at 9am on the bulletin boards outside. (Open M-Sa 10am-6pm.) Also check help-wanted columns in *Le Monde, Le Figaro,* the *International Herald Tribune,* and *France-USA Contacts* (see **Publications about Paris,** p. 75).

Teaching English

Post a sign in markets and schools stating that you are a native speaker, and scan the classifieds of local newspapers, where residents sometimes advertise for language instruction. Securing a position will require patience and legwork; teaching English is popular and competitive. Because of the high supply, visitors shouldn't expect to support themselves on teaching alone. Professional English-teaching positions are harder to get; most European schools require a bachelor's degree and experience.

International Schools Services, P.O. Box 5910, Princeton, NJ 08543 (tel. (609) 452-0990). The Educational Staffing Dept. coordinates teacher placement and publishes *Your Passport to Teaching and Administrative Opportunities Abroad.* The *ISS Directory of Overseas Schools* (US$36) is also helpful.

Office of Overseas Schools, A/OS Room 245, SA-29, Dept. of State, Washington, D.C. 20522-2902 (tel. (703) 875-7800; http://www.state.gov/www/about_state/schools/). Keeps a list of schools abroad and teacher-placement agencies.

Au Pair Positions

Primarily for single women, 18-30 years old with some knowledge of French, the au pair cares for children and does light housework for a French family while taking courses at a French school or university. Talking with children can be a great way to improve your French, but looking after them can be strenuous. Know in advance what the family expects of you. Expect to receive room, board, and a small stipend. Au pair jobs (usually 6-18 months) can be arranged through individual connections, but make sure you have a contract detailing hours per week, salary, and accommodations. Check with the French Embassy (see **French Government Information Offices,** p. 25), AIFS (see **Study,** p. 43), and the following organizations for more info.

L'Accueil Familial des Jeunes Étrangers, 23, rue du Cherche-Midi, 6ème Paris (tel. 01 42 22 50 34; fax 01 45 44 60 48). M: Sèvres-Babylone. Arranges summer and 6-10 month au pair jobs (650-700F placement fee) and will help you switch families if you are unhappy. They can also find you a room in exchange for 12hr. of work per week, or room and board for 18hr. of work (you must have a student visa).

Childcare International, Trafalgar House, Grenville Pl., London NW7 3SA (tel. (0181) 959 36 11 or 906 31 16; fax 906 34 61; email office@childint.demon.co.uk; http://www.childint.demon.co.uk). Offers long-term and summer au pair positions in France. UK£80 application fee.

InterExchange, 161 Sixth Ave., New York, NY 10013 (tel. (212) 924-0446; fax 924-0575; email interex@earthlink.net; http://www.interexchange.org), offers 2-18 month au pair and teaching opportunities. US$250-450 placement fee.

VOLUNTEERING

Volunteering can provide an opportunity to meet people and to receive free room and board. International firms, museums, art galleries, and non-profit organizations like UNESCO may have unpaid internships available.

Council Voluntary Services, 205 E. 42nd St., New York, NY 10017 (tel. (888) 268-6245; fax (212) 822-2699; email info@ciee.org; http://www.ciee.org). Offers 2-4 week community services projects. Min. age 18. US$295 placement fee.

REMPART, 1, rue des Guillemites, 4ème Paris (tel. 01 42 71 96 55; fax 01 42 71 73 00). Offers summer and year-long programs geared toward protecting the French heritage. Restores churches, monuments, and the environment. Anyone 15 or over is eligible. Programs cost 40-50F per day, plus a 220F insurance fee.

Club du Vieux Manoir, 10, rue de la Cossonnerie, 75001 Paris (tel. 01 45 08 80 40). Offers summer and year-long programs restoring castles and churches. Anyone 15 or over is eligible. Application fee 90F.

■ Specific Concerns

WOMEN TRAVELERS

While Paris is the birthplace of Simone de Beauvoir, Hélène Cixous, and the feminist movement that they pioneered, women should exercise caution, maintain a confident gait, and avoid direct eye contact with intimidating men. Parisian women often respond to verbal harassment with an icy stare, but you should do your best to avoid conflict. Don't hesitate to seek out a police officer or passerby or scream for help ("*Au secours,*" oh suh-KOOR). Otherwise let common sense prevail: stick to centrally located accommodations, avoid late-night metro rides alone (see **Personal Safety,** p. 34, for danger spots), ask women or couples for directions or aid, and carry a *télécarte* and extra money for a taxi. The following may also be helpful:

National Organization for Women (NOW), 105 E. 22nd St., Suite 307, New York, NY 10010 (tel. (212) 260-4422; email sfnow@sirius.com; http://www.sirius.com/ ~sfnow/now.html), provides lists of women's events worldwide and can refer women travelers to counseling services and crisis centers abroad.

Women's Travel in Your Pocket, Ferrari Guides, P.O. Box 37887, Phoenix, AZ 85069 (tel. (602) 863-2408; email ferrari@q-net.com; http://www.q-net.com). An annual guide for women traveling worldwide. Hotels, night life, dining, organizations, tours, cruises, outdoors, and lesbian events (US$14, plus shipping).

Women Travel: Adventures, Advice & Experience, by Miranda Davies and Natania Jansz (Penguin, US$13). Essays by women travelers in several foreign countries plus a decent bibliography and resource index. The sequel, **More Women Travel,** costs US$16.50. Both from Rough Guides, 345 Hudson St., 14th fl., New York, NY.

Handbook For Women Travellers, by Maggie and Gemma Moss (UK£9). Encyclopedic and well written. Available from Piatkus Books, 5 Windmill St., London W1P 1HF (tel. (0171) 631 07 10).

In Paris, the following women's centers can provide information on events, counselling, women's health, and birth control. Note you need a prescription from a *gynocologue* or a *généraliste* for both the pill and the morning-after pill (RU-486). Consult the groups below for a referral (also see **Health: Birth Control and Abortion,** p. 41).

Maison des Femmes, 163, rue de Charenton, 12ème (tel. 01 43 43 41 1). M: Gare de Lyon. Offers seminars, self-defense classes, and resources for women. Carries feminist journals, *Marie pas clair* and *Paris Feministe* in the center's library, which hosts a café on Fridays (8pm-midnight). Open W and F 4-7pm and Sa 5-7pm.

Librairie des Femmes, 74, rue de Seine, 6ème (tel. 01 43 29 50 75). M: Mabillon. Run in concert with Antoinette Fouque's group *Alliance des Femmes pour la Democratie,* this famous bookshop has info on women's activities and books on women's issues. Open M-Sa 11:30am-7pm.

SOS Help (tel. 01 47 23 80 80) is an English-language hotline, offering counseling services on anything from loneliness to sexual assault. Open daily 3-11pm.

SOS Viol (tel. 0 800 05 95 95) is the national **rape hotline,** which offers counseling and assistance in French. Open daily 10am-6pm.

Centre de Planification et d'Education familiale, 27, rue Curnonsky, 17ème (tel. 01 48 88 07 28). M: Porte de Champerret. Provides free consultations in French on family planning, abortion, cervical and breast cancer, and referrals for gynecologists. You must call first for an appointment. Open M-F 9am-5:30pm.

Mouvement Français pour le Planning Familial (MFPF), 10, rue Vivienne, 2ème (tel. 01 42 60 93 20). M: Bourse. Counseling and medical evaluations in French on family planning concerns. Appointment required. Open M-F 9:30am-5pm.

OLDER TRAVELERS

Senior citizens are eligible for discounts on transportation, museums, movies, theaters, concerts, restaurants, and accommodations. If you don't see a senior citizen price, ask. Agencies for senior group travel are growing in enrollment and popularity. Try **Elder-Treks,** 597 Markham St., Toronto, Ontario, CANADA M6G 2L7 (tel. (800) 741-7956 or (416) 588-5000; fax 588-9839; passages@inforamp.net; http://www.eldertreks.com) or **Walking the World,** P.O. Box 1186, Fort Collins, CO 80522 (tel. (970) 498-0500; fax 498-9100; walktworld@aol.com), which organize trips to Europe. Also consult:

AARP (American Association of Retired Persons), 601 E St. NW, Washington, D.C. 20049 (tel. (202) 434-2277). Members 50+ receive discounts on lodging, car rental, cruises, and sight-seeing. Annual fee US$8 per couple; $20 for 3 years.

Elderhostel, 75 Federal St., 3rd Fl., Boston, MA 02110-1941 (tel. (617) 426-7788; http://www.elderhostel.org). Programs at colleges and universities for those 55+.

The Globe Piquot Press, P.O. Box 833, Old Saybrook, CT 06475-0833 (tel. (800) 243-0495; fax (800) 820-2329; email info@globe-piquot.com; http://www.globe-piquot.com). Publishes *Europe the European Way: A Traveler's Guide to Living Affordably in the World's Great Cities* (US$14), which offers general hints for the budget-conscious senior considering a long stay or retiring abroad.

Pilot Books, 127 Sterling Ave., P.O. Box 2102, Greenport, NY 11944 (tel. (516) 477-1094 or (800) 79-PILOT (797-4568); fax (516) 477-0978; email feedback@pilot-books.com; http://www.pilotbooks.com). Publishes the *Doctor's Guide to Protecting Your Health Before, During, and After International Travel* (US$10).

No Problem! Worldwise Tips for Mature Adventurers, by Janice Kenyon. Advice and info on insurance, finances, security, health, packing. Useful appendices. US$16 from Orca Book Publishers, P.O. Box 468, Custer, WA 98240-0468.

Unbelievably Good Deals and Great Adventures That You Absolutely Can't Get Unless You're Over 50, by Joan Rattner Heilman. Great tips on senior discounts. US$10 from Contemporary Books or online at http://www.amazon.com.

In Paris, most museums, concerts, and sights offer reduced prices for visitors over 60. The RATP publishes a free brochure that outlines metro and city bus service for senior travelers called *Circuler sans fatigue dans le metro et le RER;* pick one up at the main RATP office or order one by phone (53ter, quai des Grands Augustins, 6ème 75271 Paris Cédex 06; tel. 08 36 68 41 14; open M-Tu 9am-4pm, W-F 9am-5pm). Tour buses and Seine-river boat tours, such as the **Bateaux Mouches** (see **Sights Introduction,** p. 135) enable you to see a large number of sights without walking great distances. *Let's Go: Paris* tries to list at least one hotel in every arrondissement that is accessible to those with a limited mobility (see **Travelers with Disabilities,** p. 50). When booking your hotel, ask for a room on the first floor or inquire about access to the lift. We've also tried to list at least one mid-priced quality hotel in each arrondissement so you can avoid the younger, noisier crowd at the youth hostels.

For those interested in the sites and monuments of **WWII,** daytrips from Paris to Normandy and the D-Day beaches are offered by the Paris USO (tel. 01 40 70 99 68). While in Normandy, don't miss the new *Musée pour la paix (Memorial for Peace Museum)* in Caen (tel. 02 32 06 06 44; http://www.unicaen.fr/memorial; email memorial@unicaen.fr; open daily 9am-7pm). The **American Battle Monuments Commission,** 68, rue 19 Janvier, 92380 Garches (tel. 01 47 01 19 76; http://www.abnc.gov), has listings for all soldiers buried in cemeteries throughout France and Northern Europe (open M-Th 8am-noon and 1-5pm, F 8am-noon and 1-4pm).

BISEXUAL, GAY, AND LESBIAN TRAVELERS

Next to London, Amsterdam, and Berlin, Paris has one of the largest gay populations in Europe. Despite homophobia and the ravages of AIDS and breast cancer, Paris' lesbian and gay communities are vibrant, politically active, and full of opportunities for *fun.* Before you go, consult the following (see also **Women Travelers,** p. 47).

Damron Travel Guides, P.O. Box 422458, San Francisco, CA 94142-2458 (tel. (415) 255-0404 or (800) 462-6654; fax (415) 703-9049 or 703-8308; email damronco@damron.com; http://www.damron.com). Publishes the *Damron Address Book* (US$15), *Damron Road Atlas* (US$16), *The Women's Traveler* (US$13), and *Damron's Accommodations* (US$19) which list bars, restaurants, services, accommodations, and bookstores catering to gay and lesbian travelers.

Ferrari Guides, P.O. Box 37887, Phoenix, AZ 85069 (tel. (602) 863-2408; fax 439-3952; email ferrari@q-net.com; http://www.q-net.com). Publishes *Gay Travel A to Z* (US$16), *Men's Travel in Your Pocket* (US$16), *Women's Travel in Your Pocket* (US$14), and *Gay Paris* (US$17.95). Available in bookstores or by mail order.

International Gay and Lesbian Travel Association, 4331 N. Federal Hwy., Suite 304, Fort Lauderdale, FL 33308 (tel. (800) 448-8550; fax (954) 776-3303; email IGLTA@aol.com; http://www.iglta.org). Over 1350 companies serving gay and lesbian travelers worldwide. Lists travel agents, accommodations, and events.

Spartacus International Gay Guides (US$32.95), published by Bruno Gmunder, Verlag GMBH, Leuschnerdamm 31, 10999 Berlin, Germany (tel. (49) 030 615 0030; fax (49) 030 615 9007; email bgvtravel@aol.com). Lists bars, restaurants, hotels, and bookstores around the world catering to gay men.

The Gay Vacation Guide: The Best Trips and How to Plan Them, by Mark Chesnut. Provides a list of tour operators, travel companies, and gay-friendly businesses, along with advice on how to avoid problems while traveling (US$14.95). Carol Publishing, 120 Enterprise Ave., Secaucus, NJ 07094 (tel. (800) 447 2665).

In Paris, visit the gay and lesbian bookstores **Les Mots à la Bouche** and **Librairie des Femmes,** two excellent resources for travelers just arriving in the city (see **Books and Magazines,** p. 265). Consult the encyclopedic **Guide Gai** (79F, at Paris news-stands), with almost 400 pages of information in French and English about gay hotels, restaurants, nightlife, organizations, and services throughout France. The hip maga-zine **Têtu** provides smart articles on fashion, culture, events, and the latest in queer *chic.* **Le Guide Paris Soirées** (29F) offers nearly 100 pages of listings for gay, lesbian, and trans clubs, restaurants, and other establishments. For information on HIV, AIDS, and safer sex, call the 24-hour free and anonymous AIDS information hotline, **SIDA Info Service** (tel. 0 800 840 800); for AIDS info in English, call **Factsline** (tel. 01 44 93 16 69; M, W and F 6-10pm). Other Parisian organizations that may be useful include:

Centre Gai et Lesbien, 3, rue Keller, 11ème (tel. 01 43 57 21 47; fax 01 43 57 27 93). M: Ledru Rollin or Bastille. Serves as an info hub of gay services and associations in Paris. Café, library, and a monthly exhibit of gay-related art. Open daily noon-8pm.

ACT-UP PARIS, 45, rue de Sedene, 11ème (tel. 01 48 06 13 89). The Paris chapter of ACT-UP (the AIDS Coalition to Unleash Power) meets Tu 7:30pm at l'École des Beaux Arts, rue Bonaparte, 6ème, to discuss HIV, AIDS, and homophobia.

Centre du Christ Libérateur (Metropolitan Community Church), 5, rue Crussol, 11ème (tel. 01 48 05 24 48 or 01 39 83 13 44). M: Oberkampf. Founded by Pasteur Doucé, this center provides advice and counseling for gay and lesbian people.

Fréquence Gaie/Radio Orient, 98.2FM (tel. 01 40 13 88 00), a 24hr. gay and lesbian radio station providing news, music, and information in French and English.

Maison des Femmes, 163, rue de Charenton, 12ème (tel. 01 43 43 41 13). Info and cultural center for lesbians and bisexual women. Open W and F 4-7pm, Sa 5-7pm. Women's café F 8pm-midnight.

S.O.S. Homophobie (tel. 01 48 06 42 41). A hotline for gay, lesbian, and bisexual concerns. Takes calls Sept.-June M-F 8-10pm; July-Aug. Tu-F 8-10pm.

Écoute Gaie (tel. 01 44 93 01 02). A gay hotline. M-F 6-10pm.

TRAVELERS WITH DISABILITIES

Many of Paris's museums and sights are fully accessible to wheelchairs and some pro-vide guided tours in sign-language. Unfortunately, budget hotels and restaurants are generally ill-equipped to handle the needs of handicapped visitors. Handicapped-accessible bathrooms are virtually non-existent among hotels in the one-to-two star range and many hotel elevators could double as shoe-boxes. Change, however is slowly coming to Paris. The invaluable brochure *Paris-Île-de-France for Everyone* (available in English for 60F at most tourist offices) lists accessible sites, hotels, and restaurants as well as indispensable practical tips. *Let's Go: Paris* tries to list at least one wheelchair-accessible hotel in each arrondissement. Please see the index for a full list of **wheelchair-accessible hotels.** But take note that the hotels described in this book as wheelchair-accessible are those with reasonably wide (but not regulation size) elevators or with ground-floor rooms wide enough for wheelchair entry. Travel-ers are encouraged to ask restaurants, hotels, railways, and airlines if they are wheel-chair accessible: *"Êtes-vous accessibles aux fauteuils roulants?"* (ET VOO ax-es-EEB-luh OH foh-TOY roo-LONT?). If transporting a **seeing-eye dog** to France, you will need a rabies vaccination certificate issued from home.

Few metro stations are wheelchair-accessible, but most RER stations are. For a guide to metro accessibility, pick up a free copy of the RATP's brochures, *Circuler sans fatigue dans le metro et le RER* and *Handicaps et déplacements en région Ile-de-France* (tel. 01 36 68 41 41 for help in English), which provide a list of stations equipped with escalators, elevators, and moving walkways. For more information on the accessibility of SNCF trains, pick up a copy of the free *Guide de Voyager à Mobil-ité* available in all stations. Public buses are not yet wheelchair accessible, but taxis are required by law to take passengers in wheelchairs. For more info, consult:

L'Association des Paralysées de France, Délégation de Paris, 22, rue de Père Guérion, 13ème (tel. 01 40 78 69 00). Publishes *Où ferons-nous étape?* (85F), which lists French hotels accessible to persons with disabilities. Open M-Th 9am-12:30pm and 2-5:30pm, F 9am-12:30pm and 2-5pm.

Comité National Français de Liaison pour la Réadaption des Handicapés (CNFLRH), 236bis, rue de Tolbiac, 13ème (tel. 01 53 80 66 66; fax 01 53 80 66 67; www.handitel.org). Publishes guides to hotels and sights with wheelchair access.

Association Valentin-Hauy, 5, rue Duroc, 7ème (tel. 01 44 49 27 27; fax 01 44 49 27 10). Houses a cassette and Braille library for vision-impaired tourists and residents. Free metro maps in Braille. Open M-Th 9am-noon, F 9am-noon and 2-5pm.

Audio-Vision guides, at Parisian theaters such as the Théâtre National de Chaillot, 1, pl. Trocadéro, 11 Novembre, 16ème (tel. 01 53 65 31 00), the Comédie Française, 2, rue de Richelieu, 1er (tel. 01 44 58 15 15), and the Théâtre National de la Colline, 15, rue Malte-Brun, 20ème (tel. 01 44 62 52 00). Spoken service for the blind or vision-impaired, which describes the costumes, sets, and theater design.

Neut Orthopedio: Orthopédie, Prothèse, Chaussures, 9, rue Léopold Bellan, 2ème (tel. 01 42 33 83 46). M: Sentier. This store sells wheelchairs, canes, and other important accessories. Open M-F 9am-6pm.

Before you leave, you may also want to consult some of the following organizations, publications, and tour providers for information on accommodations, restaurants, tour packages, and resources for travelers with disabilities.

Access Project (PHSP), 39 Bradley Gardens, West Ealing, London W13 8HE, U.K. (email gordon.couch@virgin.net). Distributes guides to Paris (UK£7.50). Researched by persons with disabilities, they cover accommodations, transport, and access to sights, entertainment, and wheelchair-accessible toilets.

Facts on File, 11 Penn Plaza, 15th Fl., New York, NY 10001 (tel. (212) 967-8800). Publishers of *Resource Directory for the Disabled,* a reference guide for travelers with disabilities (US$45 plus shipping). Available at bookstores or by mail order.

Graphic Language Press, P.O. Box 270, Cardiff by the Sea, CA 92007 (tel. (760) 944-9594; email niteowl@cts.com). Publishes *Wheelchair Through Europe,* a guide covering accessible hotels, transportation, sightseeing, and resources (US$12.95).

Mobility International USA (MIUSA), P.O. Box 10767, Eugene, OR 97440 (tel. (514) 343-1284 voice and TDD; fax 343-6812; email info@miusa.org; http://www.miusa.org). Sells *A World of Options: A Guide to International Educational Exchange, Community Service, and Travel for Persons with Disabilities* (US$35).

Society for the Advancement of Travel for the Handicapped (SATH), 347 Fifth Ave., #610, New York, NY 10016 (tel. (212) 447-1928; fax 725-8253; email sath-travel@aol.com; http://www.sath.org). Publishes *Open World* (US$13) and information sheets on accessible destinations. Membership US$45.

Twin Peaks Press, P.O. Box 129, Vancouver, WA 98666-0129 (tel. (360) 694-2462; fax (360) 696-3210; email 73743.2634@compuserve.com; http://netm.com/mall/infoprod/twinpeak/helen.htm). Publishes *Travel for the Disabled* (US$20), *Directory of Travel Agencies for the Disabled* (US$20), *Wheelchair Vagabond* (US$15), and *Directory of Accessible Van Rentals* (US$10).

DIETARY CONCERNS

Vegetarians may have trouble eating cheaply in restaurants, since *menus* usually feature meat or fish. Most restaurants have vegetarian *à la carte* selections, and some cater specifically to vegetarians. If you don't eat eggs or dairy products, you should clearly state this fact to the server. Try eating at Tunisian, Moroccan, Indian, Vietnamese, and Chinese restaurants, which offer couscous, rice, and vegetable platters. Health food stores, called *diététiques* or *maisons de régime,* are expensive. Health food products are called *produits diététiques.*

In Paris, **kosher** delis, restaurants, and bakeries abound in the 3ème and 4ème arrondissements, particularly on rue des Rosiers and rue des Écouffes. Contact the **Union Libéral Israélite de France Synagogue** (see **Religious Services,** p. 74) for more information on kosher restaurants. For a list of vegetarian and kosher restaurants, see **Restaurants by Type**, p. 107. Otherwise, the following organizations can provide comprehensive lists of dietary options in Paris.

The International Vegetarian Travel Guide (UK£2) was last published in 1991. Order copies from the Vegetarian Society of the UK (VSUK), Parkdale, Dunham Rd., Altringham, Cheshire WA14 4QG (tel. (0161) 928 0793; fax (0161) 926 9182; email veg@minxnet.co.uk; http://www.vegsoc.org). VSUK also publishes *The European Vegetarian Guide to Hotels and Restaurants.*

The Jewish Travel Guide lists synagogues, kosher restaurants, and Jewish institutions in over 80 countries. Available from Vallentine-Mitchell Publishers, Newbury House 890-900, Eastern Ave., Newbury Park, Ilford, Essex, U.K. IG2 7HH (tel. (0181) 599 88 66; fax 599 09 84). Available in the U.S. ($15) from Sepher-Hermon Press, 1265 46th St., Brooklyn, NY 11219 (tel. (718) 972-9010).

MINORITY TRAVELERS

Despite Paris's extraordinary diversity, its large African, Maghrebian, East Asian, and South Asian populations, and its wealth of multi-ethnic restaurants and cultural events, racism is as big a problem here as it is in London, Sydney, and New York. While some, like African-American writers, musicians, and performers such as Josephine Baker, Richard Wright, James Baldwin, and Sidney Bechet came to Paris for its relative freedoms, many more recent arrivals have met with difficulties. The ultra-conservative, ideologically racist *Front National,* a political party led by Jean-Marie Le Pen, emerged in the 1986 legislative elections and has since remained a leading voice of xenophobia in France. Anti-immigrant resentment escalated in 1993 when Interior Minister Charles Pasqua proposed there be "zero immigration" and initiated the "Law Pasqua," which gave the police greater freedom to interrogate (and intimidate) immigrants in France.

Paris has a number of institutes, bookstores, and community centers which can provide visitors with information on cultural events, programs, and histories of Paris's immigrant communities. The bookstore and publishing house **Présence Africaine** is most famous for having first published the Martiniquais poet Aimé Césaire's poetry in the 1920s. Today, the bookstore stocks thousands of titles on West African and Caribbean literature, politics, philosophy, and culture, and serves as an unofficial center for information on Paris's African and Caribbean communities (see **Books,** p. 265). While jazz clubs like the **Duc des Lombards** have hosted African-American jazz musicians like Ella Fitzgerald, Louis Armstrong, Thelonius Monk, and Miles Davis for decades, **Hayne's Bar,** founded by LeRoy Haynes in 1947, was (and still is) a center for African-American expatriates and a hangout for James Baldwin and Richard Wright (see **Jazz,** p. 241 and **Restaurants,** p. 118). Paris's North African communities have reshaped French identity itself. In addition to the city's Tunisian, Algerian, and Moroccan neighborhoods, mosques, restaurants, and shops, the **Institut du Monde Arabe** offers exhibitions, events, lectures, and films on Arab culture both in Paris and in the Maghreb (see **Museums,** p. 231). Paris's Vietnamese and Cambodian neighborhods share the 13ème and 19ème with their Chinese and Laotian, Indian and Pakistani neighbors.

Those of Arab, North African, or West African descent may still face suspicious or derogatory glances from passersby. Should you confront race-based exclusion or violence, you should make a formal complaint to the police. We encourage you to work through either SOS Racisme or MRAP in order to facilitate your progress through a confusing foreign bureaucracy.

S.O.S. Racisme, 1, rue Cail, 10^{ème}e (tel. 01 42 05 44 44 or 01 42 05 69 69). Occupied primarily with helping illegal immigrants and people whose documentation is irregular. They provide legal services and are used to negotiating with police.

MRAP (Mouvement contre le racisme et pour l'amitié entre les peuples), 89, rue Oberkampf, 11ème (tel. 01 43 14 83 53). Handles immigration issues and monitors racist publications and propaganda.

The good news is that immigrants, their children, and grandchildren are changing the face of France. Arabic expressions like *kif-kif* ("it's all the same") have become accepted parts of spoken French, black performers like MC Solaar and Teri Moïse top the French music charts, and multi-ethnic restaurants have changed the way Paris thinks about French cuisine. For a better idea of the racial climate in France, see **Post-Colonial French Literature,** p. 23, **Post-Colonial Paris,** p. 9, **Film,** p. 18, or rent Mathieu Kassovitz's films *La Haine* and *Café Au Lait (Métisse).*

TRAVELING WITH CHILDREN

Paris can be a wonderful place to travel with children. For those children who loved Disney's animated version of Victor Hugo's classic *Nôtre-Dame de Paris,* Nôtre Dame is the magical home of the hunchback. A climb up the cathedral's tower, with its winding stairs, its view of Paris, and its leering gargoyles, will liven up any child's tour of the cathedral. The **Jardin du Luxembourg** (see **Sights,** p. 157) is famous for its *guignol,* pony rides, go-carts, carousel, boats (to rent and sail on the ponds), and swings. In the summer, the carnival at the **Tuileries** (see **Sights,** p. 141) has rides suitable for all ages. **La Villette** (see **Museums,** p. 223), a huge science museum, aquarium, and Omnimax theater complex, offers an entire day's worth of entertainment. The **Jardin d'Acclimatation** (tel. 01 40 67 90 82), in the **Bois de Boulogne** (**Sights,** p. 203), offers a children's zoo, a hall of mirrors, and a playground for only 15F. Donkey rides and remote-control speed boats cost extra (7-10F). The **Jardin des Plantes,** with its menagerie, insect museum, and turtle- and bird-filled tropical green house (see **Sights,** p. 155) and the **Parc Zoologique** (see **Sights,** p. 207) are great for animal-lovers. When visited with children, even the most clichéd sights, such as the Eiffel Tower and the *bateaux mouches* (tour boats on the Seine; see **Sights,** p. 135) can be fun. The **Cirque de Paris** (tel. 01 47 99 40 40) gives little ones the chance to be a clown and meet the animals. And though you might not think the **Louvre** would keep your child's attention, even they have become more kid-friendly with their children's programs, some in English, at the **Atelier des Enfants** (call 01 40 20 52 63 for information and required reservations). And of course, you can always take the RER out to **Disneyland Paris** (see **Trips From Paris,** p. 291).

The Paris magazine *L'Officiel des Spectacles* (2F) has a section entitled *Pour Les Jeunes* that lists exhibits, programs, and movies appropriate for children (see **Publications about Paris,** p. 75). For more info, consult the following publications:

Take Your Kids to Europe, by Cynthia W. Harriman (US$16.95). A budget travel guide geared toward families. Published by Globe-Pequot Press, 6 Business Park Rd., Old Saybrook, CT 06475 (tel. (800) 285-4078; fax (860) 395-1418).

Travel with Children, by Maureen Wheeler (US$12). Published by Lonely Planet Publications, 150 Linden St., Oakland, CA 94607 (tel. (800) 275-8555 or (510) 893-8555, fax 893-8563; email info@lonelyplanet.com; http://www.lonelyplanet.com).

How to Take Great Trips with Your Kids, by Sanford and Jane Portnoy (US $9.95). Advice on packing and child-friendly accommodations. The Harvard Common Press, 535 Albany St., Boston, MA 02118 (tel. (888) 657-3755, fax 695-9794).

Have Kid, Will Travel, 101 Survival Strategies for Vacationing With Babies and Young Children, by Claire Tristram and Lucille Tristram. Published by Andrews & McMeel for US$9; can be had at http://www.amazon.com.

TRAVELING ALONE

With greater independence and less distractions, you can plan, travel, or write an expatriate novel like Hemingway. On the other hand, you may also be a more visible target for robbery and harassment. Try not to look lost or confused, and if questioned never admit that you are traveling alone. Maintain regular contact with someone who knows your itinerary. For more tips on going solo, check out the following resources:

American International Homestays, P.O. Box 1754, Nederland, CO 80466 (tel. (303) 642-3088 or (800) 876-2048). Lodgings with English-speaking host families.

A Foxy Old Woman's Guide to Traveling Alone, by Jay Ben-Lesser (US$11), offers advice, anecdotes, and tips for anyone interested in solitary adventure. Available from Crossing Press in Freedom, CA (tel. (800) 777-1048).

Roadrunner Hosteling Treks, 6762 A Centinela Ave., Culver City, CA 90230 (tel. (617) 984-1556 or (800) 873-5872). Inexpensive guided trips (maximum 13 travelers) to Europe in Hosteling International accommodations.

Travel Companion Exchange, P.O. Box 833, Amityville, NY 11701 (tel. (800) 392-1256; fax (516) 454-0170; email travelpals@erols.com; http://whytravelalone.com). Publishes *Travel Companions,* a newsletter for single travelers.

Traveling On Your Own, by Eleanor Berman (US$13). Lists information resources for singles and single parents. Crown Publishers, Inc., 201 East 50th St., New York, NY 10022 (tel. (212) 751-2600).

Traveling Solo: Advice and Ideas for More Than 250 Great Vacations by Eleanor Berman (US$17). Published by Globe-Pequot Press, 6 Business Park Rd., Old Saybrook, CT 06475 (tel. (800) 285-4078). Ideas on solo travel, women traveling alone, single parents, and older travelers.

■ Packing

If you want to get away from it all, don't take it all with you. Pack light: lay out what you think you'll need, and then pack half of it. Remember that you can buy almost anything you'll need in Paris. No city outdresses Paris, so plan to admire rather than compete. And leave extra room in your bags for all the fabulous new clothes and gifts you'll be bringing home. Below are some oft-overlooked items:

Daypack: Bringing a smaller bag in addition to your pack or suitcase allows you to leave your big bag in the hotel while you go sight-seeing. It can also be used as a carry-on; keep the absolute bare essentials with you to avoid the lost-luggage blues.

Walking shoes: Not a place to cut corners. Well-cushioned **sneakers** are good for walking. Bring a pair of **flip-flops** for protection against the fungi that inhabit some hostel showers. Talcum powder in your shoes and on your feet can prevent sores, and moleskin is great for blisters. Break shoes in before you leave.

Rain gear: Essential. A waterproof jacket will take care of you at a moment's notice. Gore-Tex® is a miracle fabric that's both waterproof and breathable, if expensive. Avoid cotton as outer-wear, as it is useless when wet.

Sleepsacks: If planning to stay in youth hostels, make the requisite sleepsack yourself (instead of paying the linen charge). Fold a full-size sheet in half the long way, then sew it closed along the open long side and one of the short sides.

Electrical appliances: Remember that electricity in France is 220 volts AC, enough to fry appliances made for North America's weak 110 volts. In France, sockets accommodate two-pin round plugs; get an **adapter.** If the appliance is not dual voltage, you'll also need a **converter** (US$15-18). If you have an appliance with a three-pin plug (like a laptop computer) you will also need a three-pin-American-to-two-pin-American converter. Such devices can be purchased in most hardware stores; some are unavailable in France, so buy them before you leave. Contact **Franzus,** P.O. Box 142, Beacon Falls, CT 06403 (tel. (203) 723-6664), for their free pamphlet, *Foreign Electricity is No Deep Dark Secret.*

Camera equipment: If you take expensive equipment abroad, register everything with customs at the airport before departure. Buy a supply of film and batteries before leaving; they're more expensive in France. Unless you're shooting with 1000 ASA or more, airport X-rays should not harm your pictures. Still, pack film in your carry-on, since the X-rays used for checked baggage are much stronger.

Computers: If you're bringing a laptop, have both computer and discs hand-inspected, lest X-rays wipe out your files. Officials will ask you to turn it on, so be sure the batteries are loaded. Think twice about shipping a desktop computer; most arrive in pieces, if at all. Also, you may need an adapter and converter.

GETTING TO FRANCE

■ Student and Budget Travel Agencies

Students and people under 26 ("youth") qualify for reduced airfares. These discounts are rarely available from airlines or travel agents but instead from student travel agencies which negotiate reduced rates with the airlines, then resell them to the youth market. Return-date change fees also tend to be low (around US$35 per segment through Council or Let's Go Travel). Most flights are on major airlines, although in peak season some agencies sell seats on less reliable aircraft. Student agencies can help non-students and people 26+ but may not be able to get the same low fares.

Campus Travel, 52 Grosvenor Gardens, London SW1W 0AG (http://www.campus-travel.co.uk). 46 branches in the U.K. Student and youth fares on plane, train, boat, and bus travel. ID cards for students and youths, travel insurance for students and those under 35, maps, and guides. Telephone booking: in Europe call (0171) 730 34 02; in North America call (0171) 730 21 01; worldwide call (0171) 730 81 11; in Manchester call (0161) 273 17 21; in Scotland (0131) 668 33 03.

Council Travel (http://www.ciee.org/travel/index.htm), a full-service travel agency specializing in youth and budget travel, offering discount airfares on airlines, rail-passes, hosteling cards, low-cost accommodations, guidebooks, budget tours, travel gear, and international student (ISIC), youth (GO25), and teacher (ITIC) identity cards. U.S. offices include: Emory Village, 1561 N. Decatur Rd., Atlanta, GA 30307 (tel. (404) 377-9997); 2000 Guadalupe, **Austin,** TX 78705 (tel. (512) 472-4931); 273 Newbury St., **Boston,** MA 02116 (tel. (617) 266-1926); 1138 13th St., **Boulder,** CO 80302 (tel. (303) 447-8101); 1153 N. Dearborn, **Chicago,** IL 60610 (tel. (312) 951-0585); 10904 Lindbrook Dr., **Los Angeles,** CA 90024 (tel. (310) 208-3551); 1501 University Ave. SE #300, **Minneapolis,** MN 55414 (tel. (612) 379-2323); 205 E. 42nd St., **New York,** NY 10017 (tel. (212) 822-2700); 953 Garnet Ave., **San Diego,** CA 92109 (tel. (619) 270-6401); 530 Bush St., **San Francisco,** CA 94108 (tel. (415) 421-3473); 1314 NE 43rd St. #210, **Seattle,** WA 98105 (tel. (206) 632-2448); 3300 M St. NW, **Washington, D.C.** 20007 (tel. (202) 337-6464). For U.S. cities not listed, call 800-2-COUNCIL (226-8624). Also 28A Poland St. (Oxford Circus), **London,** W1V 3DB (tel. (0171) 287 3337), **Paris** (146 55 55 65), and **Munich** (089 39 50 22).

Let's Go Travel, Harvard Student Agencies, 17 Holyoke St., Cambridge, MA 02138 (tel. (617) 495-9649; fax 495-7956; email travel@hsa.net; http://hsa.net/travel). Railpasses, HI-AYH memberships, ISICs, ITICs, FIYTO cards, guidebooks (including every *Let's Go*), maps, bargain flights, and travel gear. Call for a free catalogue.

Rail Europe Inc., 226 Westchester Ave., White Plains, NY 10604 (tel. (800) 438-7245; fax 432-1329; http://www.raileurope.com). Sells Eurail products and passes, national railpasses including Brit Rail and German Rail passes, and point-to-point tickets. Up-to-date info on rail travel including Eurostar.

STA Travel, 6560 Scottsdale Rd. #F100, Scottsdale, AZ 85253 (tel. (800) 777-0112 nationwide; fax (602) 922-0793; http://sta-travel.com). A student and youth travel organization with over 150 offices worldwide offering discount airfares, railpasses, accommodations, tours, insurance, and ISICs. Sixteen offices in the U.S. including: 297 Newbury Street, **Boston,** MA 02115 (tel. (617) 266-6014); 429 S. Dearborn St., **Chicago,** IL 60605 (tel. (312) 786-9050; 7202 Melrose Ave., **Los Angeles,** CA 90046 (tel. (213) 934-8722); 10 Downing St., Ste. G, **New York,** NY 10003 (tel. (212) 627-3111); 4341 Univ. Way NE, **Seattle,** WA 98105 (tel. (206) 633-5000); 2401 Pennsylvania Ave., **Washington, D.C.** 20037 (tel. (202) 887-0912); 51 Grant Ave., **San Francisco,** CA 94108 (tel. (415) 391-8407); **Miami,** FL 33133 (tel. (305) 461-3444). In the U.K., 6 Wrights Ln., **London** W8 6TA (tel. (0171) 938 47 11 for North American travel). In New Zealand, 10 High St., **Auckland** (tel. (09) 309 97 23). In Australia, 222 Faraday St., **Melbourne** VIC 3050 (tel. (03) 349 69 11).

Travel CUTS (Canadian Universities Travel Services Limited), 187 College St., Toronto, Ont. M5T 1P7 (tel. (416) 979-2406; fax 979-8167; email mail@travelcuts.com).

Canada's national student travel bureau with 40 offices across Canada. Also in the U.K., 295-A Regent St., **London** W1R 7YA (tel. (0171) 637 31 61). Discounted airfares, special student fares to all destinations with valid ISIC. Issues ISIC, FIYTO, GO25, and HI hostel cards, as well as railpasses. Offers free *Student Traveler* magazine, as well as information on the Student Work Abroad Program (SWAP).

Wasteels, 7041 Grand National Dr. #207, Orlando, FL 32819 (tel. (407) 351-2537; in **London** (0171) 834 70 66). 200,000 locations in Europe. Sells the Wasteels BIJ tickets, which are 30-45% off regular fare, and 2nd-class international point-to-point train tickets with unlimited stopovers (must be under 26 on the first day of travel); sold only in Europe.

■ By Plane

Understanding the airline industry's byzantine pricing system is the best way of finding a cheap fare. Very generally, courier fares (if you can deal with restrictions) are the cheapest, followed by tickets bought from consolidators and stand-by seating. Last minute specials, airfare wars, and charter flights can often beat these fares, however. Always get quotes from different sources; an hour or two of research can save you hundreds of dollars. Call every toll-free number and don't be afraid to ask about discounts, as it's unlikely they'll be volunteered. Knowledgeable **travel agents** can provide excellent guidance, but travel agents may not want to spend time finding the cheapest fares (for which they receive the lowest commissions). Students and others under 26 should never need to pay full price for a ticket. Seniors can also get great deals; many airlines offer senior traveler clubs, airline passes, and discounts. Sunday newspapers often have travel sections that list bargain fares from the local airport. Outsmart airline reps with Michael McColl's *The Worldwide Guide to Cheap Airfare* (US$15), a useful guide for finding cheap airfare.

The **Internet** offers a wealth of travel information. **TravelHUB** (http://www.travel-hub.com) provides a directory of travel agents that includes a searchable database of fares from over 500 consolidators (see **Ticket Consolidators,** below). The **Air Traveler's Handbook** (http://www.cs.cmu.edu/afs/cs.cmu.edu/user/mkant/Public/Travel/airfare.html) is an excellent source of general information on air travel. Groups such as the **Air Courier Association** (http://www.aircourier.org) offer information about traveling as a courier and provide up-to-date listings of last minute opportunities. **Travelocity** (http://www.travelocity.com) operates a searchable online database of published airfares, which you can reserve online.

Most airfares peak between mid-June and early September. Midweek (M-Th morning) round-trip flights run about US$40-50 cheaper than on weekends; weekend flights, however, are generally less crowded. Return-date flexibility is usually not an option for the budget traveler and traveling with an "open return" ticket can be pricier than fixing a return date and paying to change it. Whenever flying internationally, pick up your ticket well in advance of the departure date, have the flight confirmed within 72 hours of departure, and arrive at the airport at least three hours before your flight.

COMMERCIAL AIRLINES

The airlines' published airfares should be just the beginning of your search. Even if you pay an airline's lowest published fare, you may waste hundreds of dollars. But before shopping around it is a good idea to find out the average commercial price in order to measure just how great a "bargain" you are being offered. The commercial airlines' lowest regular offer is the **Advance Purchase Excursion Fare (APEX);** specials advertised in newspapers may be cheaper but have more restrictions and fewer available seats. APEX fares provide you with confirmed reservations and allow "open-jaw" tickets (landing in and returning from different cities). Generally, reservations must be made seven to 21 days in advance, with seven- to 14-day minimum and up to 90-day maximum stay limits, and hefty cancellation and change penalties. Book APEX fares early; by May you will have a hard time getting the departure date you want.

Look into flights to less popular destinations. **Icelandair** (tel. (800) 223-5500) has last-minute offers and a stand-by fare from New York to Luxembourg. Reservations must be made within three days of departure. **Martinair** (tel. (800) 627-8462) offers one-way only standby fares from New York to Amsterdam (you're responsible for the ticket home). **TowerAir** (tel. (800) 348-6937) offers roundtrip flights to Paris.

TICKET CONSOLIDATORS

Most airlines in the world are heavily regulated, which means that their published fares may be significantly more expensive than the market price available from a **ticket consolidator.** Ticket consolidators resell unsold tickets on commercial and charter airlines at unpublished fares; a 30-40% price reduction is not uncommon. Consolidators largely deal in international tickets; the deregulation of domestic U.S. airlines allowed them to discount their own fares. Consolidator tickets provide the greatest discounts over published fares: on short notice (you bypass advance purchase requirements, since you aren't tangled in airline bureaucracy); on a high-priced trip; to an offbeat destination; or in the peak season. Unlike tickets bought through an airline, you won't be able to use your tickets on another flight if you miss yours, and you will have to go back to the consolidator rather than the airline to get a refund. Keep in mind that these tickets are often for coach seats on connecting (not direct) flights on foreign airlines and that frequent-flyer miles may not be credited.

Not all consolidators deal with the general public; many sell tickets only through travel agents. **Bucket shops** are retail agencies that specialize in getting cheap tickets. Although ticket prices are marked up slightly, bucket shops generally have access to a larger market. Generally, a dealer **specializing** in travel to the country of your destination will provide more options and cheaper tickets. The **Association of Special Fares Agents (ASFA)** maintains a database of specialized dealers for particular regions (http://www.ntsltd.com/asfa). Look for bucket shops' tiny ads in the travel section of weekend papers; in the U.S., the Sunday *New York Times* is a good source; in Australia, use the *Sydney Times*. Kelly Monaghan's *Consolidators: Air Travel's Bargain Basement* (US$8) is an invaluable source for more info and lists of consolidators by location and destination from the Intrepid Traveler, P.O. Box 438, New York, NY 10034 (email info@intrepidtraveler.com).

Be a smart shopper; contact the local Better Business Bureau to find out how long the company has been in business and its track record. Though not necessary, it is preferable to deal with consolidators close to home so you can visit in person, if necessary. Ask to receive your tickets as quickly as possible so you have time to fix any problems. Get the company's policy in writing: insist on a **receipt** that gives full details about the tickets, refunds, and restrictions, and record who you talked to and when. It may be worth paying with a credit card (despite the 2-5% fee) so you can stop payment if you never receive your tickets. Beware the "bait and switch" gag: shyster firms will advertise a super-low fare and then tell a caller that it has been sold.

The following agents provide general services. For destinations worldwide, try **Airfare Busters** in Washington, D.C. (tel. (202) 776-0478), Boca Raton, FL (tel. (561) 994-9590), and Houston, TX (tel. (800) 232-8783); **Pennsylvania Travel,** Paoli, PA (tel. (800) 331-0947); **Cheap Tickets,** offices in Los Angeles, CA, San Francisco, CA, Honolulu, HI, Seattle, WA, and New York, NY (tel. (800) 377-1000); **Interworld** (tel. (305) 443-4929; fax 443-0351); **Travac** (tel. (800) 872-8800; fax (212) 714-9063; email mail@travac.com; http://www.travac.com). **NOW Voyager,** 74 Varick St. #307, New York, NY 10013 (tel. (212) 431-1616; fax (212) 334-5243); email info@nowvoyagertravel.com; http://www.nowvoyagertravel.com) acts as a consolidator and books discounted international flights, mostly from New York, as well as courier flights for an annual fee of US$50. For a processing fee **Travel Avenue,** Chicago, IL (tel. (800) 333-3335; fax (312) 876-1254; http://www.travelavenue.com) will search for the lowest international airfare, including consolidated prices, and will even give you a 5% rebate on fares over US$350. To **Europe,** try **Rebel,** Valencia, CA (tel. (800) 227-3235; fax (805) 294-0981; email travel@rebeltours.com; http://www.rebeltours.com), or Orlando, FL (tel. (800) 732-3588).

COURIER COMPANIES

Those who travel light should consider flying internationally as a **courier**, where ridiculously low fares often come at the price of heavy restrictions. The company hiring you will use your checked luggage space for freight; you're usually allowed to bring only carry-ons. You are responsible for the safe delivery of the baggage claim slips (given to you by a courier company representative) to the representative waiting for you when you arrive—don't screw up or you will be blacklisted as a courier. You will probably never see the cargo you are transporting—the company handles it all—and airport officials know that couriers are not responsible for the baggage checked for them. You must be over 21 (18 in some cases), have a valid passport, and procure your own visa; most flights are round-trip only with short fixed-length stays (usually one week); only single tickets are issued (but a companion may be able to get a next-day flight); and most flights out of the U.S. are from New York. Flights to Paris (during the off-season) average $200-350. You can also go directly through courier companies in New York, or check your bookstore, library, or online at http:// www.amazon.com for handbooks such as *Air Courier Bargains* and *The Courier Air Travel Handbook*.

Becoming a member of the **Air Courier Association** (tel. (800) 282-1202; http:// www.aircourier.org) is a good way to start; they give you a listing of all reputable courier brokers and the flights they are offering, along with a hefty courier manual and a bimonthly newsletter of updated opportunities ($30 one-time fee plus $28 annual dues). For an annual fee of $45, the **International Association of Air Travel Couriers,** 8 South J St., P.O. Box 1349, Lake Worth, Florida 33460 (tel. (561) 582-8320; email iaatc@courier.org; http://www.courier.org) informs travelers of courier opportunities worldwide. **NOW Voyager,** 74 Varick St. #307, New York, NY 10013 (tel. (212) 431-1616; fax 334-5243; email info@nowvoyagertravel.com; http://www.nowvoyagertravel.com), acts as an agent for courier flights primarily from New York and offers last-minute deals to Paris for as little as US$250.

STAND-BY FLIGHTS

Airhitch, 2641 Broadway, 3rd Fl., New York, NY 10025 (tel. (800) 326-2009 or (212) 864-2000; fax 864-5489) and Los Angeles, CA (tel. (310) 726-5000), offers courier flights, but complete flexibility in the dates and cities of arrival and departure is necessary. Flights to Europe cost US$159 each way when departing from the NorthEast, $239 from the West, $209 from the Midwest, and $189 from the South. Travel within the USA and Europe is also possible, with rates ranging from $79 to $139. The snag is that you buy not a ticket but the promise that you will get to a destination near where you're intending to go within a window of time (usually 5 days) from a location in a region you've specified. You call in before your date-range to hear all of your flight options for the next seven days. You then decide which flights you want to try to make and present a voucher at the airport that grants you the right to board a flight on a space-available basis. This procedure must be followed again for the return trip. Be aware that you may only receive a monetary refund if all flights are full, but future travel credit is always available. There are several offices in Europe, so you can wait to register for your return; the main one is in Paris (tel. 47 00 16 30).

AirTech.Com, 588 Broadway #204, New York, NY 10012 (tel. (212) 219-7000; fax 219-0066; email fly@airtech.com; http://www.airtech.com), offers a very similar service. Their travel window is 1 to 4 days. Rates to and from Europe are: Northeast US$169; West Coast US$229; Midwest/South US$199. Upon registration and payment, AirTech.Com sends you a FlightPass with a contact date falling soon before your travel window, when you are to call them for flight instructions. Note that the service is one-way—you must go through the same procedure to return—and that no refunds are granted unless the company fails to get you a seat before your travel window expires. AirTech.Com also arranges regular and courier flights. Be sure to read all the fine print in your agreements or call The Better Business Bureau of New York City to verify. Be warned that it is difficult to receive refunds and that clients' vouchers will not be honored when an airline fails to receive payment in time.

CHARTER FLIGHTS

Charters are flights a tour operator contracts with an airline to fly extra loads of passengers to peak-season destinations. Charters are often cheaper than flights on scheduled airlines, especially during peak seasons, although fare wars, consolidator tickets, and small airlines can often beat charter prices. Some charters operate nonstop, and restrictions on minimum advance-purchase and minimum stay are more lenient. However, charter flights fly less frequently than major airlines, make refunds particularly difficult, and are almost always fully booked. Schedules and itineraries may also change or be cancelled as late as 48 hours before the trip (without a full refund) and check-in, boarding, and baggage claim are often much slower. As always, pay with a credit card if you can; consider traveler's insurance against trip interruption.

Many consolidators, such as **Interworld, Rebel, Travac,** and **Travel Avenue** (see **Ticket Consolidators,** p. 58), offer charter options. Hunt for the best deal. **Discount clubs** and **fare brokers** offer members savings on travel, including charter flights and tour packages. **Last Minute Travel Service,** 100 Sylvan Rd., Woburn, MA 01801 (tel. (800) 527-8646 or (617) 267-9800), specializes in domestic and Caribbean packages as well as cruises. It is one of the few travel clubs that doesn't charge a membership fee. **Travelers Advantage,** Stamford, CT (tel. (800) 548-1116; http://www.travelersadvantage.com; US$49 annual fee) specializes in European travel and tour packages.

■ By Eurostar

Since the chunnel's opening a few years ago, the **Eurostar** (Paris tel. 08 36 35 35 39; London tel. 0990 186 186) has become the most convenient method of getting from London to Paris. Traveling at close to 150mph, the whole journey takes a snappy three hours. What's more, you board and exit the train right in the middle of each city—no added transportation time or cost is needed. Trains leave London Waterloo for Gare du Nord, where you can catch the metro and the RER. Given the volume of trains per day, buying a ticket the day before your journey is usually a sufficient amount of time in advance, although it is prudent to buy your ticket a week in advance. You must check-in at the station at least 20 minutes before departure. Remember to attach the nifty and required tag to all baggage items (available at terminals and travel agencies). Enquire at Eurostar ticket offices or at Campus Travel in London for special promotions. (Trains to London, approximately 15 per day. Second class tickets: one-way M-Th 1140F, round-trip 1950F; one-way F-Su 750F, round-trip 1290F; students 12-26 650F; under 12 one-way 350F, roundtrip 550F; over 60 round-trip only 890F).

■ By Ferry

Ferries link France with England and Ireland. From the French ports, you can catch a train to Paris. Le Havre has the fastest connections to Paris. The following routes are based on one-way trips. Check with travel agents or the following companies.

Brittany Ferries (tel. 08 03 82 88 28) from Portsmouth to Caen (2-3 per day; 6-7 hr; 150-250F, students 135-225F); from Poole to Cherbourg (1-4 per day; 2½ hr; 150-250F, students 135-225F); from Plymouth to Roscoff (1-4 per day; 6hr; 150-260F, students 135-234F); from Portsmouth to St-Malo (1 per day; 9hr; 160-290F, students 144-261F); Poole to Cherbourg (1-4 per day; 4hr; 150-250F, students 135-225F)

Irish Ferries (tel. (01) 661 05 11) offer year-round service from Rosslare in Ireland to Le Havre (8-13 per month; 20hr. overnight; May-June and Sept. 530F, students 450F; July 1-5 and Aug. 11-31 580F, students 500F; July 6-Aug. 10 635F, students 555F; Oct.-April 415F, students 335F), and from Rosslare to Cherbourg (June-Aug. 2 per week; Sept.-May 1 per week; 16hr. overnight; July 1-5 and Aug. 11-31 580F, students 500F; July 6-Aug. 10 635F, students 555F; May-June and Sept. 530F, students 450F; Oct.-April 415F, students 335F). During the summer, ferries also run from Cork to Le Havre (June-Aug. 1 per week; 20½hr. overnight; same prices as Rosslare-

Le Havre). Eurailpass holders travel free after paying a 30F tax. Year-round service from Rosslare to Cherbourg (20-30 per month; 16 hr.; 315-650F, students 270-550F) from Roscoff, France to Rosslare (26-30 May-Sept.; same prices as above).

P&O European Ferries (tel. 01 44 51 00 51) cross from Dover to Calais (every 45 min.; 1½ hr; one-way or 5-day return for a vehicle and 2 people 575-1245F; open return 1100-2010F; passengers on foot 175-230F) and from Porstmouth to Cherbourg (4 per day; 5hr; 9hr overnight; on foot 135-280F).

Sealink Stena Lines (tel. 01 44 94 40 40) chug from Southampton to Cherbourg (2-3 per day; 6hr; oneway or 5-day return 140-230F, students 110-190F), and from Newhaven to Dieppe (3-4 per day; 3hr.; 250, students 220F).

Traveling by **hovercraft** is quicker (50min.), but book in advance. **Hoverspeed** (tel. 08 00 90 17 77) departs for Calais or Boulogne from Dover, or to Dunkerque from Ramsgate (one-way or 5-day return 900F). Service is suspended in rough weather.

GETTING IN AND OUT OF THE CITY

■ To and from the Airports

ROISSY-CHARLES DE GAULLE

Most transatlantic flights land at **Aéroport Roissy-Charles de Gaulle,** 23km northeast of Paris. As a general rule, Terminal 2 serves Air France and its affiliates; for info call the 24-hour English-speaking passenger information center (tel. 01 48 62 22 80).

The two cheapest and fastest ways to get into the city from Roissy-Charles de Gaulle are by train or bus. To take the RER train, first take the free shuttle bus from Aérogare 1 arrival level gate 28, Aérogare 2A gate 5, Aérogare 2B gate 6, or Aérogare 2D gate 6 to the Roissy train station. From there, the **RER B3** (one of the Parisian commuter rail lines) will transport you to central Paris. To transfer to the metro, get off at **Gare du Nord, Châtelet-Les Halles,** or **St-Michel,** which are both RER and metro stops. To go to Roissy-Charles de Gaulle from Paris, take the RER B3, any train with a name starting with the letter "E," to "Roissy," which is the end of the line. Then change to the free shuttle bus (RER departs every 15min.; 5am-12:30am; train 30–35min., bus 10min.; 47F). An alternative means of airport transportation is the **Roissybus** (tel. 01 48 04 18 24) which runs from in front of the American Express office on rue Scribe, near M: Opéra, to gate 10 of Terminal 2A (which also serves terminal 2C), to gate 12 of Terminal 2D (which also serves Terminal 2B), and to gate 30 of Terminal 1, arrivals level (departs every 15min. to airport 5:45am-11pm, from airport 6am-11pm, 45min., 45F).

Daily Air France Buses (tel. 01 41 56 89 00) run to and from the Arc de Triomphe (M: Charles de Gaulle-Etoile) at 1, Av Carnot (every 12 min., 5:50am-11pm; 35. min; one-way 60F, roundtrip 105F); to and from the pl. de la Porte de Maillot/Palais des Congrès (M: Porte de Maillot), near the Air France booking agency (same schedule and prices); and to and from 13, bd. du Vaugirard, near the **Gare Montparnasse** (M: Montparnasse-Bienvenue; to the airport every 30 min. from 7am-9:30pm, one-way 70F, round-trip 120F). At Roissy, the shuttle stops between terminals 2A and 2C; between 2B and 2D; and at terminal 1 on the arrivals level, outside exit 34. **Tickets** can be purchased on the bus itself. Call 01 41 56 89 00 for recorded information, available in English, on all Air France airport shuttles.

While the RER B is likely to be the fastest means of transportation, it can be a somewhat harrowing experience to navigate the train and metro stations if you are loaded down with heavy baggage. If you are strapped with luggage, and are willing to pay for a taxi to or from the Roissybus and Air France bus depots, taxis may be your best bet. **Taxis** take at least 50 minutes to the center of Paris and cost about 250F during the day, 280F at night, although you may face being swindled during peak hours.

ORLY

Aéroport d'Orly (tel. 01 49 75 15 15 for info, in English 6am-midnight), 12km south of the city, is used by charters and many continental flights. From Orly Sud gate H or gate I, platform 1, or Orly Ouest arrival level gate F, take the shuttle bus known as **Orly-Rail** (every 15min; 5:40am-11:15pm) to the **Pont de Rungis/Aéroport d'Orly** train stop where you can board the **RER C2** for a number of destinations in Paris (every 15min., 6am-11pm; 25min.; 35F; call RATP at 08 36 68 77 14 (French) or 08 36 68 41 14 (English) for info). The **Jetbus** (every 12min.; 5:45am-11:30pm; 22F), provides a quick connection between Orly Sud-gate H-platform 2, or Orly Ouest arrival level gate C and M: Villejuif-Louis Aragon on line 7 of the metro.

Another option is the RATP **Orlybus,** which runs to and from metro and RER stop Denfert-Rochereau, 14ème. Board at Orly Sud gate H, platform 4 or Orly Ouest level O, gate J (M-F every 13min., Sa-Su every 16-20min.; 6am-11pm; 30min.; 30F). The RATP also runs **Orlyval** (tel. 01 43 46 14 14), a combination of metro, RER, and VAL rail shuttle. To get to Orly, buy an Orlyval ticket (57F), take the metro to Gare du Nord, Châtelet-les-Halles, or St-Michel and change to the RER B. Make sure that the station Antony-Orly is lit up on the changing schedule panel next to the track (see **RER,** p. 66). Get off at Antony-Orly and transfer to the VAL train. Reverse these instructions to enter the city from Orly. From the airport, buy a ticket at an RATP office (Ouest gate W level 1; sud gate K). Note that weekly or monthly cards are not valid for Orlyval. (VAL trains run from Antony to Orly M-Sa 6am-8:30pm and Su and holidays 7am-11pm; trains arrive at Orly Ouest 2min. after reaching Orly Sud. Orly to Antony every 7min. M-Sa 6am-10:30pm and Su 7am-10:57pm; 30min. from Châtelet.)

Air France Buses run between Orly Montparnasse, 36, rue Commandant Mouchotte, 6ème (M: Montparnasse-Bienvenue), and the Invalides Air France agency, pl. des Invalides (departs every 12min.; 30 min.; 45F one-way, 75 round-trip). Air France shuttles stop at Orly Sud, gate J and Orly Ouest, gate E, arrivals level. **Taxis** from Orly to town cost at least 120F during the day, 160F at night and on weekends. Allow at least 45 minutes for the trip, as traffic can be heavy.

LE BOURGET

Paris's third airport, **Le Bourget** (tel. 01 48 62 12 12), is most remembered as Charles Lindbergh's landing site after his historic transatlantic flight. In odd-numbered years, it now hosts an internationally renowned air show, the **Salon International de l'Aéronautique et de l'Espace,** otherwise known to Anglophones as the Paris Air Show. To go to Le Bourget take the RER B3 direction Roissy Charles de Gaulle from St-Michel, Châtelet, Les Halles, or Gare du Nord to the Le Bourget stop (11F). From there take the #152 bus direction Blancmenil to Le Bourget airport (8F, one metro ticket). Call RATP (tel. 08 36 68 77 14, 3F per min.) for more information.

■ From the Train Stations

Each of Paris's six train stations is a veritable community of its own, with resident street people and police, cafés, *tabacs,* banks, and shops. Locate the ticket counters *(guichets),* the platforms *(quais),* and the tracks *(voies),* and you will be ready to roll. Each terminal has two divisions: the *banlieue* and the *grandes lignes.* **Grandes lignes** depart for and arrive from distant cities in France and other countries—each of the six stations serves destinations in a particular region of France or Europe. Trains to the **banlieue** serve the suburbs of Paris and make frequent stops. Within a given station, each of these divisions has its own ticket counters, information booths, and timetables; distinguishing between them before you get in line will save you hours of frustration. **Don't forget to "composter" your ticket** (time-stamp it) at the orange machines on the platform before boarding the train, or you may be slapped with a heavy fine. All train stations are reached by at least two metro lines; the metro stop bears the same name as the train station. For **train information** or to make reservations, call the SNCF at 08 36 35 35 35 (3F per min.), or use Minitel 3615 SNCF (see

Minitel, p. 73) 7a.m to 10pm daily. The SNCF line is perpetually busy (try in the evening). You can also book tickets at a local travel agency. There is a free telephone with direct access to the stations on the right-hand side of the Champs-Elysées tourist office. In addition, there are yellow **ticket machines** known as Billetterie at every train station; if you know your PIN, you can use a Mastercard, Visa, or American Express to buy your own tickets. Mastercard and Visa are also accepted at the ticket booths. Some cities can be accessed by both regular trains and **trains à grande vitesse (TGV;** fast speed trains). TGVs are more expensive but much faster; they also require reservations that cost a small fee. Regular trains require no reservations; this means that tickets for regular trains can be used as far after purchase date as you wish, although they must be used within 24 hours of being stamped.

A number of special discounts can be applied to point-to-point tickets purchased in France. The **Carte 12-25** (270F) provides a year of cut rates (25-50%) for travelers between the ages of 12 and 25; the **Carte Senior** entitles travelers over 60 to similar discounts (285F); the **Carte Enfant** provides similar reductions for children less than 12 as well as for adults traveling with them (50F). Another reduction, **Découverte J8 and J30,** is for tickets reserved no earlier than 8 days or 30 days (respectively) before the date of departure, and no later than two months. These discounts are sold by telephone (tel. 08 36 35 35 35), automatic ticket machines, ticket counters, and travel agencies.

Note: The following prices are for one-way, second-class tickets unless otherwise noted. Summer schedules are listed. In general, prices, and number of trips per day vary according to the day of the week, season, and other criteria. A word on **safety:** each terminal shelters its share of thieves. Gare du Nord and Gare d'Austerlitz become rough at night, when drugs and prostitution emerge. It is not advisable to buy tickets in the stations except at official counters.

Gare du Nord: Trains to northern France, Britain, Belgium, the Netherlands, Scandinavia, the Commonwealth of Independent States, and northern Germany (Cologne, Hamburg). To: Brussels (18 per day (spring), 2hr., 316F); Amsterdam (15 per day, 5hr., 366F); Cologne (7 per day, 5-6hr., 428F); Boulogne (5 per day, 2½hr., 180F); Copenhagen (1 direct, 3 indirect per day, 16hr., 1343F); London (by the Eurostar chunnel, approx. 17 per day, 2hr., 350-1140F one way).

Gare de l'Est: To eastern France (Champagne, Alsace, Lorraine), Luxembourg, parts of Switzerland (Basel, Zürich, Lucerne), southern Germany (Frankfurt, Munich), Austria, and Hungary. To: Zürich (4 per day, 6hr., 429F); Munich (6 per day, 8hr., 669F); and Vienna (5 per day, 14hr., 952F).

Gare de Lyon: To southern and southeastern France (Lyon, Provence, Riviera), parts of Switzerland (Geneva, Lausanne, Berne), Italy, and Greece. To: Geneva (5 per day, 3½hr., 502F); Florence (4 per day, 11hr., 665F); Rome (4-5 per day, 12hr., 620F); Lyon (23 per day, 2hr., 295-398F); Nice (12 per day, 6½hr., 320-945F); Marseille (11 per day, 4-5hr., 170-380F).

Gare d'Austerlitz: To the Loire Valley, southwestern France (Bordeaux, Pyrénées), Spain, and Portugal. (TGV to SW France leaves from Gare Montparnasse.) To: Barcelona (2 per day, 9hr., 470-780F) and Madrid (1 per day, 12-13hr., 500-830F).

Gare St-Lazare: To Normandy. To: Caen (29 per day, 1½hr., 172F); Rouen (17 per day, 1½hr., 122F).

Gare Montparnasse: To Brittany, and the TGV to southwestern France. To: Rennes (23 per day, 2-2½hr., 273F).

■ From the Bus Stations

Most international buses to Paris arrive at **Gare Routière Internationale du Paris-Gallieni,** outside Paris at 28, av. du Général de Gaulle, Bagnolet 93170. **Eurolines** (tel. 01 49 72 51 51; Minitel 3615 Eurolines; http://www.eurolines.fr; M: Gallieni) sells tickets to most destinations. Call ahead or pick up schedules for departures.

▓ Hitchhiking and Ridesharing

While some rely on *auto-stop* (hitchhiking), don't feel pressured to save money by putting yourself at risk. Women should never hitchhike alone; even traveling in twos can be dangerous. *Let's Go* does not recommend hitchhiking, and no information in this book is intended to encourage this often dangerous practice.

For a registered and probably safer hitch, **Allostop-Provoya,** 8, rue Rochambeau, 9ème (tel. 01 53 20 42 42; Minitel 3615 Provoya; http://www.ecritel.fr/allostop; M: Cadet), will match you with a driver going your way. The following prices cover one-way trips out of Paris: to Brussels about 117F; to Frankfurt 187F; to Cologne 166F; to Geneva 188F. (Open M-F 9am-7:30pm, Sa 9am-1pm and 2-6pm).

GETTING AROUND PARIS

▓ Orientation

Surrounded by the flow of the Seine river, the Île de la Cité and Île St-Louis are the geographical heart of the city. The bridges that span the islands divide Paris into the *rive gauche* (Left Bank) to the south and the *rive droite* (Right Bank) to the north. Traditionally the Left Bank, with its older architecture and narrow streets, has been considered bohemian and intellectual while the Right Bank's grand avenues and designer shops make it more bourgeois. Paris is grouped into 20 arrondissements that spiral clockwise around the Louvre. The arrondissement system provides the organizational framework for the city and this guide. See the **Sights** chapter for a detailed description of what each arrondissement has to offer.

A **map** of Paris is essential if you plan to do any serious strolling. Convenient for a long day of touring, *Let's Go Map Guide: Paris* provides highlights from *Let's Go: Paris's* coverage along with detailed fold-out maps and a street index, all in a pocket-sized format (US$7.95). Other maps of Paris, such as *Plans de Paris par arrondissement* are available at newsstands, bookstores, or *tabacs* (60-100F). The excellent *Paris par Arrondissement* (38F), is a rather inconspicuous booklet that can easily fit into your coat pocket or bag. This guide's features include historical sites and a full street index. Pick up a free, updated metro map, that includes bus lines and the RER, in any metro station. Each metro station has a map of its neighborhood, with a street index. For more guides and maps, see **Shopping: Books,** p. 263.

■ Publc Transportation

The **RATP (Régie Autonome des Transports Parisiens)** coordinates an efficient network of subways, buses, and commuter trains in and around Paris. For information on the services of RATP, contact the **Bureau de Tourisme RATP,** pl. de la Madeleine, 8ème (tel. 01 40 06 71 44; M: Madeleine; open M-Sa 8:30am-6:45pm, Su 6:30am-1pm), or the RATP helpline (tel. 01 36 68 77 14; open daily 6am-9pm; http://www.RATP.fr). English spoken. For wheelchair or seeing-impaired metro services see **Travelers With Disabilities,** p. 50.

If you're only staying in Paris for one day but expect to do a lot of traveling, consider buying a **metro pass.** At 70F for two days, 105F for three days, and 165F for five, the **Paris Visite** tourist tickets are valid for unlimited travel on bus, metro, and RER and discounts on sightseeing trips, bicycle rentals, and more; they can be purchased at the airport or at Metro and RER stations. Zones 1-5 include RATP provided transportation from the airport. Zones 1-3 include central Paris. For one day, Zones 1-5 cost 100F; two days 175F; three days 245F; five days 300F. If you plan to purchase *Paris Visite,* you may want to coordinate it with your airport arrival or departure. Another option is the **Mobilis** pass (30-70F depending on the zone; tel. 01 53 90 20

20), which also provide unlimited metro, bus, and RER transportation within Paris. If you're staying in Paris for several days a weekly *(hebdomadaire)* **Coupon Vert** or monthly *(mensuel)* **Coupon Orange** pass can be very economical. To get your ID-style **Carte Orange**, bring an ID photo (taken by machines in most major stations) to the ticket counter, ask for a *carte orange* with its plastic case, and then purchase your handsome *coupon vert* (75F) or equally swanky *coupon orange* (255F). No matter which *coupon* you have, write the number of your *carte* on your *coupon* before you use it. These cards have specific start and end dates and may not be worthwhile if bought in the middle or end of the month or week. All prices quoted here are for passes in Zones 1 and 2 (the metro and RER in Paris and suburbs). If you intend to travel to the distant burbs, you'll need to buy RER passes for more zones (up to 5).

Metro

Inaugurated in 1898, the *Paris Métropolitain* (Metro) is one of the world's oldest and most efficient subway systems. Stations are marked with an "M" or with the *"Métro-politain"* lettering designed by Art Nouveau pioneer Hector Guimard (See **Sights,** p. 192). Trains run frequently, and connections are easy. The first trains start running around 5:30am; the last ones leave the end-of-the-line stations (the *"portes de Paris"*) for the center of the city at about 12:15am. For the exact departure times of the last trains, check the poster in the center of each station marked *Principes de Tarifica-tion* (fare guidelines). Transport maps are posted on train platforms and near turn-stiles; all have a *plan du quartier* (map of the neighborhood). Connections to other lines are indicated by orange *correspondance* signs, exits by blue *sortie* signs. Lines are numbered (1 is the oldest), but referred to by their final destinations. Transfers are free if made within a station, but it is not always possible to reverse direction on the same line without exiting the station and using another ticket.

Each trip on the metro requires one ticket. Tickets can be bought individually (8F), but a *carnet* of 10 (46F) is more practical and economical. Don't buy tickets from any-one except the people in the ticket booths. To pass through the turnstiles, insert the ticket into the small slit in the metal divider just to your right as you approach the turnstile. It disappears for a moment, then pops out about a foot farther along, and a little green or white circle lights up, reminding you to retrieve the ticket. If a small electric whine sounds and a little red circle lights up, your ticket is not valid; take it back and try another. **Hold onto your ticket** until you exit the metro, past the point marked **Limite de Validité des Billets;** a uniformed RATP *contrôleur* (inspector) may request to see it on any train. If caught without one, you must pay a hefty fine. Also, any *correspondances* (transfers) to the RER require you to put your validated (and uncrumpled) ticket into a turnstile. Otherwise you might need to buy a new ticket in order to exit. There is no longer first-class metro service; any cars still marked "1" are waiting to be repainted. A word on being helpful to people who have "lost" their ticket and need to get through an entrance or exit: while it may seem a small matter to allow someone to follow you through the gate, be warned that **thieves** often use this strategy to insinuate their way into your bag or pocket.

Do not count on buying a metro ticket home late at night. Some ticket windows close as early as 10pm, and many close before the last train is due to arrive. Always have one ticket more than you need. Stay away from the most **dangerous stations** (Barbès-Rochechouart, Pigalle, Anvers, Châtelet-Les-Halles, Gare du Nord, Gare de

That's the ticket!

Ever thought it was useless to hold on to your Metro ticket once you were actually on the Metro? Felt tempted to toss it on the tracks or in the trash? Well, resist the urge, as it will cost you. You can be sure that the one time you lose your validated Metro ticket will be the day the *contrôleurs* (inspectors) will nab you as you try to leave the station. If you think you can plead your ignorance as a tourist, guess again. The inspector's eyes will light up when he realizes he's caught a ticketless tourist and will promptly slap you with a heavy fine. Hold onto that ticket!

l'Est). Despite the good neighborhoods in which some of these stops are located, they are frequented by troublemakers looking to prey on tourists. When in doubt, take a taxi. If you choose to walk home, stay on well-lit streets.

RER

The RER *(Réseau Express Régional)* is the RATP's local suburban train system, which passes through central Paris. Introduced in 1969, the RER runs through deeper tunnels at higher speeds. Within the city, the RER travels much faster than the metro. There are four RER lines, marked A-D, with different branches designated by a number, such as the C5 line to Versailles-Rive-Gauche. The principal stops within the city, which link the RER to the metro system, are Gare du Nord, Nation, Charles de Gaulle-Étoile and Châtelet-les-Halles on the Right Bank and St-Michel and Denfert-Rochereau on the Left Bank. To check for the right train, watch the electric signboards next to each track. These signs list all the possible stops for trains running on that track. Be sure that the little square next to your destination is lit up. There are two transit classes on RER trains. Unless you indicate otherwise, you'll be sold a second-class ticket. Every RER car is marked "1" or "2"; second-class ticket holders are excluded from first-class cars under penalty of fine. First class caters to commuters, with nicer seats and more leg-room. Second-class tickets cost 8F within the city and are the same ones used for the metro or bus. First-class tickets cost 12F. To get to the suburbs, you'll need to buy special tickets (10-38F one-way). You'll need your ticket to *exit* RER stations. Insert your ticket just as you did to enter, and pass through.

Bus

Because the metro is so efficient and convenient, the Parisian bus system is often neglected by both locals and visitors. Though slower and more costly than the Metro (one ticket takes you as far as you want on one line, but connections between bus lines require a new ticket), bus rides can be cheap sight-seeing tours and helpful introductions to the city's layout. The free bus map *Autobus Paris-Plan du Réseau* is available at the tourist office and at some metro information booths. The routes of each line are also posted at each stop. Bus tickets are the same as those used in the Metro, and can be purchased either in Metro stations or on the bus. Enter the bus through the front door and punch your ticket by pushing it into the machine by the driver's seat. If you have a *carte orange*, flash it at the driver. Inspectors may ask to see your ticket, so hold onto it until the end of the ride.

Most buses run daily 7am to 8:30pm, although those marked **Autobus du Soir** continue until 12:30am. Still others, called **Noctambus**, run all night. Night buses (3 tickets needed, 4 if you use 2 buses) start their runs to the *portes* of the city from the "Châtelet" stop and leave every hour on the half hour from 1:30 to 5:30am. Buses departing from the suburbs to Châtelet run every hour on the hour 1 to 6am. Ask at a major Metro station or at Gare de l'Est for more detailed information on Noctambuses. Buses with three-digit numbers come from or are bound for the suburbs, while buses with two-digit numbers travel exclusively within Paris. Buses with numbers in the 20s come from or are bound for Gare St-Lazare, in the 30s Gare de l'Est, in the 40s Gare du Nord, in the 70s Châtelet/Hôtel de Ville (with exceptions), in the 80s Luxembourg (with exceptions), and in the 90s Gare Montparnasse. For more detailed diagrams of all bus routes, consult the *Plan de Paris par Arrondissement* (see **Orientation**, p. 64). The RATP *Grand Plan de Paris* includes legible maps of all Parisian bus routes and numbers. Some of the principle bus routes are listed below.

Bus #20: From Opéra to Montmartre-Poissonière, République, Bastille. A trip down the grands boulevards. Most have open back platform.

Bus #21: From Opéra to Palais Royal, the Louvre, Pont Neuf, Châtelet, St-Michel.

Bus #29: From Opéra to the Bibliothèque Nationale, the Centre Pompidou, Bastille. Intrepid ride through narrow streets of the Marais. Most have open back platform.

Bus #82: From Gare du Luxembourg to Montparnasse, École-Militaire, Champs-de-Mars, Tour Eiffel.

Bus #83: From pl. d'Italie, along bd. Raspail, Gare des Invalides, pl. des Ternes (34-45min.). Paris's finest real estate and views of the quais. Most have open back platform.

Bus #95: From Tour Montparnasse past St-Germain-des-Prés, the Louvre, Palais Royal, the Opéra, and to Montmartre, near Sacré-Coeur (50min.).

In addition, a special tourist bus, **Balabus,** stops at virtually every major sight in Paris (from Gare de Lyon to Bastille, St-Michel, Louvre, Musée d'Orsay, Concorde, Champs-Elysées, Charles-de-Gaulle-Etoile, Porte Maillot, Pont de Neuilly, Grande Arche de La Défense, about 1¼min.). Balabus costs 1-3 tickets and runs April 2 to September 24 on Sundays and holidays. The first bus leaves Grande Arche at 1pm and Gare de Lyon at 1:30pm; the last bus leaves Grande Arche at 8:10pm and Gare de Lyon at 8:50pm. Buses run about every 20 minutes. Each bus stop is marked Balabus (Bb).

■ Taxis

Taxi in Paris are expensive. Rates vary according to time of day and area, but they're never cheap. **Tarif A,** the basic rate, is in effect in Paris 7am to 7pm (4F per km). **Tarif B** is in effect Monday to Saturday 7pm to 7am, all day Sunday, and during the day from the airports and immediate suburbs (5F83 per km). **Tarif C,** the highest, is in effect from the airports 7pm to 7am (7F16 per km). In addition, there is a *prix en charge* (base fee) of about 13F. All taxis have lights on their roofs indicating the rate being charged. Should you call a taxi rather than getting one at a taxi stand, the base fee will increase according to how far away you are and how long it takes the driver to get there. For all cabs, stationary time (at traffic lights and in traffic jams) costs 120F per hour. Additional charges (6F) are added for luggage over 5kg, a fourth adult, or for taxis leaving from train stations and taxi stops. Taxis can refuse to take more than three people. A tip is not necessary. Taxis are cheapest on weekdays in the daytime.

If you must take a taxi, try to pick one up at a train station or taxi stand, called *arrêt taxis*, usually found near bus stops. Calling a radio-cab (**Alpha Taxis,** tel. 01 45 85 85

85; **Taxis Radio Étoile,** tel. 01 41 27 27 27; **Taxis G7,** tel. 01 47 39 47 39; **Taxis Bleus,** tel. 01 49 36 10 10; or **Taxis 7000,** tel. 01 42 70 00 42) is more expensive. If you have a complaint, or have left a personal belonging behind, contact the taxi company, or write to **Service des Taxis de la Préfecture de Police,** 36, rue des Morillons, 75015 (tel. 01 55 76 20 00; M: Convention). Ask the driver for a receipt; if you file a complaint, record and include the driver's cab license number.

■ Cars

Irwin Shaw writes, "One driver out of every twelve in Paris has killed a man. On foot, the Parisian is as courteous as the citizen of any other city. But mounted, he is merciless." The infamous rotary at the Arc de Triomphe is a nightmare for pedestrians. As a rule, the fastest and biggest car wins. **Priorité à droite** gives the right of way to the car approaching from the right, regardless of the size of the streets, and Parisian drivers make it an affair of honor to take this right even in the face of grave danger. Drivers are not allowed to honk their horns within city limits unless they are about to hit a pedestrian, but this rule is often broken. The legal way to show discontent is to flash the headlights. If you don't have a map of Paris marked with one-way streets, the city will be impossible to navigate. Parking is hard to locate and garages are expensive. Foreigners need a passport, a valid license that is at least one year old, and a credit card to rent in Paris; an international license is not required. None of the agencies in Paris will rent to drivers under 21. The following prices are for economy, standard (stick-shift) transmission cars *with* insurance.

Rent-a-Car, 79, rue de Bercy, 12ème (tel. 01 43 45 15 15; fax 01 43 45 65 00). For a Fiat Panda with unlimited miles: 199F per day during the week; 499F per weekend (F after 4pm to M 10am) with 800km free, 1F each additional km; 1819F per week (1000km included, 1F each additional km). Min. age 23 with 2-year old license. Open M-F 8:30am-7pm. Call for other locations. MC, V.

Inter Touring Service, 117, bd. Auguste Blanqui, 13ème (tel. 01 45 88 52 37; fax 01 45 80 89 30). M: Glacière. 225F per day, 450F per weekend, 1260F per week.

Autorent, 98, rue de la Convention, 15ème (tel. 01 45 54 22 45; fax 01 45 54 39 69). M: Boucicaut. Also at 35, rue Fabert, 7ème (tel. 01 45 55 12 54). M: Invalides. Rents Fiat Pandas for 280F per day (250km included), 550F per weekend (F 11am-M 10am; 700km included); 1800F with unlimited mileage. Some cars with **automatic transmission.** Open M-F 8:30am-7pm, Sa 8:30am-noon. AmEx, MC, V.

■ Two Wheelers

During the Metro strike of December 1995, bike stores sold out to car-less Parisians, and the community of cyclists dreaming of an autoless Paris became more vocal. The government promised that 1997 would bring 50km of Parisian streets reserved for motorless wheels. Nonetheless, if you have never ridden a bike in heavy traffic, don't use central Paris as a testing ground. The Bois de Boulogne and the Bois de Vincennes should be more your speed (see **Participatory Sports,** p. 246). The Metro cannot accommodate bikes. Ask for a helmet and inquire about insurance.

Paris à velo, c'est sympa! 37, bd. Bourdon, 4ème (tel. 01 48 87 60 01). M: Bastillee. Leads 3hr. tours (look out, Gilligan!) throughout Paris. Call days in advance to request tours in English and for larger groups (tours 10am, 3pm; 170F, under 26 150F; tour also at 8:30pm, 190F, under 26 160F). Rentals available with a 2500F (or credit card) deposit. 24hr. rental 150F; 9am-7pm 80F. ½day 60F.

La Maison du Vélo, 11, rue Fénelon, 10ème (tel. 01 42 81 24 72). M: Poissonière. Follow rue Lafayette in the direction of traffic. Rue Fénelon runs along the left side of the St-Vincent de Paul church. "The English speaking bike store in Paris." Sells new and used bikes, repairs all models. Rent mountain or hybrid bikes 95F for 8hr; 120F for 24hr.; 180 for 48hr.; 270 for 3 days. 2000F deposit. Open Tu-Sa 10am-7pm.

Paris-Vélo, 2, rue de Fer-à-Moulin, 5ème (tel. 01 43 37 59 22). M: Censier Daubenton. Tours in English for groups of 10 or more 150F per person, 26 and under 120F; 1 day 90F; weekend 195f; 1 week 420F. Bike rental with 2000F deposit includes accident insurance. Open M-Sa 10am-12:30pm and 2pm-7pm.

La Bicyclette Verte, (tel. 05 49 35 42 56; fax 05 49 35 42 55; http://www.bicyclette-verte.com). Leads bicycle trips lasting 1-10 days throughout the area of France outside Paris, and through other European countries. Hotels and meals are organized for you, and you will be met with bicycles at the train station. 595-4950F.

Agence Contact Location, 24, rue Arc de Triomphe, 17ème (tel. 01 47 66 19 19; M: Étoile). **Scooters** 440 per day; 1100 per weekend (Fri night-Tu morning); 2400 per week, 15,000 credit card deposit required. **Motorcycles** 580-650F per day; 3200F per week. 30,000 credit card deposit required.

USEFUL SERVICES

■ Embassies and Consulates

If anything serious goes wrong, make your first inquiry to your country's consulate in Paris. The distinction between an embassy and a consulate is significant: an embassy houses the offices of the ambassador and his or her staff and deals mostly with international business, trade, and treaty negotiation. All facilities for dealing with nationals are in the consulate. If your passport gets lost or stolen, your status in France is immediately rendered illegal—go to the consulate as soon as possible to get a replacement. A consulate is also able to lend up to 100F per day, but you will be forced to prove you are truly desperate. The consulate can give you lists of local lawyers and doctors, notify family members of accidents, and give information on how to proceed with legal problems, but its functions end there. Don't ask the consulate to investigate crimes, obtain work permits, post bail, or interfere with standard French legal proceedings. If you are arrested during your stay in France, there is little, if anything, that your own government can do to help you.

Australia: Embassy at 4, rue Jean-Rey, 15ème (tel. 01 40 59 33 00; fax 01 40 59 33 10). M: Bir-Hakeim. Open M-F 9am-6pm. **Consular services:** new passport 500F, children 250F. Open M-F 9:15am-noon and 2-4:30pm.

Canada: 35, av. Montaigne, 8ème (tel. 01 44 43 29 00). M: Franklin-Roosevelt or Alma-Marceau. Open M-F 9am-5pm. **Consulate:** ask for "consular services" for an appointment. New passport 260F. Open M-F 9:30-11:30am and 2-5pm.

Ireland: Embassy at 12, av. Foch, 16ème (tel. 01 44 17 67 48; for passport services fax 01 44 17 67 50). M: Argentine. Open 9:30am-noon. **Consular Services** at same location. Exchange passport 125F; new passport 380F, children 85F. Open M-F 9:30am-noon; telephone 9:30am-1pm and 2:30-5:30pm.

New Zealand: Embassy at 7ter, rue Léonard de Vinci, 16ème (tel. 01 45 00 24 11; fax 01 45 01 26 39). M: Victor-Hugo. New passport 900F, children 670F. Open M-F 9am-1pm and 2-5:30pm.

South Africa: Embassy at 59, quai d'Orsay, 7ème (tel. 01 53 59 23 23; fax 01 47 53 99 70). M: Invalides. New passport 110F, replacement 220F, renewal free. New passports take 6-8 weeks; renewals and replacements 7-10 days. Open M-F 9am-noon.

U.K.: 35, rue du Faubourg-St-Honoré, 8ème (tel. 01 44 51 31 00; fax 01 44 51 31 27). M: Concorde or Madeleine. **Consulate,** 16, rue d'Anjou (same phone). M: Concorde. New passport, £31, cash only. Open M-F 9:30am-12;30 and 2:30-5pm. Visa bureau open M-F 9:30am-12:30pm.

U.S.: 2, av. Gabriel, 8ème (tel. 01 43 12 22 22; fax 01 42 66 97 83), off pl. de la Concorde. M: Concorde. Open M-F 9am-6pm. **Consulate** at 2, rue St-Florentin (tel. 01 43 12 48 76, 01 43 12 23 47 for automated information, or 43 12 31 00 for automated info about passports only). Passports replacement 360F, under 16 240F. Open M-F 9am-3pm. Closed for both American and French holidays.

■ Tourist Offices

Though packed in the summer, the following offices are usually able to keep the wait down to an hour at most. Lines are worst in the afternoon. All offices stock brochures, maps, and pamphlets. For 20F, they will help you find a room in a one-star hotel, 25F for a two-star, 40F for a three-star, and 8F for hostels, but they can only arrange for a room the day of your arrival. The central branch exchanges currency at decent rates with no commission and always has English-speaking representatives.

Bureau d'Accueil Central: 127, av. des Champs-Elysées, 8ème (tel. 01 49 52 53 54). M: Charles-de-Gaulle-Étoile. English-speaking staff. Mobbed in summer. Open daily Apr.-Oct. 9am-8pm; Nov.-Mar. M-Sa 9am-8pm, Su 11am-6pm. Also call **Tourist Information** (tel. 01 49 52 53 56), where a recorded message in English (updated weekly) gives major events in Paris—call 01 49 52 53 55 for recording in French.
Bureau Gare du Nord, 10ème (tel. 01 45 26 94 82). M: Gare du Nord. Open M-Sa 8am-8pm. Brochures, maps, and tourist information.
Bureau Gare de Lyon, 12ème (tel. 01 43 43 33 24). M: Gare de Lyon. Open M-Sa 8am-8pm. Brochures, maps, and tourist information.
Bureau Tour Eiffel, Champs de Mars, 7ème (tel. 01 45 51 22 15). M: Champs de Mars. Open May-Sept. daily 11am-6pm. Brochures, maps, and tourist information.
Orly, Sud: Near gate H (tel. 01 49 75 00 90). **Orly, Ouest:** Near gate F (tel. 01 49 75 01 39). Both open daily 6am-midnight. Brochures, maps, and tourist information.
Roissy-Charles de Gaulle: Near gate 36 arrival level (tel. 01 48 62 27 29). Open daily 7:30am-10pm. Brochures, maps, and tourist information.

■ Budget Travel Offices

Accueil des Jeunes en France (AJF), 119, rue St-Martin, 4ème (tel. 01 42 77 87 80). M: Rambuteau. Across from the pedestrian mall in front of the Pompidou Center. Open M-Sa 10am-6:45pm. Also 139, bd. St-Michel, 5ème (tel. 01 43 54 95 86). M: Port-Royal. Open M-Th 10am-12:30pm and 1:45-6pm, F 10:30am-12:30pm and 1:45-6pm. Offers free maps, makes hotel and hostel reservations (10F), and sells ISICs (60F, cash only) plane, train, and bus tickets, and meal vouchers for Paris hostels. Branches are friendly, English-speaking, and absurdly crowded. Another in Gare du Nord next to Agence de Voyages SNCF (tel. 01 42 85 86 19) books accommodations only. Open M-F 8am-5pm. MC, V.
Centre Régional des Oeuvres Universitaires (CROUS), 39, av. Georges Bernanos, 5ème (general tel. 01 40 51 36 00, lodging tel. 01 40 51 37 17, or 01 40 51 36 99). RER: Port-Royal. Info on student dormitory housing in Paris (from 2 days-1 year) and on university restaurants throughout the city that offer simple but filling and cheap meals. Open M-F 9am-5pm (See **Food and Drink,** p. 106).
Council on International Educational Exchange (CIEE), 1, pl. de l'Odéon, 6ème (tel. 01 44 41 74 74; fax 01 43 26 97 45). M: Odéon. Answers questions about work abroad, and offers mail service, phone service, and computers for use in the office. The library has useful info on jobs, travel, and housing, but is only available to students registered as Council participants (Open M-F 3-6:30pm). Register in Paris (1800F) or contact your CIEE office at home before you leave. Open M-F 9am-6pm.
Council Travel, 1, pl. Odéon, 6ème (tel. 01 44 41 89 89; fax 01 40 51 89 12). M: Odéon. English-speaking travel service for people under 26. Books flights, and sells train tickets, BIJ/Eurotrain tickets, guidebooks, and ISICs (60F with current student ID). Replaces lost Council Travel tickets. Open M-F 9am-7pm, Sa 9:30am-2:30pm.
Office de Tourisme Universitaire (OTU), 2, rue Malus, 5ème (tel. 01 44 41 74 74). M: Place Monge; and 119, rue St-Martin, 4ème (tel. 01 40 29 12 12). A French student-travel agency offering reduced train and plane tickets for students under 26. Bring an official form of ID, like passport or birth certificate. Also sells ISICs (68F) and BIJ tickets. English spoken. Open M-F 10am-6:45pm.

■ Keeping in Touch

MAIL

Post offices are marked on most Paris maps by their abstract flying-letter insignia; on the streets, look for the yellow and blue PTT signs. In general, post offices in Paris are open Monday to Friday 8am to 7pm (they stop changing money at 6pm) and on Saturday 8am to noon, though the **Poste du Louvre,** 52, rue du Louvre, 1er (tel. 01 40 28 20 40 for postal info, 01 40 28 20 00 for telegrams; M: Louvre; closes daily 6:30-7:30am) is open almost 24 hours. Buy stamps at *tabacs* or from vending machines inside major post offices to save time.

Air mail between Paris and North America takes five to ten days and is fairly dependable. Send mail from the largest post office in the area. Surface mail is by far the cheapest way but takes one to three months to cross the Atlantic. It's adequate for getting rid of books or clothing you no longer need; a special book rate makes this option more economical. It is vital to distinguish your airmail from surface mail by labeling it clearly **par avion.** To airmail a 20g (about 1 oz.) letter or postcard from France to the U.S. or Canada costs 4F40, to Australia or New Zealand 5F20. The **aerogramme,** a sheet of fold-up, pre-paid airmail paper, requires no envelope and costs more (5F to the U.S. or Canada, no enclosures allowed). To airmail a package, you must complete a green customs slip. Registered mail is called *avec recommandation* and costs 26F50. To be notified of a registered letter's receipt, ask for an *avis de réception* and pay an additional 8F. In France there are two grades of express mail: **prioritaire** cost 32F40 and arrive within five days to North America; **chronopost** arrive in two to three days at a soaring cost of 240F for a letter. Chronopost is only available until 6pm in most post offices, until 7pm at major branches; call 0 800 43 11 00. For mail to the U.S., **Federal Express** (tel. 0 800 12 38 00), charges 360F to send a 500g package overnight. Call Monday through Friday until 5pm for pick up. Fedex delivers the next business day.

If you do not have a specific address in Paris, you can receive mail through the **Poste Restante** system, handled by the 23-hour Louvre post office (see above). To ensure the safe arrival of your letters, they should be addressed with your last/family name in capital letters, followed by a comma and your first name, followed by *Poste Restante,* the address of the specific post office, and Paris, FRANCE. You will have to show your passport as identification and pay 3F for every letter received. **American Express,** 11, rue Scribe, 75009, Paris (tel. 01 47 77 79 59) also holds mail for up to 30 days, after which they return it to the sender. To have it held longer, write "Hold for x days" on the envelope. The envelope should be addressed with your name in capital letters, "c/o American Express: Client Mail" printed below your name. In Paris, this service is free with presentation of your American Express traveler's checks or card.

TELEPHONES

Almost all French pay phones accept only **télécartes;** in many cafés and bars, some phones are still coin-operated. You may purchase the card in two denominations: 41F for 50 *unités,* and 97F50 for 120 *unités,* each worth anywhere from six to 18 minutes of conversation. Local calls cost one *unité* each. The télécarte is available at post offices, metro stations, and *tabacs.* Don't buy cards from street vendors who recycle discarded cards and cheat you. If you phone from a café, hotel, or restaurant, you risk paying 30% more. Country codes are posted inside most telephone booths. If your credit isn't good at home, the 96 *unités* télécarte will serve you well (call to the U.K. 20min. for 120 units; call to the U.S. or Canada 12min. for 120 units). Emergency and collect calls require neither coins nor *télécartes.*

A small digital screen on the phone issues a series of simple commands. A call is *un coup de téléphone* or *un appel;* to dial is *composer;* a collect call is made *en PCV* (pay-say-vay); a person-to-person call is *avec préavis. Décrochez* means pick up, *raccrochez* hang up. On some *télécarte* phones, you need to *fermer le volet,* pull down the lever above the card slot, and wait for a dial tone. Most pay phones receive incoming calls. The number is on a sticker inside the booth, prefaced by *ici le*.

In 1996 all the phone numbers in France changed from eight digits to 10. It has taken the country awhile to catch on; some people still provide their number in the old eight-digit format. Eight-digit numbers you see listed are wrong. Phone numbers in Paris and the Île-de-France require **01** in front, in the northwest of France **02**, in the northeast **03**, in the southeast and Corsica **04**, and in the southwest **05**. Emergency calls and numbers beginning with **0 800** (formerly 05) are free. Numbers beginning with **08** (formerly 36) are expensive (the equivalent of 900 numbers in the U.S.).

AT&T's **USA Direct** allows you to be connected instantly to an operator in the U.S. Call 00 00 11. Rates vary according to the day and time but average US$1-2 per minute. AT&T's **World Connect** facilitates calls between two countries other than the U.S. (US$2.50). For more info, call AT&T at (888) 288-4685; from abroad call (810) 262-6644 collect. **MCI World Phone** lets you call the U.S. using your MCI calling card and an access code, which you'll get before you leave. For more info, call MCI at (800) 444-4141. To call **Canada Direct** from France, dial 19, wait for the tone, then dial 0016 and the number. It will be billed as a person-to-person call. Contact **Bell Canada Direct** (tel. (800) 565 4708). Other travelers should check with their providers before they leave home. In Australia, contact **Telstra Australia Direct** (tel. 13 22 00); in New Zealand, **Telecom New Zealand** (tel. 123). In the U.K., **British Telecom BT Direct** (tel. (800) 34 51 44); in Ireland, **Telecom Éireann Ireland Direct** (tel. (800) 250 250); in South Africa, **Telkom South Africa** (tel. 09 03). **Telephone rates** are reduced M-F 9:30pm-8am, Sa 2pm-8am, and Su all day for calls to the EU; M-F 8pm-2pm, and Su afternoon to the U.S. and Canada. Remember time differences when you call—Paris is one hour ahead of Greenwich Mean Time and six hours ahead of New York (Eastern Standard Time). A brief directory:

AT&T operator: tel. 0800 99 00 11.
MCI operator: tel. 0800 99 00 19.
Directory information: tel. 12.
International information: 00 33 12 + country code (Australia 61; Ireland 353; New Zealand 64; U.K. 44; U.S. and Canada 1).
International Operator: tel. 00 33 11. **Domestic Operator:** tel. 10.

To call France, dial the **international access code** (011 from the U.S. and Canada, 00 from the U.K., 0011 from Australia, 00 from New Zealand, 09 from South Africa), 33 (France's country code), and the local number minus the initial 0.

TELEGRAMS AND FAXES

To send a **telegram** to France from the U.S., Western Union (tel. (800) 325-6000) charges US$15.88 for the first seven words and then 84 cents per each additional word and has same-day delivery. To send a telegram to the U.S. from France, the Parisian post offices charge 135F for the first 15 words and 27F40 per five words after that. Most Parisian post offices have public **fax** machines, called *télécopieurs* or *faxes* by Rates to the U.S. are approximately 45F for the first page, 25F per page after that.

MINITEL

Minitel is what the French invented while the rest of the world was working on the Internet. Today, it seems like a dinosaur: a computer system with the power of a Commodore 64 provides telephone numbers, addresses, on-screen newspapers (including the *International Herald Tribune*), the weather, train schedules, and ticket info. If you have a listed telephone number, you can lease your own from the phone company. But at 2F per minute, Minitel could break your budget before you're even aware of it. Use the little yellow Minitel machines in post offices, including the Poste du Louvre and Poste des Champs-Elysées (see **Mail,** p. 72); bring a *télécarte*.

INTERNET

While major French companies and institutions boast websites and Internet access, students are rarely given a university account. As a result, wide-spread cyber culture is still nascent in Paris. For those addicts who desire that binary fix, there are a few cybercafés (see **Internet Cafés**, p. 130). Cybercafés tend to be expensive. Your best strategy is to compose email letters on your laptop or home computer, then download and send them at the café. This will reduce your login time and your expense. Some tourist offices offer free Internet access (see **Tourist Offices**, p. 71).

Magasin Séphora, 70, rue des Champs Elysées, 8ème (tel. 01 53 93 22 50; http://www.sephora.com). M: Franklin Roosevelt. Past the cosmetic counters, a few computers at the rear of this haute fragrance shop provide slow but free access to the Net. Open M-Sa 10am-midnight, Su noon-midnight.

Web Bar, 32, rue Picardie, 3ème (tel. 01 42 72 66 55; email webbar@webbar.fr). M: Temple. Walk against traffic on rue Temple and take a left on rue du Petit-Thouars; look for the neon sign. The large and fast computers circle the hip bar and restaurant below. 1F per minute. Coffee 12F. M-Sa 11:30am-2am, Su noon-midnight.

Éspace Internet-Galeries Lafayette, 40, bd. Haussmann, 9ème (tel. 01 42 82 30 33; http://www.bistrotininternet.fr). M: Opéra. On the 5th floor. Open M-Sa 9:30am-7pm, F 9:30am-9pm.

■ English-Language Religious Services

American Church in Paris: 65, quai d'Orsay, 7ème (tel. 01 40 62 05 00). M: Invalides or Alma-Marceau. A community center and a church. Bulletin boards list jobs, rides, apartments, and personals. Publishes *Free Voice,* a free English monthly listing cultural events and classified (ads 80F for 30 words). Services Su at 11am, followed by a coffee. Counseling service (tel. 01 45 50 26 49), call for an appointment. Open M-Sa 9am-10:30pm, Su 9am-7:30pm. Free concerts Sept.-June Su 6pm. AA, AL-ANON, and FAACTS (HIV support) meetings. Orientation for newcomers to Paris in Oct. Flea market 1st Sa of each month (2-5pm).

Anglican and Episcopalian: St. Michael's Church, 5, rue d'Aguesseau, 8ème (tel. 01 47 42 70 88). M: Concorde. Services in English Su at 10:30am and 6:30pm. Bulletin boards list jobs, accommodations, and events. Open M-Tu and Th-F 10am-12:30pm and 2-5:30pm. **American Cathedral,** 23, av. George V, 8ème (tel. 01 53 23 84 00). M: George-V. English services daily at 9am. Open M-F 9am-5pm.

Catholic: St. Joseph's Church, 50, av. Hoche, 8ème (tel. 01 42 27 28 56). M: Charles de Gaulle-Étoile. Mass in English M-F 8:30am, Sa 6:30pm, Su 9:45, 11am, and 6:30pm; July-Aug. Su mass at 10am, noon, and 6:30pm. Open M-Sa 10am-6pm.

Society of Friends (Quaker), 114bis, rue de Vaugirard, 6ème (tel. 01 45 48 74 23 recorded message). M: St-Placide or Montparnasse-Bienvenue. Enter through the garage door and walk down the courtyard stairs. 11am meetings, followed by communal lunch at noon.

Buddhist Temple, Centre de Kazyn Dzong, route de la ceinture du lac Daumesnil, 12ème (tel. 01 40 04 98 06). M: Porte Dorée. A buddhist temple and meditation center. Open Tu-Su 10:30am-8pm.

Mosque de Paris, Institut Musulman (Muslim Institute), 2, Place de l'Ermite 5ème (tel. 01 45 35 97 33); M: Place Monge. A gorgeous mosque, this is also a community center with tea house, restaurant, and *hamman.* Open Sa-Th 9am-noon and 2-6pm.

Synagogue: Union Libéral Israélite de France, 24, rue Copernic, 16ème (tel. 01 47 04 37 27). M: Victor-Hugo. Services F at 6pm and Sa at 10:30am, mostly in Hebrew with a little French. English-speaking rabbi stays after the service to chat. Services in the evenings and mornings of High Holy Days; call for info. Open M-Th 9am-noon and 2-6pm, F-Sa 9am-noon.

Église Russe, also known as **Cathédrale Alexandre-Nevski,** 12, rue Daru (tel. 01 42 27 37 34; M: Ternes). Russian Eastern Orthodox. Open Tu. and F 3-5pm. Services (in French and Russian) Su at 10am.

■ Other Services

Lost Property: Bureau des Objets Trouvés, 36, rue des Morillons, 15ème (tel. 01 55 76 20 20). M: Convention. No info given by phone. Open July-Aug. M-Th 8:30am-5pm; Sept.-June M and W 8:30am-5pm, Tu and Th 8:30am-8pm.

Public Baths: 8, rue des Deux Ponts, 4ème (tel. 01 43 54 47 40). M: Pont-Marie. Shower 7F50, with soap and towel about 16F. For the same price you can also bathe at 42, rue du Rocher, 8ème (tel. 01 45 22 15 19; M: St-Lazare), and at 40, rue Oberkampf, 11ème (tel. 01 47 00 57 35; M: Oberkampf). Clean, respectable, and popular in summer. All open Th noon-7pm, F-Sa 7am-5pm, Su 8am-noon.

Libraries: Bibliothèque Publique, in the Centre Pompidou, 4ème (tel. 01 44 78 12 33). M: Rambuteau. Books in English cannot be checked out. Open M and W-F noon-10pm, Sa-Su 10am-10pm. Anybody can visit French libraries; to borrow books, you need a passport ID and two proofs of French residency (phone and electricity bills, *carte de séjour*). **The American Library,** 10, rue Général Camou, 7ème (tel. 01 45 50 25 83; email: 100142.1066@compuserve.com). M: École Militaire. The largest English library in Paris. Membership 570F per year, student 460F, summer 240F, day entry 70F. Open Tu-Sa 10am-7pm.

Weather: Allo Météo, 5-day recorded forecasts. Call from touch-tone phones. **Paris,** tel. 08 36 68 02 75; **Île de France,** tel. 08 36 68 00 00; **France,** tel. 08 36 68 01 01; **mountain regions,** tel. 08 36 68 04 04; **marine conditions,** tel. 08 36 68 08 08.

■ Publications about Paris

On those occasions when *Let's Go* falls just short, consult the following guides. *Le Petit Futé* (89F), *Paris Pas Cher* (99F), and *Paris Combines* (98F) offer advice on shops, services, and restaurants for the long-term traveler. *Connaissance de Vieux Paris* (120F) is a street-by-street guide to the history of Paris. Popular among the French is the *Guide du Routard* (77F), a French *Let's Go,* with useful info on how to live on a budget in Paris. *Gault Millau* (155F) is a respected guide to Parisian eateries. Patricia Wells's *The Food Lover's Guide to Paris* (US$15 or 120F) lists the city's best restaurants, cafés, bakeries, and food shops (see **Books and Magazines,** p. 263).

The tourist office's free monthly *Paris Sélection* highlights exhibitions, concerts, walking tours, and events. The Mairie de Paris, 29, rue de Rivoli, 4ème (tel. 01 42 76 42 42; M: Hôtel-de-Ville) publishes the free monthly *Paris le Journal* with articles about what's on around the city. The weekly *Pariscope* (3F) and *Officiel des Spectacles* (2F) list movies, plays, exhibits, festivals, clubs, and bars. *Pariscope* also includes an English-language section called *Time Out Paris.* On Wednesday *Le Figaro* includes *Figaroscope,* a supplement about what's happening in Paris. *Free Voice,* a monthly English-language newspaper published by the American Church (see **English-Language Religious Services,** p. 74), and the bi-weekly *France-USA Contacts (FUSAC)* list jobs, housing, and information for English speakers and are available for free from English-speaking bookstores, restaurants, and travel agencies throughout Paris.

French newspapers are a rich source of day-to-day politics, culture, and debate for those who read French. *Libération* (7F), a socialist newspaper, offers comprehensive news coverage of world events. Heavy on culture, including theater and concert listings, *"Libé"* has excellent, controversial, and thought-provoking editorials. Readers with a penchant for politics will disappear behind a copy of *Le Monde* (7F50), decidedly centrist with a tendency to wax socialist. *Le Figaro* (7F) leans to the right, with an entire section of financial news. *Le Parisien* (4F90) and *France-Soir* (5F) also write from the right. *La Tribune* (7F) is France's *Wall Street Journal.* The Communist Party puts out *L'Humanité* (7F) for the good of the people. Those homesick for the *Washington Post* and the *New York Times* will find solace in the *International Herald Tribune* (10F). For a run-down of the latest on rap, hip-hop, industrial, and pop, fashion trends, and Paris street–culture, pick up a copy of the way-cool magazine *Technik Art* (25F), which reports monthly (in French) on all that is hip, chic, and swank among the city's youth-culture. Gay and lesbian readers should consult *Têtu* for the latest in French Queer politics, fashion, and events.

ESSENTIALS

Accommodations

In those days the hotel was one of the many damp, plain hosteleries made for tourists, chiefly American, of very modest means who, if they were like me would always remember how the exotic bidet, positioned solidly in the drab bedroom, along with the toilet far down the ill-lit hallway, virtually defined the chasm between Gallic and Anglo-Saxon cultures.
—William Styron, *Darkness Visible,* 1989

In Paris, budget accommodations fall into three categories: hotels, hostels, and *foyers.* While hotels are comfortable and give you complete privacy and independence, hostels and *foyers* are the least expensive options, especially for people traveling alone. According to the Office du Tourisme, high season in Paris falls from May to October. The peak of high season is July and August. Be aware that the city of Paris has a *Taxe de Séjour* of 1-5F per person per day within the city. Most hostels and *foyers* include this tax in their listed prices, but hotels may or may not consider it part of the room's cost. It is advisable to check for this as well as other add-on expenses such as direct telephone service (some hotels will even charge you for collect calls) before making a reservation. Try to make a reservation in advance, but if you do arrive in Paris without one, don't panic. The **Office du Tourisme** on the Champs-Elysées or one of its other bureaus should be able to find you a room, although the lines may be long and the selections not necessarily among the cheapest in Paris (see **Tourist Offices,** p. 71). If you have difficulty finding accommodation in the popular Latin Quarter or Marais, check our listings in the outlying arrondissements. The metro commute to most sights in Paris is only 20 minutes. The following booking offices, located near major metro lines, are also frequently crowded, but their English speaking staff can arrange for stays in hostels and budget hotels throughout the city.

La Centrale de Réservations (FUAJ-HI), 4, bd. Jules Ferry, 11ème (tel. 01 43 57 02 60; fax 01 40 21 79 92). M: République. Follow the rue du Faubourg du Temple away from pl. de la République until you reach the park-like entity that divides bd. Jules Ferry in two. Cross to far side and turn right—La Centrale is half a block up on your left. One of the best ways to secure a bed in a hostel (113-125F per night per person) in Paris. Provides same-day reservations in one of their affiliated youth hostels or budget hotels—a total of 10,000 beds in and around the city. The earlier you show up the better, but they can usually help anyone any time. Books beds for groups throughout France and Europe, arranges excursions, and procures plane and bus tickets. Open M-Sa 9am-6pm. If La Centrale is closed, the 24hr. reception at the Jules Ferry Hostel, 2 doors down, has access to the same network of affiliates and may be able to find you a bed (see **11ème Arrondissement,** p. 91).

OTU-Voyage (Office du Tourisme Universitaire), 119, rue St-Martin, 4ème (tel. 01 40 12 12 29); see **Budget Travel Offices,** p. 71. Across the pedestrian mall from the Pompidou. Even in the busiest months, OTU-Voyage guarantees "decent and low-cost lodging" in Residence Bastille and hotels for same-day reservation and immediate use. You must pay the full price of the *foyer* room when making your reservation, even before seeing the room. Employees speak English and other foreign languages. 10F service charge. Open M-F 9:30am-7pm and Sa 10am-noon and 1:15-5:30pm.

TYPES OF ACCOMMODATIONS

◼ Hostels and Foyers

Paris's big-city hostels don't bother with many of the restrictions—sleepsheets, curfews, and the like—that characterize most hostels in the world, but they do have maximum stays, although even these restrictions are flexible. Accommodations usually consist of single-sex rooms with two to eight beds, but you may be asked whether you're willing to be in a co-ed room. You will certainly need to share a room with strangers.

To stay in a **Hostelling International (HI)** hostel, you must be a member. If you show up at an HI hostel without a membership card, the hostel should issue you a blank card with space for six validation stamps. Each night you'll pay a nonmember supplement (19F) and earn one Guest Stamp. Get six stamps and you're a member. Membership purchased this way costs 114F, so it's cost-efficient for prospective hostelers to become members before leaving home. Most student travel agencies issue HI cards on the spot, or you can contact a national hostel organization (see **Student and Budget Travel Agencies,** p. 55). Another benefit of an HI membership is HI's recently instituted International Booking Network, whereby you can reserve a room in advance. Information on French hostels can also be obtained through the world wide web at http://www.fuaj.fr.

Despite the hype, there are only six official HI hostels and HI affiliates in Paris. Most of the hostels and *foyers* in the city are privately run organizations, usually with services comparable to those at HI and often preferable to the HI hostels because of their more central locations. Normally intended for university students during the academic year, *foyers* offer the security and privacy of a hotel while providing the lower prices and camaraderie of a youth hostel.

■ Hotels

Of the three classes of Parisian budget accommodations, hotels may be the most practical for the majority of travelers. There is total privacy, no curfew, and (usually) concerned managers. Most important, hotels routinely accept reservations. Budget hotels in Paris are not significantly more expensive than their hostel and *foyer* counterparts. Groups of two, three, and four may find it more economical to stay in a hotel since, unlike *foyers,* hotels rent doubles by the room and not by the body.

The French government publishes a comprehensive guide that classifies hotels with a star system: 4L (luxury), 4, 3, 2, and 1, depending on the services offered, the percentage of rooms with bath, and other such indicators. Most hotels in *Let's Go: Paris* are one-star or unclassified establishments, although some two and three-star hotels offering inexpensive rooms are included. When you arrive, it is best to ask to see the room, where possible, before you register. Rooms in one and two-star hotels are sometimes rather variable. If you are not satisfied ask to change, although a brighter room may be more expensive. Most rooms come with full-size beds. In our listings, doubles refer to rooms with one full-size bed; two-bed doubles refer to the rare room with two separate (usually twin) beds. Expect to pay at least 150F for singles. If your room has no shower, you'll usually have to pay extra (15-25F) to get the key to the hall shower. Showers in your room are included in the room charge. Note: every hotel in Paris must charge a 5F per day hotel tax *(taxe du séjour)* per person; it is usually included in the listed price. Paris has a number of very nice hotels in the 150-200F range. These hotels are often small and simple and do not offer the amenities of the Sheraton or the Hilton. But the hotels listed here are clean, have well-furnished rooms, and have adequate toilet and shower facilities. Most newly renovated hotels have double-paned glass windows that insulate against cold and street noise.

A few tips about Parisian hotels: Keep in mind that the French call the ground floor the *rez-de-chaussée* and start numbering with the first floor above the ground floor *(premier étage).* Many hotels serve breakfast for 20-30F. Since local cafés often serve croissants and coffee for less, you may want to eat breakfast out. Remember that there are usually rules against bringing food into your rooms. Parisian law forbids hanging laundry from windows or over balconies to dry. Most hotels in Paris are not wheelchair accessible; in the index of this book, we list the hotels we cover that are. It is advisable to call for more information as accessibility is almost always limited to a few rooms and may require advance reservations or preparation.

RESERVATIONS

Confirm your dates before making a reservation. If you decide to leave Paris before you intended, or if you want to switch hotels, don't expect to get back all your money. Ask about a hotel's cancellation policy before giving a credit card number and whether or not your credit card will be billed. If you can avoid leaving a number (which is often times the case if you just send written confirmation or say you don't have one) do so in case you don't like the hotel upon your arrival. Make reservations at least two weeks in advance. A number of hotels claim that they are fully booked two months in advance for the summer. To help guarantee that you have a room waiting when you arrive, the following process is advised:

1. Call, write, or fax the hotel, ask for a reservation for a specific date and specify the type of room (single, double, with bathroom, shower, etc.).
2. If you write, enclose an International Reply Coupon (sold at post offices), so that the hotel need not bother with postage expenses.
3. When you receive positive confirmation, send *la caution* (a deposit) for one night. Most hotels will confirm reservations only upon receipt of a check for the first night, although some will accept a credit card number instead. The easiest way to send this deposit is to mail a traveler's check in French francs, double signed.
4. Call one or two days in advance to confirm (or cancel) and inform the manager of your intended arrival time.

■ Alternative Accommodations

STUDENT ACCOMMODATIONS

For travelers planning a summer, semester, or academic year visit to Paris, student housing is available in the dormitories of most French universities. Contact the **Centre Régional des Oeuvres Universitaires (CROUS)** for more information (see **University Restaurants,** p. 106). Additional lodging is available on a month-to-month basis at the **Cité Universitaire** (15, bd. Jourdan, 14$^{\grave{e}me}$; tel. 01 44 16 64 00; M: Cité Universitaire). Over 30 different nations maintain dormitories at the Cité Universitaire, where they board their citizens studying in Paris. In summer, dorms lodge anyone on a first-come, first-served basis. Reserve a bed months in advance—at least by April for June and July. Some kitchens ARE available. To stay in the American House write to Fondation des États-Unis, 15, bd. Jourdan, 75690 Paris Cedex 14 (tel. 01 53 80 68 82). Rates vary according to demand: in summer 2900F per month; cheaper off season. (Office open M-F 9-5pm.) For info about other dorms, write to M. le Délégué Général de Cité Universitaire de Paris, 19, bd. Jourdan, 75690 Paris Cedex 14. The **restaurant** in the Maison Internationale offers decent institutional fare at rock-bottom prices (open M-Sa 11:45am-2:30pm and 6:30-9pm, Su 11:45am-2:30pm; meal ticket 14F10 for students, with ISIC 23F50).

LONG-TERM ACCOMMODATIONS

If you plan to stay in Paris for a longer period of time, consider renting an apartment. Although rent is high and utilities are expensive, apartments offer convenience, privacy, and a kitchen. Call, fax, write, or visit **Allô Logement Temporaire,** 64, rue du Temple, 3$^{\grave{e}me}$ (tel. 01 42 72 00 06; fax 01 42 72 03 11; M: Chapelle; open M-F noon-8pm). This helpful, English-speaking association charges a membership fee of 300F if they succeed in finding an apartment for you, which is followed by an additional charge of 200F per month beginning in the second month of your stay. The company suggests writing or calling before you leave for France. Be sure to leave a phone or fax number where you can be reached easily. Vacancies come and go very quickly. Consult the French Department at your local university; it may be able to connect you with students abroad who want to sublet. Remember that short-term rentals, usually more expensive per month than longer rentals, can be difficult to procure, especially in winter months. The **Internet** can provide listings on Paris apartments, but these apartments often tend to be more expensive apartments advertised by wealthy Parisians with computers and Internet-access. Surf the web to get a sense of the housing market before you go (see **Internet Resources,** p. 26).

If possible, stay in a hotel your first week in Paris and find an apartment while you're there. This process will allow you to see what you're getting. Among the best places to look are the bulletin boards in the **American Church** (see **Essentials,** p. 74). Those upstairs tend to advertise for long-term rentals, while those downstairs list short-term, often cheaper arrangements. A smaller list of apartments to rent or share can be found at the bookstore **Shakespeare and Co.** (see **Books and Magazines,** p. 263). Check listings in any of the English-French newsletters like **Free Voice** or **France-USA Contacts (FUSAC),** a free publication found in English bookstores and restaurants throughout Paris (tel. 01 45 38 56 57; call for distribution info). FUSAC is also distributed in the U.S. (FUSAC, P.O. Box 115, Cooper Station, New York, NY 10276; tel. (212) 929 2929; fax 255 5555; fusac@club-internet.fr). It includes an extensive classifieds section, in which anglophones offer apartments for rent or sublet. An earlier generation often found cheap rooms on the top floor of regular hotels, where the cramped space under the eaves rents for less. If they haven't added elevators or renovated, some hotels still have cut rates for these simple singles and rent them for longer stays.

Let's Go doesn't recommend subletting in Paris, as it is in fact illegal; many choose to do so anyway. Those who do sublet should work out a written agreement with the landlord, defining all of their mutual expectations regarding security deposits, utilities, maintenance, and rent. This document will help to avoid any misunderstandings. The utilities and mailbox may have to remain under the original renters' name, and the subletter may need to tell the building superintendent or *concierge* that he or she is merely a guest, relative, or friend of the original renter.

HOTELS, HOSTELS, AND FOYERS

■ First Arrondissement

In the shadow of the Louvre, much of the 1er remains true to its regal past. Cartier, Chanel, and the Banque de France set an intimidating mood for the budget traveler. Don't let the financiers and ladies-who-lunch scare you away: a few budget options remain. Those who stay near Châtelet-les-Halles will revel in the central location but should use a safer metro station at night.

Henri IV, 25, pl. Dauphine (tel. 01 43 54 44 53). M: Cité. Walk toward the Conciergerie and turn right on bd. du Palais, left on quai de l'Horloge, and left at the front of the Conciergerie onto pl. Dauphine. The last outpost of cheap accommodations on Île de la Cité, the Henri IV is also among the best-located hotels in the city. Named in honor of Henri IV's printing presses that once occupied the building, the hotel has charming views of the tree-lined pl. Dauphine. First floor toilet is inconveniently located up stairs that wrap around the outside of the building. All other toilets located inside. Singles 120-125F; doubles 150-200F, with shower 265F; triples 240-260F; quads 280F. Showers 15F. Reserve 1 month in advance.

Hôtel Lion d'Or, 5, rue de la Sourdière (tel. 01 42 60 79 04; fax 01 42 60 09 14). M: Tuileries or Pyramides. From M: Tuileries walk down rue du 29 Juillet away from the park and turn right on rue St-Honoré then left on rue de la Sourdière. Carpeted, rooms are basic but quiet. You'll hear the bells toll from nearby Église St-Roch but little else. Phone and TV in most rooms. Friendly staff speaks English. Singles 230F, with shower 300F; doubles with shower 380F, with bath and toilet 420F. Extra bed 60F. Breakfast 35F. 5% discount for stays of more than 3 nights. AmEx, MC, V.

Hôtel Montpensier, 12, rue de Richelieu (tel. 01 42 96 28 50; fax 01 42 86 02 70). M: Palais-Royal. Walk around the left side of the Palais-Royal to rue de Richelieu. Clean rooms, lofty ceilings, and brightly colored decor welcome the clientele. Its good taste distinguishes it from most hotels in this region and price range. Brightly lit lounge with stained-glass ceiling. Small elevator. TVs in rooms with shower or bath. Singles 285F, with toilet 310F; doubles with toilet 310F, with shower, toilet, and sink 420F, with bath, toilet, and sink 400F. Extra bed 70F. Shower 25F. Breakfast 37F in lounge or bedroom. Reserve 2 weeks in advance. AmEx, MC,V.

Hôtel Saint-Honoré, 85, rue St-Honoré (tel. 01 42 36 20 38 or 01 42 21 46 96; fax 01 42 21 44 08). M: Louvre, Châtelet, or Les Halles. From M: Louvre, cross rue de Rivoli on rue du Louvre and turn right on rue St-Honoré. Recently renovated, with new reception, breakfast area, and comfortable rooms with firm beds and a dashing black and mauve color scheme. Friendly, English-speaking staff, and young clientele. Fridge access. All rooms have shower, toilet, and TV. Singles 290F; doubles 320-350F, with bathtub 380F; triples and quads 480F. Breakfast 29F. Reserve by fax or phone and confirm the night before. AmEx, MC, V.

Hôtel Richelieu-Mazarin, 51, rue de Richelieu (tel. 01 42 97 46 20; fax 01 47 03 94 13). M: Palais-Royal. See directions for Hôtel Montpensier, above. Plastic flowers and faux Monet prints decorate these smallish rooms with radios, phones, and a view of the bustling thoroughfare. Doubles in converted attic have an oasis of taste—muted flowered wallpaper, pine furniture, and skylight (but no view). English spoken. Singles 190-210F, with shower or bath and toilet 280-310F; doubles 230F, with shower or bath and toilet 300-330F; triples with shower and toilet 390F. Extra bed 60F. Showers 10F. Breakfast 25F in the dining room, 30F in your room. Reserve 3 weeks ahead in summer. MC, V.

Hôtel du Palais, 2, quai de la Mégisserie (tel. 01 42 36 98 25; fax 01 42 21 41 67). M: Châtelet. Located by the Seine at the corner of pl. du Châtelet and quai de la Mégisserie, all rooms (except those on top floor) have splendid views of the river and are within earshot of the traffic below. Very basic rooms with high ceilings on first floor; tiny sky-lit rooms with funky eaves on top floor. A good choice if you don't mind vertigo-inducing stairways. Singles with shower 283F, with shower and toilet 323F, with bath and toilet 353F, on top floor 183F; doubles with shower 326F, with shower and toilet 356F, with bath and toilet 386F, on top floor 236F; triples 429F; large quad 462F; quint with 2-sink bathroom and huge windows 535F. Extra bed 70F. Breakfast 30F. Reserve 3 weeks in advance. MC, V.

Hôtel de Lille, 8, rue du Pélican (tel. 01 42 33 33 42). M: Palais-Royal. From the metro walk toward the Palais-Royal, turn right onto rue St-Honoré, left on rue Croix des Petits Champs, and take your 1st right on rue du Pélican. Located on a quiet street close to the Louvre. Big, clean, and slightly worn red-carpeted rooms. Outside door locked at 9pm. Arrive before 7pm on the first day of your stay to pick up your personal and outside door keys. Singles 200F; doubles 230F, with shower 280F. Showers 30F. No breakfast. Reserve by mail with 1 night's deposit.

Hôtel du Centre, 20, rue du Roule (tel. 01 42 33 05 18; fax 01 42 33 74 02). M: Pont Neuf. From M: Pont Neuf take rue de la Monnaie toward Les Halles straight onto rue du Roule. If inexpensive accommodations and location at the center of Paris are your overriding concerns, the Hôtel du Centre is the place for you. Most rooms have mushy beds, red carpets, and TVs. Singles or doubles with shower and toilet, 350F. Extra double bed 30% extra. Breakfast 30F. Reserve 2 weeks in advance with 1 night's deposit. AmEx, MC, V.

Residence Vauvilliers, 6, rue Vauvilliers (tel. 01 42 36 89 08). M: Louvre. From the metro follow rue du Louvre away from the Seine and take the 1st right on rue St.-Honoré then the 2nd left on rue Vauvilliers; hotel is on the right. Though the Vauvillier can't boast of a grand interior, it can claim a central location, clean, medium-sized rooms, and many renovated bathrooms. Ring at the bank-telleresque window. Singles with shower 178F; doubles with shower 235F, with shower and toilet 326F. Breakfast 28F. Reserve in writing with 1 night's deposit. No credit cards.

Timhotel Le Louvre, 4, rue Croix des Petits-Champs (tel. 01 42 60 34 86; fax 42 60 10 39). M: Palais-Royal. From the metro, cross rue de Rivoli to rue St-Honoré; take a left onto rue Croix des Petits-Champs. Though part of a chain, this 2-star hotel offers the only wheelchair-accessible rooms at reasonable prices in the 1er. Clean and modern rooms with bath, shower and cable TV. Great location next to the Louvre. Singles 460F; doubles 560; wheelchair-accessible rooms 560F. AmEx, MC, V.

Hostels and Foyers

Centre International de Paris (BVJ)/Paris Louvre, 20, rue J.-J. Rousseau (tel. 01 53 00 90 90; fax 01 53 00 90 91). M: Louvre or Palais-Royal. From M: Louvre take rue du Louvre away from river then turn left on rue St-Honoré and right on rue J.-J.

Rousseau. Courtyard hung with brass lanterns and strewn with brasserie chairs. 200 beds. Bright, dorm-style rooms with 2-10 beds per room. 24hr. reception. 120F, breakfast and showers included. 2-course lunch or dinner 40F, 4-course 60F. Weekend reservations up to 1 week in advance. Rooms held only 10min. after your expected check-in time; call if you'll be late. English spoken.

Maisons des Jeunes de Rufz de Lavison, 18, rue J.-J. Rousseau (tel. 01 45 08 02 10). M: Louvre or Palais-Royal. Located next door to above hostel. During the academic year, it's a private residence for male college students. In summer (mid-June to mid-Aug.) it's a co-ed foyer, primarily for long-term stays. Quiet, spacious, and sunny rooms for 50 students. Flower-filled, open-air courtyard. 4-night min. stay. Reception 9am-7pm. No curfew. Singles 160F; doubles 280F. Monthly: singles 4,000F; doubles 6,800F. Shower and breakfast included. During winter, dinner is provided. Reservations starting June 15; 1 night's payment required.

■ Second Arrondissement

The 2ème is within easy walking distance of the Marais, the Centre Pompidou, and the Louvre. The relatively safe, animated southern half sports cobbled pedestrian streets. Nearby pl. de l'Opéra in the 9ème is lined with boutiques and theaters. But do not stray too far into the northeastern quarter, especially near seedy rue St-Denis. Below rue Réaumur, rue St-Denis glows with flashing sex shop signs and prostitution.

Hôtel Vivienne, 40, rue Vivienne (tel. 01 42 33 13 26; fax 01 40 41 98 19). M: Rue Montmartre. Follow the traffic on bd. Montmartre past the Théâtre des Variétés and turn left on rue Vivienne. From its hardwood-floored reception area to its spacious rooms with armoires, flowers, hairdryers, phones, and TVs, this hotel reconciles gracious living with budget rates. Some balconies, beamed ceilings, and views across the Paris rooftops. Elevator. Singles and doubles with shower 360-440F; doubles 505F; 3rd person under 10 free, over 10 add 30%. Breakfast 40F. MC, V.

Hôtel des Boulevards, 10, rue de la Ville Neuve (tel. 01 42 36 02 29; fax 01 42 36 15 39). M: Bonne Nouvelle. From the rue Poissonnière metro, turn right on rue Poissonnière then left on rue de la Lune and right onto rue de la Ville Neuve. This route avoids the X-rated movie theater on rue de la Ville Neuve, the one blemish in an otherwise good area. Refurbished, quiet, aqua rooms with TVs, phones, and wooden wardrobes. Showers may wet entire bathroom. Singles and doubles 220-285F; double with bath 320F; third person add 60F. Reserve 2 weeks ahead and confirm with credit card deposit. 10% discount for *Let's Go* readers. AmEx, MC, V.

Hôtel La Marmotte, 6, rue Léopold Bellan (tel. 01 40 26 26 51). M: Sentier. Follow traffic on rue Réaumur and turn right onto rue Montorgueil and then turn right again at rue Léopold Bellan. Reception located in ground-floor bar of a modern building. Clean, quiet, and spacious rooms with TVs, phones, and safe-boxes. Many restaurants nearby. Singles and doubles 180-220F, with shower 270-300F; 2-bed doubles 320F. Breakfast 25F. Shower 15F. Reserve 2-3 weeks ahead. AmEx, MC, V.

Hôtel Bonne Nouvelle, 17, rue Beauregard (tel. 01 45 08 42 42; fax 01 40 26 05 81). M: Bonne Nouvelle. From metro follow traffic down rue Poissonnière and turn left on rue Beauregard. Cozy antique-filled lobby, reasonably sized rooms of assorted retro decor. Rooms are variable, though all generally pleasant, so ask to see it beforehand where possible. All rooms have TVs, hairdryers, and tidy bathrooms with toilet, shower, or bath. Tiny elevator. Singles 330-390F; doubles 350-430F; triples 500-600F; quads 570-670F. Breakfast 30F, in room 35F. Reserve by credit card. MC, V.

Hôtel Ste-Marie, 6, rue de la Ville Neuve (tel. 01 42 33 21 61; fax 01 42 33 29 24). M: Bonne Nouvelle. Located next to Hôtel des Boulevards (see above). This little hotel has been renovated and refurbished; rooms feature candy-striped walls, electric pink bedspreads, new mattresses, and clean bathrooms. TVs in every room with a sturdy shower; all rooms with phones. Singles 200-243F; doubles 206-281F; triples with shower and toilet 392F. Showers 10F. Breakfast 25F. AmEx, MC, V.

Hôtel Tiquetonne, 6, rue Tiquetonne (tel. 01 42 36 94 58; fax 01 42 36 02 94). M: Étienne-Marcel. Walk against traffic on rue de Turbigo and turn left on rue Tiquetonne. Near Marché Montorgueil, but also near St-Denis's sex shops, this affordable 7-story hotel is a veritable study in faux finishes: from fake-marble corridors, to "I-can't-believe-it's-not-wood" doors. Elevator. Most rooms with shower and toilet. Singles 143-213F; doubles 246F. Hall showers on 2nd floor 30F. Breakfast 25F, served in room. Closed Aug. and 1 week around Christmas. MC, V.

Hôtel Favart, 5, rue Marivaux (tel. 01 42 97 59 83; fax 01 40 15 95 58). M: Richel Drout. From the metro turn left down bd. des Italiens and left on Marivaux. On a quiet street in a good location, the rooms are sizable and well decorated, and some have nice views. Large elevator. All rooms have a TV, phone, shower, toilet, and hair dryer. One handicapped accessible room on first floor with a very large bathroom. July-Aug. singles 300F; doubles 400F. Sept.-June singles 525F; doubles 655F; triples 775F. Breakfast included.

■ Third Arrondissement

Once the home of Paris's noblest families, the $3^{\grave{e}me}$'s many 17th-century mansions now house museums, boutiques, and galleries. Meanwhile, budget accommodations cluster in the $3^{\grave{e}me}$'s noisy, commercial northwest—particularly around rue de Turbigo, where hotels sidle up to Paris's garment district.

Hôtel de Roubaix, 6, rue Greneta (tel. 01 42 72 89 91; fax 01 42 72 58 79). M: Réaumur-Sébastopol or Arts-et-Métiers. From M: Réaumur-Sébastopol, walk opposite traffic on bd. de Sébastopol and turn left on rue Greneta or take bus #20 from Gare de Lyon to St-Nicolas des Champs. Run by a helpful, advice-dispensing older couple, this hotel features clean rooms with flowered wallpaper and new bathrooms. Pleasant reception, large breakfast room, 2 lounges, and a marble staircase. All rooms have shower, toilet, and TV. Some noisy rooms. Local bank changes money without commission for hotel patrons. Elevator. Singles 305-330F; doubles 390-410F; triples 415-480F; quads 500F; quints 525F. Breakfast included. MC, V.

Hôtel du Séjour, 36, rue du Grenier St-Lazare (tel. 01 48 87 40 36). M: Etienne Marcel or Rambuteau. From M: Etienne Marcel follow the traffic on rue Etienne Marcel, which becomes rue Grenier St-Lazare. One block from Les Halles and the Centre Pompidou and housed in a 300-year-old building, this hotel is being renovated. Ask for a new room. Reception 7am-10:30pm. Singles 160F; doubles 240F, with shower and toilet 300F; third person 150F extra. Showers 20F. No breakfast.

Hôtel Bellevue et du Chariot d'Or, 39, rue de Turbigo (tel. 01 48 87 45 60; fax 01 48 87 95 04). M: Etienne Marcel. From the metro, walk against traffic on rue Turbigo. A beautiful Belle Époque lobby, with bar and breakfast room, give this hotel an air of elegance. Clean, modern, and bright rooms, some on a quiet courtyard. All have phones, TVs, toilets, and baths. Singles 310F; doubles 340F; triples 410F; quads 440F. Breakfast 35F. Reserve 2 weeks ahead by fax. AmEx, MC, V.

Hôtel Picard, 26, rue de Picardie (tel. 01 48 87 53 82; fax 01 48 87 02 56). M: Temple. From the metro, walk against traffic down rue du Temple, make your first left on rue Du Petit Thouars, and at the end of the street turn right. Located on a quiet street, the hotel's simple yet tasteful rooms are 5min. from the Pompidou and the Musée Picasso. Next door to the cyber café WebBar. TVs in rooms with showers. Elevator. Mention *Let's Go* for a 10% discount. Singles 200F, with shower and toilet 250F; doubles 240-260F, with shower and toilet 320F; triples 510F. Hall showers 20F. Breakfast 30F. Apr.-Sept. reserve 1 week ahead. MC, V.

Hôtel Bretagne, 87, rue des Archives (tel. 01 48 87 83 14). M: Temple. From the metro, walk opposite traffic on rue du Temple, then turn left on rue de Bretagne and right onto rue des Archives. Steps away from a small park, the cheaper rooms are simple, while steeper ones have TVs. Many rooms are on the noisy street, others on a nondescript courtyard. Singles 160F, with bath, toilet, and TV 310F; doubles 200-360F; triples 330-500F; quads 600. Breakfast 30F, served in rooms.

Hôtel Paris France, 72, rue de Turbigo (tel. 01 42 78 00 04, reservations 01 42 78 64 92; fax 01 42 71 99 43). M: République or Temple. From M: République take rue de Turbigo. The large lobby has soft sofas and a large TV. Some noisy rooms but if you ask for one on the top floor you can get a renovated bright space with balcony, clean bathrooms, and super view. Elevator. Singles 250-330F; doubles 240-360F; triples 500F. Breakfast in sunny breakfast room 25F. AmEx, MC, V.

■ Fourth Arrondissement

On either side of rue de Rivoli, a web of narrow streets harbors galleries, shops, museums, squares, and gay cafés. The Marais is famed for its Jewish quarter, pl. des Vosges, and its many hidden courtyards. The heart of all that is chic in Paris, the 4ème is a great place to stay and an ideal base for tourists.

Grand Hôtel Jeanne d'Arc, 3, rue de Jarente (tel. 01 48 87 62 11; fax 01 48 87 37 31; http://www.hoteljeannedarc.com). M: St-Paul or Bastille. From M: St-Paul walk opposite traffic on rue de Rivoli and turn left on rue de Sévigné then right on rue de Jarente. On a quiet side-street in the Marais, the Jeanne d'Arc's stylish rooms all have showers, toilet, and TVs. 2 rooms on the ground floor are wheelchair accessible. Elevator. Singles 300-395F; doubles 305-490F; triples 530F; quads 590F. Extra bed 75F. Breakfast 35F. Reserve 2 months in advance. MC, V.

Castex Hôtel, 5, rue Castex (tel. 01 42 72 31 52; fax 01 42 72 57 91). M: Bastille or Sully-Morland. Exit M: Bastille on bd. Henri IV and take the 3rd right on rue Castex. Spotless rooms in this family-run hotel look onto the street or the courtyard. TV room. Reception 7am-noon. Check-in 1pm. All rooms with telephone and sink. Singles 240F-290F; doubles 320-360F; triples 460F. Extra bed 70F. Breakfast 25F. Reserve with 1 night's deposit 2 months in advance. MC, V.

Hôtel de Nice, 42bis, rue de Rivoli (tel. 01 42 78 55 29; fax 01 42 78 36 07). M: Hôtel-de-Ville. From the metro, walk opposite traffic on rue de Rivoli for about 4 blocks; the hotel is on the left. The lobby is like a summer day in the South of France. Many rooms have balconies with great views. Lots of sun, but hot in the summer (fans are provided). Check-in 2pm, check-out 11am. All rooms with toilet, shower, and TV. Elevator. Singles 380F; doubles 480F; triples 600F. Breakfast 35F. Extra bed 120F. Reserve with 1 night's deposit 1 month ahead for summer. MC, V.

Hôtel Andréa, 3, rue St-Bon (tel. 01 42 78 43 93; fax 01 44 61 28 36). M: Hôtel-de-Ville. Follow traffic on rue de Rivoli and turn right on rue St-Bon. On a quiet street 2 blocks from Châtelet. Clean and reasonably comfortable rooms with phones. Elevator. Rooms with shower also have TV. Singles 250F, with toilet and shower 325F; doubles 250F, with toilet and shower 360F; triples 435F; quads 500F. Hall showers 20F. Breakfast 30F. Reserve 3 weeks in advance by fax or credit card. MC, V.

Hôtel Practic, 9, rue d'Ormesson (tel. 01 48 87 80 47; fax 01 48 87 40 04). M: St-Paul. From the metro, walk opposite traffic on rue de Rivoli then turn left on rue de Sévigné and right on rue d'Ormesson. A clean modest hotel on a cobblestone square in the heart of the Marais. English spoken. Singles 200F; doubles 245F-360F. Extra bed 80F. Breakfast 25F. Reserve 2-4 weeks in advance.

Hôtel de la Place des Vosges, 12, rue de Birague (tel. 01 42 72 60 46; fax 01 42 72 02 64; http://www.france-hotel-guide.com/h75004placedesvosges.htm). M: Bastille. From the metro take the 3rd right off rue St-Antoine. Only steps away from pl. des Vosges (and once a stable for the royal horses), the location can't be beat. Plush red carpets, dark wood, and exposed beams give the small rooms lots of charm. TVs in all rooms. Very professional staff. Rooms on higher floors get a little hot in summer. Singles 350-450F; doubles 490-510F; 1 small quad 810F. Breakfast 35F. Reserve 2 months ahead with one night's deposit. MC, V.

Hostels

Hôtel des Jeunes (MIJE) (tel. 01 42 74 23 45; fax 01 40 27 81 64) books beds in Le Fourcy, Le Fauconnier, and Maubuisson (see below), 3 small hostels located on cobblestone streets in old Marais residences. The chic-est and best-located youth accommodations around. No smoking. English spoken. Public phones and free lockers (with a 2F deposit). Must be 18-30, 7-day max. stay. Reception 7am-1am. Lockout noon-4pm. Curfew 1am. Quiet after 10pm. 4- to 9-bed dorms 125F; singles 198F; doubles 304F; triples 274F. Shower, sheets, and breakfast (served 7:30-10am) included. Arrive before 3pm first day of reservation (call in advance if you'll be late). Groups may reserve 1 year in advance. Restaurant *La Table d'Hôtes* (at Le Fourcy) offers an entrée with drink and coffee and 3-course "hosteler special" (52F). Open M-F 11:30am-1:30pm and 6:30-8:30pm.

Le Fourcy, 6, rue de Fourcy. M: St-Paul or Pont Marie. From M: St-Paul, walk opposite the traffic for a few meters down rue François-Miron and turn left on rue de

Fourcy. Hostel surrounds a large courtyard ideal for meeting travelers or for open-air picnicking at one of the tables. Light sleepers should avoid rooms on the social courtyard. Elevator. Call ahead for wheelchair accessibility.

Le Fauconnier, 11, rue du Fauconnier. M: St-Paul or Pont Marie. From M: St-Paul take rue du Prevôt, turn left on rue Charlemagne, and turn right on rue du Fauconnier. Ivy-covered building steps away from the Seine and Île St-Louis. Spacious 6-bed rooms, some doubles, some singles.

Maubuisson, 12, rue des Barres. M: Hôtel-de-Ville or Pont Marie. From M: Pont Marie, walk opposite traffic on rue de l'Hôtel de Ville and turn right on rue des Barres. A half-timbered former girls' convent that looks out onto a silent street by the St-Gervais monastery. Smaller 2- to 7-bed rooms with nice views. Elevator. Call ahead for wheelchair accessibility.

■ Fifth Arrondissement

Central and popular, the 5ème has a number of great hotels near the cafés, bars, cinema, and nightlife of the *Quartier Latin*. But popularity has its price. Most hotels fill quickly in the summer. Reserve rooms at least a month in advance. In the fall, the return of students means more competition for *foyers*.

Hôtel d'Esmeralda, 4, rue St-Julien-le-Pauvre (tel. 01 43 54 19 20; fax 01 40 51 00 68). M: St-Michel. Walk along the Seine on quai St-Michel toward Nôtre-Dame then turn right at parc Viviani. Rooms with views of the park, the Seine, and Nôtre-Dame. Singles 160F; doubles 420-490F; triples 550F; quads 600F. Breakfast 40F.

Hôtel des Argonauts, 12, rue de la Huchette (tel. 01 43 54 09 82; fax 01 44 07 18 84). M: St-Michel. With your back to the Seine, take the first left off bd. St-Michel onto rue de la Huchette. Located above a Greek restaurant of the same name. Newly redecorated, clean, simple rooms. In the middle of St-Michel, the hotel is surprisingly quiet. Singles 255F; doubles 285-360F. Breakfast 25F. AmEx, MC, V.

Hôtel des Alliés, 20, rue Berthollet (tel. 01 43 31 47 52; fax 01 45 35 13 92). M: Censier-Daubenton. From the metro, walk 20min. down rue Monge toward bd. Port-Royal and turn right on rue Claude Bernard and left on rue Berthollet. In a commercial area, the Alliés offers cheap, large, well-lit rooms close to the markets of rue Mouffetard. Singles and doubles 220-300F. Hall showers 15F. Breakfast 28F. MC, V.

Hôtel Gerson, 14, rue de la Sorbonne (tel. 01 43 54 28 40; fax 01 44 07 13 90). M: Cluny-Sorbonne. From the metro turn left on bd. St-Michel, left on rue des Écoles, then right on rue de la Sorbonne. Facing the Sorbonne, the rooms are bright and clean. Singles 225F, with shower and toilet 306F; doubles with toilet 250F, with shower 330F; triples 400F. Breakfast 25F. Reserve 3 weeks in advance. MC, V.

Hôtel Gay Lussac, 29, rue Gay-Lussac (tel. 01 43 54 23 96). M: Luxembourg. From the metro walk down rue Gay-Lussac to rue St-Jacques. An old but well-preserved hotel: the floors are slightly warped and creaky, but the rooms are sunny. Some have balconies. Elevator. Singles and doubles 185F; triples 450-480F; quads 580F. Breakfast included. Reserve by phone 2-4 weeks in advance.

Hôtel St-Jacques, 35, rue des Écoles (tel. 01 44 07 45 45; fax 01 43 25 65 50). M: Maubert-Mutualité. Turn left on rue des Carmes, then left on rue des Écoles. One step up from the budget hotel, this pastel palace has bright, color coordinated rooms with balconies, large windows, and TVs. Impressive lobby with a glass chandelier and red carpet. English spoken. Elevator. Singles 250F, with shower and toilet 480F; doubles 420-580F; triples 560-650F. Breakfast 35F. AmEx, MC, V.

Hôtel le Central, 6, rue Descartes (tel. 01 46 33 57 93). M: Maubert-Mutualité. From the metro walk up rue de la Montaigne Ste-Geneviève. Great location near rue Mouffetard and the Pantheon. Long, simple rooms facing the street get brilliant sunlight. All rooms have showers. Singles 160-213F; doubles and triples 236-266F.

Hôtel Marignan, 13, rue du Sommerard (tel. 01 43 54 63 81). M: Maubert-Mutualité. From the metro turn left on rue des Carmes then right on rue du Sommerard. Quiet, simple rooms with high ceilings. The clientele ranges from backpackers to families. Breakfast room (with microwave) where residents can fix daytime meals. Singles 220-240F; doubles 320-450F; triples 410F-560F; quads 490-650F. Free laundry. Breakfast included. Reserve far in advance.

Hôtel des Médicis, 214, rue St-Jacques (tel. 01 43 54 14 66). M: Luxembourg. From the metro turn right on rue Gay-Lussac and then left on rue St-Jacques. Rock-bottom prices for lace curtains, comfortable beds, and a great location. Lots of young Americans. Reception 9am-11pm. Singles and doubles 85-180F. No reservations in summer; arrive early in the morning and hope for a vacancy.

Hostels and Foyers

Centre International de Paris (BVJ): Paris Quartier Latin, 44, rue des Bernardins (tel. 01 43 29 34 80; fax 01 53 00 90 91). M: Maubert-Mutualité. Walk with traffic on bd. St-Germain and turn right on rue des Bernardins. 162 beds. Immense ultra-modern hostel with a shiny cafeteria. A friendly, boisterous crowd congregates in the huge common area. Kitchen, TV, and message service. Showers in rooms. 24hr. reception. Check-in before 2:30pm. Check-out 9am. 2-, 4-, and 10-bed dorms 120F; singles 130F. Breakfast included. Lockers 10F. Reserve well in advance and confirm, or arrive at 9am to check for available rooms.

Young and Happy (Y&H) Hostel, 80, rue Mouffetard (tel. 01 45 35 09 53; fax 01 47 07 22 24). M: Monge. From the metro, cross rue Gracieuse and take rue Ortolan to rue Mouffetard. Clean, cheerful rooms, some with balconies and potted plants. A lively hostel in the heart of the student quarter. Small common room with blue lamps, and cheap beer. Lockout 11am-5pm. Curfew 2am. Doubles 254F; quads 428F. Breakfast included. Sheets 15F. Towels 5F. Reserve with 1 night's deposit or show up at 8am. Money exchanged for no commission. Laundry nearby. MC, V.

■ Sixth Arrondissement

The *6ème* combines the bohemian caché, intellectual panache, and thriving artistic culture of the *quartier latin*. Budget hotels are sparse in this chic neighborhood, but the following exceptions provide surprising bargains. Travelers with disabilities will find few budgets options, however, and should look to the nearby *7ème*.

Hôtel Neslé, 7, rue du Neslé (tel. 01 43 54 62 41; fax 01 43 54 31 88). M: Odéon. From the metro walk up rue de l'Ancienne Comédie, onto rue Dauphine, and take a left on rue du Neslé. Whimsical and sparkling, the Neslé stands out in a sea of nondescript budget hotels. The bright, recently renovated, ultra-clean rooms contain Moroccan tiles and murals depicting the history of Paris. Breakfast included; served in the delightful rose garden or on the covered terrace. For a special treat, book the double room with its own Turkish hammam (350F). Laundry available. Singles 275F; doubles 350-450F. Reservations recommended.

Hôtel du Lys, 23, rue Serpente (tel. 01 43 26 97 57; fax 01 44 07 34 90). M: Odéon. Go with traffic on bd. St-Germain and turn left on rue Danton, then make first right onto rue Serpente. With exposed wood beams and chintz drapes and bedspreads, this hotel feels like a warm English country house. All rooms include bath or shower, TV, phone, and hairdryer. Singles 490F; doubles 520F; triples 620F. V.

Hôtel de Chevreuse, 3, rue de Chevreuse (tel. 01 43 20 93 16; fax 01 43 21 43 72). M: Vavin. Walk up bd. Montparnasse in the direction opposite the Tour and turn left on rue de Chevreuse. Ezra Pound lived around the corner (at 70, rue Nôtre-Dame-des-Champs) and loved this neighborhood. With nearby shops, restaurants, cafés, and cinemas, the street is relatively quiet. Clean, spartan rooms. Singles 220F; doubles 270F, with shower, TV, and toilet 310-330F; triples with full bathroom and TV 510F. Breakfast 32F. Reserve one week in advance. MC, V.

Hôtel St-André des Arts, 66, rue St-André-des-Arts (tel. 01 43 26 96 16; fax 01 43 29 73 34; email hsaintand@minitel.net). M: Odéon. From the metro, take rue de l'Ancienne Comédie, walk one block, and take the first right on rue St-André-des-Arts. Centrally located, the hotel has a helpful staff who run a busy ship. The rooms aren't fancy, but the bathrooms are recently redone. High ceilings make up for smaller rooms. All rooms have showers, sinks, and toilets. Singles 360F; doubles 460-500F; triples 580F; quads 640F. Breakfast included. MC, V.

Hôtel St-Michel, 17, rue Git-le-Coeur (tel. 01 43 26 98 70; fax 01 40 46 95 69). M: St-Michel. From pl. St-Michel, walk one block on rue St-André-des-Arts and turn right on rue Git-le-Coeur. Utilitarian rooms on a quiet street close to the Seine. Friendly staff. Singles 218F, with shower 313F, with shower and toilet 353F; doubles 246F, with shower 341F, with shower and toilet 375F; 2-bed doubles with shower 471F, with shower and toilet 516F. Breakfast included. Shower 12F. Reserve with 1 night's deposit at least 2 weeks in advance. No credit cards.

Hôtel Petit Trianon, 2, rue de l'Ancienne Comédie (tel. 01 43 54 94 64). M: Odéon. Petite, sparkling rooms in a loud but central location. Negotiable prices for a week's stay or longer, youthful atmosphere, and familial staff keep the Trianon popular. 3 rooms have balconies. English spoken. Singles 170-180F; larger doubles with shower 320-350F, with shower and toilet 400-450F. Breakfast 25F. Reserve in advance with 1 night's deposit. No credit cards.

Dhely's Hotel, 22, rue de l'Hirondelle (tel. 01 43 26 58 25; fax 01 43 26 51 06). M: St-Michel. Just steps from pl. St-Michel and the Seine on a cobblestone way, the Dhely's wood paneling, flower boxes, modern facilities, and quiet location make for a pleasant stay. Singles 180F; doubles 290F, with shower 380F; triples 370F with shower 490F. Extra bed 100F. Hall showers 25F. Breakfast 30F. Each night must be paid in advance. Reserve in advance with deposit. AmEx, MC, V.

Hostels

Foyer International des Étudiantes, 93, bd. St-Michel (tel. 01 43 54 49 63). M: Luxembourg. Across from Jardin du Luxembourg. Marbled reception area, library, TV lounge, kitchenettes, laundry facilities, and spacious rooms, all fitted with elegant wood paneling and some with balconies. Breakfast and shower included. July-Sept. hotel is coed, open 24hrs; Oct.-June women only. Reception Su-F 6am-1:30am, Sa 24hr. Two-bed dorms 97F; singles 147F. Monthly: 2000F; 2950F. Reserve in writing 2 months in advance. 200F deposit if confirmed. Call ahead or arrive at 9:30am to check for no-shows. No credit cards.

Association des Étudiants Protestants de Paris, 46, rue de Vaugirard (tel. 01 43 54 31 49 or 01 43 25 98 75; fax 01 46 34 27 09; email aepp@worldnet.fr). M: Odéon or RER: Luxembourg. From the metro, go left up rue de Condé and then right on Vaugirard. Overlooking the Jardin du Luxembourg, the association lets its simple rooms to young people ages 18-26. Part summer hostel, part university residence, the building includes a kitchen, lounge area, and washing machines. Dorms 80F; singles 100-115F; doubles 174-196F. Monthly: 1550F. Breakfast included. To stay more than 5 days, make reservations 2 weeks in advance. No reservations for fewer than 5 days, but call ahead or show up at 10:30am the same day. 10F membership fee charged on arrival, plus 100F key deposit. Call, write, or email to request long-term application (due before May 30). No credit cards.

■ Seventh Arrondissement

Hotels cluster around the western edge of the 7ème all advertising (though not necessarily providing) rooms with views of the Eiffel Tower. Frequented by business travelers and older couples, hotels in this quarter are quieter and more expensive. Unfortunately, there are no hostels and few budget options. Pay a little more and enjoy telephones and TVs, breakfast in bed, bathtubs, and a short walk to the tallest thing in Paris or the big tomb of the littlest emperor.

Grand Hôtel Lévêque, 29, rue Cler (tel. 01 47 05 49 15; fax 01 45 50 49 36; http://www.interresa.ca/hotel/leveque; email hotellev@club-internet.fr). M: École Militaire. From the metro walk on av. de la Motte-Picquet and make a left onto the cobblestone pedestrian street called rue Cler. Originally a 19th-century rooming house, this 50-room hotel has just been renovated. Hairdryers and TVs in all rooms; some have balconies. Safety deposit box (10F). Singles with sink 250F; 1-bed doubles with shower, sink, and toilet 350-385F, 2-bed doubles with shower, sink, and toilet 385-420F; triples with shower and toilet 515F. Breakfast 30F. AmEx, MC, V.

Hôtel Malar, 29, rue Malar (tel. 01 45 51 38 46; fax 01 45 55 20 19). M: Latour Maubourg. From the metro, follow traffic on bd. de la Tour Maubourg, turn left on rue St-Dominique, and then right on rue Malar. Family hotel with inner courtyard, on a side street near the restaurants and shops of rue St-Dominique. All rooms have TVs, telephones, showers, and hairdryers. Renovations to be completed by Mar., 1999. Singles with shower 290F, with shower and toilet 350F, with bath and toilet 395F; doubles 330F, 450F, 480F. Extra bed 100F. Breakfast 32F. AmEx, MC, V.

If you're stuck for cash on your travels, don't panic. Millions of people trust Western Union to transfer money in minutes to 153 countries and over 45,000 locations worldwide. Our record of safety and reliability is second to none. So when you need money in a hurry, call Western Union.

WESTERN UNION | MONEY TRANSFER®

The fastest way to send money worldwide.®

MCI Spoken Here

Worldwide Calling Made Simple

For more information or to apply for a Card call: **1-800-955-0925**

Outside the U.S., call MCI collect (reverse charge) at: **1-916-567-5151**

International Calling As Easy As Possible.

The MCI Card with WorldPhone Service is designed specifically to keep you in touch with the people that matter the most to you.

The MCI Card with WorldPhone Service....

- Provides access to the US and other countries worldwide.
- Gives you customer service 24 hours a day
- Connects you to operators who speak your language
- Provides you with MCI's low rates and no sign-up fees

For more information or to apply for a Card call:
1-800-955-0925

Outside the U.S., call MCI collect (reverse charge) at:
1-916-567-5151

Pick Up the Phone, Pick Up the Miles.

You earn frequent flyer miles when you travel internationally, why not when you call internationally? Callers can earn frequent flyer miles if they sign up with one of MCI's airline partners:

- American Airlines
- Continental Airlines
- Delta Airlines
- Hawaiian Airlines
- Midwest Express Airlines
- Northwest Airlines
- Southwest Airlines
- United Airlines
- USAirways

Please cut out and save this reference guide for convenient U.S. and worldwide calling with the MCI Card with WorldPhone Service.

Your MCI Worldphone Access Numbers

COUNTRY	WORLDPHONE TOLL-FREE ACCESS #
#Singapore	8000-112-112
#Slovak Republic (CC)	00421-00112
#Slovenia	080-8808
#South Africa (CC)	0800-99-0011
#Spain (CC)	900-99-0014
#Sri Lanka (Outside of Colombo, dial 01 first)	440100
#St. Lucia ÷	1-800-888-8000
#St. Vincent	1-800-888-8000
#Sweden (CC) ◆	020-795-922
#Switzerland (CC) ◆	0800-89-0222
#Syria	0800
#Taiwan (CC) ◆	0080-13-4567
#Thailand ★	001-999-1-2001
#Trinidad & Tobago ÷	1-800-888-8000
#Turkey (CC) ◆	00-8001-1177
#Turks and Caicos ÷	1-800-888-8000
#Ukraine (CC) ÷	8▼10-013
#United Arab Emirates ◆	800-111
#United Kingdom (CC) To call using BT ■	0800-89-0222
To call using C&W ■	0500-89-0222
#United States (CC)	000-412
#Uruguay	1-800-888-8000
#U.S. Virgin Islands (CC)	000-412
#Vatican City (CC)	172-1022
#Venezuela (CC) ÷ ◆	800-1114-0
Vietnam ●	1201-1022
Yemen	008-00-102

Automation available from most locations.
(CC) Country-to-country calling available to/from most international locations.
÷ Limited availability.
▶ Wait for second dial tone.
◀ When calling from public phones, use phones marked LADATEL.
■ International communications carrier.
★ Not available from public pay phones.
◆ Public phones may require deposit of coin or phone card for dial tone.
● Local service fee in U.S. currency required to complete call.
▲ Regulation does not permit intra-Japan calls.
÷ Available from most major cities

And, it's simple to call home.

1. Dial the WorldPhone toll-free access number of the country you're calling from (listed inside).

2. Follow the voice instructions in your language of choice or hold for a WorldPhone operator.
   - Enter or give the operator your MCI Card number or call collect.

3. Enter or give the WorldPhone operator your home number.

4. Share your adventures with your family!

MCI

The MCI Card with WorldPhone Service...
The easy way to call when traveling worldwide.

For more information or to apply for a Card call:
1-800-955-0925

Outside the U.S., call MCI collect (reverse charge) at:
1-916-567-5151

Please cut out and save this reference guide for convenient U.S. and worldwide calling with the MCI Card with WorldPhone Service.

COUNTRY	WORLDPHONE TOLL-FREE ACCESS #
American Samoa	633-2MCI (633-2624)
#Antigua	1-800-888-8000
(available from public card phones only)	#2
#Argentina (CC) ◆	0800-5-1002
#Aruba ÷	800-888-8
#Australia (CC) ◆	
To call using OPTUS ■	1-800-551-111
To call using TELSTRA ■	1-800-881-100
#Austria (CC) ◆	022-903-012
#Bahamas	1-800-888-8000
#Bahrain	800-002
#Barbados	1-800-888-8000
#Belarus (CC)	
From Brest, Vitebsk, Grodno, Minsk	8-800-103
From Gomel and Mogilev	8-10-800-103
#Belgium (CC) ◆	0800-10012
#Belize	
From Hotels	815
From Payphones	557
#Bermuda ÷	1-800-888-8000
#Bolivia ◆	0-800-2222
#Brazil (CC)	000-8012
#British Virgin Islands ÷	1-800-888-8000
#Brunei	800-011
#Bulgaria	00800-0001
#Canada (CC)	1-800-888-8000
#Cayman Islands	1-800-888-8000
#Chile (CC)	
To call using CTC	800-207-300
To call using ENTEL ■	800-360-180
#China ✦	108-12
For a Mandarin-speaking Operator	108-17
#Colombia (CC) ◆	980-16-0001
Collect Access in Spanish	980-16-1000
#Costa Rica ◆	0800-012-2222
#Cote D'Ivoire	1001
#Croatia (CC) ★	0800-22-0112
#Cyprus ◆	080-90000
#Czech Republic (CC) ◆	00-42-000112
#Denmark (CC) ◆	8001-0022
#Dominica	1-800-888-8000
#Dominican Republic	1-800-888-8000
Collect Access	1121
Collect Access in Spanish	1121
#Ecuador (CC) ◆	999-170
#Egypt (CC) ◆	355-5770
(Outside of Cairo, dial 02 first)	
El Salvador	800-1767

— FOLD —

COUNTRY	WORLDPHONE TOLL-FREE ACCESS #
#Federated States of Micronesia	624
#Fiji	004-890-1002
#Finland (CC) ◆	08001-102-80
#France (CC) ◆	0800-99-0019
#French Antilles (CC)	0800-99-0019
#French Guiana (CC) (includes Martinique, Guadeloupe)	0800-99-0019
#Gabon	00-005
#Gambia ◆	00-1-99
#Germany (CC)	0-800-888-8000
#Greece (CC) ◆	00-800-1211
#Grenada ÷	1-800-888-8000
#Guam (CC)	1-800-888-8000
#Guatemala ◆	99-99-189
Guyana	177
#Haiti ÷	193
Collect Access in French/Creole	190
Honduras ÷	8000-122
#Hong Kong (CC)	800-96-1121
#Hungary (CC) ◆	00▼800-01411
#Iceland (CC) ◆	800-9002
#India (CC) ◆	000-127
Collect Access	000-126
#Indonesia (CC) ◆	001-801-11
#Iran ÷	(SPECIAL PHONES ONLY)
#Ireland (CC)	1-800-55-1001
#Israel (CC) ◆	1-800-940-2727
#Italy (CC) ◆	172-1022
#Jamaica ÷	1-800-888-8000
Collect Access	873
(From Special Hotels only)	*2
#Japan (CC) ◆	
(from public phones)	
To call using KDD ■	00539-121▼
To call using IDC ■	0066-55-121
To call using ITJ ■	0044-11-121
#Jordan	18-800-001
#Kazakhstan (CC)	8-800-131-4321
#Kenya ◆	0800-12
	009-14
#Korea (CC)	
To call using KT ■	00309-14
To call using DACOM ■	00369-14
Phone Booths÷	Press red button, 03, then *
Military Bases	550-2255
#Kuwait	800-MCI (800-624)

— FOLD —

COUNTRY	WORLDPHONE TOLL-FREE ACCESS #
#Liechtenstein (CC) ◆	600-MCI (600-624)
Collect Access	0800-89-0222
#Luxembourg (CC)	0800-0112
#Macao	0800-131
#Macedonia (CC)	99800-4266
#Malaysia (CC) ◆	1-800-80-0012
#Malta	0800-89-0120
#Marshall Islands	1-800-888-8000
#Mexico (CC)	
Avantel	01-800-021-8000
Telmex ▲	001-800-674-7000
Collect Access in Spanish	01-800-021-1000
#Monaco (CC) ◆	800-90-019
#Montserrat	1-800-888-8000
#Morocco	00-211-0012
#Netherlands (CC) ◆	0800-022-91-22
#Netherlands Antilles (CC) ÷	001-800-888-8000
#New Zealand (CC)	000-912
#Nicaragua (CC)	166
Collect Access in Spanish	
(Outside of Managua, dial 02 first)	
From any public payphone	*2
#Norway (CC) ◆	800-19912
#Pakistan	00-800-12-001
#Panama	108
#Papua New Guinea (CC)	2810-108
#Paraguay ÷	008-11-800
#Peru	0-800-500-10
#Philippines (CC) ◆	
To call using PLDT ■	105-14
To call using PHILCOM	1026-14
Collect Access via PLDT in Filipino	105-15
Collect Access via ICC in Filipino	1026-15
#Poland (CC) ÷	00-800-111-21-22
#Portugal (CC) ÷	05-017-1234
#Puerto Rico (CC)	1-800-888-8000
#Qatar ★	0800-012-77
#Romania (CC) ÷	01-800-1800
#Russia (CC) ◆ ÷	
To call using ROSTELCOM ■	747-3322
(For Russian speaking operator)	747-3320
To call using SOVINTEL ■	960-2222
#Saipan (CC) ÷	950-1022
#San Marino (CC) ◆	172-1022
#Saudi Arabia (CC) ÷	1-800-11

Royal Phare Hôtel, 40, av. de la Motte-Picquet (tel. 01 47 05 57 30; fax 01 45 51 64 41). M: Ecole Militaire. Next to the metro stop on a busy street. Blink and you'll miss the small entryway, between a cash machine and a natural food store. Small, tidy, colorful rooms with TVs, phones, and hair dryers. Friendly reception. Singles with shower and toilet 310-370F, with bath and toilet 400F; doubles 355-390F, 420F. Extra bed 100F. Breakfast 32F, served 7-10am in room or in lobby. Reserve at least 1 week ahead during the summer with 1 night's deposit. AmEx, MC, V.

Hôtel Eiffel Rive Gauche, 6, rue du Gros Caillou (tel. 01 45 51 24 56; fax 01 45 51 11 77; email eiffel@easynet.fr). M: École Militaire. From the metro, walk up av. de la Bourdonnais, turn right on rue de la Grenelle, then left on Gros Caillou. On a quiet street, this busy, family-run hotel is a favorite for anglophone travelers (the energetic owner speaks five languages). Inner courtyard is decorated like a Spanish garden. Pink, aqua, and brown rooms all with TV, radio, phone. Some with views of at least the top half of the Eiffel Tower. Singles 220-450F; doubles 270-460F; triples 440-550F. Extra bed 90F. Breakfast buffet served 8-11am in the large peach dining area (40F) or in your room (47F). Hall showers 19F. AmEx, MC, V.

Hôtel du Champ de Mars, 7, rue du Champ de Mars (tel. 01 45 51 52 30; fax 01 45 51 64 36; http://www.adx.fr/hotel-du-champ-de-mars; email stg@club-internet.fr). M: École Militaire. Just off av. Bosquet. If you are willing to pay, this hotel may be the most *chic* for your money. Flower-boxed and gardened, the entire hotel is a gem in cheerful blues, yellows, and whites, suggesting a country house in Provence. All rooms have bathtub or shower, phone, and satellite TV. Singles with shower 355F, with large bed and bath 385F; doubles with shower 360F, with bath 390-420F; triples with bath 505F. Breakfast 35F, served in rooms or elegant downstairs salon 7-10am. Reserve by phone, fax, or email and confirm with 1 night's deposit by credit card. Small elevator. AmEx, MC, V.

Hôtel Kensington, 79, av. de la Bourdonnais (tel. 01 47 05 74 00; fax 01 47 05 25 81). M: École Militaire. Walk north up av. Bosquet, turn left on rue de Grenelle and then right on av. de la Bourdonnais. Compact rooms with pastel paisley wallpaper have TV, shower or bath, and toilet. Brisk, professional service. Elevator. Singles 305F; doubles with shower 390F, with bath 420-490F. Extra bed 80F. Breakfast 30F, served 7:30-11am in dining room or bedroom. Reservations with 1 night's deposit recommended. AmEx, MC, V.

Hôtel de France, 102 bd. de la Tour Marbourg (tel. 01 47 05 40 49; fax 01 45 56 96 78). M: École Militaire. Directly across from the Hôtel des Invalides, this hotel's owners are young, energetic, and eager to give advice on Paris (in English, Spanish, or French). Beyond the hotel's purple-painted halls you'll find sparkling, clean rooms. Some rooms have spectacular views of the *Église du Dôme* and the Invalides. The hotel has two wheelchair-accessible rooms (500F), a portable ramp at the entrance, and a wide elevator. All rooms with minibar, phone, and cable. Singles 395F; doubles 500F; connecting rooms for 4-5 persons 800-860F. Breakfast 35F. AmEx, MC, V.

■ Eighth Arrondissement

The 8ème is more for jet-setters than for budget travelers. While you might spot a movie star dining at Fouquet's or hopping into a car outside Christian Dior, you'll be hard-pressed to find comfortable, affordable lodging nearby. If you must sleep near the Champs, the following shouldn't break the bank.

Hôtel d'Artois, 94, rue La Boétie (tel. 01 43 59 84 12 or 01 42 25 76 65; fax 01 43 59 50 70). M: St-Philippe de Roule. A stone's throw from the Champs-Élysées and next to a 4-star. From the metro take a left and go down on rue La Boétie. A bit worn, with high ceilings and carpets. Spacious bathrooms and large bedrooms. Plant-filled lobby and incense-scented breakfast room. English spoken. Elevator. Singles 245F, with shower 350F, with bath and toilet 395F; doubles 275F, with shower 380F, with bath and toilet 430F; 2-bed doubles with bath and toilet 450F. Extra bed 135F. Hall showers 20F. Breakfast 30F. AmEx, MC, V.

Hôtel Wilson, 10, rue de Stockholm (tel. 01 45 22 10 85). M: St-Lazare. From the metro, walk up rue de Rome and turn left on rue de Stockholm. No-frills hotel near the Gare St-Lazare, owned by an elderly couple. Bathrooms in rooms are newer than those off the halls. Occasional velvet chairs. Clean, relatively spacious rooms. Singles 185F, with shower and toilet 220F; doubles with shower 265F, with toilet 260F; triples with shower 360F; quads 365-395F. Breakfast included.

Hôtel Europe-Liège, 8, rue de Moscou (tel. 01 42 94 01 51; fax 01 43 87 42 18). M: Liège. From the metro walk down rue d'Amsterdam and turn left on rue de Moscou. Very pleasant, reasonably priced hotel with newly painted rooms. Many restaurants nearby. All rooms have TV, hairdryer, phone, showers, or baths. 2 handicapped-accessible rooms on the ground floor, though not fully wheelchair accessible. Singles 370F; doubles 480F. Breakfast 35F. Amex, MC, V.

Hôtel Madeleine Haussmann, 10, rue Pasquier (tel. 01 42 65 90 11; fax 01 42 68 07 93). M: Madeleine. From the metro walk up bd. Malesherbes and turn right on rue Pasquier. A bit expensive given the simplicity of the rooms but understandable in light of the fabulous location and close proximity to the Madeleine, pl. de la Concorde, and the Opéra. Clean, agreeable rooms with shower or bath, TV, phone, and hairdryers. A 3-star hotel. Ask for handicapped accessibility. Singles 600F; doubles 650F; triples 760F; and one quad 800F. Buffet breakfast 40F.

Hostels and Foyers

UCJF (Union Chrétienne de Jeunes Filles, YWCA), 22, rue Naples (tel. 01 53 04 37 47; fax 01 53 04 37 54). M: Europe. From the metro take rue de Constantinople and turn left onto rue de Naples. Organized, well-kept, homey environment for women only. Spacious rooms, hardwood floors, large beds. Large oak-paneled common room with fireplace, TV, VCR, books, theater space, and family-style dining room with varied daily menu. Congenial staff. June-Aug. 2-day min. stay; Sept.-May longer stays for women ages 18-26 (age flexible). All guests pay 30F YWCA membership fee, as well as 50F (for week stays) or 100F (for stays of 1 month or more) processing fee to stay in YWCA hostels. Reception open M-F 8am-12:30am, Sa-Su 9am-12:30pm and 1:30pm-12:30am. Visitors until 10pm; men not allowed in bedrooms. Curfew 12:30am (ask for key, 200F deposit). Kitchen, laundry. Singles 155F first night, 135F subsequent nights; doubles 270F; triples 405F. Weekly: singles 950F; doubles 1500F. Monthly: singles 3000F; doubles 4900F; triples 7320F. Breakfast and dinner included. Also at 168, rue Blomet, 15ème (tel. 01 53 53 63 00; fax 01 53 53 63 12); M: Convention. Men should contact the YMCA Foyer Union Chrétienne de Jeunes Gens, 14, rue de Trévise, 9ème (tel. 01 47 70 90 94).

Foyer de Chaillot, 28, av. George V (tel. 01 47 23 35 32; fax 01 47 23 77 16). M: George V. From the metro make a right down av. George V and walk about 3 blocks (on the opposite side of the street) until you see a high-rise silver office building called Centre Chaillot Galliera. The foyer is on the 3rd floor. Seeking to build a community among its residents, the foyer organizes numerous daytrips and activities in a spacious dorm-like environment for **professional women only.** Residents must be working or hold an internship and be between the ages of 18-25; min. one-month stay. Modern and impeccable rooms. Singles all have a sink, while doubles have shower and sink. Toilets and additional showers in each hall. Large common rooms equipped with stereo and TV. Fully equipped kitchens. Phones in each hall. Guests permitted until 10pm. 2000F deposit required to reserve a room together with an application and a description of your activities in Paris. Singles 3300 per month; doubles 5800F per month. Breakfast and dinner included M-F.

■ Ninth Arrondissement

The 9ème's proximity to the sights of the 2ème, 8ème, and 18ème makes it an ideal base. The hotels of the southern 9ème are generally safe and clean, while many in the north serve clients paying by the hour. Avoid the areas around M: Pigalle and M: Barbès-Rochechouart. Just a few streets south of bd. de Clichy and rue Pigalle, the neighborhood shifts from a red-light district to a quiet, diverse residential quarter.

Hôtel Beauharnais, 51, rue de la Victoire (tel. 01 48 74 71 13). M: le Peletier. From the metro, follow traffic on rue de la Victoire and look for flower boxes, since there is no Hotel sign and the lobby looks like someone's sitting room. The witty and gregarious Mme Bey dispenses helpful advice in English, German, and French and is particularly kind to young travelers. Each elegant room is dressed in antiques and mirrors. Doubles with shower 320F; triples with shower 490F. Breakfast 35F, free for *Let's Go* travelers.

Résidence Hôtel des Trois Poussins, 15, rue Clauzel (tel. 01 53 32 81 81; fax 01 53 32 81 82). M: St-Georges. Uphill on rue Nôtre-Dame-de-Lorette, turn right on rue H. Monnier and then right on rue Clauzel. Shines like a new nickel. Immaculate, spacious, freshly painted rooms with bath, phone, hairdryer, TV, and fax/modem outlet. Beautiful views from the 5th floor up. Studios with kitchenettes. 2 wheelchair-accessible rooms on the ground floor, although the 9*ème* tends to be hilly. Elevator. Singles 360F; doubles 480F; triples 740F. Studio singles: 1 week 390F, 1 month 320F; studio doubles: 1 week 520F, 1 month 360F; studio triples: 1 week 510, 1 month 480F. Reserve 2 weeks in advance. AmEx, V, MC.

Hôtel des Arts, 7, Cité Bergère (tel. 01 42 46 73 30; fax 01 48 00 94 42). M: Rue Montmartre. Walk uphill on rue du Faubourg Montmartre, turn right on Cité Bergère. A family hotel with small pleasant rooms on a quiet pedestrian street. Popular with businesspeople. All rooms have shower, TV, and hairdryer. Elevator. Singles 335-360F; doubles 380F; triples 490F. Breakfast 33F. AmEx, MC, V.

Hôtel Rex, 4bis Cité Rougement. Behind Cité Bergère, see directions for Hôtel des Arts above. A modest hotel in a quiet location full of groups of young people. All rooms have TV and shower, but no views. Small elevator. Singles 350F; doubles 450F; triples 500F.

Hostels and Foyers

Woodstock Hostel, 48, rue Rodier (tel. 01 48 78 87 76; fax 01 48 78 87 76). M: Anvers or Gare du Nord. From M: Anvers, walk against traffic on pl. Anvers, turn right on av. Trudaine and then left on rue de Rodier. From M: Gare du Nord turn right on rue Dunkerque (with the station at your back); at pl. de Roubaix, veer left on rue de Maubeuge, veer right on rue Condorcet, and turn left on rue Rodier. A 15min. walk. A nice hostel, located near Gare du Nord, Gare de l'Est, and Sacré Coeur, though distant from tourist attractions. Spotless, quiet, affordable rooms. Communal kitchen, safety deposit box, and fax. Supermarket, bakery, and laundromat on the block. June-Aug. 4-person dorms 87F; doubles 97F. Sept.-May dorms 75F; doubles 87F. Showers free (and clean). Call ahead to reserve a room. MC, V.

■ Tenth Arrondissement

Catering to the traffic that pours through the Gare de l'Est and the Gare du Nord, a number of inexpensive hotels have set up shop in the 10*ème*. This arrondissement is a good place to look if you've struck out elsewhere. After dark, beware of the Gare du Nord, rue du Faubourg St-Denis and bd. de Magenta, and near M: Barbès.

Hôtel de Milan, 17, rue de St-Quentin (tel. 01 40 37 88 50; fax 01 46 07 89 48). M: Gare du Nord. Follow rue de St-Quentin from Gare du Nord; the hotel is on the right-hand corner of the 3rd block. An antique wooden elevator ascends the center of a spiral staircase. The well-kept rooms are slightly more expensive than other 10*ème* hotels, but the location is worth the splurge. Singles 153F, with TV 173F; doubles 186-266F, triples 429F. Hall showers 18F. Breakfast 20F. MC, V.

Hôtel Moderne du Temple, 3, rue d'Aix (tel. 01 42 08 09 04; fax 01 42 41 72 17). M: Goncourt. Walk with the traffic on rue du Faubourg du Temple then turn right on rue d'Aix; the hotel is on the left. Located on a quiet street, this Czech-owned hotel has immaculate and tastefully decorated rooms, some overlooking a charming courtyard. Singles 110F; doubles 240F; triples 180-270F. Breakfast 23F.

Hôtel Palace, 9, rue Bouchardon (tel. 01 40 40 09 46 or 01 42 06 59 32; fax 01 42 06 16 90). M: Strasbourg/St-Denis. Walk against traffic on bd. St-Denis until the small arch; follow rue René Boulanger on the left, then turn left on rue Bouchardon. The privacy of a hotel with the rates of a hostel. Cheerful rooms face a green courtyard. Laundry and market next door. Singles 100F; doubles 130-280F; triples 289F; quad 362F; quints 400F. Shower 20F. Breakfast 20F. Reserve 2 weeks ahead. MC, V.

Cambrai Hôtel, 129bis, bd. de Magenta (tel. 01 48 78 32 13; fax 01 48 78 43 55). M: Gare du Nord. Follow traffic on rue de Dunkerque to pl. de Roubaix and turn right on bd. de Magenta. The hotel is on the left. A homey, family-owned hotel close to the *gare.* Clean, airy rooms with natural light and high ceilings. Singles 156-187F; doubles 211-289F; triples 376F; quads 425F. Showers 20F. Breakfast included.

Hôtel Lafayette, 198, rue Lafayette (tel. 01 40 35 76 07; fax 01 42 09 69 05). M: Louis Blanc. From the metro, walk opposite the traffic lane closest to you on rue Lafayette; hotel is on the left. Small, clean, no-frills rooms near the Canal St-Martin. Singles 120F; doubles 160-195F. Hall showers 20F. Breakfast 20F. AmEx, MC, V.

Hôtel Sibour, 14, rue Sibour (tel. 01 46 07 20 74; fax 01 46 07 37 17). M: Gare de l'Est. Go down bd. Strasbourg and then turn left on rue Sibour. Functional rooms near the Gare de l'Est. Singles 175-195F; doubles 195-310F. Breakfast 25F. MC, V.

■ Eleventh Arrondissement

The *nouveau chic* 11ème is short on sights but large on nightlife and budget accommodations. Inexpensive hotels cluster around the Opéra Bastille, providing easy access to nightclubs, bars, and cafés. More budget options cluster near pl. de la République, a transportation hub. The 11ème's hotels tend to have vacancies in July and August, although its large-sized youth hostels are popular year-round.

Hôtel de Nevers, 53, rue de Malte (tel. 01 47 00 56 18; fax 01 43 57 77 39). M: Oberkampf or République. From M: République, walk down av. de la République and take a right on rue de Malte. Spotless, spacious rooms with classy furniture. Ask for one on a high floor, away from the noise of the street. Guests have access to a refrigerator. 24hr. reception. Elevator. Singles and doubles 170F, with shower 220F; doubles with shower 260F; triples 310F; quads 380F. Hall showers 20F. Breakfast 25F, served in the rooms. Reserve 2 weeks ahead by credit card. MC, V.

Hôtel de Belfort, 37, rue Servan (tel. 01 47 00 67 33; fax 01 43 57 97 98). M: Père-Lachaise, St-Maur, or Voltaire. From M: Père-Lachaise, take the rue du Chemin Vert and turn left on rue Servan. 15min. from pl. de la Bastille. Dim corridors and clean functional rooms with industrial carpets and plain peach walls. *Let's Go* special: 100F per person per night in doubles, triples, and quads. All rooms with shower, toilet, and phone. Elevator. Breakfast (served 7:30-9:30am) 15F. MC, V.

Plessis Hôtel, 25, rue du Grand Prieuré (tel. 01 47 00 13 38; fax 01 43 57 97 87). M: Oberkampf. From the metro, walk north on rue du Grand Prieuré. 5 floors of clean, bright, renovated rooms, with hairdryers, fans, and a few balconies. TV, vending machines, and leather chairs in the comfortable lounge. 10% discount after 3rd night. Elevator. Singles 150-270F; doubles 170-315F; triples 300-335F. Hearty, "American" breakfast 35F. Open Sept.-July. AmEx, MC, V.

Hôtel Rhetia, 3, rue du Général Blaise (tel. 01 47 00 47 18; fax 01 48 06 01 73). M: Voltaire. From the metro, take av. Parmentier and turn right on rue Rochebrune then left on rue du Général Blaise. In a calm and quiet neighborhood, some rooms overlook a peaceful park; others, a peaceful courtyard. Clean rooms with lacquered furniture and narrow single beds. Reception daily 7:30am-10pm. Singles 170-210F; doubles 190-230F; triples 240-280F. Hall showers 10F. Breakfast 15F.

Hôtel de Vienne, 43, rue de Malte (tel. 01 48 05 44 42). M: Oberkampf or République. From M: Oberkampf, exit at Crussol and turn left on rue de Malte; from M: République, walk down av. de la République and turn right on rue de Malte. Peaceful rooms with flowered curtains and nice bureaus. Singles 110-135F; doubles 160F, with shower 220F. Breakfast 30F. Open Sept.-July.

Hôtel de l'Europe, 74, rue Sedaine (tel. 01 47 00 54 38; fax 01 47 00 75 31). M: Voltaire. Walk up bd. Voltaire past the Mairie du 11ème Arrondissement, and take a left on rue Sedaine. Basic, comfortable rooms with TVs. Small, dim reception area. Popular with Americans. Doubles 225-250F. Breakfast 25F. Open Sept.-July.

Hôtel Notre-Dame, 51, rue de Malte (tel. 01 47 00 78 76; fax 01 43 55 32 31). M: République. Walk down av. de la République and take a right on rue de Malte. Tidy, renovated rooms with tasteful, bright decor and decent beds. Cheerful lounge. Elevator. Singles 195-340F; doubles 190F, with shower 280F, with shower or bath and toilet 330F; 2-bed doubles 380F. Showers 20F. Breakfast served in your room or in the salon 35F. Reserve 1 month ahead. MC, V.

Luna-Park Hôtel, 1, rue Jacquard (tel. 01 48 05 65 50, reservations 01 48 05 01 21; fax 01 43 38 07 56). M: Parmentier. From the metro, turn right on rue Oberkampf and walk against traffic, then left on rue Jacquard. Colorful, clean, spacious rooms in good condition on a quiet side street near the Oberkampf nightlife. Laundromat next door. Singles 140F; doubles with TV 170F, with shower and toilet 220F; triples with shower and TV 270F; quads 320F. Showers 15F. Breakfast 25F.

Pax Hôtel, 12, rue de Charonne (tel. 01 47 00 40 98; fax 01 43 38 57 81). M: Bastille. Walk east on rue du Fbg. St-Antoine and turn left on rue de Charonne. Dim, generic rooms near the Bastille nightlife. Most rooms have TVs and bathrooms. Dark hallway, no elevator. Singles 203F, with shower and toilet 253F; doubles with shower and toilet 296F; triples 359-369F; quads 460F. Breakfast 30F in the salon, 40F in bedrooms. Reserve by credit card 15 days in advance. AmEx, MC, V.

Hôtel Beaumarchais, 3, rue Oberkampf (tel. 01 53 36 86 86; fax 01 43 38 32 86). M: Oberkampf. From the metro, exit on rue de Malte and turn right on rue Oberkampf. Newly renovated with bright, trendy furniture, whitewashed walls, clean bathrooms, and TVs. Beautiful lobby and courtyard. Small elevator. 24hr. reception. A/C. Call ahead for wheelchair access. 10% discount after the 3rd night. Singles 350F; doubles 450F. Breakfast 35F. Reserve 4 days in advance. AmEx, MC, V.

Hostels

Auberge de Jeunesse "Jules Ferry" (HI), 8, bd. Jules Ferry (tel. 01 43 57 55 60; fax 01 43 14 82 09). M: République. Walk east on rue du Fbg. du Temple and turn right on the far side of bd. Jules Ferry. Wonderfully located in front of park and next to pl. de la République. Clean rooms with 100 bunk beds and sinks. Some doubles with big beds. Crowded, friendly, party atmosphere. Friendly staff. Dining room and reception open 24hr. Lockout 10am-2pm. No curfew. 4- to 6-bed dorms 120F; doubles 250F. Showers and breakfast (served 7-9:15am) included. Laundry (20F wash, 10F dry). No reservations, so arrive by 7am. If there are no vacancies, the hostel will book you in one of its sister hostels. Flexible 4-night max. Lockers 5F. Sheets 5F. Airport shuttle 89F. Internet access in lobby (1F per min). MC, V.

Auberge Internationale des Jeunes, 10, rue Trousseau (tel. 01 47 00 62 00; fax 01 47 00 33 16). M: Ledru-Rollin. Walk east on rue du Fbg. St-Antoine and turn left on rue Trousseau. Modern building with lots of lively backpackers. Exceptionally clean, with friendly staff. Cramped 2-, 4-, and 6-bed rooms with sinks. Ground floor rooms are quiet. Upper floors look out over Paris. Luggage storage. Lounge. Lockout 10am-3pm. Internet access (1F/min). Mar.-Oct. 91F; Nov.-Feb. 81F. Breakfast (served 7-9:30am) and shower included. Sheets 5F. Show up by 8am. MC, V.

Résidence Bastille, 151, av. Ledru-Rollin (tel. 01 43 79 53 86; fax 01 43 79 35 63). M: Voltaire. Walk across the pl. Léon Blum and head south onto av. Ledru-Rollin. Modern building undergoing slow renovations. 2-4 wooden bunks per room. About 170 beds. Some triples and quads have their own bathrooms. Less crowded and more subdued than most hostels. Friendly staff. Ages 18-35 (flexible). Couples accommodated in doubles. Reception daily 7am-10pm. Flexible 1am curfew. Lockout noon-3pm. 5-nights max. stay. Wheelchair accessible. Mar.-Oct. 125F; Nov.-Feb. 110F. 10% reduction with ISIC or GO25. Showers, breakfast (7:30-10am), and sheets included. Reservations by fax 10-15 days in advance, or arrive by 8am. MC, V.

Maison Internationale des Jeunes, 4, rue Titon (tel. 01 43 71 99 21; fax 01 43 71 78 58). M: Faidherbe-Chaligny. Walk on rue Faidherbe, turn right on rue de Montreuil, then take the second left on rue Titon. In a residential area, a modern, 164-bed hostel, with single, plain cots in plain large 2- to 8-bed rooms. No social area except the breakfast room. Coed bathrooms without toilet seats. Flexible 3- to 4-night max. stay. If full, they'll find you another place. Reception daily 8am-2am. Flexible lockout 10am-5pm. Check-out 10am. Curfew 2am. Quiet hours 10pm-8am. 110F. Showers, sheets, and breakfast included.

■ Twelfth Arrondissement

The area around the Gare de Lyon has a wealth of budget hotels. This neighborhood is within walking distance of Bastille nightlife and even the Marais. However, be careful at night. In the 12ème's southeast corner, hotels are far enough from central Paris to be both cheap and quite comfortable. They also provide easy access to the Bois de Vincennes, a lovely park with gardens, a château, and a lake (see **Sights,** p. 207).

Mistral Hôtel, 3, rue Chaligny (tel. 01 46 28 10 20; fax 01 46 28 69 66). M: Reuilly-Diderot. From the metro, walk west on bd. Diderot and take a left onto rue Chaligny. One of the best deals in Paris. A spectacularly clean, mostly renovated hotel. Each room is unique, with quality furniture from chandeliers to wicker headboards. The owner's mom pays attention to detail—fresh cups and maps in the rooms. All rooms have TV and phone. Singles 205F, with shower 250F; 1-bed doubles 210F, with shower 260F; 2-bed doubles with shower 290F; triples with shower and toilet 320F; quads with shower and toilet 500F. Hall showers 15F. Breakfast 35F, served in rooms or downstairs. Call 7am-midnight to reserve 1 week in advance and confirm in writing. AmEx, MC, V.

Hôtel de Reims, 26, rue Hector Malot (tel. 01 43 07 46 18; fax 01 43 07 56 62). M: Gare de Lyon. Take bd. Diderot away from the river and make a left onto rue Hector Malot. Charming proprietress tends to this hotel, which, despite dayglo bedspreads and signs of aging, still manages to feel like a cozy French grandmother's house. Singles 180F, with shower 250F; doubles 220F, with shower 262F, with toilet 280F; triples with shower 300F. Hall showers 25F. Breakfast 30F. Reserve by phone and confirm in writing. MC, V.

Nièvre-Hôtel, 18, rue d'Austerlitz (tel. 01 43 43 81 51). M: Gare de Lyon or Quai de la Rapée. From Gare de Lyon walk away from the train station on rue de Bercy and take a right on rue d'Austerlitz. The somewhat sterile entry of the recently redone hotel belies pleasant, cheerful rooms. Resident cat presides at the entrance. High-ceilinged rooms with spotless bathrooms. Singles 160F; doubles 200F, with shower 260F, with toilet 300F. Hall showers free for *Let's Go* readers. Breakfast 20F. Call for reservations and confirm in writing. MC, V.

Hôtel Printania, 91, av. du Dr. Netter (tel. 01 43 07 65 13; fax 01 43 43 56 54). M: Porte de Vincennes. Walk west on the cours de Vincennes and turn left on av. du Dr. Netter. 25 spotless rooms with brown, office-like carpets and formica headboards. One flight climb to elevator. Doubles 160F, with shower and toilet 220F, with TV 260F. Breakfast 25F, served in rooms. Reserve by phone. MC, V.

Hôtel de l'Aveyron, 5, rue d'Austerlitz (tel. 01 43 07 86 86; fax 01 43 07 85 20). M: Gare de Lyon. Walk away from the train station on rue de Bercy and take a right on rue d'Austerlitz. On a quiet street. Small, clean, unpretentious rooms with aged wallpaper and beds. Leather and chrome lounge with a huge TV. Fridge available. Friendly staff is eager to make suggestions on local spots. Singles and doubles 185F, with shower 225F, with toilet 245F; triples 240F, with shower and toilet 290F; quads with shower and toilet 320F. Breakfast 20F. Reserve well in advance. MC, V.

Grand Hôtel Chaligny, 5, rue Chaligny (tel. 01 43 43 17 91; fax 01 43 43 18 47). M: Reuilly-Diderot. Walk west on bd. Diderot and take a left onto rue Chaligny. Screams low-budget, but some rooms have been recently redone. TVs in all 43 rooms; hair driers in most. Some dark rooms and patched bedspreads, but it's a deal. Singles 160F, with shower 230F, with bath 253F; doubles 200F, with shower and toilet 277F, with bath 280F; 2-bed doubles with shower or bath and toilet 277F; quads 372F. Extra bed 53F. Hall showers 20F. Breakfast 20F. Elevator. MC, V.

Palym Hôtel, 4, rue Émile-Gilbert (tel. 01 43 43 24 48; fax 01 43 41 69 47). M: Gare de Lyon. Rue Émile-Gilbert runs parallel off bd. Diderot, directly across from the train station. A bright, clean hotel with cheery yellow and green lobby, gleaming brass fixtures, and modern rooms. As befits a two-star, all rooms have TV and phone. Wheelchair accessible. Singles 290-380F; doubles 320-420F; quads 520F. Extra bed 100F. Breakfast 30F. MC, V.

Hostels and Foyers

Centre International du Séjour de Paris: CISP "Ravel," 6, av. Maurice Ravel (tel. 01 44 75 60 00; fax 01 43 44 45 30). M: Porte de Vincennes. Walk east on cours de Vincennes then take the first right on bd. Soult, left on rue Jules Lemaître, and right on av. Maurice Ravel. Associated with CISP "Kellerman" in the 13ème and just as cool. Large rooms (most with 4 or fewer beds), art exhibits, auditorium, and access to outdoor municipal pool next door (25F). Self-serve restaurant open daily 7:30-9:30am, noon-1:30pm, and 7-8:30pm. Full-service restaurant open noon-1:30pm and 7:30-9:30pm. 1-month max. stay. Reception daily 7:30am-1:30am. Dorms with shower 138F. Singles with shower, toilet, and phone 186F; doubles with shower, toilet, and phone 312F. Breakfast, sheets, and towels included. Reserve a few days ahead by phone. MC, V.

■ Thirteenth Arrondissement

On the cusp of revitalization, the 13ème has little in the way of established hotels. But there are some foyers and hostels with extremely reasonable prices and easy access to the metro. Many are only a short walk from the more central 5ème arrondissement.

Hostels and Foyers

CISP "Kellerman," 17, bd. Kellerman (tel. 01 44 16 37 38; fax 01 44 16 37 39). M: Porte d'Italie. From the metro cross the street and turn right on bd. Kellerman. Affiliated with CISP "Ravel" in the 12ème, this 380-bed hostel resembles a spaceship on stilts. Impeccably clean with TV room, laundry, and cafeteria (open daily noon-1:30pm and 6:30-9:30pm). 2-4 bed dorms 138F; 8-bed dorms 113F. Singles 156-186F; doubles 310F; Breakfast included (7-9:30am). Lockout 1:30-6:30am. A good place to try for last-minute reservations. Wheelchair accessible. MC, V.

Maison des Clubs UNESCO, 43, rue de Glacière (tel. 01 43 36 00 63; fax 01 45 35 05 96). M: Glacière. From the metro walk east on bd. Auguste Blanqui and take a left on rue de la Glacière. Enter through the garden on the right. Small, clean rooms. Common space is limited. Helpful management. Reception open 7am-2am. Curfew 2am. Check-out 10am, but the front desk can hold your bags for the day. Singles 165F; doubles 290F; triples 375F. Showers and breakfast included (7:45-9am). Reservations recommended.

Association des Foyers de Jeunes: Foyer des Jeunes Filles, 234, rue de Tolbiac (tel. 01 44 16 22 22; fax 01 45 88 61 84; email foyer_tolbiac.com). M: Glacière. From the metro walk east on bd. Auguste Blanqui, turn right on rue de Glacière, then left on rue de Tolbiac. Large, modern *foyer* for women (ages 18-30). Excellent facilities include kitchens, TV, laundry, gym, library, cafeteria, and garden. Helpful staff. Reception open 24hr. Sunny singles 120F. 3245F per month, breakfast and dinner included. Mostly workers, not students, here for semi-permanent stays. Showers and breakfast (M-Sa 6:30-8:30am) included. Dinner 50F. 30F registration fee (good for 1 year). There are usually vacancies in summer. For short-term reservations fax or call a few days ahead; for long-term, call 3-4 months ahead. MC, V.

■ Fourteenth Arrondissement

Just south of the *Quartier Latin*, the 14ème lured Picasso and his artistic circle from Montmartre. Today, the cafés along the **boulevard du Montparnasse,** where Einstein, Sartre, and Hemingway passed their time, are still lively and popular.

Hôtel de Blois, 5, rue des Plantes (tel. 01 45 40 99 48; fax 01 45 40 45 62). M: Mouton-Duvernet. From the metro, turn left on rue Mouton Duvernet then left on rue des Plantes. One of the better deals in Paris. Floral wallpaper, velvet chairs, and an iron spiral staircase. TVs, phones, and big, clean bathrooms. Laundromat across the street. Singles or doubles 230-270F, with shower 270F, with bath 320-360F; triples 360F. Breakfast 27F. Reserve 10 days ahead. AmEx, MC, V.

Ouest Hôtel, 27, rue de Gergovie (tel. 01 45 42 64 99; fax 01 45 42 46 65). M: Pernety. Walk against traffic on rue Raymond Losserand and turn right on rue de Gergovie. A clean hotel with excellent rates and friendly staff. Singles with small bed 120F; singles and doubles with larger bed 160F, with shower 220F; 2-bed doubles 200F, with shower 230F. Hall showers 20F. Breakfast 20F. AmEx, MC, V.

Hôtel du Parc, 6, rue Jolivet (tel. 01 43 20 95 54; fax 01 42 79 82 62). M: Edgar-Quinet. Facing the Tour Montparnasse, turn left on rue de la Gaîté, right on rue du Maine, then right on rue Jolivet. Creative color schemes and floral wallpaper. Windows open onto the courtyard or a park. Well-lit rooms with TVs. Singles and doubles 265F; triples 450F. Breakfast 30F. Shower 20F. AmEx, MC, V.

Hôtel Broussais, 3, rue Ledion (tel. 01 40 44 48 90; fax 01 40 44 96 76). M: Plaisance. Walk east on rue d'Alésia, turn right on rue Didot, and veer left onto rue Ledion. Tasteful rooms with TVs, phones, showers, and toilets. Lovely courtyard. Singles 240F; doubles 280F. Breakfast 30F. Reserve 2 weeks ahead. AmEx, MC, V.

Hôtel du Midi, 4, av. René-Coty (tel. 01 43 27 23 25; fax 01 43 21 24 58). M: Denfert-Rochereau. From the metro, take av. Général Leclerc to pl. de l'Abbé Migne, then turn right on av. René-Coty. Popular with older travelers, this professional hotel features marble bathrooms, hairdryers, and TVs. Singles or doubles with shower 298F, with shower and toilet 328-408F; large suite 598F. Breakfast 38F. MC, V.

Hostels and Foyers

FIAP Jean-Monnet, 30, rue Cabanis (tel. 01 45 89 89 15; fax 01 45 81 63 91). M: Glacière. From the metro, take bd. Auguste-Blanqui, turn left on rue de la Santé and then right on rue Cabanis. This 500-bed international student center offers well-furnished rooms with toilet and shower. The concrete complex contains a game room, TV rooms, laundry room, sunlit piano bar and café, restaurant, outdoor terrace, and *discothèque*. Lobby kiosks post events and tourist info. Some rooms wheelchair accessible. Curfew 2am. 8-bed dorms 131F; singles 281F; doubles 368F; triples 483F; quads 644F. Breakfast included. Reserve 2-4 weeks in advance. MC, V.

■ Fifteenth Arrondissement

Because of the nearby Parc des Expositions, hotels in the 15ème fill with business clients for conventions and trade shows. Many hotels consider the summer months off-season and most will have vacancies in July and August.

Hôtel Printemps, 31, rue du Commerce (tel. 01 45 79 83 36; fax 01 45 79 84 88). M: La Motte-Picquet. In the middle of a busy, bourgeois neighborhood surrounded by shops (including Monoprix) and restaurants, this hotel offers clean rooms at hostel prices. Singles or doubles 140F, with shower 170F; 2-bed doubles with shower and toilet 220F. Breakfast 20F. Hall showers 15F. Reserve 3-4 weeks ahead. MC, V.

Practic Hôtel, 20, rue de l'Ingénieur Keller (tel. 01 45 77 70 58; fax 01 40 59 43 75). M: Charles Michels. From pl. Charles Michels, walk up rue Linois, turn left on rue des 4-Frères Peignot, then turn right on rue de l'Ingénieur Keller. Possibly the most elegant budget hotel in the 15ème. Bright, clean rooms worthy of Sheraton Elevator. Singles or doubles 260-300F, with shower and toilet 345F; 2-bed doubles with shower and toilet 390F; triples 460F. Breakfast 39F. AmEx, MC, V.

Mondial Hôtel, 136, bd. de Grenelle (tel. 01 45 79 73 57 or 01 45 79 08 09; fax 01 45 79 58 65). M: La Motte-Picquet. Conveniently located next to the loud elevated metro. Ask for a room off the street. Friendly service and basic rooms, a short walk from the Eiffel Tower. Singles 153F, with shower 183F; doubles 206F, with shower 246F. Hall showers 10F. Breakfast 20F. MC, V.

Hôtel Camélia, 24, bd. Pasteur (tel. 01 47 83 76 35 or 01 47 83 69 91; fax 01 40 65 94 98). M: Pasteur. Next to the metro and surrounded by shops and cafés, this hotel offers clean rooms. Singles or doubles 210F, with shower and TV 280-300F. Extra bed 50F. Breakfast 30F. Reserve 2 weeks in advance. MC, V.

Hôtel de la Paix, 166, bd. de Grenelle (tel. 01 44 49 63 63; fax 01 45 66 45 27). M: Cambronne. On a busy street, this large hotel is frequented by British groups. The mirrored entryway gives way to brown and blue rooms. TV room. Breakfast served in North African restaurant next door (35F). Singles 185F, with shower and toilet 275F; doubles 200-290F; 3- to 4-person suites 530-550F. English spoken. MC, V.

Hôtel de l'Ain, 60, rue Olivier de Serres (tel. 01 45 32 44 33 or 01 45 32 49 36; fax 01 45 32 58 95). M: Convention. Walk down rue de la Convention and turn right on rue Olivier de Serres. A bit worn and far from a metro, this modest hotel rests on a quiet hill. Small rooms and large windows. Singles 210F; doubles 270-350F; triples 460F. Breakfast 30F. *Let's Go* travelers get free breakfast and 15% discount. MC, V.

Hostels and Foyers

Three Ducks Hostel, 6, pl. Etienne Pernet (tel. 01 48 42 04 05; fax 01 48 42 99 99). M: Félix Faure. Walk against traffic on the left side of the church; the hostel will be on your left. Paris's rowdiest summer hangout for backpackers. 15min. from the Eiffel Tower, the Three Ducks offers a kitchen, lockers, and 2- to 8-bed dormrooms. Laundromat and groceries nearby. Ivy-covered courtyard becomes a raucous café on summer nights when a young, English-speaking crowd drinks inexpensive beer from the in-house Richie's Bar. Great staff changes cash and traveler's checks at no commission. Curfew 2am. Mar.-Oct. 107F; Nov.-Feb. 87F. Sheets 15F, towels 5F. Breakfast included. Reserve with credit card deposit. MC, V.

Aloha Hostel, 1, rue Borromée (tel. 01 42 73 03 03; fax 01 42 73 14 14). M: Volontaires. Walk against traffic on rue de Vaugirard; turn right on rue Borromée. Owned by the 3 Ducks, but smaller. Music and drinks in the café. Friendly staff changes cash and traveler's checks at no commission. Kitchen and safety deposit boxes. Laundromat nearby. Lockout 11am-5pm. Reception 8am-2am. 8-bed dorms 97F; 2-bed dorms 107F. Mar.-Nov. 107F, 127F. Breakfast included. Sheets 15F, towels 10F. Curfew 2am. Reserve with credit card deposit or arrive at 8am. MC, V.

■ Sixteenth Arrondissement

Wealthy and residential, the 16ème may inconvenience budget tourists on several counts. Though close to the Eiffel Tower, it remains a 20-minute metro ride away from the more famous museums, sights, and nightlife. It also has few of the grocery stores, affordable restaurants, and cafés abundant elsewhere in the city. On the other hand, hotels here are more luxurious and have vacancies even in the high season.

Hôtel Résidence Chalgrin, 10, rue Chalgrin (tel. 01 45 00 19 91; fax 01 45 00 95 41). M: Argentine. Walk down av. de la Grande Armée toward the Arc de Triomphe, turn right on rue Argentine, then turn right on rue Chalgrin. Near the Champs-Elysées in a gorgeous neighborhood. Charming and quiet, with 19th-century tapestries, ornate woodwork, and Louis XVI chairs. The matron has found and refinished every antique lamp, armoire, and headboard herself, and no 2 spacious rooms are alike. Cheap eats and food in general may be especially hard to come by in this neighborhood, however. Most rooms have TV and phone. Singles and doubles 240-260F, with toilet and shower 280-346F; triple suite 460F. Extra bed 30F. Breakfast 30F. AmEx, MC, V.

Villa d'Auteuil, 28, rue Poussin (tel. 01 42 88 30 37; fax 01 45 20 74 70). M: Michel-Ange-Auteuil. Walk up rue Girodet and turn left on rue Poussin. At the lip of the Bois de Boulogne, on a peaceful street laced with antique shops and restaurants. A genteel and proper hotel. Spacious, high-ceilinged rooms have graceful wooden-framed beds and tasteful decor. All rooms have a shower, toilet, phone, and TV, and face the street or a garden. Singles 290-300F; doubles 340-350F; triples 415F. Breakfast 30F. Restrictive 10% discount for *Let's Go* travelers. MC, V.

Hôtel Ribera, 66, rue La Fontaine (tel. 01 42 88 29 50; fax 01 42 24 91 33). M: Jasmin. Walk down rue Ribera to its intersection with rue La Fontaine. Pink and blue rooms, some with marble fireplaces and floor-to-ceiling windows. Gender politics aside, blue rooms tend to be nicer. Rooms with shower have TV. Singles 220F, with shower 260F; doubles 250F, with shower 290-350F. Breakfast 28F. 10% discount July 15-Aug. 31. AmEx, MC, V.

Hôtel Hameau de Passy, 48, rue de Passy (tel. 01 42 88 47 55; fax 01 42 30 83 72; email hameau.Passy@wanadoo.fr; http://www.hameau.passy@wanadoo.fr). A modern, inviting hotel next to the chic boutiques that line rue de Passy. Pink rooms with views of the garden all have TV, phone, hair-dryer. 1 wheelchair-accessible room on the ground floor with a low bed and special doors. Singles 540F; doubles 590F; twins 610F; triples 695F. Breakfast included. Amex, MC, V.

ACCOMMODATIONS

■ Seventeenth Arrondissement

The 17ème combines the elegance of its western neighbor Neuilly with the sordidness of its eastern neighbor Pigalle. Some of its hotels cater to visiting businessmen, others to prostitutes. Safety is a concern where the 17ème borders the 18ème, especially on bd. des Batignolles and near pl. de Clichy. Most of the hotels listed are near the safer southern border with the 16ème. Though far from the Latin Quarter and sights, these hotels and their nearby restaurants can be wonderful bargains.

Hôtel Riviera, 55, rue des Acacias (tel. 01 43 80 45 31; fax 01 40 54 84 08). M: Charles-de-Gaulle-Étoile. From the metro, walk north on av. MacMahon, then turn left on rue des Acacias. A stone's throw from the Arc de Triomphe and Champs-Elysées, this budget hotel is one of the best located and most agreeable on the Right Bank. Don't be alarmed by the sparseness of the lobby. Modern, quiet, blue-and-pink rooms face patios and courtyards and have large, comfortable beds, TVs, and hairdryers. Elevator. Singles 240F, with shower 280F; doubles with shower or bath and toilet 370-410F; triples with shower and toilet 480F. Breakfast 27F. Reservations encouraged, by phone or fax. AmEx, MC, V.

Hôtel Belidor, 5, rue Belidor (tel. 01 45 74 49 91; fax 01 45 72 54 22). M: Porte Maillot. From the metro, go north on bd. Gouvion St-Cyr and turn right on rue Belidor. Dim halls give way to quiet rooms with floral wallpaper circa 1976 and Mondrian carpets. Most rooms face a quiet, tiled courtyard. Singles 230F, with toilet 250F, with shower 290F, with shower and toilet 340F; doubles with sink 260F, with shower and toilet 370F; 2-bed doubles with toilet 360F; with shower and toilet 450F; triples 390F. Breakfast included. Open Sept.-July. MC, V.

Hôtel Jouffrey, 28, passage Cardinet (tel. 01 47 54 06 00; fax 01 47 63 83 12). M: Malesherbes. From the metro, follow rue Cardinet across bd. Malesherbes and rue de Tocqueville and turn left into passage Cardinet. Extremely quiet, mainly residential neighborhood, which, while relatively safe, is far from the metro (10min.). Simple, clean, flowered wallpapered rooms with a modern feel. TVs and direct-line phones in every room. One room is fully handicap-accessible—once you clear the first two steps into the hotel. Dogs welcome. All rooms with shower and toilet. Singles 280F; doubles 340-350F. Breakfast 30F, in room 35F. MC, V.

Hôtel des Deux Avenues, 38, rue Poncelet (tel. 01 42 27 44 35; fax 01 47 63 95 48). M: Ternes. From the metro, walk 1 block west on av. des Ternes and turn right on rue Poncelet. Pleasant rooms with TVs and new bathrooms with hairdryers. A great location, 10min. from the Champs-Elysées and Arc de Triomphe, and nearly as much information about Paris as the tourist office. Elevator. Singles 450F; doubles 500F; 2-bed doubles 600F; triples 600-700F. Extra bed 100F. Breakfast 35F. MC, V.

Hôtel Champerret Héliopolis, 13, rue d'Héliopolis (tel. 01 47 64 92 56; fax 01 47 64 50 44). M: Porte de Champerret. From the metro turn left of av. de Villiers. Beautiful lobby matched by lovely and bright blue and peach rooms. A charming hotel. TVs, phones, hairdryers. Close to the metro, with many restaurants and cafés nearby. One fully handicap-accessible bedroom with a large and specialized bathroom. Singles 385F; doubles 450-495F; triples 580F. Breakfast 38F.

■ Eighteenth Arrondissement

As a general rule, hotels up the hill in Montmartre are safer and more expensive than those in down the hill in Pigalle. The closer you get to the Sacré Coeur, the better the hotels become. The lower you get to Pigalle, the cheaper and seedier. Do with the symbolism what you will. Up in Montmartre, you may have a view of the City of Lights glittering at night. In pl. Pigalle, hotels rent by the hour. Avoid M: Pigalle and M: Barbès-Rochechouart at night. Use M: Abbesses instead and do not walk alone at night.

Hôtel André Gill, 4, rue André Gill (tel. 01 42 62 48 48; fax 01 42 62 77 92). M: Abbesses. From the metro walk downhill on rue des Abbesses and turn right on rue des Martyrs and left on rue André Gill. On a quiet dead-end street, this family-run hotel has a reception area with faux marble and chandeliers and rooms with glittery, pastel walls; tasteful in a Liberace sort of way. Elevator. Singles 180F; singles or doubles with breakfast 240F, with shower 390F, with bath 390F; triples with bath and breakfast 530F. Hall showers 25F. Breakfast 25F. AmEx, MC, V.

Hôtel Sofia, 21, rue de Sofia (tel. 01 42 64 55 37; fax 01 46 06 33 30). M: Château-Rouge. Walk down bd. Barbès and turn right on rue de Sophia. The oak-timbered lobby leads to bright, colorful, and quiet rooms with new beds and Impressionist prints. All rooms come equipped with shower and toilet. Friendly owners speak English. Singles 220F; doubles 280F; triples 360F; quads 480F. Breakfast 20F. 24hr. reception. Call ahead or fax for reservations. MC, V.

Ideal Hôtel, 3, rue des Trois Frères (tel. 01 46 06 63 63; fax 01 42 64 97 01). M: Abbesses. Walk down rue Yvonne le Tac and turn right on rue des Trois Frères. Respectable, but the name is optimistic at best. On a lively, fairly safe street with shops and restaurants. If the lobby reminds you of a 19th-century mansion, the small, tidy rooms upstairs say "servants' quarters." Pray for their forthcoming renovations, as the hotel has potential. Singles 125-140F; doubles 190-230F, with shower 250F. Free hall showers. MC, V.

Hôtel Pax, 5, rue des Poissoniers (tel. 01 46 06 33 26; fax 01 46 06 89 41). M: Château-Rouge. With rue Custine behind you, leave M: Château-Rouge down bd. Barbès, then take a sharp left onto rue des Poissoniers. On the edge of a lively African market quarter, this recently renovated hotel is very modern, has Sheraton-esque clean rooms with new beds, peach and lime walls, and dark, wooden furniture. One wheelchair accessible room, though the region is somewhat hilly. Elevator. All rooms have toilets and TVs. Singles 165F, with shower 265F; doubles 280F, with shower 300-320F. Extra bed 80F. Hall showers 20F. Breakfast 25F. AmEx, MC, V.

Hostels and Foyers

Village Hostel, 20, rue d'Orsel (tel. 01 42 64 22 02; fax 01 42 64 22 04; email village@levillage-hostel.fr; http://www.levillage@levillage-hostel.fr). M: Anvers. From the metro, go uphill on rue Steinkerque and turn right on rue d'Orsel. This hostel is a dream and is far nicer (and usually cheaper) than many of the budget hotels in Paris, if you don't mind sharing a room or a beautiful view of Sacré Coeur from half of the rooms and from the rooftop garden terrace. On a busy little street of textile merchants and clothes shops, on the crest of Montmartre. Everything—kitchen, bathrooms, furniture, mattresses, and wallpaper—is new. Curfew 2am. TV and stereo in the lounge. Imminent Internet access. Every room has toilet and shower. 6-bed dorms 117F; 4-bed dorms 127F; 2-bed dorms 147F. 1- to 2-week max. stay. Call ahead to reserve a room, even if same day.

▓ Nineteenth Arrondissement

The 19ème is far from central. Apart from a visit to Parc de la Villette and Parc des Buttes-Chaumont, you'll have to commute to your sightseeing. However, the metro line Marie des Lilas-Châtelet will zip you quickly to the center. Parts of the 19ème are busy traffic arteries, while Belleville's winding roads and cafés are almost provincial.

Hôtel du Parc, 1, pl. Armand Carrel (tel. 01 42 08 08 37 or 01 42 08 86 89; fax 01 42 45 66 91). M: Laumière. From the metro follow rue Laumière to its end at pl. Armand Carrel (or take bus #65 or 70). Now a 3-star hotel, the pleasant Hôtel du Parc is steps away from the Parc des Buttes-Chaumont. Modern, clean, and quiet rooms come with comfy beds, A/C, TVs, phones, toilets, and hairdryers. Rec room with pool table. Top floor rooms have a great view. Elevator, handicap access. All rooms with shower Singles 350F; doubles 420F; triples 500F. Breakfast 40F in lounge or your room. Reserve 2 weeks ahead. AmEx, MC, V.

Crimée Hôtel, 188, rue de Crimée (tel. 01 40 36 75 29 or 01 40 35 19 57; fax 01 40 36 29 57). M: Crimée. By the metro, at the corner of rue de Flandre. In the northern, commercial 19ème, near many restaurants and shops and close to La Villette. Sparkling lobby doubles as a breakfast room. Modern, smallish rooms with hairdryers, TVs, radios, A/C, toilets, and showers. Elevator. Singles 280F; doubles 310F; triples 350F; quads 420F. 20% discount July-Aug. Breakfast 30F. AmEx, MC, V.

La Perdrix Rouge, 5, rue Lassus (tel. 01 42 06 09 53; fax 01 42 06 88 70). M: Jourdain. Hotel is to your left if you are facing the church at the metro exit. Perdrix's best attribute is its proximity to the metro. Small, unluxurious, but clean rooms with TV and toilet. Some rooms overlook the church. Pink formica headboards and office carpeting. Elevator. Singles with shower 265F; doubles with shower 300F; triples with bath 355F. Breakfast 26F. Reserve by fax. AmEx, MC, V.

Rhin et Danube, 3, pl. Rhin et Danube (tel. 01 42 45 10 13; fax 01 42 06 88 82). M: Danube. Steps from the metro in a residential, hilly area. Well-maintained, cheerful rooms located near a fountain. All rooms have kitchens with coffee-makers, hair-dryers, and TVs. Perfect for self-caterers and small groups. Singles with bath and toilet 250F; doubles 300-330F; triples 410F; quads 480F. MC, V.

Hôtel Polonia, 3, rue de Chaumont (tel. 01 42 49 87 15; fax 01 42 06 32 91). M: Jaurès. From the metro, walk down av. Secrétan and turn right on rue de Chaumont. Friendly Polish proprietors run this simple hotel. Popular with Eastern Europeans. Dim corridors, old mattresses, and small floral rooms. TV room. Singles 130F, with shower 161F; doubles 170F, with shower 250F; triples 250F, with shower 360F; quads 390F. Breakfast 27F. Reserve 1 month ahead.

■ Twentieth Arrondissement

Though farther from the sights of central Paris, the primarily residential $20^{\text{ème}}$ offers greater availability and cheaper prices than hotels in other *quartiers*. Despite high-rises and urban sprawl, charming streets and open-air markets cover the *quartier*. In summer, two-star hotels are often half-empty, making them a good bet if you're having trouble finding a place to stay in central Paris.

Hôtel Printana, 355, rue des Pyrénées (tel. 01 46 36 76 62). M: Jourdain. From rue du Jourdain take a left on rue des Pyrénées; hotel is on the right. Kind and devoted proprietors don't speak English but offer refurbished rooms overlooking street vendors and pastry shops. Elevator. Singles with toilet 145F; doubles with toilet 210F, with shower 245F; triples with shower and toilet 300F. Breakfast 25F.

Eden Hotel, 7, rue Jean-Baptiste Dumay (tel. 01 46 36 64 22; fax 01 46 36 01 11). M: Pyrénées. Off rue de Belleville. Turn right from the metro. Eden is an oasis of taste and hospitality, with good value for its two stars and clean rooms with TVs. Plant-filled breakfast room. Elevator. Singles 190F; doubles 235F, with shower and toilet 267-287F. Extra bed 60F. Bath 25F, free shower. Breakfast 27F. MC, V.

Hôtel Dauphine, 236, rue des Pyrénées (tel. 01 43 49 47 66; fax 01 46 36 05 79). M: Gambetta. Walk north on rue des Pyrénées. Far from luxurious on the 2-star hotel spectrum, with sparsely furnished, yet homey, pastel rooms with TV, phone, hair-dryer, and the occasional fridge. Some noise from bustling street vendors. Singles with shower 250F; doubles with shower 260F, with bath 300F. Extra bed 70F. Breakfast served 7-10am (25F). Reserve rooms 1 week in advance. AmEx, MC, V.

Hôtel Ibis Montreuil, 2, av. du Professeur André-Lemierre (tel. 01 43 63 16 16; fax 01 43 63 31 32). M: Porte de Montreuil. Exactly what you'd expect from a chain hotel: clean and efficient. Completely renovated in the last 6 months, the Ibis is one of the few wheelchair-accessible hotels in the $20^{\text{ème}}$, although those with limited mobility may not want to make the 15-minute walk from the metro, as it crosses several major roads. All rooms with TV, phone, shower/bath, and toilet. Singles 365F; doubles 395F; triples 463F. Breakfast 39F. AmEx, MC, V.

Hostels and Foyers

Auberge de Jeunesse "Le D'Artagnan" (HI), 80, rue Vitruve (tel. 01 40 32 34 56; fax 01 40 32 34 55; email d'artagnan_yh@compuserve.com). M: Porte de Bagnolet or Porte de Montreuil. From Porte de Bagnolet, walk south on bd. Davout and make a right on rue Vitruve. A big, modern complex surrounded by highrises, but with a festive, busy feel. 440 beds. Restaurant and bar (open 8pm-2am; happy hour 9-10pm, live music once a week), internet station (40F per 30min.), and a small cinema (free films nightly). Reception 8am-1am, lockout noon-3pm. 3-8 bed dorms 120F; doubles 278F. Breakfast and sheets included. Security boxes (5F per day) and large lockers (10F per day). Laundry 15F per wash, 5F per dry. Reservations a must; hostel is packed Feb.-Oct.

Food and Drink

You got very hungry when you did not eat enough in Paris because all the bakery shops had such good things in the windows and people ate outside at tables on the sidewalks so that you saw and smelled the food.
—Ernest Hemingway, *A Moveable Feast,* 1964

Eating, like love, is a Parisian obsession. With bakeries and restaurants on every corner and dozens of open-air markets, food is a high-profile, high-quality affair. The variety is astounding. *Gauche* or gourmet, French or foreign, fancy or cheap, you can dine on Tibetan soups or Thai noodles, Algerian couscous or Moroccan tea, Peruvian beans or Senegalese fish. Inexpensive French *bistros* and *crêperies* offer the breads, cheeses, wines, *pâtés, pôtages,* and pastries that are central to French cuisine.

■ French Cuisine

The aristocratic tradition of delicious food and elaborate presentation known as **haute cuisine** is actually not French at all. Catherine de Médici brought it from Italy along with her cooks, who taught the French to appreciate the finer aspects of sauces and seasonings. Great 19th-century chefs made fine food an essential art of civilized life and much of their wisdom on sauces and glazes is collected in the voluminous *Larousse Gastronomique,* a standard reference for French chefs today.

The style made famous in the U.S. by Julia Child is **cuisine bourgeoise,** quality French home-cooking. A glance through her wonderful *Mastering the Art of French Cooking I & II* will give you ideas for dishes to try in France. Simple, inexpensive meals such as *steak-frites* (steak and fries), *poulet rôti* (roasted chicken), *soupe à l'oignon, boeuf bourguignon,* and *lapin poêlé* (fried rabbit) can be found on just about every corner in Paris. Both *haute cuisine* and *cuisine bourgeoise* rely heavily on the **cuisine de province** (provincial country cooking, also called **cuisine campagnarde**) by creating sophisticated versions of simpler, traditional, regional cuisine. Trendy **nouvelle cuisine,** consisting of tiny portions of delicately cooked, artfully arranged ingredients with light sauces, became popular in the 1970s.

French **meat** is not all frogs *(grenouille)* and snails *(escargots),* although these tasty morsels both make great appetizers (frog really does taste like chicken, and snails taste like mussels; however, most of what they taste like is the garlic butter sauce in which they are usually cooked). It is true that the French tend to eat a wider variety of creatures than most Anglo-Saxons. *Tripes* (bovine stomach-lining) cooked in herbs is well-loved by many but doesn't go over as well with foreigners; the sausage version is called *andouille* or *andouillette.* Rabbit *(lapin)* is fairly common. Although not all steaks are *tartare* (raw), most red meat is served quite rare unless you request otherwise. France's many coastal provinces, such as Brittany, Normandy, and Provence have given French cuisine wonderful selections of **fish** *(poisson)* and **seafood** *(fruits de mer).* Unless clearly marked *filet,* the fish will arrive eyes, tail, and all.

Vegetables may be overcooked by some standards, but only so their full flavor can be appreciated. Usually served with vinaigrette or hollondaise, French asparagus *(asperges)* is a white, stumpy version of the matchstick you've come to love. *Haricots verts* (green beans) are a svelte and tastier cousin of the ones your mother made you eat. You may be taken aback by the cost of produce. Don't buy vegetables in the small groceries that stay open late, as the prices are exorbitant. Produce markets and stores that sell only fruits and vegetables are your best bet, but some supermarkets are reasonable as well. Restaurants often serve *frites* (french fries) or *pommes de terre gratins,* potatoes sliced, doused with cream, butter, and cheese, and baked.

Bread is served with every meal. It is perfectly polite to use a piece of bread to wipe your plate. The **baguette** is the long, crisp, archetypal French loaf, which, at about 5F, has kept many a budgeteer afloat on treks through Paris. The **bâtard** has a softer crust, the smaller **ficelle** a thicker, harder crust. **Pain de campagne,** made with whole wheat flour, is heavier inside than the baguette. **Pain complet** is a whole grain loaf, and **pain à six céréales** is made with six grains. The cheap, government-subsidized bread you buy from a nameless bakery in Paris may well be the best you have ever eaten; make it your staple.

Charles de Gaulle argued in 1951 that "the French will only be united under the threat of danger. No one can simply bring together a country that has 265 kinds of cheese." There are, in fact, over 400. With extraordinary variety, French **cheeses** *(fromages)* fall into three main categories. Cooked cheeses include *beaufort* and *gruyère*. Veined cheeses, such as *bleu* and *roquefort,* gain their sharp taste from the molds that are encouraged to grow on them. Soft cheeses, like *brie* and *camembert,* round out a basic cheese tray. Tangy *fromages de chèvre* (goat cheeses) come in two forms: the soft, moist, and crumbly *frais,* and the sharp *sec* (dry). If you're lactose- intolerant but tempted to take the risk, check out Meg Ryan in *French Kiss.*

Among **charcuterie** (cold meat products), the most renowned is *pâté,* a spread of finely minced liver and meat. Often a house specialty, it comes in hundreds of varieties, some highly seasoned with herbs. *Pâté de campagne* (from pork) is chunky, while *pâté de foie* (liver) is soft and silky. Technically, a *pâté* is baked in a pastry crust, while the variety without a crust is a *terrine.* In practice, crusted pâtés are rare, and the terms are used interchangeably.

French **pastry** is far more interesting than the mere croissant. Breakfast pastries include the delectable *pain au chocolat* (croissant or *brioche* with chocolate) and *croissant aux amandes* (almond croissant). More elaborate choices are *flans* (egg-based, custardy cakes) and fruit tartes, including the *chausson aux pommes,* a light pastry with apple filling. Many *gâteaux* (cakes) were invented in the 19th century, such as the chocolate-and-espresso *opéra* and the many-layered, cream-filled *mille-feuilles. Gâteau Paris-Brest,* a cream-filled delight, is the only dessert named for a round-trip on the SNCF. All of these pastries can be eaten in the afternoon with tea or after dinner as a dessert. Also good with tea are crumbly cookies like *macarons* and *madeleines.* Eat pastry whenever you want to. Californians and other well-toned visitors will discover little that is fat-free on Paris menus, so indulge yourself. You can hit the gym back at home. Besides, anything served cold is essentially fat-free anyway.

A note about **salads:** for many trim Parisians a salad is a regular, hefty *plat* (main dish) in itself and thus can come with more cheese, cold cuts, fish, and bread than greens and veggies. Dressing also tends to be a must, so be sure to say you want it separately or not at all. If you need food on the run, you can avoid McDonalds and its French fast-food cousin Le Quick by grabbing an easy *panini* or baguette sandwich (12-20F) at most *boulangeries, pâtisseries,* or sidewalk food stands. An excellent budget meal, baguette sandwiches are fresh and substantial and come with ham, sausage, chicken, tomato, lettuce, and different cheeses. *Panini* are a toasted Italian version. Immigrant communities have injected a dose of spice into French cuisine. In addition to ubiquitous Greek *gyro* sandwiches, there are a number of outstanding Moroccan, Algerian, Tunisian, Senegalese, Ivory Coast, and Caribbean restaurants in Paris. Many bistros have menus with foreign dishes or visiting chefs. North African couscous is the most assimilated foreign dish. Chinese, Thai, Vietnamese, Cambodian, Korean, Tibetan, Japanese, Indian, and Pakistani restaurants, especially in the "Chinatowns" of the 9ème and 13ème, offer many affordable and delicious vegetarian options.

■ Dining in Paris

The French breakfast *(le petit déjeuner)* is usually light, consisting of bread, crois-sants, or *brioches* (buttery breads) with jam and butter, plus an espresso with hot milk *(café au lait)* or a hot chocolate *(le chocolat,* often served in a bowl, or *bol).* This breakfast is the one you will receive in most hotels for 20-30F. Many people eat lunch *(le déjeuner),* the largest meal of the day, between noon and 2pm. Some shops, businesses, and government offices still close during this time. Linger over a two-hour lunch a few times and you'll be hooked too.

Dinner *(le dîner)* begins quite late. Revelers sometimes extend their meals into the early morning. Restaurants may not serve you if you want to dine at 6 or 6:30pm; 8pm is more acceptable. A complete French dinner includes an *apéritif,* an *entrée* (appetizer), *plat* (main course), salad, cheese, dessert, fruit, coffee, and a *digestif* (after-dinner drink, typically a cognac or other local brandy, such as *calvados* from Normandy). There are five major *apéritifs: kir,* a blend of white wine with *cassis,* a black currant liqueur *(kir royale* substitutes champagne for the wine); *pastis,* a lico-rice liqueur diluted with water; *suze,* which is fermented *gentiane,* a sweet-smelling mountain flower that yields a wickedly bitter brew; *picon-bière,* beer mixed with a sweet liqueur; and martinis. The French often take wine with their everyday meals. You might hear the story of the famous director who dared to order a Coke with his 1500F meal; he was promptly kicked out of the restaurant by the head chef. Of him it was said, *"Il manque de savoir vivre"*—he doesn't know how to live.

Most restaurants offer *un menu à prix fixe* (fixed-price meal) that costs less than ordering *à la carte.* The *menu* may include an *entrée* (appetizer), a main course *(plat),* cheese *(fromage),* and dessert (see **Menu Reader,** p. 321, for translations of common dishes). Some also include wine or coffee. For lighter fare, try a *brasserie,* which has a fuller menu than a café but is more casual than a restaurant. If you want to eat in true French manner, hold your fork face down in your left hand, your knife in the right and leave them there. The French also tend to cut one morsel of food and eat it right away, instead of first chopping up your entire steak or quiche and eating with the fork alone. But whatever. Does it really matter *how* you eat, as long as you aren't a vulgar pig? (see **Sweaty Freaks,** p. 243).

Mineral water is everywhere; order sparkling water *(eau pétillante* or *gazeuse)* or flat mineral water *(eau plate).* Ice cubes *(glaçons)* are rare. To order a pitcher of tap water, ask for *une carafe d'eau fraîche.* Finish the meal with espresso *(un café),* which comes in lethal little cups with blocks of sugar. When *boisson compris* is writ-ten on the menu, you are entitled to a free drink (usually wine) with the meal. You will usually see the words *service compris* (service included), which means the tip is automatically added to the check *(l'addition).* Otherwise you should tip 15%.

For an occasional 90F spree you can have a marvelous meal, but it's easy to find satis-fying dinners for under 60F or to assemble inexpensive meals yourself with staples such as cheese, *pâtés,* wine, bread, and chocolate. Having learned its lesson in the Revolu-tion, the government controls the prices of bread, so you can afford to indulge with every meal. Do as the French do: go from one specialty shop to another to assemble a picnic, or find an outdoor market *(un marché).* A *charcuterie,* the French version of the delicatessen, offers cooked meats, *pâtés,* quiches, and sausages. *Crémeries* sell dairy products, and the corner *fromagerie* may stock over 100 kinds of cheese. A *boulange-rie* sells breads. A *pâtisserie* offers pastry and candy. You can buy fruits and vegetables at a *primeur.* For the adventurous carnivore, a *chevalier* sells horse-meat (look for the gilded horse-head over the door); the more timid can stick to steaks and roasts from a regular *boucherie.* A *traiteur* is a combination of a *charcuterie* and a *boulangerie.*

Supermarchés (supermarkets) have all under one roof, although they make shop-ping less interesting. Look for chains such as Carrefour, Casino, Monoprix, Prisunic, and the ever-cheap Leader-Price. *Épiceries* (grocery stores) also carry staples, wine, produce, and a bit of everything else. Open-air markets, held at least once a week in various arrondissements, remain the best places to buy fresh fruit, vegetables, fish, and meat. Competition is fierce, prices are low. Finally, you can grab simple food items, cigarettes, and lotto tickets at any corner *dépaneur* (convenience store).

■ Wine

In France, **wine** is not a luxury, it's an everyday pleasure. During WWI, French infantry pinned down by heavy shell-fire subsisted on the barest of rations: bread and wine. When France sent its first citizen into orbit on a Soviet space craft, he took the fruit of the vine with him. Wine is an institution in France and is served at almost every occasion. The character and quality of a wine depend upon the climate, soil, and variety of grape from which it is made. Long, hot, and fairly dry summers with cool, humid nights create the ideal climate. Soil is so much a determining factor that identical grapes planted in different regions yield remarkably different wines. White wines are produced by the fermentation of grapes carefully crushed to keep the skins from coloring the wine. The fermentation of rosés allows a brief period during which the skins are in contact with the juice; this period is much longer with red wines.

Wine-producing regions are distributed throughout the country. The Loire Valley produces a number of whites, with the major vineyards at Angers, Chinon, Saumur, Anjou, Tours, and Sancerre. Cognac, farther south on the Atlantic coast, is famous for the double-distilled spirit of the same name. Centered on the Dordogne and Garonne Rivers, the classic Bordeaux region produces red and white Pomerol, Graves, and sweet Sauternes. *Armagnac*, similar to cognac, comes from Gascony, while Jurançon wines come from vineyards higher up the slopes of the Pyrénées. Southern wines include those of Languedoc and Roussillon on the coast and Limoux and Gaillac inland. The vineyards of Provence on the coast near Toulon are recognized for their rosés. The Côtes du Rhône from Valence to Lyon in the Rhône Valley are home to some of the most celebrated wines of France, including Beaujolais. Burgundy is especially famous for its reds, from the wines of Chablis and the Côte d'Or in the north to the Mâconnais in the south. Alsatian whites tend to be spicier and more pungent. Many areas produce sparkling wines, but the only one that can legally be called "Champagne" is distilled in the Champagne area surrounding Reims.

France passed the first comprehensive wine legislation in 1935, and since then the *Appellation d'Origine Controlée* regulations (*AOC*, or "controlled place of origin" laws) have ensured the quality and fine reputation of French wines. All wines are categorized according to place of origin, alcohol content, and wine-making practices; only about 16% of French wines are deemed worthy of the top classification. Categories include *Vins Délimités de Qualité Supérieure* (*VDQS*, or "restricted wines of superior quality") and *Vins de Pays* (country wines). Still, a budget traveler in France will be pleasantly surprised by even the least expensive of *vins de tables* (table wines), which are what most folk drink.

When confused about which wine to choose, simply ask. Most waiters in good restaurants and employees in wine shops will be more than happy to recommend their favorites to you. Or fall back on the *vin de maison* (house wine) of the restaurant. Don't get too self-conscious about not knowing anything about wine. Wine bars will let you sample expensive wines by the glass (see **Wine Bars,** p. 131). Realize that you are already a wine expert. Despite all the pretentious talk surrounding the color, vintage, bouquet, and year, a good wine is ultimately the wine you like.

■ Groceries

When cooking or assembling a picnic, be careful to buy before lunch: *crémeries* (dairy products), *fromageries* (cheese), *charcuteries* (meats, sausages, pâtés, and *plats cuisinés*—prepared meals), and *épiceries* (groceries) usually take a two-hour break from noon to 2pm. Épiceries also carry culinary staples: wine, produce, and a bit of everything else. *Boulangeries* sell several varieties of bread; buying in the morning, when the goods are still hot, is a memorable Parisian pleasure. *Pâtisseries* sell pastries, and a *confiserie* stocks candy and ice cream. You can buy your produce at a *primeur*. *Boucheries* sell all kinds of meat and poultry, as well as roast chicken. Note that French store owners are fantastically touchy about people touching their fruits and vegetables; unless there's a sign outside your corner store that says "libre service," ask inside before you start handling the goods displayed.

Supermarchés (supermarkets) are found in every neighborhood. In many *supermarchés*, it is up to you to weigh your produce, bag it, and label it. Electronic weighing machines can be found next to the produce bins. Simply place your fruit on the scale, press the appropriate button (with pictures of bananas, apples, etc. so that you don't need to know all of the French vocabulary) and place the sticker-ticket on the bag. If you're in the mood for a five-and-dime complete with men and women's clothing, photocopiers, telephone cards, and a supermarket, go to any of the **Monoprix** and **Prisunics** that litter the city (48 in Paris to be exact). Ask anyone to point you toward the nearest one in your arrondissement (for a listings of Monoprix and Prisunic throughout the city enter any one and ask for *Le Guide*). They are usually open during the week until 9pm, although the Prisunic at 52, av. Champs-Élysées, is open until midnight. Also look for the smaller chains such as **Franprix, Shopi,** and **Casino.** Starving students and travelers-in-the-know swear by the ubiquitous **Ed l'Épicier** and **Leader Price.** Buy in bulk and watch the pile of francs you save grow; it's possible to end up paying 30-50% less than you would elsewhere. Two of Ed's drawbacks: you can't find non-Ed brands (alas, no Nutella) and some stores do not carry produce. **Picard Surgelés,** with 50 locations throughout the city, stocks every food ever frozen—from crêpes to calamari. Most branches offer free delivery. No luck finding that special ingredient? Try the following or do not hesitate to ask random people in the street on their errands for a store selling what you are looking for.

Alléosse, 13, rue Poncelet, 17ème (tel. 01 46 22 50 45). M: Ternes. An immense and exquisite selection of cheeses, perfect for classy evenings and extravagant sandwiches. Be prepared to pay for quality to match the store's strong smell. Open Tu-Sa 9am-1pm and 4-7:15pm, Su 9am-1pm. MC, V.

Écouffes Alimentation S. Benchetrit, 16, rue des Ecouffes, 4ème (tel. 01 48 87 75 32). M: St-Paul. From the metro, walk in the direction of traffic down rue de Rivoli and turn right on rue des Écouffes. A kosher grocery store selling packaged goods, frozen meats, dairy products (including *camembert* and Philadelphia cream cheeses), and wine, much of it imported. Not too expensive. Also sells Shabbat candles. Open Su-Th 8am-8pm, F 8am-5pm. MC, V.

Fauchon, 26, pl. de la Madeleine, 8ème (tel. 01 47 42 60 11). M: Madeleine. The Rolls Royce is to the skateboard as Fauchon is to the ordinary supermarket. Tuxedoed attendants float about the store helping clients find their favorite pâté and *galettes.* The best chocolate *macarons* in the known universe. Great food items for gifts, including packaged jams and *madeleines* in fancy Fauchon tins (see **Gift Ideas,** p. 260). Like the GUM department store in Moscow, choose your items, have them written up by the walking attendants, take the slip to the cashier to pay, and then pick up your packages with the attendant. It may seem complicated, but this method is how Russian Princesses shopped in the elegant department stores of 19th-century Paris. Dressed in those fabulous hats and dresses, lugging those packages around would have been vulgar. Open M-Sa 9:40am-7pm. AmEx, MC, V.

Finkelsztajn's, 27, rue des Rosiers, 4ème (tel. 01 42 72 78 91), and 24, rue des Écouffes, 4ème (tel. 01 48 87 92 85). M: St-Paul. Grab a bagel or *piroghi* on your way through the Marais. Serving homemade Eastern European Jewish delicacies since 1946, it's the place to go for everything to-go, from strudel to latkes (14F). Gargantuan sandwiches 32-45F. Rue des Rosiers open Sept.-July Th-Tu 10am-1pm and 3-7pm; rue des Écouffes open Aug.-June, same hours.

Goldenberg, 69, av. de Wagram, 17ème (tel. 01 42 27 34 79). M: Ternes. This distinguished gourmet delicatessen sells Eastern European and Middle Eastern food, including pastrami, olives, and sausages, all priced for their chic customers. Some products are kosher, some are not; be sure to ask. Pastries (cheesecake, strudel, baklava, etc.) 10-25F each. Also doubles as an expensive café. Open daily 8:30am-11pm. MC, V.

La Grande Épicerie, 38, rue de Sèvres, 6ème (tel. 01 44 39 81 00). M: Sèvres-Babylone. This food annex to Bon Marché, one of Paris's most illustrious department stores, sells overpriced French ingredients. The produce arrangements are a work of art together with the extensive wine section. Also sells North American specialties such as maple syrup (20F). English aisle stocks Lea and Perrins Worcestershire sauce and a selection of Twinings and other teas (12-70F). Well-wrapped chocolates and bonbons make great souvenirs—if they make it home. Open M-Sa 8:30am-9pm. AmEx, MC, V.

Jardin de Vie, 13, rue Brézin, 14ème (tel. 01 45 43 54 98). M: Mouton Devernet. Stocks healthy versions of your favorite French delicacies, from wine to boxed *croque tofu* (16F). Soy drink 15F, bio-tortilla chips 14F. Small selection of organically grown vegetables and natural beauty products. Advice on health and nutrition is always available. Open in summer M-Sa 10am-7:30pm.

Paul, 4, rue Poncelet, 17ème (tel. 01 42 27 80 25). M: Ternes. Folks come to purchase this bakery's mystically aromatic crusty loaves, baked in wood-fired ovens. Bite-sized samples 4-5F. Pastries 5-14F. 25F *menu* includes a sandwich, dessert, and drink. Open M-Sa 7:30am-7:30pm, Su 7:30am-1:30pm.

Poilâne, 8, rue Cherche-Midi, 6ème (tel. 01 45 48 42 59). M: Sèvres-Babylone. Off bd. Raspail. Tiny shop that services the huge bakery responsible for Paris's most famous bread. Fragrant, crusty sourdough loaves are baked all day in wood-fired ovens. The city's finest restaurants serve pain Poilâne. Unlike the baguette, these circular loaves don't come cheap; priced by weight, a loaf usually costs 38-45F. For just a taste, ask for a *quart* (a quarter-loaf), about 11F. They're extraordinarily filling anyway. Can also be bought by the slice *(tranche)*. Open M-Sa 7:15am-8:15pm.

Aux Quatre Saisons, 5, rue Tardieu, 18ème (tel. 42 54 61 20). M: Anvers or Abbesses. From M: Anvers walk up rue Steinkerque and turn left onto pl. St-Pierre, which becomes rue Tardieu. This small health-food shop is filled with organic vegetables and a variety of snack foods to give you energy before your climb up Montmartre. Soy drink 11-13F, vegetable pasta 12F. Recipe booklets 11F. Open M 3:30-7:30pm, Tu-Sa 9:30am-1pm and 3:30-7:30pm. MC, V.

The Real McCoy, 194, rue de Grenelle, 7ème (tel. 01 45 56 98 82). An oasis for the American craving Stove Top stuffing (30F), cake mix (42F), pancake mix (30-50F), BBQ sauce (39F), H & H bagels (33F0, and Nestlé Toll House chips. Open daily 10am-8pm. AmEx, MC, V.

Tang Frères, 44 or 48, av. d'Ivry, 13ème (tel. 01 45 70 80 00). M: Porte d'Ivry. Look for no. 48 and go down a few steps to this huge grocery in the heart of Chinatown; or look for no. 44 and follow the sign through a parking lot to the much larger Tang next door. Rice, spices, soups, and noodles in bulk. Stocks canned goods and high-quality, hard-to-find Eastern and Western produce. There's also a butcher. No. 48 open daily 10:30am-8:30pm; no. 44 open daily 9am-7:30pm.

Thanksgiving, 14, rue Charles V, 4ème (tel. 01 42 77 68 29). M: St-Paul or Pont Marie. Grocery store filled with American products. Tortilla chips 17F, PopTarts 37F. Upstairs, the restaurant serves up homemade American cheesecake (33F), bagels with cream cheese (28F), and chili (81F). Store open Tu-Sa 10am-7:30pm, Su 10am-6pm. Restaurant open Tu-Sa noon-2:30pm and 7:30-10:30pm, Su 11am-4pm.

Veggie, 38, rue de Verneuil, 7ème (tel. 01 42 61 28 61). M: Rue du Bac. Follow rue de Bac toward the Seine and turn right onto rue de Verneuil. Small health-food store has been specializing in organic grains and vegetables for 25 years. Take-out options include fresh carrot juice (15F), sandwiches (15F), and vegetable pies sold by weight. Take your food to go or eat it at the tables provided in the store. Open M-F 10:30am-2:30pm and 4-7:30pm; snack bar open noon-2:30pm.

■ Food Markets and Noteworthy Streets

In the 5th century, ancient Lutèce held the first market on what is now Île de la Cité. More than a millennium and a half later, markets are not a novelty but an integral part of daily life. Both open-air and covered markets can be found around almost every corner, in every arrondissement. For more information about markets in Paris, ask at the tourist office or your local *mairie*. The freshest produce and best products are often sold by noon, when many stalls start to close up. Quality and price can vary significantly from one stall to the next; you might want to stroll through the market before selecting your purchases. Keep in mind that fruits and vegetables are cheapest and tastiest when in season. Unless there is a sign saying "libre service," you should point to what you want and ask for it; stall owners might become enraged if you touch the produce yourself, even if you do intend to purchase it.

Marché Port Royal, 5ème. M: Censier-Daubenton. Make a right on bd. du Port-Royal in front of the Hôpital du Val de Grâce and make a right. Towards the intersection of bd. du Port-Royal. Colorful, fun, and busy. Some people with limited vocabularies might call it quaint. Find your favorite fresh produce, meat, fish, and cheese here; other tables are loaded with shoes, cheap chic, and housewares. Open Tu, Th, and Sa 8am-1:30pm.

Marché Biologique, on bd. Raspail between rue Cherche-Midi and rue de Rennes, 6ème. M: Rennes. French hippies peddle everything from organic produce to 7-grain bread and tofu patties. A great place to buy natural beauty supplies, to stock up on homeopathic drugs, or just to people-watch. Prices are higher than at other markets but reflect the quality of the products. Open Su 7am-1:30pm.

Marché Raspail, on bd. Raspail between rue Cherche-Midi and rue de Rennes, 6ème. M: Rennes. Small open-air meat and produce market. A few household appliances (lampshades and the like). Open Tu and F 7am-1:30pm.

Marché St-Germain, 3ter, rue Mabillon, 6ème. M: Mabillon. Walk down rue du Four to rue Mabillon. In a rather upscale building including boutiques, sports facilities and a parking lot, the market is home to a wide variety of equally chi-chi foods. Perhaps the only *marché* in Paris to sell Corona beer. Open Tu-Sa 8:30am-1pm and 4-7:30pm, Su 8:30am-1pm.

Marché Europe, 1, rue Corvetto, 8ème. A covered food market featuring fruit, vegetables, meats, breads, and cheese. Open M-Sa 8am-1pm and 4-7pm, Su 8am-1pm.

Marché St-Quentin, 85bis, bd. de Magenta, 10ème. M: Gare de l'Est. Outside, this market is a massive construction of iron and glass, built in 1866 and covered by a glorious glass ceiling. Inside you'll find stalls of fresh fruits and vegetables, meats, cheese, seafood, and wines. Open Tu-Sa 8am-1pm and 3:30-7:30pm, Su 8am-1pm.

Marché Bastille, on bd. Richard-Lenoir from pl. de la Bastille north to rue St-Sabin, 11ème. M: Bastille. Fruit, cheese, veggies, exotic mushrooms, bread, meat, and cheap housewares stretch from M: Richard Lenoir to M: Bastille. Expect to spend at least an hour here. Popular as a Sunday morning family outing. Open Th and Su 7am-1:30pm.

Marché Popincourt, on bd. Richard-Lenoir between rue Oberkampf and rue de Crussol, 11ème. M: Oberkampf. An open-air market close to many hotels. The street fills with fresh, well-priced perishables (fruit, cheese, groceries, bread) as well as an assortment of basic goods from underwear to jewelry. Less expensive than the Bastille market. Open Tu and F 8am-1:30pm.

Marché Beauvau St-Antoine, on rue d'Aligre between rue de Charenton and rue Crozatier, 12ème. M: Ledru-Rollin. One of the largest Parisian markets, with the cheapest produce in the city. Browse before buying—the fruit and vegetable quality is wildly variable. Also visit the market's large tag sale, with scattered old clothing, fabrics, and household remnants. Produce market open Tu-Sa 8am-1pm and 3:30-7:30pm, Su 8am-1pm. Tag sale open daily 8am-1pm.

Marché de Grenelle, on bd. de Grenelle starting at rue de Lourmel to rue de Commerce, 15ème. M: Dupleix. A never-ending open-air market with the regular market fare (meat, fish, fruits, veggies, cheese) as well as cookies, candies, flowers, housewares, and clothing. Open W and Su 8am-1:30pm.

Rue de la Convention, on rue de la Convention between rue de Charonne and rue A. Dumas, 15ème. M: Convention. A bewildering array of fruits, vegetables, meat, fish, cheese, and pastries (not to mention some clothing and housewares), all at reasonable prices. Open Tu, Th, and Su 7:30am-1pm.

Marché Président-Wilson, on av. Président-Wilson between rue Freycinet and pl. d'Iéna, 16ème. M: Iéna or Alma-Marceau. An excellent alternative to the 16ème's exorbitant restaurants. Competitively priced agricultural and dairy products as well as meat and fish. Spectacular flower stalls. Clothing, table linens, and other household goods available. Open W and Sa 8:30am-1pm.

Marché St-Didier, at the corner of rue Mesnil and rue St-Didier, 16ème. M: Victor-Hugo. Walk all the way down rue Mesnil. This small market (half covered, half open-air) offers a fair selection of somewhat pricey vegetables, fish, cheese, and flowers. Gourmet salads start at 98F per kg. Open Tu-Sa 8:30am-1pm and 4-7:30pm, Su 8:30am-1pm.

Marché Gros-la-Fountain, 16ème. M: Ranelagh. Follow traffic on rue de l'Assomption then turn right on rue la Fontaine. Loads of fish, cheese, vegetables, and flowers at competitive prices. Open Tu and F 8am-1pm.

Rue de Lévis, between bd. des Batignolles and rue Legendre, 17ème. M: Villiers. A busy pedestrian marketplace with everything from bread and bananas to boots and Benetton. Friendly competition among the meat, fish, and produce markets keeps prices relatively low. Open Tu-Sa 10am-7:30pm, Su 10am-1pm.

Marché des Batignolles, 96, rue Lemercier, 17ème. M: Brochant. Turn left off rue Brochant onto rue Lemercier. An indoor market with all the usual food groups at fair, though not fantastic, prices. The complex also contains a small supermarket for the items on your shopping list that aren't animal or vegetable. Open Tu-F 8am-12:30pm and 4-7:30pm, Sa 8am-1pm and 3-7:30pm, Su 8am-1pm.

Marché Berthier, on bd. de Reims between rue de Courcelles and rue du Marquis d'Arlandes, along pl. Ulmann, 17ème. M: Porte de Champerret. Turn left off bd. Berthier onto rue de Courcelles then right on bd. de Reims. Hard-selling meat and vegetable vendors needn't try so hard—this market probably has the cheapest produce in Paris. Keep an eye out for North African and Middle Eastern specialties like fresh mint, Turkish bread, and baklava. Open W and Sa 8am-1pm.

Marché Dejean, rue Dejean, 18ème. M: Château-Rouge. Follow the rising numbers on rue Poulet and turn right on rue Dejean. A small selection of vegetables, fruit, meat, and fish catering to the mostly African neighborhood with specialties like yams and ginger roots. Surrounding streets are filled with shops selling music, fabric, and sculpture. Market open Tu-Sa 7:30am-7pm, Su 7:30am-1pm.

■ University Restaurants

For travelers or long-term visitors strapped for cash, university restaurants provide cheap and dependable meals. Students can purchase meal tickets at each restaurant location while food is being served (tickets 14F10 if you are a French or German student; 23F50 if you have an ISIC). The following university restaurants are most convenient, but the list is not nearly exhaustive. They open on a rotating schedule during the summer and on weekends; it is extremely important to get a schedule before showing up. For more information—summer and weekend schedules, a list of other restaurant locations—visit **CROUS (Centre Regional des Oeuvres Universitaires et Scolaires),** 39, av. Georges Bernanos, 5ème (tel. 01 40 51 37 10, M: Port-Royal; open M-F 9am-5pm).

Most of the following offer a cafeteria style choice of sandwiches, regional and international dishes, grilled meats, and drinks: **Bullier,** 39, av. Georges Bernanos, 5ème (M: Port-Royal; open 8am-4:30pm); **Cuvier-Jussieu,** 8bis, rue Cuvier, 5ème (M: Cuvier-Jussieu; open 9am-4:15pm); **Censier,** 31, rue Geoffroy St-Hilaire, 5ème (M: Censier-Daubenton; open 11am-3pm); **Châtelet,** 10, rue Jean Calvin, 5ème (M: Censier-Daubenton; open 8am-11am); **Assas,** 92, rue d'Assas, 6ème (M: Port-Royal or Nôtre-Dame-des-Champs; open 7:45am-6:15pm); **Mabillon,** 3, rue Mabillon, 6ème (M: Mabillon; open 11:30am-3:30pm and 6:30pm-8:30pm); **Grand Palais,** cours la Reine, 8ème (M: Champs-Élysées Clemenceau; open 11:30am-2pm and 6:15pm-7:45pm); **Citeaux,** 45, bd. Diderot, 12ème (M: Gare de Lyon; open 11:30am-2:30pm); **C.H.U. Pitié-Salpetrière,** 105, bd. de l'Hôpital, 13ème (M: St-Marcel; open 8am-4:30pm); **Dareau,** 13-17, rue Dareau, 14ème (M: St-Jacques; open 11:30am-2pm); **C.H.U. Necker,** 156, rue de Vaugirard, 15ème (M: Pasteur; open 9am-4pm); **Dauphine,** av. de Pologne, 16ème (M: Porte Dauphine; open 8am-6pm).

■ Restaurants

Do not approach French dining with the assumption that chic equals *cher*. Recent economic hard times have led to the return of the *bistro,* a more informal, less expensive, often family-run restaurant. Even more casual are *brasseries.* Often crowded and action-packed, *brasseries* are best for large groups and high spirits. The least expensive option is usually a *crêperie,* a restaurant specializing in the thin Breton pancakes filled with various meats, cheeses, chocolates, fruits, and condiments. Surprisingly, you can often eat at a *crêperie* for the price of a fast-food chain.

Note that the French sit longer at dinner than Americans do. The check (*l'addition*) may be a long time in coming—spending two hours in a restaurant is not unusual. If you are particularly pleased with the service, feel free to leave a small cash tip as a sign of your gratitude (anywhere from a few francs to 5% of the check), but don't feel obligated. The initials BC mean *boisson compris,* drink included; BNC, or *boisson non-compris,* means the opposite.

Also, consider ordering the fixed *menu* or *formule,* a *prix fixe* lunch or dinner usually offering a choice of several appetizers, main courses, and desserts. Ordering *à la carte* can be much more expensive, especially at dinner. A note about the organization of the following section: the restaurants we suggest are arranged both by type and by location. **Restaurants By Type** provides a list of restaurants followed by an arrondissement label; turn to **Restaurants By Location** for the full write-up. The latter groups restaurants by arrondissement, then lists them in order of *value:* the top entry may not be the cheapest, but it will be the best in its price range and area. See also the handy **Menu Reader** on p. 321.

RESTAURANTS BY TYPE

All-You-Can-Eat: Country Life, 2ème; Restaurant Natacha, 16ème; Lao-Thai, 19ème.
American: Elliott Restaurant, 8ème; Chesterfields Café, 8ème; Hard Rock Café, 9ème; Haynes Bar, 9ème.
Basque: Auberge de Jarente, 4ème; Chez Gladines, 13ème.
Bistro: Les Fous de l'Isle, Ile St-Louis; Pom'Cannelle, Ile St-Louis; Aux Lyonnais, 2ème; Le Petit Bolfinger, 4ème; Le Divin, 4ème; Le Temps des Cérises, 4ème; L'Estrapade, 5ème; Crémerie Restaurant Polidor, 6ème; Au Pied de Fouet, 7ème; Restaurant du Bourgogne, 10ème; Le Square Trousseau, 12ème; Le Parrot, 12ème; La Route du Château, 14ème; Le Café du Commerce, 15ème; Restaurant Perraudin, 5ème; Les Bacchantes, 9ème; Au Petit Keller, 11ème; Au Trou Normand, 11ème; Le Bistro St-Ambroise, 11ème; Chez Paul, 11ème; Le Passage, 11ème; La Route du Château, 14ème; Le Bistrot du Peintre, 11ème.
Cambodian, Thai, and Vietnamese: Le Lotus Blanc, 7ème; Lao Thai, 13ème; Tricotin, 13ème; Thiên Co. 13ème; Phetburi, 15ème; Lao Thai, 19ème; Baguette d'Or, 18ème.
Caribbean: Babylone Bis 2ème; Le Rocher du Diamant, 12ème; La Papaye, 20ème.
Chinese: Aux Délices de Széchuen, 7ème; Tricotin, 13ème.
Corsican: Sampieru Corsu, 15ème.
Crêperie: Crêperie Saint Germain, 6ème; Crêperie de Josselin, 14ème; Ty Breiz, 15ème.
Deli: Chez Jo Goldenberg, 4ème.
Eastern European: Chez Marianne, 4ème.
French: Au Gourmet de l'Isle, Ile St-Louis; L'Incroyable, 1er; Le Vieil Ecu, 1er; Le Loup Blanc, 2ème; Le Hangar, 3ème; Le Tapis Franc, 3ème; Les Lanternes du Marais, 3ème; Au Petit Fer à Cheval, 4ème; Le Vieux Comptoir, 4ème; Restaurant Perraudin, 5ème; L'Apostrophe, 5ème; Café Le Volcan, 5ème; La Cambuse, 6ème; Restaurant des Beaux Arts, 6ème; Le Petit Vatel, 6ème; La Varangue, 7ème; Le Club des Poètes, 7ème; La Menu de Margot, 8ème; Les Bachantes, 9ème; Palmier der Lorette, 9ème; Occitanie, 11ème; Le Val de Loire, 11ème; Le Passage, 11ème; Chez Paul, 11ème; Pause Café, 11ème; L'Ébauchoir, 12ème; Les Temps des Cérises, 13ème; Café du Commerce, 13ème; Le Château Poivre, 14ème; Le Colvert, 14ème; Le Jeroboam, 14ème; Restaurant Les Listine, 15ème; Chez les Fondues, 18ème; Chez Claude et Claudine, 18ème; le Baratin, 20ème.
Greek: Mozlef, 15ème; Le Colvert, 14ème.
Spanish: La Casita Tapas, 1er; Casa Tina, 16ème.
Indian: Kamala Inde, 6ème; Nirvana, 8ème; Sarangiu Anarkali, 9ème; La Route du Kashmir, 10ème; La Ville de Jagannath, 11ème.
Irish: James Joyce Pub, 17ème.e^.
Italian: La Castafiore, Ile St-Louis Pizza Sicilia, 1er; Signorelli, 1er; Saint Joseph, 3ème; Il Fiorentino Angelo, 5ème; Le Jardin des Pâtes, 5ème; Pizzéria King Salomon, 9ème; La Matta, 16ème.

Japanese: Japanese Barbecue, 2ème; Tokyorama, 6ème.

Kosher: l'As du Fallafel, 4ème; Café des Psaumes, 4ème; Chez Jo Goldenberg, 4ème; Pizzería King Salomon, 9ème.

Malaysian: Chez Foong, 15ème.

Mexican and Tex-Mex: El Pueblo, 9ème; Ay, Caramba!, 19ème.

Middle Eastern: Chez Marianne, 4ème; l'As du Fallafel, 4ème; Café des Psaumes, 4ème; Simbad, 5ème; Sannine, 9ème; Samaya, 15ème; Byblos Café, 16ème.

North African: Chez Bébert, 6ème; Le Souk, 11ème; P'tit Cahoua, 13ème; Café le Volcan, 5ème; Au Berbere Jessica, 14ème; Mozlef, 15ème; L'Atlantide, 18ème; Café Flèche d'Or, 20ème.

Open Late (midnight or later): Papou Lounge, 1er; L'Epi d'Or, 1er; Aux Lyonnais, 2ème; Le Dénicheur, 2ème; Babylone Bis, 2ème; Le Hangar, 3ème; l'As du Fallafel, 4ème; Café des Psaumes, 4ème; Chez Marianne, 4ème; Restaurant le Beautreillis, 4ème; L'Apostrophe, 5ème; Il Fiorentino Angelo, 5ème; Crêperie Saint Germain, 6ème; Le Club des Poètes, 7ème; Haynes Bar, 9ème; Hard Rock Café, 9ème; Chez Paul, 11ème; Chez Gladines, 13ème; Le Samson, 13ème; N'Zadette-M'foua, 14ème; Casa Tina, 16ème; The James Joyce Pub, 17ème; Suzon-Grisou, 18ème.

Organic: Aquarius, 4ème; Le Jardin des Pâtes, 5ème; Le Grenier de Notre Dame, 5ème; Guemaï, 6ème; Crêperie Saint Germain, 6ème; Aquarius Café, 14ème; Joy in Food, 17ème.

Outdoor Dining: Vitamine, 8ème; Le Hangar, 3ème; Saint Joseph, 3ème; Chez Jo Goldenberg, 4ème; Chez Marienne, 4ème; La Dame Tartine, 4ème; Simbad, 5ème; Aux Délices de Széchuen, 7ème; Fontaine de Mars, 7ème; Vitamine, 8ème; La Route du Kashmir, 10ème; Le Bistrot du Peintre, 11ème; Le Patio Provençal, 17ème.

Pâtisserie: Ragueneau, 1er; En Attendant Pablo, 3ème; La Maison du Chocolat, 8ème; Dalmier, 20ème.

Peruvian: Restaurant Pachamama, 3ème.

Provençale: Le Divin, 4ème; Grannie, 7ème; Fontaine de Mars, 7ème; Le Patio Provençal, 17ème.

Québecois: Équinox, 4ème.

Regional Cuisines: Aquarius, 4ème; Auberge de Jarente, 4ème; Le Divin, 4ème; Occitanie, 11ème; Chez Gladines 13ème; Crêperie de Josselin, 4ème.

Sandwich Shops: Le Dame Tartine, 12ème; Antoine's: Les Sandwichs des 5 Continents, 8ème; Vitamine, 8ème; Barry's, 8ème; Deli's Café, 9ème; Le 25ème Image, 10ème.

Spanish: Casa Tina, 16ème.

Tibetan: Pema Thang, 3ème; Le Singe d'Eau, 8ème.

Turkish: Le Cheval de Troie, 12ème; Aux Îles des Provinces, 17ème; Egée, 20ème.

Vegetarian: La Victoire Suprême du Coeur, 1er; Country Life, 2ème; Aquarius, 4ème; Piccolo Teatro, 4ème; Le Grenier de Notre Dame, 5ème; Le Jardin des Pâtes, 5ème; Guemaï, 6ème; Sannine, 9ème; Phinéas, 14ème; Aquarius Café, 14ème; Au Grain de Folie, 18ème; Joy in Food, 17ème; Rayons de Santé, 18ème.

West and East African: Paris-Dakar, 10ème; À la Banane Ivoirienne, 11ème; N'Zadette-M'foua, 14ème; Le Dogon, 10ème; Suzon-Grisou, 18ème.

RESTAURANTS BY LOCATION

■ Île St-Louis

The restaurants on Île St-Louis are everything you'd expect: expensive, romantic, and charming to a fault. In summer, rue St-Louis-en-l'Île, the island's main thoroughfare, swarms with well-heeled American strollers looking for the little restaurant they remember from last year, sticky-fingered with Berthillon ice cream. For the most part, budget travelers in search of bargain *menus* had better look elsewhere. The following establishments, however, are worthwhile splurges.

Les Fous de l'Isle, 33, rue des Deux-Ponts (tel. 01 43 25 76 67). M: Pont Marie. A café-bistro for the young neighborhood crowd, this mellow restaurant displays the work of local artists and has evening concerts every 2nd Tu. An ideal place to read. Appetizers 30-65F. Salads 50-65F. Entrées like *croustillant de saumon* and *nois de*

St. Jaques aux fruits de la passion 60-98F. Try one of the brunch *menus* (100, 130, or 150F) for a decadent Su midmorning. The blackboard lists daily specials. Open Tu-F noon-midnight, Sa 6pm-midnight, Su noon-4pm for brunch. MC, V.

Au Gourmet de l'Isle, 42, rue St-Louis-en-l'Île (tel. 01 43 26 79 27). M: Pont Marie. Exposed-beam ceilings and wooden benches create a snug, country-style setting for traditional French food. House specialties include fresh artichoke hearts and *pintadau aux lentiles vertes* (fowl with lentils). Dinner *menus* include entrée and appetizer or dessert (85 and 130F). Open W-Su noon-2pm and 7-10pm. MC, V.

Pom' Cannelle, 27, rue des Deux Ponts (tel. 01 46 34 68 59). M: Pont Marie. A straightforward place that serves up a slice of *tartes salées* (such as *quiche Lorraine*) and a salad—probably the cheapest, lightest lunch you'll find on the island (55F). Wonderful *blini chaud,* russian pancakes with salad, guacamole, and basmati rice (59-62F). Like every other place on the island, they have Berthillon ice cream. Open daily noon-midnight. MC, V.

La Castafiore, 27, rue St-Louis-en-l'Île (tel. 01 43 54 78 62). M: Pont Marie. A chic Italian restaurant looking onto a particularly lovely stretch of rue St-Louis. Salmon-colored walls and an eclectic collection of wooden chairs attract crowds for home-style Italian cuisine. Appetizers (60-78F), pastas (58-72F), meat entrées (78-98F). Lunch *menu* includes an appetizer and entrées like *soupe à l'oignon* with *penne arrabbiata* (59-62F). Dinner *formule* 98F. Prices after 8:30pm are very expensive. Open daily noon-3pm and 7-11pm. AmEx, MC, V.

■ First Arrondissement

The arcades overlooking the Louvre along rue de Rivoli are filled with the chic and expensive, but tea or *chocolat chaud* at a *salon de thé* are affordable treats. Traditional restaurants cluster around the Palais-Royal while Les Halles features cheaper, louder eateries offering everything from fast-food to four-course Italian feasts. Near Les Halles, the rue St-Denis's thoroughly respectable restaurants coexist *face à face* with sex shops. During daylight hours, travelers should consider these eateries welcome bargains, but we advise steering clear of the area after dark.

Papou Lounge, 74 rue J.-J. Rousseau (tel. 01 44 76 00 03). M: Les Halles. Walk toward the church St-Eustache, then take a right onto rue Coquillère, then a right on rue J.-J. Rousseau. With its hip young waitstaff, funky house music, black and white tile floors, and voodoo dolls on the walls, the Papou is a cross between a Tahitian lounge and a French café. Salads like endive and apple (40F) appear with substantial plates like beef brochette with tomatoes, rice, and green beans (55F). Wash down a gourmet hamburger (40-46F) or salmon burger (45F) with a cold beer (14-17F). Daily special 55F. Open daily 10am-2am with nonstop food service. MC, V.

Pizza Sicilia, 26, rue de Beaujolais (tel. 01 42 96 93 55). M: Palais-Royal. On the corner of Montpensier and Beaujolais just north of the Palais. A budget gastronomic gem. Friendly service, low prices, and absurdly good food. Try the *tortellini aux champignons* (tortellini with mushrooms, 47F), Margherita pizza (39F), or *zuppa inglese* (23F). Open M-Sa noon-2:30pm and 7-11:30pm. MC, V.

Ragueneau, 202, rue St-Honoré (tel. 01 42 61 29 76). M: Palais-Royal. From the metro, walk directly ahead toward the Palais, turning right on rue St.-Honoré. Cyrano de Bergerac used to rendez-vous here with Roxanne. Molière praised the owner's writing to get free meals. Half *pâtisserie,* half restaurant, this ultra-modern establishment with bleached wood and soothing blue walls is famous for its delicate *millefeuille* (20F), a flaky pastry layered with cream. Though a little pricey, the caliber of the cuisine is worth every franc. 2-course *menu* 115F, 3-course *menu* 154F, entrées 78F. Open M-Sa noon-3pm. AmEx, MC, V.

L'Epi d'Or, 25, rue J.-J. Rousseau (tel. 01 42 36 38 12). M: Les Halles. From the metro, walk toward St-Eustache then take the second right after the church onto rue J.-J. Rousseau. A small restaurant open to the street in the summer and decorated with tasteful antiques and fresh flowers. Frequented by journalists from the nearby Figaro offices. The staff is charming and the food is excellent. 3-course *menu* served until 9pm (105F). Main courses from 90F. Housemade *foie gras à* *canard* appetizer (26F) and *entrecôte bordelaise* (rib steak; 105F). Open Sept.-July M-F noon-2:15pm and 7:30pm-2am, Sa 7:30pm-2am. Last orders at midnight. Closed 1 week in Feb. Reservations recommended. MC, V.

L'Incroyable, 26, rue de Richelieu, or 23, rue de Montpensier (tel. 01 42 96 24 64). M: Palais-Royal. Walk along the left side of the Palais-Royal and turn left on rue de Montpensier. Look for passage Potier on your right—the restaurant has a sign above the passage. Though tiny and hidden in an alleyway, the restaurant lives up to its name ("incredible"). 3-course lunch *menu* 80F; dinner *menus* 110-130F. *Museaux* (mussels) vinaigrette and *claufoutis aux fruits* (fruit cobbler) are each 25F. Friendly, English-speaking staff. Open June-Sept. M-F noon-2:15pm and 6:30-9pm; Oct.-May Tu-Sa noon-2:15pm and 6:30-9pm.

La Victoire Suprême du Coeur, 41, rue des Bourdonnais (tel. 01 40 41 93 95). M: Châtelet. Follow traffic on rue des Halles then turn left on rue des Bourdonnais. Sit and elevate your consciousness in this bright and serene vegetarian restaurant. Run by the devotees of the guru Sri Chinmoy who have both body and soul in mind when creating dishes like *gratinée aux champignons* (mushrooms and green beans in a rich cheese sauce). All-day 3-course *formule* 89F. Entrées 47-67F. Open M-Th noon-2:30pm and 7-10pm, F-Sa noon-2:30pm and 7-10:30pm.

Signorelli, 35, rue St-Honoré (tel. 01 40 13 91 41). M: Les Halles. From Les Halles, head down rue St-Honoré toward the Louvre. The restaurant takes its name from the many copied paintings of Luca Signorelli, Michelangelo's master, that hang on its walls. Daily *menu* 78F. Pastas include homemade tortellini with prosciutto (69-82F). Desserts like chocolate fondue with orange-infused cream (49F). If you're daring, tackle *La Torre del Moro* (coffee with brandy, 54F). Open M-F and Su noon-3pm and 7-10:30pm, Sa 7-10:30pm. AmEx, MC, V.

Le Vieil Ecu, 166, rue St-Honoré (tel. 01 42 60 20 14; fax 01 42 60 02 96). M: Palais-Royal. Walk toward the Palais-Royal and turn right on rue St-Honoré. Everything you might expect from a Parisian restaurant: checkered tablecloths, lace-draped lamps, and exposed beams. Lunch *menu* (67F), dinner *menu* (72-105F), and entrées (79-83F) include dishes like stuffed eggplant gratinée and *tarte tatin.* Add a glass of Beaujolais (20F). Vegetarian entrees available. Live music upstairs M-Sa 8:30-10pm. Open M-Sa 11:30am-3pm and 6:30-11pm. MC, V.

La Casita Tapas, 34, rue Montpensier (tel. 01 40 20 44 04; fax 01 40 20 44 05). M: Palais-Royal. Step into the red-painted entry and emerge in Andalusia, España. The lunch *formule* (50F) comes with a glass of sangria and your choice of five tapas such as spicy chorizo sausage, marinated red peppers, eggplant *beignets*, or *pisto andalouse.* Desserts 28F. Spanish guitar music on weeknights. Open M noon-2:30pm, Tu-Sa noon-2:30pm and 7pm-midnight. Reservations accepted. MC, V.

■ Second Arrondissement

Wedged between the wide boulevards of the 9ème and the affluence of the 1er near the Louvre, the 2ème provides inexpensive meals to tourists exploring this and neighboring *quartiers.* Rue Montorgueil is lined with excellent bakeries, fruit stands, and specialty stores (see **Food Markets,** p. 104), and side streets like rue Marie Stuart and rue Mandar hide some charming dining options. Rue Tiquetonne is home to a number of small gay-owned restaurants. The Passage des Panoramas and Passage des Italiens offer fast, cheap food options.

Le Loup Blanc, 42, rue Tiquetonne (tel. 01 40 13 08 35). M: Étienne Marcel. Walk against traffic on rue de Turbigo and turn left on rue Tiquetonne. If you've got a wolfish appetite and are looking for great atmosphere, head to the intimate Loup Blanc. The charming owner-couple built and designed the whole place from the ground up, and you've gotta give 'em snaps for their mellow maroon and blue style. Monthly art exhibits. Specializes in grilled and marinated meats. Entrées with choice of sides 48-114F. The Loup Blanc mixed grille allows you to sample 4 different kinds of meats and sides (62-78F). The vegetarian option, *les salades mosaiques,* provides salad and 4-6 sides (48-60F). Sunday brunch 75-95F. Open M-Sa noon-3pm and 8-11:30pm, Su brunch 11am-5pm.

Aux Lyonnais, 32, rue St-Marc (tel. 01 42 96 65 04; fax 01 42 97 42 95). M: Bourse. Walk with traffic on rue Vivienne and turn left on rue St-Marc. Copious, traditional French food set with floral tiles, Victorian lamps, and antique mirrors. The ideal French restaurant for a romantic dinner. Dine on *caille rôtie* (roast quail, 75F) or *lapin aux échalotes* (rabbit with shallots, 75F). 2-course *menu* 92F. Wine 20F. Open M-F 11:30am-3pm and 6:30-11:45pm, Sa 7pm-midnight. AmEx, MC, V.

Le Dénicheur, 4, rue Tiquetonne (tel. 01 42 21 31 01). M: Étienne Marcel. Walk against traffic on rue de Turbigo and turn left on rue Tiquetonne. Lovely restaurant and *salon de thé* with funky lamps, 70s clocks, and a mascot goldfish, all for sale. 2-course *menu* 50-55F; 3-course *menu* with coffee 70F. Omelettes, sandwiches, and quiches all 35F. Large Sunday brunch (70F). Tea and brioche served all day (16F). Open daily 12:30pm-2am.

Babylone Bis, 34, rue Tiquetonne (tel. 01 42 33 48 35). M: Étienne Marcel. Walk against traffic on rue de Turbigo and turn left onto rue Tiquetonne. Popular with artists who come for Antillean and African specialties. With zebra skins and African carvings on the walls, banana leaves on the ceiling, and guests dancing on the tables to zouk and reggae, this restaurant feels like a wild Paris of the 1930s. Past patrons include Stevie Wonder, Jesse Jackson, and Marvin Gaye. Specialties include *aloko* (bananas flambéed in liqueur, 35F), *beignets de banane* (banana fritter, 50F), and *poulet braisé* (braised lime-marinated chicken, 80F). Cocktails 35F. Dinner served all night. Open M-F 8pm-7am, Sa-Su 8pm-8am. MC, V.

Japanese Barbecue, 60, rue Montorgueil (tel. 01 42 33 49 61). M: Sentier. Follow rue Réaumur and turn right on rue des Petits-Carreaux, which becomes rue Montorgueil. A Western clientele sits at the bar and watches the dextrous chef tend the grill, while some engage in people-watching seated outside on the colorfu rue Montorgueil. All *menus* with broth and rice, some with salad. Grill *menus* (73F), sushi/sashimi *menus* (80-120F), lunch *menus* (47-60F), vegetarian *menu* includes miso soup, salad and entrée (66F). Open M-Th noon-2:30pm and 7-10:45pm, F-Sa noon-2:30pm and 7-9:45pm. MC, V.

Country Life, 6, rue Daunou (tel. 01 42 97 48 51). M: Opéra. From the metro, head down rue de la Paix toward pl. Vendome and turn left on rue Daunou. Treat yourself to fresh vegetarian cuisine in the spacious but impersonal cafeteria-style dining area of this smoke-free health food store. All-you-can-eat buffet includes gorgeous fresh breads, soups, rice, and salads, as well as hot entrées (65F). Carrot juice 10F, herbal tea infusions 5F. Take-out available (fill-your-own container: small 32F, large 49F). Open M-Th 11:30am-2:30pm and 6:30-10pm, F 11:30am-2:30pm. Store open M-Th 10am-10pm, F 10am-3pm. MC, V.

▓ Third Arrondissement

Close to the 3ème's elegant *hôtels particuliers,* the restaurants of the upper Marais offer Peruvian, Tibetan, and French cuisine in the shadow of the Picasso Museum and the Musée Carnavalet. Dinner can be pricey, but lunchtime *menus* are good deals.

Le Hangar, 12, impasse Berthaud (tel. 01 42 74 55 44). M: Rambuteau. Take the Impasse Berthaud exit from the metro. Tucked in an alley near the Centre Pompidou, Le Hangar is bright and intimate, with tiger-lilies atop white tablecloths. Many French specialties, like *foie gras de canard poêlé* (fried goose liver, 88F). Appetizers 30-58F. Open M 6:30pm-midnight, Tu-Sa noon-3:30pm and 6:30pm-midnight.

Le Tapis Franc, 12, rue Pecquay (tel. 01 44 59 86 72). M: Rambuteau. From the metro, follow the traffic on rue Rambuteau, take the second right on rue Pecquay. In 1930s Paris, *les tapis* (rugs) was slang for the popular bistros of Montmartre. *Franc* described places frequented by artists and prostitutes. When the government closed Paris's brothels in 1950, bistros took over as fronts for these dislocated "employees." Today, Le Tapis sells only fine French cuisine. The place is small, but the portions are enormous. Dinner *menus* 80-105F, salads 40F, entrées 45F. Open daily noon-2:30pm and 7-11:30pm. MC, V.

Les Lanternes du Marais, 38, rue Debelleyme (tel. 01 42 72 39 24). M: Filles du Calvaire. Follow rue des Filles du Calvaire then turn right on rue de Bretagne and right on rue Debelleyme. On a quiet street, the Lanternes serves French cuisine in a warm space with tablecloths and wooden beams. Lunch and dinner *menus* 75F, appetizers 30-75F, entrées 68-120F, desserts 22F. Pitcher of wine 40F. Open Sept.-July M-Tu and Th-F 11:30am-3pm and 7-9:30pm, W and Sa noon-3pm.

En Attendant Pablo, 78, rue Vieille-du-Temple (tel. 01 42 74 34 65). M: Hotel de Ville. From rue de Rivoli, turn left on rue Vieille du Temple. Around the corner from the Picasso museum, with Picasso prints on the walls. Combination *pâtisserie*/lunch café, serving enormous salads (55F). Lunch *menu* with *tarte salée* (52F), and Sunday brunch (95F). Open W-Su 11am-6pm. MC, V.

Saint Joseph, 1, rue Perrée (tel. 01 42 71 23 08). M: Temple. Walk opposite traffic on rue Vieille-du-Temple and take the second left onto rue Perrée. On a quiet tree-lined street next to a park, this modest pizzeria has good pizza (40-52F), lunch (62F), and dinner *menus* (85F). Take-out available. Open M-Sa noon-2:30pm and 7-11pm.

Restaurant Pachamama, 2, impasse Berthaud (tel. 01 48 87 88 22). M: Rambuteau. Take the Impasse Berthaud exit. Peruvian cuisine, salsa music, and low prices make this bar/restaurant very hot. Small and intimate, run by a very friendly Peruvian couple. Generous lunch *menu* (55F). Try the spicy *Aji de Gallima* (chicken with cheese sauce, 45F). Open Tu-Su noon- 11pm.

Pema Thang, 6, rue du Parc-Royal (tel. 01 42 72 45 66). M: Chemin Vert. Opposite a beautiful park in the heart of the Marais, this simple restaurant (and *salon de thé*) offers classic Tibetan cuisine. Lunch and dinner *menus* (60F, 79F, 100F) offer a variety of vegetarian specialties such as *Bhoethouk* (57F). Refreshing yogurt desserts (32F). Open M-Sa noon to 3pm and 7-11pm, Su 7-11pm. MC, V.

■ Fourth Arrondissement

The gentrification of the 4ème has inspired many chic dining options, with old mansions, galleries, and cafés now serving *brunch*, a late-Sunday-morning meal invented by gay men in the 7th century. Several kosher bakeries, delis, and restaurants on rue des Rosiers offer Jewish and Israeli specialities, while the Marais's many gay cafés and bars overflow into the streets during warm weather.

Au Petit Fer à Cheval, 30, rue Vieille du Temple (tel. 01 42 72 47 47). M: Hôtel-de-Ville or St-Paul. Head down rue de Rivoli against traffic and turn left onto rue Vieille du Temple. One word: fabulous. A monument to all that is chic and hip in the Marais. An oasis of *chèvre*, kir, and cigarettes. The Petit Fer serves French fare to a local crowd that knows a good thing when they find it. Grab one of the streetside tables for prime viewing action or squeeze around the horseshoe bar. Invisible from the front, a few tables huddle behind the bar, where you can order the life-changing *chèvre chaud* salad with prosciutto and toasted bread (50F). Sandwiches 20-35F. Desserts 25-34F. Open M-F 9am-2am, Sa-Su 11am-2am.

Le Vieux Comptoir, 8, rue de Birague (tel. 01 42 72 55 36). M: Bastille. This tiny restaurant and wine bar, directly behind pl. des Vosges, feels like a funky artists' hangout, with a hip staff to match. Sit beneath the artwork and sky-painted ceiling to order duck with honey glaze and thyme (89F) or chocolate mousse with *grappa*, an Italian liqueur (39F). Regional wines (17F per glass). Lunch *formule* (70F), dinner *formule* (98F). Open daily noon-3pm and 7-11pm.

Équinox, 33-35, rue des Rosiers (tel. 01 42 71 92 41) M: Hôtel-de-Ville. Between Café Amésia and Au Petit Fer à Cheval, Équinox serves Québecois specialties like *tourtière* (a meat pie) and desserts made with imported *sirop d'érable* (maple syrup). Relatively new, Équinox is the latest on the hip Parisian Québecois scene, sponsoring cultural events along with the Librairie du Québec (see **Books,** p. 265) and the Association Paris-Québec (see **Festivals,** p. 251). Open M-Su 10am-2am.

Le Petit Bofinger, 6, rue de la Bastille (tel. 01 42 72 05 23). M: Bastille. Rue de la Bastille runs directly off pl. de la Bastille. Across the street from its expensive big brother, this bistro spinoff offers affordable classics. White-aproned waiters serve specials like ravioli with roast chicken or steak tartare (76F). Finish off with a dessert like poached peaches with cassis (30F). The lunch *formule* gets you an appetizer, an entrée, and a drink (89F). Open daily noon-3pm and 7pm-midnight.

Auberge de Jarente, 7, rue de Jarente (tel. 01 42 77 49 35). M: St-Paul. From the metro walk against traffic on rue de Rivoli and turn left on rue de Sévigné and then right on rue de Jarente. A cottage-like restaurant serving Basque specialties like roast *cailles* (quail, 68F) and apple *croustade* with Armagnac (45F). 3-course lunch *menu* with wine 77F, 4-course *menu* 117F. Open Tu-Sa noon-2:30pm and 7:30-10:30pm. Reservations recommended. AmEx, MC, V.

Chez Marianne, 2, rue des Hospitalières-St-Gervais (tel. 01 42 72 18 86). M: St-Paul. Follow rue de Rivoli a few steps and turn right on rue Pavée; turn left on rue des Rosiers and right on rue des Hospitalières-St-Gervais. Folksy canteen and specialty store offering Middle Eastern and Eastern European specialties. Wine bottles and pickled delicacies are stacked floor to ceiling. Sample 4, 5, or 6 specialties (55F, 65F, or 75F), including *zaziki, falafel,* and *tarama.* Homemade desserts like strudel (30F) and *vatrouchka,* a white cheese cake (35F). Arrive before 7pm to avoid the dinner crowd. Take-out available. Open daily 11am-12:30am. MC, V.

Piccolo Teatro, 6, rue des Écouffes (tel. 01 42 72 17 79). M: St-Paul. From the metro, walk with the traffic down rue de Rivoli and take a right on rue des Écouffes. A romantic vegetarian hideout. Appetizers (22-45F), entrées (60-70F), lunch *menu* (52F), and dinner *menus* (90-115F) feature *tempeh au curry* (solid grains sauteed in a curry sauce with assorted veggies, 70F) and charlotte rhubarb (35F). A *kir* on the house for *Let's Go* readers. Open W-Su noon-3pm and 7-11pm. AmEx, MC, V.

Le Divin, 41, rue Ste-Croix-de-la-Bretonnerie (tel. 01 42 77 10 20). M: Hôtel-de-Ville or Rambuteau. Walk away from the Hôtel de Ville on rue du Temple and turn right on rue Ste-Croix-de-la-Bretonnerie. A taste of Provence. House specialties include *terrine du Divin* (pâté with scallops, 38F). Gourmet *menu* (136F) offers such specialties as *dos de saumon au champagne* (salmon cooked with champagne). Open Tu-Sa noon-2pm and 7:30-11:30pm, Su 7:30-11pm. AmEx, MC, V.

Restaurant le Beautreillis, 18, rue Beautreillis (tel. 01 48 04 99 29). M: Bastille. Exit the metro on rue St-Antoine and take the 5th left onto rue Beautreillis. Located across from where Jim Morrison died (no. 17), the restaurant hosts readings of Jim's poetry, tarot readings, and musicians Dec. 8-July 3. Traditional French cuisine like *chèvre* in puff pastry and *cuisse de canard gras confit maison* (glazed duck leg) fills the lunch *menus* (49F-78F). Open M-Sa 10am-2am. MC, V.

Le Temps des Cérises, 31, rue de la Cerisaie (tel. 01 42 72 08 63). M: Bastille or Sully-Morland. From M: Bastille exit on bd. Henri IV and turn right onto rue de la Cerisaie. A neighborhood bistro, café, and wine bar run by campy Marie-Claire and Gérard, who've emblazoned themselves on postcards and calendars. Situated in the former banquet hall of a Celestine convent, the Cérises serves a hearty 3-course lunch *menu* (68F), *pot au feu* (a rich beef stew, 65F), sandwiches (12F), and coffee (10F). Open for lunch M-F 11:30am-2:30pm; bar open M-F 7:45am-8pm.

L'As du Falafel, 34, rue des Rosiers (tel. 01 48 87 63 60; http://www.notresite.com/as-du-falafel). M: St-Paul. From the metro, go with the traffic a few steps down rue de Rivoli, make a right on rue Pavée; turn left on rue des Rosiers. This kosher falafel stand and restaurant displays pictures of Lenny Kravitz, who credited this cheerfully decorated place with "the best falafel in the world, particularly the special eggplant falafel with hot sauce." Go his way with the falafel special (25F), lamb *schawerma* (32F), or sauteed chicken with curry sauce (32F). Pay first at the cashier and give your ticket to the falafel chef. Open Su-Th 10am-midnight. MC, V.

Café des Psaumes, 14-16, rue des Rosiers (tel. 01 48 04 74 77). M: St-Paul. Next to l'As du Falafel, above. A kosher restaurant in the heart of the Jewish quarter with a mural of rue des Rosiers as it was in 1905. Falafel plate (59F) or falafel sandwich (25F). *Couscous douceur* (couscous with beef, raisins, chick peas, almonds, and cinnamon, 85F). Open Su-Th 11am-midnight, F noon-sundown. MC, V.

Chez Jo Goldenberg, 7, rue des Rosiers (tel. 01 48 87 20 16). M: St-Paul. See directions for l'As du Falafel. In the heart of the Marais's Jewish quarter, Goldenberg's (est. 1920) has become a landmark. It suffered a 1982 terrorist attack that took the life of the owner's son. A site for tourists and celebrities from Moshe Dayan to Harry Belafonte, but still a neighborhood, family place serving kosher soups (20-32F), *blinis* (18F), stuffed cabbage or beef goulash (80F), and pastries galore. Take-out available: borscht (25F per L), gefilte fish (45F), bagels (6F). English menu. Outdoor tables. Deli open daily 8:30am-11pm; restaurant open daily noon-midnight.

FOOD AND DRINK

Aquarius, 54, rue Ste-Croix-de-la-Bretonnerie (tel. 01 48 87 48 71). M: Hôtel-de-Ville. Walk away from the Hôtel de Ville on rue du Temple and turn right on rue Ste-Croix-de-la-Bretonnerie. Also at 40, rue de Gergovie, 14ème (tel. 01 45 41 36 88). Potted plants, smoke-free air, an occult library, and fresh vegetarian dishes like homemade yogurt (62F). Lunch or dinner *menu* (92F) features a cold dish, hot dish, and dessert. The *assiette paysanne* (64F) includes *chèvre chaud*, bread, mushrooms, and potatoes. Open M-Th noon-10:15pm, F-Sa noon-10:30pm. MC, V.

■ Fifth Arrondissement

Foraging for food in the 5ème requires no special skills. Cheap restaurants and a lively open-air market (see **Food Markets,** p. 104) cluster on rue Mouffetard, the main culinary artery of the arrondissement. The highest density of cheap restaurants is found on the pedestrian streets off rue de la Huchette, near pl. St-Michel.

Le Jardin des Pâtes, 4, rue Lacépède (tel. 01 43 31 50 71). M: Jussieu. From the metro, walk up rue Linné and turn right on rue Lacépède. This bright Mediterranean restaurant makes organic gourmet pastas with a variety of sauces, including *pâtes de seigle* (ham, white wine, and sharp *comté* cheese; 56F). Many vegetarian offerings. Appetizers 19-34F, entrées 39-77F. Reservations recommended. Open daily noon-2:30pm and 7-11pm. MC, V.

Restaurant Perraudin, 157, rue St-Jacques (tel. 01 46 33 15 75). M: Luxembourg. From the metro, take rue Royer Collard to rue St-Jacques. A warm burgundy and wood interior and classic French dishes like *sautée d'agneau aux flageolets* (sauteed lamb with white beans, 59F). Come early to avoid crowds. 3-course lunch *menu* (98F). Appetizers 41F, entrées 59F, desserts 28-36F, wine 9F. Open Tu-F noon-2:15pm and 7:30-10:15pm, M and Sa 7:30-10:15pm.

L'Apostrophe, 34, rue de la Montagne Ste-Geneviève (tel. 01 43 54 10 93). M: Maubert-Mutualité. From the metro, walk down bd. St-Germain toward the Institut du Monde Arabe and turn right on rue de la Montagne Ste-Geneviève. This small, candle-lit restaurant offers traditional French food at reasonable prices. Lunch (65F) and dinner (85F) *menus*. Open M-Th 5pm-12:30am, F-Sa 5pm-2am. MC, V.

Café Le Volcan, 10, rue Thouin (tel. 01 46 33 38 33). M: Cardinal Lemoine. Turn left on rue Cardinal Lemoine, right on rue Thouin. Offbeat posters of French kitsch and film stars and French cuisine. Dinner *menus* (59-145F). Open Tu-Su noon-2:15pm and 6:30-11:30pm. MC, V.

L' Estrapade, 15, rue de l'Estrapade (tel. 01 43 25 72 58). M: Luxembourg. From pl. du Panthéon turn right on rue Clotaire and left on rue de l'Estrapade. Near the Panthéon, this tiny *fin de siècle* bistro specializes in French cuisine like *fricassée de volaille* and *soupe à l'oignon*. Lunch *menu* 67F. Dinner *menu* 122F. Entrées 65-89F. Open Su-F noon-2:30pm and 7-11pm, Sa 7-11pm. MC, V.

Le Grenier de Nôtre Dame, 18, rue de la Bûcherie (tel. 01 43 29 98 29). M: St-Michel. Walk along quai St-Michel to quai de Montebello; turn right on rue Lagrange and left on rue de la Bûcherie. Macrobiotic and vegetarian specialties. 3-course *menus* (75F, 78F, and 105F). Delicious polenta with stir-fried vegetables (75F). Open M-Th noon-2:30pm and 7-11pm, F-Su noon-11pm. MC, V.

Il Fiorentino Angelo, 3, rue Mouffetard (tel. 01 46 34 71 61). M: Cardinal Lemoine. From the metro, walk southwest on rue du Cardinal Lemoine, turn right on rue Thouin and left on rue Mouffetard. Italian restaurant with a variety of pasta offerings (50-65F) and meat dishes (75-105F). Lunch (58F) and dinner (85F) *menus*. Open M-F noon-3pm and 7pm-midnight, Sa-Su 7pm-midnight. MC, V.

Simbad, 7, rue Lagrange (tel. 01 43 26 19 05). M: Maubert-Mutualité. Take your pick of *tabouli, hummus,* and stuffed grape-leaf sandwiches (18-20F) and platters (20-45F). If the terrace is full, bring your food to the parc Viviani across the street and gaze at Nôtre Dame. Delivery available (20F) in the 1er-8ème arrondissements with a 75F minimum. Open daily 10am-midnight.

FOOD AND DRINK

■ Sixth Arrondissement

Tiny restaurants with rock-bottom prices jostle each other for space and customers in the area bounded by bd. St-Germain, bd. St-Michel, and the Seine, making this area an excellent quadrangle to wander in search of a filling meal. Rue de Buci harbors bargain Greek restaurants and a rambling daily street market, while rue Gregoire de Tours has the highest density of cheap restaurants (think greasy spoons, not 4-star gems). More options can be found along the streets near the Odéon metro stop.

Crêperie Saint Germain, 33, rue St-André-des-Arts (tel. 01 43 54 24 41). M: St-Michel. This *crêperie* is young, funky, and far from conventional. Jazz plays amid a Moroccan-mosaic of disco balls, beaded lampshades, terra cotta tables, and earthenware plates. The house specializes in filling wheat-flour *crêpes noirs,* like the *Chihuahua* (guacamole, black olives, and salad, 39F) or the *Manhattan* (ground beef, cheese and tomatoes topped with a fried egg, 56F), and sweet dessert crêpes (26-56F). A 49F *menu* (served until 6pm) includes 2 simple *crêpes* and a glass of *cidre,* but bring a friend; there's a 110F minimum. Open daily noon-1am. AmEx, MC, V.

La Cambuse, 8, rue Casimir Delavigne (tel. 01 43 26 48 84). M: Odéon. Veer right off pl. de l'Odéon. This 6-table family restaurant serves up ample amounts of *soupe à l'oignon, boeuf bourguignon,* or *coq au vin.* Expect hearty servings. The 3-course *menu* (100F) includes a starter, a daily *plat* like duck terrine, and desserts such as *crème caramel.* Open M-Sa noon-2:30pm and 7-10:30pm. Reservations accepted and a good idea. May be closed in Aug. MC, V.

Guemaï, 6 rue Cardinale (tel. 01 43 26 03 24). M: Mabillon. Turn right off bd. St-Michel onto rue Cardinale. A combination store and lunch-only restaurant serving vegetarian, *biologique* (organic), and macrobiotic food (no eggs, butter, or refined sugars) alongside freshly squeezed juices and organic wines. Robust house-made *gratin de tofou* (26F) and vegetable tart (24F) highlight the *plats du jour* (64F). Go early to be guaranteed a spot in this ultra-popular place. Store (which sells all-natural products and some organic fruits and vegetables) open M-Sa 9am-8:30pm. Restaurant open M-Sa 11:45am-3:30pm. No reservations. MC, V.

Tokyorama, 9, rue Monsieur-le-Prince (tel. 01 43 54 37 04). M: Odéon. At the Carrefour de l'Odéon, take the left-most prong of the fork onto rue Monsieur-le-Prince, and walk one block up on your left. A youngish crowd dines on a wide selection of sushi and Japanese grilled meats. Most menus include miso soup, salad, and rice. The 36F *menu* features four chicken shish kabobs; the sushimi *menu* (62F) offers slices of tuna and salmon; the *menu Pacifique* (96F) includes four choices of sushi and sashimi and a maki roll. Open daily noon-3pm and 6pm-midnight. MC, V.

Restaurant des Beaux Arts, 11, rue Bonaparte (tel. 01 43 26 92 64). M: St-Germain-des-Prés. Follow traffic on bd. St-Germain and turn left onto rue Bonaparte. Few frills, but full of character and just across from the École des Beaux Arts. Starting in the late 19th century, students from the art school would pay for meals by painting the frescos that still decorate the restaurant walls. The clientele is a bit older since the School of Architecture moved out of the Beaux Arts, but you'll still find art students there enjoying a late-night meal. 95F *menu* and vegetarian options. *Plat du jour* 65F. Large salads 25-35F. Open daily noon-2:15pm and 7-10:45pm.

Crémerie Restaurant Polidor, 41, rue Monsieur-le-Prince (tel. 01 43 26 95 34). M: Cluny-Sorbonne. From the metro, walk down bd. St-Michel away from the river, take a right on rue Racine and the first left on rue Monsieur-le-Prince. Rimbaud and Verlaine used to eat here together amid the Polidor's mirrors and polished wood. Faithful regulars keep their cloth napkins (as Hemingway and Joyce did) in the numbered wood drawers in the back of the restaurant. Comforting French bistro cuisine like *escargots* (74F) and *bavarois au cassis* (a cake soaked in blackberry liqueur, 25F) supplement a 2-course lunch *menu* (55F), 3-course dinner *menu* (100F), and a 3-course *à la carte* option (120-130F). Open M-Sa noon-2:30pm and 7pm-12:30am, Su noon-2:30pm and 7-8:30pm.

Chez Bébert, 71, bd. Montparnasse (tel. 01 42 22 55 31; fax 01 42 81 97 02). M: Montparnasse. Right by the metro, on the corner of bd. Montparnasse and rue de Rennes. A North African oasis on the busy boulevard, Chez Bébert serves up Tuni-

FOOD AND DRINK

sian specialties in an atmosphere that doesn't feel budget. Sink into plush velvet banquettes surrounded by glittering tile and glass while attentive waiters bring heaping plates of couscous (70F) and succulent *tajines* (a North African stew) like lamb with prunes and almonds (98F). Lunch *menu* (75F), mint tea (15F), and Turkish coffee (20F). Open daily noon-4pm and 6pm-2am. AmEx, MC, V.

Kamala-Inde, 13, rue Monsieur-le-Prince (tel. 01 40 51 73 27). M: Odéon. An incense-scented refuge near St-Germain-des-Prés, Kamala's ample portions bring in neighborhood regulars such as Gérard Depardieu for well-priced fare. The 49F lunch *menu* consists of either chicken or vegetable korma with dessert, and 50F buys chicken tandoori, naan (an Indian bread), and salad. Other specialties include lamb curry (72F) and basmati with saffron, veggies, almonds, and raisins (65F). Open daily noon-2:30pm and 7-11pm.

Le Petit Vatel, 5, rue Lobineau (tel. 01 43 54 28 49). M: Mabillon. From the metro, follow traffic on bd. St-Germain, turn right on rue de Seine, and then take the second right onto rue Lobineau. With four small tables, Le Petit Vatel still makes a big impression with Mediterranean French specialties such as *pamboli* (bread with puréed tomatoes, ham, and cheese). The 60F lunch *menu* includes appetizer, main course, and dessert. The friendly owner/chef Sixte (he was the 6th one in the family) offers different daily entrées, and there is always a vegetarian option. Take-out available. Open Tu-Sa noon-3pm and 7-11pm. MC, V.

▓ Seventh Arrondissement

Restaurants are some of the only touristed spots in the militaristic 7*ème* not consecrated to the memory of Napoleon. The emperor himself never allowed more than 20 minutes to dine. Unfortunately, you might need an emperor's fortune to eat in this arrondissement. Those seeking cheaper options should look elsewhere. Despite the pricey menus, the following restaurants provide wonderful meals and atmosphere.

La Varangue, 27, rue Angereau (tel. 01 45 05 51 22). M: École Militaire. Turn right on rue de Grenelle from av. de la Bourdonnais, then take a left onto rue Angereau. Intimate atmosphere and homestyle cuisine in a little restaurant with a staff of two and seating for less than two dozen. The *menu* is short but varied and changes daily: a testament to the freshness of their ingredients and the careful preparation of every dish. The 77F lunch and dinner *formule* includes dishes such as eggplant, chicken, and tomato tart, wine or cider, and dessert. *Grandes salades* with fresh vegetables (45F) and other vegetarian meals are always available. Open M-F noon-10pm. Dinner reservations recommended. AmEx, MC, V.

Le Club des Poètes, 30, rue de Bourgogne (tel. 01 47 05 06 03; fax 01 45 55 65 79; http://www.franceweb.fr/poesie). M: Varenne. Walk up bd. des Invalides toward the esplanade, turn right on rue de Grenelle and then left onto rue de Bourgogne. With a fisted salute and a *"Vive la poésie,"* Jean-Pierre Rosnay welcomes you to his club, established in 1961 to "make poetry contagious and inevitable." Beginning at 10pm, a troupe of readers including Rosnay and his wife grace your ears with the great French poets. If you find the food simple and the prices high (100-150F for dinner with wine), remember that you're also paying for Apollinaire, Rimbaud, and Aragon. 96F lunch *menu*. Open M-Sa noon-3pm and 8pm-1am. AmEx, MC, V.

Grannie, 27, rue Pierre Leroux (tel. 01 43 34 94 14; http://www.infenst.fr/verna/grannie). M: Vaneau. A colorful breath of country in the grind and grim of Paris. Cheerful, rustic decor and provincial victuals transport you from the city to the South of France. Lunchtime *formules* include meat or fish of the day with salad and coffee (58F) or with salad, appetizer, and wine (80F). Wine 15-30F per glass. Open M-F noon-1:30pm and 7:30-10pm, Sa 7:30-10:30pm. MC, V.

Aux Délices de Széchuen, 40, av. Duquesne (tel. 01 43 06 22 55). M: St-François-Xavier. On the corner of av. Duquesne and av. Breteuil behind the Église St-François-Xavier. An elegant, family-run Chinese restaurant that has been serving Szechuan specialties for two decades, like the **poulet sauté aux champignons noirs** (chicken sauteed with black mushrooms, 50F). 3-course *menu* offered M-Sa (100F). Plenty of vegetarian options served on the large, shaded outdoor terrace in summer. Open Tu-Su noon-2:30pm and 7-10:30pm.

Fontaine de Mars, 129, rue St-Dominique (tel. 01 47 05 46 44; fax 01 47 05 11 13). M: École Militaire. Walk north on av. Bosquet and turn left on rue St-Dominique. A splurge but worth every *centime,* this picture-perfect restaurant with plaid curtains, pine interior, and red-checkered tablecloths is one of the best places in the 7ème for healthy helpings of southwestern French food. The terrace overlooks the restaurant's fountain namesake. Specialties such as goat cheese with nuts (67F), roast duck with garlic potatoes (95F), and marinated plums in Armagnac supplement a lunch *menu* (90F) of steak tartare, potatoes, salad, and dessert. English menu available. Open daily noon-3pm and 7:30-11pm. AmEx, MC, V.

Le Lotus Blanc, 45, rue de Bourgogne (tel. 01 45 55 18 89). M. Varenne. This Vietnamese restaurant, replete with banquettes in burgundy velvet and warm polished wood, is a neighborhood favorite as yet undiscovered by the throngs visiting the nearby Musée Rodin. For 59F the lunchtime *formule* serves up filling main dishes like caramelized pork or ginger chicken with rice, and dessert. Other dishes include spicy shrimp and cashews (63F) and curried squid (47F). Menu available in English. Open M-Sa noon-2:30pm and 7:30-11pm.

Au Pied de Fouet, 45, rue de Babylone (tel. 01 47 05 12 27). M. Vaneau. A small, neighborhood bistro serving simple and affordable fare such as *confit de canard* (duck casserole, 60F). Open M-F noon-2:30pm and 7-9:45pm, Sa noon-2:30pm.

■ Eighth Arrondissement

The 8ème is as glamorous and expensive as one might expect of Paris. In fact, most of the charm of this arrondissement lies in its gratuitous extravagance. If you're not interested in participating in such exuberant wastefulness, there are some affordable restaurants to be found, especially on side streets around rue La Boétie.

Vitamine, 20, rue de Bucarest (tel. 01 45 22 28 02). M: Liège. From the metro, walk up rue de Moscou. The restaurant is on the 1st corner on your right. Overlooking the lively pl. Dublin, with an outdoor summer terrace. Straightforward self-serve place with light, low-priced sandwiches and salads. English spoken. Sandwiches with excellent bread 13-20F, salads 22-40F. *Plats du jour,* such as moussaka with salad 35F. Several vegetarian selections. Open M-F 8am-4pm.

Nirvana, 6, rue de Moscou (tel. 01 45 22 27 12). M: Liège. So, you're sick of French food and want something a bit spicier. You also want real tablecloths, impeccable service, high-backed velvet chairs, and a clientele that speaks in hushed tones. If you are seeking to cultivate a state of serenity and happiness from a meal, this may be the place to do it, provided you've got some cash to plunk down. Indian cuisine in a schmancy setting with a classy crowd. Lunch *menu* includes chicken or fish tikka, salad, and naan bread (79 and 95F). Dinner *menus* (119, 129, 159F) offer an appetizer, entrée, naan, and dessert. Open M-Sa noon-2pm and 7:30-11pm.

Barry's, 9, rue de Duras (tel. 01 40 06 02 27). M: Champs Elysées-Clemenceau. From the metro, cross the Champs-Élysées and walk straight up av. Marigny to pl. Beauvau, take a sharp right onto rue du Faubourg St-Honoré and turn left on rue de Duras. Head to Barry's to refuel after window-shopping on rue Fbg. St-Honoré. A clean, quiet, airy sandwich emporium with *panini* (26-32F), sandwiches (25-28F), and salads (39-55). An incredible deal for the 8ème. Open M-F 11am-3pm.

Elliott Restaurant, 166, bd. Haussmann (tel. 01 42 89 30 50). M: Miromesnil. Walk up av. Percier and turn left on bd. Haussmann. Bistro-style restaurant with slick decor and boxing motif. Buffalo wings (45F), hamburgers (63-73F), and selected beers (35F). Huge American brunch Sa-Su includes eggs Benedict (99F). Open M-Sa noon-3pm and 8pm-midnight, Su noon-4pm. AmEx, V.

Antoine's: Les Sandwichs des 5 Continents, 31, rue de Ponthieu (tel. 01 42 89 44 20). M: Franklin D. Roosevelt. Walk toward the Arc de Triomphe on the Champs-Elysées then turn right on av. Franklin D. Roosevelt and left on rue de Ponthieu. This hip sandwich shop features specialties like the Buffalo sandwich (barbecued chicken and melted cheese on hearty bread, 27F). Desserts and ice-cream bars 12-18F. Beer 12-18F. Take-out available. Open M-Sa 8am-7pm.

Le Singe d'Eau, 28, rue de Moscou (tel. 01 43 87 72 73). M: Europe. Opened in 1992, the year of the water monkey *(singe d'eau),* this restaurant serves Tibetan cuisine in a colorful dining room. Appetizers 18-40F, entrées 45-55F. Lunch *menu* 65F. Plenty of vegetarian options available. English spoken. Open Sept.-July M-Sa noon-3pm and 7-11pm.

Chesterfields Café, 124, rue la Boétie (tel. 01 42 25 18 06). M: Franklin D. Roosevelt. From the metro walk up the Champs-Élysées and turn right on rue la Boétie. A crowded bar and restaurant frequented by a predominantly 20-something anglo crowd. Serves great burgers (59-69F) and club sandwiches (68F). Live rock music Tu-Sa at 11:30pm. Open daily 10am-5am.

La Table de Margot, 40, rue Ponthieu (tel. 01 53 96 06 88). M: Franklin D. Roosevelt. From the metro walk up the Champs-Élysées and turn right on rue la Boétie then right on rue Ponthieu. Head here with your parents or to impress a date. Meat and fish entrées 67-69F, salads 56-58F. *Menu de nos provinces* includes appetizer or salade, kir, and a choice of an entrée (89F). *Menu de la mer* offers seafood entrées (99F). Open daily 11:30am-3pm and 7-10:30pm.

La Maison du Chocolat, 52, rue Francois 1er (tel. 01 47 23 38 25). M: George V. From the metro walk down George V, turn left on Francois 1er, and walk to the intersection of av. Pierre Charonne. For chocolate-lovers seeking to splurge, this is an essential stop while in the 8ème. *Guayaquil* and *Caracas* are two fabulous cold chocolate drinks (both 40F). *L'assitude découverte* (35F) provides you with a platter of your choice of 6 chocolates. A wide array of chocolates to bring home as gifts or for yourself. Open M-Sa 9:30am-7pm.

▓ Ninth Arrondissement

Except for a few gems, meals close to the Opéra cater to the after-theater and -movie crowd and can be quite expensive. For truly cheap deals, head farther north. Displaced by the projectile force of the city's skyrocketing prices, many immigrants have found a home here, providing visitors to the 9ème with affordable North and West African, Latin American, and Middle Eastern delicacies.

Haynes Bar, 3, rue Clauzel (tel. 01 48 78 40 63). M: St-Georges. Head uphill on rue Nôtre-Dame-de-Lorette and turn right on rue H. Monnier and then right on rue Clauzel to the end of the block. In 1947, the late LeRoy Haynes opened the first African American owned restaurant in Paris, what would soon become a center for expatriates and a hangout for the likes of Louis Armstrong, James Baldwin, and Richard Wright. History, hospitality, and very generous portions for under 100F. African-American soul food like fried chicken and fresh-baked cornbread (70F), Sister Lena's BBQ spare ribs (80F), and T-bone steak (90F): all served with creole rice, and red or string beans. New Orleans jazz piano F nights. Open Sept. to early Aug. Tu-Sa 7:30pm-12:30am. AmEx, MC, V.

Sarangui, Anarkali, 4, pl. Gustave Toudouze (tel. 01 48 78 39 84). M: St-Georges. Walk uphill on rue Nôtre-Dame-de-Lorette and branch right onto rue H. Monnier. On a secluded cobblestone square. This north Indian restaurant is best in the summer when you can sit outside on the plaza. Tandoori, curry, *biryani* dishes (50-80F), chicken and lamb (55-75F), and veggie dishes (30-40F). Lunch *menus* 60-72F. Open June-Aug. Tu-Sa noon-2:30pm and 7-11:30pm, Su-M 7pm-11:30am; Sept.-May Tu-Sa noon-2:30pm and 7-11:30pm. AmEx, MC, V.

Pizzéria King Salomon, 46, rue Richer (tel. 01 42 46 31 22). M: Cadet or Bonne Nouvelle. From M: Cadet descend rue Saulner and turn right on rue Richer. A popular kosher pizzeria in the heart of the 9ème's small Jewish community. The King Salomon (58F) is topped with tomato, cheese, artichoke hearts, egg, basil, mushrooms, and olives. Individual pizzas 42-58F. Take-out available. Open Su-Th 11:30am-3pm and 6:30pm-midnight, Sa 6:30pm-midnight.

Sannine, 32, rue du Faubourg-Montmartre (tel. 01 48 24 01 32). M: Rue Montmartre. Walk uphill on rue du Faubourg-Montmartre to its corner with rue Richer. A small, Lebanese family affair specializing in kebabs, falafel, and tabouli that come with wheat rice or salad (58-78F). Traditional music and painted murals of the Lebanon that once was. Lunch *menu* 49F, dinner *menu* 69F. Vegetarian *menu* of 10 assorted hors-d'oeuvres 75F. Take-out available. Open M-F noon-2:30pm and 6-11pm, Sa-Su 6-11:30pm. AmEx, MC, V.

Deli's Café, 6, rue du Faubourg-Montmartre (tel. 01 48 24 24 04). M: Rue Montmartre. Walk uphill on rue du Faubourg-Montmartre. A small, affordable café with great sandwiches (16-21F), *panini* (18-23F), *brioches* (25F), and *la brucetta* (35F). Open daily 7am-2am.

Les Bacchantes, 21, rue de Caumartin (tel. 01 42 65 25 35). M: Havre-Caumartin. As you come up from the metro walk back and go in the direction away from Au Printemps on rue de Caumartin. Hearty portions of French favorites and wine amid dark wood and lacy chandeliers. Specials include *pommes de terre au munster et au lard paysan* (potatoes with melted munster cheese and bacon, 60F) and *pêches au vin à la cannelle* (peaches in red wine, 25F). Very crowded around lunchtime. Wine 13-30F. Open M-Sa 11:30-12:30am. AmEx, V.

Le Palmier de Lorette, 19, rue de Châteaudun (tel. 01 48 78 34 41). M: Nôtre-Dame-de-Lorette. Across from the church, this family-run brasserie has plush interiors and farm-fresh French classics. Lunch and dinner *menus* (95F) include a kir. Entrées 75-128F. Open noon-3pm and 7-11pm. MC, V.

Hard Rock Café, 14, bd. Montmartre (tel. 01 42 46 10 00). M: Richelieu Drouot. Just in case you wanted the address. Happy hour M-F 6-8pm. Open daily 11:30am-2am. AmEx, MC, V (100F minimum). Almost next door is **TGI Friday's** (tel. 01 47 70 27 20). Open daily 11:30am-midnight.

El Pueblo, 16, rue du Faubourg de Montmartre (tel. 01 42 47 04 47). Bright and festive, this Mexican restaurant offers *parilladas* (meats dishes, 78-86F), *tacos* (62-68F), *fajitas* (74F), and terrific margaritas (30-38F). *Menu Chihuahua*: chile and burritos or enchiladas and a dessert (125F). Open M-Th noon-2pm and 6:30-11:30pm; F-Su 7pm-12:30am.

■ Tenth Arrondissement

While many tourists never see more of the 10ème than their Gare du Nord layover allows, those who venture out will find French, Indian, and African restaurants with reasonable prices. Catering to locals rather than tourists, these restaurants offer some of Paris's more colorful culinary fruits. Passage Brady overflows with cheap Indian *restaux* and rue Lafayette with Japanese delights.

Paris-Dakar, 95, rue du Faubourg St-Martin (tel. 01 42 08 16 64). M: Gare de l'Est. Senegalese cuisine served with West African charm. Lunch *menu* (59F), dinner *menu* (129F), and African *menu* (179F) feature *tiébou dieune* (fish with rice and veggies) and the house drink *bissap,* made from the African flower *oseil rouge* and fresh mint. Open Tu-Th and Sa-Su noon-3pm and 7pm-2am, F 7pm-2am. MC, V.

Restaurant du Bourgogne, 26, rue des Vinaigres (tel. 01 46 07 07 91). M: Jacques Bonsergent. Walk with traffic on rue de Lancry, bear left on rue Jean and turn left on rue des Vinaigres. With wood-beam ceilings, red-checkered tablecloths, and family-style seating, this classic bistro specializes in meat dishes. Lunch *menu* (50F) and dinner *menu* (55F). Open M-F noon-2:15pm and 7-11pm, Sa noon-2:15pm.

La Route du Kashmir, 24, passage Brady (tel. 01 42 40 44 86). M. Château d'Eau. Walk against traffic on bd. de Strasbourg; enter passage Brady at no. 34. One of the many Indian-Pakistani hybrids, this pink palace of spices has large portions of rich curries. Lunch *menu* (30F), dinner *menus* (49F and 89F), entrées (59-95F), desserts (18-22F). Open daily noon-3pm and 6-11:30pm. MC, V.

Le Dogon, 30, rue René Boulanger (tel. 01 42 41 95 85). M: République. Follow bd. St-Martin from the metro; rue René Boulanger is on your right. Named after the owner's hometown in Mali, this West African restaurant is steps away from pl. de la République. White walls, batiks, and animal pelts serve as the backdrop for curries, couscous, and affordable lunch *menus* (55F). Popular bar in the evening. Open M-F 11:30am-3pm and 7pm-midnight, Sa-Su 12:30-7pm. MC, V.

La 25ème Image, 9, rue Récordects (tel. 01 40 35 80 88). M: Gare de l'Est. Near the Canal St-Martin, this colorful café-gallery offers light salads and creative sandwiches (38-50F) for those waiting for a train. Open daily 9am-1am. MC, V.

■ Eleventh Arrondissement

Like trailer-trash to a hog-fry, TexMex-, burger-, and pizza-chains have sprung up around the mall-like Opéra Bastille. Trendy restaurants along rue Charonne, rue Keller, rue de Lappe, and rue Oberkampf, however, fill with hip regulars. Reflecting the 11ème's status as Paris's latest in chic, some of its bars and cafés have been featured in recent films, including Pause Café in Klapisch's *Chacun cherche son chat* (1996; see **Film**, p. 18). Don your sunglasses and hang with the stars.

Au Petit Keller, 13, rue Keller (tel. 01 47 00 12 97). M: Charonne. From the metro, walk down rue Charonne and turn left on rue Keller. Hip bistro in the heart of the Bastille. Bright yellow interior and tortured art produce a slick, retro vibe. Lunch *menus* (50 and 70F) include endive salad with roquefort cheese. Open M-Sa noon-2:30pm and 7pm-midnight. MC, V.

À la Banane Ivoirienne, 10, rue de la Forge-Royale (tel. 01 43 70 49 90). M: Faidherbe-Chaligny. From the metro, walk west on rue du Fbg. St-Antoine and turn right on rue de la Forge-Royale. African prints from the Ivory Coast complement West African specialties, such as *attieke* and *aloko*. Entrées 60-80F. Live African music every Friday. Dinner *menus* (95-140F). Open Tu-Sa 7pm-midnight. MC, V.

Occitanie, 96, rue Oberkampf (tel. 01 48 06 46 98). M: Parmentier. In the heart of the Oberkampf district. Named after the southern region of France whose cuisine it serves. Lunch *formule* 52F. Dinner *menus* 65 and 93F. Entrées 66-110F. Open mid-Aug. to mid-July M-F noon-2pm and 7-11pm, Sa 7-11pm. AmEx, MC, V.

Au Trou Normand, 9, rue Jean-Pierre Timbaud (tel. 01 48 05 80 23). M: Oberkampf. From the metro, walk north on rue de Malte until it intersects rue Jean-Pierre Timbaud. Possibly the cheapest bistro in Paris, the Norman attracts youthful regulars for its *steak frites* (38F). Appetizers 15-18F, *plats du jour* 35F, desserts 10-14F. Open Sept.-July M-F noon-2:30pm and 7:30-11pm, Sa 7:30-11pm.

Le Val de Loire, 149, rue Amelot (tel. 01 47 00 34 11). M: Filles du Calvaire. From the metro, walk toward the Cirque d'Hiver and turn left on rue Amelot. Locals share tables with tourists from nearby hotels. French fare at good prices. Dinner *menus* (50 and 59F) feature *frites*, *coq au vin*, and *flan*. Open Sept.-July M-Sa noon-2:30pm and 7-10:30pm. AmEx, MC, V.

Le Bistro St-Ambroise, 5, rue Guillaume Bertrand (tel. 01 47 00 43 50). M: St-Maur. From the metro, walk against traffic on rue St-Maur and turn left on rue Guillaume Bertrand. Old ads from French magazines cover the walls of this small, hidden bistro. Wonderful desserts (20-40F). Lunch *menu* (69F) include *Travers de porc au miel* (honeyed pork). Open M-F noon-2:30pm and 7-11pm, Sa 7-11pm. MC, V.

Le Bistrot du Peintre, 116, av. Ledru-Rollin (tel. 01 47 00 34 39). M: Ledru-Rollin. From the metro, walk up av. Ledru-Rollin. The original Art Nouveau dark-wood and mirror interior complements the omelettes (32-35F), entrées (48-82F), and desserts (18-33F) of this classic bistro. The house specialty is duck with sauteed potatoes (69F). Open M-Sa 9am-2am, Su 10am-9pm. MC, V.

Le Passage, 18, passage de la Bonne-Graine (tel. 01 47 00 73 30). M: Ledru-Rollin. From the metro, walk east on rue du Fbg. St-Antoine and take a near-hidden left on passage de la Bonne-Graine. Famous for *andouillettes* (sausages) with potatoes and pureed peas or lentils (80-110F). Daily specials (60F). Ask about wine-tasting events. Open M-F noon-2:30pm and 7:30-11:30pm, Sa 7:30-11:30pm. AmEx, MC, V.

Chez Paul, 13, rue de Charonne (tel. 01 47 00 34 57). M: Bastille. From the metro, go east on rue du Fbg. St-Antoine and turn left on rue de Charonne. Late-night crowds fill this small restaurant with a 1920s zinc bar and black-and-white-tiled floor. Friendly staff. *Escargots* (38F), steak with pears, cognac, and potatoes (78F), rabbit thigh stuffed with goat cheese and mint leaves (72F). Open Sept.-July daily noon-3pm and 7pm-2am, food served until 12:30am. AmEx, MC, V.

Le Souk, 1, rue Keller (tel. 01 49 29 05 08). M: Ledru-Rollin. Bags of spices, mud walls, oil lamps, and blue pottery amid Arabic specialties. Entrées 78-120F; grilled meat dishes 85-88F. The Souk is also a late-afternoon *salon de thé*. Open Tu-Su noon-2:30pm and 7:30pm-midnight. Tea 3-9pm. Amex, MC, V.

La Ville de Jagannath, 101, rue St-Maur (tel. 01 43 55 80 81). M: St-Maur. Near Oberkampf, this Indian restaurant serves vegetarian lunch (50F) and dinner (75-145F) *menus* with curries, daal, rice, and yogurt. Open M 7:30-10:30pm, Tu-Th noon-2pm and 7:30-10:30pm, F-Sa noon-2pm and 7:30-11:30pm. Amex, MC, V.

Pause Café, 41, rue de Charonne (tel. 01 48 06 80 33). M: Ledru-Rollin. While you aren't busy people-drooling, name-dropping, or terrace-posing you will be frantic trying to get a place to sit. This ultra-hip bar had a starring role in the recent film *Chacun cherche son chat* (see **Film,** p. 18). Excellent salads (40-80F) and cheap beer (20F). Open Tu-Sa 8:30am-2am, Su 8:30am-8:30pm. MC, V.

■ Twelfth Arrondissement

Although the area around the Gare de Lyon provides unimaginative fare for travelers on a train layover, the areas away from the station reflect the global population of the area's residents. The 12th is a good place to give your wallet a break. Hip new spots are always springing up, while prices remain low.

Le Cheval de Troie, 71, rue de Charenton (tel. 01 43 44 24 44). M: Bastille. Sneak into this restaurant like the famed Trojan horse, its namesake, and pillage the menu. Serving savory Turkish food in an authentic setting, the Cheval's lunch *formule* can't be beat. For only 55F, feast on an appetizer like *Coban Saleta,* with fresh cucumbers, tomatoes, and feta; a main course like *Imam Bayildi* (stuffed eggplant); and dessert such as rice pudding and *Sigara Bogregi* (feta, egg, and mint fried inside flaky pastry, 54F). Open M-Sa noon-2:30pm and 7-11:30pm. MC, V.

Dame Tartine, 59, rue de Lyon (tel. 01 44 68 96 95). M: Bastille. This saucy dame's got everything to satisfy you, and her prices can't be beat. Try the imaginative *tartines* (open-faced sandwiches) like lamb with eggplant and red pepper (45F) or duck with orange sauce and wilted lettuce (40F). Finish with a dessert like the caramelized pear tart (25F). Child's menu (49F) includes a *croque-monsieur* sandwich, chocolate cake, and soda or juice. Open daily noon-1:30am.

Le Square Trousseau, 1, rue Antoine-Vollon (tel. 01 43 43 06 00). M: Ledru-Rollin. This beautiful Belle Époque bistro is well worth the small splurge that gets you fabulous and innovative French cuisine. Sample roast chicken with 3 marinades (85F) or duck with olive purée (95F) with a glass of wine (15F and up). Save room for desserts like Grand Marnier soufflé with raspberry *coulis* (40F). Watch for the movie crews; the Trousseau has appeared in more than a few French films. Open daily noon-2:30pm and 8-11:15pm. AmEx, MC, V.

L'Ebauchoir, 45, rue de Citeaux (tel. 01 43 42 49 31). M: Faidherbe-Chaligny. Walk down the Rue de Faubourg St-Antoine, turn left on rue de Citeaux. Great balance of young, funky (check out the mural of the neighborhood), and sophisticated French food. 3-course lunch *menus* with drink 68-88F. Try the *foie de veau au miel et au coriandre* (veal liver with honey and coriander, 80F). Appetizers 25-60F, main courses 75-120F, desserts 25-35F. Open M-Th noon-2:30pm and 8-10:30pm, F-Sa noon-2:30pm and 8-11:30pm.

Le Rocher du Diamant, 284, rue de Charenton (tel. 01 40 19 08 78). M: Daumesnil or Dugommier. From Daumesnil, walk down rue Claude Decaen, take your first right on rue de la Brèche-aux-Loups, and walk until it intersects rue de Charenton. Stuffed turtles in the windows suggest the tropical, palm-and-sea decor of this Antillean outpost. 3-course lunch *menu* 94F. Dinner *menu* 120F. *Colombos* (Caribbean curry dishes) around 60-75F. Appetizers 25-40F, main courses 59-80F, seafood 60-135F, desserts 30-40F. Open daily 11am-2:30pm and 7pm-midnight. MC, V.

Le Parrot, 5, rue Parrot (tel. 01 43 43 05 64). M: Gare de Lyon. Walk against traffic on rue de Lyon and take a right on rue Parrot. A cheap, old-fashioned place to go for typical bistro fare, with standards like grilled rabbit (60F) and mussels and fries (48F). 60F menu includes appetizer, main course, and dessert. Try various big salads (e.g. lettuce, potato, mushrooms, radish, apples, carrots) and dessert (48F). Open M-Sa 11:30am-10:30pm with continuous service. AmEx, MC, V.

■ Thirteenth Arrondissement

The 13ème is a budget gourmand's dream. Scores of Vietnamese, Thai, Cambodian, Laotian, and Chinese restaurants cluster here in Paris's "Chinatown," south of pl. d'Italie on av. de Choisy. Many restaurants in this neighborhood are open all day. Haven for artists and intellectuals, the Butte aux Cailles's restaurants and bars fill with the young and high-spirited. A large North African community offers Moroccan, Tunisian, and Algeria specialties in the restaurants near the St-Marcel metro.

Chinatown

Thiên Co, 41, av. de Choisy (tel. 01 45 85 55 00). M: Porte de Choisy. Through the green-trim and glass patio lies a long dining room serving homestyle Vietnamese food. Friendly staff, and popular with local Vietnamese residents. House specialty *Bo Bún* (rice vermicelli, vegetables, and grilled beef, 39F), *Phô* soup specialties (36-41F), desserts (7-17F), and Vietnamese coffee (14F). Open M and W-F 11am-4pm and 6:30-11pm, Sa-Su 11am-11pm. MC, V.

Tricotin, 15, av. de Choisy (tel. 01 45 84 74 44 or 01 45 85 51 52). M: Porte de Choisy. 2 locations on either side of the arcade labeled "le Kiosque de Choisy." One side specializes in Chinese dishes while the other takes on Thai, Vietnamese, and Cambodian. Exhaustive menu highlights *canard au cinq parfums* (38F) and curried shrimp with coconut juice (41F). *Phô* soups (25-30F). Chinese side open daily 9am-11:30pm; Vietnamese side open M and W-Su 9am-11:30pm.

Lao Thai, 128, rue de Tolbiac (tel. 01 44 24 28 10). M: Tolbiac. Asian and French regulars come for Thai and Laotian food in an austere, traditional setting. Two-person dinner *menus* (136F, 156F, or 176F) allow you to try a few dishes, soup, and dessert. Open Th-Tu noon-2:30pm and 7-11pm. Reservations recommended. MC, V.

Butte aux Cailles

Le Temps des Cérises, 18-20, rue de la Butte aux Cailles (tel. 01 45 89 69 48). M: pl. d'Italie. Take rue Bobillot and turn right on rue de la Butte aux Cailles. Locals discuss art and (left) politics at this restaurant cooperative with lace curtains, warm red walls, and specials displayed on a wall-sized blackboard. Solidly unpretentious lunch (58F) and dinner (78-118F) *menus* include *pâté de foie* and *boudin* sausage with apples and *crème fraîche;* served M-Th until 9pm. Open M-F noon-2pm and 7:30-11:45pm, Sa 7:30-11:45pm. AmEx, MC, V.

Le Samson, 9, rue Jean-Marie Jégo (tel. 01 45 89 09 23). M: pl. d'Italie. Take rue Bobillot and turn right on rue de la Butte aux Cailles and then right on rue Jean-Marie Jégo. Jam-packed with artsy hipsters. Homemade sausages flambéed in whiskey (38F) and *tagliatelle* with smoked salmon (49F). Lunch (63F) and dinner (73F) *menus.* Open M-F noon-2pm and 7:30pm-1am, Sa 7:30pm-2am.

Chez Gladines, 30, rue des Cinq Diamants (tel. 01 45 80 70 10). M: pl. d'Italie. Take bd. Auguste Blanqui and turn left onto rue des Cinq Diamants; on the corner of rue Jonas. Serves southwestern French and Basque specialties on long wooden tables with red-checked tablecloths. Hearty main courses like *escalope de veau montagnarde* (country ham with cheese and mushroom sauce, 58-72F), salads (28-50F), and *escargots* (55F). Wines by the glass (14-16F). Open Sept.-July daily 9am-2am.

Café du Commerce, 39, rue des Cinq Diamants (tel. 01 53 62 91 04; email cafe-du-commerce@horeca.tm.fr). M: pl. d'Italie. Near Chez Gladines, above. One of the newest arty/intellectual hangouts, the Commerce serves French food to young crowds discussing labor strikes and gallery openings. Art and photography by area artists and African music complement lunch *menus* (50F), *morteaux* sausages sautéed with apples (65F), *camembert* and salmon sandwiches (20-25F), and regional wines (15-20F per glass). Open daily 11:30am-3pm and 7pm-2am. AmEx, MC, V.

St. Marcel

P'tit Cahoua, 39, bd. St-Marcel (tel. 01 47 07 24 42). M: St-Marcel. Underneath a tented ceiling and surrounded by Moroccan ceramics, decorative tiles, and lace-cut woodwork, this restaurant feels like a world away from Paris. Featuring Moroccan and *maghrebin* cuisine, the lunch *menu* (65F) offers *tabouli* or *briouats au thon* (tuna in a flaky pastry), chicken, olive and lemon *tajine,* or *couscous merguez* (a spicy sausage). Various *tajines* (85-95F) and couscous (85-115F) entrées. Finish with fig, date, and apricot pastries (40F for a plate). Open M-F and Su noon-3pm and 7:30-11pm, Sa 7:30-11pm. MC, V.

■ Fourteenth Arrondissement

The budget traveler is forever indebted to the Bretons who flooded Paris at the turn of the century and settled in Montparnasse. Breton *crêpes* and *galettes* (a larger, buckwheat version) are easy to find, easy to eat, and even easier on the wallet. The *crêperies* on rue de Montparnasse and the 14ème's bistros provide great dining options.

Le Château Poivre, 145, rue du Château (tel. 01 43 22 03 68). M: Pernety. Walk with traffic on rue Raymond Losserand and turn right on rue du Château. Intimate dining room serves generous portions and over 60 varieties of wine. Dinner *menu* (89F) features *mousse de saumon* (salmon mousse) and *gigot d'agneau* (grilled leg of lamb). Open M-Sa noon-2:30pm and 7-10:30pm. AmEx, MC, V.

Phinéas, 99, rue de l'Ouest (tel. 01 45 41 33 50). M: Pernety. Follow the traffic on rue Pernety and turn left on rue de l'Ouest. Specializing in *tartes sucrées et salées* made before your eyes, this delightful restaurant doubles as a shrine to comic books. Look for the bust of Tintin. Entrées include vegetarian options (58-80F). Desserts include *tarte citron* (10-36F). Open Tu-Sa noon-11:30pm. AmEx, MC, V.

Le Colvert, 129, rue du Château (tel. 01 43 27 95 19). M: Pernety. Follow traffic on rue Raymond Losserand and turn right on rue du Château. French mediterranean cuisine such as *confit de canard aux baies roses* (duck pâté with bayberries, 85F). Affordable lunch (65F) and dinner *menus* (89F). Open M-F noon-3pm and 7-11:30pm, Sa 7-11:30pm. MC, V.

La Route du Château, 123, rue du Château (tel. 01 43 20 09 59). M: Pernety. Walk with traffic on rue Raymond Losserand until it crosses rue du Château. The romantic Parisian bistro *par excellence:* mood lighting, lace curtains, courteous service, and exquisite food. Specialties include *lapin* (rabbit) sautéed in cider and mustard (80F). Wonderful dinner *menu* (85F). Appetizers 32-50F, entrées 80-95F. Open M 7pm-midnight, Tu-Sa noon-2pm and 7pm-midnight. AmEx, MC, V.

Le Jeroboam, 72, rue Didot (tel. 01 45 39 39 13). M: Plaisance. Off of rue d'Alésia. Intimate French restaurant with traditional fare. Lunch (65-82F) and dinner (98-129F) *menus* feature *bavette grillé au poivre vert* (grilled steak with pepper sauce). Open M noon-2:30pm, Tu-Sa noon-2:30pm and 7-10:30pm. AmEx, MC, V.

N'Zadette-M'foua, 152, rue du Château (tel. 01 43 22 00 16). M: Pernety. Walk with the traffic on rue Raymond Losserand, and turn right on rue du Château. Congolese cuisine in an African setting. *Sourire Congolais* (fish, tomato, pineapple, cream, and cucumber appetizer, 42F) and *maboke* (meat or fish cooked in banana leaves, 69F) served with a smile. Entrées (54-88F). Open daily 7pm-1am. MC, V.

Aquarius Café, 40, rue de Gergovie (tel. 01 45 41 36 88). M: Pernety. Walk against traffic on rue Raymond Losserand and turn right on rue de Gergovie. A vegetarian oasis. The "mixed grill" smorgasbord includes tofu sausages, wheat pancakes, brown rice, and vegetables in a mushroom sauce (65F). Aquarius salad with goat cheese, vegetable pâté, and potato salad (55F). Desserts 16-35F. Open M-Sa noon-2:15pm and 7-10:30pm. AmEx, MC, V.

Au Berbere Jessica, 50, rue de Gergovie (tel. 01 45 42 10 29). M: Pernety. Walk against traffic on rue Raymond Losserand and turn left on rue de Gergovie. North African specialties at low prices: appetizers (17-42F), entrées (57-62F), and couscous dishes (48-87F). Lunch *menu* (55F). Open daily 10am-3pm and 7-11pm.

Crêperie de Josselin, 67, rue du Montparnasse (tel. 01 43 20 93 50). M: Edgar Quinet. On a street full of *crêperies,* this small restaurant stands out. Locals crowd the wood-panelled dining room with Breton lace coverings and table lamps. Le Petit Josselin next door accommodates the overflow. Outstanding food at reasonable prices: *crêpes salées* (22-70F) and *crêpes sucrées* (22-42F). Open Tu-F noon-3pm and 6-11:30pm, Sa-Su noon-midnight.

FOOD AND DRINK

■ Fifteenth Arrondissement

Traditional French bistros, complete with oak bars and mirrored walls, pepper the
area around rue du Commerce. The streets radiating from bd. de Grenelle offer North
African, Asian, Middle Eastern, and Basque cuisine.

Restaurant Les Listines, 24, rue Falguière (tel. 01 45 38 57 40). M: Falguière. Fresh
cut flowers complement the grilled ostrich special (60F) and monkfish with leeks
and cream (79F). Entrées (60F), desserts (28-36F), and Loire Valley wines (14-21F).
Open M-F noon-2:30pm and 7-10pm, Sa noon-2:30pm. AmEx, MC, V.

Sampieru Corsu, 12, rue de l'Amiral Roussin. M: Cambronne. Walk into the pl. Cambronne and take a left on rue de la Croix Nivert, then turn left on rue de l'Amiral
Roussin. A Corsican types out copies of his communist journal while his wife
warmly invites you to share a table. Eat your fill of roast chicken salad and pay
according to your means, though the suggested price for the copious 3-course
menu is cheap (41F, wine included). Open M-F 11:45am-1:30pm and 6:30-9:30pm.

Chez Foong, 32, rue Frémicourt (tel. 01 45 67 36 99). M: Cambronne. Walk across
pl. Cambronne and turn left on rue Frémicourt. In one of Paris's only Malaysian restaurants, hand-made batiks and kites adorn the walls. Entrées like *ikan pais berny-
iur* (grilled fish in banana leaves with coconut, 59F) and desserts such as coconut
crêpes, sweet potato balls, and coconut tarts (35F) grace the dinner *menus* (56-
85F). Open M-Sa noon-2:30pm and 7-11pm. MC, V.

Ty Breiz, 52, bd. de Vaugirard (tel. 01 43 20 83 72). M: Pasteur. A taste of Brittany in
the shadows of Tour Montparnasse, this *crêperie* is hung with cookware and
embroidery. Dinner crêpes (17-51F) like the *forestière* (fried egg, tomato, and
mushroom in a Provençale sauce). The dinner *formule* includes 3 crêpes and a clay
bowl of *Breton* cider (59F). Show them your *Let's Go* and get a free *kir breton*.
Open M-Sa 11:45am-2:45pm and 7-10:45pm. MC, V.

Café du Commerce, 51, rue du Commerce (tel. 01 45 75 03 27). M: Commerce.
Since 1921, this brasserie has offered great food for less. The 3-level, open-air interior surrounds courtyard with vines and flowers. The bistrot *menu* (82F) and dinner *menu* (117F) feature *saumon cru mariné à l'aneth* (raw salmon in dill), *côtes
d'agneau aux herbes* (lamb with herbs), and *mousse au chocolat*. Reservations
recommended on weekends. Open daily noon-midnight. AmEx, MC, V.

Samaya, 31, bd. de Grenelle (tel. 01 45 77 44 44). M: Dupleix. Decorated with bun-
dles of wheat on the wall for good luck, this Lebanese restaurant offers *menus* with
tabouli, laban concombre (yogurt, cucumber and mint), hummus, and lamb (68-
105F). More than 24 vegetarian dishes. Open daily noon-midnight. MC, V.

Phetburi, 31, bd. de Grenelle (tel. 01 40 58 14 88). M: Dupleix. An elegant restaurant
serving Thai dishes on porcelain. Specialties include steamed fish with banana
leaves (55F) and shrimp salad flavored with lemon grass (42F). Lunch *menu* (72F)
and dinner *menus* (92F and 125F) include 3 courses and a portion of rice. Takeout
available (at 10% off). Open M-Sa noon-2:30pm and 7-10:45pm. AmEx, MC, V.

Mozlef, 18, rue de l'Arrivée (tel. 01 45 44 76 63). M: Montparnasse-Bienvenue. Facing the Tour Montparnasse with the train station at your back, cross the street on
your left, descend the shallow stairs, and turn right on rue de l'Arrivée. This Tuni-
sian-Greek deli serves the cheapest meals near the *tour*. Generous portions of couscous, grilled meats, and Tunisian salads (35–50F). Open daily noon-midnight.

■ Sixteenth Arrondissement

If you are staying in the 16ème, eat elsewhere. If you are visiting, bring a picnic. Or
buy lunch at the open-air markets on av. du Président Wilson, rue St-Didier, and at the
intersection of rue Gros and rue La Fontaine (see **Food Markets,** p. 104). A good bet
for restaurants is on rue de l'Annonciation, running perpendicular between rue de
Passy and rue de Raynouard or on rue de Lauriston, closer to Étoile, running parallel
to av. Kleber and av. Victor Hugo.

Casa Tina, 18, rue Lauriston (tel. 01 40 67 19 24). M: Charles-de-Gaulle-Étoile. Walk up av. Victor Hugo, turn left on rue Presbourg and right on rue Lauriston going uphill. An upbeat Spanish restaurant—think bullfights, Hemingway, Gypsy Kings—decorated with painted tiles. Serves up tapas (18-68F), sangria (pitcher 110F), and Andalusian *paella* (98-150F). Appetizers 18-28F, entrées 68-124F. Open daily noon-2:30pm and 7-11pm. Reservations recommended. AmEx, MC, V.

Byblos Café, 6, rue Guichard (tel. 01 42 30 99 99). M: La Muette. Walk down rue Passy one block and turn left on rue Guichard. A Lebanese café/restaurant dressed with bright flowers. Hors d'oeuvres (30-48F), *tabouli,* and *moutabal* (pureed eggplant with sesame paste), and a variety of hummus dishes. 2-person dinner *menu* (230F) is a filling 7-dish sampler. The *assiette Byblos Café* offers an assortment of 8 appetizers (85F). Grilled meats and chicken 70-86F. Vegetarian meals include beautiful salads like the moussaka (eggplant in olive oil, tomato sauce, hummus, and onions, 34F). Takeout available for 10-20% less. Open daily noon-2:30pm and 7-10:30pm. AmEx, MC, V.

La Matta, 23, rue de l'Annonciation (tel. 01 40 50 04 66). M: Passy. From the metro, walk up rue de Passy; at pl. de Passy, turn left on rue de l'Annonciation. A small Venetian restaurant with straw-bottomed chairs, paintings of Venice, and empty chianti casks. The waiters and owners speak in Italian and provide fair fare at relatively low prices. Pizza 47-74F, pasta 50-68F, meat dishes 70-102F, antipasti 25-60F. Takeout available. Open daily noon-2:30pm and 7-11pm. MC, V.

■ Seventeenth Arrondissement

Formed from a patchwork of isolated neighborhoods, the 17$^{\grave{e}me}$ can't lay claim to any single, unifying quality, much less a characteristic meal. This identity deficit creates a sumptuous smorgasbord of meal options. Francophiles should investigate av. des Ternes and the streets that lead away from the Arc de Triomphe for traditional French fare. Small bistros pepper the Village de Batignolles between rue de Rome and the av. de Clichy. Rue de la Jonquière (M: Guy Môquet) is lined with Moroccan, Tunisian, and Algerian shops and restaurants.

Le Patio Provençal, 116, rue des Dames (tel. 01 42 93 73 73). M: Villiers. Follow rue de Lévis away from the intersection and turn right on rue des Dames. On the sunny terrace, indoors among green arbors, vines, and dried lavender, this restaurant serves staples of southern French cuisine: tomatoes, eggplants, olives, thyme, fish, and wine. Ample *grandes assiettes* (57-65F) or half-portions (37-45F). Desserts like chocolate draped with raspberry purée (34-37F). Enjoy a *pastis* (an anis flavored liqueur), the staple *apéritif* of the south (25-26F). Reservations recommended. Open M-F noon-2:30pm and 7pm. MC, V.

Restaurant Natacha, 35, rue Guersant (tel. 01 45 74 23 86). M: Porte Maillot. Take bd. Gouvion St-Cyr past the Palais de Congrès and turn right on rue Guersant. Follow the gray flannel suits to this local favorite. Extraordinary lunch selection: all you can eat buffet with hors d'oeuvres, fish, grilled meat, and desserts (85F). Smaller 2-course *menu* 65F. Dinner *formule* 100F. All *menus* include unlimited wine, so belly up to the wooden barrels and help yourself. Open M-F noon-2:30pm and 7:30-11pm, Sa 7:30-midnight. Call for reservations. MC, V.

Joy in Food, 2, rue Truffaut (tel. 01 43 87 96 79), on the corner of rue des Dames. M: Rome. Walk one block up rue Boursault and turn right on rue des Dames. Some of the best vegetarian meals in Paris, prepared by a friendly chef named Naema in the open kitchen of this 7-table restaurant. Large bowls of fresh fruit, vegetables, and spices grace the interior. Selection of entrées (45F) changes daily but includes quiches, bean dishes, salads, and couscous. Lunch and dinner *menus* (58-71F). Organic beer and wine or one of Naema's frothy fruit and vegetable shakes (16F). There's even a coffee substitute *café de céréale* made from dates, figs, and other magical ingredients (6F). Open M-Sa 11:30am-3pm. Will open in the evening with reservations for groups of 10 or more. No smoking.

The James Joyce Pub, 71, bd. Gouvion St-Cyr (tel. 01 44 09 70 32). M: Porte Maillot. Take bd. Gouvion St-Cyr past Palais de Congrès. Upstairs from the pub itself is a restaurant with stained-glass windows depicting scenes from Joyce's novels. Food, furniture, and staff are imported directly from Ireland. It is no surprise that this Irish pub is the busiest in Paris. The spectacular brunch on Sundays (noon-3pm) is a full Irish fry: eggs, bacon, sausage, mushrooms, black and white puddings, beans, chips, and coffee (65F). Regular menu selections include Bunratty Boxty potatoes (30F), Ballybunion bacon with cabbage (55F) and Cu Chulann's chicken (75F). Downstairs, the pub pulls pints of what Joyce called "... Ghinis. Foamous bomely brew bebattled by bottle gagerne de guergerre..." Also serves as a tourist office for English speaking ex-pats (they even sell bus tickets). Televised sporting events and monthly concerts bring crowds; weekly advertisement in *Pariscope* lists times. Open daily 6am-2am. MC, V.

Aux Îles des Princes, 96, rue de Saussure (tel. 01 40 54 01 03). M: Wagram. Turn left off av. de Villiers onto rue Jouffroy then left again onto rue de Saussure. A hopping Turkish dinner spot decorated in a strange pastiche of bottles, oil paintings, foliage, and foreign currency. Specializes in charcoal-grilled lamb, beef, and chicken brochettes (40-70F). The moustachioed owner speaks a bit of French and no English, but hand gestures and patience will get you lunch and dinner *menus* (45-90F). Bottles of Turkish wine 60-65F. Turkish tea 6F. Reservations recommended. Open M-F noon-3:30pm and 6-11pm, Sa 6pm-midnight, Su noon-3:30pm. V, MC.

■ Eighteenth Arrondissement

During the siege of Paris in 1814, Russian cossacks occupied Montmartre, an ideal location to keep an eye on wily Napoleon, and came to call the restaurants where they grabbed quick bites between battles *bistro* (Russian for "quick"). While the Russians are gone, the *butte* is now liberally sprinkled with tiny, charming bistros, especially along the streets between M: Abbesses and pl. St-Pierre. The heavily touristed cafés and restaurants around pl. du Tertre are perfect for coffee breaks but pricey for meals. In addition to the listings below, **Chez Louisette** and **Au Baryton,** which are located within the Puce St-Ouen flea market just north of the 18*ème*, offer *moules marinière, frites,* and live French *chanson* entertainment (see **Markets,** p. 268).

Chez les Fondues, 17, rue des Trois Frères (tel. 01 42 55 22 65). M: Abbesses. From the metro stop, walk down rue Yvonne le Tac and take a left on rue des Trois Frères. A narrow, red-painted room with two long tables and an ambiance somewhat like a cabaret or a mead hall. Only two main dishes served: *fondue bourguignonne* (meat fondue) and *fondue savoyarde* (cheese fondue). The wine is served in baby-bottles with rubber nipples; leave your Freudian hang-ups at home. Perhaps the most raucous dinner you'll ever eat in a restaurant. *Menu* with *apéritif,* wine, appetizer, fondue, and dessert (87F). Call ahead to reserve or show up early. Open W-M 5pm-2am, dinner served after 7pm. Closed for part of July and Aug.

Au Grain de Folie, 24, rue la Vieuville (tel. 01 42 58 15 57). M: Abbesses. Eating here is like dining in the kitchen of an unpretentious French family. Serves a vast array of vegetarian dishes, from couscous and hummus to salads and cheese, in portions so huge that eating *à la carte* may be cheaper than the 2-course *menu* (100F). Appetizers, including avocado in roquefort sauce, 20-40F. Entrées 50-70F. Desserts, like frozen bananas in hot chocolate, 25-40F. Glass of wine 15-45F. Open M-F 12:30-2:30pm and 7-10:30pm, Sa-Su 12:30-2:30pm and 7-11pm.

Suzon-Grisou, 96, rue des Martyrs (tel. 01 46 06 10 34). M: Abbesses. Follow rue Yvonne le Tac away from the metro and turn left on rue des Martyrs. If you see frogs, you're in the right place. Frog figurines, toys, and cuckoo clocks decorate this welcoming African restaurant. Entrées include *n'dole* beef with African leaves and *mafe* chicken cooked in ground-nuts, 70-80F. Appetizers include stuffed crab, 30-70F. Several vegetarian options include vegetarian couscous (75F), fried bananas (20F), and *igname* root (20F). Dinner *menus* 79-110F. Frequent live African music. Open Tu-Su 7pm-2am. MC, V.

Chez Claude et Claudine, 94, rue des Martyrs (tel. 01 46 06 50 73). M: Abbesses. From the metro walk down rue Yvonne le Tac and turn right on rue des Martyrs. Decorated like a knick-knack cabinet and lit by lace-covered hanging lamps, this plant-filled restaurant serves large portions of solid, standard French fare. 3-course *menu* (79F) includes choices like onion soup, *boeuf bourgignon,* and *poulet à l'éstragon* (chicken with tarragon). Open daily noon-2:30pm and 6-11:30pm. MC, V.

Rayons de Santé, 8, pl. Charles Dullin (tel. 01 42 59 64 81). M: Abbesses or Anvers. Follow rue Yvonne le Tac away from M: Abbesses and turn right on rue des Trois Frères and left into pl. Charles Dullin. This homey restaurant on a quiet square offers palatable and very cheap vegetarian meals. On any given day you might find artichoke mousse (27F) or wholewheat couscous and soy sausage (35F). All main dishes are served with boiled vegetables and grains. 2-course *formule* (48F) and 3-course *menu* (63F) served at lunch and dinner. Desserts include the house soy yogurt (8F) or *clafoutis* (fruit flan, 16F). Non-alcoholic wine 15-16F; carrot juice 17F. Open Aug.-June Su-Th 9:15am-3pm and 6:30-10pm, F 9am-3pm.

■ Nineteenth Arrondissement

The ethnically diverse 19ème offers great dining options, especially in "Little Chinatown" where Chinese, Vietnamese, Thai, and Malaysian restaurants cluster near M: Belleville. Greek sandwich shops line av. Jean Jaurès and rue de Crimée. The Parc des Buttes-Chaumont is a romantic spot for a picnic lunch and a worthy place to jog it off.

Lao-Thai, 34, rue de Belleville (tel. 01 43 58 41 84). M: Belleville. Thai and Laotian specialties on an all-you-can-eat buffet with 12 different dishes, rice, and dessert. Perfect for the poor and hungry traveler. Lunch M-F 49F, Sa-Su 55F. Dinner Su-Th 74F, F-Sa 80F. Open Tu-Su noon-2:30pm and 7-11:15pm. MC, V.

Baguettes d'Or, 61, rue de Belleville (tel. 01 44 52 02 95). M: Belleville. Don't be fooled by the name—there is no golden bread to be found at this Thai restaurant (*baguettes* is French for chopsticks). Two menus 52F, *assiète rapide* (appetizer, main dish, and rice) 39F. Soups 22-30F, entrées 30-40F. Open M 11am-3pm, Tu-Su 11am-3pm and 6pm-midnight. MC, V.

Ay, Caramba!, 59, rue de Mouzaïa (tel. 01 42 41 23 80; fax 01 42 41 50 34). M: Pré-St-Gervais. From the metro, turn right on rue Mouzaïa. With piñatas and a Mariachi band, Ay, Caramba! seems a little out of place on the quiet rue de Mouzaïa. Good Mexican menu includes *fajitas* and *tacos* (79-84F), *Nachos caramba* (chips, cheese, *pico de gallo,* guacamole, and choice of beef, chicken, or chile; 43F). Margaritas 39F. Adjoining Tex-Mex grocery and liquor store. Restaurant open M-Th 7:30-11pm, F-Sa noon-2:30pm and 7:30-11pm. AmEx, MC, V.

L'Atlantide, 7, av. de Laumière (tel. 01 42 45 09 81). M: Laumière. Exotic rugs and lattice wooden screens welcome you to this elegant Algerian restaurant. Starters 30-45F, *couscous* 56-102F, *semolina* 60-107F, veggies 70-80F. Open Tu-Th 7-11pm, F-Su noon-3pm and 7-11pm. MC, V.

■ Twentieth Arrondissement

Dominated by hideous highrises, the 20ème may not seem appetizing. A traditional meal amid Belleville's cobblestones, however, may be a welcome breath of fresh air from Paris's crowded center. In addition, the busy Arab, Greek, Turkish, and Asian markets of rue de Ménilmontant may yield the perfect picnic items for an al fresco lunch at Père Lachaise cemetery.

Egée, 19, rue de Ménilmontant (tel. 01 43 58 70 26). M: Ménilmontant. Turn right on rue Ménilmontant, and the restaurant is down on your left. Serving Greek and Turkish specialties, the Egée doesn't look like much from the outside, but is well worth the extra metro stop if you're visiting Père Lachaise. Huge portions of *kanarya* (eggplant, yogurt, and paprika) and brochettes of chicken, beef, or lamb are served with baskets of warm, homemade pita bread. Lunch *menu* comes with main dish, appetizer, and dessert (47F). Wash it down with a half-bottle of *retsina,* a pungent Greek wine (32F). Open daily noon-2:30pm and 7:30-11pm.

La Papaye, 71, rue des Rigoles (tel. 01 43 66 65 24). M: Jourdain. Turn left on rue des Rigoles from rue du Jourdain. A mix of Caribbean and South American specialties, the cuisine here reflects the French/Panamanian background and wide travels of

FOOD AND DRINK

the owner and chef. Lunch *menu* (61F) and dinner *menus* (89F and 129F) feature *colombos* (Caribbean curry dishes) like mussels and shrimp, grilled fish, and Brazilian coconut cake (35F). Other entrees 50-95F. Open M-Tu and Th-F noon-2pm and 7pm until last customer leaves, Sa-Su 7pm-closing. MC, V.

Café Flèche d'Or, 102, rue de Bagnolet (tel. 01 43 72 04 23). M: Alexandre Dumas. From metro, follow rue de Bagnolet until it crosses rue des Pyrénées; café is on right. Near the Porte de la Réunion gate of Père Lachaise cemetery, this bar, performance venue, and café is housed in a defunct train station and sits on a windowed terrace overlooking the old tracks. The funky *menu* highlights North African, Caribbean, and South American cuisine. Lunch *formule* 69F, entrees 70-80F. Nightly jazz and samba concerts (10-25F). Open daily 10am-2am; lunch served Tu-Su noon-3pm, dinner served daily 8pm-midnight. MC, V (100F minimum).

Dalmier, 29, rue St.-Blaise (tel. 01 42 72 16 95). M: Porte de Bagnolet. From the metro, follow rue de Bagnolet, then turn left on rue St-Blaise. Nestled into a cobbled street in the old Charonne neighborhood, Dalmier is a combination *pâtisserie* and restaurant where you can squeeze in with the midday regulars for some good, down-home *cuisine familiale*. Lunch *menu* 62F. Open M-Sa noon-7pm.

Le Baratin, 3, rue de Jouye-rouve (tel. 01 43 49 39 70). M: Belleville. From Belleville walk uphill and turn right on rue de Jouye-rouve. This intimate neighborhood wine bar serves hearty, home-style meals like *canard roti* (roast duck, 68F). Appetizers 30-50F, entrees 65-85F, dessert 35F. Wine by the glass (8-16F) or bottle (75-350F). Open Tu-F noon-4pm and 6pm-1:30am, Sa 6pm-1:30am. MC, V.

CAFÉS

When you think of Paris, your thoughts inevitably turn to that perfect little sidewalk café with its struggling writers and embracing lovers. But to Parisians, café culture is a way of life. Contrary to its American counterpart, the coffee shop, the French café has long been associated with strong coffee and long hours of conversation. But cafés are not merely about leisure and caffeine. They provide a place to meet friends, to watch the world, to read and write, to argue and discuss, and to plan revolutions—both in art and in politics. On July 12, 1789, Camille Desmoulins leaped onto a café table in the Palais Royale and urged his fellow citizens to arm themselves, shouting, "I would rather die than submit to servitude." In the 1940s and 50s, Surrealists, Existentialists, and expatriates including Picasso, Sartre, de Beauvoir, and Hemingway argued, wrote, and drank in the cafés of the 6ème. At this very moment, today's politics and tomorrow's novels are erupting over espressos across the city.

Café drinks are cheaper at the *comptoir* (or *zinc*) than seated inside the *salle* or on the *terrasse*. Both of these prices should be posted. Aside from coffee, other popular café drinks include *citron pressé*, freshly squeezed lemon juice (with sugar and water on the side), and *kir*, made with white wine and cassis (a *kir royal* is made with champagne). Cafés also serve *croques monsieur* (grilled ham-and-cheese sandwiches), *croques madame* (the same with a fried egg), and assorted omelettes.

CLASSIC CAFÉS

The following is a list of Paris's most famous cafés. Think of these cafés as museums, where the often expensive coffee is comparable to the average admission fee.

La Closerie des Lilas, 171, bd. du Montparnasse, 6ème (tel. 01 40 51 34 50). M: Port-Royal. Exit the metro and walk one block up bd. du Montparnasse. This lovely flower-filled café was home to Hemingway (a scene in *The Sun Also Rises* takes place here), the Dadaists, and the Surrealists. Picasso came here weekly to hear Paul Fort recite poetry. In summer, soak up the sun among the plants on the terrace. Steak tartare (90F), *crêpes* (90F) and rum cake (45F) fill out the menu. Open daily noon-2:30pm and 7pm-1:30am. AmEx, MC, V.

La Coupole, 102, bd. du Montparnasse, 6ème (tel. 01 43 20 14 20). M: Vavin. Half-café and half-restaurant, La Coupole's Art Deco mirrors, chairs, tiled floors, and tables have hosted Lenin, Stravinsky, Hemingway, and Einstein. The menus are expensive, but you can probably still afford coffee (11F), hot chocolate (21F), a *croque monsieur* (28F), and the daily special (98F). Open M-Th 7:30am-2am, F 9:30pm-4am, Sa 3-7pm and 9:30pm-4am. Dancing on the weekends. MC, V.

Les Deux Magots, 6, pl. St-Germain-des-Prés, 6ème (tel. 01 45 48 55 25). M: St-Germain-des-Prés. Sartre's second-choice café and Simone de Beauvoir's first, it was here that the couple first met. Home to literati since 1885, Les Deux Magots is now a favorite among chic Left Bank youth and tourists. Named after 2 Chinese porcelain figures *(magots)*, this café has high ceilings, gilt mirrors, and Art Deco café decor. Coffee (22F), *café crème* (25F), hot chocolate (32F), goose *rillette tartine* (40F), and pastries (12-24F). Open daily 7am-1:30am. AmEx, MC, V.

Le Dôme, 108, bd. du Montparnasse, 14ème (tel. 01 43 35 25 81). M: Vavin. The elegant 1920s marble tables, gilded mirrors (with engravings of flappers), and Victorian stained glass make it one of the best and most expensive cafés in town. Coffee 18F, sandwiches 25F. Open daily noon-3pm and 7pm-12:30am. AmEx, MC, V.

Café du Flore, 172, bd. St-Germain, 6ème (tel. 01 45 48 55 26). It was here, in his favorite hangout, that Jean-Paul Sartre composed *L'être et le néant (Being and Nothingness)*. Apollinaire, Picasso, Breton, and James Thurber also sipped their brew here. Enjoy your drink on the terrace, Brigitte Bardot's favorite spot. Espresso 34F, tea 34F, *salade Flore* 68F, pastries 31-50F. Open daily 7am-2am.

Le Fouquet's, 99, av. des Champs-Elysées, 8ème (tel. 01 47 23 70 60). M: George V. Opened in 1899 in the shadow of the Arc de Triomphe, Le Fouquet's is the premier café for Parisian *vedettes* (stars) of radio, television, and cinema. It seems more like Planet Hollywood with classic French decor and snobbery. James Joyce dined here. Bank-breaking coffee and a chance to be seen 25F. Entrées 90-140F. Open daily 8am-1am; food served noon-3pm and 7pm-midnight. AmEx, MC, V.

Café de la Paix, 12, bd. des Capucines, 9ème (tel. 01 40 07 32 32). M: Opéra. On the left as you face the Opéra. This institution just off rue de la Paix (the most expensive property on French Monopoly) has drawn a classy crowd since it opened in 1862. Coffee 26F, *café crème* 31F, ice cream 40-59F. The restaurant inside is twice as *cher,* with *menus* around 300F. Open daily noon-midnight.

Le Procope, 13, rue de l'Ancienne Comédie, 6ème (tel. 01 43 26 99 20). M: Odéon. Founded in 1686, making it the first café in the world. Voltaire drank 40 cups per day here while writing *Candide.* Marat came here to plot the Revolution and dodge the police. Figurines of other famous regulars line the café's back wall. History has its price—a 299F *menu.* The café also offers *coquille de crevettes* (shrimp cocktail) and steak tartare (72-99F). Coffee 14F, beer 21-28F. Open daily 11am-2am.

Le Sélect, 99, bd. du Montparnasse, 6ème (tel. 01 45 48 38 24). M: Vavin. Across the street from La Coupole. Trotsky, Satie, Breton, Cocteau, and Picasso all frequented this swank bistro/café. Today the maudlin still gather. Coffee 12-15F, *café au lait* 35F, teas 22-25F, and hot chocolate 35F. Open daily 7am-3am. MC, V.

HIP CAFÉS

If you prefer your coffee *en vogue* (in fashion), then head to one of these hangouts, where the in-the-know crowd sips the day away, not caring where Sartre or Hemingway sat. While these suggestions will get you started, remember that half the fun of being in Paris is discovering your own favorite café.

Café Beaubourg, 100, rue St-Martin, 4ème (tel. 01 48 87 63 96). M: Hôtel de Ville. This would be your neighborhood café if the boy next door was a Calvin Klein model. But oh what fun to pretend, which is what most of these people are doing anyway. Outside, rattan chairs line up to scan the passing scene outside the Centre Pompidou, while inside the look is minimalist. Legendary bathrooms. Coffee 16F, hot chocolate 26F, breakfast 65F. Open daily 8am-1am. AmEx, MC, V.

Le Fumoir, 6, rue de l'Amerat Coligny, 1er (tel. 01 42 92 05 05). M: Louvre. Directly across from the Louvre sits this chic café, where pretty posers drink their chosen brew in deep green leather sofas. A kind of funky, jazz-filled gentlemen's club, Le Fumoir serves tuna sashimi with potatoes and fennel (62F), smoked-salmon sandwiches (37F), and coffee (15F). Fight for a seat outside, with views of the Louvre. Open Su-Th 11am-midnight, F-Sa 11am-2am. AmEx, MC, V.

Café de la Mosquée, 39, rue Geoffrey St-Hilaire, 5ème (tel. 01 43 31 38 20). M: Censier Daubenton. In the Mosquée de Paris, this cool café, with decorative tiles, white-marble floors, and tropical shade trees offers mint tea (22F) and *Maghrebin* pastries such as *kadaïf* (10F). Indulge yourself with an afternoon in the *hammam* (Men on Tu and Su; Women M, Tu, Th, Sa). Café open daily 10am-midnight.

L'Apparement Café, 18, rue des Coutures St-Gervais, 3ème (tel. 01 48 87 12 22). M: St-Paul. Next to the Picasso Museum, this hip café offers coffee (12F), designer salads (45F), and Sunday brunch served in comfortable cushioned chairs. Open M-F noon-2am, Sa 4pm-2am, Su 12:30pm-midnight. MC, V.

Amnésia Café, 42, rue Vieille du Temple, 4ème (tel. 01 42 72 16 94). M: Hôtel de Ville. In the heart of the Marais, the Amnésia's wood interior, plush sofas, and beautiful people attract a largely gay crowd on Saturday nights and a mixed scene for Sunday brunch (70-130F). Other options include the swank smoked salmon *Salade Nordique* (65F), espresso (11F), and *kir* (20F). Open daily 10am-2am. MC, V.

CYBER CAFÉS

Café Orbital, 13, rue du Médicis, 6ème (tel. 01 43 25 76 77; email info@orbital.fr; http://www.orbital.fr). M: Odéon. France's first cyber café offers telnet, newsgroups, the Web, and a Webcam so you can wave to your friends across cyberspace. No need to order cyberwiches (45F) to use the computers. Internet 1F per min., 55F per hr. Students may get a *Carte Sidérante:* 200F per 5hr., 300F per 10hr. Open M-Sa 10am-10pm, Su noon-8pm.

Hammam Café, 4, rue des Rosiers, 4ème (tel. 01 42 78 04 45). M: St-Paul. This café replaced a *hammam* in 1996. Salads, pasta, and Ben and Jerry's ice-cream. Internet 1F per min. Live music 2-3 times per week. Saunter downstairs to link up or upstairs for music. Open Su-Th noon-2am, F noon-4pm, Sa sundown-2am.

WebBar, 23, rue de Picardie, 3ème (tel. 01 42 72 66 55; email webbar@webbar.fr; http://www.webbar.fr). M: République. With leather chairs and a funky bar, one of coolest spots to surf. Live music, debates, poetry nights, and salsa dancing on Mondays. Internet 40F per hr., 250F for 10hr. Open M-F 8:30am-2am, Sa-Su 11am-2am.

Le Jardin de l'Internet, 79, bd. St-Michel, 5ème (tel. 01 44 07 22 20; email jardinnet@wanadoo.fr; http://perso.wanadoo.fr/jardin.internet). RER: Luxembourg. Friendly English-speaking staff. Coffee 7F, hot chocolate 10F, sandwiches 12-19F. 8 computers with 7 more on the way. Internet 1F per min., 28F for 30min., 50F for 1hr., 230F for 5 hours. Open M-Sa 9am-10pm, Su noon-9pm.

SALONS DE THÉ

T'ien Yi Heng said, "one drinks tea to forget the sound of the world." Paris's *salons de thé* (tea rooms) provide low-key refinement and an afternoon respite not only for the ladies-who-lunch but also for an increasingly younger set. Service is often slow, so relax over a *tisane* (herbal tea), or sip an invigorating *menthe* (mint) or *tilleul-menthe* (lime blossom and mint). And don't forget the pastries.

Angelina's, 226, rue de Rivoli, 1er (tel. 01 42 60 82 00). M: Concorde or Tuileries. Audrey Hepburn's favorite. Belle Époque paintings, gold-leaf interiors, and an atmosphere of propriety dampen all sounds but the clink of teacups. Afternoon tea (33F) and pastries (6-35F). The *chocolat africain* (hot chocolate, 36F) and *Mont Blanc* (meringue with chestnut cream, 36F) are house specialties. Open M-F 9am-7pm, Sa-Su 9:30am-7:30pm. AmEx, MC, V.

Ladurée, 16, rue Royale, 8ème (tel. 01 42 60 21 79). M: Concorde. Frescoed ceilings, antique tables, and green gilt pillars. World-famous chocolate, pistachio, coffee, vanilla, and lemon macaroons (22F). Pay less if you carry your goodies away. Lunch served daily 11:30am-3pm. Open M-Sa 8:30am-7pm, Su 10am-7pm. AmEx, MC, V.

Le Loir Dans la Théière, 3, rue des Rosiers, 4ème (tel. 01 42 72 90 61). M: St-Paul. Named "The doormouse in the teapot" after the character in *Alice in Wonderland*, this bohemian salon serves caramel and jasmine tea (20F), coffees (12-30F), cakes and tarts (38-48F), and Sunday brunch (115F). Open daily noon-7pm.

Marriage Frères, 30, rue du Bourg-Tibourg, 4ème (tel. 01 42 72 28 11). M: Hôtel de Ville. Also at 13, rue des Grands Augustins, 6ème (tel. 01 40 51 82 50; M: St-Michel). Founded by 2 brothers who found British tea shoddy, this elegant salon offers 400 varieties of tea (35-41F), sandwich plates (55F), and cakes (40F). Tea *menu* (sandwich, pastry, and tea, 115F). The **Musée de Thé** upstairs chronicles Marriage Frères's imperialist forays into the Orient. Museum and salon open daily 10:30am-7:30pm; lunch M-Sa noon-4pm, brunch Su noon-6:30pm. AmEx, MC, V.

Max Poilâne, 29, rue de l'Ouest, 14ème (tel. 01 43 27 24 91). M: Gaîté. Follow av. du Maine away from the Tour Montparnasse and turn right on rue de l'Ouest. Since the 1940s, this salon boasts the famous *pain Poilâne,* on which they serve their *croque monsieur* (30F). Sandwiches 17-36F, desserts 13F. Open July-Aug. M-F 10am-7pm, Sa 10am-noon; Sept.-June M-Sa 9am-7:30pm.

Muscade, 36, rue de Montpensier, 1er (tel. 01 42 97 51 36). M: Palais-Royale. In the Palais-Royale's northwest corner, Muscade is an expensive restaurant that becomes an affordable *salon de thé* in the afternoon. With mirrored walls and art by Cocteau (who lived above), Muscade is ideal for Sunday afternoons. 26 kinds of tea (22F) and an assortment of pastries (30F). Open daily 3-7pm.

LIBATIONS

▓ Wine Bars

Although wine bistros have existed since the early 19th century, the modern wine bar emerged only a few years ago with the invention of a machine that pumps nitrogen into the open bottle, protecting wine from oxidation. Rare wines, expensive by the bottle, have become affordable by the glass. Expect to pay 20F for a glass of high-quality wine. The owners carefully select the wines that constitute their *caves* (cellars) and are usually available to help out less-knowledgeable patrons. The wine shops in the **Nicolas** chain are reputed for having the world's most inexpensive cellars, although Nicolas himself owns the fashionable and expensive wine bar **Jeroboam,** 8, rue Monsigny, 2ème (tel. 01 42 61 21 71; M: Opéra). For a crash-course on French wine, see **French Cuisine,** p. 99. But remember that *everyone* is a wine expert. Despite all the snobbery surrounding wine-tasting, fine vintages, delicate bouquets, and "very good years," a good wine is the wine you like.

Au Sauvignon, 80, rue des Sts-Pères, 7ème (tel. 01 45 48 49 02). M: Sèvres-Babylone. At the corner of rue de Sèvres and rue des Sts-Pères. Specializes in wines from the Loire valley. Articles and caricatures paper the walls to show the national recognition received by the owner for wines sold here. Lively crowd of well-groomed thirty-somethings. Come here the third Thursday in Nov. to sample the newest Beaujolais. Wine from 22F per glass. Open M-Sa 8:30am-10pm. MC, V.

Le Bar du Caveau, 17, pl. Dauphine, 1er (tel. 01 43 26 81 84), facing the front steps of the Palais de Justice. M: Cité. Luscious cheeses and wines attract fashionable Parisians to this traditional brass and wood *caveau.* The cuisine is simple and delicious. Wines by the glass 12-23F. Plate of cheese 47F. Open M-F 8:30am-8pm.

Le Franc Pinot, 1, quai de Bourbon, 4ème (tel. 01 46 33 60 64). M: Pont Marie. A fixture on Île St-Louis since the 17th and 18th centuries when it was a meeting place for enemies of the state. The exterior's metal grillwork was installed in 1642 to prevent prisoners from escaping once trapped inside. The labyrinthine caves have been preserved as a bistro/jazz club. A wine bar occupies the main floor. Burgundy wines are a specialty, by the glass 15-36F. Pricey *menus* (150-200F). Open Tu-Sa 10am-2am, Su 2pm-2am. Jazz club open W-Sa 10pm-2am. MC.

Jacques Mélac, 42, rue Léon Frot, 11ème (tel. 01 43 70 59 27). M: Charonne. A family-owned wine bar and bistro. In Sept., Mélac lets children harvest, tread upon, and extract wine from grapes grown in vines hanging from the bar's storefront—call ahead for the exact date and don't miss the party. The Mélac wines sold here, however, come from his vineyard. Wine 18F per glass. Entrées include *gigot d'agneau* (69F). Lovely atmosphere. Open Sept.-July M 9am-5pm, Tu-F 9am-10:30pm. MC, V.

Le Relais du Vin, 85, rue St-Denis, 1er (tel. 01 45 08 41 08). M: Châtelet-Les-Halles or Etienne-Marcel. Amid Les Halles, this low-key wine bar is a place to sit terrace-side with a glass of Bordeaux and people-watch. Wines by the glass 12-35F. Copious French *menus* (67 and 85F). Extensive desserts. Open daily 11:45am-2am. MC, V.

Le Rouge Gorge, 8, rue St-Paul, 4ème (tel. 01 48 04 75 89). M: St-Paul or Pont-Marie. From M: St-Paul, take rue St-Antoine and turn right on rue St-Paul. Once the home of the Marquise De Brin Villiers (beheaded in 1676 for poisoning her husband, her lover, and her father), this tiny and pleasant bar changes its wine menu every 2-4 weeks. Wines from different regions are served with regional dishes. Wine 22-35F per glass. Entrees 68-88F. Cheese 28F. Open daily 11am-2am. V.

Willie's Wine Bar, 13, rue des Petits Champs, 1er (tel. 01 42 61 05 09; fax 01 47 03 36 93). M: Palais-Royale. Behind the Palais. This classy English bar has been popular since opening in 1980. Exposed wood beams, chic decor and huge windows looking out onto the Palais and apartment of author Colette (see **Literature,** p. 20). International clientele. Huge selection of French wines (20-75F). Open M-Sa noon-2:30pm and 7pm-1am. MC, V.

■ Bars and Pubs

Bars make the arrondissement. The arrondissement makes the bar. In the 5ème and 6ème, bars cater to Anglophone students, while the Bastille and Marais teem with Paris's young and hip, gay and straight gettin' jiggy wid'it. In the Bastille, rue de la Roquette and rue de Lappe are *phat* while rue Vieille du Temple in the 4ème is *all that.* The 11ème and 20ème's working-class bars avoid all pretension. Draft beer (*bière pression*) is served in full- or half-pints (*un demi*). *Kir* is a mix of white wine and cassis. Like cafés, prices at the bar are cheaper than table service and rise after 10pm.

Le Merle Moqueur, 11, rue de la Butte aux Cailles, 13ème (tel. 01 45 65 12 43). M: Corvisart. Take rue Bobillot south until rue de la Butte-aux-Cailles branches right. Psychedelic graffiti exterior and walls peppered with Beatles posters. Super-cheap beer (12-30F) and food (nothing over 50F). No table service, no frills, and few tourists. Most customers head for the terrace but the back room is cooler. Happy hour 5-8pm. Open daily 3pm-2am. MC, V.

Les Oiseaux de Passage, 7, rue Barrault, 13ème (tel. 01 45 89 72 42). M: Corvisart. From rue de la Butte aux Cailles, turn right on rue des Cinq Diamants then left on passage Barrault. Young, hip, and laid-back. Art openings, live music, and multiple board-games. Beer and *kir* 12F; food all under 55F. Open Tu-Su 10am-2am.

Le Sous-Bock Tavern, 49 and 51, rue St-Honoré, 1er (tel. 01 40 26 46 61). M: Châtelet. Follow rue des Halles toward Les Halles, and turn left on rue St-Honoré. Bar is just before rue du Pont Neuf. Low on atmosphere, but high on variety and value. If there's a beer in the world you've got a hankering for, they've got it (400 bottled beers 30-90F, 12 on tap 20-36F, and 50 whiskeys). Food includes *Moules à la Marinière* (mussels marinara, 62F) and Su brunch (70F). Open daily 11am-5am.

Au Caveau Montpensier, 15, rue Montpensier, 1er (tel. 01 47 03 33 78). M: Palais-Royale. Walk around the Comédie Française to the left of the Palais, make a sharp left off Richelieu and left up Montpensier. A dark, basement-level Irish bar with Guinness, Murphy's, and Kilkenney (37F). Blues band on Tu. Open M-Sa. 6pm-2am.

Jip's, 41 rue St-Denis, 1er (tel. 01 42 33 00 11). M: Châtelet-Les Halles. Overflowing with Afro-Cuban music and clients, this bar features cheap and very strong rum-based cocktails. Carved wood interior, sun mirror, and neon exterior. Cocktails 35-45F, beer 15-25F. Open M-Sa 11am-2am, Su 4pm-2am. MC, V.

Café Oz, 184, rue St-Jacques, 5ème (tel. 01 43 54 30 48). M: Luxembourg. From the metro, take any street off bd. St-Michel away from the metro, then turn left on rue St-Jacques; look for the rainbow. An Australian bar in the heart of the Latin Quarter. Relaxed Aussie atmosphere with baby croc over the bar attracts Anglos and Parisians. Beer 22-35F, cocktails 38-45F; happy hour daily 6:30-9:30pm. Open daily 11am-2am. Also at 18, rue St-Denis, 1er. MC, V.

Finnegan's Wake, 9, rue des Boulangers, 5ème (tel. 01 46 34 23 65). M: Cardinal Lemoine. From the metro, walk up rue des Boulangers to this Irish pub set in a renovated 14th-century wine cellar with low, black-beamed ceilings. Caters to a thirty-something crowd, pours the best pints of Guinness in the city (25-35F), and hosts a variety of Irish cultural events, including poetry readings, jig, and Gaelic and Breton lessons. Open M-F 11am-2am, Sa-Su 4pm-2am.

Lou Pascalou, 14, rue des Panayaux, 20ème (tel. 01 46 36 78 10). M: Ménilmontant. Follow bd. de Ménilmontant; make a left on rue des Panayaux. An out-of-the-way Provençal bar, Lou Pascalou features open-air terrace seating, a pool table, occasional concerts, and art displays. Beer 30F. Open daily 10am-2am.

Au Petit Fer à Cheval, 30, rue Vieille-du-Temple, 4ème (tel. 01 42 72 47 47). M: Hôtel-de-Ville. A Marais institution with a horseshoe zinc bar, sidewalk terrace, and small, intimate restaurant in the back. Paradise on earth. Charming and handsome barmen. Coffee 6-11F, beer 14-18F, cocktails 48F. For more on food at the Petit Fer, see **Restaurants,** p. 112. Open M-F 9am-2am, Sa-Su 11am-2am.

Le Piano Vache, 8, rue Laplace, 5ème (tel. 01 46 33 75 03). M: Cardinal Lemoine or Maubert-Mutualité. 80s indie-pop standards energize this poster-plastered alterna-grotto, hidden in the winding streets near the Panthéon. Popular with French university students. Beer 20-30F. Open daily July-Aug. 6pm-2am; Sept.-June noon-2am.

Chez Richard, 37, rue Vieille-du-Temple, 4ème (tel. 01 42 74 31 65). M: Hotel-de-Ville. Inside a courtyard off rue Vieille-du-Temple, this Marais goth-bar features mosaic-tile stairs, goblins, and techno in its swank central bar with plush red-leather cushions and handsome staff. Upstairs and downstairs lounges have swank couches and mini-bars. Beer 22-40F. Cocktails 45-55F. Open M-Sa 5pm-2am. MC, V.

Lizard Lounge, 18, rue du Bourg-Tibourg, 4ème (tel. 01 42 72 81 34). M: Hotel-de-Ville. A split-level steel-sleek space full of cocktails, this Marais bar also serves Sunday brunch. The underground cellar has a happy hour (8-10pm) where all cocktails are 25F. Drinks 45-55F, beer 20-35F. Open daily 11am-2am. MC, V.

Le Bar sans Nom, 49, rue de Lappe, 11ème (tel. 01 48 05 59 36). M: Bastille. A deep red front distinguishes this bar from the others along the packed rue de Lappe. Tall walls hung with tapestries, dolls, plants, cherubs, and huge candles. Trendy people sit in odd chairs and sofas. Famous for its inventive cocktails: some are even flambé. Beer 30-40F, cocktails 50F. Open M-Sa 7pm-2am.

Café Charbon, 109, rue Oberkampf, 11ème (tel. 01 43 57 55 13). M: Parmentier or Ménilmontant. This beautiful, *fin de siècle* dance hall, with mirrors, dark-wood bar, vintage booths, and chandeliers, is like a Brassaï photograph. In the hip *quartier* Oberkampf. Expect large crowds. Beer 15-20F, salads 35-40F, *entrecôte grillée* 59F. Daily newspapers with your coffee (6-8F). Open daily 9am-2am. MC, V.

La Flèche d'Or, 102bis, rue de Bagnolet, 20ème (see **Restaurants,** p. 128). Live music from ragga hip hop to Celtic rock every night, art videos, dance classes, Sunday *bals,* and crazy theater on the tracks below the terrace. Open daily 10pm-2am.

China Club, 50, rue de Charenton, 12ème (tel. 01 43 43 82 02). M: Ledru-Rollin or Bastille. A swank Hong Kong gentlemen's club with a speakeasy-style cellar, mile-long bar, and a lacquered *fumoir chinois* look. High-class prices, but a Chinatown (gin fizz with mint) is hard to resist. Cocktails (70-90F) and jazz. Open M-Th 7pm-2am; F-Sa 7pm-3am. AmEx, MC, V.

SWEETS

Paris's pastries and chocolates, fail-safe cure-alls for the weary traveler, are generally made where you buy them. Recently, American desserts—like brownies and cookies (koo-KEES)—have gained a strong following among Parisians young and old, but more traditional vices like the *tarte au chocolat* deservedly remain local favorites. Neighborhood *pâtisseries* or *confiseries* will satisfy any sweet-tooth, but for serious sugar lovers, the *crème de la crème* in specialty sweets can be found sprinkled throughout the city.

Berthillon, 31, rue St-Louis-en-l'Île, 4ème (tel. 01 43 54 31 61), on Île-St-Louis. M: Cité or Pont Marie. The best ice cream and sorbet in Paris. Choose from dozens of *parfums* (flavors), ranging from passionfruit and gingerbread to the standard chocolate. Singles 9F; doubles 16F; triples 20F. Sitting down is more expensive (double 32F). Since lines are quite long in summer, look for stores nearby that sell Berthillon products; the wait is shorter and they're open in late July and Aug., when the main Berthillon shuts down. A list of participating stores is posted on the Berthillon window after it closes. Open Sept.-July 14 W-Su 10am-8pm. Also closed 2 weeks both in Feb. and Apr.

Debauve et Gallais, 30, rue des St-Pères, 7ème (tel. 01 45 48 54 67). M: St-Germain-des-Près. Also at 33, rue Vivienne, 2ème (tel. 01 40 39 05 50). M: Bourse. A "chocolate pharmacy" founded in 1800 by confectioner Sulpice Debauve. Need something for your nerves? They prescribe two almond milk chocolates, from among 40 flavors. Select your own *bouchée* (mouthful) for 18F. Open M-Sa 9am-6pm.

Fauchon, 24-30, pl. de la Madeleine, 2ème (tel. 01 47 42 60 11). M: Madeleine. Tucked in the brightly lit bottom level of the flagship store the pastry shop, where the most melt-in-your-mouth chocolate macaroons (19F) and pastries (15F and up) await. When you decide you can't live without them, head upstairs to the excellent food hall, where *madeleines* and *galettes* are packaged to take home to mom (or keep for yourself). Open M-Sa 9:40am-7pm. AmEx, MC, V.

Jeff de Bruges, 95, rue du Commerce, 15ème (tel. 01 40 43 07 06). M: Commerce. Excellent homemade candies—like *pâtes de fruits* (fresh-fruit gumdrops, 19F per kg) or *dragées aux amandes* (almonds covered in hard candy; 18F per 100g). Gift baskets make good presents. Open Tu-Sa 10am-2pm and 3-7:30pm. MC, V.

Gérard Mulot, 76, rue de Seine, 6ème (tel. 01 43 26 85 77). M: Odéon or St-Sulpice. Outrageous selection of handmade pastries, from flan to marzipan with virtually any kind of fruit. Individual *tartes* 18F; *éclairs* 13F. Open Th-Tu 6:45am-8pm.

Maison du Chocolat, 8, bd. de la Madeleine, 9ème (tel. 01 47 42 86 52). M: Madeleine. Every imaginable kind of chocolate, plus delicious ice cream and sorbets (2 scoops for 21F). For a decadent splurge try the champagne truffles (155-584F). Open M-Sa 9:30am-7pm. MC, V.

Le Nôtre, 48, av. Victor Hugo, 16ème (tel. 01 45 02 21 21). M: Victor Hugo. Also at 15, bd. de Courcelles, 8ème (tel. 01 45 63 87 63); and 121, av. de Wagram, 17ème (tel. 01 47 63 70 30). A small chain that sells wonderful pastries (17-30F) throughout the city. Join the local children pointing out their choices to *maman*. Buttery croissants (5F). Gourmet meat and fish selections available for take-out (30-125F). Most branches open daily 9am-9pm. AmEx, MC, V.

Peltier, 66, rue de Sèvres, 7ème (tel. 01 47 83 66 12 or 01 47 34 06 62). M: Vaneau or Duroc. Also at 6, rue St-Dominique, 7ème (tel. 01 47 05 50 0). M: Solférino. A famous and famously self-congratulatory *chocolatier*. Nonetheless, great desserts. The house specialty, a *tarte au chocolat*, is more gooey than rich (16F). Melt into a chair in the *salon de thé*. Open M-F 9:30am-8pm, Sa 9am-8pm, Su 8:30am-6:45pm. Credit cards require 150F minimum.

Pierre Mauduit, 54, rue du Faubourg St-Denis, 10ème (tel. 01 42 46 43 64). M: Château d'Eau. From the metro, walk against traffic on rue du Château d'Eau and left on rue du Faubourg St-Denis. Mauduit catered a party for Madonna in 1992 and now her photo is one among many in Mauduit's photo album. Can you guess that the place is expensive? Try the *opéra* (30F) or *mille-feuilles* pastry (25F). The mini macaroons (245F per kg) are the house specialty. Open daily 8am-8pm. MC, V.

Sights

Paris is an ocean. Sound it: you will never touch bottom.
Survey it, report on it! However scrupulous your surveys and
reports, however numerous and persistent the explorers of
this sea may be, there will always remain virgin places,
undiscovered caverns, flowers, pearls, monsters—there will
always be something extraordinary.

—Honoré de Balzac, *Père Goriot*, 1834

No matter how many times you've seen Gene Kelly dance by the Seine, Audrey Hepburn glide through the Louvre, or Jean Seberg run breathlessly down the Champs-Elysées, you're never fully prepared for that moment of utter amazement when you see the sights of Paris for the first, second, or hundredth time. From the Eiffel Tower to the corner café, Paris is always new, exciting, eternal.

For all its grandeur, Paris is a small city. In just a few hours you can walk from the heart of the Marais in the east to the Eiffel Tower in the west, passing many of the city's principal monuments. You don't have a true sense of Paris until you know how close medieval Nôtre Dame is to the modern Centre Pompidou, or the *Quartier Latin* of students to the Louvre of kings. With a map and comfortable shoes, you are ready to see Paris from ground-zero. The city is particularly manageable if explored by arrondissement, and *Let's Go: Paris* is arranged this way to make things easier.

Although walking is one of the best ways to see the city, buses may be just the thing for tired feet. **Parisbus** (tel. 01 42 30 55 50) runs bus tours with English-language commentary that last over two hours. The ticket is good for unlimited trips on two consecutive days; you can spend as much time as you want at any of the sights (Trocadéro, Eiffel Tower, Louvre, Nôtre Dame, Musée d'Orsay, Opéra, Champs-Elysées, and the Grand Palais) then hop on the next bus (tickets 125F, students 100F, children 60F). For a fraction of the cost, some public bus lines offer less formal tours of Paris's sights (see **Buses**, p. 66).

The Seine is the life-blood of Paris, and one of the most scenic ways to see the city is on board a tour boat. **Bateaux-Mouches** (tel. 01 42 25 96 10; info line 01 40 76 99 99; M: Alma-Marceau) provide 1½-hour tours in English. *(Departures every 30min. 10am-11:30pm from the Right Bank pier near Pont d'Alma. Tickets 40F, ages 4-14 20F, under 4 free.)* The ride is particularly beautiful at night, when riverside buildings and monuments are illuminated. **Vedette Pont-Neuf** boats (tel. 01 53 00 98 38; M: Pont-Neuf or Louvre) are another option, with commentaries in French and English. *(1hr. Departures every 30min. 9:30am-10:30pm from the Pont Neuf landing. Tickets 50F, under 13 25F.)*

🖐 SUGGESTED ITINERARIES

- **One Day.** Arrive early at Nôtre Dame and climb the tower for one of the best views of the city. Have lunch in the Marais before spending a few hours at the Louvre. After dinner in the Latin Quarter, stroll the Champs-Élysées, climb the Arc de Triomphe, and finish the evening in the glow of the Eiffel Tower.
- **Three Days.** Spend the first day as suggested. On the second day, take the train to Versailles and bask in the opulance of the Sun King and Marie-Antoinette. Return to the city and spend the evening in a Marais café or a Latin Quarter jazz club. On day three, climb Montmartre to Sacré Coeur, spend the afternoon in the Musée d'Orsay, and eat a leisurely dinner on the Île-St-Louis.
- **One week.** After three hectic days, indulge yourself with a late morning *déjeuner* and an early afternoon steam-bath at the Mosquée de Paris's luxuriant *hammam*. During your remaining days, visit the stunning Institut du Monde Arabe, picnic in the Jardin du Luxembourg, marvel at the Ste-Chappelle, explore La Défense and La Villette, make a pilgrimage to Père Lachaise, and shop like a Chanel warrior.

■ Seine Islands

■ Île de la Cité

If any place could be called the heart of Paris, it is this slip in the river. Île de la Cité sits in the very center of the city and indeed at the very center of the Île de France, the geographical region surrounding Paris and bordered by the Seine, the Marne, and the Oise Rivers (see the map for **Trips from Paris,** p. 269). All distance points in France are measured from the *kilomètre zéro*, a circular sundial on the ground in front of Nôtre-Dame. The island was first inhabited by a Gallic tribe of hunters, sailors, and fishermen called the Parisii, who settled on the island in the 3rd century BC. The first certifiable record left by the Parisii was, sadly, their defeat by Caesar's legions in the year 52 BC (see **History,** p. 1). The island became the center of the Lutèce colony, languishing for four centuries under the rule of the crumbling Roman empire. In the early 6th century, Clovis crowned himself king of the Franks and adopted the embattled island as the center of his domain. At that time, Clovis ordered that work begin on the Église St-Etienne, the island's first Christian church, constructed over the ruins of a Roman temple. The basilica, built into the wall that surrounded the island-fortress, was finished in the late 6th century under Clovis's son, Childebert I, but was completely destroyed two centuries later by Norman invaders. It was rebuilt but razed again to make room for Nôtre-Dame. During the Middle Ages, the island began to acquire the features for which it is best known and loved today. In the 12th century work commenced on Nôtre-Dame and the Ste-Chapelle under the direction of Bishop Maurice Sully. Completed in the 14th century, the cathedral is one of the most famous and beautiful examples of medieval architecture. For an overview of this area, refer to the color **map** of the **Fifth and Sixth Arrondissements** in the front of this book.

NÔTRE-DAME

> We climbed the spiral staircase. Atop this cathedral, I
> expected to see Quasimodo around some corner. "It's
> marvelous, marvelous," I kept exclaiming to myself.
> "Isn't it sir?" the fat woman replied, brimming with pride at
> being the concierge of Nôtre-Dame. "You don't see that
> anywhere else. We're at the heart of Paris. It beats the
> Eiffel Tower, doesn't it?"
>
> —Georges Brassaï, *Paris of the 30s,* 1932

Tel. 01 42 34 56 10. **M:** Cité. **Open** daily 8am-6:45pm. **Towers** open Apr.-Sept. 10am-6pm, Oct-Mar. 10am-5pm; last ticket sold 30min. before closing. Admission 32F, students 12-25 21F, under 12 free. **Tours:** in English begin at the booth to the right as you enter, W and Th at noon; in French M-F at noon, Sa at 2:30pm. Free. **Confession** can be heard in English. **Roman Catholic masses** celebrated daily. **Treasury** open M-Sa 9:30am-6pm; last ticket at 5:30pm. Admission 15F, students 10F, ages 12-17 10F, 6-12 5F, under 6 free. **High Mass** with Gregorian chant is celebrated Su at 10am, with music at 11:30am, 12:30, and 6pm. **Crypt** open daily Apr.-Sept. 10am-6pm; Oct.-Mar. 10am-5pm; last ticket sold 30min. before closing. Admission 32F, students 21F, under 12 free.

In 1163, Pope Alexander III laid the cornerstone for the **Cathédrale de Notre-Dame-de-Paris** over the remains of a Roman temple. The most famous and most trafficked of the Cité's sights, this massive structure was completed 200 years later in 1361. Around this time, three other cathedrals also dedicated to the Virgin Mary were built in the Paris basin. Among its peers, Nôtre-Dame was perhaps the site of the fewest events of major historical significance during its first few centuries of existence; royal burials were reserved for St-Denis (see **Trips From Paris,** p. 284), coronations for Reims (although Henri VI was crowned at Nôtre-Dame in 1431), and the most important relics to Ste-Chappelle (see below, p. 138). Ordinarily used as a place of assembly for the public, the cathedral nevertheless saw much history. Joan of Arc (Jeanne d'Arc), for example, was tried here in 1455 for heresy. Revolutionary secularity renamed the cathedral Le Temple de la Raison (The Temple of Reason). During this time the Gothic arches were hidden behind plaster façades of virtuous Neoclassical design. Though reconsecrated after the Revolution, the building fell into disrepair and was used to shelter livestock. Victor Hugo's wildly popular 1831 novel *Nôtre-Dame-de-Paris (The Hunchback of Notre-Dame)* revived the cathedral's popularity enough to inspire Napoleon III and Haussmann to devote time and money into its restoration. The modifications by Eugène Viollet-le-Duc (including a new spire, the gargoyles, and a statue of himself admiring his own work) restored and reinvigorated the cathedral. Nôtre-Dame became a valued symbol of civic unity after its renovation. In 1870 and again in 1940 thousands of Parisians attended masses to pray for deliverance from the invading Germans. On August 26, 1944, Charles de Gaulle braved Nazi sniper fire to come here and give thanks for the imminent liberation of Paris. All of these upheavals seem to have left the cathedral unmarked, as have the hordes of tourists who invade its sacred portals every day. In the words of e. e. cummings, "The Cathedral of Nôtre-Dame does not budge an inch for all the idiocies of this world."

Today, thousands of visitors flood through the doors of the cathedral, depriving themselves of one of the most glorious aspects of the structure: the **façade**. "Few architectural pages," Hugo proclaimed, "are as beautiful as this facade...a vast symphony in stone." Though begun in the 12th century, the façade was not completed even in the 17th, when artists were still adding Baroque statues. Highly symbolic, the carvings were designed to instill a fear of God and desire for righteousness in a population of which less than 10% were literate. Revolutionaries, not exactly regular churchgoers, wreaked havoc on the façade of the church during the ecstasies of the 1790s. Not content to decapitate Louis XVI, they attacked the stone images of what they thought were his royal predecessors above the doors. The heads were found in the basement of the Banque Française du Commerce in 1977 and were installed in the Musée de Cluny (see **Museums,** p. 222). Chips of paint on the heads led to a surprising discovery: Nôtre-Dame was once painted in garish colors, a far cry from the smog-gray that most people associate with medieval churches. Replicas of the heads (unpainted) now crown the severed bodies.

From the inside, the cathedral seems to be constructed of soaring light and seemingly weightless walls. Behind this effect are the spidery **flying buttresses** that support the vaults of the ceiling from outside, allowing the walls to be opened up for stained glass. The effect is increased by a series of subtle optical illusions, including the placement of smaller pillars around the bigger ones, which diminishes their apparent size. The most spectacular features of the interior are the enormous stained-glass **rose windows** that dominate the transept's north and south ends. Originally, similarly masterful artistry adorned the windows on the ground level, but "Sun King" Louis XIV tried to live up to his nickname by ordering that the lower-level stained glass be smashed and replaced by clear windows. More recent and unimpressive stained-glass panels now take their place.

Outside again, the two **towers**—home to the cathedral's most famous fictional resident, Quasimodo the Hunchback—stare with grey solemnity across the square below. There's usually a line to make the climb, but it's well worth it. The perilous and claustrophobia-inducing staircase emerges onto a spectacular perch, where rows of gargoyles survey a rewarding view over the heart of the city. The climb generally deters the bus-load tourists, and you may even have the towers to yourself if you come early. Although this point is not the highest in Paris, it affords you a detailed view of both the Left Bank's *Quartier Latin* (in the 6ème) and the Marais on the Right Bank (in the 4ème). On to the south tower, a tiny door gives access to the 13-ton bell that even Quasimodo couldn't ring: it requires the force of eight people to move. For a striking **view** of the cathedral, cross Pont St-Louis (behind the cathedral) to Île St-Louis and turn right on quai d'Orléans. At night, the buttresses are lit up, and the view from here is beautiful. The Pont de Sully, at the far side of Île St-Louis, also affords an impressive view of the cathedral.

The cathedral's **treasury,** south of the choir, contains an assortment of glittering robes, sacramental cutlery, and other gilded souvenirs from the cathedral's past. Far below the cathedral towers, in a cool excavation beneath the pavement of the square in front of the cathedral, the **Crypte Archéologique,** pl. du Parvis du Nôtre-Dame (tel. 01 43 29 83 51), houses artifacts unearthed in the construction of a parking garage. Essentially an archeological dig, the *crypte* offers a self-guided tour through the history of Île de la Cité, allowing you to wander among architectural fragments from Roman Lutèce up through the 19th-century sewers.

THE REST OF THE ISLAND

At the very tip of the island on pl. de l'Île de France, behind the cathedral, and down a narrow flight of steps, is the **Mémorial de la Déportation**, a haunting memorial erected for the French victims of Nazi concentration camps. *(Open M-F 8:30am-9:45pm, Sa-Su and holidays 9am-9:45pm. Free.)* Two hundred thousand flickering lights represent the dead, and an eternal flame burns close to the tomb of an unknown deportee. The names of all the concentration camps glow in gold triangles that recall the Stars of David that French and European Jews were forced to wear on their clothing. A series of quotations is engraved into the stone walls—most striking of these phrases is the injunction, *"Pardonne. N'Oublie Pas"* (Forgive. Do Not Forget) engraved over the exit. Old men frequent the memorial and chant the *kaddish,* the Jewish prayer for the dead.

The nearby **Hôtel Dieu** was a hospital built in the Middle Ages to provide aid to foundlings. *(Open daily 7:30am-10:30pm.)* It became more a place to confine the sick than to cure them. Guards were posted at the doors to keep the patients from getting out and infecting the city. More recently, Pasteur did much of his pioneering research inside. In 1871, the hospital's proximity to Nôtre-Dame saved the cathedral—communards were dissuaded from burning the cathedral for fear that the flames would engulf their hospitalized wounded. The hospital's serene gardens lies within the inner courtyard. Across the street is the **Préfecture de Police,** where at 7am on August 19, 1944, members of the Paris police force began an insurrection against the Germans that lasted until the Allies liberated the city six days later.

Spanning the western side of the island, the **Palais de Justice** (tel. 01 44 32 51 51), harbors the infamous Conciergerie, a Revolutionary prison, and the Ste-Chapelle, the private chapel of St. Louis. Since the 13th century, the buildings between the Conciergerie and the Ste-Chapelle have housed the **district courts** of Paris. *(Courtrooms open M-F 1:30-4pm; trials M-F 9am-noon and 1:30-5pm. Free.)* After WWII, Pétain was convicted in Chambre 1 of the Cour d'Appel. All trials are open to the public, but don't expect a *France v. Dreyfus* every day. Even if your French is not up to legalese, the theatrical sobriety of the interior, with lawyers dressed in archaic black robes, makes a quick visit worthwhile.

At the heart of the *palais,* the **Ste-Chapelle** (tel. 01 53 73 78 50) remains one of the foremost examples of flamboyant Gothic architecture and a triumph of medieval stained glass. *(Open daily Apr.-Sept. 9:30am-6:30pm; Oct.-Mar. 10am-5pm. Last admission 30min. before closing. Admission 32F, twin ticket with Conciergerie 50F, students and seniors 21F, ages 12-17 21F, under 12 free.)* Crowded into an inner courtyard of the *palais,* the church appears plain and unassuming from the outside, a simple structure topped with a 33m cedar steeple from the 19th century. The Lower Chapel echoes this architectural modesty with a low vaulted ceiling, blank arcades, and painted walls. Inside, however, the Upper Chapel is an extraordinary fusion of space, color, and light. Construction began on the church in 1241 to house the most precious of King Louis IX's possessions: the crown of thorns from Christ's Passion. Bought by the Emperor of Constantinople in 1239 along with a section of the Cross for the ungodly sum of 135,000 livres, the crown required an equally princely chapel. Although the crown—minus a few thorns that St. Louis gave away as political favors—has been moved to Nôtre-Dame, Ste-Chapelle still remains a masterpiece—"the pearl among them all," as

Marcel Proust called it. In the Upper Chapel, formerly reserved for royalty and their court, the brilliantly colored stained-glass windows have a lace-like delicacy. Their blues and reds combine to produce a claret-colored lighting, giving rise to the saying "wine the color of Ste-Chapelle's windows." The windows are the oldest stained glass in Paris, tastefully restored in 1845. The glass you see is for the most part the same under which St. Louis prayed to his own personal holy relic. Check weekly publications for occasional concerts held in the Upper Chapel mid-March through October, or ask at the information booth.

Around the corner of the Palais de Justice from the entrance to the Ste-Chapelle, the **Conciergerie**, 1, quai de l'Horloge (tel. 01 53 73 78 51), lurks ominously over the Seine, brooding over the memories of the prisoners who died here during the Revolution. *(Open daily Apr.-Sept. 9:30am-6:30pm; Oct.-Mar. 10am-5pm. Last ticket 30min. before closing. Admission (with guided tour in French at 11am and 3pm) 28F, students 21F. For English tours, call in advance.)* The northern façade looks like a gloomy medieval fortress. At the farthest corner on the right, a stepped parapet marks the oldest tower, the **Tour Bonbec** (good beak), which once housed the prison's torture chambers where the accused were made to "sing." The modern entrance lies between the **Tour d'Argent,** stronghold of the royal treasury, and the **Tour de César,** which housed the Revolutionary tribunal.

Besides its beautifully restored stonework, the Conciergerie's exhibits on daily life in the prison during the Revolution are worth a visit, especially for those who can read the French explanations. If you choose to tread the same stones as Queen Marie-Antionette and the 2700 people sentenced to death between 1793 and 1794 who spent their final days in the Conciergerie, you'll follow the "rue de Paris," the corridor leading from the entrance, named for "Monsieur de Paris," the executioner during the Revolution. Past the hall, stairs lead to facsimiles of prisoners' cells, now inhabited by glum-looking mannequins. The most desperate mannequins are in the *pailleux* cell, where prisoners who weren't rich enough to bribe their jailers for bedding were forced to sleep on straw. Farther down the hall is the cell where Maximilien de Robespierre, the mastermind behind the Reign of Terror, awaited his death. The cell has been converted into a display of his letters, and engraved on the wall are Robespierre's famous last words: *"Je vous laisse ma Mémoire. Elle vous sera chère, et vous la défendrez"* ("I leave you my memory. It will be dear to you, and you will defend it"). Brought back to Paris from Vincennes while trying to escape with her husband and her hairdresser Léonard, Marie-Antoinette was imprisoned in the Conciergerie before her head has ignobly shaven and severed from her body by the guillotine on October 16, 1793.

You can leave Île de la Cité from here by the oldest bridge in Paris, ironically named the **Pont Neuf** (New Bridge). Completed in 1607, the bridge broke tradition by not having its sides lined by houses. Before the construction of the Champs-Elysées, the bridge was Paris's most popular thoroughfare, attracting peddlers, performers, thieves, and street physicians. More recently, Christo, the Bulgarian performance artist, wrapped the entire bridge in 44,000 square meters of nylon. Unfortunately, the bridge itself is not of particular architectural interest, although it does have individual gargoyle capitals on its supports that can be viewed by craning your neck over the side or, better yet, from a *bateau-mouche.* Alternatively, you can follow the directions below to **Ile St-Louis.**

■ Île St-Louis

From Île de la Cité, a short walk across the Pont St-Louis will take you to the elegant neighborhood of **Île St-Louis.** Originally two small islands—the Île aux Vâches (Cow Island) and the Île de Nôtre-Dame—it was considered suitable for duels, cows, and little else throughout the Middle Ages. In 1267, Louis IX departed for the Tunisian Crusade from the Île aux Vâches, never to return, and the island was later named in memorian. It became habitable in the 17th century due to a contractual arrangement between Henri IV and the bridge entrepreneur Christophe Marie, after whom the

Pont Marie is named. Virtually all of the construction on the island happened within a few short decades in the mid-17th century, giving Île St-Louis an architectural unity lacking in most Parisian neighborhoods. For an overview of this area, refer to the color map of the **Fifth and Sixth Arrondissements** in the front of this book.

Today, the island looks much as it did 300 years ago, with only two small streets altered in any significant sense. Its *hôtels particuliers* and townhouses have attracted an elite that now includes Guy de Rothschild and Pompidou's widow. Voltaire, Mme de Châtelet, Daumier, Ingrès, Baudelaire, and Cézanne number among its past residents. Floating somewhere between a small village and an exclusive *quartier,* the island retains a certain remoteness from the rest of Paris. Older residents say *"Je vais à Paris"* ("I'm going to Paris") when leaving by one of the four bridges linking Île St-Louis and the mainland. In a rare burst of vigor, inhabitants even declared the island an independent republic in the 1930s. While you may not be able to afford the rent, you can afford the view. Many a literary personage has watched the passage of the *bateaux-mouches* down this stretch of the Seine and past the Île St-Louis, notably Jake Barnes in Hemingway's *The Sun Also Rises.*

Wrapping around the northwest edge of the island (to the left immediately after crossing the Pont St-Louis) is the **quai de Bourbon.** Camille Claudel lived and worked at no. 19 from 1899 until 1913, when her brother, the poet Paul Claudel, had her incarcerated in an asylum. Because she was the protégée and lover of sculptor Auguste Rodin, Claudel's most striking work is displayed in the Musée Rodin (see **Museums,** p. 219). At the intersection of the quai and rue des Deux Ponts sits the café **Au Franc-Pinot,** whose wrought-iron and grilled façade is almost as old as the island itself. The grapes that punctuate the ironwork gave the café its name; the *pinot* is a grape from Burgundy. Closed in 1716 after authorities found a basement stash of anti-government tracts, the café-cabaret reemerged as a treasonous address during the Revolution. Cécile Renault, daughter of the proprietor, mounted an unsuccessful attempt on Robespierre's life in 1794. A young admirer of Charlotte Corday, she was guillotined the following year.

The island's most beautiful old *hôtels* line the **quai d'Anjou,** between Pont Marie and Pont de Sully. No. 29 once housed Ford Madox Ford's *Transatlantic Review,* the expatriate lit rag to which Hemingway frequently contributed. At no. 17, the **Hôtel Lauzun,** built in 1657 by Le Vau (and currently under construction for the next few years), features gold filigree on the iron balcony and on the fish-shaped drainpipes. In the 1840s, the *hôtel* became the clubhouse for the *Hachischiens,* a bohemian literary salon with a hookah-heavy bent. Baudelaire and Théophile Gautier reclined with hookahs at its evening gatherings. Baudelaire lived here for a while and is said to have spotted from his window his future mistress Jeanne Duval—the famous "Black Venus"—bathing in the Seine. He later housed her nearby on rue Le Regrattier. No. 9, quai d'Anjou, was the address of Honoré Daumier, realist painter and caricaturist, from 1846 to 1863.

Loop around the end of the quai and walk down **rue St-Louis-en-l'Île,** the main thoroughfare of Île St-Louis, which harbors shops, art galleries, and traditional French restaurants as well as the famous Berthillon *glacerie* (see **Sweets,** p. 133). The **Hôtel Lambert,** at no. 2, was designed by Le Vau in 1640 for Lambert le Riche and was home to Voltaire and Mme de Châtelet, his mathematician mistress. **Église St-Louis-en-l'Île,** 3 rue Poulletier (tel. 01 46 34 11 60), is another Le Vau creation built between 1664 and 1726. *(Open Tu-Sa 9am-noon and 3-7pm.)* Get beyond the sooty, humdrum façade and you'll find one of the airiest and lightest of Rococo interiors, decorated with gold leaf, marble, and statuettes and lit by more windows than seemed to exist on the outside. Legendary for its acoustics, the church hosts concerts throughout the year and every night in July and August (check with FNAC for details or call the church at 01 46 34 11 60). Currently a four-star hotel, no. 54 was frequented by sports-lovers during the 17th and early 18th centuries when *jeu de paume* was in vogue. The ancestor of modern tennis, the game was originally played in rectangular halls painted black so the white leather ball could be more visible. On either side of rue St-Louis-en-l'Île, residential streets lead to the quais. Follow rue Budé to the **Musée Adam Mickiewicz**, 6, quai d'Orléans, the former home of the Polish poet, which now displays exhibits on his circle of exiled Polish artists, including Chopin (see **Museums**, p. 231). Marie Curie lived on the other side of rue des Deux Ponts at 36, quai de Béthune, until she died of radiation-induced cancer in 1934. Proust fans should remember that Swann lived nearby on **quai d'Orléans**. And, although Proust's Aunt Léonie found the island "a neighborhood most degrading," naughty Marcel found its streets, *bordels,* and beautiful boys amusing enough.

■ First Arrondissement

In the shadow of the Louvre, former seat of royal power and home to kings and queens, stretches the first arrondissement. But today the bed-chambers and dining rooms of innumerable rulers house the world's treasures. Glittering royal crowns have been replaced by Cartier diamonds and clothes fit for the fabulous in the shops of the rue St-Honoré. The Sun King's well-tended gardens are now filled with sun-bathers, cafés, and carnival rides. While the Ritz stands in the regal pl. Vendôme, less-ritzy souvenir shops crowd rue du Louvre and Les Halles. Farther west, smoky jazz clubs pulse on bd. Sebastopol, while hopping gay bars crowd rue des Lombards. Just blocks from the Louvre, the Queens still hold court. For a **map** of this area, refer to the color map of the **First and Second Arrondissements** in the front of this book.

TO THE WEST: TUILERIES AND PLACE VENDÔME

Sweeping down from the **Louvre** to the **place de la Concorde**, the **Jardin des Tuileries** (tel. 01 40 20 90 43) celebrates the victory of geometry over nature. *(Open daily Apr.-Sept. 7am-9pm; Oct.-Mar. 7:30am-7:30pm. Free tours in French W-Su at 3pm from the Arc de Triomphe du Carrousel.)* Missing the public promenades of her native Italy, Catherine de Médici had the gardens built in 1564. In 1649, André Le Nôtre (designer of the gardens at Versailles) imposed his preference for straight lines and sculpted trees upon the landscape of the Tuileries. It is fitting that Louis XIV's mistress was responsible for the completion of the park, now a major pick-up area when the sun goes down. During the day the pleasures are more subdued. The elevated terrace by the Seine offers remarkable views of the Louvre, the gardens, the Eiffel Tower, and the Musée d'Orsay (across the river). From the central path, you can see the Obélisque de Luxor (in pl. de la Concorde), the Arc de Triomphe, and, on a clear day, the Grande Arche de La Défense. Turn around to face the **Arc de Triomphe du Carrousel** and the glass **pyramid** of the Louvre's Cour Napoléon. Sculptures by Rodin and others stand amid the gardens' cafés and *pétanque* courts. In the summer, the rue de Rivoli terrace becomes an **amusement park** with children's rides, food stands, and a huge ferris wheel. *(Open late June to mid-Aug. and Dec. to early Jan. Rides 20F, under 12 15F.)*

Flanking the pathway at the Concorde end of the Tuileries are the **Galérie National du Jeu de Paume** and the **Musée de l'Orangerie** (see **Museums**, p. 230 and p. 231). If the Orangerie is swamped in Monet's Water Lilies and the people who come to see them, the Jeu de Paume is a breath of fresh air. Constructed as a *jeu de paume* (an ancestor of tennis) court for Napoleon III, the building now serves as a space for contemporary art. When the Nazis took over Paris, they sent plundered art here, where much of it was labeled "degenerate" and burned.

At the other end of the gardens once stood the **Palais des Tuileries,** which stretched along the Jardin du Carrousel, forming the western wall of the Louvre. In 1791, Louis XVI and Marie-Antoinette attempted to flee this palace, where they had been kept after a mob of Parisian housewives dragged them back from Versailles. Napoleon lived here before his exile. Louis XVIII was chased out upon Napoleon's return in 1814. Louis-Philippe fled in similar haste during the Revolution of 1848, and in 1870, the Empress Eugénie scrambled out as the mob crashed in the main entrance. Nine months later, as forces streamed into the city to crush the Commune, a *communard* packed the palace with gunpowder, tar, and oil, and set it on fire. The ruins survived until 1882 when the Municipal Council had them flattened.

Stately **Place Vendôme**, three blocks north along rue de Castiglione from the Tuileries, was begun in 1687 by Louis XIV. Designed by Jules Hardouin-Mansart, the *place* was built to house embassies, but bankers created lavish private homes for themselves within the elegant façades. Today, the smell of money is still in the air: bankers, perfumers, and jewelers, including Cartier (at no. 7), line the square. Founded by César Ritz at the turn of the century, the unaffordably opulent **Ritz** hotel (no. 15) stands as a monument to both wealth and misery. It was here where Princess Diana had her last meal in 1997, where American Ambassador Pamela Harriman died in 1997 while swimming in the pool, and where Hemingway escaped the grind of the Left Bank to drink (and drink, and drink some more). After riding into Paris with the U.S. Army in 1944, Hemingway gathered Resistance troops and went off to liberate the Ritz. Greeted by his old chum, the assistant manager, Hemingway proceeded to order 73 dry martinis. You can raise an expensive glass in his memory at the bar **Hemingway** (tel. 01 43 16 33 65). *(Open Tu-Sa 7pm-1am. Suitable attire required.)*

In the center of pl. Vendôme, Napoleon stands atop a large **column**, dressed as Caesar. In 1805, Napoleon erected the work, modeled after Trajan's column in Rome, and surrounded it with reliefs of military exploits. After Napoleon's exile, the Royalist government arrested the sculptor and forced him, on penalty of execution, to get rid of it. For all his pains, the return of Napoleon from Elba soon brought the original statue back to its perch. Over the next 60 years it would be replaced by the white flag of the ancient monarchy, a renewed Napoleon in military garb, and a classical Napoleon modeled after the original. During the Commune, a group led by Gustave Courbet toppled the entire column, planning to replace it with a monument to the "Federation of Nations and the Universal Republic." The original column was recreated with new bronze reliefs and the Emperor still presides over the square.

PALAIS-ROYAL AND SURROUNDINGS

The once regal and racy **Palais-Royal** lies farther down rue de Rivoli, across from the Louvre. Constructed in 1632 by Jacques Lemercier as Cardinal Richelieu's Palais Cardinal, it became a Palais Royal when Richelieu gave it to Louis XIII, a few years before both of them died. Louis's widow moved in after his death, preferring the place to the Louvre, and gave the home its current name. Louis XIV was the first king to inhabit the palace, and it was from here that he fled when the Fronde broke out (see **History**, p. 4). In 1784, the broke Duc de Chartres rented out the elegant buildings that enclose the palace's formal garden, turning the complex into an 18th-century shopping mall with boutiques, restaurants, theaters, wax museums, and gambling joints. Its covered arcades were a favorite for prostitutes and lewd encounters. On July 12, 1789, 26-year-old Camille Desmoulins leaped onto a café table here and urged his fellow citizens to arm themselves, shouting, "I would rather die than submit to servitude." The crowd filed out and was soon skirmishing with cavalry in the Tuileries garden. The Revolutions of 1830 and 1848 also began with angry crowds in these gardens. In the second half of the 19th century, Haussmann's boulevards re-gentrified the area and moneyed aristocrats moved back in.

Today, the 1er's galleries contain shops and cafés with splendid views of the palace fountain, flower beds, and **gardens**. *(Open daily June-Aug. 7am-11pm; Sept. 7am-9:30pm; Oct.-Mar. 7am-8:30pm; Apr.-May 7am-10:15pm.)* In the summer, the fountain becomes a mecca for tourists in need of a therapeutic foot bath. The floors above the cafés and shops are occupied by the Ministry of Culture and the Conseil d'État. In the central courtyard, the **colonnes de Buren**—a set of black and white striped pillars—are as controversial today as they were when installed by artist Daniel Buren in 1986. On the southwestern corner of the Palais-Royal, facing the Louvre, the **Comédie Française** is home to France's leading dramatic troupe (see **National Theaters**, p. 234). Built in 1790 by architect Victor Louis, the theater became the first permanent home for the Comedie Française troupe, which was created by Louis XIV in 1680. The entrance displays busts of famous actors by celebrated sculptors, including Mirabeau by Rodin, Talma by David, and Voltaire by Houdon. Ironically, Molière, the company's founder, took ill here on stage while playing the role of the Imaginary Invalid.

The chair onto which he collapsed can still be seen. At the corner of rue Molière and rue Richelieu, Visconti's **Fontaine de Molière** is only a few steps from where Molière died at no. 40. When the Burgundians and the English occupied Paris in 1429, Joan of Arc was hit by an arrow while attempting to liberate the city at what is now 163, rue St-Honoré. Her troops carried her back to pl. André-Malraux, but the wound was serious and the attack was called off. A shining **statue of Joan of Arc** commemorates the saint on pl. des Pyramides.

Stretching north from the Comédie Française into the 2ème and 9ème arrondissements is the glittering **Avenue de l'Opéra.** Haussmann leveled the butte de Moulins and many old homes to connect the old symbol of royalty, the Louvre, to the new symbol of imperial grandeur, the Opéra. The grand creation was intended to bear the name avenue Napoléon III, but the Franco-Prussian war interrupted this scheme, and when finished, the avenue was named for its terminus instead.

TO THE EAST: LES HALLES AND SURROUNDINGS

Between rue du Louvre and the Forum des Halles, the large round **Bourse du Commerce** (tel. 01 55 65 55 65; fax 01 55 65 70 67; www.ccip.fr; M: Châtelet Les Halles) brokers commodities trading, while its cousin the Bourse des Valeurs in the 2ème serves as the stock exchange. *(Open M-F 9am-6pm. Tours in French and English.)* The Bourse du Commerce's recently restored iron-and-glass cupola is surrounded by paintings and frescoes. In the Middle Ages, a convent of repentant sinners occupied the site. Catherine de Médici threw out the penitent women in 1572, when a horoscope convinced her that she should abandon construction of the Tuileries and build her palace here instead. Catherine's palace was demolished in 1748, leaving only the observation tower of her personal astrologer as a memorial to her superstition. Louis XV replaced the structure with a grain market. It was transformed into a commodities market in 1889.

The **Église de St-Eustache** (tel. 01 42 36 31 05; M: Les Halles) towers over Les Halles. *(Open June-Aug. M-F 9am-8pm, Sa 9am-12:30pm and 2:30-8pm; Sept.-May M-F 9am-7pm. High Mass with choir and organ, Su 11am. Organ tickets 90-150F.)* Eustache (Eustatius) was a Roman general who is said to have adopted Christianity upon seeing the sign of a cross between the antlers of a deer. As punishment, the Romans locked him and his family into a brass bull that was placed over a fire until it became white-hot. Construction of the church in his honor began in 1532 and dragged on for over a century. In 1754, the unfinished façade was demolished and replaced with the Romanesque one that stands today—incongruous with the rest of the Gothic building but appropriate for its Roman namesake. Richelieu, Molière, and Madame de Pompadour were all baptized here. Louis XIV received communion in its sanctuary, and Mozart chose to have his mother's funeral here. The chapels contain paintings by Rubens, American artist Keith Haring's glittering triptych, *Life of Christ,* and British artist Raymond Mason's *Departure of the Fruits and Vegetables from the Heart of Paris,* commemorating the closing of the market at Les Halles in February, 1969. Summer concerts are played on the exquisite organ, commemorating St-Eustache's premiers of Berlioz's *Te Deum* and Liszt's *Messiah* in 1886. In front of the church, Henri de Miller's 1986 sculpture *The Listener* features a huge human head and hand.

Émile Zola called **Les Halles** (M: Les Halles, Châtelet Les Halles) *"le ventre de Paris"* ("the belly of Paris"). A sprawling food market since 1135, Les Halles received a much-needed face-lift in the 1850s with the construction of large iron-and-glass pavilions to shelter the vendors' stalls. Designed by Victor Baltard, the pavilions resembled the one that still stands over the small market at the Carreau du Temple in the 3ème. In 1970, authorities moved the old market to a suburb near Orly. Politicians and city planners debated how to fill *"le trou des Halles"* ("the hole of Les Halles"), 106 open acres that presented Paris with the largest urban redesign opportunity since Haussmannization. Most of the city adored the elegant pavilions and wanted to see them preserved. But planners destroyed the pavilions to build a subterranean transfer-point between the metro and the new commuter rail, the RER. The city retained architects Claude Vasconti and Georges Penreach to replace the pavilions with a subterranean shopping mall, the **Forum des Halles.** If the markets of Les Halles were once Paris's belly, then this underground maze is surely its bowels. Descend on one of the four main entrances to discover over 200 boutiques and three movie theaters. Putting the mall underground allowed its designers to landscape the vast Les Halles quadrangle with greenery, statues, and fountains. Striking a delicate balance between hypermodernity and *verdure,* the gardens avoid some of the aesthetic pitfalls of the forum beneath them. Both forum and gardens, however, present the danger of pickpockets. Hold onto your wallet and stay above ground at night.

Southeast of the forum along rue St-Honoré is **rue de la Ferronnerie.** In 1610, as Henri IV passed no. 11 in his carriage, he was assassinated by François Ravaillac, who leaped into the coach and stabbed the king for his tolerance of French Protestants. Ravaillac was seared with red-hot pincers, scalded with boiling lead, and then torn to pieces by an angry mob. Built in 1548 and designed by Pierre Lescot, the nearby **Fontaine des Innocents** is the last trace of the Église and Cimetière des St-Innocents, which once bordered and overlapped Les Halles. Until its demolition in the 1780s, the edges of the cemetery were crowded by tombstones, the smell of rotting corpses, and vegetable merchants selling their produce. The cemetery was closed during the Enlightenment's hygienic reforms, and the corpses were relocated to the city's catacombs (see **Sights,** p. 185). Once attached to the church, the fountain is now a huge rendezvous for punks with spiked hair and the overflow crowd from McDonald's.

Tucked behind the Louvre near the Pont Neuf is the Gothic **Église St-Germain l'Auxerrois.** *(Vespers nightly 5pm. Mass with organ Su 11am.)* On August 24, 1572, the church's bell functioned as the signal for the St. Bartholomew's Day Massacre (see **History,** p. 3). Thousands of Huguenots were rounded up by the troops of the Duc de Guise and slaughtered in the streets, while King Charles IX shot at the survivors from the palace window. Today, visitors are allowed a quiet visit inside to view the gorgeous violet stained-glass windows or listen to the Sunday evening vespers The **Pont Neuf,** the oldest and most famous of the Seine bridges, connects the 1er to the Île de la Cité. On its left and spanning three blocks along rue de Rivoli, **Samaritaine** is one of the oldest department stores in Paris. Founded in 1869, it ushered in the modern age of consumption. The building began as a delicate iron and steel construction in 1906 and was revamped in the Art Deco style of 1928. The roof has one of the best free views of Paris in the city (see **Department Stores,** p. 259).

■ Second Arrondissement

Since the 19th century, the 2ème has been a commercial district. From stocks and bonds trading at the Bourse des Valeurs to 19th-century shopping in the arrondissement's numerous glass-covered *passages* to the prostitution on rue St-Denis and rue d'Aboukir, the 2ème has a long history of trade and commerce. Abundant fabric shops and cheap women's clothing stores hover between rue du Sentier and rue St-Denis, while theaters crowd the streets in the arrondissement's western half. For more of a laugh, the Opéra Comique is found in between bd. des Italiens and rue de Richelieu. For an overview of the area, refer to the color **map** of the **First and Second Arrondissements** in the front of this book.

GALLERIES, PASSAGES, & THE BIBLIOTHÈQUE NATIONALE

In the early 19th century, speculators profiting from the Revolutionary confiscation of property from the church and the aristocracy began to build numerous glass-housed *galeries* or *passages* between the Grands Boulevards. Under these structures, pedestrians could be safe from the cold, rain, and mud of Paris's street before Haussmannization. Designed in the same glass and steel atrium-style of Paris's main train stations, over 100 of these galeries existed in the early 1800s, whereas fewer than 20 survive today. Galerie Colbert and Galerie Vivienne, near the Palais Royal, were the most fashionable *galeries* of the 1820s. Within these marbled pedestrian walkways, which were built within city blocks, shops, cafés, and *flâneurs* mingled. Today, the *galeries* continue to house shops, boutiques, and antique stores. Like others of their kind, these two recently-restored *galeries* are the predecessors of the modern shopping mall. Enter **Galerie Vivienne** at 4, rue des Petits Champs, or 2, rue Vivienne, and you'll encounter a spectacular showcase of pastel luxury, dainty shops, and *trompe l'oeil* faux-marble columns. One of Madonna's preferred designers, **Jean-Paul Gaultier,** is found inside at 6, rue Vivienne (tel. 01 42 86 05 05). Turn left at the end of the corridor to visit the Galerie Colbert's bronze sculptures and rotunda. Part of the Galerie Colbert is used by the Bibliothèque Nationale as a storage annex and **exhibition space.** This portion comprises three small rooms displaying temporary exhibits, with at least one dedicated to contemporary photography. *(Open M-Sa noon-6pm. Free. Call 01 47 03 85 71 for exhibit info.)*

Previously the largest library in Continental Europe, the **Bibliothèque Nationale site Richelieu,** 58, rue de Richelieu (tel. 01 47 03 81 26), lies just north of the two galleries. *(Open only to qualified researchers M-Sa 9am-4:30pm.)* Its collection of 12 million volumes includes two Gutenberg Bibles and assorted other first editions dating from the 15th century to the present. Since 1642, a year before Richelieu founded the Académie Française, every book published in France has been legally required to enter the national archives, which evolved out of the Bibliothèque du Roi, the royal book depository, and sizeable donations from noted bibliophiles and authors such as Victor Hugo and Émile Zola. To accommodate the ever-increasing volume of books, annexes were purchased near the library, notably in the Galerie Vivienne. In the late 1980s, the French government eschewed annexes as a short-term solution and resolved to build the mammoth Bibliothèque de France in the 13ème (see **Sights,** p. 184), where the collections from the Richelieu branch were relocated between 1996 and 1998. Scholars must pass through a strict screening process to gain access to the main reading room; plan to bring a letter from your university, research advisor, or editor stating the nature of your research, and two pieces of photo ID. Contact the main office for info (tel. 01 47 03 81 26).

Open to the public, however, are the library's **Galerie Mazarin** and **Galerie Mansart,** which host excellent temporary exhibitions of books, prints, and lithographs from the Bibliothèque Nationale archives. (Mansart gallery open Tu-Su 10am-7pm. Admission 35F, students, 24F. Call 01 47 03 81 10 for info.) Upstairs, the **Cabinet des Médailles** displays coins and medallions as well as 18th-century armoires and other treasures (open M-Sa 1-5pm, Su noon-6pm; admission 22F, reduced 15F). Across from the library's main entrance, pl. Louvois's sculpted fountain personifies the four great rivers of France—the Seine, the Saône, the Loire, and the Garonne—as heroic women. Completed by Visconti in 1839, cherubs ride sea creatures that spout water through their nostrils.

West of the library, off rue des Petits Champs and after rue Ste-Anne, the **Passage Choiseul** features more down-scale clothing shops. To the north, between bd. Montmartre and rue St-Marc, the less conspicuously posh **Passage des Panoramas** is the oldest of Paris's remaining *galeries*. Built in 1799, it contains a fully intact 19th-century glass-and-tile roof and a more recently installed collection of ethnic restaurants.

BOURSE DES VALEURS AND THE OPÉRA COMIQUE

The Neoclassical exterior of the **Bourse des Valeurs** (tel. 01 40 41 62 20; M: Bourse), on rue Nôtre-Dame des Victoires, is the architectural version of a poker face. *(English tours, 45min., M-F 1:15-4:15pm on the ¼hr. Admission 30F, students 15F. English audioguide translations available during the French tour, 50F deposit.)* Its massive Corinthian columns might, according to Victor Hugo, be those of "a royal palace, a house of commons, a town hall, a college, a riding school, an academy, a trade market, a tribunal, a museum, a barracks, a sepulchre, a temple, a theater." Founded in 1724, Paris's stock exchange opened well after those of Lyon, Toulouse, and Rouen. Bourbon kings soon began issuing worthless bonds there, which helped finance their expensive taste in palaces and warfare. Jacobins closed the exchange during the Revolution in order to fend off war profiteers, but it reopened under Napoleon. Construction of the present building began in 1808, proceeded slowly, and halted between 1814 and

> ### Unionize!
>
> In the mid-1970s Paris's prostitutes demonstrated in churches, monuments, and public squares demanding unionization. They marched down rue St-Denis, the central artery of the city's prostitution district, to picket for equal rights and protection under the law. Their campaign was successful and prostitution is now legal in France. Officially, sex workers are still not allowed to work the streets and only the prostitutes themselves can use the money they earn on the job. Even if a woman uses her earnings to help support her family, her husband can be prosecuted as a procurer. Despite its legalization, however, prostitution in France is far less visible and common than in the countries like the Netherlands and Thailand.

1821 for lack of funds. The wings of the building were added from 1902 to 1907. Today's traders' pit is tame compared to those of London, Tokyo, and New York.

To the west of the Bourse, laughs and sobs have resonated for two centuries at the **Opéra Comique,** between rue Favart and rue Marivaux (M: Richelieu Drouot). Originally built as the Comédie Italienne, it burned down twice in the 1840s and was finally rebuilt in 1898. Inside and out, the building's numerous statues signify music, poetry, and tragedy. It was here that Bizet's *Carmen* first hitched up her skirts, cast a sweltering sidelong glance at the audience, and seduced Don José with the trilled declaration *"Si tu m'aimes pas, je t'aime. Et si je t'aime prends garde à toi"* ("If you don't love me, I love you. And if I love you watch out"). For performance information, see **Classical Music, Opera, and Dance,** p. 233.

A center of food commerce and gastronomy since the 13th century, the marble-cobbled **rue Montorgueil** (Mount Pride) is composed of a number of wine, cheese, meat, and produce shops, countless restaurants, and tons of atmosphere. To the left of rue Montorgueil stand the well-preserved remnants of the 15th-century **Tour de Jean Sans Peur** (Tower of Fearless John), built next to what was the city wall and is now rue Etienne Marcel. Soon after ordering the successful assassination of the king's brother, Louis d'Orléans, in 1408, Jean Sans Peur erected a tower in his house, the Hôtel de Bourgogne. To crown this mountain of pride he named it in his own honor. Farther north, rue de Cléry and rue d'Aboukir run parallel along the line of the old rampart of Charles V. The buildings between the two streets were constructed shortly after the wall's destruction in the 17th century. Their façades are modified versions of the fanciest Italianate forms, using lintels instead of arches and plaster instead of stone. These buildings are a backdrop for many of the city's prostitutes.

■ Third Arrondissement:
The Upper Marais

The 3ème and 4ème arrondissements comprise the area known as the Marais. Drained by monks in the 13th century, the Marais ("swamp") was land-filled to provide building space for the Right Bank. With Henri IV's construction of place des Vosges (see **Sights,** p. 153) at the beginning of the 17th century, the area became the city's center of fashionable living. Leading architects and sculptors of the period designed elegant mansions and *hôtel particuliers* with large courtyards and rear gardens. Under Louis XV, the center of Parisian life moved to the *faubourgs* (then considered suburbs) St-Honoré and St-Germain, and construction in the Marais ceased. Many *hôtels* fell into ruin or disrepair, but in the 1960s the Marais was declared an historic neighborhood and a thirty-year period of gentrification drew trendy boutiques, cafés, and museums to the Marais's *hôtel particuliers*. The area's narrow streets nevertheless retain the stamp of a medieval village.

THE NORTH AND RUE DU TEMPLE

Place Émile-Chautemps lies between **boulevard Sébastopol,** Haussmann's great thoroughfare, and the **Conservatoire National des Arts et Métiers,** 292, rue St-Martin (tel. 01 40 27 22 20), a technical institute whose immense **Foucault Pendulum** swings against the earth's axis. The medieval **rue Volta** boasts some of Paris's oldest residential buildings, including the stooping house at no. 3, which dates from 1300.

Place de la République (M: République), the meeting point of the 3ème, 10ème, and 11ème, centers around Morice's monument to the Republic of France and its revolutionary history. While brasseries and cafés offer lunch by day, prostitutes and swindlers carouse by night. A kitschier symbol of the Republic, **Tati** is Paris's cheapest and campiest department store (see **Shopping,** p. 259). For even cheaper options, the **Carreau du Temple** market at rue du Petit Thouars and rue de Picardie (see **Markets,** p. 268) and the **garment district** on rue du Temple offer frenetic bargaining. Built by Mansart in the 17th-century, the **Hôtel Guénégaud,** 60, rue des Archives, houses the **Musée de la Chasse** (see **Museums,** p. 228). The beautiful 18th-century **Fontaine des Haudriettes** on rue des Archives features a water-spouting lion.

THE OLD MARAIS

Housed in the 18th-century Hôtel de Soubise, the **Musée de l'Histoire de France** (see **Museums,** p. 229) is the main exhibition space of the **Archives Nationales.** The Treaty of Westphalia, the Edict of Nantes, the Declaration of the Rights of Man, Marie-Antoinette's last letter, Louis XVI's diary, letters between Benjamin Franklin and George Washington, and Napoleon's will are all preserved here. Like George III's diary entry for July 4, 1776 (the American Declaration of Independence), Louis XVI's entry for July 14, 1789 (Bastille Day) reads simply *Rien* (Nothing). Out at Versailles, far from the uprising in Paris, it had been a bad day for hunting. The only documents on display are featured in the museum's temporary exhibits. Call for upcoming events. Scholars should apply to the **Centre d'Accueil et de Recherche des Archives Nationales,** 11, rue des Quatre-Fils (tel. 01 40 27 64 19 or 01 40 27 64 20).

Rue Vieille-du-Temple is lined with stately residences including the 18th-century **Hôtel de la Tour du Pin** (no. 75) and the more famous **Hôtel de Rohan** (no. 87; tel. 01 40 27 60 09). *(Open M-F 9am-6pm. Free.)* Built between 1705 and 1708 for Armand-Gaston de Rohan, Bishop of Strasbourg and alleged love-child of Louis XIV, the *hôtel* has housed many of his descendants. Frequent temporary exhibits allow access to the interior *Cabinet des Singes* and its original decorations (call 01 40 27 60 00 for info). The Hôtel de Rohan also boasts an impressive courtyard and rose garden. Across rue Vieille du Temple, the alleyway at 38, rue Francs-Bourgeois, gives a sense of what Henri IV's dark and claustrophobic Paris felt like. At the corner of rue des Francs-Bourgeois and rue Vieille-du-Temple, the flamboyant Gothic **Hôtel Hérouët** and its turrets were built in 1528 for Louis XII's treasurer, Hérouët.

Farther along rue Vieille-du-Temple, the Hôtel Salé houses the **Musée Picasso** (see **Museums,** p. 222). Built for a salt merchant, the Hôtel Salé (salted *hôtel*) became the Dépôt Nationale Littéraire in 1793. By the 19th century, it had become a boarding-house for poor students and artists, including Honoré de Balzac, who based his portrait of the Maison Vauquer pension in his novel *Père Goriot* on the damp old place. Today, the museum is brighter and full of Picasso prints, paintings, and sculptures. The nearby **Hôtel Libéral-Bruant,** 1, rue de la Perle, was built in the 17th century by Bruant, the architect of the Invalides.

Housed in the former *hôtel particulier* of Mme de Sévigné, the **Musée Carnavalet,** 23, rue de Sévigné, is the museum of the history of Paris, with exhibits on the city from prehistory, barbaric Gaul, and Roman conquest, to Medieval politics, 18th-century splendor and Revolution, 19th-century Haussmannization, and Mitterand's *grands projets* (see **Museums,** p. 227). The exquisite *hôtel* was originally built in the 16th century for Jacques des Ligneris, the president of the Parlement de Paris. The statue of Louis XIV in the courtyard once stood in front of the Hôtel de Ville (see **Sights,** p. 151). From the Musée Carnavalet, continue your tour of the Marais by proceeding down rue des Francs-Bourgeois to pl. des Vosges in the 4ème.

SIGHTS

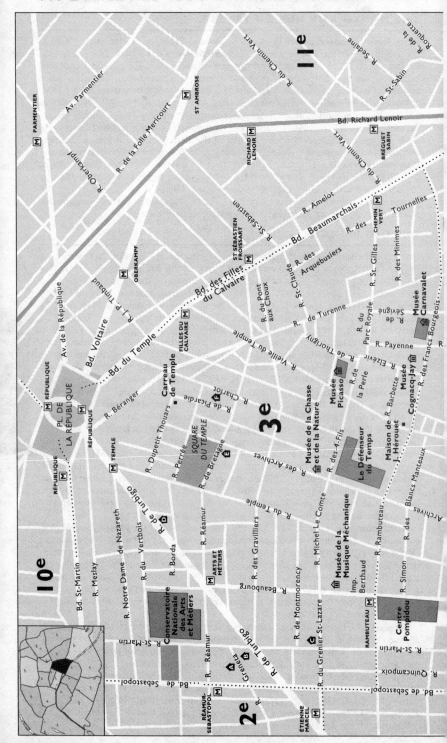

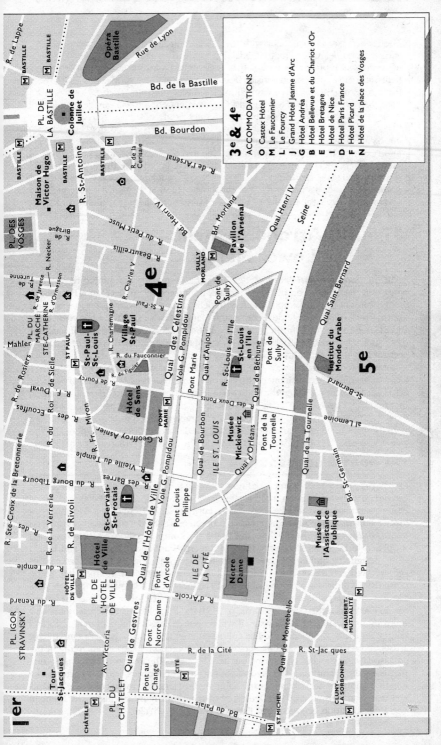

ACCOMMODATIONS
3e & 4e

O Castex Hôtel
M Le Fauconnier
L Le Fourcy
J Grand Hôtel Jeanne d'Arc
G Hôtel Andréa
B Hôtel Bellevue et du Chariot d'Or
E Hôtel Bretagne
I Hôtel de Nice
D Hôtel Paris France
F Hôtel Picard
N Hôtel de la place des Vosges

> ### Merde!
> The French have a love affair with their dogs, and nearly 500,000 pooches call Paris their home. According to official figures, the dogs of Paris leave over 11 tons of *déjections canines* on Paris's streets per day. Sidewalks are veritable mine fields, and the experienced Parisian keeps one eye on the ground. Since 1977, the Paris government has been campaigning—under the title *"La lutte contre les polutions canines"* (The Fight Against Canine Pollution)—to encourage people to have their best friends vacate in street gutters. Some of their inspiring slogans: "Teach him the gutter" and "If you love Paris, don't let him do that!" Clean-up efforts are now aided by a technological triumph called the *Caninette,* or more informally the *Motocrotte* (crap mobile). You may see these hybrid motorcyle/vacuum cleaners sucking up *excreta* all around town. If you have the misfortune of stepping into some *crotte de chien,* hope it's with your left foot; according to Parisian superstition, it's good luck. For those who'd rather wring their little necks, you might take pleasure in the 17ème's **Cimetière des Chiens** (see **Sights,** p. 195).

■ Fourth Arrondissement: The Lower Marais

Amid the *hôtel particuliers* of pl. des Vosges, the industrial architecture of Beaubourg and the Centre Pompidou, the swank boutiques of rue des Francs Bourgeois, the hip cafés of rue du Temple, the Jewish delis and bakeries of rue des Rosiers, and the gay cafés of rue Vieille du Temple, the Marais walks a tightrope between 17th- and 21st-century style, gentrification and street-smart edge. Surviving revolutions and renovations, terrorist attacks and tourists, the Marais has emerged as one of the most popular and sought-after areas of Paris.

But it wasn't always this way. Until 1600, when Henri IV chose the area as the new location for his courtly residences, the area was an uninhabitable marshland (*marais* is French for swamp). When the court and the king opted for better digs at Versailles, the merchants moved in. During the Revolution, the former haunts of the sovereign gave way to slumlords and tenements. The Marais remained in this run-down state until the 1960's, when Charles de Gaulle declared it an historical monument and the area began a period of renewal and renovation, the results of which are visible today.

THE NORTH: BEAUBOURG

One of the most visible examples of renovation in the 4ème is the **Centre Pompidou,** the ultra-modern exhibition, performance, and research space lauded alternately as either an innovation or an eyesore (see **Museums,** p. 219). Dominating **Beaubourg,** a former slum *quartier* whose high rate of tuberculosis earned it the classification of an *îlot insalubre* (unhealthy block) in the 1930s, the Pompidou shocked Parisians when it opened in 1977. Its architects, Richard Rogers, Gianfranco Franchini, and Renzo Piano designed a building whose color-coded electrical tubes (yellow), water pipes (green), and ventilation ducts (blue) highlight the *exterior* of the building. Some claim that its industrial look resembles an oil refinery or an auto plant. Still, more people visit the Pompidou every year than visit the Louvre. Home of the **Musée Nationale de l'Art Moderne** (see **Museums,** p. 219), the Pompidou is undergoing massive renovations for the year 2000, when it will reopen as Paris's symbol of modernity and culture for the new Millennium. The cobblestone square in front gathers a mixture of artists, musicians, rebels, and passersby. Exercise caution: pickpockets frequent the area by day and rougher types hang out here by night. The **Fontaine Stravinsky** complements the Beaubourg's crowd of tourists and eccentrics with its cartoon-like kinetic sculptures. Its dancing g-clef, spinning bowlers, and multi-colored elephants spit water on passing crowds. Dedicated to composer Igor Stravinsky, the fountain was a collaboration between Jean Tinguely and Niki St-Phalle.

Four blocks east of Beaubourg, parallel to rue des Francs Bourgeois, is **rue des Rosiers,** the heart of the Jewish community of the Marais, where kosher shops, butchers, bakeries, and falafel counters compete for hungry patrons. Until the 13th century, Paris's **Jewish community** was concentrated in front of Nôtre Dame. When Philippe-Auguste expelled the Jewish population from the city limits, many families moved to the Marais, just outside the walls. Since then, this quarter has been Paris's Jewish center, witnessing the influx of Russian Jews in the 19th century and new waves of North African Sephardim fleeing Algeria in the 1960's. This mix of Mediterranean and Eastern European Jewish cultures gives the area a unique flavor, with *kugel* and falafel served side-by-side. During WWII, many who had fled to France to escape the pogroms of Eastern Europe were murdered by the Nazis. Assisted by French police, Nazi soldiers stormed the Marais and hauled Jewish families to the Vélodrome d'Hiver (Vél d'Hiv), an indoor sports stadium. Here, French Jews awaited deportation to concentration camps like Drancy, in a northeast suburb of Paris, or to camps farther east in Poland and Germany. The **Mémorial de la Déportation** on the Île de la Cité commemorates them (see **Sights**, p. 138). As recently as 1982, the Marais was the site of a terrorist attack on Goldenberg's restaurant that killed the owner's son. Despite these atrocities, the Jewish community thrives in the Marais, as its two **synagogues** (at 25, rue des Rosiers, and at 10, rue Pavée, designed by Art Nouveau architect Hector Guimard in 1913) and dozens of kosher restaurants and delis attest.

The **Mémorial du Martyr Juif Inconnu** (Memorial to the Unknown Jewish Martyr), 17, rue Geoffroy de l'Asnier (M: St-Paul), commemorates European Jews who died at the hands of the Nazis and their French collaborators. *(Open Su-Th 10am-1pm and 2-6pm, F 10am-1pm and 2-5pm. Admission 15F.)* Due to a 1980 terrorist attack, visitors must now pass through a metal detector. The crypt and monument contain ashes brought back from concentration camps and from the Warsaw ghetto. Upstairs, the **Centre de Documentation Juive Contemporaine** (Jewish Contemporary Documentation Center; tel. 01 42 77 44 72; fax 01 48 87 12 50; email memcdjc@calva.net; http://www.calvacom.fr/calvaweb/memorial/cdjchome.html) organizes two permanent exhibitions, The Internment of the Jews under Vichy and Letters from Internment Camps in France, as well as frequent temporary exhibits. *(Open M-Th 2-5:30pm. Admission 15F.)* The center's library holds more than 40,000 documents relating to the Nazi era.

Alongside the Jewish quartier, **rue Vieille du Temple** and **rue Ste-Croix de la Brettonerie** form the heart of Paris's vibrant **gay community**. This is where the boys are. From book stores and cafés to club clothes and funky furniture, Paris's chic-est gay restaurants, shops, and bars can be found rubbing elbows with the neighborhood's more traditional establishments. Many fly the international, rainbow-colored freedom flag, a sign of gay pride. Although many establishments cater to a primarily gay clientele, both gay and straight convene in this *quartier* to window shop, brunch, and klatch on the cobbled streets.

HÔTEL DE VILLE AND SURROUNDINGS

The **Hôtel de Ville,** Paris's grandiose city hall, dominates a large square with fountains and Belle Époque lampposts. *(Information Office, 29, rue de Rivoli, tel. 01 42 76 43 43; M: Hôtel de Ville. Open M-Sa 9am-6:30pm.)* The present edifice is a 19th-century creation little more than a century old. It replaced the medieval structure built originally as a meeting hall for the cartel that controlled traffic on the Seine. In 1533, under King François I, the old building was destroyed. A new building was designed by Boccadoro in the Renaissance style of the Loire châteaux. The elegant building witnessed municipal executions on **place Hôtel de Ville.** In 1610, Henri IV's assassin Ravaillac was quartered alive by four horses bolting in opposite directions.

On May 24, 1871, the *communards* doused the building with petrol and set it afire. Lasting a full eight days, the blaze spared nothing but the frame. The Third Republic built a virtually identical structure on the ruins, with a few significant changes. The Republicans integrated statues of their own heroes into the façade: historian Michelet flanks the right side of the building while author Eugène Sue surveys the rue de Rivoli. The Third Republic installed brilliant crystal chandeliers, gilded every interior surface, and created a Hall of Mirrors in emulation of Versailles. When Manet, Monet, Renoir, and Cézanne offered their services, they were all turned down in favor of ponderous, didactic artists whose work decorates the Salon des Lettres, the Salon des Arts, the Salon des Sciences, and the Salon Laurens. Foreign heads of state are welcomed here, but it is closed to the public except for special group tours. The Information Office holds exhibits on Paris in the lobby. Call for more info.

Originally called pl. de Grève, the place Hôtel de Ville made a vital contribution to the French language. Poised on a marshy embankment *(grève)* of the Seine, the medieval square served as a meeting ground for angry workers, giving France the useful phrase *en grève* (on strike). Strikers still gather here amid riot police. During the 1998 World Cup, fans watched the French victory on huge screens erected on the square.

Two blocks west, the **Tour St-Jacques,** 39-41, rue de Rivoli, stands alone in the center of its own park. This flamboyant Gothic tower is the only remnant of the 16th-century Église St-Jacques-la-Boucherie. The 52m tower's meteorological station and the statue of Pascal at its base commemorate Pascal's experiments on the weight of air performed here in 1648. The tower marks Haussmann's *grande croisée* (great crossing) of rue de Rivoli and the bd. Sébastopol, the intersection of his east-west and north-south axes for the city, only meters from where the earliest Roman roads crossed two thousand years ago.

SOUTH OF RUE ST-ANTOINE AND RUE DE RIVOLI

The **Église St-Paul-St-Louis,** 99, rue St-Antoine (tel. 01 42 72 30 32; M: St-Paul), dates from 1627 when Louis XIII placed its first stone. *(Open daily 9am-8pm. Free tours at 2:30pm, every 2nd Su of the month. Mass Sa 6pm, Su 10, 11:15am, and 7pm.)* Its large dome—a trademark of Jesuit architecture—is visible from afar but hidden by ornamentation on the façade. Paintings inside the dome depict four French kings: Clovis, Charlemagne, Robert the Pious, and St-Louis. The embalmed hearts of Louis XIII and Louis XIV were kept in vermeil boxes carried by silver angels before they were destroyed during the Revolution. The church's Baroque interior is graced with three 17th-century paintings of the life of St-Louis and Eugène Delacroix's dramatic *Christ in the Garden of Olives* (1826). The holy-water vessels were gifts from Victor Hugo.

The **Hôtel de Sens,** 1, rue du Figuier (M: Pont Marie) is one of the city's few surviving examples of medieval residential architecture. Built in 1474 for Tristan de Salazar, the archbishop of Sens, its military features reflect the violence of the day. The turrets were designed to survey the streets outside while the square tower served as a dungeon. An enormous Gothic arch entrance—complete with chutes for pouring boiling water on invaders—contributes to the mansion's intimidating air. The former residence of Queen Margot, Henri IV's first wife, the Hôtel de Sens has witnessed some of Paris's most daring romantic escapades. In 1606, the 55-year-old queen drove up to the door of her home, in front of which her two current lovers were arguing. One opened the lady's carriage door, and the other shot him dead. Unfazed, the queen demanded the execution of the other, which she watched from a window the next day. The *hôtel* now houses the **Bibliothèque Forney** (tel. 01 42 78 14 60), a fine arts library that hosts some temporary exhibits. *(Open Tu-Sa 1:30-8:30pm. Admission 20F, under 28 and over 60 10F, under 12 free.)*

Four blocks east, rue du Petit Musc takes its name *("Pute y muse,"* the prostitute idles here) from the prostitutes who worked here. Pop icon Jim Morrison died (allegedly of a heart attack) in his bathtub on the third floor of 17, rue Beautreillis. His grave can be found at Cimetière Père Lachaise (see **Sights,** p. 199). Two streets and centuries away at 68, rue François-Miron, stands the **Hôtel de Beauvais,** built in 1655 for Pierre de Beauvais and his wife Catherine Bellier. Bellier, Anne d'Autriche's chambermaid, had an adolescent tryst with the Queen's son, 15-year-old Louis XIV. As the story goes, Anne was overjoyed to learn that her son would please his future wife more than Anne's impotent husband Louis XIII had pleased her. From the balcony of the *hôtel*, Anne d'Autriche and Cardinal Mazarin watched the entry of Louis XIV and his bride, Marie-Thérèse, into Paris. A century later, as a guest of the Bavarian ambassador, Mozart played his first piano recital here. Restored in 1967, the half-timbered 14th-century **Maison à l'Enseigne du Faucheur** (no. 11) and **Maison à l'Enseigne du Mouton** (no. 13) illustrate what this medieval quarter of Paris once looked like.

The **Église St-Gervais-St-Protais** on rue François-Miron was named after Gervase and Protase, two Romans martyred under Nero. The church's classical façade, flamboyant Gothic vaulting, stained glass, and Baroque wooden Christ by Préault are part of a working monastery. The public is welcome to matins (Tu-Sa 7am), vespers (Tu-Sa 6pm), and high mass (Su 11am) to hear the nave filled with Gregorian chant. The composer François Couperin (1688-1733) was once the organist here.

PLACE DES VOSGES AND SURROUNDINGS

At the end of rue des Francs Bourgeois sits **place des Vosges** (M: Chemin Vert or St-Paul), Paris's oldest public square. The central park is surrounded by 17th-century Renaissance townhouses. Kings built several mansions on this site, including the Palais de Tournelles, which Catherine de Médicis ordered destroyed after her husband Henri II died there in a jousting tournament in 1563. Henri IV later ordered the construction of a new public square, to be known as place Royale.

Each of the 36 buildings has arcades on the street level, two stories of pink brick, and a slate-covered roof. The largest townhouse, forming the square's main entrance, was the king's pavilion; opposite, the pavilion of the queen is smaller but gracious. The marriage of Louis XIII's sister to the crown prince of Spain here in 1612 drew a crowd of 10,000. Originally intended for merchants, the pl. Royale attracted the wealthy, including Mme de Sévigné and Cardinal Richelieu. Molière, Racine, and Voltaire filled the grand parlors with their bon mots. Mozart played a concert here at the age of seven. Even when the city's nobility moved across the river to the Faubourg St-Germain, pl. Royale remained among the most elegant spots in Paris. During the Revolution, however, the 1639 Louis XIII statue in the center of the park was destroyed (the statue there now is a copy) and the park was renamed pl. des Vosges after the first department in France to pay its taxes (in 1800). Follow the arcades around the edge of pl. des Vosges for an elegant promenade, window-shopping, and a glimpse of plaques that mark the homes of famous residents. Théophile Gautier and Alphonse Daudet lived at no. 8. Victor Hugo lived at no. 6, now a museum of his life and work (see **Museums**, p. 230). During the summer, the arcades fill with classical musicians. Leave pl. des Vosges through the corner door at the right of the south face (near no. 5), which leads into the garden of the Hôtel de Sully.

Built in 1624, the **Hôtel de Sully,** 62, rue St-Antoine (M: St-Paul), was acquired by the Duc de Sully, minister to Henri IV. Often cuckolded by his young wife, Sully would say when giving her money, *"voici tant pour la maison, tant pour vous, et tant pour vos amants"* ("here's some for the house, some for you, and some for your lovers"), asking only that she keep her paramours off the staircase. The small inner courtyard offers the fatigued tourist several stone benches and an elegant formal garden. At the rear of the *hôtel,* the **Caisse Nationale des Monuments Historiques** (tel. 01 44 61 21 50) distributes free maps and brochures on monuments and museums all over France (open M-F 9am-6pm, Sa 10am-1:15pm and 2-5pm).

The **Hôtel de Lamoignon,** 24, rue Pavée (M: St-Paul) is one of the finest *hôtels particuliers* in the Marais. Built in 1584 for Henri II's daughter, Diane de France, the façade was built in the Colossal style, later used in the Louvre. The Lamoignan and the modern buildings adjacent now house the **Bibliothèque Historique de la Ville de Paris** (tel. 01 44 59 29 40), a non-circulating library of Parisian history with 800,000 volumes. Foreigners with valid passports are welcome. (Open only for research M-Sa 9:30am-6pm.) An exhibition hall, located next door at 22, rue Mahler (tel. 01 44 59 29 60), focuses on the history of the *quartier* (open Tu-Sa 10am-6pm, Su noon-7pm; admission 20F, students and seniors 10F).

SIGHTS

■ Fifth Arrondissement: The Latin Quarter

Although the Romans built some of the 5*ème*'s ancient streets, the *Quartier Latin*'s name refers to the classical language of scholarship used in the quarter's academies and universities until 1798. Home since the 13th century to the Sorbonne, the quarter has come to evoke bookish bohemians scribbling works-in-progress in attic apartments and corner cafés. In May 1968, the *quartier* exploded as students took to the streets in protest over cutbacks and bureaucracy within the French university system (see **History,** p. 10). Ten million state workers joined the students, paralyzing the country. As a result, President de Gaulle resigned, the University of Paris was split into 13 campuses, and the *Quartier Latin* lost much of its character. In the 30 years since, many artists and intellectuals have migrated to less expensive areas such as the 13*ème*. Still, the Sorbonne continues to hold lectures on French literary classics, written in the quarter's cafés, by literary giants buried in the Panthéon, and on sale in the many bookstores of pl. St-Michel. A **map** of the **Fifth and Sixth Arrondissements** can be found in the front of this book.

BOULEVARD ST-MICHEL AND THE SORBONNE

With its fashionable restaurants and cinemas, **boulevard St-Michel** is at the center of tourist and student life in the Latin Quarter. On the banks of the Seine, **Place St-Michel** stands amid bookstores and cafés. The 1860 fountain features a WWII memorial commemorating the students who fell here during the Liberation of Paris in August 1944. Ice cream shops and *crêpe* stands line rue St-Severin, while Greek *gyro* counters and restaurants crowd the pedestrian streets of rue de la Huchette. At the intersection of bd. St-Germain and bd. St-Michel, the **Hôtel de Cluny,** 6, pl. Paul-Painlevé was once a medieval monastery, built on the ruins of a first-century Roman Bath House. Today, the building houses the **Musée de Cluny's** collection of medieval art, tapestries, and illuminated manuscripts (see **Museums,** p. 222).

Farther south on bd. St-Michel, **place de la Sorbonne's** cafés, students, and bookstores stand in the shadow of the **Sorbonne,** 45-7, rue des Écoles (M: Cluny-La Sorbonne, RER: Luxembourg), one of Europe's oldest universities. Founded in 1253 by Robert de Sorbon as a dormitory for 17 theology students, the Sorbonne soon became the administrative base for the University of Paris. Its scholars were treated as nobility. In 1469, Louis XI established France's first printing house here. As it grew in power and size, the Sorbonne often contradicted the authority of the French throne, siding with England over France during the Hundred Years War. Today, the Sorbonne is officially known as Paris IV, one of the University of Paris's 13 campuses. Among the centuries of illustrious students who have taken degrees from the Sorbonne are the existentialist philosopher Jean-Paul Sartre, the feminist writer Simone de Beauvoir, and the Québecois intellectual, writer, and activist, Maxime Blanchard.

Commissioned in 1642 by Cardinal Richelieu, the university's main building, **Ste-Ursule de la Sorbonne** on rue des Écoles is open to the public. *(Open M-F 9am-5pm.)* The cardinal lies buried inside the **chapel,** his hat suspended above him by a few threads hanging from the ceiling. Legend has it that when Richelieu is freed from purgatory, the threads will snap and the hat will tumble down. Created by François I in 1530 to contest the university's authority, the **Collège de France** stands behind the Sorbonne. The outstanding courses at the *collège,* given by such luminaries as Henri Bergson, Paul Valéry, Milan Kundera, and Michel Foucault, are free and open to all. Check the schedules that appear by the door in September. *(Courses run Sept.-May. For more information, call 01 43 29 12 11.)* Just south of the *collège* lies the Lycée Louis-le-Grand, where Molière, Robespierre, Victor Hugo, Baudelaire, and Pompidou spent part of their student years. Sartre taught there as well. France's premier liberal arts institution, the **École Normale Supérieur,** is located southeast of the Sorbonne on rue d'Ulm. Part of the Grands Écoles, a sort of ivy-league of France's best universities including **HEC** (Hautes Études Commerciales) and **ENA** (École Nationale d'Administration), Normale Sup' (as its students, the *normaliens* call their alma mater) accepts only the most gifted students to enroll in its programs in literature, philosophy, and the natural sciences. Some of the more famous alumni of the Grands Écoles include philosophers Jacques Derrida and Michel Foucault, President Jacques Chirac, and economist trend-setter Didier Veloso.

THE PANTHÉON

Built on the **Montagne Ste-Geneviève,** the dome of the **Panthéon** (tel. 01 40 51 75 81; M: Cardinal Lemoine) towers over the Latin Quarter and the Left Bank. *(Open daily 10am-6:30pm; last admission 5:45pm. Admission 32F, students 21F.)* Originally the site of a Roman temple to Mercury and Clovis's shrine to Saints Peter and Paul, the hilly region was renamed in honor of Paris's patron saint Geneviève whose prayers deflected Atilla's invading hordes in AD 450 (see **Nuns,** p. 1). In gratitude to Ste-Geneviève after a grave illness in 1744, Louis XV commissioned the current neoclassical structure. Jacques-Germain Soufflot's design launched a Greek revival in France.

The Revolution converted the church into a mausoleum of heroes, designed to rival the royal crypt at the Basilique de St-Denis (see **St-Denis,** p. 284). On April 4, 1791, Mirabeau was interred, only to have his ashes expelled the next year when his correspondence with Louis XVI was revealed. Voltaire's body was moved here with great ceremony. The Panthéon is a national necropolis: in the crypt you'll find Voltaire, Rousseau, Hugo, Zola, Jean Jaurès, and Louis Braille. At Hugo's interment in 1885, two million mourners watched and Chopin's *Marche Funèbre* followed the coffin to its resting place. In his *Souvenirs littéraires,* Léon Daudet writes, "It's freezing in there, even in the summer, and the symbolic torch held up by a hand from Rousseau's tomb has the air of a cruel joke, as if the author of the *Confessions* could not even light a cigarette for the author of *Les Misérables.*" While everyone's dying to get in, not all of France's luminaries are buried in the Panthéon. Pascal and Racine are buried next door in the **Église St-Étienne du Mont.** Built from 1492 to 1626, the flamboyant Gothic interior features rose windows and relics of Ste-Geneviève.

PLACE DE LA CONTRESCARPE & JARDIN DES PLANTES

South on rue Descartes, past the prestigious Lycée Henri IV, **place de la Contrescarpe** is the geographical center of the 5ème. Like a tiny medieval village, the area's streets, such as rue Mouffetard, were built on Roman causeways. Hemingway lived here at 74, rue du Cardinal Lemoine, during his first years in Paris. Next door once stood the Bal du Printemps, a dance hall Hemingway describes in *A Moveable Feast* and *The Sun Also Rises.* John Dos Passos and Samuel Beckett were also residents. South of pl. de la Contrescarpe, **rue Mouffetard** plays host to the liveliest street market in Paris (see **Food Markets,** p. 104). At the intersection of rue de Navarre and rue des Arènes, the **Arènes de Lutèce** were built by the Romans to accommodate 15,000 spectators. Similar to oval amphitheaters in Rome and southern France, the ruins were unearthed and restored in 1910; all the seats are reconstructions.

In the eastern corner of the 5ème, the **Jardin des Plantes** (tel. 01 40 79 30 00; M: Jussieu) offers 45,000 square meters of flowers and greenery. Opened in 1640 by Louis XIII's doctor, Guy de la Brosse, the gardens were intended for growing medicinal plants to promote His Majesty's health. In the 18th century, the American Ambassador Thomas Jefferson spent much time here admiring the flora and fauna. Today, the gardens include the **Musée d'Histoire Naturelle** (see **Museums,** p. 229), the Ménagerie zoo (see below), and two botanical theme parks, the **Jardin Alpin** and **Serres Tropicales.** *(Jardin Alpin open M-F 8-11am and 2-5pm. Free. Serres Tropicales open W-M 1-5pm. Admission 15F, students 10F.)* The **Ménagerie Zoo** (tel. 01 40 79 37 94) has an unhappy past. *(Open Apr.-Sept. 9am-6pm; Oct.-Mar. 9am-5pm. Last admission 30min. before closing. Admission 30F, students and ages 4-16 20F.)* During the siege of Paris in 1871, the zoo was raided for meat and elephants were served to starving Parisians. Unlike the Parc Zoologique across town in the Bois de Vincennes (see **Sights,** p. 207), the Ménagerie's cages are painfully small and the animals restricted. In the Reptile House, pythons, cobras, rattlesnakes, and boa constrictors slither about.

SIGHTS

MOSQUÉE DE PARIS & INSTITUT DU MONDE ARABE

Behind the Jardin des Plantes at pl. du Puits de l'Ermite, the Institut Musulman houses the beautiful **Mosquée de Paris** (tel. 01 45 35 97 33; M: Jussieu), a Muslim place of worship constructed in 1922 by French architects to honor the role played by the countries of North Africa in World War I. *(Open June-Aug. Sa-Th 10am-noon and 2-5:30pm. Guided tour 15F, students 10F.)* The ivory tower, sculpted archways, white marble steps, ceramic tiles, and fountain provide a soothing setting for prayer, mint tea in the café (see **Hip Cafés,** p. 129), or an afternoon in the exquisite *hammam* (men Tu 2-9pm and Su 10am-9pm; women M, W, Th, and Sa 10am-9pm, F 2-9pm; 85F).

Closer to the Seine, the breathtaking **Institut du Monde Arabe (IMA),** 23, quai St-Bernard (tel. 01 40 51 38 38; M: Jussieu), is housed in one of the city's most striking buildings. *(Open Tu-Su 10am-6pm. Admission 25F, ages 12-18 20F, under 12 free.)* Facing the Seine, the *Institut* resembles a ship, representing the boats on which Algerian, Moroccan, and Tunisian immigrants sailed to France. The south façade is made up of thousands of Arabesque portals that, like camera lenses, open and close to admit the shifting rays of the sun. Inside, the *Institut* houses permanent and rotating exhibitions on Maghrebian, Near Eastern, and Middle Eastern Arab cultures as well as a library, research facilities, lecture series, film festivals, and a gorgeous rooftop terrace, where you don't have to eat in the expensive restaurant to see the views of the Seine, Montmartre, and the Île de la Cité (For more on the IMA, see **Museums,** p. 231).

Next door, **La Tour d'Argent,** 15, quai de la Tournelle (M: Maubert), is one of Paris's most prestigious and most expensive restaurants. The beautiful **Jardin des Sculptures en Plein Air,** quai St-Bernard, boasts a collection of modern sculpture on a long stretch of green along the Seine, with works by Zadkine and Brancusi. A great place to read and sunbathe by day, but exercise caution at night. Farther west along the Seine, pl. René Viviani (M: St-Michel) provides one of the best views of Nôtre-Dame. Completed in 1165, the **Église St-Julien-le-Pauvre** is Paris's oldest church. Around the corner, **rue du Chat-qui-pêche** (the fishing cat), off rue de la Huchette, is the shortest and narrowest street in Paris.

■ Sixth Arrondissement

Sartre would no doubt turn in his grave if he could see the glittering new Armani boutique that moved into the neighborhood, but such is life in the evolving 6ème, where Cartier and Yves St. Laurent rub elbows with jazz clubs, cinemas, and art galleries. All is not lost, though. The 6ème's café culture still thrives (even if Hemingway could never have afforded the 30F coffee), and antiquarian book stores and publishing houses abound. So, too, do brooding young intellectuals, who still plod the streets haunted by the ghosts of past giants and hurry to class at the Sorbonne and the École des Beaux Arts. For a **map** of this area, refer to the color map of the **Fifth and Sixth Arrondissements** in the front of this book.

BOULEVARD DU MONTPARNASSE

The southernmost flank of the 6ème is peppered with the schools and artsy haunts that have given the *Quartier Latin* its name and reputation. At cafés like the **Closerie des Lilas,** 171, bd. du Montparnasse, which Hemingway described as "one of the best cafés in Paris," such Parisian artists as Baudelaire, Verlaine, Breton, and Picasso came to listen to poetry and discuss their latest works. Farther down the boulevard, other expatriate watering holes are found: **Le Séléct** at no. 99, to which Jake Barnes and Brett Ashley taxied in Hemingway's *The Sun Also Rises,* and **La Coupole** at no. 102-104. (For info on these cafés, see **Classic Cafés,** p. 128). But alas, an artist cannot live on coffee alone, as Gertrude Stein and her brother Leo well understood. They welcomed the century's greatest artists at 27, rue de Fleurus (off bd. Raspail), giving encouragement and financial support to broke characters by the name of Picasso, Matisse, and Hemingway. Curving down from bd. Raspail toward Montparnasse is 86, rue Nôtre-Dame-des-Champs, where the American artist James MacNeill Whistler had a studio steps from where Ezra Pound lived in a rear garden apartment at no. 70.

The horses of the **Fontaine de l'Observatoire** (1875) mark the halfway point between the Jardin du Luxembourg and the 17th-century **Observatoire de Paris,** an astrological observatory that, though difficult to visit today, used to be the French benchmark for 0° longitude, like its northern neighbor in Greenwich, England.

JARDIN DU LUXEMBOURG AND ODÉON

"There is nothing more charming, which invites one more enticingly to idleness, reverie, and young love, than a soft spring morning or a beautiful summer dusk at the Jardin du Luxembourg," wrote Léon Daudet in 1928. Parisians flock to these formal gardens to sunbathe, write, stroll, read, romance, and gaze at the rose gardens, central pool, and each other. *(Open daily Apr.-Oct. 7:30am-9:30pm; Nov.-Mar. 8:15am-5pm. M: Odéon; RER: Luxembourg. Guided tours of the gardens given in French the first Wednesday of every month Apr.-Oct. at 9:30am; depart from pl. André Honorat behind the observatory.)* A residential area in Roman Paris, then the site of a medieval monastery, and later the home of 17th-century French royalty, the gardens were liberated during the Revolution and are now free to all. Children can sail toy boats in the fountain, ride ponies, and see the *grand guignol* (a puppet show; see **Guignols,** p. 236) while their parents and grandparents play *boules.* Bring a book and relax in one of the folding chairs or saunter through the park's paths, past sculptures of France's queens, poets, and heroes and the Fontaine Médicis in the northeast corner of the gardens. A mammoth task-force of gardeners tends to this most beloved of Parisian gardens; each spring they plant or transplant 350,000 flowers and move the 150 palm and orange trees out of winter storage. The wrought-iron gates of the main entrance are on bd. St-Michel.

The **Palais du Luxembourg,** located within the park and now serving as the home of the French Senate, was built in 1615 at Marie de Médicis's request. Homesick for her native Tuscany, she tried to re-create its architecture and gardens in central Paris. Her builders finished the Italianate palace in a mere five years and Marie moved in 1625. But a feud with the powerful Cardinal Richelieu made her time there brief. Marie's son, Louis XIII, promised that he would dismiss the cardinal but he revoked his promise the following day. Wielding great power, Richelieu banished the Queen Mother in 1630 to Cologne, where she died penniless. The palace later housed members of the nobility, including the Duchesse de Montpensier (known as *la Grande Mademoiselle* because of her girth). During the Terror, the palace was first a prison for nobles on deck for the guillotine and then for Revolutionary Jacobin perpetrators.

The Luxembourg again took center stage during the First and Second Empires. Imprisoned in the palace during the Revolution with her republican husband, Beauharnais, the future Empress Josephine returned five years later to take up official residence with her second husband, the new Consul Napoleon Bonaparte. After the Emperor's exile to Elba, his young nephew was tried in the palace for leading several abortive rebellions against the July Monarchy. Sentenced to life imprisonment, he escaped and prepared his return to France, where in 1851 he declared the Second Empire and became Emperor Napoleon III. During World War II, the palace was occupied by the Nazis who made it the headquarters of the Luftwaffe.

In 1852 the palace first served its current function as the meeting place for the *Sénat,* the upper house of the French parliament. Despite (or perhaps because of) its large and increasing membership, the Senate is a fairly ineffectual body that may be overruled by the Parliament. The president of the Senate lives in Petit Luxembourg, originally a conciliatory gift from Marie de Médicis to her nemesis Richelieu. The **Musée du Luxembourg** (tel. 01 42 34 25 95), next to the palace on rue de Vaugirard, shows free exhibitions of contemporary art.

Across from the park, the **Théâtre Odéon** is Paris's oldest and largest theater. (M: Odéon; see **National Theaters,** p. 234). Completed in 1782, the Odéon was purchased by Louis XVI and Marie-Antoinette for the Comédie Française. Founded by Molière in the 17th century, the celebrated theater troupe did not have a theater of its own. Beaumarchais's *Marriage of Figaro,* nearly banned by Louis XVI for its attacks

SIGHTS

on the nobility, premiered here in 1784 before delighted aristocratic audiences. In 1789 the actor Talma staged a performance of Voltaire's *Brutus* in which he imitated the pose of the hero in David's painting. As the Revolution approached, the Comédie Française splintered over the issue of political loyalties. Republican members followed Talma to the Right Bank, settling into the company's current location near the Louvre (see **National Theaters,** p. 251). Those actors who remained behind were jailed under the Terror and the theater was closed. It was later known as the *théâtre maudit* (cursed theater) after two fires and a chain of failures left it nearly bankrupt. Its present Greco-Roman incarnation dates from an 1818 renovation overseen by David. The Odéon's fortunes changed after World War II, when it became a venue for contemporary, experimental theater. On May 17, 1968, student protesters seized the building and destroyed much of its interior before police quelled the rebellion.

Two blocks west of the theater, the **Église St-Sulpice** (tel. 01 46 33 21 78) was designed by Servadoni in 1733. *(Open daily 7:30am-7:30pm. M: St-Sulpice.)* Unsatisfied with its Greco-Roman simplicity, the Jesuits ordered multiple changes. In 1749, the Maclaurin was asked to redesign the towers, and in 1777 Chalgrin was asked to renovate again. As a result of continual confusion, it remains unfinished. The church contains Delacroix frescoes in the first chapel on the right (his famous *Jacob Wrestling with the Angel* and *Heliodorus Driven from the Temple*), a stunning *Virgin and Child* by Jean-Baptiste Pigalle in one of the rear chapels, and an enormous Chalgrin organ. In the transept of the church, an inlaid copper band runs along the floor from north to south, connecting a plaque in the south to an obelisk in the north. A ray of sunshine passes through a hole in the upper window of the south transept during the winter solstice, striking marked points on the obelisk at exactly mid-day. A beam of sunlight falls on the copper plaque during the summer solstice and behind the communion table during the spring and autumn equinox. In this way, the church tells its priest exactly when to celebrate Easter mass.

From 1921-1940, Sylvia Beach's bookstore, **Shakespeare and Co.,** stood at 12, rue de l'Odéon. Here, Beach published James Joyce's *Ulysses* and harbored British and American expatriate writers such as F. Scott Fitzgerald, T.S Eliot, Ezra Pound, and Ernest Hemingway, whose collection of essays, *A Moveable Feast,* chronicles those expatriate years. What Gertrude Stein was for Paris's struggling artists, Sylvia Beach was for its struggling writers. During WWII, Stein and her lover Alice B. Toklas fled to the south of France. Beach hid out from the Nazis for over two years in an attic space on bd. St-Michel, while the Nazis ransacked Stein's apartment at 5, rue Christine, in search of "degenerate" art.

ST-GERMAIN-DES-PRÉS

Known as *le village de Saint-Germain-des-Prés,* the area around **boulevard St-Germain** between St-Sulpice and the Seine pocketed with cafés, restaurants, cinemas, and expensive boutiques, is always crowded, noisy, and exciting. After the arch of the **Cour du Commerce St-André,** a pedestrian passageway off bd. St-Germain, stands the **Relais Odéon,** a Belle Époque bistro whose stylishly painted exterior, decked with floral mosaics and a hanging sign, is an excellent example of art Nouveau (see **Fine Arts,** p. 17).

Farther down this passageway, on the top floor of the building on your left, was the site of the Revolutionary-era clandestine press that published Marat's *L'Ami du Peuple.* Marat was assassinated by Charlotte Corday in the bathtub of his home, which once stood where the courtyard meets rue de l'Ancienne Comédie. The poet Baudelaire was born at 15, rue Hautefeuille, just off pl. St-André-des-Arts.

The bd. St-Germain's cafés have long been gathering places for literary and artistic notables. **Les Deux Magots,** 6, pl. St-Germain-des-Prés, is named for two porcelain figures that adorned a Chinese silk and imports store at this spot in the 19th century. Converted into a café in 1875, the Deux Magots had become, by 1885, a favorite hangout of Verlaine, Rimbaud, and Mallarmé (see **Classic Cafés,** p. 128). Forty years later, it attracted Surrealists Breton and Artaud as well as Picasso, Léger, and Gide.

Established in 1890, **the Café du Flore**, 172, bd. St-Germain, was made famous in the 1940s and 50s by literati Sartre, Camus, and Prévert (see **Classic Cafés**, p. 128).

The nearby **Église de St-Germain-des-Prés**, 3, pl. St-Germain-des-Prés (tel. 01 43 25 41 71), is the oldest standing church in Paris. *(Open daily 8am-7:30pm. Information office open Tu-Sa 10:30am-noon and 2:30-6:45pm. M: St-Germain-des-Prés.)* King Childebert I commissioned the first church on this site to hold relics he had looted from the Holy Land. Completed in 558, it was consecrated by St. Germain, Bishop of Paris, on the very day of King Childebert's death—and not a moment too soon: the king had to be buried inside the church's walls.

The rest of the church's history reads like an architectural Book of Job. Sacked by the Normans and rebuilt three times, the present-day church dates from the 11th century. It served as a Benedictine monastery long before it was turned into a state prison in 1674. On June 30, 1789, the Revolution seized the prison in a sort of dress rehearsal for the storming of the Bastille. The church then did a brief stint as a saltpeter mill and in 1794, 15 tons of gunpowder that had been stored in the abbey exploded. The ensuing fire devastated the church artwork and treasures, including much of its renowned monastic library. Baron Haussmann destroyed the last remains of the deteriorating abbey walls and gates when he extended rue de Rennes to the front of the church and created place St-Germain-des-Prés. Yet the church has maintained an air of sanctity throughout, despite its centuries of wear. The magnificent interior, painted in shades of terra-cotta and deep green with gold, was restored in the 19th century. There is a millennium's worth of clashing architectural detail: the Romanesque pillars, hidden stonework in the side chapels, medieval shrines, and 17th-century vaulting. In the second chapel on the right inside the church you'll find a stone marking the interred heart of 17th-century philosopher René Descartes (see **Language and Literature**, p. 20), who died of pneumonia at the frigid court of Queen Christina of Sweden, and an altar dedicated to the victims of the September 1793 massacre, in which 186 Parisians were slaughtered in the courtyard. Pick up one of the free maps of the church with information in English on St-Germain's history, artifacts, and frequent concerts. As in most medieval churches, built to accommodate an age without microphones, the acoustics are wonderful. (See **Classical Music, Opera, and Dance**, p. 239).

Moving north from bd. St-Germain toward the Seine, you'll come upon some of the most tangled streets in central Paris. Haussmann retired before he could figure out a way to extend rue de Rennes across the Seine to meet up with rue de Louvre. Today the maze of streets on the rue de Seine, rue Mazarine, rue Bonaparte, and rue Dauphine is home to art galleries and specialty stores featuring decorative arts, home furnishings, books, manuscripts, and comics.

France's most acclaimed art school, the **École Nationale Supérieure des Beaux Arts** (ENSBA), 14, rue Bonaparte (tel. 01 47 03 50 00; http://www.ensba.fr; M: St-Germain-des-Prés), at quai Malaquais, was founded by Napoleon in 1811 and soon became the stronghold of French academic painting and sculpture. The current building, the Palais des Études, was finished in 1838 in a gracious style much like that of the nearby Institut de France. The public is not permitted to tour the building itself nor to prowl around its gated courtyard, but you can get a look at the next Léger or Delacroix at the changing public shows in the Exhibition Hall at 13, quai Malaquais. If you have the talent to be the one on display, the school admits foreign students (call 01 47 03 50 65 for application information).

Just one block to the east on the quais, the **Palais de l'Institut de France**, pl. de l'Institut (M: Pont-Neuf), broods over the Seine beneath its famous black and gold-topped dome. This one-time school (1688-1793) and prison (1793-1805) was designed by Le Vau to lodge a college established in Cardinal Mazarin's will. The glorious building has housed the *Institut de France* since 1806. Founded in 1795, the institute was intended to be a storehouse for the nation's knowledge and a meeting place for France's greatest scholars. During the Restoration, appointment to the institute depended more on political position than talent, but since 1830 the process has been slightly more meritocratic.

SIGHTS

Academy O' Words

One of the branches of the Institut de France is the prestigious **Académie Française,** which, since its founding by Richelieu in 1635 (see p. 20), has assumed the tasks of compiling the official French dictionary and serving as guardian of the French language. Having already registered its disapproval of *le weekend (la fin de semaine), le parking (le stationnement), le walkman (le balladeur),* and other "Franglais" nonsense, the Academy recently triumphed with the passage of a constitutional amendment affirming French as the country's official language. It is so difficult to become elected to this arcane society, limited to 40 members, that Molière, Balzac, and Proust never made it. In 1981 the first woman, novelist Marguerite Yourcenar, gained membership. Influenced by the presence of more women, the Academy decided in 1998 to allow the use of feminine forms of normally masculine nouns, such as *avocat* (*avocat,* lawyer), reflecting the role of women in professions from which they were once *barred.*

Once the mint for all French coins, **Hôtel des Monnaies** next door proudly displays its austere 17th-century façade to the heart of the Left Bank. The footbridge across from the *Institut,* appropriately called the **Pont des Arts,** is celebrated by poets and artists for its delicate ironwork, its beautiful views of the Seine, and its spiritual locus at the heart of France's most prestigious Academy of Arts and Letters. Built as a toll bridge in 1803, the *pont* was first bridge to be made of iron and was built for pedestrians only. On the day it opened, 65,000 Parisians paid to walk across it; today, it is less crowded, absolutely free, and still lovely. Come here at dusk to watch the sun go down against the silhouette of Paris's most famous monuments.

■ Seventh Arrondissement: Eiffel Tower

There is virtually no Parisian glance it fails to touch at some time of day. Whatever the season, through mist and cloud, in sunshine, in rain— wherever you are, whatever the landscape, the Tower is there.

—Roland Barthes

Since the 18th century, the 7ème has stood its ground as the city's most elegant residential district. Home to the National Assembly, countless foreign embassies, the Invalides, the Musée d'Orsay, and the Eiffel Tower, this section of the Left Bank is a medley of France's diplomatic, architectural, and military achievements. You might be the only one without a uniform, gun, or cellular phone on some streets in the 7ème, where policemen and soldiers guard the area's consulates and ministries.

TO THE WEST: THE EIFFEL TOWER

Tel. 01 44 11 23 44. **Web** http://www.eiffel-tower.com. **M:** Bir Hakeim. **Open** daily June-Aug. 9am-midnight; Sept. to May 9:30am-11pm. Last lift at 10:30pm. **Admission** to 1st floor 20F, under 12 11F; 2nd floor 42F, under 12 21F; 3rd floor 59F, under 12 30F. Under 4 free.

Of the Eiffel Tower, its engineer Gustave Eiffel wrote in 1889: "France is the only country in the world with a 300m flagpole." Designed in 1889 as the tallest structure in the world, the Eiffel Tower was conceived as a monument to engineering and industry, to surpass the Egyptian pyramids in size and notoriety. Yet before construction had even begun, shockwaves of dismay reverberated through the city. In February of 1887, one month after builders broke ground on the Champ de Mars, French writers and artists, such as Guy de Maupassant, Dumas *fils,* Charles Garnier (architect of the Opéra), and the composer Gounod, published a scathing letter of protest in *Le Temps* condemning the "useless and monstrous Eiffel Tower." After the building's completion, Maupassant ate lunch every day at its ground-floor restaurant—the only place in Paris, he claimed, from which he couldn't see the offensive thing.

Nevertheless, when it was inaugurated in March, 1889, as the centerpiece of the Universal Exposition, it brought popular, if not critical, acclaim; nearly 2,000,000 people ascended the tower during the event. Numbers dwindled by comparison during the following decades. As time wore on and the 20-year property lease approached expiration, Eiffel faced the imminent destruction of his masterpiece. It survived because of its importance as a communications tower, a function Eiffel had helped cultivate in the 1890s. The radio-telegraphic center on the top of the tower worked during WWI to intercept enemy messages, including the one that led to the arrest and execution of Mata Hari, the Danish dancer accused of being a German spy.

With the 1937 World Exposition, the Eiffel Tower again became a showpiece. Eiffel himself walked humbly before it, remarking: "I ought to be jealous of that tower. She is more famous than I am." Since then, Parisians and tourists alike have reclaimed the monument, and over 150,000 people have visited this iron maiden. But while Eiffel's creation stands in part as a symbol of Paris as it once was, it is also leading the city's efforts to count down the days until the year 2000. Since April 5, 1997, exactly 1000 days before the start of the new millennium, a 100m-high clock counting down the days was placed on the Seine side of the tower. In addition, the Tower's website has links to year 2000 events in Paris and around the world.

On everything from postcards to neckties and umbrellas, Eiffel's wonder still takes the heat from some who see it as Maupassant did: an "excruciating nightmare" overrun with tourists and their trinkets. Don't believe the anti-hype, though. The tower is a wonder of design, and all those kitschy replicas are nothing like the tower in the lattice-iron flesh. It is a soft brown, not the metallic steel gray that most visitors anticipate. And despite the 18,000 pieces of iron, 2,500,000 rivets, and 9,100,000 kilograms of sheer weight that compose it, the girders appear light and elegant, especially at night, when artfully placed spotlights turn the tower into a lacy hologram.

The cheapest way to ascend the tower is by walking up the first two floors (14F). The Cinemax, a relaxing stop midway through the climb on the first floor, shows films about the tower. Posters chronicling its history are a good excuse to catch your breath and rest your legs. Visitors must take an elevator to get to the third story. Tickets can be bought from the caisse or from the coin-operated dispenser (18F). The top floor offers the obvious reward of an unparalleled view of the city, and captioned aerial photographs (in English) help you locate landmarks.

Across the river (and the **Pont d'léna**) from the Eiffel Tower are the **Trocadéro** and the **Palais de Chaillot.** Built for the 1937 World's Fair, the Palais de Chaillot's elegant, expansive terrace and gardens provide the city's best views of the tower. Save your pictures for here (see **Sights,** p. 191).

NEAR THE TOWER

Though close to the 7ème's military monuments and museums, the **Champ de Mars** (Field of Mars) celebrates the god of war in name alone. The park's name comes from its previous function as a drill ground for the adjacent École Militaire. This flower-embroidered carpet stretching from the École Militaire to the Eiffel Tower is a great place to view the tower. You'll find many groups of backpackers sprawled on the grass with bottles of wine in their hands. Travelers don't get a full night's sleep here, regardless of what you've heard; *gardiens* kick them off the grass at 3am. In 1780, Charles Montgolfier launched the first hydrogen balloon (with no basket attached) from here. During the Revolution, the park witnessed infamous civilian massacres and political demonstrations. At the champ's 1793 Festival of the Supreme Being, Robespierre proclaimed Reason the new Revolutionary religion. During the 1889, 1900, and 1937 expositions, the space was used for fairgrounds. After the 1900 Exhibition, the municipal council considered parceling off the Champ de Mars for development. They concluded that Paris needed all the open space it could get.

Louis XV created the **École Militaire** at the urging of his mistress, Mme de Pompadour, who hoped to make educated officers of "poor gentlemen." Jacques-Ange Gabriel's building first accepted students in 1773, when lottery profits and a tax on playing cards financed the school's completion. In 1784, the 15-year-old Napoleon

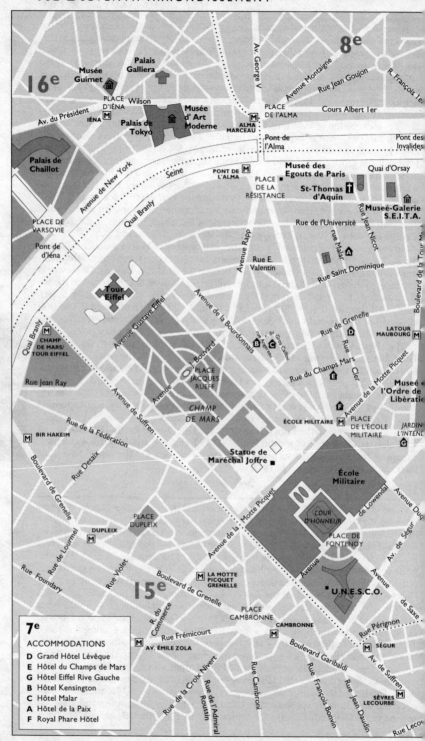

16e

Musée Guimet

Palais Galliera

PLACE D'IÉNA

IÉNA Ⓜ

Wilson

Palais de Tokyo

Musée d'Art Moderne

ALMA MARCEAU Ⓜ

Av. du Président

Palais de Chaillot

8e

Av. George V

Avenue Montaigne

Rue Jean Goujon

R. François 1er

PLACE DE L'ALMA

Cours Albert 1er

Pont de l'Alma

Pont des Invalides

PONT DE L'ALMA Ⓜ

PLACE DE LA RÉSISTANCE

Museé des Egouts de Paris

St-Thomas d'Aquin

Quai d'Orsay

Musée-Galerie S.E.I.T.A.

Avenue de New York

Seine

Quai Branly

Rue de l'Université

Rue de l'Université

Rue Jean Nicot

Rue Malar

PLACE DE VARSOVIE

Pont de d'Iéna

Avenue Rapp

Rue E. Valentin

Rue Saint Dominique

A

Boulevard de la Tour M

Tour Eiffel

Avenue Gustave Eiffel

Avenue de la Bourdonnais

Rue de Grenelle

D

Rue

LATOUR MAUBOURG Ⓜ

Quai Branly

CHAMP DE MARS/ TOUR EIFFEL Ⓜ

B

Rue du Champs Mars

Cler

E

Rue de la Motte Picquet

Musée de l'Ordre de Libératio

Rue Jean Ray

Av. de Bouvard

PLACE JACQUES RUEFF

CHAMP DE MARS

Avenue

Avenue de Suffren

F

Avenue de la Motte Picquet

JARDIN L'INTEND

G

BIR HAKEIM Ⓜ

Rue de la Fédération

ÉCOLE MILITAIRE Ⓜ

PLACE DE L'ÉCOLE MILITAIRE

Rue Desaix

Statue de Maréchal Joffre

École Militaire

Boulevard de Grenelle

PLACE DUPLEIX

DUPLEIX Ⓜ

Rue de la Motte Picquet

COUR D'HONNEUR

de Lowendal

Avenue Duq

Rue de Lourmel

Rue Violet

PLACE DE FONTENOY

Av. de Ségur

Avenue

Rue Foundary

Boulevard de Grenelle

LA MOTTE PICQUET GRENELLE Ⓜ

Avenue

U.N.E.S.C.O.

de Saxe

15e

R. du Commerce

Rue Frémicourt

PLACE CAMBRONNE

Rue Pérignon

SÉGUR Ⓜ

AV. ÉMILE ZOLA Ⓜ

CAMBRONNE Ⓜ

Boulevard Garibaldi

Av. de Suffren

Rue de la Croix Nivert

Rue de l'Admiral Roussin

Rue Cambroni

Rue François Bonvin

Rue Jean Daudin

SÈVRES LECOURBE Ⓜ

Rue Lecou

7e

ACCOMMODATIONS

D Grand Hôtel Lévêque
E Hôtel du Champs de Mars
G Hôtel Eiffel Rive Gauche
B Hôtel Kensington
C Hôtel Malar
A Hôtel de la Paix
F Royal Phare Hôtel

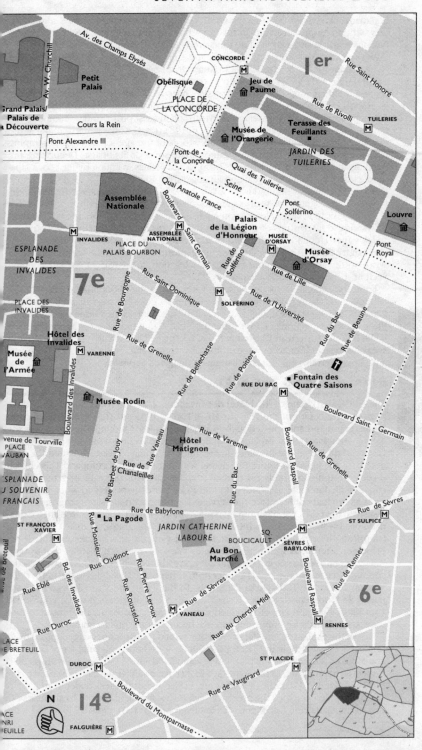

Av. des Champs Elysés

Av. W. Churchill

Rue Saint Honoré

Petit Palais

CONCORDE Ⓜ

I er

Obélisque

Jeu de 🏛 Paume

Rue de Rivoli

PLACE DE LA CONCORDE

Grand Palais/ Palais de a Découverte

Cours la Rein

Pont Alexandre III

Musée de 🏛 l'Orangerie

Terasse des Feuillants

TUILERIES Ⓜ

JARDIN DES TUILERIES

Pont de la Concorde

Quai des Tuileries

Seine

Quai Anatole France

Boulevard Saint Germain

Assemblée Nationale

Pont Solférino

Louvre 🏛

INVALIDES Ⓜ

ASSEMBLÉE NATIONALE Ⓜ

PLACE DU PALAIS BOURBON

Palais de la Légion d'Honneur

MUSÉE D'ORSAY

Pont Royal

Musée d'Orsay 🏛

ESPLANADE DES INVALIDES

Rue de Solférino

Rue de Lille

7e

Rue Saint Dominique

PLACE DES INVALIDES

Rue de Bourgogne

SOLFÉRINO Ⓜ

Rue de l'Université

Rue du Bac

Rue de Beaune

Hôtel des Invalides

VARENNE Ⓜ

Rue de Grenelle

Rue de Bellechasse

Rue de Poitiers

RUE DU BAC Ⓜ

🛈

Fontain des Quatre Saisons

Musée de l'Armée 🏛

Boulevard des Invalides

Musée Rodin 🏛

Rue Barbet de Jouy

Rue Vaneau

Hôtel Matignon

Rue de Varenne

Boulevard Raspall

Boulevard Saint Germain

Rue de Grenelle

venue de Tourville PLACE VAUBAN

Rue de Chanaleilles

Rue du Bac

Rue de Sèvres

SPLANADE U SOUVENIR FRANCAIS

Rue de Babylone

ST SULPICE

ST FRANÇOIS XAVIER Ⓜ

Rue Monsieur

La Pagode

JARDIN CATHERINE LABOURE

SQ. BOUCICAULT

SÈVRES BABYLONE Ⓜ

Rue Eblé

Rue Oudinot

Rue Pierre Leroux

Au Bon Marché

Rue de Rennes

6e

Bd. des Invalides

Rue Rousselot

Rue de Sèvres

Boulevard Raspall

Rue Duroc

VANEAU Ⓜ

Rue du Cherche Midi

RENNES Ⓜ

LACE E BRETEUIL

DUROC Ⓜ

ST PLACIDE Ⓜ

Rue de Vaugirard

N

14e

Boulevard du Montparnasse

ACE NRI EUILLE

FALGUIÈRE Ⓜ

Bonaparte arrived from Corsica to enroll. A few weeks later he presented administrators with a comprehensive plan for the school's reorganization. The building still belongs to the army today, and no tours are available to the public.

As the École Militaire's architectural and spiritual antithesis, **UNESCO** (United Nations Educational, Scientific, and Cultural Organization), 7, pl. de Fontenoy (tel. 01 45 68 03 59 or 01 45 68 16 42; http://www.unesco.org; M: Ségur), occupies the Y-shaped building across the way. *(Bookstore open M-F 9am-1pm and 2-6pm. Exhibition hours vary.)* Established to foster science and culture throughout the world, the agency developed a reputation for waste, cronyism, and Marxist propaganda, prompting the U.S., the U.K., and Singapore to withdraw in 1984 (the U.K. has plans to rejoin at the end of 1998). In so doing, they withdrew 30% of the agency's budget, cramping UNESCO's propensity for spending inordinate sums on its image. Decorating the building and its garden are ceramics by Miró and Artigas, painting by Picasso, a Japanese garden, a meditation area, and an angel from the façade of a Nagasaki church destroyed by nuclear bomb during WWII. UNESCO often mounts free rotating exhibitions of photography as well as exhibits on art, science, and culture.

If your visit to UNESCO leaves you ready to serve a greater cause, the organization offers unpaid internships of three to six months for university graduates. You must speak either French or English and be a citizen of a member country; if you aren't, you can try through a university. (For more information check the website above or write, to the attention of your country's delegation, to UNESCO PER-Staff Training Section, 1 rue Miollis, 75732 Paris).

From the École Militaire, av. Bosquet takes you to rue St-Dominique's myriad restaurants and *pâtisseries,* while rue Cler features a colorful street market (see **Food Markets,** p. 104). At the end of av. Bosquet, by the Seine, is the **Musée des Égouts de Paris** (Sewer Museum; see **Museums,** p. 244). A few blocks west along the river you'll find the **American Church in Paris,** 65, quai d'Orsay, which helps out English speakers in search of accommodations, jobs, counseling, cultural programs, sports, and support groups (see **English-Language Religious Services,** p. 74).

INVALIDES AND THE EAST

The gold-leafed dome of the **Hôtel des Invalides,** 2, av. de Tourville (M: Invalides), shines at the center of the 7ème. In 1670, Louis XIV decided to "construct a royal home, grand and spacious enough to receive all old or wounded officers and soldiers." Architect Liberal Bruand's building accepted its first wounded in 1674, and veterans still live in the Invalides today. Jules Hardouin-Mansart provided the final design for the **Église St-Louis,** the chapel within the Invalides complex. This church received Napoleon's body for funeral services in 1840, 19 years after the former emperor died in exile. His body was said to be perfectly preserved when exhumed from its original coffin before the service. Napoleon's ornate sarcophagus, now on display in the *hôtel,* wasn't completed for 20 more years. The green, tree-lined **Esplanade des Invalides** runs from the *hôtel* to the **Pont Alexandre,** a bridge (with gilded lampposts) from which you can catch a great view of the Invalides and the Seine. **Napoleon's tomb,** as well as the **Musée de l'Armée, Musée d'Histoire Contemporaine,** and **Musée de l'Ordre de Liberation,** are housed within the Invalides museum complex (see **Museums,** p. 221). Enter from either pl. des Invalides to the north or pl. Vauban and av. de Tourville to the south. To the left of the Tourville entrance, the **Jardin de l'Intendant** provides a shady place to rest on a bench when you've had your fill of guns and emperors. Lined with foreign cannons, the ditch used to be a moat and still makes it impossible to leave by any but the official entrance.

East of the Esplanade, the **Palais Bourbon** would probably not be recognized by its original occupants. Built in 1722 for the Duchesse de Bourbon, daughter of Louis XIV and Mme de Montespan, the palace was remodeled after 1750 to align with pl. de la Concorde, directly across the Seine (see **Eighth Arrondissement,** p. 166). Sold to the Prince of Cond in 1764, the building grew in size and ornateness under its new ownership. Napoleon erected the present Greek revival façade in 1807 to harmonize with that of the Madeleine (see **Eighth Arrondissement,** p. 166). From 1940 to 1944, the

Nazis occupied the palace. During the Liberation, parts of it were damaged and many of the library's books were destroyed. Today, the palace is the well-guarded home of the French parliament, the **Assemblée Nationale,** 33, quai d'Orsay (tel. 01 40 63 63 08; http://www.assemblée-nat.fr). *(Open Oct.-June while the Assembly is in session. Tours Sa 10am, 2, and 3pm. Free.)* Machine-gun-toting police stationed every few yards are ostensibly there to prevent a replay of the unsuccessful 1934 Fascist coup, during which rioters stormed the building. Today visitors are allowed to attend parliamentary sessions, but foreigners need to write in advance for permission, should expect a one-hour security check before entering the chamber, and will be required to present their passports. Appropriate dress is required. The security check does not apply to those who take free guided tours (in French, with pamphlet in English) of the Assembly's chambers, which includes a visit to the **Salon Delacroix** and the library (both spectacularly painted by Eugène Delacroix). The library's holdings include the original transcripts of Joan of Arc's trial. The tour continues in the Assembly chamber, the **Salle de Séances,** where the *Président du conseil* presides. Behind him, a framed tapestry of Raphael's *School of Athens* depicts the republic of philosopher-kings. Members of the political right and left sit to the right and left of the president's seat. The **Kiosque de l'Assemblée Nationale,** 4, rue Aristide-Briand (tel. 01 40 63 61 21), provides more information as well as the standard collection of souvenirs. *(Open Sept.-July M-F 9:30am-7pm, Sa 9:30am-1pm; Aug. M-F 10am-noon and 2-5pm. AmEx, MC, V.)*

At the corner of rue de Lille and rue de Bellechasse is the elegant **Hôtel de Salm,** built in 1786 by the architect Rousseau for the Prince de Salm-Kyrbourg. Unable to make payment, the prince later returned it to Rousseau but continued to live there as a tenant until he was decapitated in 1794. The state raffled the *hôtel* the following year to a wealthy wig maker named Lieuthraud who presented himself as Count Beauregard until 1797, when he was jailed as a forger. The mansion was then purchased by the Swedish ambassador and his wife, *salonnière* Mme de Staël. Purchased by Napoleon in 1804, the *hôtel's* current name bears the mark of its most recent owner. Now called the **Palais de la Legion d'Honneur,** it houses the **Musée National de la Legion d'Honneur** (see **Museums,** p. 230). Although the museum's display of medals and military honoraria may not spark the interest of many tourists, admission allows a look at the 18th- and 19th-century interiors. Across the street stands the world-famous **Musée d'Orsay,** a former train station now known for its glass-and-steel elegance and immense collection of Impressionist works (see **Museums,** p. 215).

At 75, rue de Lille, Montesquieu and Marivaux frequented the literary salon of Mme de Tencin. Famous for her adventurous parties during the Regency, she once hosted a "soirée d'Adam" for which guests arrived dressed only in fig leaves. Continue down rue de Lille and turn right on rue du Bac. In the 18th century, this street marked the boundary between town and country; now it's lined with specialty stores.

The 17th-century **Église St-Thomas d'Aquin** (tel. 01 42 22 59 74), stands on rue de Gribeauval, off rue du Bac. *(Open M-F 9am-7pm, Su 9am-noon.)* Originally dedicated to St. Dominique, it was reconsecrated by Revolutionaries as the Temple of Peace. Farther south, at 55-57, rue de Grenelle, the **Fontaine des Quatre Saisons** (Fountain of Four Seasons) features a personified, seated version of the city of Paris near reclining figures of the Seine and the Marne. Bouchardon built the fountain in 1739-45 to provide water to this part of the city. Nearby at 202, bd. St-Germain, the poet Guillaume Apollinaire lived and died.

At 57, rue Varenne, which stretches toward the Invalides parallel to rue de Grenelle, you'll find the **Hôtel Matignon,** once owned by Talleyrand and now the official residence of the prime minister. The nearby **Hôtel Biron** at no. 77 was built by Gabriel in 1728. In 1904 it became an artists' pension. The French sculptor Auguste Rodin rented a studio on its ground floor in 1908. When the Ministry of Fine Arts evicted all tenants in 1910, Rodin offered to donate his works to make the *hôtel* an art museum, on the condition that he be permitted to spend his last years there. The Hôtel Biron now houses the **Musée Rodin** (see **Museums,** p. 219).

South of the Musée Rodin, at the intersection of rue de Babylone and rue Monsieur, stands **La Pagode,** a Japanese pagoda built in 1895 by the Bon Marché department store magnate M. Morin. A gift to his wife, it endures as a testament to the 19th-century Orientalist craze in France. Incidentally, the marriage lasted as long as the orientalist fad: Mme Morin left her husband for his colleague's son just prior to WWI. The building then became the scene of Sino-Japanese soirées, although these years saw a period of tension between the two countries (which deepened with Japan's conquest of Manchuria). In 1931, la Pagode opened its doors to the public, becoming a cinema and swank café where the likes of silent screen star Gloria Swanson were known to raise a glass. The theater closed during the Nazi occupation, despite the Axis allegiance. Although it reopened in 1945, it was again closed in 1998 due to a lack of funds to maintain it. A campaign to save la Pagode is underway, but for now visitors must content themselves with the pagoda's exteriors. South of rue Monsieur, along the southern edge of the 7ème, the **Bon Marché** department store that inspired the pagoda (see **Shopping,** p. 259) has no fear of closing its doors.

■ Eighth Arrondissement: The Champs-Elysées

Full of expansive mansions, expensive shops and restaurants, grand Haussmann boulevards like the Champs-Élysées, and grandiose monuments like the Arc de Triomphe, the 8ème is the area circumscribed by bd. Haussmann to the north and west and the Seine to the South. Well-known salons and boutiques of *haute couture* line fashionable streets such as the rue du Faubourg St-Honoré. Embassies crowd around the Palais de l'Elysée, the state residence of the French president. Already attractive to the bourgeoisie of the early 19th century, the neighborhood took off with the construction of boulevards Haussmann, Malesherbes, Victor Hugo, Foch, Kléber, and the others that shoot out from the Arc de Triomphe in a radiating formation known as l'Étoile (the star). The grand symmetry of the **Axe Historique,** the line that stretches from the Arc de Triomphe du Carrousel in front of the Louvre, down the Champs-Élysées to the Arc de Triomphe, and down bd. de la Grande Armée to La Défense, reflects the largesse of the 8ème's big streets, big money, and big attitude.

ARC DE TRIOMPHE AND AVENUE DES CHAMPS-ELYSÉES

Looming gloriously above the Champs-Elysées at pl. Charles de Gaulle-Étoile, the **Arc de Triomphe** (tel. 01 55 37 73 77; M: Charles-de-Gaulle-Étoile), commemorates France's military victories and military history. *(Open daily Apr.-Sept. 9:30am-11pm; Oct.-Mar. 10am-6pm. Last entry 30min. before closing. Admission 35F, ages 12-25 and seniors 23F, under 12 free. Expect lines even on weekdays. Buy your ticket in the pedestrian underpasses before going up to the ground level.)* The world's largest triumphal arch and an internationally recognized symbol of France, this grand arch was commissioned by Napoleon in 1806. When construction began, the Étoile marked the western entrance to the city through the *fermiers généraux* wall. Napoleon was exiled before the monument was completed, but Louis XVIII ordered the completion of the work in 1823 and dedicated the arch to the war in Spain and to its commander, the Duc d'Angoulême. Designed by Chalgrin, the Arc de Triomphe was consecrated in 1836, 21 years after the defeat of the Napoleon's great army. There was no consensus on what symbolic figures could cap the monument, and so it has retained its simple unfinished form. The names of Napoleon's generals and battles are engraved inside; those generals underlined died in battle. The most famous of the Arc's allegorical sculpture groups depicting the military history of France is François Rude's *Departure of the Volunteers of 1792,* commonly known as *La Marseillaise,* to the right facing the arch from the Champs-Elysées.

The Arc is primarily a military symbol. As such, the horseshoe-shaped colossus has proved a magnet to various triumphal armies. The victorious Prussians marched through in 1871, inspiring the mortified Parisians to purify the ground with fire. On July 14, 1919, however, the Arc provided the backdrop for an Allied celebration parade headed by Maréchal Foch. His memory is now honored by the boulevard that bears his name and stretches out from the west side of the Arc into the 16ème. In 1940, shocked Parisians shed tears of defeat as the Nazis goose-stepped through the Arc and down the Champs-Elysées. After four years of Nazi occupation, France was liberated by British, American, Canadian, Québecois, and French troops who marched through the Arc de Triomphe on August 26, 1944, to the roaring cheers of thousands of grateful Parisians. The **Tomb of the Unknown Soldier** has rested under the Arc since November 11, 1920. The **eternal flame** is rekindled every evening at 6:30pm, when veterans lay wreaths decorated with blue, white, and red. De Gaulle's famous cry for *Résistance,* broadcast over the BBC from his WWII exile in London in 1940, is inscribed on a brass plaque in the pavement below the Arc.

The Arc de Triomphe sits in the center of the Étoile, which in 1907 became the world's first traffic circle. Rather than risk an early and painful death by crossing the street to reach the Arc, use the underpasses on the even-numbered sides of both the Champs-Elysées and av. de la Grande-Armée. Inside the Arc, climb 205 steps up a winding staircase to the *entresol* and then 29 more to the *musée,* or tackle the lines at the elevator for a lift. The museum explains (in French) the Arc's architecture and history. Just 46 steps beyond, the **terrasse observation deck** at the top of the Arc provides an brilliant view of the Champs-Elysées, the tree-lined avenue Foch (see **Sights,** p. 189), and the Axe Historique from the Arc de Triomphe du Carrousel and the Louvre Pyramid at one end to the Grande Arche de la Défense at the other. This view is especially stunning at night.

The **avenue des Champs-Élysées** is the most famous of the 12 symmetrical avenues radiating from the huge rotary of pl. Charles de Gaulle-Étoile. No one can deny that this 10-lane wonder, flanked by cafés and luxury shops and crowned by the world's most famous arch, deserves its reputation. Le Nôtre planted trees here in 1667 to extend the Tuileries vista, completing the work begun under Marie de Médici in 1616. In 1709, the area was renamed the "Elysian Fields" because of the shade provided by the trees. During the 19th century, the Champs (as many Parisians call it) developed into a fashionable residential district. Mansions sprang up along its sides, then apartments and smart boutiques, making this strip of pavement the place to see and be seen in Paris. Balls, café-concerts, restaurants, and circuses drew enormous crowds. The *Bal Mabille* opened in 1840 at no. 51, and, at no. 25, in a somewhat more subdued setting, the charming hostess and spy Marquise de Païva entertained her famous guests.

Today, you can escape the crowds and watch the modern-day circus of tourists walk by while relaxing at **Fouquet's** (M: George V), a famous and outrageously expensive café-restaurant where French film stars ostensibly hang out. Paris's answer to Hollywood's Sunset Strip, a square in front of Fouquet's bears golden plaques with the names of favorite French recipients of the coveted César award (the French equivalent to the Oscar). Among those with names emblazoned here are Isabelle Adjani, Catherine Deneuve, and Louis Malle, director of *Au Revoir Les Enfants.* Street performers move in at night all along the Champs-Élysées, jamming to an industrial beat. During the day, anyone can enjoy the Champs's many restaurants, cinemas, and overpriced stores, planted next to airline and other commercial offices. At night, Paris's hottest dance club, **Le Queen,** 102 Champs-Élysées, features the fattest house music on the Right Bank and the most beautiful and best-dressed people in the city (and their straight friends).

FROM FASHION HOUSES TO THE GRAND & PETIT PALAIS

Six big avenues radiate from the Rond Point des Champs-Elysées. Avenue Montaigne runs southwest and shelters the houses of *haute couture* of **Christian Dior** (no. 30), **Chanel** (no. 42), and **Valentino** (nos. 17 and 19). **St-Laurent,** 77, av. George V, along with **Dolce & Gabbana** (no. 2) and **Prada** (no. 10), hold sway nearby. You may not be able to afford even the smallest bottle of Chanel (445F per 7mL), but it's fun to look. Built by the Perret brothers in 1912 with bas-reliefs by Bourdelle, the **Théâtre des Champs-Élysées,** 15, av. Montaigne (tel. 01 49 52 50 00; M: Alma-Marceau), is best known for staging the controversial premiere of Stravinsky's *Le Sacre du Print-*

SIGHTS

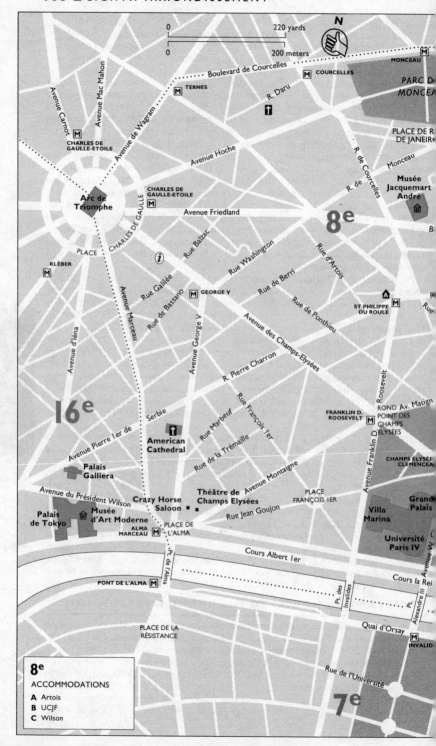

0   220 yards

0   200 meters

N

Boulevard de Courcelles

MONCEAU

COURCELLES

PARC D
MONCEA

TERNES

R. Daru

PLACE DE R
DE JANEIR

Avenue Mac Mahon

Avenue Carnot

Avenue de Wagram

CHARLES DE
GAULLE-ETOILE

Avenue Hoche

R. de Courcelles

Monceau

R. de

Musée
Jacquemart
André

Arc de
Triomphe

CHARLES DE
GAULLE-ETOILE

8e

B

PLACE

CHARLES DE GAULLE

Avenue Friedland

KLÉBER

Rue Balzac

PLACE

Rue Washington

Rue d'Artois

Rue de Berri

Rue Galilée

GEORGE V

Rue de Ponthieu

Rue

Avenue d'Iéna

Avenue Marceau

Rue de Bassano

Avenue George V

ST PHILIPPE
DU ROULE

A

P

Avenue des Champs-Elysées

R. Pierre Charron

Roosevelt

16e

Serbie

Rue Marbeuf

Rue François 1er

FRANKLIN D.
ROOSEVELT

ROND Av. Matign
POINT DES
CHAMPS
ELYSEES

Avenue Pierre 1er de

American
Cathedral

Rue de la Trémaille

Avenue Franklin D

CHAMPS ELYSÉE
CLEMENCEA

Palais
Galliera

Avenue Montaigne

PLACE
FRANÇOIS IER

Grand
Palais

Avenue du Président Wilson

Crazy Horse
Saloon

Théâtre de
Champs Elysées

Rue Jean Goujon

Villa
Marina

Palais
de Tokyo

Musée
d'Art Moderne

ALMA
MARCEAU

PLACE DE
L'ALMA

Université
Paris IV

PONT DE L'ALMA

Pt. de l'Alma

Cours Albert 1er

Pt. des Invalides

Cours la Rei

Avenue W. C

Alexandre III

Pt.

Quai d'Orsay

INVALID

PLACE DE LA
RÉSISTANCE

Rue de l'Université

7e

8e

ACCOMMODATIONS

A Artois
B UCJF
C Wilson

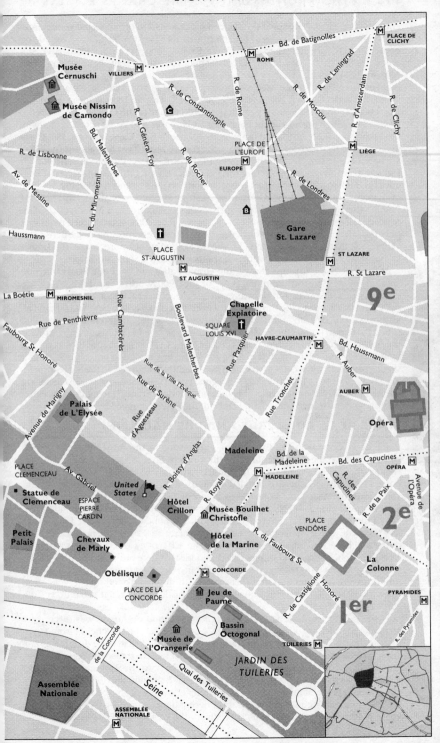

emps, where Nijinsky humped the stage in mock imitation of carnal and vernal eroti-cism. The three large *salles* still host performances (tickets 60-500F). Around the corner from the theater, the **Crazy Horse Saloon,** long famous for its cabaret, still entertains fans of the "Art du Nu" (art of the nude). **Pershing Hall,** 49, rue Pierre Char-ron, is a 113-year-old, five-story piece of America. Given to the U.S. government, the building has allegedly been used as a brothel, a brawling bar, a casino, a black-market exchange, and a Council Travel office. Now closed, it awaits its next incarnation.

Avenue Montaigne's counterpart on the northern side of the Champs-Elysées is the high-fashion, high-priced **rue du Faubourg St-Honoré.** You could spend hours win-dow-shopping at the lavish and outrageous vitrines of **Karl Lagerfeld** (no. 19), **Cart-ier** (no. 23), **Hermès** (no. 24), **Guy Laroche** (no. 30), and **Yves St-Laurent** (no. 38).

The guards pacing around the house at the corner of av. de Marigny and rue du Faubourg St-Honoré are protecting the **Palais de l'Élysée** (M: Champs-Elysées-Clem-enceau). Built in 1718, the *palais* was later home to the Marquis de Marigny, brother of Madame de Pompadour. During the Restoration, July Monarchy, and Second Empire, the Elysée was used to house royal guests. Since 1870, it has served as state residence of the French president, now Jacques Chirac. Although entrance requires a personal invitation, the persistent visitor can catch a glimpse of the gardens. The Union Jack flying overhead at no. 35, rue du Faubourg-St-Honoré, marks the British Embassy. At 2, av. Gabriel, the American Embassy flies the Stars and Stripes.

At the foot of the Champs-Elysées, the **Grand Palais** and the **Petit Palais** face one another on av. Winston Churchill. Built for the 1900 World's Fair, both *palais* are examples of Art Nouveau architecture; the glass over steel and stone composition of the Grand Palais makes the top look like a giant greenhouse. The Petit and Grand Pal-ais host exhibitions on architecture, painting, sculpture, and French history. The Grand Palais also houses the **Palais de la Découverte** (see **Museums,** p. 231). Around the time that the palaces were built, the first stone of Pont Alexandre III was placed by the czar's son, Nicholas II. It made a stir as the first bridge to cross the Seine in a single span. Today it is considered the most beautiful bridge across the Seine, provid-ing a noble axis with the Invalides (see **Sights,** p. 164). The statues on pilasters facing the Right Bank represent Medieval France and Modern France; facing the Left Bank, they show Renaissance France and France of the Belle Époque.

PLACE DE LA CONCORDE AND THE MADELEINE

Place de la Concorde (M: Concorde), Paris's largest and most infamous public square, forms the eastern terminus of the Champs-Elysées. With your back to Av. Gabriel, the Tuileries Gardens are to your left, while across the river you see the gold-domed Invalides and the Greek-styled columns of the Assemblée Nationale. Behind you stands the Madeleine. Constructed between 1757 and 1777 to provide a home for a monument to Louis XV, this vast area soon became place de la Révolution, the site of the guillotine that severed 1,343 necks. On Sunday, January 21, 1793, Louis XVI was beheaded by guillotine on a site near where ˙e Brest statue now stands. The celebrated heads of Louis XVI, Marie-Antoinette, Cl .otte Corday (Marat's assassin), Lavoisier, Robespierre, and others rolled into bask╵ ╷ here and were held up to the cheering crowds who packed the pavement. In 19╵3, hundreds of French (and the American ambassador) honored this event with flowers placed on the very spot. After the Reign of Terror, the square was optimistically renamed place de la Con-corde (place of Harmony).

At the center of pl. de la Concorde, the **Obélisque de Luxor** was offered by Mehemet Ali, Viceroy of Egypt, to Charles X in 1829. Getting the obelisk from Egypt to the center of Paris was no simple task; a canal to the Nile had to be dug, the mono-lith had to be transported by sea, and a special boat built to transport it up the Seine. Erected in 1836, Paris's oldest monument dates back to the 13th century BC and recalls the deeds of Ramses II. At night the obelisk, fountains, and turn-of-the-century cast-iron lamps are illuminated, creating a romantic glow. Don't be surprised if you see a commercial being shot on location here. Much favored by film crews for its views of Paris's monuments (and especially for the view of the Eiffel Tower in relief against the Paris sky), this square has been featured in many films, such as the famous dream sequence in Gene Kelly and Stanley Donen's *An American in Paris*. On Bastille Day (July 14) a military parade marches through pl. de la Concorde (usually around 10am) and down the Champs-Élysées to the Arc de Triomphe led by the President of the Republic. In the evening, a marvelous fireworks display lights up the sky over pl. de la Concorde. If you try to ask a French person about "Bastille Day," you may encounter a blank stare. In France, July 14 is known as La Fête Nationale. At the end of August, the Tour de France finalists pull into the home stretch on the Champs-Élysées and the pl. de la Concorde. Get there early for a view of the cyclists.

Flanking the Champs-Elysées at pl. de la Concorde stand the Guillaume Coustou 18th-century **Cheveaux de Marly,** which were originally designed for Marly, Louis XIV's château near Versailles. Also known as *Africans Mastering the Numidian Horses,* the original sculptures are now in the Louvre to protect them from the effects of city pollution. Perfect replicas graciously hold their places on the Concorde. Eight large statues representing France's major cities also grace the *place*. Juliette Drouet, Victor Hugo's mistress, allegedly posed for the town of Strasbourg.

Directly north of pl. de la Concorde, like two sentries guarding the gate to the Madeleine, stand the **Hôtel de Crillon** (on the left) and the **Hôtel de la Marine** (on the right). Architect Jacques-Ange Gabriel built the impressive colonnaded façades between 1757 and 1770. On February 16, 1778, the Franco-American treaties were signed here, making France the first European nation to recognize the independence of the United States of America. Chateaubriand lived in the Hôtel de Crillon between 1805 and 1807. Today it is one of the most expensive, elegant hotels in Paris, with guests such as Michael Jackson. Whatever. If you're dressed for the occasion, you can step inside and have an espresso (30F) in the plush salon and check out the decor by Sonia Rykiel. At 9, rue Royale, **Christofle** has been producing works in gold and crystal since 1830. Next door, at 11, rue Royale, stands the famed crystal shop **Lalique,** named after the Art Nouveau artist who foreshadowed it. World-renowned **Maxim's** restaurant, 3, rue Royale, won't even allow you a peek into what was once Richelieu's home. On the other side of the Crillon **Le Buddha Bar,** 8, rue Boissy d'Anglas, boasts outrageous prices and an equally exclusive clientele of models, designers, and actors, including Naomi Campbell and Isabelle Adjani.

Mirrored by the Assemblée Nationale across the Seine, the **Madeleine** (tel. 01 44 51 69 00; M: Madeleine), formally called Église Ste-Marie-Madeleine (Mary Magdalene), was begun in 1764 by Louis XV and modeled after a Greek temple. *(Open daily 7:30am-7pm. Occasional organ and chamber concerts.)* Construction was halted during the Revolution, when the Cult of Reason proposed transforming the building into a bank, a theater, or a courthouse. Completed in 1842, the structure stands alone in the medley of Parisian churches, distinguished by its four ceiling domes that light the interior in lieu of windows, 52 exterior Corinthian columns, and the lack of even one cross. An immense sculpture of the ascension of Mary Magdalene, the church's namesake, adorns the altar. Marcel Proust spent most of his childhood nearby at 9, bd. Malesherbes, which might explain his penchant for his aunt Léonie's *madeleines* with tea (see **Illiers-Combray,** p. 289). You can stop and eat a few *madeleines,* pick up some chocolate *macarons,* or buy some French honey and jam at the world-famous foodshop, **Fauchon,** 24-30, pl. de la Madeleine, just behind the church (see **Gift Ideas,** p. 260). Do not mistake the Madeleine with Ludwig Bemelman's 1939 children's classic, *Madeline,* who lived in Paris with Miss Clavel and twelve girls, all in a line.

CHAPELLE EXPIATOIRE AND PARC MONCEAU

Place Louis XVI, on rue Pasquier below bd. Haussmann, includes the improbably large **Chapelle Expiatoire** (tel. 01 42 65 35 80), its monuments to Marie-Antoinette and Louis XVI, and a lovely park with benches. *(Open Apr.-Sept. Tu 9:30am-1pm and 2-6pm; Oct.-Nov. Tu 10am-1pm and 2-5pm; Nov.-Jan. Tu 10am-1pm and 2-4pm.)* Once affiliated with the Madeleine, a cemetery was opened on the site in 1722. During the Revolution, victims of the guillotine, including the King and Queen, were dumped here. Although Louis XVIII had his brother and sister-in-law's remains removed to St-Denis in 1815, Marat's assassin Charlotte Corday and Louis XVI's cousin Philippe-Égalité (who voted for the king's death only to be beheaded himself) are buried on either side of the staircase. Statues of the expiatory King and Queen, with their crowns at their feet, stand inside the Chapelle. Their last letters are engraved in French on the base of the sculptures.

A few blocks north, the **Gare St-Lazare's** romantic platforms and iron-vaulted canopy are not to be missed by train riders and fans of Monet's impressionist painting *La Gare St-Lazare* (now at Harvard's Fogg Art Museum) and Émile Zola's novel about the station and its trains, *La Bête Humaine*. To the north of the train station is pl. de Dublin, the setting for Gustave Caillebotte's famous urban impressionist painting, *A Rainy Day in Paris* (now at the Art Institute of Chicago).

The **Parc Monceau** (M: Monceau or Courcelles), an expansive natural urban refuge guarded by gold-tipped, wrought-iron gates, borders the elegant bd. de Courcelles. *(Open Apr.-Oct. 7am-10pm; Nov.-Mar. 7am-8pm. Gates close 15min. earlier.)* While the Jardin du Luxembourg emphasizes presentation over relaxation, the Parc Monceau is a pastoral setting for kids to play and parents to unwind or read in the shade. This park is also popular with joggers. The painter Carmontelle designed the park for the Duc d'Orléans, and it was completed by Haussmann in 1862. The *Rotonde de Monceau* is a remnant of the *fermiers généraux* wall of the 1780s. A tollhouse designed to enforce customs duties rather than to keep out invaders, the wall and its fortifications reflected their creator's penchant for ornament. An array of architectural follies—a pyramid, a covered bridge, an East Asian pagoda, Dutch windmills, and Roman ruins—make this spot one of Paris's most whimsical for lunch on a bench or for an afternoon with your children. As in other Parisian parks, frolicking, laying, or playing on the grass is forbidden and you are likely to be told to move *tout de suite* by the strangely clairvoyant park police.

In the days of pre-revolutionary Russia, many Russian aristocrats owned vacation homes in France. Built in 1860, the onion-domed **Église Russe,** also known as **Cathédrale Alexandre-Nevski,** 12, rue Daru (tel. 01 42 27 37 34; M: Ternes), is a Russian Eastern Orthodox church. *(Open Tu and F 3-5pm. Services Su at 10am.)* The gold domes, spectacular from the outside, are equally beautiful on the inside. They were intricately painted by artists from St. Petersburg. Restoration is expected to resume in the near future.

■ Ninth Arrondissement: Opéra

The boulevards and *quartier* surrounding the Opéra Garnier are simply called *l'Opéra*. On the southernmost border of the 9ème, the Opéra is the arrondissement's most prosperous and visited area with a big city feel. For those less interested in the high art offerings of the Garnier's ballets, concerts, and opera, the 9ème is filled with cinemas and is home to the legendary Olympia, one of Paris's most famous concert stages for American, European, and Brazilian pop, jazz, and rock performances. Near the Opéra, many large banks and chic boutiques greet their affluent clientele while the American Express office exchanges traveler's checks and cash for centime-less travelers (see **Money,** p. 35). Perhaps the busiest sites of the 9ème, however, are the arrondissement's department stores Au Printemps and Galeries Lafayette, where thousands of Parisians and tourists seek out the fairest of the(m)all (see **Department Stores,** p. 259).

OPÉRA GARNIER AND SURROUNDINGS

Emerging from the Opéra metro station, your eyes will be quickly drawn to the grandiose and grand **Opéra Garnier** (tel. 01 44 73 13 99; for recorded information 08 36 69 78 68; for reservations 08 44 73 13 00; M: Opéra) in the middle of pl. de l'Opéra. *(Open daily 10am-5pm, last entry 4:30pm. Admission 30F, ages 10-16, students and 60 and over 20F. Tours 60F; students, ages 10-16, or above 60 45F; under 10 25F. For info on tours, call 01 40 01 25 14. For concert info, see* **Classical Music, Opera, and Dance,** *p. 239.)*

Designed by Charles Garnier under Napoleon III in the showy eclecticism of the Second Empire, the Opera is perhaps most famous as home to the legend of the Phantom of the Opéra. Towering high above the *grands boulevards* of the southern 9ème, the building epitomizes both the Second Empire's ostentation and its rootlessness; a mix of styles and odd details ties it to no formal tradition. Queried as to whether his building was in the style of Louis XIV, Louis XV, or Louis XVI, Garnier responded that his creation belonged to Napoleon III. The interior of the Opéra, with its grand staircase, golden foyer, and five-tiered auditorium, was designed as a stage for not only opera performance but also for 19th-century bourgeois social life. As Mary Cassat's paintings and Edith Wharton's novels illustrate, the balconies and galleries were designed so that audience members could watch each other as much as the action on stage.

Garnier's design outshined hundreds of competing plans in an 1861 competition, including the entry of the "Pope of Architects" Viollet-le-Duc, who restored Nôtre-Dame. Garnier was virtually unknown at the time, and the commission made him famous. Opened in 1875, the magnificent interiors are adorned with Gobelin tapestries, gilded mosaics, and a six-ton chandelier that fell on the audience in 1896. In 1964, Chagall was commissioned to paint the ceiling. Since 1989, when the new Opéra de la Bastille was inaugurated, most opera have been performed at the Bastille, while the Opera Garnier has been used mainly for ballets. In 1992, Rudolf Nureyev made his last public appearance here shortly before his death.

Guided tours are available in several languages, but they are in high demand during the summer months so it is best to call ahead. Ask about availability at the entrance when you arrive. It is suggested that you call up to three months in advance. The Opéra also houses a **library** and **museum** on the history of opera and dance that focus particularly on Nijinksy and the Ballet Russe, Diaghilev's innovative troupe that liberated classical dance from fluffy Romanticism with such controversial, erotic 20th-century works as Stravinsky's *Firebird* and *Rite of Spring* (open daily 10am-noon and 2-5pm).

For a filmic introduction to Paris's monuments before you strike out across the city, the nearby **Paristoric,** 11bis, rue Scribe (tel. 01 42 66 62 06), is a high-tech slide show montage showing highlights of Paris's monuments and cultural history with narrative and musical accompaniment. *(Shows daily on the hour 9am-8pm. Admission 50F, students and children 30F.)* Covering two-millennia in 45 minutes, the show really does a good job of contextualizing the city within history, art, and architecture.

To the right of the Opéra, the **Café de la Paix,** 12, bd. des Capucines, is the quintessential 19th-century-café. Like the Opéra, it was designed by Garnier and today caters to the after-theater crowd and anyone else who doesn't mind paying 30F for coffee (see **Classic Cafés,** p. 128). Cartier's jewels glitter at 11, bd. des Capucines. Farther down bd. des Capucines, the giant red glowing letters of the **Olympia** music hall (tel. 01 47 42 25 49) signal the place where Edith Piaf achieved her fame. Popular artists, like the Brazilian musician Gilberto Gil, still perform here. Check posters for concerts. Boulevard des Capucines, bd. des Italiens, and bd. Montmartre overflow with popular restaurant, cafés, cinemas, and shops. In the 1780s, the American ambassador, Thomas Jefferson, lived near what is now the intersection of bd. Haussmann and rue du Helder. The carnivalesque **Musée Grévin,** 10, bd. Montmartre, is a French wax museum (see **Museums,** p. 229), with figures from Royalty and the Revolution. West of the Opéra, the department stores **Au Printemps** and **Galeries Lafayette** stand on the bd. Haussmann amid other clothing and shoe shops (see **Department Stores,** p. 259).

NORTH OF OPÉRA

Built at the end of the 19th century in Italian Renaissance style, **Église de la Sainte-Trinité** on rue de la Chaussée (M: Trinité) has beautiful, painted vaults and is surrounded by a fountained park with tree-shaded benches. The **Musée Gustave Moreau,** 14, rue de La Rochefoucauld, is housed in the painter's house and studio (see **Museums,** p. 231). Farther east, on pl. Kossuth, **Église Nôtre-Dame-de-Lorette** (M: Nôtre-Dame-de-Lorette) was built in 1836 to "the glory of the Virgin Mary." This

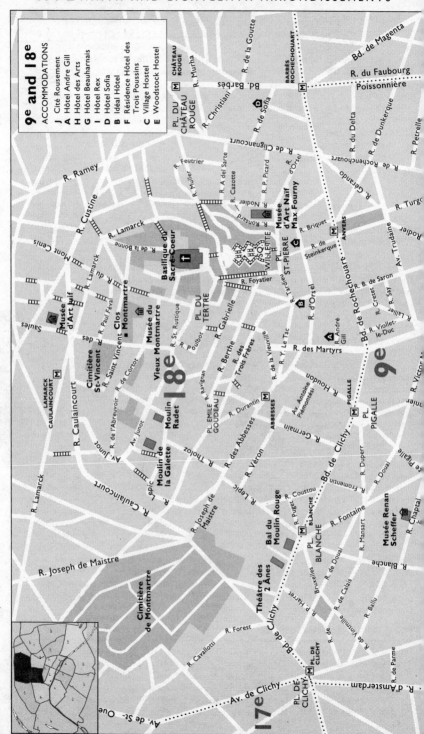

9e and 18e

ACCOMMODATIONS

- J Cité Rousement
- A Hôtel Andre Gill
- H Hôtel des Arts
- G Hôtel Beauharnais
- I Hôtel Rex
- D Hôtel Sofia
- B Idéal Hôtel
- F Résidence Hôtel des Trois Poussins
- C Village Hostel
- E Woodstock Hostel

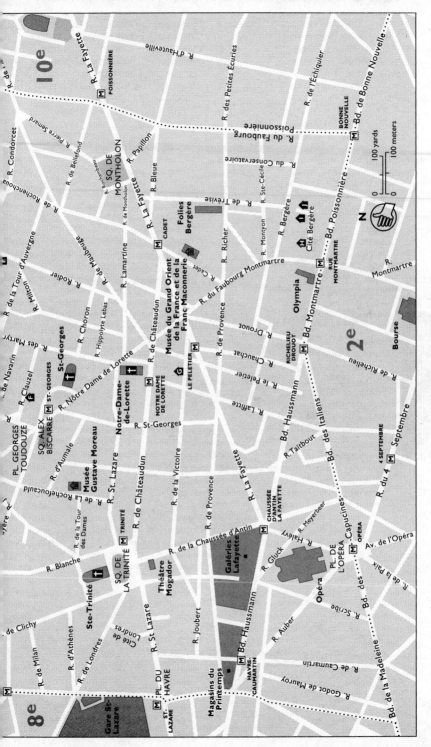

10e

R. La Fayette
POISSONNIÈRE

R. d'Hauteville

R. de l'Échiquier

Bd. de Bonne Nouvelle

R. des Petites Écuries

R. Condorcet

R. Pierre Semard

SQ. DE MONTHOLON

R. de Bellefond

R. de Rochambeau

R. de Montholon

R. Papillon

R. La Fayette

R. Bleue

R. du Conservatoire

R. du Faubourg Poissonnière

BONNE NOUVELLE

Bd. Poissonnière

R. de la Tour d'Auvergne

R. de Maubeuge

R. Rodier

R. Lamartine

Folies Bergère

CADET

R. de Trévise

R. Ste-Cécile

R. Richer

R. Montyon

Cité Bergère

Bd. Montmartre

N

R. de Navarin

R. des Martyrs

R. Choron

R. Hippolyte Lebas

R. de Châteaudun

Musée du Grand Orient de la France et de la Franc Maçonnerie

R. Cadet

R. du Faubourg Montmartre

R. de Provence

R. Drouot

Olympia

RICHELIEU DROUOT

Bd. Montmartre

RUE MONTMARTRE

R. Montmartre

100 yards
100 meters

R. Clauzel

St-Georges

ST. GEORGES

Notre-Dame-de-Lorette

NOTRE DAME DE LORETTE

LE PELETIER

R. de Provence

R. de Châteaudun

R. de la Victoire

R. Le Peletier

R. Chauchat

R. de Richelieu

2e

Bourse

PL. GEORGES TOUDOUZE

SQ. ALEX BISCARRE

R. Notre Dame de Lorette

R. St-Georges

R. Laffitte

R. Taitbout

Bd. Haussmann

Bd. des Italiens

R. d'Aumale

Musée Gustave Moreau

R. de La Rochefoucauld

R. St. Lazare

R. de la Victoire

R. La Fayette

R. de la Tour des Dames

Théâtre Mogador

R. de la Chaussée d'Antin

CHAUSSÉE D'ANTIN LA FAYETTE

R. Meyerbeer

R. du 4 Septembre

4 SEPTEMBRE

R. Blanche

Ste-Trinité

TRINITÉ

SQ. DE LA TRINITÉ

Galeries Lafayette

R. Gluck

R. Halévy

OPÉRA

PL. DE L'OPÉRA

Av. de l'Opéra

de Clichy

R. de Milan

R. d'Athènes

R. de Londres

Cité de Londres

R. St. Lazare

R. Joubert

Opéra

R. Scribe

R. Auber

Bd. des Capucines

R. de la Paix

8e

Gare St-Lazare

ST. LAZARE

PL. DU HAVRE

Magasins du Printemps

Bd. Haussmann

HAVRE-CAUMARTIN

R. de Caumartin

R. Godot de Mauroy

Bd. de la Madeleine

Neoclassical church is filled with statues of the saints and frescoes of scenes from the life of Mary. Built in 1840, rue Nôtre-Dame-de-Lorette was less saintly than its name. A thoroughfare of ill-repute in the late 1960s, this street became the debauched hang-out of Émile Zola's *Nana* (whose name is now slang for chick or babe). The term *lorette* came to refer to the quarter's young prostitutes. The mere mention of Nôtre-Dame-de-Lorette made men look away and good girls blush. **Rue des Martyrs,** once home to bars and restaurants for the kind of crowd that rents hotel rooms by the hour, revelled in an equally bad reputation. Now filled with fruit stands, cheese shops, and *épiceries,* the street has mended its sordid ways.

North of rue de Châteaudun is a quiet, residential area with a large student population and many small, well-priced ethnic restaurants. The streets are narrow and quiet, full of small shops, *tabacs,* small hotels, and modest private residences. Farther north, at the border of the 18ème, is the infamous area called Pigalle, the so-called un-chastity belt of Paris. During World War II, American servicemen aptly called Pigalle "Pig-alley." Stretching along the bd. de Clichy from pl. Pigalle to pl. Blanche is a salacious, voracious neighborhood. Sex-shops, brothels, porn stores, lace, leather, and latex boutiques line the streets. In Pigalle, people look one another in the eye, usually with money, sex, or drugs in mind. As a result, the area swarms with policemen. Although Pigalle is undergoing a slow gentrification, tourists (especially women) should be wary of walking alone here at night. The areas to the north of bd. Clichy and south of pl. Blanche are comparatively calmer. This neighborhood is experiencing a retro-kitsch revival with trendy restaurants and bars, fashionable nightclubs, and numerous artists' studios.

■ Tenth Arrondissement

Far from most tourist itineraries, the 10ème's working-class neighborhoods offer hidden sights. The tree-lined Canal St-Martin is a refreshing break from the city while the Faubourg St-Denis features North and West African markets, restaurants, and shops. Europe's train lines converge at the Gare de l'Est and the Gare du Nord, and the 3ème, 10ème, and 11ème converge at pl. de la République. One word of caution: bd. Magenta and bd. Faubourg tend to be risky at night. Be careful of pickpockets.

Designed by Jacques-Ignace Hittorf in 1863, the **Gare du Nord's** grandiose, beige neoclassical exterior is topped by statues representing the cities of France. Inside, the platforms are covered by a vast vault of glass and steel, which Napoleon III called the station's *parapluie* (umbrella). Across from the station, a fringe of *brasseries* and cafés cater to the thousands of travelers who go through here every day.

The neoclassical **Église St-Vincent de Paul** on rue de Belzunce was also built in the 19th century by Hittorf. *(Open M-Sa 8am-noon and 2-7pm, Su 8am-noon and 4:30-7:30pm. Mass with Gregorian chant Su at 9:30am.)* Resembling a Greek temple, the façade is topped with a sculpted pediment of the *Glorification of St. Vincent de Paul* by Leb-oeuf-Nanteuil. Inside, the somber nave is adorned with a frieze by Hippolyte Flandrin representing 160 saints. Built in 1866, the **Marché St-Quentin,** 85, bd. de Magenta, houses a flower, butcher, and produce market in its cavernous iron and glass spaces (see **Food Markets,** p. 104). Similarly, the **Gare de l'Est's** 19th-century glass and iron-work spins a delicate fan-like façade and latticed roof. Surrounding the station on pl. du 11 Nov. 1918 and bd. de Strasbourg, Alsatian restaurants serve Franco-Germanic specialties brought to this quartier by WWI refugees from Alsace-Lorraine. Shops on **rue de Paradis** display china and crystal produced at the famous **Cristalleries Baccarat,** 30-32, rue de Paradis, suppliers of fine crystal for Europe's royal houses since 1764 (see **Museums,** p. 227). On **rue du Faubourg St-Denis,** shops owned by African, Arab, Indian, and Pakistani vendors specialize in seafood, cheese, bread, and produce. Intersecting bd. de Strasbourg and rue du Faubourg St-Martin, the tiny **passage Brady** is a sea of tables each night, as Parisians enjoy a spicy meal outside.

At the end of rue Faubourg St-Denis, the grand **Porte St-Denis** (M: Strasbourg/St-Denis) looms triumphantly. Built in 1672 to celebrate the victories of Louis XIV in Flanders and the Rhineland, the gate imitates the Arch of Titus in Rome. Once the site

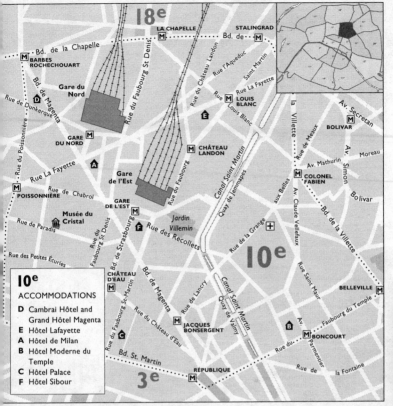

18e

LA CHAPELLE

STALINGRAD

Bd. de

Bd. de la Chapelle

BARBES
ROCHECHOUART

Rue de Dunkerque

Bd. de Magenta

Rue du Faubourg St Denis

Rue du Château Landon

Rue de l'Aqueduc

Saint Martin

Rue La Fayette

LOUIS
BLANC

Rue Louis Blanc

Av. Secretan

BOLIVAR

Gare du
Nord

la Villette

Rue de Meaux

Av. Simon

Moreau

GARE
DU NORD

Rue La Fayette

Rue du Poissonnière

Rue de Chabrol

POISSONNIÈRE

Gare
de l'Est

Rue du Faubourg

CHÂTEAU
LANDON

Canal Saint Martin

Quay de Jemmapes

Av. Mathurin

COLONEL
FABIEN

Av. Claude Vellefaux

Bolivar

Bd. de la Villette

GARE
DE L'EST

Musée du
Cristal

Rue de Paradis

Rue du Faubourg St Denis

Bd. de Strasbourg

Rue des Récollets

Jardin
Villemin

Rue de la Grange

10e

Rue Saint Maur

BELLEVILLE

Rue des Petites Écuries

10e
ACCOMMODATIONS

D Cambrai Hôtel and
 Grand Hôtel Magenta
E Hôtel Lafayette
A Hôtel de Milan
B Hôtel Moderne du
 Temple
C Hôtel Palace
F Hôtel Sibour

CHÂTEAU
D'EAU

Bd. de Magenta

Rue du Château d'Eau

Rue de Lancry

Rue du Faubourg St-Martin

Canal Saint Martin

Quay de Valmy

JACQUES
BONSERGENT

Faubourg du Temple

Av. Parmentier

BONCOURT

Bd. St. Martin

3e

RÉPUBLIQUE

Rue du

Rue de

la Fontaine

SIGHTS

of a medieval entrance to the city, the present arch serves only as a rotary for traffic. In the words of André Breton, *c'est très belle et très inutile* (it's very beautiful and very useless). On July 28, 1830, it was the scene of intense fighting as revolutionaries scrambled to the top and rained cobblestones on the monarchist troops below. Two blocks down bd. St-Denis, the 1674 **Porte St-Martin** is a smaller copy with a silly Herculean Louis XIV on the façade in nothing but a wig and a smile.

The stretch from Porte St-Martin to pl. de la République along rue René Boulanger and bd. St-Martin served as a lively theater district in the 19th century and has recently begun to retrieve some of its former sparkle. A shining example is the **Théâtre de la Renaissance,** with its sculpted façade of griffins and arabesques by Carrier-Belleuse. Newly refurbished, it has breathed new life into the neighborhood. **Place de la République** (M: République) is the meeting point of the 3ème, 10ème, and 11ème arrondissements. At its center, Morice's sculpture of *La République* glorifies France's many revolutionary struggles. Buzzing with crowds during the day, the area can be dangerous at night. (See **Sights,** p. 147, for more on the *place*.)

The most pleasant area of the 10ème is the tree-lined **Canal St-Martin.** Measuring 4.5km, the canal connects to the Seine and has several locks, which can be traveled by boat on one of the **canauxrama** trips (see **Sights,** p. 135). East of the canal, follow rue Bichat to the **Hôpital St-Louis.** Built in 1607 by Henri IV as a sanctuary/prison for victims of the plague, it was located across a marsh and downwind of the rotting Buttes-Chaumont (see **Sights,** p. 198). Its distance from any water-source suggests that it was intended more to protect the city from contamination than to help the unfortunates inside. Today, the hospital specializes in dermatology and boasts the

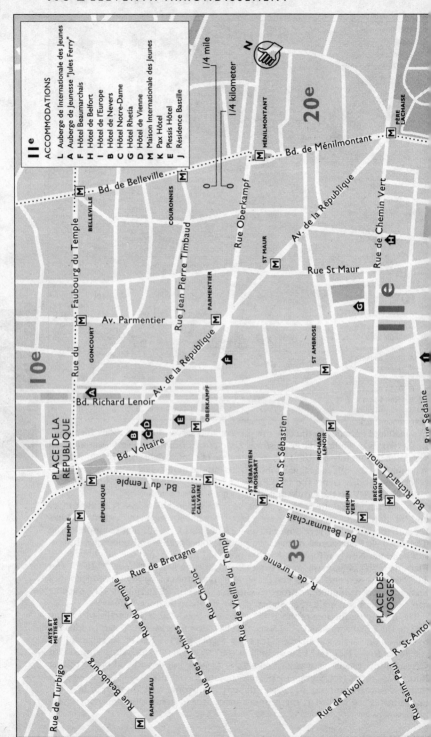

 ACCOMMODATIONS
L Auberge de Internationale des Jeunes
A Auberge de Jeunesse "Jules Ferry"
F Hôtel Beaumarchais
H Hôtel de Belfort
I Hôtel de l'Europe
B Hôtel de Nevers
C Hôtel Notre-Dame
G Hôtel Rhetia
D Hôtel de Vienne
M Maison Internationale des Jeunes
K Pax Hôtel
E Plessis Hôtel
J Résidence Bastille

1/4 mile
1/4 kilometer

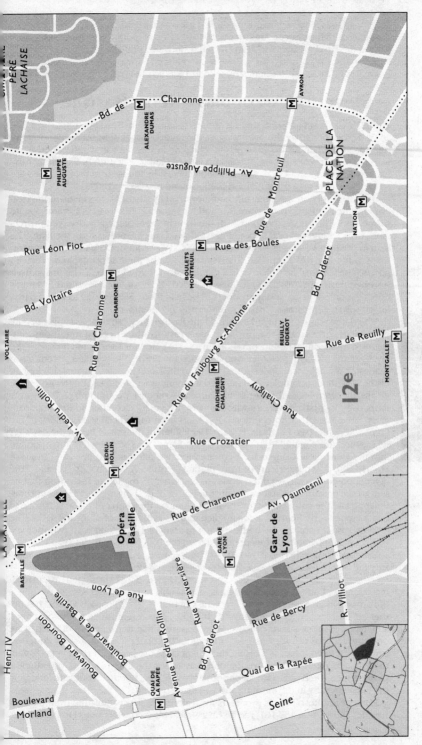

PÈRE LACHAISE

Bd. de Charonne

ALEXANDRE DUMAS

Av. Philippe Auguste

PHILIPPE AUGUSTE

AVRON

PLACE DE LA NATION

Rue de Montreuil

NATION

Rue Léon Fiot

Rue des Boules

BOULETS MONTREUIL

Bd. Diderot

Bd. Voltaire

CHARRONE

Rue de Charonne

Rue du Faubourg St-Antoine

REUILLY DIDEROT

Rue de Reuilly

VOLTAIRE

FAIDHERBE CHALIGNY

Rue Chaligny

MONTGALLET

12e

Av. Ledru Rollin

Rue Crozatier

LEDRU-ROLLIN

Av. Daumesnil

Rue de Charenton

GARE DE LYON

Gare de Lyon

BASTILLE

Opéra Bastille

Rue de Lyon

Rue Traversière

Rue de Bercy

R. Villiot

Henri IV

Boulevard Bourdon

Boulevard de la Bastille

Avenue Ledru Rollin

Bd. Diderot

QUAI DE LA RAPÉE

Quai de la Rapée

Boulevard Morland

Seine

gorgeous **Quadrilatère Historique de St-Louis,** a flowered courtyard. North of the hospital, the **Montfaucon Gallows**—famous for its hanging capacity of 60—once hanged medieval prisoners with an efficiency unrivaled until the invention of the guillotine. In the 14th century, the gallows were replaced with a more efficient design by Pierre Rémy, treasurer to Charles IV, who in 1328 was hanged by his own creation.

▓ Eleventh Arrondissement: Bastille

The 11ème is most famous as the site of the storming of the **Bastille** on July 14, 1789, an event celebrated as the beginning of the French Revolution. Although nothing remains of the famous debtors' prison, **place de la Bastille's** new opera house has inspired new revolts by architects and citizens alike. Place de la Bastille is now packed with bars and cafés, whose trendy clients, including Jean-Paul Gaultier, are sparking entirely new revolutions in fashion, fabulousness, and style.

The Bastille prison was originally commissioned by Charles V to safeguard the eastern entrance to Paris. A royal treasury under Henri IV, the fortress became a state prison under his successor Louis XIII. Internment there, generally reserved for religious heretics and political undesirables, followed specific orders from the king. The man in the iron mask languished here at Louis XIV's request. Despite imprisonment, many titled inmates furnished their suites, brought their servants, and received guests. The Cardinal de Rohan held a dinner party for 20 in his cell. The prison itself provided fresh linen. Notable prisoners included Mirabeau, Voltaire, and the Marquis de Sade, one of the last seven prisoners to be held there. Seldom one to miss a party, he left July 7, 1789, just a week before the prison's liberation.

When Revolutionary militants stormed the Bastille, they came for its supply of gunpowder. Having sacked the Invalides for weapons, they needed munitions. Surrounded by an armed rabble, too short on food to entertain a siege, and unsure of the loyalty of the Swiss mercenaries who defended the prison, the Bastille's governor surrendered. While he was under armed escort to the Hôtel de Ville, the mob hacked off his head with a pocketknife and paraded it around on a pike. Despite the gruesome details, the storming of the Bastille has come to symbolize the triumph of liberty over despotism. Its first anniversary was the cause for great celebration in Revolutionary Paris. Since the late 19th century, July 14 has been the official state holiday of the French Republic (see **Festivals,** p. 246). Demolition of the prison began the day after its capture and concluded in October 1792. Some of its stones were incorporated into the **Pont de la Concorde.** A commemorative pile can also be found in **place Henri Galli,** down bd. Henri IV from pl. de la Bastille. A certain Citizen Palloy, the demolition contractor, used the stones to construct 83 models of the prison that he sent to the provinces as reminders of "the horror of despotism." In 1831 King Louis-Philippe laid the cornerstone for the July Column at the center of pl. de la Bastille to commemorate the Republicans who died in the Revolutions of 1789 and 1830. The column's vault contains the bodies of 504 martyrs of 1830 along with two mummified Egyptian pharaohs that were moved from the Louvre when they began to rot.

The **Opéra Bastille** (tel. 01 40 01 19 70), a space-age conversation piece, is regularly the butt of jokes. *(Tours 50F, students, under 16, and over 60 30F. Call for tour schedule. For concert info, see* **Classical Music, Opera, and Dance,** *p. 239.)* Designed by Canadian mall architect Carlos Ott, the building is second only to Disneyland Paris in the minds of Parisians as an example of architectural Chernobyl. The "People's Opera" has further been described as a huge toilette, because of its resemblance to the coin-operated facilities in the streets of Paris. Many complain that the acoustics of the hall are defective. Worse yet, the "people," for whom the opera was supposedly designed, can't afford to go there; as a result, the Opéra costs the people of Paris in taxes a lot more than it returns. Tours are the only way to see the interior unless you attend a performance. On Bastille day, all performances are free, but the queues are long. Join the line very early in the morning and you may get a seat.

Many of the Revolution's profiteers lived along the streets radiating from pl. de la Bastille. The *hôtel* at 157-161, rue de Charonne, housed the infamous Dr. Belhomme, whose **Maison de Retraite et de Santé** sheltered condemned aristocrats with ready cash during the Terror (1792-1795). For 1000 livres a month, Dr. Belhomme would let a room in his sham sanatorium and certify his clients as too ill to brave the scaffold. Arrested himself after word got out, the savvy Dr. Belhomme holed up in a similar establishment on rue de Picpusin in the 12ème.

In the early 1990s, the neighborhood near the Opéra Bastille was touted as the next Montmartre, Montparnasse, and *Quartier Latin:* the city's latest Bohemia. But the Bastille's 15 minutes are over. In the scramble to find the next, new, "in" place crowds have surged north toward **Oberkampf** and **Ménilmontant.** To preserve the area's older buildings, the **Ateliers de Ménilmontant,** 42, rue Alexandre Dumas, holds open studios and brings artists together to paint outdoor frescoes. **Glassbox,** 113bis rue Oberkampf, attracts politically engaged artists. Plans are also being laid to build a **Centre de Danse Africaine et Culture du Monde.** To meet the new 11ème scene, check out the curvy rue de la Roquette, a 17th-century byway that was home to Verlaine (at no. 17), and is now lined with shoulder-to-shoulder cafés and bars. Off rue de la Roquette, the narrow rue de Lappe is crammed with bars and tapas joints. Somewhat deserted by day, the party scene here at night is as intense as it gets in 1999 Paris. **Le Bar Sans Nom,** 49, rue de Lappe (see **Bars and Pubs,** p. 132), is a good start, but you should shop around. In the Oberkampf *quartier,* the crowded **Café Charbon,** 109, rue Oberkampf (see **Bars and Pubs,** p. 132), exemplifies the new scene. Running parallel to rue de Lappe a bit farther from pl. de la Bastille, rue Keller's cafés meet the needs of the urban underground. At the end of rue de Lappe, rue de Charonne features art galleries and funky boutiques. Jean-Paul Gaultier's gallery is at 30, rue Faubourg-St-Antoine.

■ Twelfth Arrondissement

The 12ème is a study in dynamic contrasts, where artists and tourists, working class and upper crust all meet at the bustling crossroads of the **Gare de Lyon.** Drawing on the hip, youthful energy of the neighboring 11ème, the broad avenues of this eastern arrondissement make space for both **Jean-Paul Gaultier** boutiques and sex shops, trendy furniture designers and tanning salons. But while its fringes are decidedly funky, its core is solidly working class, with a large **immigrant** population.

Once known as the "red belt" around Paris because of its participation in both the 1830 and 1848 Revolutions, the 12ème also saw its residents make up large sectors of the Parisian Resistance during WWII. The only rebellions staged these days are over the **Opéra Bastille** (tel. 01 44 73 13 00; M: Bastille), one of Mitterand's *Grands Projets.* Presiding over the **pl. de la Bastille** and designed by Carlos Ott, a Canadian mall architect, the Opéra opened in 1989 to protests over its unattractive and questionable design (nets still surround parts of the building to catch falling tiles). The Opéra has not struck a completely sour note, though, and has helped renew local interest in the arts. The Opéra Bastille is but one of the 12ème's recent architectural additions. East of the **Gare de Lyon,** the **Bercy** quarter (M: Bercy) has seen the rapid construction of Mitterand's new **Ministère des Finances** building, the mammoth **Palais Omnisports** concert and sports complex, and Frank Ghery's brilliant 1994 **American Center,** which offers cultural programs and events on American culture.

Opened in 1995 in a renovated railway viaduct, the **Viaduc des Arts,** 15-121, av. Daumesmil (M: Bastille) provides workspace and showrooms for potters, painters, and weavers. Above the viaduct runs the **Promenade Plantée,** Paris's longest and skinniest park and probably the only one in the world accessible solely by train, elevator, or stairs. Trees, roses, and shrubs line an old railroad track high above the avenue, the traffic, and the stores below. Farther down the promenade and to the north is **place Aligre,** where the busy North African street market takes place. **Place de la Nation's** current reputation as a red-light district belies the fact that it was once the site of a royal wedding between Louis XIV and Marie-Thérèse in 1660. During the Revolution, 1300 nobles were executed on this spot. It became pl. de la Nation on July 14, 1880. At the eastern edge of the 12ème stands the beautifully green **Bois de**

SIGHTS

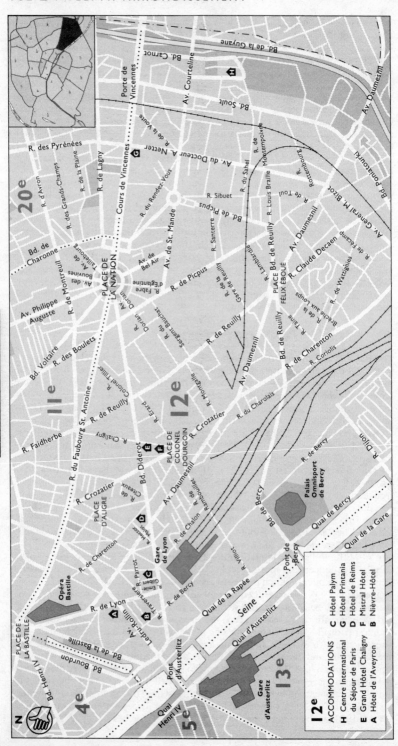

12e

ACCOMMODATIONS
H Centre International du Séjour de Paris
E Grand Hôtel Chaligny
A Hôtel de l'Aveyron
C Hôtel Palym
G Hôtel Printania
D Hôtel de Reims
F Mistral Hôtel
B Nièvre-Hôtel

SIGHTS

12e

Palais Omnisports de Bercy

Quai de Bercy

Quai de la Rapée

Pont de Bercy

Pont de Tolbiac

Quai de Tolbiac

Bibliothèque Nationale

The Seine

Quai de la Gare

Quai d'Austerlitz

R. Witt

R. Camagrel

R. E. Oudine

R. de Pasay

R. du Dessous des Berges

Av. de la porte de Vitry

R. Chevaleret

R. Albert

R. Regnault

Bd. Massena

Av. Boutroux

Av. Regaud

de Vitry

Gare d'Austerlitz

Hôpital Salpétrière

R. Jenner

CHEVALERET

R. du Chevaleret

Charcot

R. Dunois

R. Clisson

R. Domrémy

R. Jeanne d'Arc

PLACE JEANNE D'ARC

R. Jean Colley

R. du Château des rentiers

R. de Tolbiac

R. National

Av. d'Ivry

PORTE D'IVRY

R. de la Pointe d'Ivry

Bd. de l'Hôpital

ST-MARCEL

R. Esquirol

R. Pinel

Campo Formio

R. Pichon

R. Pirandello

R. Le Brun

R. du Banquier

PLACE PINEL

Av. Vincent Auriol

NATIONALE

PLACE NATIONALE

13e

R. Edison

Richet

R. Baudricourt

Av. de Choisy

R. de la Visule

R. Caillaux

R. Candon

Av. d'Italie

5e

R. Monge

R. Mouffetard

Av. des Gobelins

LES GOBELINS

R. Claude Bernard

R. Pascal

R. Rubens

R. Coypel

Rubens

R. Abel Hovelacque

Véronèse

Vulpian

PLACE D'ITALIE

PL. DE L'ITALIE

PL. DE L'ITALIE

Av. d'Italie

TOLBIAC

R. du Moulin de la Pointe

R. du Tage

Av. d'Italie

R. Damesme

R. du Dr. Tuffier

R. de Dr. Tuffier

Bd. Kellerman

R. de Croulebarbe

CORVISART

R. Corvisart

R. du Molin des Pres

R. Bobillot

R. de la Butte aux Cailles

R. Barrault

R. de Tolbiac

R. Charles Fourier

R. de la Colonie

R. des Peupliers

R. Brillat

PLACE DE RUNGIS

Cacheux

C

R. Deslandes

R. d'Arago

GLACIÈRE

R. de la Glacière

R. Vergniaud

R. Wurtz

P. A. Lançon

R. Boussingault

Bd. de Port Royal

R. de la Santé

A

B

Bd. Arago

Bd. Auguste Blanqui

Hôpital St-Anne

R. d'Alésia

N

14e

13e

ACCOMMODATIONS
B Association des Foyers de Jeunes:
   Foyer des Jeunes Filles
C CISP "Kellerman"
A Maison des Clubs UNESCO

Vincennes (see **Sights,** p. 207). Once a royal hunting ground, the Bois now contains the premier zoo in France, the **Parc Zoologique** (see **Sights,** p. 207), and the royal **Château de Vincennes.**

■ Thirteenth Arrondissement

A working-class immigrant neighborhood, the 13ème is now poised to surface as an important axis of French intellectual and cultural life. From the new **Bibliothèque de France** (Library of France) and the modern architecture of pl. d'Italie to Chinatown and the Butte aux Cailles, Parisians are rediscovering the 13ème and you can too. Until the 20th century, the 13ème was one of Paris's poorest neighborhoods. Victor Hugo used parts of the 13ème as a setting for *Les Misérables.* Traversed by the **Bièvre,** a stagnant stream clogged with industrial refuse, it was notoriously the city's worst-smelling district. Environmentalists eventually won their campaign to close its tanneries and paper factories, and in 1910 the Bièvre was filled in. The **Manufacture des Gobelins,** 42, av. des Gobelins (tel. 01 44 61 21 69; M: Gobelins), a tapestry workshop over 300 years old, is all that is left of the 13ème's industrial past. *(Tours in French with free English-language handout, 1½hr., Tu-Th 2 and 2:45pm; 45F, ages 7-24 25F, under 7 free.)* In the mid-17th century the Gobelins produced some of the priceless tapestries now displayed in the Musée de Cluny (see **Museums,** p. 222). Still an adjunct of the state, the factory receives commissions from French ministries and foreign embassies. Guided tours (the only way inside) explain the intricacies of the weaving process.

Farther southwest, the **Butte aux Cailles** (Quail Knoll) district features cobblestone streets, tree-shaded sidewalks, and street lamps. One of the first areas to fight during the Revolution of 1848, the area around rue des Cinq Diamants was the unofficial headquarters of the *soixante-huitards,* the student and intellectual activists of the 1968 riots. Today the fight continues in the Butte's cooperative bar, **La Folie en Tête,** 33, rue de la Butte aux Cailles, and intellectual hang-out, **Le Temps des Cérises** (see **Food and Drink,** p. 122). The nascent gentrification of the 13ème has attracted trend-setters, artists, and intellectuals, but residents are worried that once-affordable real estate may go the way of the now unaffordable Marais.

The Byzantine **Église Sainte-Anne de la Maison Blanche** on rue Tolbiac owes its completion to the Lombard family who in 1898 donated funds from their chocolate store on av. de Choisy to complete the construction. The front of the church is nicknamed *la façade chocolat* in their honor. East of Ste-Anne on av. de Choisy and av. d'Ivry lies Paris's **Chinatown,** home to large Chinese, Vietnamese, and Cambodian communities. Asian restaurants, shops, and markets like **Tang Frères** on rue d'Ivry offer embroidered slippers, exotic fruits, fresh vegetables, and Asian specialties.

Opened in 1996, the **Bibliothèque de France** is the last and most expensive of Mitterand's *Grand Projets.* *(Open Tu-Sa 10am-7pm, Su noon-6pm. 20F per day, yearly pass 200F, students and children 100F.)* Replacing the old Bibliothèque Nationale in the 2ème (still open to scholars), the new library is open to the public and houses 10 million volumes. Designed by Dominique Perrault, the four L-shaped towers are designed to look like open books from above. The library is just one piece of the 13ème's urban renewal. A new project called **ZAC** (Zone d'Aménagement Concerte) plans to build a new university, five schools, a sports complex, a public garden, and a new metro.

On the northern edge of the 13ème near the **Gare d'Austerlitz** stands the **Hôpital de la Salpêtrière,** 47, bd. de l'Hôpital (tel. 01 42 16 00 00; M: Austerlitz or St-Marcel). The enormous hospital was built by Louis XIII in the 17th century and later converted into a shelter for disadvantaged women and orphans. Many women were imprisoned here for "hysteria," a term that described anything from mild depression and PMS to genuine mental illness. Through the hospital and the large inner courtyard stands the austere **Chapelle St-Louis.** *(Open M-Sa 8:30am-6:30pm, Su 9:30am-3:30pm. Free.)* By the 19th century, the Salpêtrière had evolved into one of the world's premier psychiatric institutions. It was here that Princess Diana was taken after her tragic accident in the Pont d'Alma tunnel in 1997 and where she later died.

■ Fourteenth Arrondissement

Like Montmartre and the *Quartier Latin,* the 14ème has long been a haven for 20th-century artists and writers like Man Ray, Modigliani, and Henry Miller. While gentrification has forced struggling artists out of those *quartiers,* the 14ème's affordability and café culture still attract starving bohemians. While young painters chat in the Parc Montsouris and student writers debate at the Cité Universitaire, their illustrious predecessors rest peacefully in the Cimetière Montparnasse.

MONTPARNASSE

Generations of newly arrived immigrants have called Montparnasse home. The first to arrive were Bretons, who left Brittany in the 19th century after failed harvests. Arriving en masse at the **Gare de Montparnasse,** they settled around the station, now known as Petite Bretange. Breton *crêperies,* handicraft shops, and cultural association line the **rue du Montparnasse.** In the early 20th century, Montparnasse became a center for avant-garde artists including Modigliani, Utrillo, Chagall, and Léger who migrated from Montmartre. Political exiles like Lenin and Trotsky planned new strategies over cognac in the cafés along the **boulevard Montparnasse.**

After WWI, Montparnasse attracted American expatriates. Man Ray transformed an apartment into a photo lab; Calder worked on his first sculptures; Hemingway did some serious writing (and drinking); and Henry Miller produced the steamy *Tropic of Cancer* at Seurat's villa with the amorous help of Anaïs Nin. But the Spanish Civil War and WWII ended this golden age of bohemia. To see where Lenin, Hemingway, and Sartre sat and racked their brains, check out the café **La Coupole** (see **Classic Cafés,** p. 128). Surrounding Montparnasse's residential neighborhoods are rue d'Alésia's clothing stores, rue de la Gaité's porn shops, and rue Daguerre's restaurants.

Dominating the landscape is the **Tour Montparnasse,** an ode to modern design (see **Fifteenth Arrondissement,** p. 188). In its shadow, the beautiful **Cimetière Montparnasse,** 3, bd. Edgar Quinet (tel. 01 44 10 86 50; M: Edgar Quinet), brings repose to writers Guy de Maupassant, Samuel Beckett, Simone de Beauvoir, Jean-Paul Sartre, and Charles Baudelaire, who wrote in *Les Fleurs du Mal,* "O Death, old captain, it is time! Lift the anchor!" *(Open daily 9am-5:30pm. Free.)* Filmmaker François Truffaut and his favorite actress Jean Seberg are also buried here, along with artists Man Ray, Brancusi, and Frédéric Bartholdi, the sculptor of the Statue of Liberty. Ironically, the accused-traitor Alfred Dreyfus and the anti-Semitic WWII traitor Maréchal Pétain lie just feet away from each other. Composer Camille Saint-Saëns is buried not far from the 70s French pop singer, Serge Gainsbourg, whose graffitied grave resembles Jim Morrison's across town at Père Lachaise (see **Sights,** p. 199). With a free *Index des Célébrités* (available to the left of the entrance), you can pay your respects.

Southwest of the cemetery, the **Église Nôtre-Dame du Travail,** 59, rue Vercingétorix (tel. 01 44 10 72 92), was built by labor organizer Father Soulange-Boudin and architect Jules Astrac for the workers of the parish. *(Open M-F 8:30am-noon and 2-7pm, Sa 2-8pm, Su 8:30am-noon.)* The Roman exterior belies the industrial iron-girder interior. Painted flowers remind the working faithful that they've left the factory.

DENFERT-ROCHEREAU

At the intersection of six avenues, a lion sculpted by Bartholdi (who created the Statue of Liberty) dominates **place Denfert-Rochereau.** Most visitors observe Bartholdi's Leo from their place in the line to visit **Les Catacombs,** 1, pl. Denfert-Rochereau (tel. 01 43 22 47 63; M: Denfert-Rochereau), a series of subterranean tunnels 20m below that were originally excavated to provide stone for building the city. *(Open Tu-F 2-5pm, Sa-Su 9-11am and 2-4pm. Admission 27F, under 25 19F, under 7 free.)* By the 1770s, much of the Left Bank was in danger of caving in and digging promptly stopped. The former quarry was then used as a mass grave to relieve the stench emanating from Paris's overcrowded cemeteries. The entrance warns "Stop! Beyond Here Is the Empire of Death." In 1793, a Parisian got lost in here and became a perma-

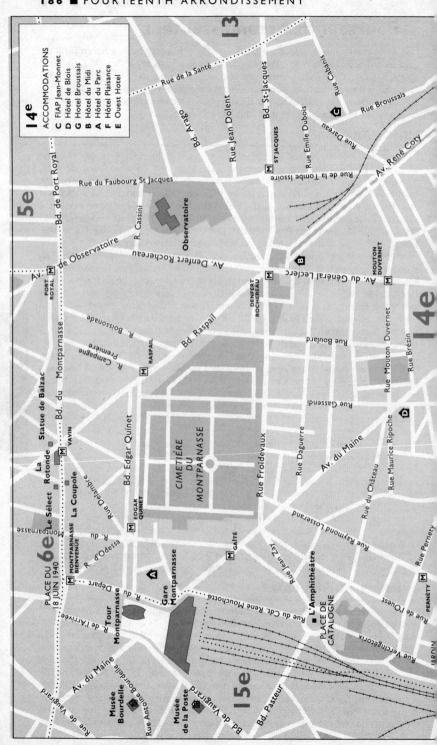

14e

ACCOMMODATIONS

- **C** FIAP Jean-Monnet
- **D** Hôtel de Blois
- **G** Hôtel Broussais
- **B** Hôtel du Midi
- **A** Hôtel du Parc
- **F** Hôtel Plaisance
- **E** Ouest Hotel

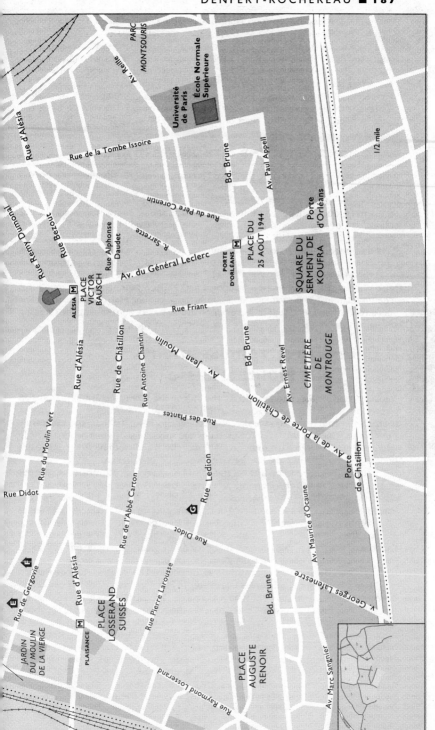

nent resident, so stick to the tour! During WWII, the Empire of Death was full of life when the Resistance set up headquarters among the departed.

The catacombs are like an underground city, with street names on walls lined with femurs and craniums. The ghoulish arrangement features rooms with cheery proverbs—*"Pensez le matin que vous n'irez peut être pas jusques au soir et au soir que vous n'irez pas jusques au matin"* ("Think each morning that you may not be live 'til evening, and each evening that you may not be live 'til morning"). Beware the low ceilings and bring a sweater (and a flashlight if you have one). The catacombs are not recommended for the faint of heart or leg; there are 85 steep steps to climb on the way out.

PARC MONTSOURIS AND CITÉ UNIVERSITAIRE

Begun in 1867 by Haussmann, the **Parc Montsouris** features hundreds of rare and unusual trees, a gaggle of ducks and snow geese splashing on the pond, and bright flowers in the summer. *(Open M-F 7:30am-10pm, Sa-Su 9am-10pm.)* Sunbathers and children stretch out on the grass. Across bd. Jourdan, thousands of students from 122 countries study, argue, and drink themselves silly in the **Cité Universitaire**, a 40-hectare residential campus with 30 dorms, two of them designed by Le Corbusier. The **Pavilion Suisse** (1932) reflects the architect's dream of a vertical city, although its roof-garden housed anti-aircraft guns during WWII. In 1959, Le Corbusier returned to build the **Maison du Brasil**. While the **Maison des États-Unis** houses Americans in prison-like squalor, the **Maison Suédoise** and **Maison Japonaise** offer delightful accommodations. The swankiest addition is the luxurious **Maison d'Espagne**. (For long-term housing, see **Student Accommodations,** p. 78). Surrounding the Cité Universitaire, joggers, bikers, and frisbee ultimates occupy the lawns.

■ Fifteenth Arrondissement: Tour Montparnasse

A mostly residential quarter, the 15ème has little in the way of sights but presents an elegant picture of daily middle-class Parisian life. Board at M: Trocadéro and ride the **metro's elevated tracks** to La Motte-Picquet-Grenelle. From the train, there's a lovely view of the Seine and the Eiffel Tower. Cafés and specialty shops line bd. de Grenelle while rue du Commerce overflows with flower shops and clothing stores, and cafés huddle at the corner of rue de la Convention and rue de Vaugirard.

The modern **Tour Montparnasse** (tel. 01 45 38 52 56; M: Montparnasse-Bienvenue) dominates the *quartier*'s northeast corner. *(Open May-Sept. daily 9:30am-11:30pm; Oct.-April M-F 9:30am-10:30pm. Admission 42F, seniors 36F, students 33F, under 14 26F.)* Standing 59 stories tall and completed in 1973, the controversial building looks out of place amid the 19th-century architecture of Montparnasse. Shortly after it was erected, the city passed an ordinance forbidding further skyscraping, designating La Défense (see **Sights,** p. 208) the sole home for future *gratte-ciels*. Ride the elevator to the 56th floor, then climb three flights to the rooftop terrace for a fabulous view of the city. Enjoy the panorama over drinks at the chic, yet *cher* bar, **Le Ciel de Paris.**

In front of the Tour Montparnasse, **place du 18 juin** commemorates two important events from WWII. On June 18, 1940, General de Gaulle broadcast from London his first BBC radio address, urging France to resist the Nazi occupiers and the collaborationist Vichy regime of Maréchal Pétain (the entire speech is engraved by the Tomb of the Unknown Soldier under the Arc de Triomphe; see **Sights,** p. 166). It was also here that General Leclerc, the leader of the French forces, accepted the surrender of General von Choltitz, the Nazi commander of the Paris occupation, on August 25, 1944. It is due to von Choltitz that the Tour Montparnasse is not Paris's only monument. Despite orders from Hitler to destroy Paris and retreat, von Choltitz disobeyed and saved the city (see **Paris Is Burning,** p. 9). The nearby **Musée Bourdelle** houses works by French sculptor Émile-Antoine Bourdelle (see **Museums,** p. 227).

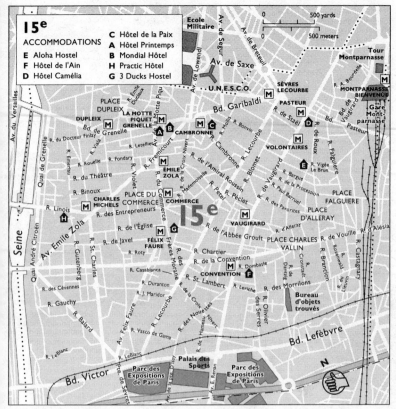

Founded by the French scientist Louis Pasteur in 1887, the **Institut Pasteur,** 25, rue du Dr. Roux (tel. 01 45 68 82 82 or 01 45 68 82 83; M: Pasteur), is now a center for biochemical research, development, and treatment. *(Open Sept.-July M-F 2-5:30pm. Admission 15F, students 8F.)* It was here that Pasteur, a champion of 19th-century germ theory, developed pasteurization, his technique for purifying milk products and beer. It was also here in 1983 that Dr. Luc Montaigner (in conjunction with Robert Gallo) first isolated HIV, the virus that causes AIDS. The institute's small museum houses Pasteur's projects, lab, awards, living quarters, and grave.

Designed by Gustave Eiffel, the brick compound called **La Ruche,** 52, rue Dantzig (M: Convention), used to house struggling artists like Chagall and Soutine. Today the Foundation La Ruche offers grants, studios, and housing to young artists. Sculptures by La Ruche residents line the garden, but beware the Linden trees. Near M: Félix Faure, many buildings sport **Art Nouveau façades,** such as 24, pl. Étienne Pernet, and 31 & 40, av. Félix Faure, whose front depicts Aesop's *The Crow and the Fox.*

■ Sixteenth Arrondissement

On January 1, 1860, the wealthy villages of Auteuil, Passy, and Chaillot banded together and joined Paris, forming what is now the 16ème arrondissement. More than a century later, the area's original aristocratic families continue to hold their ground, making the 16ème a stronghold of conservative politics, fashion, and culture. It is rumored that some members of the local nobility forbid their children to sing *La Marseillaise,* the anthem of the Revolutionaries who beheaded their ancestors. In

SIGHTS

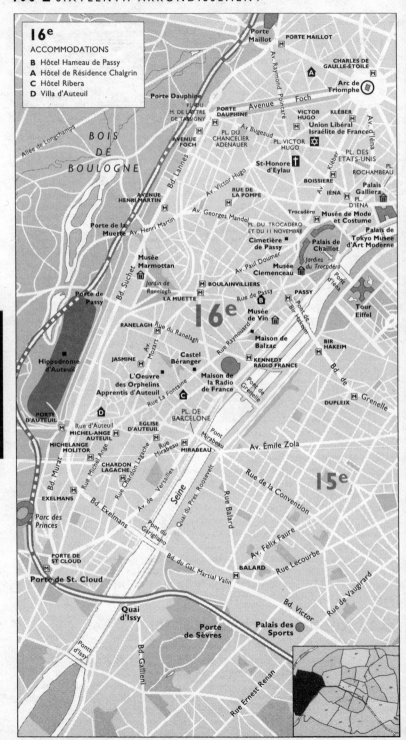

16ᵉ

ACCOMMODATIONS

- **B** Hôtel Hameau de Passy
- **A** Hôtel de Résidence Chalgrin
- **C** Hôtel Ribera
- **D** Villa d'Auteuil

Porte Maillot

PORTE MAILLOT

CHARLES DE GAULLE-ÉTOILE

Arc de Triomphe

Av. Raymond Poincaré

Avenue Foch

Allée de Longchamps

BOIS DE BOULOGNE

Porte Dauphine

PL. DU M. DE LATTRE DE TASSIGNY

PORTE DAUPHINE

VICTOR HUGO

KLÉBER

AVENUE FOCH

Av Bugeaud

PL. DU CHANCELIER ADENAUER

PL. VICTOR HUGO

Union Libéral Israélite de France

Bd. Lannes

St-Honore d'Eylau

PL. DES ETATS-UNIS

PL. ROCHAMBEAU

AVENUE HENRI MARTIN

Av. Victor Hugo

RUE DE LA POMPE

BOISSIERE

IÉNA

Palais Galliera

PL. D'IENA

Porte de la Muette

Av. Henri Martin

Av. Georges Mandel

Trocadéro

Musée de Mode et Costume

PL. DU TROCADERO ET DU 11 NOVEMBRE

Cimetière de Passy

Palais de Chaillot

Palais de Tokyo Musée d'Art Moderne

Musée Marmottan

Av. Paul Doumer

Musée Clemenceau

Jardins du Trocadéro

Pont d'Iéna

Jardin de Ranelagh

LA MUETTE

BOULAINVILLIERS

Rue de Passy

PASSY

Tour Eiffel

Porte de Passy

Bd. Suchet

16ᵉ

Musée de Vin

Pont de Bir Hakeim

RANELAGH

Rue du Ranelagh

Av. Mozart

Rue Raynouard

Maison de Balzac

BIR HAKEIM

JASMINE

Castel Béranger

KENNEDY RADIO FRANCE

Bd. de Grenelle

Hippodrome d'Auteuil

L'Oeuvre des Orphelins Apprentis d'Auteuil

Rue La Fontaine

Maison de la Radio de France

Pont de Grenelle

DUPLEIX

Grenelle

PORTE D'AUTEUIL

Rue d'Auteuil

MICHEL-ANGE AUTEUIL

EGLISE D'AUTEUIL

PL. DE BARCELONE

Pont Mirabeau

Av. Émile Zola

15ᵉ

MICHELANGE MOLITOR

Rue Michel Ange

CHARDON LAGACHE

Rue Mirabeau

MIRABEAU

Rue de la Convention

Bd. Murat

Rue Chardon Lagache

Av. de Versailles

Seine

Quai du Prés Roosevelt

Rue Balard

EXELMANS

Bd. Exelmans

Pont du Garigliano

Av. Félix Faure

Rue Lecourbe

Parc des Princes

PORTE DE ST CLOUD

Bd. du Gal. Martial Valin

BALARD

Bd. Victor

Rue de Vaugirard

Porte de St. Cloud

Quai d'Issy

Porte de Sèvres

Palais des Sports

Pont d'Issy

Bd. Gallieni

Rue Ernest Renan

this lavish residential neighborhood, *hôtels particuliers* (mansions and gardened townhouses) retire graciously from wide, quiet streets. Businesses, storefronts, and tackiness are at a minimum. Instead, this quarter has over 60 embassies, about half of Paris's museums (get ready to flip back and forth between these pages and the **Museums** chapter), the Trocadéro, and the Bois de Boulogne (see **Bois de Boulogne,** p. 203). Metro stops are few and far between, and inexpensive restaurants are difficult to find. Cafés near av. du Président Wilson and Trocadéro are particularly scarce and you may find yourself wandering for hours from museum to museum feeling overheated and hungry. Plan ahead, bring a lunch, and picnic on the steps of the Trocadéro while watching the best view of the Eiffel Tower.

TO THE NORTH: AVENUE FOCH AND TROCADÉRO

A good point of entry to the 16ème is M: Porte Dauphine, whose entrance is one of few surviving examples of Hector Guimard's Art Nouveau Paris metro designs. If you don't remember it from photographs, it's recognizable by its green, spidery, winged metal frame. The **Bois de Boulogne** is west of here. **Avenue Foch** stretches east to the Arc de Triomphe. One of Haussmann's finest creations, this avenue's expansive width (about 120m) features stretches of lawn running up each of its sides and through its center. Fashionable 19th-century Parisians drove carriages down av. Foch on their way to the Bois de Boulogne. The stately *hôtels particuliers* lining both sides of the avenue are some of the city's most expensive addresses. At no. 59 you'll find the **Musée d'Ennery** (see **Museums,** p. 229). While enjoyable for a stroll during the day, the avenue becomes a cruising strip for prostitutes at night.

Many of the 16ème's busiest avenues radiate from pl. Charles de Gaulle-Étoile, home to the Arc de Triomphe in the 8ème (see **Sights,** p. 166). Following the commercial av. Marceau down to the Seine takes you past the **Église St-Pierre de Chaillot,** between rue de Chaillot and av. Pierre-1er de Serbie. *(Open M-Sa 9:30am-12:30pm and 3-7pm, Su 9:30am-12:30pm.)* In the former heart of the village of Auteuil, St-Pierre boasts neo-Romanesque architecture, brilliantly lit stained glass, and Henri Bouchard sculptures. (The **Musée Henri Bouchard,** 25, rue de l'Yvelette, is also in the 16ème. See **Museums,** p. 227.) Free organ concerts are given inside St-Pierre. At the end of av. Marceau is pl. de l'Alma and a replica of the torch of Bartholdi's Statue of Liberty, one of several tributes in the 16ème to France's most famous gift to the United States.

The **Palais de Tokyo,** 11, av. du Président Wilson, houses the **Musée d'Art Moderne de la Ville de Paris** (see **Museums,** p. 226), which, in addition to its own permanent collection, will also display the collection from the **Pompidou Center Museum of Modern Art** until it reopens on December 31, 1999. Built for the 1937 World Expo, the palace took its name from the adjacent quai de Tokyo. After WWII, in which Japan fought as an Axis power, it was renamed the quai de New York. The gardens of the **Palais Galliera,** across from the Palais de Tokyo, draw young children and sculpture enthusiasts to contemplate the three allegorical figures representing painting, architecture, and sculpture. If you've packed a lunch, the gardens are a good place to relax while avoiding the area's expensive restaurants. The Palais Galliera was built for the Duchess of Galliera by Louis Ginain as a repository for her collection of Italian Baroque art, but the collection was sent to Genoa instead. The Italianate structure, completed in 1892, now houses the more contemporary and international **Musée de la Mode et du Costume** (see **Museums,** p. 231). To enter the museum, follow either of the streets next to the garden to av. Pierre-1er de Serbie. Farther down the avenue at pl. d'Iéna, the **Musée Guimet** (see **Museums,** p. 226) contains a spectacular collection of Asian art.

A museum and cinema temple, the **Palais de Chaillot** houses the **Musée du Cinéma Henri-Langlois** (see p. 228), the **Musée de l'Homme** (see p. 229), the **Musée de la Marine** (see p. 246), the **Musée National des Monuments Français** (see p. 231), the **Théâtre National de Chaillot** (see p. 234) and the **Cinémathèque Française** (see p. 238). Built for the 1937 World Exposition, Jacques Carlu's design features two curved wings cradling a gorgeous Art Deco courtyard and terrace overlooking spectacular cannon-fountains. Surveyed by the 7.5m tall bronze Henri Bouchard Apollo, the terrace attracts tourists, vendors, skateboarders, and rollerbladers and offers brilliant views of the Eiffel Tower and Champs de Mars. This spot is where most postcards of the tower are taken, so bring your camera and take a photo of yourself with the Millennium Countdown Clock to show to your grandchildren. From this angle the Eiffel Tower looks deceptively close. The walk down the Trocadéro steps, by the fountains, and across the Pont d'Iéna takes about 15 minutes. Be aware of pickpockets and traffic as you gaze upwards. At night, the Trocadéro is less crowded and the Eiffel Tower is illuminated. As always, be careful and go with a friend.

The Palais de Chaillot is actually the last of a series of buildings built on this site. Catherine de Médicis had a château here, later transformed into a convent by Queen Henrietta of England. Napoleon razed the old château and planned to build a more lavish one on the same site for his son until his rotten luck at Waterloo brought construction to a screeching halt. In the 1820s, the Duc d'Angoulême built a fortress-like memorial to his Spanish victory at Trocadéro—hence the present name. That in turn was replaced in 1878 by the pavilion on Islamic architecture for the World Exposition, also since demolished. Below the palace, the **Jardins du Trocadéro** extend to the Seine. The **fountains** lining the central av. Gustave V de Suède and Albert 1er de Monaco are particularly striking when lit at night. After a day of sight-seeing, children might enjoy the *carrousel* (merry-go-round, 10F) in pl. de Varsovie in front of the Eiffel Tower or a crêpe from one of the many outdoor stands.

TO THE SOUTH: PASSY AND AUTEUIL

Located south and southwest of Trocadéro, **Passy** was once famous for its restorative waters, although it's more recently known as the set for *Last Tango in Paris.* Running along the northern walls and shaded by a chestnut bower, the small **Cimetière de Passy,** 2, rue de Commandant Schloesing (M: Trocadéro), contains the tombs of Claude Debussy, Gabriel Fauré, and Édouard Manet. *(Open M-F 8am-6pm, Sa 8:30am-6pm, Su 9am-6pm, Nov. 6-Mar. 15 closes at 5:30pm.)* Ask the concierge at the entrance for directions to the grave sites.

Rue Benjamin Franklin commemorates the elder statesmen's one-time residence in Passy. Franklin, who built France's first lightning rod, lived at 66, rue Raynouard, from 1777 to 1785 while negotiating a treaty between the new United States and the old Louis XVI; the present building was built long after his stay. Located in former Prime Minister Clemenceau's own home (see **Museums,** p. 228), the **Musée Clemenceau** 8, rue Benjamin Franklin, chronicles the life and times of France's hardline negotiator of the WWI Treaty of Versailles. While completing the last volumes of *La Comédie Humaine,* Honoré de Balzac lived at what is now the **Maison de Balzac,** 47, rue Raynouard (see **Museums,** p. 227). The large, white, round building at the end of rue Raynouard is the **Maison de Radio France** (see **Museums,** p. 232). Just past it, rue de Boulainvilliers will take you down to the miniature Bartholdi **Statue of Liberty** near the pont de Grenelle. Donated by a group of American expatriates in 1885, it was moved to this spot for the 1889 World Exposition. It's larger cousin stands on Liberty Island in New York harbor, with the ironic inscription *Give me your Poor, your Tired, your Huddled Masses Yearning to Breathe Free.* For more on the Statue of Liberty, see *Let's Go: New York 1999,* Rachel Farbiarz, Editor.

The end of rue Raynouard marks the boundary of Passy and **Auteuil,** a 17th-century meeting-place for men of letters such as Racine, Molière, and Boileau and home to beautiful *hôtels particuliers* with Art Nouveau and Modernist architecture. A number of Hector Guimard buildings line rue La Fontaine (an extension of rue Raynouard). The award-winning **Castel Béranger** (1898), at no. 14, flaunts its Art Nouveau flourishes, swooping arabesque balconies, staircases, and rooftops. Guimard himself lived here briefly before moving to his building at 122, av. Mozart. Other Guimard buildings cluster on rue La Fontaine, including no. 17 (1911) and 9-10, rue Agar, an odd, T-shaped street that is Art Nouveau down to its street sign. **L'Oeuvre des Orphelins Apprentis d'Auteuil** (Society of Apprenticed Orphans), 40, rue la Fontaine, was founded in 1866 to provide a home and future for local orphans, who now perform apprenticeships in 30 occupations throughout France (the Auteuil campus does printing). Apprentice gardeners tend the beautiful grounds. **Proust** fans might want to visit 96, rue Fontaine, where the writer was born on July 10, 1871.

Seventeenth-century *hôtels particuliers* line rue d'Auteuil. John Adams and his son John Quincy Adams lived at no. 43-47. On rue Raffe, pink stucco, black marble, and mosaic-covered townhouses adjoin more familiar-looking gray façades and iron grill-work. Around the corner and set back behind 55, rue du Docteur-Blanche, stand two **Le Corbusier** villas, completed in 1925. **Villa La Roche** and **Villa Jeanneret** are stark, white structures that now house the **Fondation Le Corbusier.** Villa La Roche contains a small collection of 20th-century paintings, sculpture, and furniture, although the masterpiece of the collection is the building itself (see **Museums,** p. 228).

Boulevard de Beauséjour is the continuation of bd. Montmorency as it approaches the La Muette metro stop. Northwest of the metro once stood the Château de la Muette, where Louis XV entertained his mistresses. In 1783 Pilâtre de Rozier and the Marquis d'Arlandes became the first two humans to defy gravity, lifting off from the castle's lawn in a Montgolfier balloon and landing 20 minutes later in what is now the 13ème. West of M: La Muette, past the playgrounds, *carrousel,* and *guignol* (puppet show) of the **Jardin de Ranelagh,** the **Musée Marmottan,** 2, rue Louis-Boilly, displays exquisite Impressionist paintings and medieval illuminations (see **Museums,** p. 230).

■ Seventeenth Arrondissement

If you believe the hype, you'd think it wasn't even there. In Michael Bay's 1998 summer blockbuster film *Armageddon,* an enormous meteor smashes into what looks like the 17ème and reduces the arrondissement, the southern 8ème, and the northern 16ème to meteor dust. Miraculously, the impact just misses the Arc de Triomphe and the Champs-Élysées, but the 17ème is scorched flat. Hugging the northwestern edge of the city and sandwiched in between more luxurious and famous arrondissements, the 17ème suffers from a bit of an inferiority complex. Or is it multiple personality disorder? Like its aristocrat southern neighbors in the 8ème and 16ème and its suburban western neighbors in Passy and Neuilly, the arrondissement's southern border looks like old money. Like its more tawdry eastern neighbors, Pigalle and the 18ème, the arrondissement's eastern border can be seedy, especially around pl. de Clichy. In between these two extremes, the 17ème is a predominantly working-class residential neighborhood. At least until the meteor comes.

While barricades were erected, nobles beheaded, and novels written in the heart of the city, **les Batignolles** was little more than farmers' fields until the mid-19th century. If you happen to be staying in the center of the 17ème, though, the **Musée Jean-Jacques Henner,** 43, av. de Villiers, might be worth a look (see **Museums,** p. 229). Nearby, the **Banque de France,** 1, pl. Général Catroux (tel. 01 42 27 78 14), is housed in a neo-Gothic house, built in 1884 for the bank's regent. *(Open M-F 8:45am-noon and 1:45-3:30pm.)* The building features a small garden, mosaic brickwork, and a façade with leering gargoyles and serpentine iron drainpipes that slither down the walls, spiralled with gold paint and capped with spitting-fish spouts. Inside, the lobby's vaulted ceilings rise to impossible heights.

Rue des Batignolles is considered the center of the **Village Batignolles,** a quiet village of shops and residences starting at av. des Batignolles and extending to pl. du Dr. Felix Lobligeois. To the west, restaurants and cafés line rue des Dames, while shops stand on rue des Lévis (M: Villiers). On the other side of rue des Batignolles, rue Lemercier (M: Brochant) has a daily covered market filled with meat, cheese, flowers, produce, and old women who've shopped here since WWII. Farther down, at no. 45, is yet another of Verlaine's Parisian addresses. Several blocks north, rue de la Jonquière (M: Guy Môquet) is lined with Moroccan, Tunisian, and Algerian shops and restaurants. **La Cité des Fleurs,** 59-61, rue de la Jonquière, boasts a row of exquisite private homes and gardens straight out of a Balzac novel. Created in 1847, this prototypical condominium required each owner to plant at least three trees in the gardens. Don't miss the elegantly sculpted façades at no. 29 and no. 33.

SIGHTS

18e

8e

17e

16e

LEVALLOIS PERRET

500 yards
500 meters

17e
ACCOMMODATIONS
A Hôtel Belidor
B Hôtel Camperret Héliopolis
C Hotel Riviera
D Hôtel des Deux Avenues
E Hôtel Jouffrey

R. Guy Moquet
R. Jean Leclaire
R. de la Jonquière
R. Davy
R. Legendre
R. Lacroix
Av. de St. Ouen
Av. de Clichy
R. d'Amsterdam
R. Biot
R. St. Pétersbourg
R. Darcy
R. de Moscow
Bd. de Batignolles
R. Sauffroy
R. des Moines
R. Pouchet
R. Berzelius
Cité des Fleurs
Av. de Clichy
R. de la Condamine
R. Lemercier
R. Nollet
R. Truffaut
R. Brochant
R. des Batignolles
R. Boursault
R. des Dames
R. de Rome
R. Constantinople
R. du Rocher
R. de Madrid
R. du Gal Foy
R. de Naples
R. de Lisbonne
Bd. Malesherbes
R. de Levis
VILLIERS
R. de Moncean
Av. de Messine
Av. de la porte de Clichy
R. de Saussure
R. Cardinet
R. de Toqueville
R. Legendre
MALESHERBES
R. Jouffroy
R. Cernuschi
COURCELLES
Bd. de Courcelles
R. de Courcelles
Bd. Haussmann
Av. de Villiers
R. Fortuny
R. de Prony
R. Michel
Av. Hoche
Av. de Friedland
Av. de la Porte d'Asnières
Av. Brunetière
Bd. Berthier
Av. Gourgaud
PEREIRE
R. Ampère
WAGRAM
R. de Courcelles
Av. de Wagram
R. Fourcroy
D
R. Laugier
R. Poncelet
R. d'Alsace
PTE CHAMPERRET
R. Héliopolis
B
R. Stéphane Mallarmé
PORTE DE CHAMPERRET
Bd. de la Somme
Bd. Pereire
R. Pierre Demours
Av. Niel
C
Av. Macmahon
Arc de Triomphe
R. des Ternes
R. d'Armaillé
Av. Carnot
R. de Colonel Moll
Av. de la Grand Armée
R. Bayen
Bd. de Gouvion St-Cyr
R. Ferdinand Flocon
R. St. Ferdinand
Air France Terminal
A
Porte Maillot
Av. de Malakoff
Bd. Dixmude
Bd. Bineau
Bd. Victor Hugo
Av. du Roule
Bd. de Gaulle
Bd. de l'Amiral Bruix
Av. de la Grande Armée

N

The **Cimetière des Batignolles,** 8, rue St-Just (tel. 01 46 27 03 18; M: Porte de Clichy), sandwiched between a noisy *lycée* and the car horns of the Périphérique in the northwest corner of the 17ème, contains the graves of André Breton, Paul Verlaine, and Benjamin Peret. *(Open M-F 8am-6pm, Sa 8:30am-5:30pm, Su 9am-5:30pm. Free.)* The guards at the entrance give out maps and can refer you to other sources of information on the resident stars. To get to the cemetery from the metro, follow av. de Porte de Clichy toward the highway, then turn right onto av. du Cimetière des Batignolles. Across the Seine, the less famous, somewhat comic, and touching **Cimetière des Chiens,** 4, Pont de Clichy, in Asnières (tel. 01 40 86 21 11; M: Gabriel Péri Asnières-Gennevilliers), is the final resting spot for countless Parisian pets. *(Open W-M 10am-6pm; Oct. 15-March 15 W-M 10am-noon and 2-5pm. Free.)* Names like Fifi, Jean-Pierre, Jack, and Chérie mark small stones and tiny graves. From the metro, take rue Gabriel Péri to bd. Voltaire to the *cimetière.*

Back within the city limits, the enormous and ultra-modern **Palais des Congrès** stands at the western end of the 17ème (M: Porte Maillot). The glass tower's upper-crust restaurants, shopping galleries, and conference halls house a year-round convention center, keeping guests entertained with the Palais's in-house disco and cinema. When not welcoming a variety of business groups, the conference hall hosts music, theater, and dance performances with the likes of Ray Charles and the Red Army Chorus. (For show info call 01 40 68 00 05.) The open-air terrace on the seventh floor offers a free view of the sprawling Bois de Boulogne to the south and of La Défense to the west. Nearby, the lovely **place des Ternes** (M: Ternes), on the border of the 8ème, hosts a number of cafés and a daily flower market. From pl. des Ternes, it's a quick walk down bd. des Courcelles to the **Parc Monceau** (M: Monceau; see **Sights,** p. 172).

■ Eighteenth Arrondissement: Montmartre

Built high above the rest of Paris on a steep butte, Montmartre gets its name from its history of Roman occupation and Christian martyrdom and a series of etymological coincidences. A site of worship since before the arrival of the Druids, the hilltop was once home to an altar dedicated to Mercury and a shrine in honor of Mars. At different points in the Roman era, it was referred to as *Mons Mercurii* or *Mons Martis.* The mini-mountain suffered from this confused identity until a bishop named Dionysus, now known as St. Denis, came to introduce Christianity to the Gauls in the late 3rd century. Unimpressed, the Romans eschewed constructive criticism and cut off his head. St. Denis then picked up his head and carried it north, until he collapsed 7km away in St-Denis on the spot that is now the Basilique de St-Denis (see **St-Denis,** p. 284). To honor his gumption, the hill's name was changed to *Mont Martyrum* (Hill of Martyrs), which then became **Montmartre.** During the Revolution, the hill was renamed *Montmarat* after the Revolutionary martyr Marat, but the change was so subtle—a virtual play on words and their martyr namesakes—that the name Montmartre stuck and has been used ever since.

Along with the Montagne Ste-Geneviève in the 5ème (see **Sights,** p. 155), Montmartre is one of the two Parisian hills and few Parisian neighborhoods Baron Haussmann left intact when he redesigned the city and its environs. A rural area outside the city limits until the 20th century, the butte used to be covered with vineyards, wheat fields, windmills, and gypsum mines. Its picturesque beauty and low rents attracted notable bohemians like Toulouse-Lautrec and Eric Satie as well as performers and impresarios like Aristide Bruant. Toulouse-Lautrec, in particular, immortalized Montmartre through his paintings of life in disreputable nightspots like the Bal du Moulin Rouge (see below). A generation later, just before WWI smashed its spotlights and destroyed its crops, the butte welcomed Picasso, Modigliani, Utrillo, and Apollinaire into its artistic circle. As years passed, Montmartre grew in reputation but diminished in rural charm as city blocks replaced wheat fields. The last quaint traces of rural Montmartre are those profitably maintained by area residents and businesses. The neighborhood's reputation for countrified bohemia is now a memory. Parts of the butte are charming preserves of what Montmartre once was. You'll see windmills on tops of restaurants, a few vineyards, another generation of painted ladies, women in high-kicking chorus lines, and so on. The butte also provides a dramatic panorama of Parisian rooftops. Musicians, mimes, and peddlers gather in front of Sacré-Coeur and portrait artists sketch amid the cafés in the adjacent pl. du Tertre. At dusk, gas lamps trace the stairways up the hillside to the basilica.

MOUNTING MONTMARTRE

One does not merely visit Montmartre; one climbs it. Entering this *quartier* all along its southern boundary at M: Barbès-Rochechouart, M: Anvers, M: Pigalle, M: Blanche, or M: Clichy, you can wander slowly upward through any of the butte's small streets. The walk up rue Steinkerque from M: Anvers will carry you through a bustling fabric and clothing district, while approaching the hill from M: Château-Rouge along its eastern border gives you the chance to explore the African cloth, food, and gift shops that gather around rue Doudeauville and rue des Poissonniers. At night, use safer M: Abbesses even if it makes for a more roundabout route. It has the distinction of being the deepest metro station in Paris, with a large elevator, delightful murals, and a long spiral staircase that provides a warm-up for the climb ahead. To ascend from M: Abbesses to Sacré Coeur, follow rue la Vieuville to rue des Trois Frères, then continue straight up the stairs along rue Drevet, turning right on rue Gabrielle and left up the stairs to rue du Cardinal Dubois, directly below Sacré-Coeur. For a more scenic, if circuitous, route, walk up rue des Abbesses, turn right on rue Tholozé, and take rue Lepic through pl. Marcel Aymé to rue Norvins.

For the classic approach to Sacré-Coeur, climb up the switchbacked stairs leading away from pl. Willette up the disreputable rue Steinkerque from M: Anvers. Though steep, the walk is pleasant. Day and night, students and tourists mingle in the square to play guitars, drink wine, and smoke whatever's handy. To the east of the square, the **Musée d'Art Naïf Max Fourny** houses neoprimitivist art in a 19th-century iron and glass market-pavilion (see **Museums**, p. 226). For a less difficult ascent to the basilica, take the glass-covered **funicular** from the base of rue Tardieu (from M: Anvers, walk up rue Steinkerque and take a left on rue Tardieu). Reminiscent of a ski lift or a San Francisco cable car, the funicular is operated by the metro service and can be used with a normal metro ticket. In 45 seconds, you are miraculously whisked up an impressive 45-degree gradient while the city below comes almost immediately and spectacularly into sight. (Open 6am-12:45am. 8F.)

ONCE ATOP: SACRÉ COEUR AND PLACE DU TERTRE

However you choose to get there, the **Basilique du Sacré-Coeur** (Basilica of the Sacred Heart), 35, rue du Chevalier de la Barre (tel. 01 42 51 17 02; M: Anvers, Abbesses, or Château-Rouge), is like an exotic headdress or a white meringue floating above Paris. *(Open daily 7am-11pm. Free. Dome and crypt open daily 9am-6pm. Admission 16F, students 8F.)* In 1873, the Assemblée Nationale selected the birthplace of the Commune as the location for the Sacré-Coeur, "in witness of repentance and as a symbol of hope," although politician Eugène Spuller called it "a monument to civil war." It was hoped by the Catholic establishment that the Sacré-Coeur would "expiate the sins" of France after the bloody civil war in which thousands of *communards* (leftists who proclaimed a new populist government, known as the Commune of Paris) were massacred by the Thiers government troops sent from Versailles. After a massive fund-raising effort, the basilica was completed in 1914 and consecrated in 1919. Both its Romanesque-cum-Byzantine styles (a hybrid of onion domes and arches) and its white color sets it apart from the gray, smoky grunge of most Parisian buildings. The church's bleached look is a quirk of its stone, which secretes white lime when wet. As a result, the parts of the building sheltered from rain are noticeably darker than more exposed ones. While accordion players compete with mimes and illegal street vendors outdoors, the interior of the church is hushed, cool, and quiet. The mosaics inside the basilica are striking, especially the depiction of Christ on the ceiling and the mural of the Passion at the back of the altar. The narrow climb up the 112m bell tower offers the highest vantage point in Paris and a view that stretches as far as 50km on clear days. Farther down, the crypt contains a relic of what many believe to be a piece of the sacred heart of Christ.

As you exit the basilica, turn right on the winding rue du Mont to arrive at **place du Tertre.** Impossibly crowded with cafés, restaurants, and portrait and silhouette artists, the *place* can be a lovely spot for coffee or a photograph. At 21, pl. du Tertre, the **tourist office** (tel. 01 42 62 21 21) changes money and gives out annotated maps (5F) and information about the area (open daily Apr.-Sept. 10am-10pm; Oct.-Mar. 10am-7pm). Around the corner, the **Musée Salvador Dalí,** 11, rue Poulbot, displays a collection of the mustachio'd artist's lithographs and sculptures (see **Museums,** p. 228).

Moving away from the overpopulated pl. du Tertre you'll find narrow, winding streets, hidden gardens, and other remnants of the old bohemian-pastoral Montmartre. The **Clos Montmartre** stretches and twines its vines along rue des Saules. The only remaining vineyard on the butte, the Clos was planted in 1933 to emulate the vineyards and pastures that once covered the hill. It hosts an annual **harvest festival** in October (see **Festivals,** p. 249). Below the vineyard at 22, rue des Saules, is the **Lapin Agile,** a popular cabaret that welcomed Verlaine, Renoir, Modigliani, Max Jacob, and Maxime Blanchard (see **Chansonniers,** p. 236). In the 1860s, the establishment was known as the "Cabaret des Assassins" until André Gill decorated its façade with a *lapin* (rabbit) striking a pose as it leaps out of a pot while balancing a hat on its head and a bottle on its paw. The cabaret immediately gained renown as the "Lapin à Gill," (Gill's rabbit). By the time Picasso began to frequent the establishment, walking over from his first studio at 49, rue Gabrielle, the name had contracted to "Lapin Agile." In a zany satire of Picasso's work, other regulars at the café borrowed the owner's donkey, tied a canvas to its back and a paintbrush to its tail, and exhibited the resulting mess as the work of an unknown Italian artist (the painting received favorable reviews and fetched a respectable sum when sold). Overlooking the vineyard at 12, rue Cortot, the **Musée du Vieux Montmartre** presents a history of the neighborhood and has one of the few zinc bars to have escaped metal rationing during WWI (see **Museums,** p. 232).

DOWNHILL: PIGALLE AND THE MOULIN ROUGE

Walking down rue de l'Abreuvoir and left on rue Girardon to rue Lepic will carry you past the **Moulin Radet,** one of the last remaining windmills on Montmartre. Farther down are the **Moulin de la Galette,** depicted by Renoir during one of the frequent dances held there, and one of Van Gogh's former homes at 54, rue Lepic. These days, restaurants, antique stores, and *boulangeries* crowd this corner of Montmartre along rue des Abbesses, rue des Trois Frères, and rue Lepic. Tall iron gates hide the beautiful gardens of 18th-century townhouses. Parallel to rue Lepic, rue Caulaincourt leads downhill to the landscaped, secluded **Cimetière Montmartre,** 20, av. Rachel (tel. 01 43 87 64 24; M: Pl. de Clichy or Blanche), where writers such as Alexandre Dumas and Théophile Gautier, painters like Édgar Degas and Gustave Moreau, physicist André Ampère, and composer Hector Berlioz are buried. *(Open daily 8am-5:30pm.)* Émile Zola also reposed here until his corpse joined the Panthéon in 1908. In 1871, this cemetery became the site of huge mass graves after the siege of the Commune.

Along the bd. de Clichy and bd. de Rochechouart, you'll find many of the cabarets and nightclubs that were the definitive hangouts of the Belle Époque, including the infamous cabaret **Bal du Moulin Rouge** (tel. 01 46 06 00 19; fax 01 42 23 02 00; M: Blanche) immortalized by the paintings of Toulouse-Lautrec and the music of Offenbach. After WWI, Parisian bohemians relocated to the Left Bank and the area around pl. Pigalle became a world-renowned seedy red-light district (see **Sights,** p. 176). At the turn of the century, Paris's upper bourgeoisie came to the Moulin Rouge to play at being bohemian. Today, the crowd consists of tourists out for an evening of

SIGHTS

sequins, tassels, and skin. The revues are still risqué, but the admission is prohibitively expensive. **Place Pigalle** hosts several discos and trendy nightspots for Parisian and foreign youth. Other than that, it offers a seedy selection of peep-shows, prostitutes, and XXX movie theaters. Farther down bd. de Clichy, at the edge of the 17ème, **place de Clichy** is resplendent in the glowing neon of popular restaurants and cinemas. Busy during the day, it can (like Pigalle) be dangerous at night.

■ Nineteenth Arrondissement

Like Paris's other periphery arrondissements, the 19ème is a predominantly working-class, residential quarter. A host of recent emigrés from East and South Asia have settled here, making this neighborhood culturally diverse but poor and crowded. The notable exception to this rule is rue de Mouzaïa near the Parc des Buttes, where wealthy Parisians pay handsomely for houses with small gardens. The only major sight in the 19ème is the amazing **Parc de la Villette** (see **Museums,** p. 223), which features huge grassy areas for frisbee and soccer, paths for jogging and biking, wacky sculpture gardens, and the futuristic **Cité des Sciences et de l'Industrie** complex that includes the **Géode** omnimax theater, the **Explora** and **Technocité** science museums, the **Argonaute** oceanic museum, and the **Cinaxe** film complex.

To the south, **Parc des Buttes-Chaumont** (M: Buttes-Chaumont) is a mix of man-made topography and transplanted vegetation. *(Open daily May-Aug. 7am-11pm; Oct.-Apr. 7am-9pm.)* Nostalgic for London's Hyde Park, where he spent much of his time in exile, Napoleon III added four public parks to Paris: the Bois de Boulogne, the Bois de

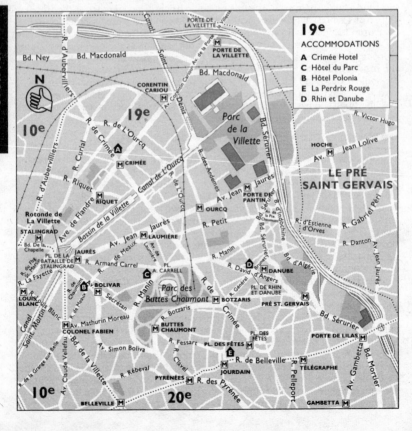

Vincennes, the Parc Montsouris, and the Parc des Buttes-Chaumont. All English gardens, they are filled with artificial lakes and tangled trees instead of the immaculately trimmed, rigidly geometrical forms of traditional French gardens like the Jardin du Luxembourg, the Tuileries, and Versailles. Before the construction of the Buttes-Chaumont, the *quartier* had been (since the 13th century) the host to a gibbet (an iron cage filled with the rotting corpses of criminals), a dumping-ground for dead horses, a breeding-ground for worms (sold as bait), and a gypsum quarry (the source of "plaster of Paris"). Making a park out of this mess took four years and 1000 workers. Designer Adolphe Alphand had all of the soil replaced and the quarried remains built up with new rock to create fake cliffs surrounding a lake, waterfalls, caves with stalactites, and a Roman temple, from which there is a great view of the *quartier*.

The park is policed at night and is one of the rare spots in Paris where you can sit on the grass and do serious exercise. The park offers *Sport et Nature* activities every Sunday morning 9:30am to noon. Just east of the park, on the western and southern sides of pl. de Rhin et Danube, pleasant villas line the cobbled rue Miguel Hidalgo and rue de l'Egalité of **Belleville,** one of Paris's new "in" neighborhoods, especially the part bordering the 11ème near rue Oberkampf. The 19ème is also home to Paris's Chinatown, full of wonderful, inexpensive restaurants. At night, avoid rue David d'Angiers, bd. Indochine, and av. Corentin Cariou.

■ Twentieth Arrondissement

As Haussmannization expelled many of Paris's workers from the central city, thousands migrated east to **Belleville** (the northern part of the 20ème), **Ménilmontant** (the southern), and **Charonne** (the southeastern). By the late Second Republic, the 20ème had come to be known as a "red" arrondissement, solidly proletarian and radical. In January 1871, just before the lifting of the Prussian siege, members of Belleville's National Guard stormed a prison to demand the release of leftist political leaders—an omen of the civil war to come. Some of the heaviest fighting during the suppression of the Commune took place in these streets, where the *communards* made desperate last stands on their home turf. Caught between the *Versaillais* troops to the west and the Prussian lines outside the city walls, the Commune fortified the Parc des Buttes-Chaumont (see **19ème** above) and the **Cimetière Père-Lachaise** but soon ran out of ammunition. On May 28, 1871, the *communards* abandoned their last barricade and surrendered (see **History,** p. 6).

After the Commune, the 20ème kept on as the fairly isolated home of those workers who survived the massacres. "Many a workman's child," historian Eugene Weber has observed, "grew to adolescence before World War I without getting out of Ménilmontant or Belleville." Today, the arrondissement has a similar feel, with busy residential areas and markets that cater not to visitors but to regulars. The area is also the home to large Greek, North African, Russian, and Asian communities.

PÈRE LACHAISE CEMETERY

16, rue du Repos. **Tel.** *01 43 70 70 33;* ***http://www.cemetary.org/lachaise/lachaise.intro.html.*** **M:** *Père-Lachaise.* **Open** *Mar.-Oct. M-F 8am-6pm, Sa 8:30am-6pm, Su and holidays 9am-6pm; Nov.-Feb. M-F 8am-5:30pm, Sa 8:30am-5:30pm, Su and holidays 9am-5:30pm. Last entrance 15min. before closing.* **Free.** *Free* **maps** *supposedly available at guard booths by main entrances, but they're usually out; it may be worth the 10F or so to buy a detailed one from a nearby tabac before entering. 2hr.* **guided tour** *(in French only) Tu and Sa at 2:30pm, W and F at 3pm; 35F, students 25F; meet at the bd. de Ménilmontant entrance (tel. 01 40 71 75 23 for more info).*

With its winding paths and elaborate sarcophagi, Cimetière Père Lachaise has become the final resting place of French and foreign giants. Balzac, Colette, David, Delacroix, La Fontaine, Haussmann, Molière, and Proust are buried here, as are Chopin, Jim Morrison (see below), Gertrude Stein, and Oscar Wilde. With so many tourists, they're hardly resting in peace. The land for Père Lachaise was bought by Napoleon's government in 1803 from Père de la Chaise, Louis XIV's confessor, to cre-

SIGHTS

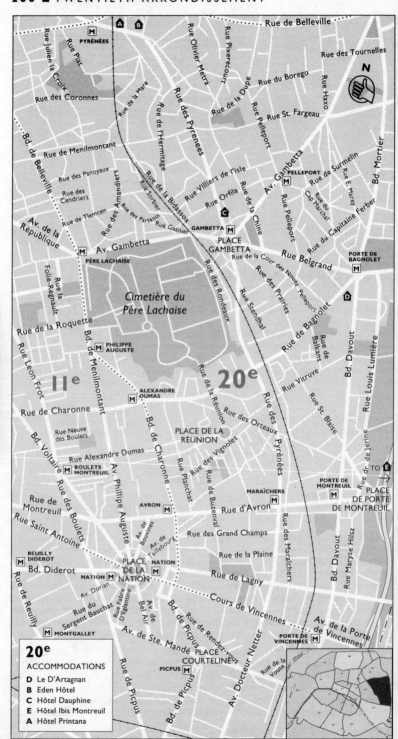

20ᵉ

ACCOMMODATIONS

- **D** Le D'Artagnan
- **B** Eden Hôtel
- **C** Hôtel Dauphine
- **E** Hôtel Ibis Montreuil
- **A** Hôtel Printana

Dying to Get In

How did Jim Morrison and Oscar Wilde end up here? Simply by dying in Paris (that is, if Jim is really dead and not hiding out in South America). Anybody who was born in or who died in Paris has the right to burial in a Parisian cemetery. Because of overcrowding, however, city policy now requires a family to pay a hefty fee for a departed member to be inhumed in a popular cemetery like Père Lachaise. Still, if you're looking for a unique gift for that special someone, a gravesite near a path is 38,395F, one away from a path only 23,595F. If these prices are beyond your reach, you can rent shelf space for your cremated ashes in the columbarium: 50 years 9000F, 30 years 6000F, 10 years 2000F. Pax vobiscum.

---

ate a "modern and hygienic necropolis" that would relieve the overcrowding of city cemeteries. At first, Parisians were reluctant to bury their dead so far from the city. To increase the cemetery's popularity, Napoleon ordered that the remains of a few famous figures be dug up and reburied in Père Lachaise. Thus abruptly arrived the remains of Molière, La Fontaine, those sexy medieval lovers Abélard and Héloïse, and several other luminaries.

The antithesis of the church cemetery, Père Lachaise is like a 19th-century garden party for the dead. Many of the tombs in this landscaped grove strive to remind visitors of the dead's many worldly accomplishments: the tomb of French Romantic painter Géricault wears a reproduction of his *Raft of the Medusa;* on Chopin's tomb sits his muse Calliope with a lyre in her hand. Oscar Wilde's grave is marked by a life-sized streaking Egyptian figure. The well-endowed likeness of journalist Victor Noir that stands atop his tomb is said to have magical fertility powers. You can figure out the rest. Haussmann, the man of the boulevards, wanted to destroy the cemetery as part of his urban-renewal project, but obviously relented; he occupies a mausoleum in Père Lachaise. Remembered by plaques here are dancer Isadora Duncan, author Richard Wright, opera diva Maria Callas, and artist Max Ernst. The most-visited grave is that of Jim Morrison, the former lead singer of The Doors. His graffiti-covered bust was removed from the tomb, leaving his fans to fill the rest of the cemetery with their messages. In summer, dozens of young people bring flowers, joints, beer, poetry, and Doors paraphernalia to leave on his tomb; the sandbox in front of the stone is now the sanctioned site for the creative expression of those pensive mourners. At least one guard polices the spot at all times.

Over one million people are buried in the cemetery. Curiously, there are only 100,000 tombs. The discrepancy is due to the old practice of burying the poor in mass graves. Corpses are removed from these unmarked plots at regular intervals to make room for new generations of the dead. This grisly process is necessary in a densely populated city like Paris. Even with such purges, the 44 hectares of Père Lachaise are filled to bursting, so the government makes room by digging up any grave that has not been visited in a certain number of years. To avoid this fate, some hire an official "mourner," much as wealthy patrons used to hire choirs to sing their funeral masses.

Perhaps the most moving sites in Père Lachaise are those that mark the tragic deaths of collective groups. The **Mur des Fédérés** (Wall of the Federals) has become a site of pilgrimage for left-wing sympathizers. In May 1871, a group of *communards* murdered the Archbishop of Paris, who had been taken hostage at the beginning of the Commune. They dragged his mutilated corpse to their stronghold in Père Lachaise and tossed it in a ditch. Four days later, the victorious *Versaillais* found the body. In retaliation, they lined up 147 Fédérés against the eastern wall of the cemetery, shot them, and buried them on the spot. Since 1871, the Mur des Fédérés has been a rallying point for the French Left, which recalls the massacre's anniversary every Pentecost. Ironically, Republican Adolphe Thiers, who ordered their execution, shares the cemetery with them; he died of natural causes in 1877. Near the wall, a number of moving monuments containing human remains commemorate both Resistance fighters from WWII as well as Nazi concentration camp victims.

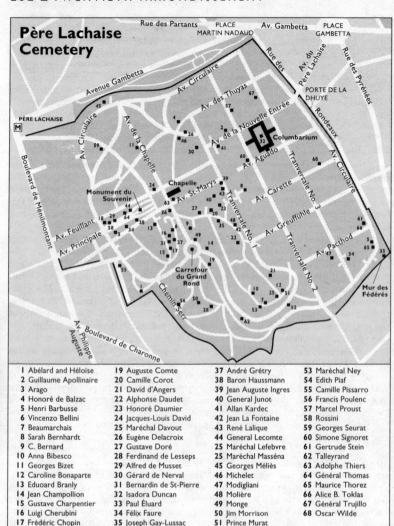

Père Lachaise Cemetery

1 Abélard and Héloïse	19 Auguste Comte	37 André Grétry	53 Maréchal Ney
2 Guillaume Apollinaire	20 Camille Corot	38 Baron Haussmann	54 Edith Piaf
3 Arago	21 David d'Angers	39 Jean Auguste Ingres	55 Camille Pissarro
4 Honoré de Balzac	22 Alphonse Daudet	40 General Junot	56 Francis Poulenc
5 Henri Barbusse	23 Honoré Daumier	41 Allan Kardec	57 Marcel Proust
6 Vincenzo Bellini	24 Jacques-Louis David	42 Jean La Fontaine	58 Rossini
7 Beaumarchais	25 Maréchal Davout	43 René Lalique	59 Georges Seurat
8 Sarah Bernhardt	26 Eugène Delacroix	44 General Lecomte	60 Simone Signoret
9 C. Bernard	27 Gustave Doré	25 Maréchal Lefebvre	61 Gertrude Stein
10 Anna Bibesco	28 Ferdinand de Lesseps	25 Maréchal Masséna	62 Talleyrand
11 Georges Bizet	29 Alfred de Musset	45 Georges Méliès	63 Adolphe Thiers
12 Caroline Bonaparte	30 Gérard de Nerval	46 Michelet	64 Général Thomas
13 Eduoard Branly	31 Bernardin de St-Pierre	47 Modigliani	65 Maurice Thorez
14 Jean Champollion	32 Isadora Duncan	48 Molière	66 Alice B. Toklas
15 Gustave Charpentier	33 Paul Éluard	49 Monge	67 Général Trujillo
16 Luigi Cherubini	34 Félix Faure	50 Jim Morrison	68 Oscar Wilde
17 Frédéric Chopin	35 Joseph Gay-Lussac	51 Prince Murat	
18 Colette	36 Thédore Gericault	52 Nadar	

CHARONNE, MÉNILMONTANT, AND BELLEVILLE

Of all the old neighborhoods in the 20ème, **Charonne** has been swallowed up least by the concrete and metal of urbanization. The best-preserved vestige of Charonne is the **Église de St-Germain-de-Charonne**, 4, pl. St-Blaise (tel. 01 43 71 42 04; M: Porte de Bagnolet), a 13th-century church ravaged by fire in 1737 and restored in the 18th century. *(Open daily 9am-noon and 2-7pm. Cemetery open daily Mar. 15-Nov. 5 9am-7pm; Nov. 6-Mar. 15 9am-5:30pm.)* The church cemetery is the burial site of the murdered *communards,* who were accidently dug up in 1897 during the building of a reservoir. Inside, you'll find the original organ, a 19th-century depiction of St-Germain by Suvée, and a contemporary pietà given to the church in 1995 by local artist Paul Rambé. Directly opposite, the cobbled rue St-Blaise gives a taste of what Charonne used to be.

Along the western edge of Pére Lachaise, rue de Ménilmontant's busy ethnic markets, cafés, alleyways, housing projects, and small parks reveal little of the flavor of the old **Ménilmontant** quartier. The same is true of the old village and quartier **Belleville.** But Belleville is now home to one of Paris's largest Asian communities. Just south of rue de Belleville, is 72, rue des Pyrénées—the site where the legendary Edith Piaf was abandoned as a child (see **Music,** p. 19). The **Parc de Belleville** at the corner of rue de Piaf and rue des Envierges is the best-kept secret of the arrondissement. A good example of urban renewal gone right, the terraced park is a green oasis nestled in among the stark grey of the surrounding housing projects. Squeaky clean and constantly patrolled by authorities, the park is replete with waterfalls, fountains, gorgeous views of Paris, and the fascinating **Maison de l'Air** (see **Museums,** p. 231).

■ Bois de Boulogne

The **Bois de Boulogne** (M: Porte Maillot, Sablons, Pont de Neuilly, Porte Dauphine, or Porte d'Auteuil) is an 846-hectare green canopy at the western edge of Paris and a popular place for walks, jogs, and picnics. Formerly a royal hunting ground, the *bois* was given to the city of Paris by Napoleon III in 1852. The Emperor had become a dilettante landscape-architect during his exile in England and wanted Paris to have something comparable to Hyde Park. Acting on these instructions, Baron Haussmann filled in sand-pits, dug artificial lakes, and cut winding paths through thickly wooded areas. This attempt to copy nature marked a break with the tradition of French formal gardens, rectilinear hedges, and flower beds established by Le Nôtre.

When Paris annexed Auteuil in 1860, the park, though outside the city walls, became part of the $16^{\grave{e}me}$. In 1871, it was the site of a massacre of *communards*. General Gallifet shot the most politically and socially undesirable people he could discern among the prisoners bound for Versailles—men with gray hair, watches, glasses, or with "intelligent faces." At the turn of the century, the park became fashionable for carriage rides. Aristocratic families rode weekly to the park to spend a Sunday afternoon "in the country." Balzac's *Nana*, Colette's *Gigi*, and Vincente Minnelli's film *Gigi* with Leslie Caron, Louis Jourdan, and Maurice Chevalier feature Belle Époque carriage rides through the *Bois*. Picture parasol'd ladies in enormous wide-brimmed and plumed hats (*à la* Audrey Hepburn in *My Fair Lady* or Barbara Streisand in *Hello Dolly*) and men with canes in gray top hats, gloves, and morning coats.

The Bois de Boulogne contains several stadiums, the most famous of which are the **Hippodromes de Longchamp** and **d'Auteuil.** During the Belle Époque, the Grand Prix at Longchamp in June was one of the premier events of the social calendar. Also within the *bois,* the **Parc des Princes** hosts football (soccer) matches. The **Stade Roland Garros** is home of the **French Open** tennis tournament (see **Sports,** p. 248). The *bois*'s boathouses rent rowboats (see below).

Until a couple of years ago, the *bois* by night was a bazaar of sex and drugs, where transvestite prostitutes would stand along the roads and violent crime was quite common. In 1991, a flood of newly liberated Eastern Europeans visiting Paris camped out in the park, in odd imitation of the Cossacks who bivouacked here after Waterloo. All lawn-crashers have been nudged out (for better or for worse) and police are now especially attentive to the *bois*, closing the roads at night and stepping up patrols. Nonetheless, the boulevards around the periphery of the *bois* continue to be lined with prostitutes at night. It is a bad idea to come here for a moonlight stroll.

The **Jardin d'Acclimatation** (tel. 01 40 67 90 82), at the northern end of the *bois* (M: Sablons), offers a small zoo, mini-golf course, carousels, kiddie motorcycle race-track, bumper cars, pony rides, and outdoor jazz concerts. *(Open daily 10am-6pm. Ticket office closes 5:45pm. Admission 12F, under 3 free. No dogs allowed.)* Within the park, the **Musée en Herbe** (tel. 01 40 67 97 66; M: Porte Maillot), is a modern art museum designed for children ages 4 to 11. *(Open Su-F 10am-6pm, Sa 2-6pm. Admission 16F. Studio sessions July-Aug. daily at 2 and 4pm; Sept-June W, Sa, and Su at 2 and 4pm. Call to make reservations. Participation 25F.)* Previous shows have featured Chagall and Picasso. The museum also offers a studio workshop. A participatory theater company for children

SIGHTS

Bois de Boulogne

← TO LA DÉFENSE

Seine

Île de Puteaux

M PONT DE NEUILLY

Av. Charles de Gaulle

M LES SABLONS

PORTE MAILLOT M

Bd. Maurice Barrés

Jardin d'Acclimatation

Musée National des Arts et Traditions Populaires

Bd. du Général Koenig

Rue de Longchamp

Bd. du Cdt. Charcot

Mare St-James

Rue du Mahatma Gandhi

Cercle du Bois de Boulogne

PORTE DAUPHINE/ AV. FOCH M

Musée de la Contrefaçon

Bd. Richard Wallace

Université Paris IX

Bd. Lannes

Parc de Bagatelle

Allée de Longchamps

Rte. de Sévres Neuilly

Allée de la Reine Marguerite

Rte. de Suresnes

M AV. HENRI-MARTIN

Lac Inférieur

Racing Club de France

Pelouse de la Muette

Bd. Suchet

Stèle de Santos Dumont

Pré Catelan

Rte. de la Grande Cascade

Musée Marmottan

Château de Longchamp

Lac Supérieur

Rte. de l'Hippodrome

Hippodrome d'Auteuil

Rte. de Suresnes

Av. de St-Cloud

Bd. Suchet

Hippodrome de Longchamp

Rte. de la Seine à la Butte Mortemart

Av. de St-Cloud

PORTE D'AUTEUIL M

N

0 ____ 1/4 mile

0 ____ 1/4 kilometer

Av. de la Pte. d'Auteuil

Bd. Anatole France

Jardin des Serres d'Auteuil

stages plays (Oct.-July W and Sa-Su) and puppet shows (W, Sa-Su, and daily during school vacations at 3:15 and 4:15pm; free). From the metro, go to the big house marked l'Orée du Bois and follow the brown signs that point to the right of the building, or take the little train to the left of the building. (Trains W, Sa-Su, and public holidays every 10min. 1:30-6:30pm, 5F, under 3 free.)

Hear pins drop at the **Bowling de Paris** (tel. 01 40 67 94 00), near the route Mahatma Gandhi entrance of the Jardin d'Acclimatation. (Admission 25F, students and children 17F, shoe rental 12F. See **Sports**, p. 246). On the edge of the garden, the **Musée National des Arts et Traditions Populaires** focuses on French pre-industrial life (see **Museums**, p. 227). The **Pré Catelan** (tel. 01 46 47 73 20) is a neatly manicured meadow supposedly named for a troubadour who died in these woods. (Open daily 8:30am-8pm.) Arnault Catelan, who rode from Provence to Paris in order to deliver gifts to Philippe le Bel, hired a group of men to protect him on his journey. The men robbed and murdered him in the dead of night, believing that Arnault carried valuable parcels. In fact, Arnault carried only rare perfumes and essences. Authorities later captured the marauders, who, doused in scent, were easily identified. The huge purple beech on the central lawn is almost 200 years old. You can sit on the grass, except where there are *pelouse interdite* signs. Inside the Pré Catelan, the **Jardin de Shakespeare** features plants mentioned by the bard, grouped by play—there is a collection of Scottish highland vegetation in the **Macbeth** area, a Mediterranean section for **The Tempest**, etc. In the center, a lovely 300-person open-air **Théâtre de Verdure du Jardin Shakespeare** (tel. 01 40 19 95 33) gives popular summer performances of Shakespeare's and others' plays in French. (F at 6:30pm, Sa 3:30 and 6:30pm, Su 3:30 and 5:30pm. Tickets 100F, students and seniors 60F, can be reserved by phone at 06 60 10 04 15 or purchased at the entrance to the garden 15 minutes before the show. Pré Catelan open 8:30am-7:30pm. Jardin de Shakespeare open daily 3-3:30pm and 4:30-5pm; admission 5F, students 3F, under 10 2F. For more info, see **Private Theaters**, p. 235.) Take the metro to Porte Maillot then take bus #244 to Bagatelle-Pré-Catelan.

The **Parc de la Bagatelle** (tel. 01 40 67 97 00; same bus stop as Pré Catelan) was once a private estate within the *bois*, which became a public park in 1905. (Open daily Jan. 1-15 9am-4:30pm; Jan. 16-Feb. 15 and Oct. 16-Nov. 30 9am-5:30pm; Feb. 16-28 and Oct. 1-15 9am-6pm; March 1-15 8:30am-6:30pm; March 16-April 30 and Sept. 8:30am-7pm; June-July 8:30am-8pm. Ticket office closes 30min. earlier. Admission to park 10F, ages 6-10 5F. Why they made it this complicated, we don't know.) In 1777, the future Charles X employed 900 workers to toil night and day to build the little **Château de la Bagatelle** when Marie Antoinette, his sister-in-law, bet him that he could not have it ready to receive her in 60 days. The Anglo-Chinese garden is famous for its stunning June rose exhibition (35F, seniors 25F, plus 10F park admission; call for specific dates) and for its water lilies, which the gardener added in tribute to Monet. Do not walk on the grass. They really care about this—enough to put up signs in English. The two artificial **lakes** stretching down the eastern edge of the Bois feature the manicured islands of **Lac Inférieur** (M: Porte Dauphine), which can be reached by rented rowboat only. Lake Superior, on the other hand, requires an airplane. (Boathouses open late Feb. to early Nov. daily 10am-7pm, weather permitting. Rentals 45F per hr., 400F deposit; with insurance against damage to boat 52F per hr., 200F deposit.)

The **Jardin des Serres d'Auteuil** (Greenhouse Garden) is full of hothouse flowers and trees. (Open daily May-Aug. 10am-6pm; Sept.-Apr. 10am-5pm. Admission 3F.) Enter at 1, av. Gordon-Bennett, off bd. d'Auteuil (M: Porte d'Auteuil or Michel Ange Molitor). Free and prettier, if something of a make-out spot, is the neighboring **Jardin des Poètes**. Poems are attached to each flower bed: scan Ronsard, Corneille, Racine, Baudelaire, and Apollinaire. Rodin's sculpture of Victor Hugo is partially obscured by a thicket. Bicycles can be rented from the boathouse at the northern end of the Lac Inférieur and in front of the entrance to the Jardin d'Acclimatation (tel. 06 07 35 40 17). (Both open from Apr.16-Oct. daily 10am-7pm; Oct. 16-Apr. 15 W and Sa-Su 10am-7pm. Organized rides through the park 3-5pm, 100F. To rent a bicycle without a guide 130F, half day 70F; deposit for rides limited to the bois 1000F, for rides outside 1500F. Call for reservations.)

Bois de Vincennes

N

Av. de la Dame Blanche

M FONTENAY-SOUS-BOIS

M NOGENT-SUR-MARNE

Jardin Tropical

Av. de la Belle Gabrielle

Av. de Nogent

Lac des Minimes

Fort de Vincennes

PARC FLORAL DE PARIS

Av. du Tremblay

Institut National des Sports

Stade Pershing

Rte. Mortemart

M JOINVILLE LE PONT

École d'Horticulture

ARBORÉTUM

Hippodrome

M CHÂTEAU DE VINCENNES

Château de Vincennes

Av. de Paris

Esplanade St-Louis

Caserne

Stade Municipal de Vincennes

Rte. de Pyramide

Rte. Saint Hubert

Rte. du Pesage

Rte. Bourbon

Rte. Dauphine

Rte. de la Faluère

Allée Royale

Rte. de la Demi Lune

1/4 mile

1/4 kilometer

0   0

Av. des Minimes

Rte. de la Tourelle

Rte. de la Tourelle

Rte. de la Tourelle

M ST-MANDÉ TOURELLE

Av. Foch

Av. Victor Hugo

Lac de St-Mandé

Rue de la République

Av. Daumesnil

PARC ZOOLOGIQUE

Lac Daumesnil

Temple Bouddhique

Cimitière de Charenton

Av. de Gravelle

Bd. Périphérique

Bd. Soult

Musée des Arts Africains et Océaniens

M PORTE DORÉE

M LIBERTÉ

Vélodrome J. Anquetil

Rue de Paris

It's Not Easy Being Green

London has Hyde Park, New York has Central Park, but Paris has Woods *(Bois)* and Gardens *(Jardins)*. While Haussmann and Napoleon III's 19th-century **Bois de Boulogne** and **Bois de Vincennes** keep politely on the western and eastern edges of town, the 18th-century **Jardin des Tuileries** and **Jardins du Luxembourg's** formal geometric French gardens offer relief in the center of Paris. In truth, Paris also has its **Parcs:** Haussmann and Napoleon III's **Buttes-Chaumont, Monceau,** and **Montsouris** green the city-scene. Since the 1980s, Mitterrand and Chirac have lobbied for even more flowers, grass, and trees. Opened in 1985, **La Villette's** exquisite urban park mixes nature and technology. The **Jardin de l'Atlantique** (M: Montparnasse Bienvenue) is an engineering feat of tress and bamboos suspended 18m over the busy railway tracks of Montparnasse. The **Promenade Plantée** (M: Bastille) features roses and shrubs amid the railway tracks above the Viaduc des Arts. Opened in 1993, the **Parc André Citroën** (M: Citroën) sprawls on the site of the former car factory. And the latest project for Paris 2000 is the proposed **Tour de la Terre** (Tower of Earth or Tree House), a 200m high, 3000 square-meter mountain of earth, topped by cafés, restaurants, and Millennium exhibitions, which will symbolize Paris's commitment to the environment. Critics argue that it will take thousands of felled trees to build this millennial monument. So much for the future.

■ Bois de Vincennes

Like the Bois de Boulogne, the Bois de Vincennes (M: Chateau de Vincennes or Porte Dorée) was once a royal hunting forest. Today it is the largest expanse of greenery in Paris. Since it lay outside the city limits and beyond the reach of Parisian authorities, it was also a favorite ground for dueling. The elder Alexandre Dumas dueled a literary collaborator here who claimed to have written the *Tour de Nesle*. Dumas's pistol misfired and the author had to content himself with using the experience as the basis for a scene in *The Corsican Brothers*. Like the Bois de Boulogne, the Vincennes forest was given to Paris by Napoleon III, to be transformed into an English-style garden. Not surprisingly, Haussmann oversaw the planning of lakes and pathways. Annexed to a much poorer section of Paris than the Bois de Boulogne, Vincennes was never quite as fashionable or as formal. As one fin-de-siècle observer wrote, "At Vincennes, excursionists do not stand on ceremony, and if the weather is sultry, men may be seen lounging in their shirt sleeves, and taking, in other respects, an ease which the inhabitants of the boulevards, who resort to the Bois de Boulogne, would contemplate with horror." Today, the Bois de Vincennes's bikepaths, horsetrails, zoo, and Buddhist Temple are wonderful escapes from the grind of the city.

Considered the best zoo in France, the **Parc Zoologique de Paris,** 53, av. de St-Maurice (tel. 01 44 75 20 10; fax 01 43 43 54 73; M: Porte Dorée) is the Bois de Vincennes's most popular attraction. *(Open May-Sept. M-Sa 9am-6pm, Su 9am-6:30pm; Oct.-Apr. M-Sa 9am-5pm, Su 9am-5:30pm. Ticket office closes 30min. before zoo. Admission 40;, ages 4-16, students 16-27, and over 60 30F; under 4 free. Kiddie train tour leaves from restaurant 12F, under 10 10F. Guidebook to the zoo 30F.)* Unlike their brethren in the Jardin des Plantes, animals promenade in relatively natural surroundings. Recently, the zoo has been working hard to improve the animals' environment. The *phoques* (the French word for *seal* that is pronounced just as you think it is) are fed daily at 4:30pm. And, oh, those crazy baboons! The park is also home to the privately owned **Grand Rocher,** an observatory. The 20F fee is a bit exorbitant, but the view is lovely.

If you're with the kids, or just feel the need for some heavy petting, head to the Bois de Vincennes's **Ferme de Paris** (Paris Farm, tel. 01 43 28 47 63). *(Open Sa-Su and holidays in summer 1:30-7pm; in winter 1:30-5:30pm. Admission 22F, under 18 11F.)* Full of barnyard animals and fields of produce, the farm encourages kids and adults to do some hands-on learning. If you'd rather watch flowers grow, the City of Paris offers over 20 different flora and fauna tours starting from the **Parc Floral de Paris,** within the *bois* (5F). Joggers, cyclists, and people-watchers share the turf around **Lac Daumesnil.** Others row boats. (Boat rental Mar.-Nov. daily 10:30am-5:30pm. 1-2 people 50F per hr., 3-4 people 56F per hr., 50F deposit plus recommended tip.) Penetrate farther into the park for running and cycling paths. The **Vélodrome Jacques Anquetil,** the **Hippodrome de Vincennes,** and other sports facilities await you (see **Participatory Sports,** p. 246).

The **Château de Vincennes** (M: Chateau de Vincennes), on the northern edge of the park, is called "the Versailles of the Middle Ages." *(Open daily May-Sept. 10am-6pm; Oct.-Apr. 10am-5pm. Admission by guided tour only, 25F, students 15F.)* French kings held court here as early as the 13th century, and although the Louvre was royalty's principal home, every French monarch from Charles V to Henri IV spent at least part of his time at Vincennes. On the spot that Philippe-Auguste chose for a royal hunting residence, Charles V built up a medieval fortress. Henri III found it a useful refuge during the Wars of Religion, and Mazarin and the court found its defenses useful in the wake of the Fronde. In the 18th century, Vincennes became a country-club prison for well-known enemies of the state. Mirabeau spent 3½ years here, killing time by writing lecherous letters to his (married) mistress. When Diderot was imprisoned in the château, Rousseau walked through the forest to visit. In the 19th century, the complex resumed its military functions, serving as fortress, arsenal, and artillery park. In 1917, the infamous Mata Hari, convicted of spying for the Germans, faced a firing squad within its walls. In 1940, the château was headquarters for General Maurice Gamelin, Supreme Commander of French Land Forces. De Gaulle criticized Gamelin for holing up in Vincennes, without even a radio to connect him with the front.

Built between 1360 and 1370, the 52m-high **donjon** is a striking example of medieval architecture. It has been closed for restoration for the past five years, however, and unfortunately will probably not be open until early in the next millennium. The **Sainte-Chapelle** was founded as a church in 1379, but the building was not inaugurated until 1552. *(French language tours of the church, 4 per day, 32F. Tours of the church and château, 5 per day, 32F; students, ages 18-25, and seniors 14F, under 12 free.)* Dainty in its decor and especially beautiful in late afternoon, the Ste-Chapelle is looking even better these days after restoration of the exterior. Guided tours are the only way to get in, but the church, stripped down to its bare bones over the centuries, is more impressive from the outside. There are archaeological digs to survey in the main courtyard, and the ramparts offer a pleasant, if unexciting, view of the area.

One of the gems of the Bois de Vincennes is the **Parc Floral de Paris,** Esplanade du Château (tel. 01 43 43 92 95; M: Chateau de Vincennes), reached by walking down rue de la Pyramide from the castle. *(Open daily Apr.-Sept. 9:30am-8pm; Oct.-Mar. 9:30am-5pm. Admission 10F, ages 6-18 5F, under 6 free.)* The park has a library, a butterfly garden, miniature golf, and assorted games for kids. Picnic areas, restaurants, and open-air concerts make it a center of summer entertainment.

■ La Défense

Located just outside the city limits, **La Défense** is a comic-book city come to life. A brilliant and gleaming center of modern architecture, glass, and steel, La Défense is, in effect, Paris's newest arrondissement. Home to 14 of France's top 20 corporations, many of the buildings in this modernist metropolis house businesses, corporate offices, and law firms. Great efforts have been made since La Défense's initial development in 1958, especially by Mitterrand and his *Grands Projets* program, to interject social spaces, monuments, and art into La Défense's commercial landscape. Shops, galleries, trees, and sculptures by **Miró, Calder,** and **César** cluster around the **Grande Arche de la Défense,** a breathtaking 35-story building in the shape of a white hollow cube. *(Open daily 10am-7pm; roof closes 1hr. after ticket office. Admission 40F, under 18, students, and seniors 30F.)*

After the construction of the Tour Montparnasse in 1973 (see **Sights,** p. 188), Parisian authorities restricted the further construction of skyscrapers *(gratte-ciel)* within the 20 arrondissements for fear that new highrises would alter the Paris skyline. As a result, new building projects moved to La Défense, and modern Paris was born. To maintain the symmetry of the **Axe Historique** (the line that stretches from the Arc de Triomphe du Carrousel in front of the Louvre, down the Champs-Élysées to the Arc de Triomphe, and down the bd. de la Grande Armée to La Défense), and to connect La Défense with the rest of Paris, I.M. Pei suggested in 1969 a plan for a monument to anchor the Défense end of the axis. Ultimately, Pei was asked instead to design the eastern terminus in the courtyard of the Louvre. French Presidents Pompidou, Giscard d'Estaing, and Mitterrand sponsored international contests for a monument. Of 424 projects, four were presented anonymously to the president, who chose Danish architect Otto von Spreckelsen's Grande Arche for its "purity and strength." Spreckelsen backed out of the project before its completion, disheartened by red tape and by his own design, which he deemed a "monument without a soul." Others celebrated the arch as a "window to the world," whose slight asymmetry gives the empty cube a dash of humanity. British engineer Peter Rice finished the work and designed the canvas "clouds" suspended to soften the arch's austere angles.

The Grande Arche de la Défense was inaugurated on the French Republic's bicentennial, July 14, 1989, when it hosted a G7 summit. The roof of this unconventional office building covers 2.5 acres—Nôtre-Dame could nestle in its hollow core. The arch's walls are covered with white marble that shines brilliantly in sunlight. Ride the outdoor glass elevators for an unparalleled view at the top.

Despite La Défense's 20th-century architecture and modernist look, the area dates from the 19th century. In 1871, Louis-Ernest Barrias's design beat 100 other proposals (including one by Auguste Rodin) in a contest to commemorate the defense of Paris against the Prussians. The name has caused some confusion: the Managing Director of La Défense was once refused entry to Egypt when he was mistaken for a military official.

Other Défense buildings include the **Bull Tower,** the tent-like **Palais Défense,** and the **CNIT building,** a center for congresses, exhibitions, and conferences that, at 37 years old, is La Défense's oldest building. The **Musée de l'Automobile,** 1, pl. du Dôme, features car-related accessories, exhibits on the history of the automobile, and 110 vintage *voitures. (Open daily noon-7pm. Admission 30F, students, seniors, and under 16 25F.)* The globe-shaped **Dôme IMAX** houses a huge-screen omnimax theater (see **Cinema,** p. 237). Across from Joan Miró's popsicle (iced-lolly) sculpture on pl. de la Défense, Alexander Calder's linear, spidery red steel sculpture provides a fitting counterpart. Next door, beyond the small lawn, the **Info Défense** booth (tel. 01 47 74 84 24) offers free maps, guides, and a permanent exhibit on the architectural history and future of La Défense (open M-F 9am-6pm, Sa-Su 10am-6pm). For French tours of La Défense, call **Défense-Évenement** (tel. 01 46 92 17 50; tours 35F, students 25F) or take the *petit train. (Tours every 40min. Apr.-Oct. daily 10am-6:30pm from under the Grande Arche; 27F, under 10 15F.)* To the right of the booth, the **Galerie de l'Esplanade** features temporary art exhibits (open daily noon-7pm).

If you want to eat or shop, the huge **Quatre Temps** shopping center—one of the largest shopping malls in Europe—contains cafés, supermarkets, and 30 restaurants. Enter from the Grande Arche metro stop, from doors behind the Miró sculpture, or from next to the Musée de l'Automobile. The info desk on the first floor near the escalator to the metro distributes maps of the complex. *(Shops open M-Sa 10am-8pm. Supermarkets open M-Sa 9am-10pm.)* The CNIT building contains six restaurants, including a café and sandwich shop with outdoor seating and views of the Grande Arche.

To get to La Défense from Paris, take the metro or RER. The RER is faster, but the metro is cheaper. If you do take the RER, buy the RER ticket before going through the turnstile. A normal metro ticket may get you into the RER station in Paris, but won't get you out without a fine at La Défense.

Museums

Since Charles de Gaulle appointed France's first Minister of Culture in 1956, thousands of hours and millions of francs have been spent shaking the dust off the reputation of the Parisian museum. Paris's national museums are multi-purpose, user-friendly institutions shaped by public interest and state funds. Serving as forums for lectures, art films, concerts, and the occasional play, the museums here—most prominently the Louvre, Orsay, and Pompidou—broadcast Paris, past and present.

Paris's *grands musées* cater to an international public and are mobbed, particularly in summer. Take advantage of evening hours, avoid weekends and reduced admission days where possible, and be forewarned: the *Mona Lisa* will be obscured by raised cameras and clamoring schoolchildren. If you tire of dangling from chandeliers for a better view, look for Paris's smaller museums, which display specialized collections often comparable in content to wings of their larger cousins. For listings of temporary exhibits, consult the bimonthly *Bulletin des Musées et Monuments Historiques,* available at the tourist office, 127, av. des Champs-Elysées (tel. 01 49 52 53 54). *Paris Museums and Monuments* not only provides phone numbers, addresses, and hours but also describes the museums (including wheelchair access). *Pariscope* and *l'Officiel des Spectacles* contain weekly updates of hours and temporary exhibits (see **Publications About Paris,** p. 75).

If you are in Paris for a short period of time or are generally hoping to do a sightseeing blitz, you may want to invest in a **Carte Musées et Monuments,** which offers admission to 65 museums in the Paris area. This card will probably save you money if you are planning to visit more than 3 museums/sights in one day and will enable you to sail past all of the frustrated tourists standing in line. In summer, lines can be more than half an hour long. You may want to coordinate your purchase of this card with a visit to Versailles, where the card is indispensable: you will skip the hour and a half line in the summer heat. The card is available at major museums and in almost all metro stations. Ask for a brochure listing participating museums and monuments. A pass for one day is 80F; for three consecutive days 160F; for five consecutive days 240F. For more information, call **Association InterMusées,** 25, rue du Renard, 4ème (tel. 01 44 78 45 81; fax 44 78 12 23; http://www.intermusees.com).

Larger museums often offer group tours in various languages. Prices are typically around 500F for a group of adults, 250F for students and visitors 60 years and older. In the past few years, many of Paris's museums have turned their attention toward a national audience, foregoing regularly scheduled English-language tours for more extensive programs in French. This shift is particularly the case in smaller museums with major collections. Relatively inexpensive English pamphlets can usually be found at bookstores within these museums.

Visiting Paris's galleries is the best way to see what's new in contemporary art. Most of the city's 200 galleries specialize in one type of art, such as neoprimitive painting, modern sculpture, prints, or photography. The 8ème is loaded with Old Master galleries. Those near M: Franklin Roosevelt on the Champs-Elysées, av. Matignon, rue du Faubourg St-Honoré, and rue de Miromesnil focus on Impressionism and post-Impressionism. Thanks to the new opera house, the Bastille area has become a haven for artists and galleries with an *épater-les-bourgeois* (shock-the-bourgeoisie) spin. The highest concentration of galleries is in the Marais, especially on rue Quincampoix and rue des Blancs-Manteaux. In St-Germain-des-Prés, rue Mazarine, rue de Seine, rue des Beaux-Arts, and rue Bonaparte also contain an assembly of small galleries focusing on 20th-century art. Walk right in and don't feel intimidated. You're not usually expected to buy. Most galleries are closed Sunday and Monday and are open until 7pm on other days, often with a break at lunch. The galleries that require appointments are not appropriate for casual browsing.

MAJOR MUSEUMS

▓ Musée du Louvre

Tel. 01 40 20 50 50. *Web* http://www.louvre.fr. *M:* Palais-Royal/Musée du Louvre. *Open* M and W 9am-9:45pm, Th-Su 9am-6pm. Last entry 45min. before closing, but people are asked to leave 30min. before closing. *Admission* W-Sa 9am-3pm 45F, 3pm-close and all day Su 26F, under 18 and first Su of the month free. *Temporary exhibitions* in the Cour Napoléon: Open at 10am; additional admission 30F, under 18 free. Ticket to both regular and temporary expositions 60F before 3pm, 40F after 3pm and on Su. *English Tours:* "Discover the Louvre," M and W-Sa 17F; call 01 40 20 52 09 for exact times. *Bookstore:* Open W-M 9:30am-10pm.

Built on the foundations of a medieval castle to house French kings for nearly four centuries, restructured by a 20th-century Socialist politician and a Chinese-American architect, and filled with priceless objects from the tombs of Egyptian pharaohs, the halls of Roman emperors, the studios of French painters, and the walls of Italian churches, the Louvre is an enormous intersection of time, space, and national boundaries. Explore the endless exhibition halls, witness new generations of artists at work on easels in the galleries, and see the Louvre's most famous residents: the Mona Lisa, the Venus de Milo, and the Winged Victory of Samothrace.

PRACTICAL INFORMATION

The **surface entrance** to the Louvre is through I.M. Pei's center glass pyramid, where an escalator descends into the Cour Napoléon. From the metro, you can reduce your wait in lines and enter directly by following signs through the Carrousel du Louvre, a new subterranean mall under the museum, whose food court, gift shops, and inverted pyramid reflect the architecture on the surface. A Mastercard- and Visa- compatible ATM is located on the main floor of the mall. **Tickets** for the museums are sold in the Cour Napoléon. If you are buying full-priced tickets, save time by using coins or a credit card in one of the automatic ticket machines. You can also buy your tickets before you leave home and save yourself the hassle once in Paris. Simply go to the Louvre's website, order by credit card, and the tickets will be mailed to you. Website tickets are valid through the end of the calendar year in which they are purchased. Holders of a *Carte Musée et Monuments* (see **Museums,** p. 210) can skip the line by entering the Louvre from the Richelieu entrance (in the passage connecting the Cour Napoléon to the rue de Rivoli). To avoid heat and crowds, visit on weekday afternoons or on Monday and Wednesday evenings, when the museum stays open until 9:45pm.

Because of the ongoing Grand Louvre project, scheduled to be finished by the end of 1999, curators are relocating 80% of the museum's collection. Until then, some galleries will be closed for renovations. All of this juggling means that no guidebook can give you a completely accurate walking tour of the museum. Be sure to pick up an updated map at the circular information desk in the center of the Cour Napoléon or take a guided tour. Whatever your visiting pace, consider purchasing *The Guide for the Visitor in a Hurry* (20F), an English-language brochure available in the bookstore of the Cour Napoléon. **Audioguides,** available at the top of both the Denon and Sully escalators (rental 30F; deposit of driver's license, passport, or credit card), describe over 100 of the museum's highlights. **Tours** fill up quickly. Make frequent use of the free plastic info boards *(feuillets)* found in gallery corners, which provide intelligent, detailed commentary and historical context on art work in each gallery.

There are three **places to eat** in the Cour Napoléon. Two cafés are located on the upper and main floors (sandwiches 22-55F). A pricier restaurant is on the main floor. Far better than all of these establishments is the Universal Restaurant food court located on the second floor of the Carrousel du Louvre mall, on the other side of the inverted pyramid. Here, you can get a cup of coffee for 8F or eat a decent, fast meal for 35-60F.

The Louvre is fully **wheelchair-accessible.** You may borrow a wheelchair for free at the central information desk (passport deposit). The Louvre has begun a series of workshops for children in English (see the information desk in the Cour Napoléon for info). The auditorium in the Hall Napoléon hosts concerts (65-130F), films, lectures, and colloquia (all 25F). For more information, call 01 40 20 51 12. There is also a small theater in the hall with free one-hour films relating to the museum (M-F 10am, Sa-Su every 1½hr. from 11am).

If you're under 26 years old and plan to visit the Louvre more than twice in the next twelve months, consider buying the *Carte Louvre Jeunes.* An amazing deal at 100F, it entitles its holder to one year's unlimited entrance (without waiting in line) to the permanent collection and temporary exhibits and visits with a guest on Monday nights from 6 to 9:45pm, as well as discounts on all books, tours, concerts, movies, and classes offered at the Louvre. For more information call 01 40 20 51 04 or inquire at the information desk for an application.

THE LAYOUT

When visiting the Louvre, strategy is everything. Think like a four-star general; the goal is to come and see without being conquered. The reality is that you can't *do* the Louvre, not all of it anyway. Pick a few areas you'd like to see, and take the time to see them well. If the Cour Napoléon leaves you confused, consider the tour, guidebook, or audioguide resources above. Otherwise, relax, pick a department for a first meander and let serendipity take care of the rest.

The Louvre is organized into three different wings—Sully, Richelieu, and Denon—each leading off of the center of the Cour Napoléon. Each wing is divided into different sections according to the artwork's date, national origin, and medium (for example, "18th-century French Painting"). The color-coding and room numbers on the Louvre's free maps correspond to the colors and numbers on the plaques at the entrances to every room within the wing. Getting lost is an inevitable part of the Louvre experience, but there are plenty of blue-jacketed docents (many who speak English) who can point you in the right direction. The collection itself is divided into seven departments that spread out over the three wings: Oriental Antiquities; Egyptian Antiquities; Greek, Etruscan, and Roman Antiquities; Painting; Sculpture; Decorative Arts; and Graphic Arts.

THE BUILDING

Construction of the Louvre began in 1190 and isn't finished yet. King Philippe-Auguste built the original structure to protect Paris while he was away on a crusade. In the 14th century, Charles V extended the city walls beyond what is now the Jardin des Tuileries (see **Sights,** p. 141), thus stripping the Louvre of its defensive utility. Not one to let a good castle go to waste, Charles converted the austere fortress into a residential château. Later monarchs avoided the narrow, dank, and rat-infested building. In 1527, however, François I returned to the Louvre in an attempt to flatter the Parisian bourgeoisie, whom he hoped to distract from their raised taxes. François razed Charles's palace and commissioned Pierre Lescot to build a new royal palace in the open style of the Renaissance. All that remains of the old Louvre are its foundations, unearthed in the early stages of Mitterrand's renovations and displayed in an underground exhibit called "Le Louvre Mediéval" (admission included in museum ticket).

François I started work on the **Cour Carrée** (Square Courtyard) in 1546. Most of the Cour owes its ponderous classicism to Louis XIV, who hired a trio of architects—Le Vau, Le Brun, and Perrault—to transform the Louvre into the grandest palace in Europe. Louis XIV eventually abandoned the Louvre in favor of Versailles, and construction did not get past the Cour Carrée. The main courtyard is the **Cour Napoléon,** begun by Catherine de Médicis 200 years before it was completed by Napoléon III. The two wings stretching into the distance were once connected by the Palais des Tuileries, a royal residence begun in 1563 to grant Catherine privacy (it was burned by the *communards* in 1871; see **History,** p. 6). Henri IV completed the Tuileries and embarked on what he called the Grand Design—a project to link the

Louvre and the Tuileries with the two large wings you see today. He only built a fraction of the project before his death in 1610.

In 1725, after years of relative abandonment, the Academy of Painting inaugurated annual salons in the halls to show the work of its members. For over a century, French painting would revolve around the salons, and, in 1793, the Revolution made the exhibit permanent, thus creating the Musée du Louvre. Napoleon filled the Louvre with plundered art from continental Europe and Egypt. With his defeat at Waterloo, however, most of this art had to be returned to the countries from which it had been "borrowed." More durably, Napoleon built the **Arc de Triomphe du Carrousel,** a copy of Rome's Arch of Septimus Severus, to commemorate his victories.

In 1857, Napoleon III continued work on Henri IV's Grand Design, extending the Louvre's two wings to the Tuileries palace and remodeling the façades of the older buildings. The François I wing gained a new face on its west side but retained its original design on the Cour Carrée side. Only 14 years after the completion of the Grand Design, the Tuileries palace was burned to the ground by the Paris Commune. Ever since, the Louvre's Denon and Richelieu wings reach out to grasp only empty space.

For most of the 20th century, the Louvre was a confusing maze of government offices and inaccessible galleries. Until 1989, the Finance Ministry occupied the Richelieu wing of the Louvre. Mitterrand's *Grands Projets* campaign transformed the Louvre into an accessible, well-organized museum. Internationally renowned Chinese-American architect I.M. Pei came up with the idea of moving the museum's entrance to the center of the Cour Napoléon, on an underground level surmounted by his stunning and controversial **glass pyramid.** At first, Pei's proposal met with intense disapproval. Others consider Pei's pyramid a stroke of genius. An enlarged reception area facilitates welcoming services, and escalators provide ready access to the palace's three wing. The Cour Napoléon glows in the sun streaming through the glass pyramid. There are 666 panes of glass on the Pyramid.

PAINTINGS

The Louvre's painting collection begins with the Middle Ages and includes works dating up to the mid-19th century. The **Flemish Gallery** (second floor, Richelieu) houses such masterworks as **Van Hemessen's** *Young Tobias Gives Sight to His Father,* **Hieronymous Bosch's** *Ship of Fools,* and **Jan Van Eyck's** *Madonna of Chancellor Rolin,* remarkable for the minute detail of the countryside that can be seen beyond the window of the foreground and thought to be one of the first oil paintings. **Peter Paul Rubens's** 24-paneled *Médicis Cycle* (1621-25) occupies its very own room. Returning from an exile imposed by her son Louis XIII, Marie de Médicis hired Rubens to retell her personal history to the world (or at least to the treacherous French court). These wall-sized Baroque canvases depict a mythical Marie de Médicis as well as Rubens's famous buxom maidens, nymphs, muses, and goddesses.

French works, which stretch from the Richelieu wing through the entire Sully wing and part of the Denon wing, include paintings from the Neoclassical, Rococo, and Romantic schools of 16th- through 19th-century painting. The Rococo works of **Antoine Watteau, Jean-Honoré Fragonard,** and **François Boucher** showcase aristocratic styles of architecture and dress that culminated in the reign of Louis XIV, the Sun King. Watteau's unsettling *Gilles* (also called *Pierrot*) illustrates an awkward boy in a clown suit staring uncomfortably out at the observer while other characters mock him. **Jacques-Louis David's** pivotal 1785 work, *The Oath of the Horatii,* is as stimulating visually as it was politically. It focuses on three Roman brothers swearing allegiance to their father and country before going off to battle, an ominous theme for Paris on the eve of the Revolution. His other paintings, the dramatic *Rape of the Sabine Women* and the homoerotic *Defeat at Thermopylae* also hang in the Denon wing (for more on David, see **Fine Arts,** p. 15). **Jean-Auguste-Dominique Ingres,** one of David's students, abandoned his mentor's hard, sculptural physiques in favor of the fleshy roundness of the Italian Renaissance master Raphael. Ingres's *Grand Odalisque* incorporates exoticized Oriental themes. **Théodore Géricault's** *Raft of the Medusa* (1819) tells the true story of the survivors of the sunken ship Medusa, who lashed together a raft to avoid drowning but were forced to resort to cannibalism to make it through two weeks on the open sea. Salon-goers were horrified by the portrayal of half-eaten corpses (Géricault studied real ones in preparation for this work) tumbling into the sea as the survivors struggle to catch the attention of a ship on the horizon. **Delacroix's** *Liberty Leading the People* personifies Liberty as a woman on the barricades of the French Revolution. Louis-Philippe thought it so dangerous that he bought the painting and hid it from the public. Delacroix's *The Death of Sardanapalus* depicts the final scene of a play by Lord Byron in which King Sardanapalus slaughters his horses and concubines as the enemy surrounds his palace.

The **Italian Renaissance** collection (on the first floor of the Denon wing) is rivaled only by that of the Uffizi museum in Florence. For the best in Renaissance portraiture, look to **Raphael's** *Portrait of Balthazar Castiglione* and **Titian's** *Man with a Glove.* Titian's *Fête Champêtre* inspired Manet's *Déjeuner sur l'Herbe* (see **Musée d'Orsay,** p. 217). **Veronese's** gigantic *Wedding Feast at Cana* occupies an entire wall. A few years ago it was accidentally dropped while being restored; the fall caused a meterlong tear in the canvas, since then repaired. The models for the apostles were 16thcentury aristocratic Venetians, with Veronese himself playing the cello. Bought by François I during the artists's visit to Paris, **Leonardo da Vinci's** *Mona Lisa* (or *La Joconde,* The Smiling One; 1503) smiles mysteriously at millions of guests each year. In the struggle to elbow your way to a close-up view, don't forget to look at her remarkable neighbors. Da Vinci's *Virgin of the Rocks* displays the *sfumato* (smoky) technique for which he is famous.

Ms. Mona's Wild Ride

The lovely Mona is fortunate to be here at all. Louvre curators discovered her missing one morning in 1911. Guillaume Apollinaire warned his friend Pablo Picasso, who owned two statues stolen from the Louvre, that a search for the *Mona Lisa* might uncover the contraband sculptures. The pair panicked, and at midnight struck out into the darkness with the statues packed into a suitcase, intending to dump them in the Seine. Near the *quais,* they suspected they were being followed and decided to leave the statues anonymously with a local newspaper. But the police soon tracked down and jailed Apollinaire as a suspect in the *Mona Lisa* heist. After two days of intense questioning, Apollinaire's resolve broke and the loyal friend accused Picasso of stealing the painting. In spite of this treachery, Picasso cleared his name with a convincing plea. Only through the efforts of local artists, who attested to the fine quality of Apollinaire's character, was the poet released. The *Mona Lisa* turned up two years later in the possession of a former Louvre employee who had snuck it out of the museum under his overcoat, leaving only the frame and a fine impression of his left thumb. Unfortunately, the museum had recorded employees' right thumb prints only. The joyful, albeit embarrassed, museum directors returned the smiling lady to her proper place, where she now resides securely within a glass enclosure.

GREEK, ETRUSCAN, AND ROMAN ANTIQUITIES

Although most visitors stumble into this section looking for two of the museum's most famous pieces, the **Venus de Milo** and the **Winged Victory of Samothrace,** the rest of the Louvre's collection of ancient sculpture is extraordinary. Despite yearly requests from the Greek Minister of Culture to return its collection of antiquities, the Louvre maintains that these sculptures are better off in Paris. The Louvre's collection of **Greek vases** is one of the finest in the world. Beautiful black and red *kylix's* and *kraters* (used to mix wine and water) depict nymphs and satyrs doing things for which you could be arrested in some Southern American states. The collection, acquired in 1861 by Napoleon III, includes the **Melos Amphora** with its painting of Hercules and Athena, surrounded by the rest of the Olympian bratpack.

Greek and Roman sculpture at the Louvre covers too many floors and periods to be tackled by all but the classics junkies, but there are some standouts if you're in a hurry. The **Winged Victory of Samothrace** dominates the landing between the Denon and Sully wings. Despite the thousand pictures you've seen of her (most nota-

(say yes)

and use **AT&T Direct**^{SM} Service
to tell everyone about it.

It's all within **AT&T** your reach.

You pop the question in Paris, you better have an

AT&T Direct^{SM} Service wallet guide in your pocket.

It's a list of access numbers you need to call home

fast and clear from around the world, using an AT&T Calling Card or credit card.

So you can give everyone back home a ring.

For a list of **AT&T Access Numbers,**
take the attached wallet guide.

It's   all   within      your   reach.

www.att.com/traveler

For your calling convenience tear off and take with you!

AT&T Direct℠ Service

WALLET GUIDE

Inside you'll find simple instructions on how to use AT&T Direct Service to place calling card or collect calls from outside the U.S.

All you need are the AT&T Access Numbers when you travel outside the U.S., because you can access us quickly and easily from virtually anywhere in the world. And if you need any further help, there's always an AT&T English-speaking Operator available to assist you.

www.att.com/traveler

Calling From Specially Marked Telephones

Throughout the world, there are specially marked phones that connect you to AT&T Direct℠ Service. Simply look for the AT&T logo. In the following countries, access to AT&T Direct Service is *only* available from these phones: Ethiopia, Mongolia, Nigeria, Seychelles Islands.

Public phones in Europe displaying the red 3C symbol also give you quick and easy access to AT&T Direct Service. Just lift the handset and dial ✱60 (in France dial M60) and you'll be connected to AT&T.

Pay phones in the United Kingdom displaying the New World symbol provide easy access to AT&T. Simply lift the handset and press the pre-programmed button marked AT&T.

Customer Care

If you have any questions, call 800 331-1140, Ext. 707.

When outside the U.S., dial the AT&T Access Number for the country *you are in* and ask the AT&T Operator for Customer Care.

108-25   © AT&T 6/98

Printed in the U.S.A. on recycled paper.

To Call the U.S. and Other Countries Using Your AT&T Calling Card* or credit card∞, Follow These Steps:

1. Make sure you have an outside line. (From a hotel room, follow the hotel's instructions to get an outside line, as if you were placing a local call.)

2. If you want to call a country other than the U.S., make sure the country *you are in* is highlighted in blue on the chart like this: ▢

3. Enter the AT&T Access Number listed in the chart for the country *you are in.*

4. When prompted, enter the telephone number you are calling as follows:
   - For calls to the U.S., dial the Area Code (no need to dial 1 before the Area Code) + 7-digit number.
   - For calls to other countries,† enter 01+ the Country Code, City Code, and Local Number.

5. After the tone, enter your AT&T Calling Card* or credit card number (not the international number). If you need help or wish to call the U.S. collect, hold on for an AT&T Operator.

   * You may also use your AT&T Corporate Card, AT&T Universal Card, or most U.S. local phone company cards.
   † The cost of calls to countries other than the U.S. consists of basic connection rates plus an additional charge based on the country you are calling.
   ∞ Credit card billing subject to availability.

Special Features

Just dial the AT&T Access Number for the country *you are in* and follow the instructions listed below.

- To call U.S. 800 numbers: Enter the 800 number you are calling. (Note: Based upon the 800 number dialed, calls may be toll-free or AT&T Direct℠ Service charges may apply for the duration of the call; some numbers will be restricted.)

- To set up conference calls: Dial AT&T TeleConference Services at 800 232-1234. (Note: One conferee must be in the U.S.)

- To access language interpreters: Dial AT&T Language Line® Services at 408 648-5871.

- To record and deliver messages: Dial #123 if you get a busy signal or no answer, or dial AT&T True Messages® Service at 800 562-6275.

Here's a time-saving tip for placing additional calls: When you finish your conversation, or if there is a busy signal or no answer, don't hang up – press # and wait for the voice prompt or an AT&T Operator.

AT&T Access Numbers

(Refer to footnotes before dialing.) From the countries highlighted in blue below, like this ☐, you can make calls to the U.S. location in the world, and from *all* the countries listed, you can make calls to the U.S.

It's all within your reach.

Country	Access Number
Albania ●	00-800-0010
American Samoa	633 2-USA
Angola	0199
Anguilla +	1-800-872-2881
Antigua +	1-800-872-2881
(Public Card Phones)	#1
Argentina	0-800-54-288
Armenia ●▲	8◆10111
Aruba	800-8000
Australia	1-800-881-011
Austria ○	022-903-011
Bahamas	1-800-872-2881
Bahrain	800-001
Bahrain	800-000
Barbados+	1-800-872-2881
Belarus ×—	8◆6001011
Belgium ●	0-800-100-10
Belize ▲	811
(From Hotels Only)	555
Benin ●	102
Bermuda +	1-800-872-2881
Bolivia ●	0-800-1112
Bosnia ▲	00-800-0010
Brazil	000-8010
British V.I. +	1-800-872-2881
Brunei ●	800-1111
Bulgaria ■▲	00-800-0010
Cambodia ✶	#1
Canada	1 800 CALL ATT
Cape Verde Islands	112
Cayman Islands +	1-800-872-2881
Chile	800-225-288 or 800-800-288
(Easter Island)	800-800-311
China, PRC ▲	10811
Colombia	980-11-0010
Cook Island	09-111
Costa Rica	0-800-0-114-114
Croatia ▲	99-385-0111
Cyprus ●	080-90010
Czech Rep.●	00-42-000-101
Denmark	8001-0010
Dominica +	1-800-872-2881
Dom. Rep. ●✶□	1-800-872-2881
Ecuador ▲	999-119
Egypt ● (Cairo)	510-0200
(Outside Cairo)	02-510-0200
El Salvador ○	800-1785
Estonia	8-00-8001001
Fiji	004-890-1001
Finland ●	9800-100-10
France ●	0800 99 00 11
French Antilles	0800 99 0011
French Guiana	0800 99 0011
Gabon ●	00+001
Gambia ●	00111
Georgia ▲	8◆0288
Germany	0130-0010
Ghana	0191
Gibraltar	8800
Greece ●	00-800-1311
Grenada +	1-800-872-2881
Guadeloupe +✶ (Marie Galante)	0800 99 00 11
Guam	1 800 CALL ATT
Guantanamo Bay ✝ (Cuba)	935
Guatemala O✶	99-99-190
Guyana ✶	165
Haiti	183
Honduras	800-0-123
Hong Kong	800-96-1111
Hungary ●	00◆800-01111
Iceland ●	800 9001
India ×▼	000-117
Indonesia→	001-801-10
Ireland✓	1-800-550-000
Israel	1-800-94-94-949
Italy ●	172-1011
Ivory Coast ●	00-111-11
Jamaica □	1-800-872-2881
Jamaica ○	872
Japan IDC ●▲	0066-55-111
Japan KDD ●	005-39-111
Kazakhstan ●	8◆800-121-4321
Korea ✦	0072-911 or 0030-911
Korea ↑	550-HOME or 550-2USA
Kuwait	800-288
Latvia (Riga)	7007/007
(Outside Riga)	8◆27007007
Lebanon ○ (Beirut)	426-801
(Outside Beirut)	01-426-801
Liechtenstein ●	0-800-89-0011
Lithuania ×—	8◆196
Luxembourg†	0-800-0111
Macao	0800-111
Macedonia, F.Y.R. of ●, ○	99-800-4288
Malaysia ○	1-800-80-0011
Malta	0800-890-110
Marshall Isl.	1 800 CALL ATT
Mauritius	01
Mexico ▽¹	01-800-288-2872
Micronesia	288
Monaco ●	800-90-288
Montserrat +	1-800-872-2881
Morocco	002-11-0011
Netherlands ●	0800-022-9111
Netherlands Antilles ✦	001-800-872-2881
New Zealand	000-911
Nicaragua	174
Norway ●	800-190-11
Pakistan ▲	00-800-01001
Palau	02288
Panama	109
Papua New Guinea	0507-12980
Paraguay ■▲ (Asuncion City)	008-11-800
Peru ●	0-800-50000
Philippines ●	105-11
Poland	0◆0-800-111-1111
Portugal ▲	05017-1-288
Qatar	0800-011-77
Reunion Isl.	0800 99 0011
Romania ●	01-800-4288
Romania ↑	01-801-0151
Russia ●) ▲ (St. Petersburg)	325-5042
(Outside St. Petersburg)	8-812-325-5042
Russia ●) ▲ (Moscow)	755-5042
(Outside Moscow)	8-095-755-5042
St. Kitts/Nevis & St. Lucia +	1-800-872-2881
St. Pierre & Miquelon	0800 99 0011
St. Vincent △■	1-800-872-2881
Saipan ▲	1 800 CALL ATT
San Marino ●	172-1011
Saudi Arabia ◇	1-800-10
Senegal	3072
Sierra Leone	1100
Singapore ■	800-0111-111
Slovakia ▲	00-42-100-101
Solomon Isl.	0811
So. Africa	0-800-99-0123
Spain	900-99-00-11
Sri Lanka ■	430-430
Sudan	800-001
Suriname △	156
Sweden	020-795-611
Switzerland ●	0-800-890011
Syria	0-801
Taiwan	0080-10288-0
Thailand ✓	001-999-111-11
Trinidad/Tob.	0800-872-2881
Turkey ●	00-800-12277
Turks & Caicos +	1-800-872-2881
Uganda	800-001
Ukraine ▲	8◆100-11
U.A. Emirates ◇	0800-121
U.K.▲+✦	0800-89-0011 or 0500-89-0011
U.S. ▼	1 800 CALL ATT
Uruguay ■	000-410
Uzbekistan	8◆641-7440010
Venezuela	800-11-120
Vietnam ●	1-201-0288
Yemen	00 800 101
Zambia	00-899
Zimbabwe ▲	110-98990

● Public phones require coin or card deposit. 2Press red button. 3 Additional charges apply when calling outside of Moscow. ■ AT&T Direct® calls cannot be placed to this country from outside the U.S. ✖ Available from public phones only. ✶ Not available from public phones.
① From St. Maarten or phones at Bobby's Marina, use 1-800-872-2881.
⑪ From St. Maarten or phones at Bobby's Marina, use 1-800-872-2881.
Phnom Penh and Siem Reap only. ✖ Not available from public phones.

◇ From this country, AT&T Direct® calls terminate to designated countries only.
✝ From U.S. Military Bases only. —— Not yet available from all areas. ○ Select hotels.
▲ May not be available from every phone/public phone. ✝Collect calling from public phones. ▼ Available from phones with international calling capabilities or from most Public Calling Centers. ✓ From Northern Ireland use U.K. access code.

★ Collect calling only. ○ Public phones require local coin payment through the call duration. ◆ Await second dial tone. ▽ When calling from public phones, use phones marked "Ladatel." If call does not complete, use 001-800-462-4240.
▲ Available from public phones only. ✦ Public phones and phones marked Lenso. ✖ When calling from public phones, use phones marked Lenso.
—— Use phones allowing international access. ✦ Including Puerto Rico and the U.S. Virgin Islands.
✶ AT&T Direct® Service only from telephone calling centers in Hanoi and post offices in Da Nang, Ho Chi Minh City and Quang Ninh. ✝ If call does not complete, use 0800-013-0011.
□ Calling Card calls available from select hotels.

bly with Audrey Hepburn in *Funny Face*), she is still breathtaking, especially from the staircase below. Originally situated on a rocky precipice overlooking the sea, the *Winged Victory* was excavated in 1863 on the Greek island of Samothrace by a French archaeologist (you can still sign the petition to bring her back at Samothrace's 2-room museum). The statue commemorates a Rhodian naval victory and is one of the most important examples of Hellenistic sculpture. The recently restored **Borghesian Gladiator** pulses with ripples of Roman musculature and was imitated widely in works of the 17th and 18th century. Found in 1820 on the Greek island of Milos, the **Venus de Milo** (on the ground floor of the Sully wing) depicts the goddess of love wrapped in sculpted folds of cloth. The 8th century BC Etruscan **Sarcophagus of a Married Couple** (in the Denon wing) depicts a couple reclining at a banquet, the husband's arm wrapped around his wife's shoulder. Resting atop their coffin, this funerary sculpture illustrates their love for each other, together in life as in death.

OTHER COLLECTIONS

The **Oriental Antiquities** department houses an impressive collection of pre-Christian antiques and sculpture from the Fertile Crescent region. This collection includes the world's oldest legal document, a basalt slab from the 18th century BC on which is inscribed the **Code of King Hammurabi.** Room 4 presents the reliefs from the Palace of Khorsabad built by Sargon II in the 7th century BC and five winged bulls, which guarded the palace doors. The **Islamic Art** collection (in Richelieu and Sully) features rugs, tapestries, armor, swords, and scientific instruments. Half of the first floor of the Louvre stands as a showcase for **Objets d'Art**—the jewelry, tapestries, statuettes, furniture, dishes, and decorations belonging to centuries of ruling classes. The **Sculpture** department includes everything after the Roman period until the 19th century. The stars of the collection are **Michelangelo's** *Slaves.* Michelangelo said that he attempted to free each of his sculptures from the marble block in which it was imprisoned. Originally meant to decorate the tomb of Pope Julius II, the homoerotic slave-boys are sculpted peeling their moist tank-tops from tortured-torsos. But the pope wasn't gay at all. Really.

SPECIAL EXHIBITIONS

In addition to its regular collections, the Louvre features rotating exhibits in the Cour Napoléon and the three main wings. In April, 1999, the museum will celebrate the 1**0th anniversary of the Pyramid,** Pei's glass wonder, with special concerts, lectures, and films related to the structure. Temporary exhibits will include **Eternal Monuments to Ramses II,** from February to May 1999, which draws on the Louvre's rich collection of Egyptian artifacts. The **Essence of Architecture** will be displayed in the Sully wing from April to July, 1999. Though the Louvre will not stage an official celebration to ring in the year 2000, the museum is staging a special exhibition called **The Invention of Time** to begin in January of the new **millennium.**

■ Musée d'Orsay

Tel. *01 40 49 48 48; recorded information tel. 01 45 49 11 11.* **Web** *http://www.musee-orsay.fr.* **M:** *Solférino.* **RER:** *Musée d'Orsay.* **Open** *June 20-Sept. 20 Tu-W and F-Su 9am-6pm, Th 9am-9:45pm; Sept 21-June 19 Tu-W and F-Su 10am-6pm, Th 10am-9:45pm. Last ticket sales 30min. before closing.* **Admission** *40F; ages 18-25, seniors, and all on Su 30F; under 18 free.* **Tours** *in English M-Sa, 90min., 36F.* **Bookstore and Boutique:** *Open Tu-W and F-Su 9:30am-6:30pm, Th 9:30am-9:30pm.*

While the Musée d'Orsay, 62, rue de Lille, 7*ème*, has established itself as *the* Impressionist museum, those who come only to see the soft strokes of Monet, Degas, Manet, and Pissarro will miss the breadth and excitement of its full collection. Paintings, sculpture, decorative arts, architecture, photography, and cinema are presented in this former Beaux Arts railway station, with works spanning the period from 1848 until the First World War. Beneath the great steel roof-beams and ornate clocks that took the city's breath away during the Universal Exposition, the Impressionists' and their descendants' work is displayed in elegant galleries.

MUSEUMS

PRACTICAL INFORMATION

The museum is least crowded on Sunday mornings and on Thursday evenings when it is open late. Avoid visiting on a Tuesday if at all possible, since this is the day the Louvre closes. The *Guide to the Musée d'Orsay* by Caroline Mathieu, the museum's curator, is excellent (95F), or you can buy the practical condensed *Guide for the Visitor in a Hurry* (20F). **Audioguides,** available in English and other languages, provide anecdotal histories and analyses of 60 masterpieces throughout the museum. These hand-held devices permit you to dial up descriptions of the featured works at your leisure. The recording lasts two hours, but you should set aside at least three to visit all the rooms (30F; driver's license, passport, credit card, or 500F deposit required). **Tours** leave regularly from the group reception. In addition to the permanent collection, seven **temporary exhibition** spaces, called *dossiers,* are dispersed throughout the building. Call or pick up a free copy of *Nouvelles du Musée d'Orsay* to find out which temporary exhibitions are currently installed. The museum also hosts conferences, special tours, and concerts. Call 01 40 49 49 66 for more information.

The **Café des Hauteurs** is situated on the upper level behind one of the train station's huge iron clocks (sandwiches 28-65F, salads 42-52F, coffee 22F). There is also a self-service concession stand directly above the café. Weather permitting, you can take your food to the adjoining outdoor terrace, which offers a beautiful view of the Seine and Right Bank. The **Restaurant du Palais d'Orsay** on the middle floor is worth a peek, even if you don't plan on lunching. A stylish artifact of the Belle Époque designed by Gabriel Ferrier, the restaurant offers a view of the Seine, gilt ceilings, and magnificent chandeliers, as well as dining options: all-you-can-eat buffet (96F), one-course *menu* (89F), *plat du jour* (68F), and children's *menu* (45F). (Open M and Th 11:30am-3:30pm, Tu-W and F-Sa 11:30am-5:30pm; lunch served until 2:30pm.) The **bookstore** downstairs offers reproductions, postcards, art books, and historical and architectural guides to Paris. The museum's **boutique** offers jewelry, scarves, and sculptures inspired by the museum's collection.

THE BUILDING

Built for the 1900 Universal Exposition, the Gare d'Orsay's industrial function was carefully masked by architect Victor Laloux behind glass, stucco, and a 370-room luxury hotel, so as to remain faithful to the station's elegant surroundings in the prestigious 7ème. For several decades, it was the main departure point for southwest-bound trains, but newer trains were too long for its platforms, and it closed in 1939. After WWII, the station served as the main French repatriation center, receiving thousands of concentration camp survivors and refugees. Orson Welles filmed *The Trial* here in 1962. The Musée d'Orsay opened in 1986.

For all its size and bustle, the d'Orsay may be the friendliest museum in Paris. A specially marked escalator at the far end of the building ascends directly to the Impressionist level, and a slew of maps and English-language pamphlets cover the information desks. Statues here meet their visitors at eye-level, paintings are well-organized, and the Impressionist galleries on the upper level are lit by natural light from the glass ceiling above. The museum's visit begins on the ground floor, then proceeds to the top floor and the mezzanine, as signs and maps clearly indicate.

GROUND FLOOR: CLASSICISM TO PROTO-IMPRESSIONISM

Triumphant Napoleons and toga-clad figures line the central aisle's collection of sculpture from 1850 to 1870. **Jean-Baptiste Carpeaux's** massive *Ugolino* (1963) depicts the punishment of the condemned count and his four children in Dante's *Inferno.* Carpeaux's *La Danse* (1869) illustrates five female figures dancing around a leaping male spirit. Academic paintings and portraiture from the Second Empire fill the galleries along the right side of the ground floor. **Jean-Auguste-Dominique Ingres's** *La Source* (1820-56) features the soft, rounded curves that defined Classical style. **Eugène Delacroix's** *La Chasse aux Lions* herald the dawn of Fauvism (see Fine

Arts, p. 17). In the rooms to the left of the aisle, **Jean-François Millet, Jean-Baptiste-Camille Corot,** and **Théodore Rousseau** are delegates of the Barbizon school of painting, known for its nostalgic depiction of rural life (see **Trips from Paris,** p. 278). While they shared a common subject matter, Realists like **Gustave Courbet** did not depict as idyllic a version of humanity as did the Barbizon painters. "How can it be possible to paint such awful people?" one critic demanded upon viewing the tired, imperfect faces of the funeral-goers in Courbet's *Un Enterrement à Ornans* in 1850.

Édouard Manet's *Olympia* (1863) caused a scandal at the 1865 salon. Inspired by Titian's *Venus of Urbino* (1538), a standard for female nudes in Western art, Manet asked a famous courtesan to pose for this painting. The classical reference to Titian mixed with the vulgar subject of the Paris *demi-monde* drew great controversy. Caricatures of the painting covered the pages of Paris's newspapers and art journals, while Manet himself was accused of creating pornography and insulted in the streets. Charles Baudelaire and Émile Zola, on the other hand, were enthusiastic supporters. Manet's *Portrait of Zola* can be seen to the right of Olympia. The **decorative arts** and **architecture** galleries focus on industrial design from 1850 to 1900. Here you can stand above the Paris Opéra thanks to scale models and drawings.

UPPER LEVEL: IMPRESSIONISM AND POST-IMPRESSIONISM

Chosen for its soft, natural light, the upper level of the d'Orsay features a series of rooms devoted to **Impressionists** and their heirs, such as **Van Gogh, Gauguin,** and **Seurat.** Though considered mainstream today, Impressionism began as a movement against the establishment. When a group of young radicals lead by **Claude Monet** exhibited this new style in 1874, they were derided as *"Impressionistes."* Artists like **Renoir, Bazille, Manet, Pissarro, Dégas,** and **Caillebotte** adopted the name and a new era in Art History was born (see **Fine Arts,** p. 16).

Manet's *Déjeuner sur l'Herbe* (*Luncheon on the Grass,* 1863), in which two bourgeois gentleman picnic with a nude lady, is exhibited at the first room of the Upper Level. **Monet's** *La Gare St-Lazare* (1877) and **Renoir's** *Le bal du Moulin de la Galette* (1876) capture the iron train stations, crowded boulevards, and society balls of the industrialized Paris of the 1870s. Like most Impressionist paintings, Monet's *Rouen Cathedral* series (1892-93) plays with light and color. Paintings by **Alfred Sisley, Camille Pissarro,** and **Berthe Morisot** provide tranquil glimpses of daily life in the countryside around Paris. **Edgar Dégas's** dancers in *La classe de danse* (1874) scratch their backs, massage their tense necks, and cross their arms while listening to their teacher. The *Petite danseuse de quatorze ans* (*Little fourteen-year-old dancer,* 1881) was the only one of Dégas's sculptures exhibited before his death. At the time of the exhibition, the public was scandalized by its realism; she had doll hair, real ballet slippers, a real tutu, and polychrome skin. Dégas's *Absinthe* (see **The Green Pary**) highlights the loneliness and isolation of life in the city.

James Whistler, the American artist associated with French Realism, is represented by his *Portrait of the Artist's Mother,* a painting of a seated old woman in a black dress and white bonnet staring blankly, hands folded. Everyone crowds around **Vincent Van Gogh's** tormented *Portrait de l'Artiste* (1889), although the artist's anguish is also suggested by the twisted lines and shifting perspective of his landscapes and still lifes. **Paul Cézanne's** still lifes, portraits, and landscapes experiment with the soft colors and geometric planes that would open the door to Cubism.

The north wing focuses on the late 19th-century avant-garde. **Pointillists** like **Paul Signac** and **Georges Seurat** strayed from the blur of Impressionism to the dot-matrix precision of Pointillism. Like photography and film, their paintings are made up of thousands of tiny dots of color. Henri de Toulouse-Lautrec left his aristocratic family behind to paint dancers and prostitutes. **Paul Gauguin** left his family and job as a stockbroker to join the School of Pont Aven, an artists colony in Brittany. His *Belle Angèle* (1889) sets a Breton wife against a background reminiscent of Japanese art.

The Green Party

Dégas's *L'absinthe* (1875) features the green concoction being downed at a café in Pigalle. Van Gogh, some think, owed much of his inspiration (and madness) to it. Like Baudelaire and Verlaine, Hemingway wrote about absinthe, calling it "that opaque, bitter, tongue-numbing, brain-warming, stomach-warming, idea-changing liquid alchemy." Picasso, Toulouse-Lautrec, and hoards of Parisians loved and drank it fanatically. Much romanticized, the liquor absinthe made a big emerald splash on the Paris scene in the 19th century. First distilled in 1792 from the wormwood plant *(Artemisia absinthium)* and chlorophyll that makes it green, the 120-proof, licorice-like drink was initially used by French soldiers in Algeria to foil dysentery. They came back to France in the 1830s with a taste for the stuff, and soon it seemed that all of Paris was riding the green wave. Bars had *l'heure vert* (green hour), where water was poured onto a sugar cube and into the clear green liquor, turning it a darker, cloudy hue. Drinkers talked about the *fée verte* (green fairy—she's all over Art Nouveau posters) that stole the drinker's soul, while others warned of *le peril vert,* and in 1915 absinthe was outlawed in France. Most countries followed suit, although it's still available in Spain and the Czech Republic. *Pernod* tastes similar, but for the real thing most of us will probably have to settle for anecdotes. "After the first glass," wrote Oscar Wilde, "you see things as you wish they were. After the second, you see things as they are not. Finally you see things as they really are, and that is the most horrible thing in the world." (See the **Musée d'Absinthe** in **Auvers-sur-Oise,** p. 296.)

MIDDLE LEVEL: BELLE ÉPOQUE & ART NOUVEAU

Once the elegant ballroom of the Hôtel d'Orsay, the neo-Rococo *Salle des Fêtes* on the middle level displays late 19th-century salon sculpture, painting, and decorative arts. These salon works show what was going on in the sanctioned art world, while Impressionists were rebelling against the Academy. Nearly one-third of the middle level's terrace is devoted to **Auguste Rodin.** Commissioned in 1880 to be the main doors to the new École des Arts Décoratifs, the unfinished *Porte de l'Enfer (Gates of Hell)* is encrusted with figures from Dante's *Inferno;* Rodin recast many of these in larger bronzes such as *Le Penseur (The Thinker),* who sits atop the gates, surveying the hellish misery below, and Ugolino, whose starvation in hell tempts him to eat his own sons. On the terrace stands *l'Age Mûr (The Ripe Age,* 1899) a sculpture by Rodin's lover, Camille Claudel. (For more on Rodin, see the **Musée Rodin,** p. 219.)

Most of the western half of the middle level is devoted to the works of **Art Nouveau.** Modeled after the English Arts and Crafts movement, Art Nouveau's mantra was "unity in design": Art Nouveau techniques and styles sought a marriage of function and form. Doing away with heavy ornamentation, the pieces were now animated by the grain of the wood or the play of light on metal. Artists from various disciplines— carpenters, glassblowers, and painters—joined together in close collaboration. One example of this joint effort can be seen in the Belle Époque Dining Room of **Charpentier, Bigot,** and **Fontaine,** which was commissioned by the banker who financed much of the Paris metro. Art Nouveau had an often tortured relationship with the general public. Concerned with the accessibility of artisanal works and committed to the fair distribution of its creations to the underprivileged classes, Art Nouveau eventually became the domain of private patrons and bankers. Objects like **René Lalique's** delicately wrought *Flacon à odeurs* (scent bottle, 1900), with a gold-leafed stopper, was a thing of beauty, but not an affordable one. Walk forward into the 20th century with the large-scale decorative works by the **Nabis** artists (a name that means "prophets" in Hebrew), which combine elements of theater decor, Japanese art, and Symbolism. The visit ends with the **Birth of Cinematography** display.

■ Centre Pompidou

After two years of renovations, the Centre Pompidou will reopen on December 31, 1999, in time to ring in the **Millennium.** Ever controversial, the Pompidou will continue to symbolize culture and modernity for Paris 2000 and into the 21st century. While the **Atelier Brancusi** is open during renovations, you should head to the **Musée d'Art Moderne de la Ville de Paris** (see **Museums,** p. 226) and the **Musée Picasso** (see **Museums,** p. 222) to satisfy your cravings for modern art.

Often called the Beaubourg, the **Centre National d'Art et de Culture Georges Pompidou,** 4ème (tel. 01 44 78 12 33 or 01 44 78 14 63; M: Rambuteau), has inspired architectural controversy ever since its inauguration in 1977. Named after French president Georges Pompidou, it fulfills his desire for Paris to have a cultural center embracing music, cinema, books, and the graphic arts. Chosen from 681 competing designs, Richard Rogers and Renzo Piano's building-turned-inside-out bares its circulatory system to all. Piping and ventilation ducts in various colors run up, down, and sideways along the outside (blue for air, green for water, yellow for electricity, red for heating). Framing the building like a cage, huge steel bars support its weight. The Centre Pompidou attracts more visitors per year than any other museum or monument in France—eight million annually compared to the Louvre's three million.

The **Musée National d'Art Moderne,** the Pompidou's main attraction, houses a rich selection of 20th-century art, from the Fauves and Cubists to Pop and Conceptual Art. Most of the works were contributed by the artists themselves or by their estates; Joan Miró and Kandinsky's wife number among the museum's founding members. The **Salle Garance** hosts adventurous film series, and the **Bibliothèque Publique d'Information** is a free, non-circulating library. The **Institut de la Recherche et de la Coordination Acoustique/Musique (IRCAM)** is a musical institute where the public can do research using a database of 20th-century music (for info call 01 44 78 47 44).

■ Musée Rodin

Address 77, rue de Varenne, 7ème **Tel.** 01 44 18 61 10. **Fax** 01 45 51 17 5. **Web** http:// www.musee-rodin.fr. **M:** Varenne. **Open** Apr.-Sept. Tu-Su 9:30am-5:45pm; Oct.-Mar. Tu-Su 9:30am-4:45pm. Last admission 30min. before closing. **Admission** 28F, students, seniors, under 18, and all on Su 18F. Park alone 5F. Temporary exhibits housed in the chapel, to your right as you enter. Entrance included in the price of museum admission. Persons who are blind or vision-impaired may obtain advanced permission to touch the sculptures.

Located in the elegant 18th-century **Hôtel Biron,** in which the artist lived and worked at the end of his life, the **Musée Rodin** highlights the work of one of France's greatest sculptors. During his lifetime, Auguste Rodin (1840-1917) was among the country's most controversial artists, classified by many as Impressionism's sculptor (Monet, incidentally, was a close friend and admirer). Today, almost all acknowledge him as the father of modern sculpture. Born in a working-class district of Paris, Rodin began study at the Petite École, a trade school for technical drawing. He tried three times to get into the famous École des Beaux-Arts (see **Sights,** p. 156) and failed each time. Frequenting the Louvre to study Classical sculpture, he later worked as an ornamental carver, eventually setting up a small studio of his own. His travels away from Paris allowed him to articulate a definitive, powerful style, completely unlike the flowery academic style then in vogue. He refused the standard of "ideal beauty" for a more expressive style of realism. One of his first major pieces, *The Age of Bronze* (1875), was so anatomically perfect that he was accused of molding it directly from the body.

The museum houses many of Rodin's better known sculptures in plaster, bronze, and marble, such as *The Hand of God* (1902) and *The Kiss* (1888-98), along with nearly 500 lesser-known works. *The Cathedral* shows two hands twisted around each other, palms facing and fingertips touching; look twice and you'll notice that both of the hands are right hands, one a man's and one a woman's. Rodin's training in drawing is evident everywhere; as he said, "my sculpture is but drawing in three dimensions." One room on the first floor is dedicated to a rotating display of drawings and studies. In addition, the museum has several arresting works by **Camille Claudel,** Rodin's muse, collaborator, and lover. Claudel's *L'Age Mûr* (The Ripe Age) has been read as her response to Rodin's decision to leave her for Rose Beuret, here depicted as an angel of death; Claudel, on her knees, begs the aging Rodin to stay.

The *hôtel*'s expansive garden is a museum unto itself. Flowers, trees, and fountains frame outdoor sculptures. If you're short on time or money, consider paying the smaller admission fee for the grounds only. You won't miss the collection's star; just inside the gates sits Rodin's most famous work, *The Thinker* (1880-1904). *Balzac* (1891-1897), to the right of *The Thinker,* was commissioned in 1891 by the Société des Gens de Lettres. A battle over Rodin's design and his inability to meet deadlines raged for years. Unlike the flattering portrait the Société expected, the finished product shows a dramatic, haunted artist with hollow eyes. The plasticity of the body and the distortion of the author's well-known face enraged artists and non-artists alike. Rodin canceled the commission and kept the statue himself. Later in his life, he noted, "Nothing that I made satisfied me as much, because nothing had cost me as much; nothing else sums up so profoundly that which I believe to be the secret law of my art." On the other side of the garden, a cast of the stunning *Burghers of Calais* (1884-95) somberly recreates a moment in the Hundred Years War. Beyond stands one version of Rodin's largest and most intricate sculpture, the unfinished *Porte de l'Enfer* (The Gates of Hell, 1880-90). A bronze cast of the gates towers inside the Musée d'Orsay. Inspired by Dante's *Inferno,* the figures emerge from and disappear back into an endless whirlwind. Presiding above it all is the small *Thinker,* representing the author (and protagonist) as he sits and contemplates man's fate. Originally commissioned as the entrance doors for the new École des Arts Décoratifs, the sculpture was never finished. Rodin replied to his critics, "Were the cathedrals ever finished?" The first bronze cast of the gates was made in 1977 through the generous support of the Iris and B. Gerald Cantor Foundation in Beverly Hills (http://www.cantorfoundation.com). Philanthropists and patrons of the arts, Mr. and Mrs. Cantor have, through their collaboration with the Rodin Museum in Paris, acquired and donated hundreds of Rodin pieces to the Met and the Brooklyn Museum in New York, the L.A. County Museum in Los Angeles, and Stanford University.

A small, upscale **cafeteria** is tucked away in a leafy and shaded part of the garden to the right, behind the Hôtel Biron. *(Open Apr.-Sept. 10am-6pm; Mar. 10am-4:30pm.)* A superb place for lunch, it offers an extensive salad bar (40F), desserts (10-30F), packaged sandwiches (25-30F), and plenty of tables along the shaded west walkway, although you will have to fend off brazen birds with designs on your lunch.

If you need more Rodin, you can visit the smaller Rodin museum, the **Villa des Brillants,** 19, av. Auguste Rodin (tel. 01 45 34 13 09), in Meudon. *(Open F-Su 1:30-6pm; last ticket sold at 5:30pm. Admission 10F, students 5F.)* The country house where Rodin spent his final years now contains most of his minor works and the plaster models for *The Thinker, The Gates of Hell,* and his other major bronze works. In the garden, another bronze cast of *The Thinker* sits contemplatively above the tombs of Rodin and his wife, Rose Beuret, whom he married here after 53 years as companions and only 2 weeks before her death. Take the RER line C to Meudon-val-Fleury. Be sure to take a train that stops at all stations; some express trains zoom right by. When you exit the train station, take your first right then your next right onto av. A. Rodin. The museum is on the left-hand side (15min. walk). Or take bus #169 from the station and get off at the Paul Bert stop. Alternatively, you can take metro line 12 (direction: Mairie d'Issy) to the end of the line, board bus #190, and get off at the Hôpital Percy stop.

■ The Invalides Museums

Tel. 01 44 42 37 72. **Web** http://www.invalides.org. **M:** Invalides. **Open** daily Apr.-Sept. 10am-7pm; Oct.-Mar. 10am-5pm. **Admission** 37F, students under 26 and ages 12-17 27F, under 12 free. Accepts MC, V for sales of 50F or more. Ticket also permits entry to the Musée de l'Armée, Musée des Plans-Relief, and the Musée de l'Ordre de la Libération.

The **Hôtel des Invalides** stands in the center of the 7ème and guards a series of museums within its walls that revolve around France's military glory. Lying under the massive gilded cupola of the **Église du Dôme,** constructed by Jules Hardouin-Mansart, is Napoleon's tomb. Finished in 1861, the Emperor's tomb actually consists of six concentric coffins, made of materials ranging from mahogany to lead—perhaps to make sure he doesn't escape again, like he did from Elba. The tomb is placed on the lower level and viewed first from a round balcony above, forcing everyone who visits to bow down to the emperor even in his death. (This delighted Adolf Hitler on his visit to Paris in 1940.) Names of significant battles are engraved in the marble surrounding the coffins; oddly enough, Waterloo isn't there. Ten bas-reliefs recall Napoleon's institutional reforms of law and education. Bonaparte himself is depicted as a Roman emperor in toga and laurels. The tiny *Roi de Rome,* Napoleon's only son, is buried at his feet. Six chapels dedicated to different saints lie off the main room, sheltering the tombs of famous French Marshals. Bring a 10F coin to the Tomb for a five-minute recorded explanation in English.

More war trophies are housed in the **Musée de l'Armée** (tel. 01 44 42 37 72; email ma@invalides.org), which celebrates French military history. *(Open daily Apr.-Sept. 10am-6pm; Oct.-Mar. 10am-5pm. Admission included in ticket for Napoleon's tomb.)* The museum is housed in two wings on opposite sides of the Invalides's cobblestone main courtyard, the Cour d'Honneur. The East Wing *(Aile Orient)* houses war paraphernalia from the 17th, 18th, and 19th centuries and culminates in the First Empire exhibit on the second floor, with a special focus on Napoleon. The West Wing *(Aile Occident)* holds 20th-century exhibits revolving around Charles de Gaulle and the two World Wars. Be prepared for more detail than you ever wanted to know. The **Musée des Plans-Reliefs** (tel. 01 45 51 95 05) on the fourth floor is a collection of about 100 models of fortified cities. *(Open daily Apr.-Sept. 10am-6pm; Oct.-Mar. 10am-5pm. Admission included in price for Napoleon's tomb. No wheelchair access.)* Spanning the period from 1668 to 1870, the exhibit is of special interest to architects, urban planners, and historians. A free English brochure is available at the museum's entrance.

The **Musée de l'Ordre de la Libération,** 51bis, bd. de Latour-Maubourg (tel. 01 47 05 04 10), in the west wing and accessible both from the street and from the Cour d'Honneur, tells the story of those who fought for the liberation of France. *(Open daily Apr.-Sept. 10am-6pm; Oct.-Mar. 10am-5pm. Free.)* A diverse collection of de Gaulle-related paraphernalia is complemented by tributes to the Resistance fighters of Free France. The exhibit also juxtaposes journals and prisoners' drawings with camp uniforms and instruments of Nazi torture in an attempt to document the mental and physical horror endured by POWs, Holocaust victims, and survivors.

Independent from its neighboring museums but housed in a gallery off the Invalides's Cour d'Honneur, is the **Musée d'Histoire Contemporaine** (tel. 01 44 42 54 91 or 01 44 42 38 39). *(Call for information regarding temporary exits and hours. Admission 30F, students and ages 12-17 20F, under 12 free.)* Originally constructed in 1914 by benefactors M. and Mme Henri Leblanc to create a library and museum to hold documents about the history of the unfolding World War, the three-room museum today mounts two temporary exhibits per year, probing recent history, propaganda, and popular culture. Cutting-edge shows (with subjects like the history of TV) incorporate everything from posters and photos to furniture and period objects. The exhibits are in French, but the visual nature of the exhibits helps transcend the language barrier.

MUSEUMS

■ Musée Picasso

Address: 5, rue de Thorigny, 3*ème*. **Tel.** 01 42 71 25 21 or 01 42 71 70 84. **M:** Chemin Vert.
Open Apr.-Sept. W-M 9:30am-6pm, last entrance 5:15pm; Oct.-Mar. 9:30am-5:30pm, last
entrance 4:45pm. **Admission** 30F, ages 18-25 and Su 20F, under 18 free. **Tours** Sa and Su in
French 36F, ages 7-18 25F.

The **Musée Picasso** catalogues the life, work, and 70-year career of one of the most
prolific and inventive artists of the 20th century. The museum leads the viewer chro-
nologically through Picasso's earliest work in Barcelona to his Cubist and Surrealist
years in Paris and his Neoclassical work on the French Riviera. Each room covers one
period of Picasso's life, detailing the progression of both his technique and his personal life, from his many mistresses to the two World Wars. Born in Málaga, Spain in
1881, Picasso loved Paris and lived in the studios of the Bateau-Lavoir in Montmartre
(see **Sights,** p. 195), where he painted the *Demoiselles d'Avignon* in 1907 (now at
the Museum of Modern Art in New York). In the late 20s, Picasso moved to Montparnasse (see **Sights,** p. 185), where he frequented the Café Sélect and La Closerie des
Lilas (see **Classic Cafés,** p. 128) along with Cocteau, and Breton. Unable to return to
Spain during the Franco régime, Picasso adopted France as his permanent home in
1934. Later, he moved to the French Riviera, where he died in Cannes in 1973.

The collection begins with Picasso's arrival in Paris from Spain, when he experi-
mented with various styles including Impressionism. The first floor shows work from
his Blue and Pink periods, including a haunting blue and black *Self-Portrait* (1901).
The great break for Picasso was with collage and Cubism. His guitar and musician col-
lages, such as *Violin with Sheet Music* (1912), moved his art toward abstraction. In
his post-Cubist painting *Two Women Running on the Beach* (1922), Picasso painted
thick-limbed, Neoclassical bodies reminiscent of Roman statues but whose movement and color celebrates vitality. Picasso's friendship with Cocteau in the 1920s
inspired him to experiment with Surrealism in paintings like *Painter with Palette
and Easel* (1928). Picasso's dear friend, poet Paul Éluard, wrote in 1926 that "Picasso
loves intensely, but he kills what he loves." Many works highlight both his experiments with abstraction and his many love affairs, including *Woman Reading* (1932),
a portrait of his lover Marie-Thérèse Walter, and *The Kiss* (1969), painted later in his
life while he was married to Jacqueline Roque. By the time Picasso married Roque,
Clouzot's film *Le Mystère Picasso* and retrospectives at the Petit Palais were already
celebrating his life's work.

When Picasso died in 1973, his family paid the French inheritance tax in artwork.
The French government opened the Musée Picasso in 1986 to display the collection.
Housed in the 17th-century *Hôtel Salé*, the former home of a salt merchant, the
museum's large and breezy rooms and Giacometti light fixtures display Picasso's
large, turbulent works, while the courtyard and fountain below provide a quiet spot
for rest and reflection. Behind the *hôtel*, through the central courtyard, a sculpture
garden features Picasso's abstract series of *Bathers* (1956).

■ Musée de Cluny

Tel. 01 43 25 62 00. **M:** Cluny-Sorbonne. **Open** W-M 9:15am-5:45pm. **Admission** 30F; students, under 25, over 60, and Su 20F; under 18 free. **Tours** in English W 12:30pm; 54F; students, under 25, and over 60 44F; under 18 16F. **Concerts** F 12:30pm, Sa 5pm, and summer
evenings; 55F, students and seniors 45F, under 18 15F. For information, call 01 53 73 78 00.

The **Hôtel de Cluny**, 6, pl. Paul Painlevé, 5*ème*, houses the **Musée National du Moyen
Âge,** one of the world's finest collections of medieval art, jewelry, sculpture, and tapestries. The *hôtel* itself is a flamboyant Gothic 14th-century medieval manor built on
top of first-century Roman ruins. One of three ancient *thermae* (public baths) in
Roman Lutèce, the baths were purchased in 1330 by the Abbot of Cluny, who built
his residence upon them. In the 15th century, the *hôtel* became home to the monastic Order of Cluny, led by the powerful Amboise family. In 1843 the state converted

the hôtel into the medieval museum. Excavations after WWII unearthed the baths. Roman bathing was an important social ritual. After working out in the *palestre*, bathers would take a hot bath in the *caldarium*, then dip in the lukewarm *tepidarium*, before plunging into the cold *frigidarium*. Only the *frigidarium* and swimming pool remain intact and open to visitors.

The medieval museum's collection includes art from Paris's most important medieval structures, the Ste-Chapelle, Nôtre Dame, and St-Denis. Panels of brilliant stained glass in ruby-reds and royal blues from the Ste-Chapelle line the ground floor. The brightly lit *gallerie des rois* contains sculptures from Nôtre Dame. Discovered in 1977, these 13th-century stone heads of Judean and Israelite kings were severed from Nôtre-Dame's portals in 1793 when the Revolution mistook them for ancestors of Louis XVI. A collection of medieval jewelry includes royal crowns, courtly brooches, and jewelled daggers.

The museum's collection of 15th- and 16th-century tapestries includes the famous series entitled *La Dame et la Licorne* (The Lady and the Unicorn). The first five panels represent the five senses. The sixth panel, emblazoned with the dedication *À mon seul désir*, depicts a lady holding a necklace from a jewelry box. Some hold that the lady is removing her necklace, locking it away, and rejecting the material, sensual world of the first five tapestries. In this way, *À mon seul désir* could mean "by my own volition," a wish to abandon the body and retreat to the spiritual. Others argue that the lady is donning the necklace and accepting the pleasures of the next five tapestries. In this way, the dedication is to "my only desire." One also wonders why mi'lady strokes the unicorn's horn, but it's certainly not worth a dissertation. The museum sponsors chamber music concerts in its Roman and medieval spaces.

■ La Villette

La Villette, 19ème (M: Porte de la Villette), is a gorgeous, highly successful urban renewal project in the northeastern corner of Paris. Its 55 hectares enclose a beautifully landscaped park, science museum, Omnimax cinema, conservatory, exhibition hall, jazz club, concert and theater space, and a high-tech music museum surrounded by sparkling canals. A former meat-packing district, the area used to contain slaughterhouses that provided Paris with most of its pork and beef. With the advent of refrigerated transport in 1969, it became more economical to kill cattle in the countryside and deliver the meat directly to butchers. The government closed down the 19ème's meat industry in 1974. Work began on La Villette in 1979, and in 1985, president Mitterrand's inaugurated the complex with the motto, "The place of intelligent leisure." Appropriately, La Villette has an extensive program of Millennium activities planned for 1999 and 2000 (see **Paris 2000,** p. 252).

CITÉ DES SCIENCES ET DE L'INDUSTRIE

The **Cité des Sciences et de l'Industrie** (tel. 01 40 05 80 00) perches on the northern end of La Villette, next to the Porte de la Villette metro station. Dedicated to bringing science to the layperson, the star attraction is the **Explora** science museum. *(Open daily 10am-6pm. A one-day Cité-Pass covers entrance to Explora, the planetarium, the Louis Lumière cinema, and the aquarium Su-F 50F, Sa 35F. Reduced admission M-F for seniors, teachers, large families, and under 25. Combined ticket for Children's Cité and the Cité des Sciences 55F; Techno Cité and the Cité des Sciences 55F; Géode and Cité des Sciences 92F, reduced 79F.)* Even when you know the scientific principles behind the displays, you'll be dazzled by the ingenious ways they are presented. There are close to 300 separate exhibits, ranging from astronomy and mathematics to computer science and sound. The museum also features a **planetarium** (Floor 2), the **Cinéma Louis Lumière** with 3D movies, a modest **aquarium** (Floor S2), and the **Médiathèque,** a multimedia scientific and technical library that has over 4000 films (open daily noon-8pm; free).

If you're traveling with children, the Explora's **Cité des Enfants** offers one set of programs for kids ages 3-5 and another for ages 5-12. *(Children's programs on Tu, Th, and F 11:30am, 1:30, and 3:30pm; W, Sa, and Su 10:30am, 12:30, 2:30, and 4:30pm. 25F, Cité des Enfants and Cité des Sciences combined admission 55F.)* Both require adult accompani-

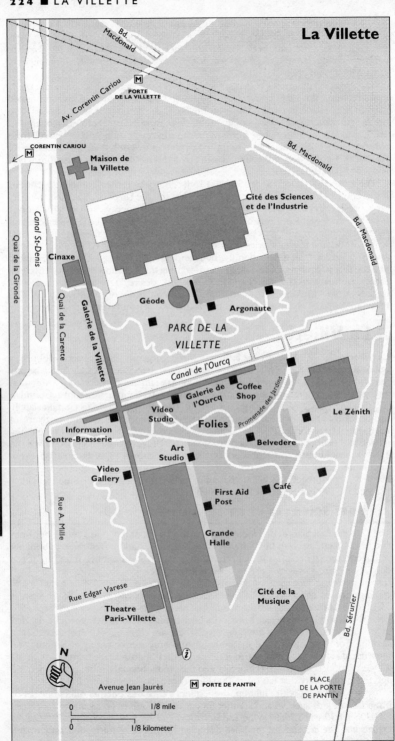

La Villette

Bd. Macdonald

PORTE
DE LA VILLETTE

Av. Corentin Cariou

Bd. Macdonald

CORENTIN CARIOU

Maison de
la Villette

Cité des Sciences
et de l'Industrie

Bd. Macdonald

Canal St-Denis

Quai de la Gironde

Cinaxe

Quai de la Carence

Galerie de la Villette

Géode

Argonaute

PARC DE LA
VILLETTE

Canal de l'Ourcq

Galerie de
l'Ourcq

Coffee
Shop

Promenade des Jardins

Le Zénith

Video
Studio

Folies

Information
Centre-Brasserie

Belvedere

Art
Studio

Video
Gallery

Café

Rue A. Mille

First Aid
Post

Grande
Halle

Rue Edgar Varese

Cité de la
Musique

Theatre
Paris-Villette

Bd. Sérurier

N

Avenue Jean Jaurès

PORTE DE PANTIN

PLACE
DE LA PORTE
DE PANTIN

0   1/8 mile
0   1/8 kilometer

MUSEUMS

ment, but no more than two adults per family are admitted. Although programs are in French, the interactive exhibits are just as fun for English-speaking explorers. The vestiare on the ground floor rents strollers and wheelchairs. Also located on the ground floor, **Technocité** (for those age 11 and older) challenges visitors to program their own computer games, design a custom bicycle, work with computer animation, and experiment with lasers and industrial art (hours vary wildly; inquire at the front desk for scheduling; visits 1½hr.; admission 25F).

Outside the Cité, the enormous **Géode** (tel. 01 40 05 12 12) is a huge mirrored sphere mounted on a water basin, like a disco ball in a birdbath. The exterior is coated with 6433 polished stainless-steel triangles that reflect every detail of their surroundings. Inside, Omnimax movies on volcanoes, glaciers, and other natural phenomena are shown on a 1000-square-meter hemispheric screen (see **Cinema,** p. 238 for more info). To the right of the Géode, the **Argonaute** submarine details the history of submersibles from Jules Verne to present-day nuclear-powered subs. *(Open Tu-F 10:30am-5:30pm, Sa-Su 11am-6:30pm. Admission 25F, under 7 free.)* This 400-ton, 50m-long fighter submarine was designed in 1950 as part of the French national fleet. An audioguide tour of the submarine (in English or French) is included. Between the Canal St-Denis and the Cité, **Cinaxe** (tel. 01 40 05 12 12) features inventive movies filmed in first-person perspective from vehicles like Formula One cars, low-flying planes, and Mars land-rovers, while hydraulic pumps simulate every curve and bump (open Tu-Su 11am-6pm; shows every 15min; tickets 34F, reduced 29F).

CITÉ DE LA MUSIQUE

At the opposite end of La Villette from the Cité des Sciences is the **Cité de la Musique** (tel. 01 44 84 44 84; fax 01 44 84 45 01; M: Porte de Pantin). Designed by Franck Hammoutène and completed in 1990, the Cité de la Musique has been an overwhelming success. The complex of buildings is visually stunning, full of curves, grand open spaces, and glass ceilings. The highlight of the Cité de la Musique is the **Musée de la Musique,** a collection of paintings, sculptures, and 900 instruments. *(Open Tu-Th noon-6pm, F-Sa noon-7:30pm, Su 10am-6pm. Admission 35F, reduced 25F, children 6-18 10F, under 6 free. Guided tours in French Sa at 2:30pm, thematic tours F at 7pm, kiddie tour Su at 11am. Tours 60F, reduced 45F, children 6-18 20F, under 6 free.)* Visitors don a pair of headphones that tune into musical excerpts and explanations of each instrument. You can relax on well-placed stools as you enjoy the music.

The Cité de la Musique's two performance spaces—the enormous 1200-seat **Salle des Concerts** and the smaller 230-seat **Amphithéâtre**—host an eclectic range of shows and concerts year round (see **Music,** p. 239). The Cité de la Musique also contains a **music and dance information center** (open M-Sa noon-6pm, Su 10am-6pm) and the **Médiathèque Hector-Berlioz** (tel. 01 40 40 45 40) with 90,000 books, documents, music journals, and photographs (open M-F 12:30-5:30pm; all free).

PARC DE LA VILLETTE

Cut in the middle by the **Canal de l'Ourcq** and the **Canal St-Denis,** the **Parc de la Villette** separates the Cité des Sciences from the Cité de la Musique. Rejecting the 19th-century notion of the park as natural oasis, Bernard Tschumi designed a 20th-century urban park, "based on cultural invention, education, and entertainment." Constructed in 1867 as the La Villette beef building, the park's steel-and-glass **Grande Halle** (tel. 0 803 306 306 or 0 803 075 075) features frequent plays, concerts, temporary exhibitions, and films. Unifying the park is a set of red cubical structures that form a grid of squares, known as **Folies.** One houses a fast-food restaurant, three are day-care centers, and one, at the park's entrance near M: Pte. de Pantin, is an **information office** (tel. 01 40 03 75 10; open daily 10am-7pm). Every summer there is a free open-air **film festival** that shows foreign, art, and generally funky movies from July to August next to the Grande Salle. The **Zénith** concert hall (tel. 01 42 08 60 00) hosts major rock bands. Nirvana played one of their last concerts here in February 1994. Directly behind Zénith is the **Hot Brass** jazz club (tel. 01 42 00 14 14). The park's phenomenal yearly jazz festival is extraordinarily popular (see **Festivals,** p. 246).

MUSEUMS

Finally, the park's **Promenade des Jardins** links several thematic gardens, such as the **Mirror Garden,** which uses an array of mirrors to create optical illusions, the **Garden of Childhood Fears,** which winds through a wooded grove resonant with spooky sounds, and the rollercoaster **Dragon Garden.** The promenade ends at the Cité de la Musique fountain, shaped like a wedding cake with lion icing. At night the Promenade, which begins near the Cinaxe on the northern end, is lit up in cyber blue.

FROM AIR TO ZADKINE

La Maison de l'Air, 27, rue Piat, 20ème (tel. 01 43 28 47 63). This brand-new municipal museum allows you to touch, hear, and smell your way into a broader understanding of the air around you. Exhibits investigate the wonders of flight, the atmosphere, meteorology, and the evils of air pollution (a growing problem in Paris). One memorable exhibit allows you to sniff different samples of Parisian air: flowers, traffic, and the metro! Open Oct.-Mar. Tu-Su 1:30-5pm, Apr.-Sept. Tu-Su 1:30-6pm. Admission 22F, ages 11-10 and over 60 11F, ages 6-10 5F.

Musée des Arts Africains et Océaniens, 293, av. Daumesnil, 12ème (tel. 01 44 74 84 80). M: Porte Dorée. On the western edge of the Bois de Vincennes. A stunning collection of several millennia of African and Pacific art. Highlights include the immense display of African statues, masks, jewelry, and wedding dresses from the Maghreb. Built for the 1931 Colonial Exposition, the building is still decorated with its original Eurocentric murals and friezes. Families and young schoolchildren crowd downstairs to the tropical fish aquarium and crocodile room. Open M and W-F 10am-noon and 1:30-5:20pm, Sa-Su 12:30-6pm. Last entry 30min. before closing. Admission 38F, students and seniors 28F, under 18 free.

Musée National des Arts Asiatiques (Musée Guimet), 6, pl. d'Iéna, 16ème (tel. 01 45 05 00 98). M: Iéna. A large collection of Asian art representing 17 different countries. Closed until 2000 for renovations, much of the museum's collection has been placed in storage. Some pieces, however, have been moved to the Musée Guimet's annex, the **Musée du Panthéon Bouddhique** (below).

Musée du Panthéon Bouddhique, 19, av. d'Iéna (tel. 01 45 05 00 98), located just a few steps away in the Hôtel Heidelbach. Housed in a turn-of-the-century Neo-Baroque *hôtel particulier,* the Panthéon traces the religious history of Japan and China through a collection of sculpture, painting, and sacred figures dating from the 4th-19th centuries. Beautiful Japanese garden behind the *hôtel.* Open W-M 9:45am-5:45pm. Admission 16F, students and seniors 12F, under 18 free.

Musée de l'Art et d'Histoire du Judaism, 71, rue de Temple, 3ème (tel. 01 53 01 86 53). M: Hotel de Ville. The museum celebrates Judaism through pictures, objects used in Jewish rituals, and an enormous model of King Solomon's Jerusalem. The library displays beautifully illustrated texts and works by artists including Marc Chagall. Scholars can call to inquire about access to the museum's library. After renovations, the museum will reopen in Dec. 1998. Open Su-Th 3-6pm. Closed on Jewish holidays. Admission 30F, students and groups 20F, children 10F.

Musée d'Art Moderne de la Ville de Paris, 11, av. du Président Wilson, 16ème (tel. 01 53 67 40 80). M: Iéna. Housed in the Palais de Tokyo (see **Sights,** p. 191), this museum contains one of the world's foremost collections of 20th-century modern art together with much of the collections from the Centre Pompidou until Dec. 31, 1999. Matisse's *The Dance* and Picasso's *Jester* are on permanent display while temporary exhibits vary dramatically. What the collection lacks in overall coherence it makes up for in quality. Open Tu-F 10am-5:30pm, Sa-Su 10am-6:45pm. Admission 27-35F, student and seniors 17-25F.

Musée d'Art Naïf Max Fourny, 2, rue Ronsard, 18ème (tel. 01 42 58 72 89). M: Anvers. From the metro, walk up rue de Steinkerque, turn right at pl. St-Pierre, then left onto rue Ronsard. Installed within the impressive iron and glass structure of what used to be a Parisian marketplace, the museum is dedicated to presenting neoprimitivist art ranging from child-like scrawls to raw, moving tableaux. Participatory games for visitors ages 3-12. Open Sept.-July daily 10am-6pm. Admission 40F, students 30F. The Halle St-Pierre also contains a quiet *salon de thé* open the same hours as the museum, with assorted teas (15F) and tables for readers.

Musée National des Arts et Traditions Populaires, Bois de Boulogne (tel. 01 44 17 60 00). M: Sablons. Enter from the Jardin d'Acclimation or from route Mahatma Gandhi. Exhibits tools and everyday artifacts from French pre-industrial life. Open W-M 9:30am-5:45pm. Admission 22F, ages 18-25, over 60, and Su 12F.

Cristalleries Baccarat, 30-32, rue de Paradis, 10ème (tel. 01 47 70 64 30). M: Gare de l'Est. Walk against traffic on bd. Strasbourg and turn right on rue de la Fidelité, which becomes rue de Paradis. The façade, built under the Directory between 1798 and 1799, covers the ugly steel interior that houses both the Baccarat crystal company and the Baccarat museum. Since its founding in 1764 by Louis XV, Baccarat has become one of the most prestigious of crystal makers, patronized by kings, czars, and shahs. The glittering display of every imaginable crystal object looks like a magic ice palace, or a scene from Balzac's *La Peau de Chagrin.* Open M-Sa 10am-6pm. Admission 15F, students and groups 8F, under 12 free.

Maison de Balzac, 47, rue Raynouard, 16ème (tel. 01 42 24 56 38). M: Passy. Honoré de Balzac (1799-1850), one of France's greatest novelists, lived in this house (1840-1847) while finishing *La Comédie Humaine.* To evade bill collectors, Balzac required all visitors to recite a password such as *"la saison des prunes est arrivée"* (plum season has arrived) before gaining admittance. The museum's collection includes portraits, personal memorabilia, manuscripts, a plaster cast of Balzac's hand, and Victor Hugo's description of his death and funeral. The museum is more fun if you've read a Balzac novel or two. Great reason to read *Père Goriot* or *Cousin Bette* before you come. Both novels paint vivid pictures of Paris in the 19th century. Open Tu-Su 10am-5:40pm. Admission 18F, students 9F, over 60 free.

Musée Henri Bouchard, 25, rue de l'Yvette, 16ème (tel. 01 46 47 63 46). M: Jasmin. Housed in the workshop of Henri Bouchard (1875-1960), sculptor of the Palais de Chaillot's *Apollo,* this museum illustrates his dexterity with bronze, tin, plaster, clay, stone, and wood. Bouchard's son and daughter-in-law are the friendly curators. The first Saturday of the month, Mme Bouchard guides a free tour at 3pm. Open July-Sept. 15, Oct.-Dec. 15, Jan. 2-March 15, and April-June 15 W and Sa 2-7pm. Admission 25F, students 15F. Call about lectures on sculpting technique.

Musée Bourdelle, 18, rue Antoine Bourdelle, 15ème (tel. 01 49 54 73 73). M: Montparnasse. From av. du Maine, turn left onto rue Antoine Bourdelle. A pupil of Rodin and mentor of Giacometti, Richier, and da Silva, Émile-Antoine Bourdelle (1861-1929) sculpted the reliefs that adorn the Théâtre des Champs-Élysées (see **Music,** p. 240) and the Opera House in Marseilles. The museum presents 500 works in marble, plaster, and bronze, including Bourdelle's masterpiece, *Heracles as Archer,* and an impressive series of 40 busts of Beethoven. Visit the 3 intimate sculpture gardens, the artist's studio, and Bourdelle's private collection of paintings. Open Tu-Su 10am-5:40pm. Last entry 5:15pm. Admission 18F, students 9F.

Musée Carnavalet, 23, rue de Sévigné, 3ème (tel. 01 42 72 21 13; fax 01 42 72 01 61). M: Chemin-Vert. Housed in Mme de Sévigné's 16th-century *hôtel particulier,* this museum traces Paris's history from its origins to the present. The collection includes Gallo-Roman and medieval archaeological collections, paintings, and objects from the Revolution. There are rooms that reconstitute Parisian homes from the 16th-19th centuries, including the Art Nouveau *Bijouterie Fouquet.* Open Tu-Su 10am-5:40pm. Admission 27F, students 15F, seniors and under 18 free.

Fondation Cartier pour l'Art Contemporain, 261, bd. Raspail, 14ème (tel. 01 42 18 56 50; fax 01 42 18 56 52). M: Raspail or Denfert-Rochereau. Surrounded by wildflowers and an outdoor performance space, the Fondation hosts exhibitions on subjects ranging from Warhol to the history of birds. Held on Thursdays at 8:30pm Sept.-June, the *Soirées Nomades* series offers films, lectures, music, dance, and art performances linked with the current exhibition. Open Tu-Su noon-8pm. Admission 30F, students and seniors 20F, under 10 free.

Musée Cernuschi, 7, av. Velasquez, 8ème (tel. 01 45 63 50 75), outside the gates of Parc Monceau. M: Villiers or Monceau. A magnificent collection of Asian art housed in a villa that belonged to financier Henri Cernuschi (1820-96). Second only to the Musée Guimet (see above) in Asian art, the Cernuschi contains a rich collection of ancient to 18th-century Chinese and Japanese pieces such as a three-ton Buddha. Open Tu-Su 10am-5:40pm. Admission 18F, students 9F, seniors and under 18 free.

MUSEUMS

Musée de la Chasse, 60, rue des Archives, 3ème (tel. 01 42 72 86 43). M: Rambuteau. Housed in the spacious, 17th-century Hôtel Guénégaud, the appalling hunting museum's stuffed animals stare glassy-eyed for hunting and taxidermy fans. If you cried when Bambi's mother died, this may not be the place for you. Highlights include slaughtered rhinos and bears. Open W-M 10am-12:30pm and 1:30-5:30pm. Admission 30F, students and seniors 15F, ages 5-16 5F.

Musée du Cinéma Henri Langlois, pl. du Trocadéro, 16ème (tel. 01 45 53 74 39). M: Trocadéro. Closed for renovations until 2000. In the Palais de Chaillot, the museum features over 3000 versions of projectors and cameras as well as demonstrations of how they work. Exhibits trace the history of film from its beginnings in 1895. Tours in French W-Su at 10, 11am, 2, 3, 4, and 5pm. Admission 30F, students 20F.

Musée Clemenceau, 8, rue Benjamin Franklin, 16ème (tel. 01 45 20 53 41). M: Passy. Through a small courtyard. The museum thoroughly documents the life of revered and vilified journalist and statesman Georges Clemenceau (1841-1929). As a journalist, Clemenceau published Émile Zola's *J'accuse*. As mayor of Montmartre, Prime Minister of France, Président du Conseil, Minister of War during WWI, and the much-criticized negotiator of the Treaty of Versailles, Clemenceau distinguished himself as one of 20th-century France's most prolific political leaders. On the ground floor, Clemenceau's apartment has been left as it was when he died, including a portrait of Clemenceau by his friend Monet and a withered bouquet of flowers given to him by a soldier. Open Tu, Th, and Sa-Su 2-5pm. Admission 20F, students and seniors 15F.

Musée Cognacq-Jay, 8, rue Elzévir, 3ème (tel. 01 40 27 07 21). M: St-Paul. Walk up rue Pavée and take a left on rue des Francs-Bourgeois and a right on rue Elzévir. This peaceful museum in the 16th-century Hôtel Donon, formerly owned by department-store mogul Ernest Cognacq, houses a collection of Enlightenment art, including minor works by Rembrandt, Ingres, and Rubens. Occasional plays and concerts. Museum open Tu-Su 10am-5:40pm. Admission 18F, students and under 25 9F, seniors and under 18 free. Gardens open May-Sept. 10am-5:40pm.

Fondation le Corbusier, 10, sq. du Docteur-Blanche, 16ème (tel. 01 42 88 41 53). M: Jasmin. Walk up rue de l'Yvette and turn left on rue du Docteur-Blanche and left again at no. 55 into pl. du Docteur-Blanche. The foundation is located in Villas La Roche and Jeanneret, both designed and furnished by Le Corbusier. Originally commissioned by the young banker La Roche to house his collection of Cubist art, Le Corbusier trademarks include his use of light, artifice, nature, curved forms and ramps. The Villa Jeanneret next door holds the library and the foundation's offices. Open Sept.-July M-Th 10am-12:30pm and 1:30-6pm, F 10am-12:30pm and 1:30-5pm. Admission 15F, students 10F.

Musée Salvador Dalí (Espace Montmartre), 11, rue Poulbot, 18ème (tel. 01 42 64 40 10). M: Anvers or Abbesses. From pl. du Tertre follow rue du Calvaire toward the view, then turn right onto rue Poulbot. Dedicated to the "Phantasmic World of Salvador Dalí," the museum is full of lithographs and sculptures by the Spanish surrealist. Laid out in "Surrealist surroundings," which amount to wonderful spacing, interesting lighting, erotic artwork, and space-music in the background. Open daily 10am-6pm, last ticket at 5:30pm. Admission 35F, students 25F.

Musée Delacroix, 6, pl. Furstenberg, 6ème (tel. 01 44 41 86 50). M: St-Germain-des-Prés. Behind the Église St-Germain off rue de l'Abbaye. At the courtyard, follow the sign to the atelier Delacroix. Located in the 3-room apartment in which he lived until his death in 1863. One of the leaders of French Romanticism, Delacroix is most famous for his painting *Liberty Leading the People* (see **Musée du Louvre,** p. 211). Sketches, watercolors, engravings, and letters to Théophile Gautier and George Sand belie a gentler artist than a visitor to the Louvre might expect. Other works include two Manet watercolors. Open W-M 9:30am-5pm, last entry 4:30pm. Admission 30F, ages 18-25 and over 60 23F, under 18 free.

Musée des Égouts de Paris (The Sewers of Paris), 7ème (tel. 01 47 05 10 29). M: Pont de l'Alma. Inside the sewers, at the corner of the quai d'Orsay and pl. de la Résistance. In *Les Misérables,* Victor Hugo wrote, "Paris has beneath it another Paris, a Paris of sewers, which has its own streets, squares, lanes, arteries, and circulation." The French Resistance used these hidden arteries during WWII. You can visit, but don't breath deep—the smell can be overwhelming. Tours and brochures in English. Open May-Sept. Sa-W 11am-5pm; Oct.-Apr. Sa-W 11am-4pm. Closed last 3 weeks of January. Admission 25F, students and under 10 20F. Under 5 free.

MUSEUMS

Musée d'Ennery, 59, av. Foch, 16ème (tel. 01 45 53 57 96). M: Porte Dauphine. Like the Musée Guimet (see above), the Musée d'Ennery features treasures of East Asian art. The museum houses the collection of Clémence d'Ennery (wife of author Adolphe d'Ennery), who scavenged the city's flea markets and antique shops for Orientalist art during the 19th century. Open Sept.-July Th and Su 2-5:45pm. Free. On the ground floor, the **Musée Arménien** (tel. 01 45 56 15 88) displays Armenian jewelry, paintings, and religious decoration. Closed for renovations until 2000.

Galerie d'Entomologie (Insect Museum), 45, rue Buffon, 5ème (tel. 01 40 79 34 00). M: Censier-Daubenton or Gare d'Austerlitz. Across the street from the Galerie de Minéralogie in the Jardin des Plantes. Insects, bugs, and beetles. Most of the small gallery is dedicated to various specimens of beetles and butterflies in different colors and sizes. Open M and W-F 1-5pm. Admission 15F, students 10F.

Musée du Grand Orient de France et de la Franc-Maçonnerie, 16, rue Cadet, 9ème (tel. 01 45 23 20 92). M: Cadet. This one-room museum tells the story of the Masons from their early Scottish brotherhood. Folksy captioning, handwritten in French, accompanies pamphlets, medals, portraits, and busts of renowned freemasons, including Voltaire and Talleyrand. Housed in the Hôtel Cadet, which was built in 1852 as the headquarters for French freemasonry. During WWII, Vichy officials used its resources to persecute Masons. Open M-Sa 2-6pm. Free.

Grand Palais, 3, av. du Général Eisenhower, 8ème (tel. 01 44 13 17 30 or 01 44 13 17 17). M: Champs-Élysées-Clemenceau. Designed for the 1900 Universal Exposition. Most of the building houses the **Palais de la Découverte** (see below), but the *palais* also hosts temporary exhibits. Open Th-M 10am-8pm, W 10am-10pm. Last entry 45min. before closing. Admission varies with the exhibit, and some require reservations. Anticipate something like 50F, students and M 35F, under 13 free.

Musée Grévin, 10, bd. Montmartre, 9ème (tel. 01 42 46 13 26). M: Rue Montmartre. This wax museum's ornate halls feature Marie-Antoinette awaiting her execution in the Conciergerie, the cannibals from Géricault's *Raft of the Medusa,* and the King of Pop. Open daily 1-7pm, last entry 6pm. Admission 55F, ages 6-14 36F. Who's who guide booklet, 10F. AmEx, V, MC (130F minimum). The smaller branch at level "-1" of the Forum des Halles, near the Porte Berger, 1er (tel. 01 40 26 28 50; M: Châtelet-Les Halles), presents figures from Paris's Belle Époque.

Musée Jean-Jacques Henner, 43, av. Villiers, 17ème (tel. 01 47 63 42 73). M: Malsherbes. This museum displays the *études* and paintings of Jean-Jacques Henner (1829-1905), who painted his soft-focus subjects with haunting, luminous, bone-white skin. Open Tu-Su 10am-noon and 2-5pm. Admission 20F, students and seniors 15F, under 18 free.

Musée de l'Histoire de France, 60, rue des Francs Bourgeois, 3ème (tel. 01 40 27 60 96). M: Rambuteau. Walk up rue Rambuteau, which becomes rue de Francs Bourgeois. Housed in the Hôtel de Soubise, this museum is the main exhibition space of the Archives Nationales and exhibits important French documents, including an edict drafted by Richard the Lionhearted, an extract from Louis XVI's diary on the day he was arrested by Revolutionaries, and a letter from Napoleon to Josephine. For more about the Hôtel Soubise and the Archives Nationales, see **Sights,** p. 147). Open M and W-F noon-5:45pm, Sa-Su 1:45-5:45pm. Admission 15F, students, seniors, and Su 10F, under 18 free.

Musée d'Histoire Naturelle, in the Jardin des Plantes, 5ème (tel. 01 40 79 39 39). M: Gare d'Austerlitz. Two science museums in one. The **Gallery of Comparative Anatomy and Paleontology** houses a dinosaur exhibit, whose triumph is the 7m skeleton of an iguanodon. The rest of the gallery is devoted to more familiar, though equally large skeletons (like those of elephants and whales) as well as a small collection of fossils. In the Grande Galerie next door, the **Musée de Minéralogie,** surrounded by luscious rose trellises, contains diamonds, rubies, and sapphires along with assorted *objets d'art* including two Renaissance Florentine marble tables inlaid with lapis lazuli, amethyst, and other semi-precious stones. Both museums share hours and prices. Open M and W-F 10am-5pm, Sa-Su 10am-6pm, last admission 30min. before closing. Admission 30F, students 20F.

Musée de l'Homme (Museum of Man), pl. du Trocadéro, 16ème (tel. 01 44 05 72 00 or 01 44 05 72 72). M: Trocadéro. In the Palais de Chaillot. A painted cart from Sicily, a Turkish store, a birth-control exhibit, and a pre-colombian totem pole are all elements of the museum's multimedia presentations and glass-cased exhibits covering cultures worldwide since prehistory. Open W-M 9:45am-5:15pm. Admission 30F, under 27 and seniors 20F, under 4 free. Films W and Sa at 3 and 4pm.

Maison de Victor Hugo, 6, pl. des Vosges, 4ème (tel. 01 42 72 10 16). M: Chemin Vert or Bastille. Dedicated to the father of the French Romantics and housed in the building where he lived from 1832 to 1848, the museum displays Hugo memorabilia. One room is devoted to *Les Misérables,* another to *Nôtre-Dame de Paris.* A desk containing the inkwells of Lamartine, Dumas, Sand, and Hugo as well as a reconstruction of the room where Hugo died. Open Tu-Su 10am-5:40pm. Admission 18F, students 9F, under 18 free.

Musée Jacquemart-André, 158, bd. Haussmann, 8ème (tel. 01 42 89 04 91). M: Miromesnil. As you wander through the music room, smoking room, reception area, and boudoir of this opulent mansion, you will surely ask yourself, "How did two people (Nélie Jacquemart and her husband) have so much time and money?" The building dates from the 19th century, while the works of art are mostly French and Italian Renaissance and Baroque pieces: Rembrandt, Botticelli, Bellini, and others. Well-done audioguide included with admission. Open daily 10am-6pm; last visitors admitted at 5:30pm. Admission 47F, students and ages 7-17 35F, under 7 free.

Galérie Nationale du Jeu de Paume, 1er (tel. 01 47 03 12 50; recorded info at 01 42 60 69 69; fax 01 47 03 12 51). M: Concorde. Huge windows bathe this spectacular exhibition space in afternoon sunlight. Connoisseurs and tourists alike come to appreciate the changing contemporary art exhibitions. Shows scheduled for 1999 feature works by Pierre Alechinsky and Jean-Pierre Raynaud. There is a café with sandwiches (25F) and tarts (48-52F). Open Tu noon-9:30pm, W-F noon-7pm, Sa-Su 10am-7pm. Admission 38F, students under 26, seniors, and ages 13-18 28F, under 13 free. Tours in French Tu-Sa 9am and noon; call ahead to reserve a place.

Musée National de la Légion d'Honneur et des Ordres de Chevalerie, 2, rue de Bellechasse, 7ème (tel. 01 40 62 84 25; fax 01 47 53 74 50). M: Solférino. Housed in an 18th-century mansion, this museum displays medals, ribbons, and uniforms of the French Legion of Honor, created by Napoleon in 1802. Across from the Musée d'Orsay. Open Tu-Su 2-7pm. Admission 25F, students and seniors 15F.

Mémorial de la Libération de Paris, 23, allée de la D-B, Jardin Atlantique, 15ème, (tel. 01 40 64 39 44). M: Montparnasse-Bienvenue. Above the tracks of the Gare Montparnasse. Follow signs to the Jardin Atlantique from the train station, pl. du Pont des Cinq Martyrs du Lycée Buffon, or rue Commandant René Mouchotte. Officially the Mémorial du Maréchal Leclerc de Hauteclocque. From Africa to the beaches of Normandy and from a liberated Paris to the capture of Berchtesgaden, this museum traces the military maneuvers of Leclerc and the liberation of Paris with a wealth of rare film footage, posters, and photographs. Open Tu-Su 10am-5:40pm, last ticket 5:15pm. Admission 27F, students and seniors 19F.

Musée de la Marine (Museum of the Navy), pl. du Trocadéro, 16ème (tel. 01 53 65 69 69). M: Trocadéro. In the Palais de Chaillot. A fleet of model and real boats from the 17th-19th centuries are anchored here, including the golden dinghy built for Napoleon in 1810. Other neptunian novelties include a huge nautical rope, lighthouse windows, and antique divers' suits. Open W-M and holidays 10am-6pm. Last entry at 5:30pm. Admission 38F, under 25 and seniors 25F.

Musée Marmottan, 2, rue Louis-Boilly, 16ème (tel. 01 42 24 07 02). M: La Muette. Follow Chausée de la Muette, which becomes av. Ranelagh, through the Jardin du Ranelagh park. Having inherited from his father a hunting lodge near the Bois de Boulogne and a passion for artwork, Paul Marmottan transformed the lodge into a stately mansion and furnished it with Empire furniture and art. At his death in 1932, the building, his own collection, and his father's group of primitive German, Flemish, and Italian paintings were bequeathed to the Académie des Beaux-Arts. Later, Michel Monet contributed roughly 100 of his father's paintings, many from the later years at Giverny. Other Impressionist canvases by Renoir. The Wildenstein room houses 228 medieval illuminations. Open Tu-Su 10am-5pm. Admission 40F, students and seniors 25F, under 8 free.

Centre de la Mer et des Eaux, 195, rue St-Jacques, 5ème (tel. 01 44 32 10 90). M: Luxembourg. More than just the requisite tanks of colorful fish—a multimedia marine experience. Interactive exhibits on fish disguises and algae life cycles. Films and exhibitions change, but most come from the adventures of late sea czar Jacques Cousteau. Open Tu-F 10am-12:30pm and 1:15-5:30pm, Sa-Su 10am-5:30pm. Admission 30F, students 18F.

Musée Adam Mickiewicz, 6, quai d'Orléans, 4ème (tel. 01 55 42 83 83), on the Île-St-Louis. M: Pont Marie. Ring the doorbell and enter to your left in the courtyard. Located in the **Bibliothèque Polonaise de Paris,** the museum is dedicated to the Polish poet Adam Mickiewicz (1798-1835), including letters from Goethe and Hugo and a sketch by Delacroix on George Sand's letter-head. In the same building are the **Musée Boleslas Bregas,** with work by the sculptor and the **Salon Chopin,** with manuscripts, letters, and his death mask. Library open Tu-F 2-6pm and Sa 10am-1pm. Tours at 2, 3, 4, and 5pm. Admission 30F, students 15F, children free.

Musée de la Monnaie, 11, Quai de Conti, 6ème (tel. 01 40 46 56 66; http://www.monnaideparis.fr). M. Odéon. See more money than you'll ever make honestly. Located in the Hôtel des Monnaies, where coins were minted until 1973, the museum displays coins, medals, and documents on the history of money-making in France. Open Tu-Su noon-5:30pm. Admission 20F, students free.

Musée de la Mode et du Costume (Museum of Fashion and Clothing), in the Palais Galliera, 10, av. Pierre 1er-de-Serbie, 16ème (tel. 01 47 20 85 23). M: Iéna. With 30,000 outfits and 70,000 accessories, the museum has no choice but to rotate in temporary exhibitions showcasing fashions of the past 3 centuries. A fabulous place to visit to see the history of Paris fashion, haute couture, and society. Visit and get ideas before you head off to the Vintage Stores (see **Shopping,** p. 259). Open Tu-Su 10am-5:40pm. Last entry at 5:15pm. Admission 45F, students and seniors 35F.

Musée de la Mode et du Textile, 107, rue de Rivoli, Palais du Louvre, 1er (tel. 01 44 55 57 50). M: Palais-Royal. Housed in the Louvre with the Musée des Arts Décoratifs, the Musée de la Mode et du Textile is a huge collection of all that has been en vogue since the 18th century. Exhibits rotate every 6 months and tell changing stories of the history of costume, from 17th century brocade evening dresses to pointy latex bras by Jean-Paul Gaultier. A research center is available by appointment. Open Tu and Th-Su 11am-6pm, W 11am-9pm. Admission 25F, students 16F.

Institut du Monde Arabe, 23, quai St-Bernard, 5ème (tel. 01 40 51 38 38). M: Jussieu. Established in 1987, the Institute of the Arab World is the most architecturally innovative of Parisian museums. The riverside façade is shaped like a boat, representing the migration of Arabs to France. The opposite side has ingenious camera-lens windows with Arabic motifs and pupil-like blinds that open and close in response to the sunlight. The museum assembles 3rd- to 18th-century art from 3 Arab regions: the Maghreb (Morocco, Tunisia, Algeria, and Spain), the Near East, and the Middle East. Level 4 is devoted entirely to contemporary Arab artists. Extensive public library. From Sept.-June the auditorium hosts Arab movies (subtitled in English and French; 25F, students 20F) and theater (80-100F). The rooftop terrace has a fabulous and free view of Montmartre, the Sacré Coeur, the Seine, and the Île de la Cité. Museum and library open Tu-Su 10am-6pm. Museum admission 25F, ages 12-18 20F, under 12 free. 90min. tours Tu-F at 3pm, Sa-Su at 2 and 4pm; 50F.

Musée National des Monuments Français, pl. du Trocadéro, 16ème (tel. 01 44 05 39 05). M: Trocadéro. In the Palais de Chaillot. A scholarly museum appealing to artists, architects, and medievalists, the collection features models of façades and tombs from medieval churches around France. Open W-M 10am-6pm. Last ticket at 5:30pm. Admission 22F, students ages 18-25 and seniors 14F, under 13 free.

Musée Gustave Moreau, 14, rue de La Rochefoucauld, 9ème (tel. 01 48 74 38 50). M: Trinité. Housed in the 19th-century home of symbolist painter Gustave Moreau, the museum contains thousands of his drawings and paintings, including the celebrated painting of Salomé dancing before the severed head of John the Baptist. Open M and W 11am-5:15pm, Th-Su 10am-12:45pm and 2-5:15pm. Admission 17F, students, children, and Su 9F.

Musée de l'Orangerie, southwest corner of the Jardin des Tuileries, 1er (tel. 01 42 97 48 16). M: Concorde. Opened in 1927, the museum is home to works by Renoir, Cézanne, Rousseau, Matisse, Picasso, and Monet's *Les Nymphéas (Water Lilies).* Finished before his death in 1926, these 4 murals of Monet's Giverny lilies were the artist's gift to France on the day of the Armistice, *"comme un bouquet des fleurs."* Open W-M 10am-5pm. Admission 30F, ages 18-25 20F, under 18 and over 60 free.

Palais de la Découverte, 8ème (tel. 01 01 40 74 80 00). M: Franklin Roosevelt. In the Grand Palais, entrance on av. Franklin D. Roosevelt. Less flashy than the Cité des Sciences, this Palace of Discovery, housed in the Petit Palais, features interactive science exhibits. Kids tear around pressing buttons that start comets on celestial trajectories, spinning on seats to investigate angular motion, and glaring at all kinds of cleverly camouflaged creepy-crawlies. Planetarium shows 4 times per day. Call for info on lectures and movies. Open Tu-Sa 9:30am-6pm, Su 10am-7pm. Admission 27F, students, seniors, and under 18 17F.

Petit Palais, av. Winston Churchill, 8ème (tel. 01 42 65 12 73). M: Champs-Elysées-Clemenceau. Also called the **Palais des Beaux-Arts de la Ville de Paris.** Built for the 1900 Universal Exposition, the *palais* houses 17th- to 20th-century Flemish, French, and Dutch painting and sculpture, including Jean-Baptiste Carpeaux's *Young Fisher with the Shell,* Camille Claudel's *Bust of Rodin,* and Monet's *Sunset at Lavacourt* as well as works by Rubens, Rembrandt, Cézanne, Pissarro, and Renoir. Call ahead for wheelchair access. Open Tu-Su 10am-5:40pm, last entry 5pm. Admission to temporary collection 27F, students 14F, seniors and under 18 free. Regular admission includes both permanent and temporary exhibits, 45F, students 35F, seniors and under 18 free.

Musée de la Poupée, Impasse Berthaud, 3ème (tel. 01 42 72 73 11). M: Rambuteau. Follow signs off rue Beaubourg near the Centre Pompidou. 400 glass eyes staring out of 200 porcelain faces, many with diabolical pointed teeth. Dolls from 1860 to 1960 are shown in 42 glass cases. Each room is from a different era. Open Tu-Su 10am-6pm. Admission 35F; students, under 26, and over 60 25F, ages 3-18 20F.

Maison de Radio France, 116, av. du Président Kennedy, 16ème (tel. 01 42 30 15 16). M: Passy; RER: (C) Av. du Pt. Kennedy/Maison de Radio France. Head for the Seine and enter through Door A of the big, white, round building. The museum, visited only by guided tour, presents a whirlwind trip through the evolution of communications. Attractions range from classic radio specimens to full TV studios and concert halls. Inquire about attending free tapings of TV programs. Season tickets to concerts with the resident Orchestre National de France are also available. Ask for the free English-language brochure at the information desk. Open M-Sa; tours at 10:30, 11:30am, 2:30, 3:30, and 4:30pm. English tours at 3pm during the summer, but call for info. Admission 20F, students and seniors 15F.

Musée-Galerie de la SEITA (Société d'Exploitation Industrielle des Tabacs et All-umettes), 12, rue Surcouf, 7ème (tel. 01 45 56 60 17). M: Invalides. On the corner of rue de l'Université and rue Surcouf. Holy smokes! While non-smoking grows in other countries, France celebrates its love affair with tobacco. Smokers can learn the story of tobacco while peering at tobacco-related documents and pipe and cigarette holders depicting everything from nudes to nuns. Learn smoker trivia like the fact that "nicotine" is named after Jean Nicot, who introduced tobacco to France in 1561. Open M-Sa 11am-7pm. Free

Musée du Vieux Montmartre, 12, rue Cortot, 18ème (tel. 01 46 06 61 11). M: Lamarck-Caulaincourt. From the metro turn right on rue Larmarck, right again up steep rue des Saules, then left onto rue Cortot. Dedicated to the political, artistic, cultural, and religious past of the *butte,* the museum occupies a beautiful 17th-century house overlooking a pleasant garden and Paris's only vineyard. Once home to artists like Renoir and Utrillo, the museum features maps, paintings, photographs, and a wooden model of the *quartier,* as well as a re-created turn-of-the-century café, complete with one of the few zinc bar counters left after the metal rationing during WWI. Open Tu-Su 11am-6pm. Admission 25F, students and seniors 20F.

Musée du Vin, rue des Eaux, or 5-7, sq. Charles Dickens, 16ème (tel. 01 45 25 63 26). M: Passy. From the metro, go down the stairs, turn right on pl. Alboni, and then turn right on rue des Eaux. Set up in a former limestone quarry, this mildly entertaining museum is filled with wax models engaged in the process of wine making. Real connoisseurs will learn little, but others might enjoy the paraphernalia and the wax model of Honoré de Balzac fleeing his creditors. You may have to remind the receptionist to give you your free tasting of red, rosé, or white. Open Su-Sa 10am-6pm. Admission 35F, seniors 30F, students 29F.

Musée Zadkine, 100bis, rue d'Assas, 6ème (tel. 01 43 26 91 90). M: Port-Royal. Just south of the Jardin du Luxembourg. Installed in 1982 in the house and studio where he worked, the museum highlights the work of Russian sculptor Ossip Zadkine (1890-1967), whose work spans from the extremes of Cubism to neo-Classicism. Lovely gardens feature the artist's works, including his two-faced *Woman with the Bird.* Open Tu-Su 10am-5:30pm. Admission 27F, students 19F.

MUSEUMS

Entertainment

Paris loved Porgy & Bess. We were originally supposed to stay at the Théâtre Wagram for three weeks, but were held over for months. One evening after the theater, a group of Black American entertainers who lived in Paris came backstage. Bernard Hassel worked at the Folies-Bergères and Nancy Holloway sang at the Colisée. Bernard invited me to see the nightlife of Paris.
"Alors, something groovy, you know?"
—Maya Angelou, 1976.

Crawling with swank nightlife, hopping dance clubs, and smoky bars and bursting with theater, dance, music, film, and cultural programs, Paris can satisfy all tastes and desires. When looking for something to do, consult the bibles of Paris entertainment, the weekly bulletins **Pariscope** (3F) and **Officiel des Spectacles** (2F), both on sale at any newsstand. For nightlife listings pick up the free *Time Out* issues found in most anglo-friendly bars. Even if you don't understand French, you should be able to decipher the listings of times and locations. Contact **Info-Loisirs,** a recording that keeps tabs on what's on in Paris (English tel. 01 49 52 53 56; French tel. 01 49 52 53 55).

You don't need to speak fluent French to enjoy the theater scene. Paris's two opera houses, five national theatres, and many private theaters present productions whose music, physical comedy, and experimental abstraction lend themselves to any audience. The comedy-oriented *café-théâtres* and the music-oriented *chansonniers* perpetuate the ambiance of 1930s Parisian cabarets. Paris's ballet and modern dance companies often host performances by visiting companies, including the Kirov Ballet, the Alvin Ailey Dance Company, and the Dance Theater of Harlem. Gay and straight, the fabulous and the fashion disasters all flock to Paris's dance-clubs. Despite a plethora of straight clubs, most hets head to **Queen** on the Champs-Élysées, where Paris's Queens are gettin' jiggy wid'it *à la Cent Deux*. For the butcher types among us, Paris's new **Stade de France** and other athletic venues offer spectator sports.

Among Paris's many treasures, film and jazz top the list. Since the 1930s, Paris has been one of the world's jazz capitals, and big-name American, Brazilian, and French artists make frequent stops here. More recently, Paris has witnessed the fusion of West African music, Caribbean calypso and reggae, Latin American salsa, North African raï, European house, techno, and rap. Classical concerts are staged both in expensive concert halls and more affordable churches, particularly during the summer. To get more information and to buy tickets for rock, rap, jazz, or classical concerts, head to **FNAC Spectacles** (see below, p. 234). Parisians are inveterate film-goers, greedy for film from all over the world, but particularly American, French, and Italian classics. Frequent English-language film series and festivals make Parisian cinema accessible, inventive, challenging, and entertaining. After-cinema talks range from laughter to tears, from the intellectual to the silly. Don't believe the hype: you don't need a course in film theory or deconstruction to discuss the film and have a good time.

Paris is crammed full of cafés, clubs, and bars. Each *quartier* has a wide range of intimate places to discover. Keep in mind that the neighborhoods around some popular night-spots, such as Pigalle, Gare St-Lazare, and Beaubourg, are not always safe. Some fill nightly with prostitutes and drug dealers. Also keep an eye on the time in order to avoid expensive, late-night taxis; although the metro doesn't stop running until 1am, hop on a train by about 12:30am if you have to make a connection.

■ Theater

Parisian theater offers something for every taste and budget, from classically staged spectacles to avant-garde productions, from shoebox spaces to ornate venues like the Comédie Française. Intimate performance spaces like *café-théâtres* and *chanson-*

niers book anything from Vaudevillian comics to accordionists. The slapstick *grands guignols* (puppet shows) are intended for children but fun for adults as well. Many theaters do not offer performances on Mondays, and many close in July and August. *Pariscope* and *l'Officiel des Spectacles* (see **Publications,** p. 75) provide complete listings of current shows. Partial 1999 schedules for major theaters are listed below.

TICKET SERVICES

Kiosque Info Jeune, 25, bd. Bourdon, 4ème (tel. 01 42 76 22 60). M: Bastille. Also at 101, quai Branly, 5ème (tel. 01 43 06 15 28). M: Bir Hakeim. A youth information service provided by the *Mairie.* Sells theater tickets at half-price and distributes free passes to concerts, plays, and exhibits. You must be under 26 for discounts. Bastille branch open M-F noon-7pm; quai Branly branch open M-F 12:30-6pm.

Kiosque-Théâtre, 15, pl. de la Madeleine, 8ème. M: Madeleine. Also in 1er, M: Châtelet-les-Halles. *The* best discount box office, selling discount tickets the day of the show. 16F per seat commission. Open Tu-Sa 12:30-8pm, Su 12:30-4pm. MC, V.

Alpha FNAC: Spectacles, 136, rue de Rennes, 6ème (tel. 01 49 54 30 00). M: Montparnasse-Bienvenue. Also at Forum des Halles, 1-7, rue Pierre Lescot, 1er (tel. 01 40 41 40 00), M: Châtelet-Les Halles; 26-30, av. des Ternes, 17ème (tel. 01 44 09 18 00), M: Ternes; and 71, bd. St-Germain, 5ème (tel. 01 44 41 31 50). Tickets for theater, concerts, and festivals. Open M-Sa 10am-7:30pm. AmEx, MC, V.

Virgin Megastore, 52, av. des Champs-Elysées, 8ème (tel. 01 49 53 52 45; box office tel. 01 44 68 44 08). M: Franklin D. Roosevelt. Like FNAC, easy ticket pick-up but no discounts. On the lower level. Open M-Sa 10am-6pm. AmEx, MC, V.

NATIONAL THEATERS

Four of France's five national theaters are located in Paris (the fifth is in Strasbourg). With the advantages of giant auditoriums, great acoustics, veteran acting troupes, and centuries of prestige, they stage popular and polished productions of Molière, Racine, Goethe, and Shakespeare (all in French). Unless you're banking on last-minute rush tickets, make reservations 14 days in advance.

La Comédie Française, 2, rue de Richelieu, 1er (tel. 01 44 58 15 15). M: Palais-Royal. Founded by Molière, now the granddaddy of all French theaters. Much pomp and prestige, with red velvet and chandeliers. Expect wildly gesticulated slapstick farce in the much-parodied style of the Comédie Française. You don't need to speak French to understand the jokes. Performances take place in the 892-seat Salle Richelieu. 1999 will feature Molière's *Les Femmes Savantes* and Goethe's *Faust,* among others. Box office open daily 11am-6pm. Tickets 45-120F, under 27 60-70F (remainders). Rush tickets (30F) available 45min. before show; line up an hour in advance. The *comédiens français* also mount plays in the 330-seat

Théâtre du Vieux Colombier, 21, rue du Vieux Colombier, 6ème (tel. 01 44 39 87 00 or 01 44 39 87 01; recorded info 08 36 68 01 50). M: St-Sulpice. 1999 will feature works by Shakespeare and Genet. Tickets 130F; rush tickets 60F sold 45min. before performances, available to students under 27 and anyone under 25.

Odéon Théâtre de l'Europe, 1, pl. Odéon, 6ème (tel. 01 44 41 36 36). M: Odéon. Programs in this elegant neoclassical building range from classics to avant-garde, but the Odéon specializes in foreign plays in their original language. 1042 seats. Also Petit Odéon, an affiliate with 82 seats. Open Sept.-July. Box office open M-Sa 11am-6:30pm. Tickets 30-170F for most shows; student rush tickets 60F, available 45min. before performance. Petit Odéon 70F, students 50F. MC, V.

Théâtre National de Chaillot, pl. du Trocadéro, 16ème (tel. 01 53 65 30 00). M: Trocadéro. In the Palais de Chaillot. Plays, music, and dance concerts take place in 2 rooms, one with 1000 and the other with 400 seats. 1999 season includes: *Les Bas-fonds* by Maxime Gorki and *Variations Goldberg* by Georges Tabore. Call to arrange wheelchair access. Box office open M-Sa 11am-7pm, Su 11am-5pm. Tickets 160F, under 25 and seniors 120F, same-day student rush 80F. MC, V.

Théâtre Nationale de la Colline, 15, rue Malte-Brun, 20ème (tel. 01 44 62 52 00, for reservations tel. 01 44 62 52 52; fax 01 44 62 52 92; minitel 3615 La Colline). M: Gambetta. The Grand Théâtre has 754 seats, the Petit Théâtre 240 seats. Founded in 1988, this fledgling national theater features French and foreign contemporary plays. 1999 season includes works by Sarraute and Sleisser. Call ahead for wheelchair access or braille plot summaries. Open Sept.-June. Informal debate/soirée W before show in lounge. Box office open M-Sa 11am-7pm, Su 2-5pm. Call to reserve tickets M-Sa 11am-7pm, until 9pm on show days. Tickets 160F, over 60 130F, students and under 26 110F; W performances 110F.

PRIVATE THEATERS

Paris's private theaters, though less celebrated than their state-run counterparts, often stage outstanding productions. In this realm of the weird and wonderful, risky performances sometimes misfire. Check the reviews in newspapers and entertainment weeklies before investing in a seat. Watch for schedules on the green, cylindrical spectacles notice boards posted throughout the city; also, check *Pariscope* or *l'Officiel des Spectacles*, or pick up a schedule from the theater itself.

Bouffes du Nord, 37, bd. de la Chapelle, 10ème (tel. 01 46 07 34 50). M: La Chapelle. This experimental theater, headed by the British director Peter Brook, produces cutting-edge performances and occasional productions in English. Box office open M-Sa 11am-6pm. Tickets 130F, students 100F.

Jardin Shakespeare du Pré Catelan (recorded info tel. 01 40 19 95 33; reservations 06 60 10 04 15), in the center of the Bois de Boulogne, west of the Lac Inférieur. Take bus #244 from Porte Maillot. 450 seats. Summertime Shakespeare (and other classics) in French, set in a garden of plants mentioned by the bard. Tickets at the door or at FNAC. Evening shows F-Sa, matinees Sa-Su. Buses stop running before late shows end, and walking in the Bois de Boulogne is dangerous even if you know your way out. Take a taxi to Porte Maillot. Tickets 100F, reduced 60F.

Théâtre de la Huchette, 23, rue de la Huchette, 5ème (tel. 01 43 26 38 99). M: St-Michel. 100 seats. Tiny historic theater where Ionesco's *La cantatrice chauve (The Bald Soprano)* and *La leçon (The Lesson)* premiered and continue to play today, 41 years later. A bastion of Left Bank intellectualism, but still a good choice for people with functional high school French. Shows M-Sa. Box office open M-Sa 5-7pm. *La cantatrice chauve* starts at 7pm, *La leçon* at 8pm. No one admitted after curtain. Tickets 100F, students M-F 80F; both shows 160F, students M-F 120F.

Théâtre Mogador, 25, rue de Mogador, 9ème (tel. 01 53 32 32 00). M: Trinité. With 1792 seats, one of the largest theaters in Paris, staging national and international productions on its colossal stage. 1999 highlights include a staged ballet of *Don Quixote* and the American sensation *Tap Dogs.* Box office open M-Sa 11am-7pm. Ticket prices vary, though most are 100-260F, matinees 100-230F.

Théâtre du Rond Point, Salle Renaud-Barrault, 2bis, av. Franklin D. Roosevelt, 8ème (tel. 01 44 95 98 00; fax 01 40 75 04 48). M: Franklin D. Roosevelt. 750 seats. Smaller Salle Jean Vautier has 150 seats. Main stage features anything from musical comedy to Beckett. The smaller stage is more experimental. 1999 will see plays by Francois Billetdoux and Isaac Babol. Open Sept.-July. Box office open Tu-Sa noon-5pm. Tickets 180F, students and under 26 80F, seniors 130F. MC, V.

Théâtre de la Ville, 2, pl. du Châtelet, 4ème (tel. 01 42 74 22 77). M: Châtelet. 1000 seats. Excellent productions, including classical music concerts and ballets. Box office open M-F 11am-7pm; open for telephone sales M 9am-6pm, Tu-Sa 9am-8pm. Tickets 95-140F, student same-day rush tickets half-price. MC, V.

CAFÉ-THÉÂTRES

Visit one of Paris's *café-théâtres* for an evening of word play and social satire in mostly black-box theater settings. Expect low-budget, high-energy skits filled with political puns and double-entendres. In general, knowledge of French slang and politics is a must for audience members. One-person shows are a mainstay.

Au Bec Fin, 6, rue Thérèse, 1er (tel. 01 42 96 29 35). M: Palais-Royal. A tiny, 60-seat theater featuring 2-3 shows per night. Dinner and 1 show from 178F, Sa 200F. Dinner and 2 shows from 300F. Shows at 7, 8:30, and 10:15pm. Tickets 80F, students

80F (except Saturdays); M-Tu 50F. Seats for auditions open to the public every M at 9:30pm, 50F. The show is free on your birthday when you purchase a meal.

Café de la Gare, 41, rue du Temple, 4ème (tel. 01 42 78 52 51). M: Hôtel-de-Ville. Couched in the Centre de Danse du Marais, where its line-up includes solo comics and Addams Family Goth seances. Box office open daily 3-7pm and 30min. before the show. Shows W-Sa at 8pm. Tickets 100F, 25 and under 70F. MC, V.

Petit Casino, 17, rue Chapon, 3ème (tel. 01 42 78 36 50). M: Arts-et-Métiers. Once a plumbing store, now a basement dinner-theater with a stage that's 4 paces wide. Performances tend toward low comedy and require a fairly high level of French. Dinner starts at 7:30pm, 1st show at 9pm, 2nd show at 10:30pm. Box office open daily 9am-midnight. Dinner and 2 shows 140F, Sa 170F. Shows alone 100F. MC, V.

Le Point Virgule, 7, rue Ste-Croix-de-la-Bretonnerie, 4ème (tel. 01 42 78 67 03). M: Hôtel-de-Ville. Built by the actors and comedians themselves, Le Point Virgule is as intimate and interactive as theater can be, with crowds of 130 sitting shoulder-to-elbow on benches. Frequent slapstick acts ideal for non-French speakers. Reservations suggested. 3 shows daily at 8, 9:15, and 10:15pm. Tickets to 1 show 80F, students 65F; 2 shows 130F; 3 shows 150F. Open daily 5pm-midnight.

CHANSONNIERS

The *chansonnier*, the musical cousin of the *café-théâtre*, is popular music in the best sense of the word, a mix of nostalgia, biting commentary, and tunes everyone knows. Think cabaret with an edge. In the spirit of old Paris, audience members usually sing, and you'll join in, too, by the end of the night. The better your French, the better the time you'll have. Admission usually includes one drink, to loosen the vocal chords.

Au Lapin Agile, 22, rue des Saules, 18ème (tel. 01 46 06 85 87; fax 01 42 54 63 04). M: Lamarck-Coulaincourt. From the metro, turn right on rue Lamark, then right again up rue des Saules. Picasso, Verlaine, Renoir, and Apollinaire hung out here during the heyday of Montmartre; now a mainly tourist audience crowds in for comical poems and songs. Originally called the *Cabaret des Assassins*, this *chansonnier* inspired Steve Martin's 1996 hit play *Picasso at the Lapin Agile*. In 1875, when the artist André Gill painted a rabbit on the theater's façade, it came to be known as *le lapin à Gill* (Gill's Rabbit), a name that eventually morphed into *Le lapin agile* (the nimble rabbit). Shows at 9:15pm. Admission and first drink 110F, students 80F. Subsequent drinks 30-35F. Open Tu-Su 9pm-2am.

Caveau de la République, 1, bd. St-Martin, 3ème (tel. 01 42 78 44 45; fax 01 42 78 52 09). M: République. A Parisian crowd fills the 482 seats of this 96-year-old venue for political satire. Shows consist of 6 separate comedy and song acts; the sequence is called the *tour de champs* (tour of the field). Good French skills and knowledge of French politics needed to get the gags. Tickets sold up to 6 days in advance, daily 11am-6pm. Shows mid-Sept. to June Tu-Sa 5 and 9pm, Su 3:30pm. Admission M-Th 140F, F-Sa 180F, Tu-Th students and over 60 110F. MC, V.

Deux Ânes, 100, bd. de Clichy, 18ème (tel. 01 46 06 10 26). M: Blanche. More music and comedy; Sept.-June M-Sa 9pm. Tickets sold up to 2 weeks in advance. Reservations by phone or in person daily 11am-7pm. Admission 200, students 100F.

GUIGNOLS

Grand guignol is a traditional Parisian marionette theater featuring the *guignol*, its classic stock character, like *Punch and Judy*. These antic performances have long thrilled adults as well as children. Although the puppets speak French, you'll have no trouble understanding the slapstick, child-geared humor. Nearly all parks, like the popular Jardin du Luxembourg (see **Sights**, p. 157) have *guignols;* check *Pariscope* for more information (see **Publications,** p. 75).

Marionettes des Champs-Elysées, Rond-Point des Champs-Elysées, 8ème (tel. 01 42 56 18 22), at the intersection of av. Matignon and Gabriel. M: Champs-Elysées-Clemenceau. The classic adventures of the *guignol* character. Shows Sept. to mid-July W and Sa-Su at 3, 4, and 5pm. Admission 13F.

ENTERTAINMENT

Marionettes du Luxembourg, Jardin du Luxembourg, 6ème (tel. 01 43 26 46 47). M: Odéon or RER: Luxembourg. The best *guignol* in Paris. This theater plays the same classics it has since it opened in 1933: *Little Red Riding Hood, The Three Little Pigs,* and so on. Running time is about 45min. Arrive 30min. early for good seats. Shows M and F at 10:30am, W at 3pm and 4:30pm, Sa at 4pm. Admission 23F.

Théâtre Guignol du Parc des Buttes Chaumont, 19ème (tel. 01 43 98 10 95). M: Laumière. Puppets gladly interact with excitable children. 7 different 40min. shows. W at 3pm and 5:30pm, Sa, Su and holidays at 3, 4, and 5pm. Call before going, as shows are often added or cut. Admission 15F.

■ Cinema

With a tradition that goes back to the very birth of cinema, Paris is a cinophile's silver-screened heaven. Invented by the Frenchmen Auguste and Louis Lumière, cinema also had its world debut in Paris. When the first movie about a train pulling up into a station premiered at the **Grand Café,** 14, bd. des Capucines, in 1895 the audience ran screaming in terror of being run over. At the time, Louis belittled his innovation as "an invention without a future." The French film industry has always seen itself as an artistic house first, an industry second. But despite all the pretentious talk of Hollywood capitalism and French cinematic vision, both film industries continue to produce films that are engaging *(Schindler's List, The Color Purple, Au revoir les enfants, La Haine)* and entertaining *(Chacun cherche son chat, La cage au folles, Father of the Bride, The X Files).* For more on French film and cinema, see **Film,** p. 18.

The French love affair with cinema is reflected in the fact that there are more films shown in Paris—over 300 a week—than in probably any other city in the world. You'll find scores of cinemas throughout the city, particularly in the *Quartier Latin* and on the Champs-Élysées. Many theaters in Paris specialize in programs featuring classic European film, current independent film, Asian classics, American classics, and current Hollywood blockbusters. The two big theater chains—**Gaumont** and **UGC**—offer *cartes privilèges* for frequent customers (Gaumont 175F for 5 entries; UGC 132F for 4 entries, 195F for 6). In late June, the wonderful two-day **Fête du Cinéma** offers great discounts and interesting films (see **Festivals,** p. 246).

Check **Pariscope** or **l'Officiel des Spectacles** (available at any kiosk or newsstand, 3F) for weekly film schedules, prices, and reviews. The notation V.O. *(version originale)* after a non-French movie listing means that the film is being shown in its original language with French subtitles; watching an English-language film with French subtitles is a great way to pick up new vocabulary. V.F. *(version française)* means that the film has been dubbed—an increasingly rare phenomenon. French cinemas sell tickets with specific **seat assignments.** Paris's cinemas offer student, senior, and family discounts. On Monday and Wednesday, prices drop about 10F for everyone. Many theaters show a series of commercials and previews *(séance)* that roll for as long as half an hour. The *séance* is often as entertaining as the film itself, and French ads are creative and witty. However, the film begins at the listed time.

Musée du Louvre, 1er (tel. 01 40 20 51 86 for info; 01 40 20 52 99 for schedules and reservations). M: Musée du Louvre. Art films, films on art, and silent movies with live musical accompaniment. Admission 25-70F, students 15-50F. Open Sept.-June.

Le Grand Rex, 1, bd. Poissonnière, 2ème (tel. 01 42 36 83 93). M: Bonne-Nouvelle. This 2800-seat behemoth is the largest theater in Paris. Amazing sound and a truly *grand écran* (big screen). Mostly 1st-runs. Last show starts around 9:30pm. Admission 46F, students and M 36F. Shows at 11am 27F. A UGC affiliate.

MK2 Beaubourg, 50, rue Rambuteau, 3ème (tel. 01 40 30 30 31 for schedules and film descriptions). 6 theaters screen 1st-run films. Cannes submissions and prize-winners run May-June. Films competing in Deauville festival screened in Sept. Matinée repertory of cult favorites like *Blade Runner* and *Blue Velvet* changes weekly. All foreign films in V.O. Admission Tu-Su 49F, M 37F, before noon daily 33F; students, under 18, and over 60 Tu-Th and F until 6:30pm 37F.

ENTERTAINMENT

Studio Galande, 42, rue Galande, 5ème (tel. 01 43 26 94 08). M: St-Michel. A 1-screen theater with independent and cult films, mostly prior releases. Don your best fishnets for the *Rocky Horror Picture Show,* F-Sa night in English. Admission 44F, students, seniors, and kids 34F.

Les Trois Luxembourg, 67, rue Monsieur-le-Prince, 6ème (tel. 01 46 33 97 77). M: Odéon. High-quality independent, classic, and foreign films, all in V.O. Popular. Purchase tickets early for a good seat. Admission 40F, students 30F.

Action Christine, 4, rue Christine, 6ème (tel. 01 43 29 11 30). M: Odéon. Off rue Dauphine. Plays an eclectic, international selection of art and cult films from the 40s and 50s. Always V.O. Admission 40F, early show (usually 6 or 7pm) 25F; M and students 30F. For 180F, buy a 1-year pass for 6 movies. One of the 2 rooms is wheelchair accessible; descend a steep staircase to reach the other.

L'Arlequin, 76, rue de Rennes, 6ème (tel. 01 45 44 28 80). M: St-Sulpice. A revival cinema with occasional visits from European directors and first-run preview showings. Some films in V.O., others are dubbed. Buy tickets in advance. Admission 45F, students M-F 35F, W all tickets 35F. Su matinée 30F. MC, V.

La Pagode, 57bis, rue de Babylone, 7ème (tel. 01 36 68 75 07). M: St-François-Xavier. From bd. des Invalides, turn right on rue de Babylone. A monument to 19th-century Parisian orientalism, La Pagode's intimate *Salle Japonaise,* with velvet seats and painted screens, makes this Paris's most charming cinema. Specializing in contemporary art films, the Pagode is a well-disguised outpost of the Gaumont chain. Admission 45F, students and seniors M-F before 6pm and everyone on W 38F. Discuss the film afterwards in the *salon de thé,* whose terrace spills into the Japanese garden. Tea and pastries 22F. *Salon de thé* open M-Sa 4-9:45pm, Su 2-8pm.

Gaumont Grand Écran Italie, 30 pl. d'Italie, 13ème (tel. 08 36 68 75 13). M: pl. d'Italie. Paris's newest and largest screen (24m by 10m), designed by Japanese architect Kenzo Tange. Hollywood blockbusters. See the world destroyed by asteroids and aliens, or watch the damn boat sink to the sounds of that damn song.

Le St-Germain-des-Prés, 22, rue Guillaume Apollinaire, 6ème (tel. 01 42 22 87 23). M: St-Germain-des-Prés. A big, beautiful theater screening independent, classic, and foreign films. Admission 40F, students, seniors, M, W, and noon show 30F.

L'Entrepôt, 7-9, rue Francis de Pressensé, 14ème (tel. 01 45 40 78 38). M: Pernety. Turn right off rue Raymond Losserand. An international venue for independent films, this cinema organizes week-long festivals, sometimes with director and actor forums. 3 screens show films in V.O. Admission 40F, students and seniors 30F. The delightful restaurant/bar (tel. 01 45 40 60 70) serves meals on the secluded garden terrace. Lunch *menu* 69F. Beer 20-25F. Restaurant open M-F 10:30am-1am, Sa-Su 12:30-3pm. Bar open daily 3pm-1am. Great for a date.

Cinémathèque Française, pl. du Trocadéro, 16ème (tel. 01 45 53 21 86). M: Trocadéro. At the Musée du Cinéma in the Palais de Chaillot; enter through the Jardins du Trocadéro. Also 18, rue du Faubourg-du-Temple, 11ème. M: République. Recording (tel. 01 47 04 24 24) lists all shows. A must for film buffs. 2-3 classics, near-classics, or soon-to-be classics per day. Foreign films usually in V.O. Buy tickets 15-20 min. early. Open W-Su 5-9:45pm. Admission 28F, students 17F.

La Géode, 26, av. Corentin Cariou, 19ème (tel. 01 40 05 12 12; recorded schedule 08 36 68 29 30, 3F per min.). M: Porte de la Villette. In La Villette (see **Museums,** p. 238). Science and nature movies on a huge spherical screen in a building that looks like a giant silver alien ship. Shows Tu-Su on the hour 10am-9pm. Admission 57F, students M-F 44F. Reserve well in advance.

14 Juillet sur Seine, 14, quai de la Seine, 19ème (tel. 08 36 68 47 07). M: Stalingrad. This huge new addition to the waterfront has 6 screens, a restaurant, exhibition space, and shops. 1st-run films in V.O. Admission 47F, students 37F.

Dôme IMAX, pl. de la Défense (tel. 01 46 92 45 45). M: Grande Arche de la Défense. The big dome to the right with your back to the Grand Arche. An IMAX cinema with huge-screen documentary films like *The Fires of Kuwait* and *Antarctica.* Documentaries are in French, but since what you see is of primary importance, non-French speakers can attend without a problem. Admission 55F, students, seniors, and under 16 40F. For 2 shows 75F, students, seniors, and under 16 65F.

■ Music

CLASSICAL MUSIC, OPERA, AND DANCE

Paris toasts the classics under lamppost, spire, and chandelier. The city's squares, churches, and concert halls feature world-class performers from home and abroad. Acclaimed foreign and provincial dance companies visit Paris frequently; watch for posters and read *Pariscope*. Connoisseurs will find the thick and indexed *Programme des Festivals* (free at *mairies* and at tourist offices) an indispensable guide to seasonal music and, to a lesser extent, dance series and celebrations in and around Paris. The monthly publication *Paris Selection*, free at tourist offices throughout the city, also keeps track of concerts in churches and museums, many of which are free or reasonably priced. In general, Paris offers cheap tickets to high culture in great quantities, thanks to a decade of socialism that offered the arts to the masses. Beware, however, of rock-bottom prices. The Opéra Bastille allegedly suffers from poor acoustics. And while Balanchine may have said "see the music, hear the dance," you may not be able to do either from the upper eaves of the Opéra Garnier, Paris's ballet-only theater. Try to check a theater floor plan and ask about the obstructed views whenever possible before purchasing a ticket. **Alpha FNAC** is the most popular booking agent (see **Theater,** p. 234). For more information about seasonal events, consult **Festivals and other Seasonal Events,** p. 249.

Free concerts are often held in churches and parks, especially during summer festivals. These concerts are extremely popular, so get there early. Check *Pariscope* and *L'Officiel des Spectacles* and the Alpha FNAC offices for concert notices. The **American Church in Paris,** 65, quai d'Orsay, 7ème (tel. 01 40 62 05 00; M: Invalides or Alma Marceau), sponsors free concerts (Sept.-June Su at 5pm). **Église St-Merri,** 78, rue St-Martin, 4ème (M: Hôtel de Ville), is also known for its free concerts (Sept.-July Sa at 9pm and Su at 4pm); contact Accueil Musical St-Merri, 76, rue de la Verrerie, 4ème (tel. 01 42 71 40 75 or 01 42 71 93 93; M: Châtelet). Sunday concerts take place in the **Jardin du Luxembourg** band shell, 6ème (tel. 01 42 34 20 23); show up early for a seat or prepare to stand. Infrequent concerts in the **Musée d'Orsay,** 1, rue Bellechasse, 7ème (tel. 01 40 49 49 66; M: Solferino), are occasionally free with a museum ticket but usually cost 20-130F. The **Maison de Radio France** (see **Museums,** p. 232) hosts concerts, some free.

Many churches stage frequent concerts that are somewhat expensive but feature fantastic acoustics and atmosphere (tel. 01 42 50 70 72). Check schedules at **Église St-Germain-des-Prés,** 3, pl. St-Germain-des-Prés, 6ème (tel. 01 44 62 70 90; M: St-Germain-des-Prés); **Église St-Eustache,** 2 rue du Jour, 1er (tel. 01 42 36 31 05; M: Les Halles); **Église de la Trinité,** pl. Estienne d'Orves, 9ème (tel. 01 48 74 12 77; M: Trinité); **Église St-Louis-en-l'Île,** 19bis, rue St-Louis-en-l'Île, 4ème (tel. 01 46 34 11 60; M: Pont Marie); and **Église St-Julien-le-Pauvre,** 23, quai de Mortebello, 5ème (tel. 01 43 54 52 16). Arrive 30-45 minutes ahead for good seats. Ste-Chapelle also hosts fabulous concerts a few times per week in the summer. Contact the box office at 4, bd. du Palais, 1er (tel. 01 53 73 78 50; M: Cité).

IRCAM, Institut de Recherche et Coordination Acoustique/Musique, Centre Pompidou, 1, pl. Igor-Stravinsky, 4ème (tel. 01 44 78 48 16; http://mediatheque.ircam.fr/). M: Rambuteau. This institute, which invites scholars, composers, and interpreters to come together in the study of music, often holds concerts. Contemporary works sometimes accompanied by film or theater. Stop by the office at the Stravinsky fountain or at the information desk in the Centre Pompidou for schedules. There are 2 computers in the lobby that allow you to "visit" IRCAM and play musical games. The institute also houses a music library for scholars. IRCAM will not be closing along with the Centre Pompidou. The music library, or médiathèque, is open mid-Aug. to mid-July M and W-F 10am-7pm, Th noon-7pm, Sa 1pm-7pm. 20F per afternoon; 300F per year, students 150F.

Musée du Louvre, 1er (tel. 01 40 20 51 86 for information, 01 40 20 52 99 for schedule, 01 40 20 84 00 for reservations; http://www.louvre.fr). M: Palais-Royal or Musée du Louvre. Classical music in the classy Louvre auditorium. Ten concerts

ENTERTAINMENT

130F, students 100F; individual concerts 25F, students 17F. Music-film combos 25F. Open Sept.-June.

Opéra de la Bastille, pl. de la Bastille, 11ème (tel. 01 44 73 13 99). M: Bastille. The Opéra de la Bastille staged its first performance on July 14, 1989, during the bicentennial jubilee. Hailed by some as the hall to bring opera to the masses, decried by others as offensive to every aesthetic sensibility, this huge theater features elaborate opera and ballet, often with a modern spin. The Bastille Opera is said to have acoustical problems spread democratically throughout the theater, so it's probably not the place to go all-out for front row seats. Subtitles in French. The '99-'00 season will feature *Don Carlo, Carmen, Macbeth,* and *La Bohème.* Tickets 45-650F. Call, write, or stop by for a free brochure of the season's events. Tickets can be purchased: by writing (foreigners can pay on arrival in Paris by presenting their letter of confirmation); by phone (tel. 01 44 73 13 00; open M-Sa 11am-6pm); or in person M-Sa 11am-6:30pm. Tickets on sale 14 days in advance of performance. Reduced rush tickets for students under 25, and anyone over 65 often available 15min. before show; 120F for operas, 70F for ballets, and 50F for concerts. Wheelchair access: call (tel. 01 44 73 13 73) at least 15 days in advance. MC, V.

Opéra Comique, 14, rue Favart, 2ème (tel. 01 42 44 45 46; fax 01 49 26 05 93). M: Richelieu-Drouot. Operas on a lighter scale—from Rossini to Offenbach. It was here that Bizet's *Carmen* first scandalized the Parisian public. The '99-'00 season will include: *La Finita Semplice* (Mozart) Feb. 22-Mar. 4; *La Sonnambula* (Bellini) April 24-May 6; *La Bohème* (Puccini) June 24-July 10. Buy tickets at the box office M-Sa 11am-7pm or reserve by phone. Tickets 35-550F, student cut-rate tickets are available 15min. before show starts, 50F.

Opéra Garnier, pl. de l'Opéra, 9ème (tel. 01 44 73 13 99 for information, 01 44 73 13 00 for reservations). M: Opéra. Although the renovations of this historic Opéra will not be finished until 2002, it will be open for the 1999 season. The Garnier also hosts the Ballet de l'Opéra de Paris. Tickets available at the box office 2 weeks before each performance M-Sa 11am-6pm. The '99-'00 season will feature *Alcina* and *La Clémence de Titus.* Ballet tickets 45-405F; opera tickets up to 650F. Lowest-end tickets often have obstructed views. Show up an hour before to buy leftover tickets at remarkable discounts (especially in summer). MC, V.

Cité de la Musique, at La Villette, 20ème (tel. 01 44 84 44 84; http://www.cite-musique.fr). M: Porte de Pantin. Hosts everything from lute concerts to American gospel year round in its enormous *salle des concerts* and smaller *amphithéâtre.* Concerts planned for 1999 include Bach (Mar. 17-27) and Music from Brazil (May 12-16). Tickets run 60-200F. One particularly good deal offered by the Cité is a *carnet* of 4 tickets for 150F. There are free concerts throughout the year in both spaces; call for information. Shows at 8pm, box office opens 30min. prior.

Orchestre de Paris, 252, rue du Faubourg St-Honoré, 8ème (tel. 01 45 61 65 65). M: Ternes. The internationally renowned orchestra delivers first-class performances under Semyon Bychkov. 1999 season includes Schubert, Stravinsky, Mozart, Brahms, and Beethoven. Season runs Oct.-June; call or stop by for concert calendar. 2 concerts per week, usually W-Th. Box office open M-Sa 11am-6pm and until 8pm shownights not including Sunday. Shows at 7:30. Tickets 60-320F. Student rush tickets 30min. before show for 50F. MC, V.

Théâtre des Champs-Elysées, 15, av. Montaigne, 8ème (tel. 01 49 52 50 50). M: Alma Marceau. Top international dance companies and orchestras, from world music to chamber music. To play here is to "arrive" on the highbrow music scene. When asked by a passerby, "How do I get to the Théâtre des Champs-Elysées?", Horowitz replied, "Practice. Lots and lots of practice." Season runs Sept.-June. Buy tickets 3 weeks in advance. Reserve by telephone M-F 10am-noon and 2-6pm; box office open M-Sa 11am-7pm. Tickets 60-690F.

Théâtre Musical de Paris, pl. du Châtelet, 1er (tel. 01 42 33 00 00). M: Châtelet. A superb 2300-seat theater featuring orchestras, ballet companies, opera, and dance. Magnificent acoustics. Closed until Oct. 1998. Call in Feb. '99 for schedule information. Tickets usually 60-775F. Last-minute reduced rate tickets sold 15min. before performance (opera 100F, all others 50F). AmEx, MC, V.

JAZZ

Jazz began to trickle into Paris with U.S. servicemen during WWI. By the 1940s Paris had emerged as a jazz hot spot. Jazz is commonly recognized by Parisian intellectuals as one of America's few totally unique and worthy cultural contributions. American jazz musicians flocked to Paris, as they were accorded great respect and appreciation by the French. Since then, French jazz musicians, including pianist and native Parisian Michel Petrucciani, have themselves become fixtures of the international scene. In Paris, pianist Laurent de Wilde won France's Django Prize in 1993. Funk leader and guitarist Hervé Krief is well loved by French crowds, as is the old-guard blues organist Eddy Louis. From the American scene, Herbie Hancock, McCoy Tyner, Benny Baily, Duffy Jackson, and Kenny Garrett frequent the Paris circuit, and you can find nearly every type of jazz in Paris, from New Orleans to cool jazz, from acid jazz to hip-hop and fusion. Brazilian samba and bossa nova are steadily growing in popularity together with music from the West Indies and Francophone Africa. In Paris you pay for jazz clubs either through inflated drink prices or via a cover charge. Once you have paid your cover, you are not required to drink and will likely not be disturbed should you choose to nurse one drink for the rest of the night.

Frequent summer festivals sponsor free or nearly free jazz concerts. The **Fête du Marais** often features free Big Band jazz, while the **La Villette Jazz Festival** offers very big names and a few free shows (see **Festivals,** p. 249). In the fall, the **Jazz Festival of Paris** comes to town as venues high and low open their doors to celebrity and up-and-coming artists. French mags *Jazz Hot* (45F) and *Jazz Magazine* (35F) are both great sources of information, as is the hard-to-find, bimonthly *LYLO (Les Yeux, Les Oreilles;* free). If you can't find it in bars or FNACs, try the main office, 55, rue des Vinaigriers, 10ème. *Pariscope* and *l'Officiel des Spectacles* also have jazz listings.

Au Duc des Lombards, 42, rue des Lombards, 1er (tel. 01 42 33 22 88). M: Châtelet. Murals of Ellington and Coltrane swathe the exterior of this premier jazz joint. The best in French jazz, with occasional American soloists, and hot items in world music. Excellent acoustics, dark and smoky atmosphere. Cover 80-100F, music students 50-80F. Beer 28-48F, cocktails 55F. Music starts around 10pm and wails on until 3am (4am on weekends). Open daily 7:30pm-4am. V.

Le Baiser Salé, 58, rue des Lombards, 1er (tel. 01 42 33 37 71). M: Châtelet. Cuban, African, Antillean music featured together with modern jazz and funk upstairs on the first floor. Month-long African music festival Oct.-Nov.; bass festival June. Concerts start at 10pm, music until 3am (typically 3 sets). Cover 35-80F, depending on performers; mainly new talent. Free Monday jam sessions with 1 drink min. Beer 24F, cocktails 52F. Open daily 4pm-2am.

Blue Note, 38, rue Mouffetard, 5ème (tel. 01 45 87 36 09). M: Monge. Take rue Monge north and turn left on rue Lacépède then left on rue Mouffetard at pl. de la Contrescarpe. Brazilian music, jazz, and blues in a small, laid-back, albeit warm, setting. Excellent samba guitarists and new groups. Play along yourself with the make-shift percussion implements on each table. Try the house drink *caipirinha* (*caçhaça* and lime 50F). No cover. Drinks Su and Tu-Th 25-45F, F-Sa 40-55F. Music starts F-Sa 11pm, Su and Tu-Th 10pm. Open daily from 6:30pm.

Caveau de la Huchette, 5, rue de la Huchette, 5ème (tel. 01 43 26 65 05). M: St-Michel. For those who have always felt jazz was meant to be danced to. Come prepared to listen, watch, and dance the jitterbug, be-bop, swing, and jive in this extremely popular jazz club. Be-bop dance lessons offered M-F evenings before club opens; call 01 42 71 09 09. Excellent music, matched by a terrific atmosphere and varied age-group (ages 20-60). The caves have a gruesome history. They served as tribunal, prison, and execution rooms for Danton, Marat, St-Just, and Robespierre during the Revolution. When the club moved into this space in the late 40s, they found 2 skeletons chained together. Crowded on weekends. Cover Su-Th 60F, F-Sa 70F. Students always 55F. Drinks 22-30F. Open M-Th 9:30pm-3am, F 9:30pm-2:30am, Sa 9:30pm-4am.

Le Franc Pinot, 1, quai de Bourbon, 4ème (tel. 01 46 33 60 64; see **Wine Bars,** p. 131, for full review). Jazz W-Sa 10am-2am. Admission 40F, drinks start at 30F. MC.

New Morning, 7-9, rue des Petites-Ecuries, 10ème (tel. 01 45 23 51 41). M: Château d'Eau. 400-seat former printing plant with the biggest American headliners in the city. Dark, smoky, and crowded, it's everything a jazz club should be. Sit in the lower front section or near the wings for the best acoustics. All the greats have played here—from Chet Baker to Stan Getz and Miles Davis—and the club still attracts big names like Wynton Marsalis, Betty Carter, John Scofield, and Archie Shepp. Open Sept.-July from 8pm; times vary; concerts usually at 9pm. Tickets available at box office, the FNAC, or Virgin Megastore; 110-140F. Drinks 30-55F. MC, V.

Le Petit Journal St-Michel, 71, bd. St-Michel, 5ème (tel. 01 43 26 28 59; http://www.jazzfrance.com/pjsm). M: Luxembourg. A crowded though somewhat dry establishment for those who mainly limit jazz to New Orleans and Big Band. First-class performers play in this Parisian center of the "Old Style." Open M-Sa 8:30pm-1:30am. Obligatory 1st drink 110F, subsequent drinks 45F.

Le Petit Journal Montparnasse, 13, rue du Commandant-Mouchotte, 14ème (tel. 01 43 21 56 70). M: Gaîté or Montparnasse-Bienvenue. Look for the large, animated neon sign featuring a horn player. An elegant club, popular with a well-to-do, older clientele. Very good piano and sound system at the service of the best contemporary mainstream French jazz. Obligatory first drink 100-150F, depending on the show. Open M-Sa 8:30pm-2am; music begins at 10pm.

Le Petit Opportun, 15, rue des Lavandières-Ste-Opportune, 1er (tel. 01 42 36 01 36). M: Châtelet. A relaxed, unpolished pub with some of the best modern jazz around, including many American performers. Hidden in an ancient stone-walled cellar, this popular club has only 60 seats—show up early. Cover 50-80F depending on act. Drinks 25-60F. Open Sept.-July Tu-Sa 9pm-5am; music begins at 10:30pm.

Slow Club, 130, rue de Rivoli, 1er (tel. 01 42 33 84 30). M: Châtelet. In a cellar that used to be a banana-ripening warehouse, Slow Club—an old favorite of Miles Davis—hosts Big Band, Dixieland, and rock and roll in a rock-around-the-clock vein. Playful but painfully tacky old-time setting. Older crowd than la Huchette. Lessons offered (tel. 01 42 53 14 49). Expect dancing and a crowd in their 30s. Weekday cover 60F, students 55F; weekend cover from 75F. Drinks from 25F. Open Tu-Th 10pm-3am, F-Sa 10pm-4am.

Le Sunset, 60, rue des Lombards, 1er (tel. 01 40 26 46 60). M: Châtelet. An easy-going club with an old and widespread reputation, Le Sunset is where musicians come to unwind and jam into the wee hours after their gigs around Paris. The room resembles the metro in shape but also in its acoustics, so sit close. Mostly French and European acts. W-Sa international jazz, Su jazz vocalists, M jam sessions, Tu new generation jazz. Cover 50-100F, with a 20% discount for *Let's Go* travelers; drinks 26-56F. Open daily 10pm-dawn; hang around past 2am to catch the jam scene. Restaurant upstairs not really connected to club (82F 2 course *menu*) serves food until 2am (3am on weekends).

Aux Trois Mailletz, 56, rue Galande, 5ème (tel. 01 43 54 00 79). M: St-Michel. The basement houses an exceptional jazz café featuring world music. Leans toward Latin and Afro-Cuban, but also has jazz, blues, and gospel musicians from Europe and the U.S. 70F admission to club, admission to bar is free. Beer 38-50F, cocktails 65F. Bar open daily 5pm-dawn; cave 8:30pm to dawn.

La Villa, 29, rue Jacob, 6ème (tel. 01 43 26 60 00). M: St-Germain-des-Prés. Downstairs from 4-star Hôtel La Villa, this exclusive and expensive club can afford to fly American artists here for week-long engagements. Stars that have appeared include Shirley Horn and Joshua Redman. The sort of place with drinks like "Night and Day" and "So What." First drink M-F 120F, Sa-Su 150F. Special musician price 60F. Open M-Sa 10pm-2am. AmEx, MC, V.

▓ Dance Clubs

In the City of Lights, some of the brightest rays are flashing on the dance floor. Some Parisian clubs are small and nearly impossible to find unless you're a native. Others are larger-than-life and outrageously flashy. The discos that are "in" (and in business) change drastically from year to year. Many Parisian clubs are officially private, which means they have the right to pick and choose their clientele. The management evaluates prospective customers before they let them past the bouncers. The admissions process is tougher than those at most Ivy-League schools. Parisians tend to dress up more than North Americans, Australians, and Kiwis for a night on the town. So, as RuPaul says, girl, you better *work*. And above all: **Wear Black.**

The current recession and 16% unemployment rate has hit the previously chic Paris club scene badly. As a result a few stylish, lucky rich visit their private, exclusive clubs. The rest of the party public makes do with roving parties and raves (called *soirées*) that move from location to location, sometimes even to the outskirts, and are announced only weeks before. The regular, easy to locate, booming, booty-shaking clubs are crowded, expensive, and outrageously flashy. Last year, a controversial drug scandal drove the reactionary French *flics* (cops) to shut down many major clubs, of which a few like **Le Cox** and **Le Queen** resurfaced, while others went bankrupt. Hard to find, many small clubs are also quick to harass those not properly attired or suitably colored. If you're a fashion victim, or more seriously, a victim of racist bouncers, you may want to try the more friendly and varied bar scene instead. There are a number of hip lounges and bars that become raging clubs on the weekend (see **Bars and Pubs,** p. 132).

In general, word of mouth and weekly journals (such as *Pariscope* or club flyers) are the best guide to the current scene. Some of the smaller places in the *Quartier Latin* admit almost anyone who is sufficiently decked out (in black). To access one of the more exclusive places, you may need to accompany a regular (and wear black). Women often get a discount or get in free, but don't go alone unless you're looking for lots of amorous attention from sweaty freaks (see **Vulgar Pigs,** p. 101). Weekdays are cheaper and less crowded, but most action happens on weekends and very, very late. As a rule 2 to 3am is the peak period in any club. May the party spirit be with you.

Le Queen, 102, av. des Champs-Elysées, 8ème (tel. 01 53 89 08 90). Come taste the fiercest funk in town where drag queens, superstars, models, moguls, and buff Herculean go-go boys get down to the rhythms of a 10,000 gigawatt sound system. Her majesty is open 7 days a week, midnight to dawn. M Disco (50F cover plus 50F drink); Tu Gay House and gallons of soap suds (very hot, 50F cover, 50F drink); W Latin House (no cover); Th house (no cover); F-Sa House (80F entry, plus 50F drink); Su 80s Retro (no cover). All drinks 50F. Le Queen is at once the cheapest and most fashionable club in town, and thus the toughest to get in to. Dress fabulously and pray to Madonna that you get in.

L'Arapaho, 30, av. d'Italie, Centre Commercial Italie 2, 13ème (tel. 01 53 79 00 11). M: pl. d'Italie. It's the gray door on the right, just past Au Printemps. Since 1983, this place has built up a reputation for hosting some of the best hard-core, rap, pop, and metal bands to come through Paris. A pitstop on most indie rock bands' tour itineraries. Past acts have included Pavement, Sebadoh, Shellac, Bim Skala Bim, and Soul Asylum. Tickets usually around 60-130F. Beer 20F. New dance nights: 11pm-dawn; F Asian, Sa Cuban. Cover 80F, cocktails 50F.

Les Bains, 7, rue du Bourg l'Abbé, 3ème (tel. 01 48 87 01 80). M: Réaumur-Sébastopol. Ultraselective, super-crowded, and very expensive. The Artist Formerly Known as Prince boosted its reputation with a surprise free concert here a few years back. It used to be a public bath, visited at least once by Marcel Proust. More recently, Mike Tyson, Madonna, and Jack Nicholson have stopped in, but to bathe only in their glory. Lots of models on the floor and on-stage as gogo dancers. House and garage grunge. Mirrored bar upstairs. Cover and 1st drink 100F. Subsequent drinks 100F. Open daily midnight-6am. AmEx, MC, V.

Le Bataclan, 50, bd. Voltaire, 11ème (tel. 01 47 00 39 12). M: Oberkampf. A concert space cum café-bar that hosts indie rock bands like Guided By Voices and Beck. Young, artsy crowd. Tickets start at 100F and vary with show. Th (free) is low-key. F (80F) is gay night, and Sa (80F) is house. Open Sept.-July, Th-Sa 11pm-dawn.

Le Cithéa, 114, rue Oberkampf, 11ème (tel. 01 40 21 70 95). M: Parmentier. Somewhat similar to What's Up, this place is more of a bar with live music and an intimate floor than a pulsing, flash-dancing club. In the very hip Oberkampf *quartier* and full of young, artsy folk, Le Cithéa often has jazz, hip hop, and free jack fusion bands. No cover. Drinks 25F-60F. Open daily 9:30pm-5:30pm. MC, V.

244 ■ BISEXUAL, GAY, & LESBIAN ENTERTAINMENT

Divan du Monde, 75, rue des Martyrs, 18ème (tel. 01 44 92 77 66). M: Pigalle. Not quite global, but this grungy den does try with Brazilian music, live bands, English DJs, and funk evenings. Youngish crowd varies depending on the nightly program. Su is gay tea dance. Open daily 7:30pm-dawn. Cover 40F-100F. Drinks from 20F. MC, V.

Folies Pigalle, 11, pl. Pigalle, 9ème (tel. 01 40 36 71 58). M: Pigalle. This club is the largest and most popular in the once-sleazy Pigalle *quartier*. A former strip joint, the Folies Pigalle is popular among gay and straight clubbers, with some special girls-only events. Mostly house and techno. Very crowded at 4 in the morning. Open Th-Sa 11pm-7am, Su 3-8pm. Cover 100F. Drinks 50F. AmEx, MC, V.

Pulp!, 25, bd. Poissonnière, 2ème (tel. 01 40 26 01 93). M: Rue Montmartre. The legendary lesbian club L'Entracte has cleaned up its act and is now the swanky, glamorous Pulp! W lounge, easy listening; Th house, disco, and techno. Women-only weekends, but open to all during the week. Open W-Th 11pm-5am, F-Sa midnight-5am. Cover free-50F. Drinks 30-60F. AmEx, MC, V.

Rex Club, 5, bd. Poissonnière, 2ème (tel. 01 42 36 10 96). M: Bonne-Nouvelle. Good news: this is not a selective club. Bad news: this is not a selective club. The crowd varies from clueless tourists to young break-dancers and veteran clubbers. Usually keen on house and techno, this large club does have one of the best music systems in Paris. Open Th-Sa 11:30pm-6am. Cover 70F. Drinks 60-80F. MC, V.

Le Saint, 7, rue St-Séverin, 5ème (tel. 01 40 20 43 23). M: St-Michel. Plays a wide range of music (from reggae to techno to R&B). A small comfortable club set in 13th-century caves and filled with chic regulars who come to dance. Cover Tu-Th 60F, F 80F, Sa 90F. Drinks 15-50F. Open daily 11pm-6am.

Scala de Paris, 188bis, rue de Rivoli, 1er (tel. 01 42 61 45 00). M: Palais-Royal. Halfway between a disco (with 2 disco balls above the 2-story dance floor) and a rollercade, La Scala could be straight out of *Saturday Night Fever* were it not for the thumping house and techno. Caters to a sometimes rough-looking 18-24 crowd. Looks like a Xanadu production number. There's a smaller dance floor and a Baywatch pinball machine to boot on the 3rd floor. Cover Su-Th 80F, women free, 1-drink min.; F-Sa and holidays 100F for men and women, 1 drink included. Additional drinks 45-60F. Open daily 10:30pm-dawn.

What's Up Bar, 15, rue Daval, 11ème (tel. 01 48 05 88 33). M: Bastille. One of those rare Paris miracles: a place that is free and funky. Set up in a concrete bunker, with plenty of places to chill and chat and check out people, this bar/club has DJ competitions and its own magazine. M house, W Electronic, F Garage, Sa Freestyle. Open M-F 6:30pm-2am, Sa-Su 5pm-4am. Cover M-Th free; F-Sa 50F. Drinks 15F and up. MC, V.

■ Bisexual, Gay, & Lesbian Entertainment

It was nearly two in the morning, the Manhattan was about to close. I had collected my things at the coat-check and was looking for a quieter place to put on my sweater and leather jacket. He was sitting on a bench upstairs. Apparently he had been there a long time; in any case, I don't remember having seen him downstairs. (Yes I do.)
—Renaud Camus, Tricks, 1978.

This is Gay Paree, where the boys wear Gaultier, the drag queens sing Piaf, and where everybody's still recovering from EuroPride 1997, when Paris played host to hundreds of thousands of gay, bi, and lesbian visitors for the annual pan-European gay pride fest. Echoing Piaf, Paris is ever the Ville en Rose, with an active **Centre Gai et Lesbien** (see **Bisexual, Gay, and Lesbian Travelers,** p. 49), a politically and socially active queer community, and many lesbian and gay bars and cafés.

The center of lesbian and gay life is still the Marais, known throughout Paris as the chicest part of the city (see the **4ème Arrondissement,** p. 150). Here, amid the winding streets and *hôtel particuliers* of such famous lesbian and gay Parisians as Marie-Antoinette, Mme de Sévigné, and the Cardinal de Rohan, you will find gay and lesbian cafés, bars, bookstores, shops, and restaurants. Most gay establishments cluster around rue du Temple, rue Ste-Croix de la Bretonnerie, rue des Archives, and rue Vie-

ENTERTAINMENT

ille du Temple in the 4ème. Anyone seeking the hippest club scene in Paris will want to drop in at **Le Queen** on the Champs-Élysées. **Pulp!** is the glamorous gal alternative. Other clubs such as **Les Bains, Folies Pigalle,** and **Le Bataclan** also host gay nights (see **Dance Clubs**, p. 242). The biggest party every year is the annual Gay Pride celebration when thousands of *gais, pédés, folles, travellaux, lesbiens, gouines,* and *cammioneuses* fill the streets of the city with parades, demonstrations, and celebrations.

For the most comprehensive listing of gay and lesbian restaurants, clubs, hotels, organizations, and services, consult Gai Pied's *Guide Gai* (79F at any kiosk), *Illico* (free at gay bars and restaurants), *Le Guide Paris* (28F at gay shops). *Lesbia* (25F), and the hip new queer magazine, *Têtu* (25F at newsstands). *Pariscope* has an English-language section called *A Week of Gay Outings.* The magazines *3 Keller* and *Exit,* available at the Centre Gai et Lesbian and at many bars and clubs, can also help you find the hot spots. **Les Mots à la Bouche,** Paris's largest gay and lesbian bookstore and **La Libraire des Femmes,** Paris's premier women's bookstore serve as unofficial information centers for queer life and can also tell you what's hot and where to go (see **Bisexual, Gay, and Lesbian Travelers,** p. 49, **Women Travelers,** p. 47, and **Bookstores,** p. 263).

MOSTLY MALE

> Around two-fifteen in the morning, I climbed over the fence into the Place Jean XXIII, behind Nôtre Dame. As I walked toward the river, on my right were the bushes that are planted along the fence of the parish garden, and to my left were two men in motorcycle outfits, holding their helmets and standing with their legs wide apart.
> —Renaud Camus, *Tricks,* 1978

Le Quetzal, 10, rue de la Verrerie, 4ème (tel. 01 48 87 99 07). M: Hôtel-de-Ville. Nicknamed *l'Incontournable* (a Must), this neon, techno bar is packed with a 20s-30s crowd. Small but stylish, the Quetzal is opposite the appropriately named rue des Mauvais Garçons. Beer 16F, cocktails 15-45F. Open daily 5pm-8am.

Open Café, 17, rue des Archives, 4ème (tel. 01 42 72 26 18). M: Hôtel-de-Ville. Recently redone, the Open Café is the most popular of the Marais gay bars. Grit your teeth, grip your handbag, and bitch your way onto the terrace. Beer 18F, cocktails 35F. Open daily 10am-2am; Su brunch (70-105F). AmEx, MC, V.

Cox, 15, rue des Archives, 4ème (tel. 01 42 72 72 71). M: Hôtel-de- Ville. As the name suggests, this is a buns-to-the-wall men's bar with bulging and beautiful boys; So crowded, the boys who gather here block traffic on the street. Very cruisy; this isn't the place for a quiet cocktail. Beer 16-29F. Happy hour (with beer ½ off) M-Sa 6-8pm, Su 6-9pm.Open daily 2pm-2am.

Amnésia Café, 42, rue Vieille-du-Temple, 4ème (tel. 01 42 72 16 94). M: Hôtel-de-Ville. A classy, relaxed bar where friends gather and gossip. Crowded, but less cruisy, the Amnésia will help you forget your troubles. Beer 18-45F. Open daily 10am-2am. Su brunch noon-4pm (50-70F). MC, V.

Banana Café, 13 rue de la Ferronerie, 1er (tel. 01 42 33 35 31). M: Châtelet-Les-Halles. Around the corner from Les Halles, the *très branché* (way hip) Banana Café is the most popular gay bar in the 1er. Two floors include a popular piano bar. Beer 20F (before 10pm), 30-35F (after 10pm). Open daily 4:30pm-dawn. AmEx, MC, V.

Le Bar, 5, rue de la Ferronerie, 1er (tel. 01 40 41 00 10). M: Châtelet. Just down the street from the Banana Café, Le Bar is dark and filled with mirrors, throbbing techno, and a tiny, underground disco. If you're looking for a break from the muscle-boys, Le Bar offers a crowd with all shapes, sizes, and ages. Happy hour 6-9pm. Beer 16F until 10:30pm, 18F after. Open daily 5pm-3am.

Le Piano Zinc, 49, rue des Blancs Manteaux, 4ème (tel. 01 42 74 32 42). M: Rambuteau. A non-cruisy, mature crowd gathers nightly to enjoy the hysterical cabaret performances of the gifted bar staff. Campy homage is paid to Liza, Eartha, Madonna, Bette, Barry, and (of course) Edith Piaf. All are welcome to perform (though coming to 10pm rehearsals is recommended). Happy hour 6-8pm. Beer 10-14F, cocktails 37-44F. Open Tu-Su. 6pm-2am. AmEx, MC, V.

Le Bar Central, 33, rue Vieille-du-Temple, 4ème (tel. 01 48 87 56 08). M: Hôtel-de-Ville. Across from Amnésia, this small neighborhood gay bar is in the middle of the

Marais. A 30-something, mostly French crowd. Check out the torso sculpture. Beer 15-18F. Open Su-Th 2pm-1am, F-Sa 2pm-2am. MC, V.

WOMEN

> Satin persuaded Nana to dine at Laure's, a table d'hôte in the rue des Martyrs where dinner cost three francs. Nana's attention was drawn by a young man who was keeping a whole tableful of enormous women breathlessly attentive to his slightest caprice. But when the young man began to laugh, his chest swelled out. "God, it's a woman!" Nana blurted. Satin looked up and murmured, "Oh yes, I know her. A real good looker, eh? You ought to see them fighting for her."
>
> —Émile Zola, *Nana*, 1880

Le Champmeslé, 4, rue Chabanais, 2ème (tel. 01 42 96 85 20). M: Pyramides or Quatre Septembre. This intimate lesbian bar is Paris's oldest. Comfortable couches, small tables, dim blue lighting, and a yuppie clientele. Cabaret show every Th and first Su of every month at 10pm. On your birthday month, you get a free drink. No cover. Drinks 25-45F. Open M-W 5pm-2am, Th-Sa 5pm-5am. AmEx, MC, V.

Pulp!, 25 bd Poissonnière, 2ème (tel. 01 40 26 01 93). M: Rue Montmartre. The legendary lesbian L'Entracte has cleaned up its act and is now the swanky, glamorous Pulp!. Weekdays are mixed and het-oriented. Weekends are women-only. Open W-Th 11pm-5am, F-Sa midnight-5am. Cover free-50F. Drinks 30F-60F. AmEx, MC, V.

L'Unity, 176/178 rue St Martin, 4ème (tel. 01 42 72 70 59). M: Rambuteau. Bright punk graffiti audacious fronts this large and loud bar. Walk down rue Rambuteau and look right. Next to the Pompidou, Unity features a pool table and music ranging from reggae to rock to techno. Drinks 17-40F. Happy hour M-F 4-8pm. Open daily 4pm-2am. MC, V.

Le Sceud, 35, rue St.-Croix de la Bretonnerie, 4ème (tel. 01 40 29 44 40). M: Hôtel de Ville. Sceud means *disque* (album) in verlan (French backwards slang). A gay DJ bar with colorful and funky decor, Sceud is brand new. Techno and house music liven up the dance floor. Beer 18F, cocktails 38-50F. Open daily 3pm-2am.

SOMEWHAT MIXED

Le Bar du Palmier, 16, rue des Lombards, 4ème (tel. 01 42 78 53 53). M: Châtelet. From bd. Sébastopol turn right on rue des Lombards. Amid palm trees and piña coladas, a friendly mixed crowd overflows on the terrace, while jazz, soul, and techno keep the mood light. Beer 20-33F, cocktails 34-47F. Happy hour daily 6-8pm. Open daily 5pm-dawn. MC, V.

Day Off, 10 rue de l'Isly, 8ème (tel. 0145 22 87 90). M: St. Lazare. Off rue de Rome, near the Gare St. Lazare this small and mellow pub/restaurant features a dark wood interior, long bar, and walls covered with the luscious Marilyn Monroe. Relax to smoky French *chansons* by the divine Edith. Drinks 18-45F. Entrées 69-75F. Open M-F 11am-3pm, 5pm-3am.

■ Sports

PARTICIPATORY SPORTS

You might find it hard to believe while pounding the city's pavement, but Paris and its surroundings teem with indoor and outdoor sports opportunities. For more info call the Mairie de Paris's sports hotline, **Allô-Sports** (tel. 01 42 76 54 54; open M-Th 10:30am-5pm, F 10:30am-4:30pm). Many of the courses offered by the city are for residents only. *Pariscope* (see **Publications About Paris,** p. 75) has a *Sports et Loisirs* section with pages of facilities, hours, and prices for a variety of sports locations. Also see *Paris Pas Cher* for lists of affordable gyms geared toward the long-term visitor.

Jogging: Running is difficult in the city, where traffic is dangerous and drivers are not used to looking out for sprinters. Many joggers head to one of Paris's many public parks. Remember that running in deserted or unknown areas is dangerous, especially after dark. **In Central Paris:** the **Champs de Mars,** 7ème (M: Bir Hakeim), is a popular in-city jogging spot, with a 2.5km path around the outside, and with gardens that are broken up into 200m lengths; the leafy **Jardin du Luxembourg,** 6ème (M: Cluny-La Sorbonne), offers a 1.6km circuit and a huge crowd; the **Parc Monceau,** 8ème (M: Monceau), crawls with kids but remains serenely green; 1km loop. **On the Periphery:** the **Parc des Buttes-Chaumont,** 19ème (M: Buttes Chaumont). Labyrinthine paths great for hill-work. A swooping path (1.6km) rings the park; the **Bois de Boulogne,** 16ème, has 35km of trails. Maps are to be found at regular intervals on the periphery of the park; less renowned, but no less runable, is the **Bois de Vincennes,** 12ème; begin at the northwest corner of the park at the medieval **Château de Vincennes** (M: Château de Vincennes). Peripheral path, marked in red and yellow on park maps, is 11km; inside path (marked in blue and white) is 8km. Avoid the southwest corner of the park, especially if you're alone.

Swimming: The Mairie de Paris has created a network of public-access pools. Opening hours vary, but all are open in summer (most open M 2-7pm, Tu-Sa 7am-7:30pm, Su 8am-5pm). Call Allô-Sports to have a copy of *Les Piscines à Paris* sent to you, or pick one up at a *mairie*. It lists hours and services available at each pool. Entry to any **municipal pool** 14F; under 17, over 64, or those accompanying children but not swimming 7F. Ask about 1-year passes and discounts. Under 8 must be accompanied. Last entry 30min. before closing; pools are cleared 15min. before closing. Some pools have a *"nocturne"* 1-2 nights a week, when they're open past 8pm.

Tennis: Paris boasts 170 municipal tennis courts in 45 "tennis centers," each open to the individual player. You must have your own equipment for municipal courts. Free intro lessons for children. To use municipal courts, apply for a free **Carte Paris Tennis,** which enables you to reserve space through Minitel. Reservation is crucial, especially in summer. Pick up an application at tennis centers scattered throughout the city. Cards take 5 weeks to process. Municipal courts 34F per hr.

Gyms and Fitness: Alésia Club, 143, rue d'Alésia, 14ème (tel. 01 45 42 91 05; M: Alésia), has a gym, sauna, and other facilities and will sell you a membership for the day (200F), or for longer. Students 300F for 1 month, 1200F for 6 months, 1800F for 1 year; 100F for required insurance. Open M-F 11:30am-9pm, Sa 11:30am-8pm, Su 2-8pm. Or try the **Espace Vit'Halles,** 48, rue Rambuteau, 3ème (tel. 01 42 77 21 71), near Les Halles in pl. Beaubourg. With a weight room, a sauna, and aerobics and step classes, Vit'Halles offers both long-term and short-term memberships. Students 100F per day, 640F per month. Open M-F 8am-10pm, Sa 10am-7pm, Su 11am-4pm. **Gymnase Club,** 149, rue de Rennes, 6ème (tel. 01 45 44 24 35). There are at least 20 spread throughout Paris. Call for a free brochure. Each one has different classes and equipment. Most have pools, aerobics, weights, and sauna. Some have martial arts and tennis. 140F per day. With 350F membership card good for 1 year, pay 700F per month, 1500F for 3 months; student membership 2680F per year. If you feel the need for a beach, perhaps a jacuzzi, wavepool, and waterslide will do at **Aquaboulevard,** 4, rue Louis Armand, 15ème (tel. 01 40 60 10 00). M: Balard. Come early to avoid the crowds. Admission 69F for 4hr., 79F on weekends, 50F and 56F for under 12; 600F for Sept.-June; 1300F for 1 year. Open M-Th 9am-11pm, F 9am-midnight, Sa-Su 8am-11pm. Associated fitness club gives access to sauna, gym, tennis and squash courts, aerobic classes, and a golf course, as well as water park. Open M-F 8am-10pm, Sa-Su 9am-8pm. 160F per day, 2120F per year.

Cycling: The city is not a good place for a leisurely afternoon pedal, although the highway along the Seine near Châtelet is closed to cars on Sundays. Cyclists peddle away the hours in the **Bois de Vincennes,** 12ème (M: Porte Dorée), around Lac Daumesnil or deeper into the woods. The **Bois de Boulogne,** 16ème, officially boasts 8km of bike paths, but any cyclist can make up an original route among the innumerable trees. The **Canal de l'Ourcq** passes through the Parc de la Villette, 30, av. Corentin Cariou, 19ème (M: Porte de la Villette), and has a bicycle path alongside. For information about bike rentals, consult **Two Wheelers,** p. 68, or see **Sights,** p. 205, for info on the Bois de Boulogne. Long-distance cyclists may want to try the 109km ride out to **Ferté Milon** in the province of Aisne. Also consider the **Forêt de Fontainebleau** (see **Fontainebleau,** p. 276).

Roller Skating: Rollerblades are catching on in Paris streets. The **Jardins du Tro-cadéro,** in front of the Palais de Chaillot, fill with motorless Evil Knievals. Rent Roll-erblades at **FranScoop,** 47, rue Servan, 11ème (tel. 01 47 00 68 43). M: St- Maur. 45-90F per day, 85-150F per weekend, 170-300F per week. Open M-Sa 9:30am-7:30pm. Or check out **La Main Jaune,** pl. de la Porte-de-Champerret, 17ème (tel. 01 47 63 26 47). M: Porte de Champerret. A roller disco with non-skate dancing, it's popular with the high school crowd. Open W and Sa-Su 2:30-7pm, F-Sa and holi-days 10pm-dawn. Admission W and Sa-Su 50F (includes a drink), skate rental 10F; F-Sa night it becomes a disco with Portuguese music and non-skating clientele.

Fishing: Contact the **Annicale des Pêcheurs de Neuilly, Levallois, et environs,** Base Halientique de la Jatte, 19, bd. de Levallois Prolongé, 92000 Levallois-Perret (tel. 01 43 48 36 34). They'll fill you in on angling in the Bois de Boulogne.

Golf: Golf enthusiasts must reach deep into the suburbs for a real 18-hole game. Nev-ertheless, Paris contains a number of putting greens. Including club and ball rental, expect to pay about 100F. Try **Golf Club de l'Étoile,** 10, av. de la Grande Armée, 17ème (tel. 01 43 80 30 79), or **Aquagolf École de Golf de Paris,** 26, rue Colonel Pierre Avia, 15ème (tel. 01 45 57 43 06), 9 holes (practice space 70F).

Bowling: Bowling de Paris (tel. 01 40 67 94 00), in the Bois de Boulogne near the route Mahatma Gandhi entrance of the Jardin d'Acclimatation. After the park closes, you have to enter through the park's Mahatma Gandhi entrance, which remains open. Games M-F 9am-noon 5F, noon-8pm 22F; F late hours 8pm-2am, Sa-Su 9am-2am 34F. Obligatory bowling shoe rental 10F. Because the Bowling de Paris is inside the garden, you must also pay the garden's admission fee (10F). **Bowling International Stadium,** 66, av. d'Ivry, 13ème (tel. 01 45 86 55 52), M: Tolbiac, is a joint bowling alley and billiard hall. American billiards require a 100F deposit, a 5F supplementary fee, and cost 50F per hr. Bowling in any of the 12 lanes costs 16-33F depending on the time of day, the day of the week, and who you are (reduced prices for students and seniors); shoe rental 7F. Open daily 2pm-2am.

SPECTATOR SPORTS

If you think that Parisians are obsessed with only the very highest of high culture, think again. Parisians follow sports with fierce interest, reading between the lines of their own sports daily, *l'Équipe* (6F), and the sports sections of other newspapers. The **Palais Omnisports Paris Bercy,** 8, bd. de Bercy, 12ème (tel. 01 44 68 44 68; M: Bercy), hosts everything from beach volleyball to figure skating, horse jumping, and surfing beneath its radical, sod-covered roof. Ticket prices vary wildly with the event.

Football/Soccer: Unless you're American (and even then), you would have to have been in a coma last year not to realize that France hosted and won the **1998 World Cup** in the final match over Brazil in Paris's new **Stade de France** in St-Denis. Called *le football,* France's hands-down national sport consumes Paris, especially during the World Cup (*La Coupe du Monde*). The **Club de Football Paris St-Ger-main** (PSG; tel. 01 40 71 91 91) is Paris's own professional *football* team, splitting its time between road games and matches at the enormous **Parc des Princes** (box office tel. 01 49 87 29 29; M: Porte de St-Cloud), the city's premier outdoor stadium venue. Tickets to all events can be purchased at the Parc des Princes box office, 24, rue du Commandant-Guibaud, 16ème (M: Porte d'Auteuil), and go on sale anywhere from 2 days to 2 weeks in advance. Games on weekends and some weekday eve-nings. Prices 50-300F, depending on the seat and the event. Box office open M-F 9am-8pm, Sa 10am-5pm. MC, V.

Cycling: The women's **Tour de France** leaves Paris in mid-Aug. near the Eiffel Tower. Call 01 43 57 02 94 for information. Held in July, the men's **Tour de France** pits 200 of the world's best male cyclists against the Alps, the elements, and each other for 21 grueling stages. Call *l'Équipe* (tel. 01 41 33 15 00), one of the tour's sponsors, for information about the race's itinerary. Spectators turn out in droves along the way, stationed at bends in highways to cheer their favorites to vic-tory. Parisians and tourists alike line the Champs-Elysées for the triumphal last stage, usually between noon and 6pm. Show up early and be prepared for a mob scene. The **Grand Prix Cycliste de Paris** is an annual time trial competition held in June in the Bois de Vincennes, 12ème (tel. 01 43 68 01 27; tickets 50F).

Tennis: The *terre battue* (red clay) of the **Stade Roland Garros**, 2, av. Gordon Bennett, 16ème (M: Porte d'Auteuil), has ended more than one champion's quest for a Grand Slam. Two weeks each year during May and June, **Les Internationaux de France de Tennis (the French Open)** welcomes the world's top players to Paris. Write to the **Fédération Française de Tennis** (tel. 01 47 43 48 00), located at the stadium, in February for information on tickets for the next spring's tournament. Call in March for prices; seats generally range 45-295F. Also, write or call your national tennis association; they sometimes have an extra supply of tickets.

Horse Racing: The numerous hippodromes in and around town host races of all kinds throughout the year. Far from seedy, an afternoon at the track is a family outing. The level of classiness climbs a notch or two for the season's championship races. **Hippodrome de Vincennes**, 2, route de la Ferme, in the Bois de Vincennes, 12ème (tel. 01 05 11 21 14). M: Château de Vincennes. A hike through the woods from the metro stop takes you to the home of Parisian harness racing since 1906. Prix d'Amérique (late Jan.), Prix de France (early Feb.), and Prix du Président de la République (late June). Tickets 15-30F, even for the big races. **Hippodrome d'Auteuil**, in the Bois de Boulogne, 16ème (tel. 01 45 27 12 24). M: Porte d'Auteuil. Steeplechases since 1873; the stands date from 1921. For big races in June and July, shuttles run from the metro and RER stations. Open Sept.-Nov. and Feb.-June. Tickets M-F 25F, Su 40F, major events 50F. No reservations.

■ Festivals and Other Seasonal Events

The Millennium cometh and Paris prepareth (see **Paris 2000,** p. 252). In addition, Paris is a city where nearly every art form, historical event, or celebrity has a corresponding festival or cultural event, offering year-round opportunities to celebrate with various degrees of pomp and libation. While the city-wide **Fête de la Musique** and the **Bastille Day** are difficult to miss—even if you want to—some of the smaller festivities need some explanation. The **Office de Tourisme** (see **Practical Information,** p. 71) distributes the multilingual **Saisons de Paris,** a booklet listing all the celebrations. The English information number (tel. 01 49 52 53 56) gives a weekly summary of current festivals, as does *Pariscope.* You can also get a listing of festivals before you leave home by writing the French Government Tourist Office (see **Practical Information,** p. 25).

Ateliers d'Artistes-Portes Ouverts, May-June. Call tourist office for details. For selected days during the year, each *quartier's* resident artists open their workshops to the public for show-and-tell. For the '99 season, openings will include: *Ateliers d'Artistes de Belleville* in the 10ème, 11ème, 19ème, and 20ème (May) and *D'Anvers aux Abbesses* in the 9ème and 18ème (late May-early June). Free.

Bals Concerts, end of July to Aug. (tel. 08 03 30 63 06; http://www.la-villette.com). A month-long series of concerts held at the Kiosque à Musique at Parc de la Villette, featuring "musique exotique" such as rhumba, salsa, and various kinds of African music. Join the crowds and boogie. Free.

Bastille Day (Fête Nationale), July 14. Vive la République and pass the champagne. Festivities begin the night before France's independence day (see **Sights,** p. 180), with traditional street dances at the tip of Île St-Louis. The *Bals Pompiers* (Firemen's Balls) take place inside every Parisian fire station the night of the 13th, with DJs, bands, and cheap alcohol. Free of charge, these *bals* are the best of Paris's Bastille Day celebrations. Here you can meet, drink, and dance with people from the *quartier* in what is perhaps your first opportunity of being invited to a French party and feeling like you're part of the family. The ones in the 4ème, 6ème, and 10ème are pretty lively. July 14 begins with the army parading down the Champs-Elysées and ends with fireworks. The fireworks can be seen from any bridge on the Seine or from the Champs de Mars. Groups also gather in the 19ème and 20ème (especially in the Parc de Belleville) where the hilly topography allows a long-distance view to the Trocadéro. Unfortunately, the entire city also becomes a nightmarish combat zone with firecrackers under foot; avoid the metro and deserted areas if possible. *Vive la France!*

Christmas (Noël), Dec. 24-25. At midnight on Christmas eve, Nôtre-Dame becomes what it only claims to be the rest of the year: the cathedral of the city of Paris. Midnight mass is celebrated with pomp and incense. Get there early to get a seat. Christmas Eve is more important than Christmas Day in France. Families gather to exchange gifts and eat wonderful Christmas food, including *bûche de Noël* (Christmas Yule Log), a rich chocolate cake. During the season leading up to Dec. 24, the city illuminates the major *boulevards,* including the Champs-Élysées, in holiday lights and decorations. A huge *crèche* (nativity scene) is displayed on pl. Hôtel de Ville. Restaurants offer Christmas specialties and special *menus.* If you're stuck alone in Paris for Christmas (and even if you're not Christian), try to get invited home with one of your French friends to Christmas Eve dinner. The experience will be heart-warming. If not, gather some fellow holiday misfits and go out to a bistro for a nice dinner and some cheer. *Joyeux Noël!*

Le Festival International de Danse de Paris, Sept.-Oct.'99 (tel. 01 45 22 28 74 for information and auditions). Classical and contemporary dance festival at the Théâtre des Champs Elysées, 8ème (M: Alma-Marceau). Tickets 70-350F.

Course des Serveuses et Garçons de Café, 1 day in mid-June (tel. 01 42 96 60 75). If you thought service was slow by necessity, let this race change your mind. In Paris, those who serve you at your table are not necessarily students or teenagers doing part-time work. Many servers take pride in their work as a respected and time-honored career. This race reminds Paris to appreciate the city's café and restaurant staff while having some mildly competitive laughs. Tuxedoed waiters and waitresses sprint through the streets carrying a full bottle and glass on a tray. Starts and finishes at Hôtel de Ville, 4ème. An extraordinarily fun and uniquely Parisian event. If you're in town, do not miss it. Look for posters.

Tour de France, 4th Su in July. The Tour de France, the world's premier long-distance bicycling event, ends in Paris and thousands turn out at the finish line to see who will win the *chemise d'or.* Expect huge crowds at pl. de la Concorde as well as along the av. des Champs-Elysées. You may never see calves this strong again in your life.

Festival d'Art Sacré, Nov.-Dec. (tel. 01 44 70 64 10). Sacred music in churches and cultural centers throughout Paris. Ticket prices vary according to venue.

Festival d'Automne, mid-Sept. to late Dec. (tel. 01 53 45 17 00; http://www.festival-automme.com). Drama, ballet, and music arranged around a different theme each year. Many events held at the Théâtre du Châtelet, 1er, the Théâtre de la Ville, 4ème, and the Cité de la Musique, 19ème. Ticket prices vary according to venue.

Festival Chopin, mid-June to mid-July (tel. 01 45 00 22 19 or 01 45 00 69 75). Route de la Reine Marguerite. From M: Porte Maillot, take bus #244 to Pré Catelan stop 12. Concerts and recitals held at the Orangerie du Parc de Bagatelle in the Bois de Boulogne. Not all Chopin, but all piano music, arranged each year around a different aspect of the Polish francophile's *oeuvre.* Times and prices vary (usually 80-150F).

Festival du Cinéma en Plein Air, mid-July to late Aug. (tel. 01 40 03 76 92). M: Porte de la Villette or Porte de Pantin, at the Parc de la Villette, 19ème. A fabulous outdoor summer film festival and a great way to meet new people. Seats are arranged in the Prairie du Triangle. Movies usually focus on one theme, although exceptions are made for certain cult classics and major action and blockbuster films. Rent a chair for 40F or bring a blanket. All films shown in v.o. Tu-Su 10pm.

Festival Foire St-Germain, June (tel. 01 40 46 75 12). Antique and book fair in pl. St-Sulpice; theater, cinema, and concerts in the Auditorium St-Germain, 4, rue Félibien, 6ème (tel. 01 46 33 87 03). Free.

Festival de Paris, mid-July to mid-Aug. (tel. 01 44 94 98 00; http://www.quartierd'ete.com). This city-wide, multifaceted festival features dance, music of the world, a giant parade, promenade concerts, and jazz. Locations vary, but many events are usually held in the Jardin des Tuileries, Jardin du Luxembourg, and Parc de la Villette. This festival is one of Paris's largest and includes both world class (i.e. international ballet companies and top-10 rock bands) and local artists, musicians, and performers. Prices vary, but much is free. Pick up a brochure at the tourist office or call for more info.

Festival de St-Denis, early June to early July (tel. 01 48 13 06 07). A 4-week concert series featuring baroque as well as classical and contemporary works. Held in the magnificent Basilique St-Denis, and the Legion d'Honneur. Tickets 50-275F.

Festival Musique en l'Île, mid-July to Aug (tel. 01 44 62 70 90). Chamber and classical music in some of Paris's most exquisite churches, including the Ste-Chapelle, Église St-Louis, and Église St-Germain-des-Près. Fabulous acoustics. Tickets 100-150F.

Festival de l'Orangerie de Sceaux, mid-July to Sept. (tel. 01 46 60 07 79). A weekend series of chamber music concerts held in l'Orangerie du Château de Sceaux, in Sceaux (RER B). Concerts at 5:30pm; tickets 100-140F. Call for info.

Festival d'Orgue à St-Eustache, mid-June to early July (tel. 01 42 36 31 05). M: Châtelet-Les Halles. Organ concerts in the beautiful Église St-Eustache, 2, rue du Jour, 1er. Tickets 70-120F, on sale on site the day of the concert or at ARGOS, 3 rue de Bernes, 8ème (M: St-Augustin).

Festivals du Parc Floral de Paris, May-Sept. (tel. 01 43 43 92 95; http://www.quartierd'ete.com). Three separate festivals held at the Kiosque Géand de la Vallée des Fleurs (Route de la Pyramide, Bois de Vincennes). *Festival Jeune Public* offers kids a different show every W at 2:30pm. The *Festival à Fleur de Jazz* offers jazz concerts Sa at 4pm. And the *Festival Classique au Vert* offers classical concerts Su at 4:30pm. All shows free with 10F park entrance. Pick up a schedule at the tourist office or see *Pariscope,* as the schedule will not be released over the phone.

Fête du Cinéma, around June 28. A Parisian institution, this festival is one of the city's best—don't miss it. Purchase 1 ticket at full price and receive a passport that admits you to an unlimited number of movies for the duration of the 3-day festival for 10F each. Choose your first film carefully; full-price tickets vary considerably from cinema to cinema. Expect long lines and get there at least 30min. early for popular movies. Hundreds of films are shown during the festival, from major blockbusters to classics and experimental flics. If any of the films mentioned in our Film section entice you (see **Film,** p. 18), it will probably be shown in one of Paris's hundreds of cinemas during the festival. Look for posters in the metro or ask at cinemas for the specific dates.

Fête de l'Humanité, 2nd or 3rd week of Sept. (tel. 01 49 22 72 72 or 01 49 22 73 86). At the Parc de la Courneuve. Take the metro to Porte de la Villette and then one of the special buses. The annual fair of the French Communist Party. Entertainers in recent years have included Charles Mingus, Marcel Marceau, the Bolshoi Ballet, and radical theater troupes. A cross between the Illinois State Fair and Woodstock; you don't have to be Communist to enjoy it. But don't admit that you attended at your next U.S. Congressional Hearing.

Fête de la Musique, June 21 (tel. 01 40 03 94 70). Also called "faîtes de la musique" (get it—make music?), this summer solstice celebration gives everyone in the city the chance to make as much racket as possible; noise laws don't apply on this day. Closet musicians fill the streets, strumming everything from banjos and *ukuleles* to Russian *balalaikas.* Major concerts at La Villette, pl. de la Bastille, pl. de la République, and the Latin Quarter. This festival is one of Paris's best, and everyone comes out for the music and the camaraderie. If you're not humming by noon, you need to reprioritize. Partying in all open spaces. Before you join that samba or hari krishna parade, put your wallet in a safe place. Avoid the metro. Free.

Fête des Tuileries, late June to late Aug. (tel. 01 46 27 52 29). M: Tuileries. A big fair held on the terrace of the Jardin des Tuileries. Huge ferris wheel with views of nighttime Paris. Open 11am-midnight, F-Sa 11am-1am. Free entrance, ferris wheel around 20F. (see **Sights,** p. 144).

Fête des Vendanges à Montmartre, first weekend in Oct. Rue des Saules, 18ème (tel. 01 42 62 21 21). M: Lamarck-Caulaincourt. A celebration of the wine grape harvest from Montmartre's own vineyards. Folksongs, wine tasting, and costumed picking and tromping of grapes. Much wine is consumed. *À Vôtre Santé!*

Feux de la St-Jean, June 24 (tel. 01 45 08 55 61). Magnificent fireworks at 11pm in the Jardin de Tino Rossi at quai St-Bernard, 5ème, honoring the Feast of St. John the Baptist. For a bird's-eye view of the spectacle, stand in front of Sacré-Coeur. Also the **Fête Nationale du Québec** (la Fête St-Jean Baptiste), the day is celebrated by Paris's Québecois community with dancing, *drapeaux fleurs-de-lys,* and music at the Librairie Québecoise, 5ème (see **Books,** p. 263); the Délégation Générale du Québec, 66, rue Pergolèse, 16ème; the Association Paris-Québec, 5, rue de la Boule Rouge, 9ème (tel. 01 48 24 97 27); and the Centre Culturel Québecois, 5, rue de Constantine, 7ème (M: Invalides). With a referendum on Québecois Sovereignty likely by 2000, this year's Fête St-Jean Baptiste may ring in the birth of a new, independent, francophone Québec. As Charles de Gaulle said, *Vive le Québec Libre!*

Foire du Trône, late Mar. to early June (tel. 01 46 27 52 29). M: Porte Dorée. On Reuilly Lawn, Bois de Vincennes, 12ème. A gigantic amusement park. Open Su-Th 2pm-midnight, F-Sa and holidays 2pm-1am.

Gay Pride (Fierté), June. Gay Paree celebrates its annual Pride celebration with parties, special events, film festivals, demonstrations, art exhibitions, concerts, and a huge Pride Parade through the Marais and the streets of Paris. For specific dates and events, call the Centre Gai et Lesbien (tel. 01 43 57 21 47), Les Mots à la Bouche bookstore (tel. 01 42 78 88 30) or check Marais bars and cafés for posters.

Grandes Eaux Musicales de Versailles, early May to mid-Oct. (tel. 01 39 50 36 22). Weekly outdoor concerts and fountain displays every Sunday at Parc du Château de Versailles, RER C7. A magical event when you will see the splendors of Versailles's gardens in all their excess and glory. Marie-Antoinette costumes and wigs are optional. Tickets 25F, reduced 15F.

Journées du Patrimoine, 3rd weekend of Sept. (tel. 01 44 61 21 50). The few days each year when national palaces, ministries, monuments, and some townhouses are opened to the public. The Hôtel de Ville should be on your list. Free.

Musique au Carrousel du Louvre, last week in Aug. (tel. 01 43 16 48 38). At 99, rue de Rivoli. Classical concerts at the Louvre followed by a buffet-meeting with the musicians. Of food, sex, and art, you get 2 (and maybe 3) out of 3. Tickets 90-125F.

Musique en Sorbonne, Oct.-Nov. (tel. 01 42 62 71 71 for info and to audition). At 47, rue des Ecoles, 5ème. M: Maubert-Mutualité. Classical music by students at the Sorbonne (this is very intelligent music). Admission 70-165F.

New Year's Eve and Day. December 31, 1999-January 1, 2000. Join *Let's Go: Paris 1999*'s editor in Paris for the beginning of the New Millennium. Forget the stories of doom, gloom, aliens, and armageddon. It's gonna be one big fabulous party. For more on what to do and see at the dawn of the 21st century in the City of Millennial Lights, see **Paris 2000,** p. 252.

Rallye Paris-Deauville, Friday in early Oct. (tel. 01 47 32 15 59). More than 100 vintage Parisian cars assemble at the Trocadéro fountains at 7am to leave for the long automotive pageant to Deauville, in Normandy.

Le Temps des Livres, mid- to late Oct. (tel. 01 49 54 68 64). Debates, open-houses, lectures, and celebrations with books, poets, and writers throughout France.

Théâtre de Verdure du Jardin Shakespeare, July-Sept. (tel. 01 40 19 95 33). At route de la Reine-Marguerite, Bois de Boulogne. Each year this theater hosts a festival dedicated to a particular playwright. Tickets around 80F.

La Villette Jazz Festival, late June to early July (tel. 01 40 03 75 75 or 01 44 84 44 84; http://www.la-villette.com). M: Porte de Pantin. At Parc de la Villette. A week-long celebration of jazz from big bands to new international talents, as well as seminars, films, and sculptural exhibits. 1998 saw McCoy Tyner, Olodum, Ravi Coltrane, Taj Mahal, and B.B. King. Marching bands parade every day and an enormous picnic closes the festival. Some concerts are free; call for info and ticket prices. A *forfait-soirée* gives access to a number of events for one night of the festival for 170F, students, under 26, and seniors, 145F.

■ Paris 2000: The Millennium

Like Madonna's *Ray of Light,* Paris will shine in 1999. In 1889 and 1900, Paris kicked off the 20th century with the Universal Exposition, the new Eiffel Tower, Gare d'Orsay, Grand and Petit Palais, and Pont Alexandre III. Quite a feat to beat. To signal the beginning of the next Millennium (or the end of the world as we know it), Paris will take centerstage with a year-long program of celebrations, events, exhibitions, and festivals all centered around the theme *Paris, City of Lights.* Think big, bright, and glamorous. With monuments cleaned, the Seine scented, and the streets draped in flowers, Paris will be decked out like a drag queen. Our cover for *Let's Go: Paris*

1999 reflects the spirit of this Parisian festival of lights, uniting the monuments of the past with the shimmering, shaking, exploding light of the dawning Millennium.

A BRIEF HISTORY OF THE FUTURE

From Nostradamus to Jules Verne, France has flirted for centuries with visions of the future. The Gothic portals of **Nôtre Dame** depict the Apocalypse as the **Last Judgment,** when Christ will come to judge the living from the dead. Illiterate medieval pilgrims looked on the sculptures of Christ and the gargoyles atop the cathedral with millennium fear and trembling. In the 16th century, Michel de Nostradame, an astronomer and doctor popularly known as **Nostradamus,** published his prophetic quatrains in the seven-volume *Centuries*. Despite accusations of heresy by the Inquisition, Nostradamus became Catherine de Médici's court advisor when he predicted in 1556 the death of her husband Henry II in a jousting accident at the place des Vosges's Palais des Tournelles in 1563. According to some interpretations of his quatrains, Nostradamus predicted the rise of Napoleon and Hitler, WWII, the Cold War, and the Nuclear Holocaust of WWIII, beginning in March, July, or September of 1999 and killing two thirds of the planet before ending in 2028. But don't worry. That bit about nuclear holocaust might only be an asteroid colliding with the earth *à la Deep Impact* or *Armageddon* or massive alien invasion *à la Independence Day*.

In addition to his fantastic adventures in *Journey to the Center of the Earth* (1864), *Twenty-thousand Leagues Under the Sea* (1870), and *Around the World in Eighty Days* (1873), **Jules Verne's** visions of space flight in *From the Earth to the Moon* (1865) inspired imaginations of 19th-century explorers and future cosmonauts. Georges Méliès's extraordinary *fin de siècle* film, *Voyage à la lune* (1902), used the emerging magic of motion pictures to dramatize Verne's lunar tale. It would take only a century for technology to catch up to Verne's imagination, when Buzz Aldrin and Neil Armstrong landed on the moon on July 16, 1969.

From the 1860s to the 1960s, French science fiction moved from lunar landings to darker dystopias and intergalactic adventures. François Truffaut's film adaptation of Ray Bradbury's *Fahrenheit 451* (1966) paints a world where fire-fighters burn illegal books. More optimistically, Roger Vadim's *Barbarella* (1967) used the creative energy of the cinematic New Wave (see **Film,** p. 18) and psychedelic scenery to project Jane Fonda into space. Traveling from planet to planet in fabulous patent leather moon boots and cosmo-bustiers, Barbarella is seduced by a handsome French galactic explorer named Duran-Duran (hence the name of the rock band), who proves that even in the 24th century, French men are great lovers. Remember, it's science fiction. Incidentally, this film wasn't the first time that French science fiction combined futurism and male fantasy. Auguste Villiers de l'Îsle-Adam's novel, *Ève Futur* (1886) took Shelley's *Frankenstein* and Shaw's *Pygmalion* to a cyborg level with a mad inventor who creates a cybernetic, bionic, android woman.

Pierre Boulle's *La Planète des Singes* (*Planet of the Apes,* 1963) and the 1968 film it inspired painted the future in a more pessimistic light. In an ominous vision of evolution, humans regress and become slaves to their gorilla and orangutang captors. The ruins of Paris's beloved gift to New York, Bartholdi's Statue of Liberty, lie half-sunk in the sand like Shelley's *Ozymandias.* Marc Caro's films *Delicatessen* (1991) and *City of Lost Children* (1995) portray a dark, post-apocalyptic Paris where food is scarce, genetic mutants terrorize orphans, and the Resistance occupies the sewers and catacombs, much like their 20th-century WWII ancestors. Luc Besson's *Fifth Element* (1997) interjected humor and fashion into this dystopic tradition, pitting chaotic urban violence and planetary destruction against alien opera, high camp, and Jean-Paul Gaultier's fabulous, retro-galactic fashion including pink-pillboxed spaceship stewardesses, tight synthetic muscle-T's, and 23rd-century gangsta-wear.

In Gene Roddenberry's 24th-century world of *Star Trek: The Next Generation,* erudite Frenchman Jean-Luc Picard is at the helm of humanity's flagship, the starship *Enterprise.* In addition, Paris is the future home of Star Trek's United Federation of Planets, an alliance of hundreds of alien worlds and species that work for the common intergalactic good. Most importantly, Star Trek's 24th-century France still makes wine, and Paris's cafés still serve merlot in the shadow of the Eiffel Tower. Apparently, 2342 will be a very good year.

To believe the sci-fi hype of the past two years, you'd think Paris wouldn't make it much beyond the Millennium. Roland Emmerich's blockbuster film *Independence Day* (1996) showed an alien space-saucer poised ominously over the Eiffel Tower, ground-zero for total Parisian destruction. In Michael Bay's *Armageddon* (1998), Paris is pummeled by merciless meteors that lay waste to the 17ème and the northern 8ème, right up to the Arc de Triomphe, which triumphantly, Napoleonically defies the blast and clears the dust standing. The film shows the meteor's impact from the classic Georges Brassaï viewpoint of the medieval gargoyles atop Nôtre Dame. Paris's oldest demons watch the arrival of its newest.

Outside the world of cinema, visions of the future are all over Paris. Architecturally, the future is already here. The industrial Centre Pompidou, the geodesic structures of La Villette, the gleaming futurism of La Défense, and the stargate symmetry of the Louvre Pyramid all seem to come right out of the 21st century. It's as if no one would be shocked if the Pyramid lifted off the Cour du Louvre, or if the Grande Arche de la Défense was a gateway to another dimension. The City of Lights will continue to illuminate the future. But for now, many of those rays of light are flickering across computer screens and cyberspace. Internet cafés are opening up across the city, merging café culture with cyber style, websites with waiters, servers with *serveurs*.

Starmania

Michel Berger and Luc Plamondon's wildly popular rock opera **Starmania** (1978) paints a dark and moving picture of the fictional dystopia **Monopolis,** *une ville de l'an deux mille* (a city of the year 2000), where orphan *zonards* (zonies) grow up on the streets of the dismal *Banlieue du Nord* (Northern Suburb). With songs like *Enfant de Pollution* (Child of Pollution), Starmania's Monopolis is an Orwellian urban nightmare where tattooed zombie-workers like the *Serveuse Automate* (the automated/automaton waitress) struggle to live and love in gray-blue streets where neon has replaced the sun. While Monopolis could be any city, its French and Québecois co-writers paint a particularly Francophone urban vision, where *Le Monde est Stone* (The World is Stone). Paris 2000? Not likely. But Paris 2050?

NEW YEAR'S EVE 1999

Focusing on the themes of time, light, history, art, and the environment, *Paris, City of Lights* will feature hundreds of events that celebrate our achievements of the past and our hopes for the future. On September 3, 1999, a floating concert will sail down the Seine with twenty barges and hundreds of percussionists drumming in the Millennium. On April Fool's Day (April 1), the Seine will be filled with 2000 giant fish sculptures. And during the **Fête du Parfum,** the Seine will be scented with France's finest fragrances as large flower-covered barges float down the river to kick off the opening of the new **Musée du Parfum.** Two new footbridges, similar to the Pont des Arts, will be built across the Seine joining the Musée d'Orsay to the Tuileries and the Bibliothèque de France to the Parc de Bercy. And a 12-kilometer walkway will be built along the length of the Seine for Millennial joggers, sprinters, and strollers.

Enormous clocks will count down the hours and minutes to the Millennium in celebration of Paris's place in time and history. The Eiffel Tower's **Countdown Clock** has already begun the digital countdown to January 1, 2000. From the summer solstice to the autumnal equinox (June 21-Sept. 22, 1999), an enormous **Sun Dial** will be constructed on the place de la Concorde, using the ancient Egyptian Obélisque de Luxor as the center. And the twelve *grandes avenues* that span out from the Arc de Triomphe at place Charles-de-Gaulle-Étoile will be lit up with powerful lights and lasers, creating a huge **Millennium Clock** that will count down the last hours of the Millennium starting at 6pm. At the stroke of midnight, the star of streets will shine in a spectacular Millennial explosion.

During the months of December 1999 and January 2000, the City of Lights' **Itinerance** light festival will illuminate the Eiffel Tower, the Arc de Triomphe, the Louvre, La Défense, the Grande Mosqué, and over 200 churches and monuments to mark the opening of the Millennium. A companion program **Phosphorescences** will provide small **modulum** orbs that can be purchased by Parisians and lit at nighttime events. Extra moduli will float in the Seine and float down from airplanes in the sky. Lights will be placed along the length of the Seine and inside Nôtre Dame to illuminate the stained-glass rose windows by night. Amid the space-age structures of La Villette, fireworks will rise and burst for two whole nights, from December 31 to January 1.

In one of the more bizarre Millennium spectacles, it is rumored that the Eiffel Tower will give birth to a gigantic, luminous **Millennium Egg** that will descend from the tower amid television screens underneath that will broadcast Millennium parties from all the capitals of the world. In another controversial move, Paris will build a huge 200m **Tour de la Terre** (Earth Tower) near the Seine on the east side of the city. Sponsored by UNESCO, the top of the tower will be decked in huge metallic petals, transforming the tower into a giant flower. Echoing the construction of the Eiffel Tower for the 1900 Universal Exposition and celebrating the Earth and the Environment, Paris's Tour de la Terre will feature exhibitions on technology, history, and culture, as well as restaurants and cafés. The only problem with this environmental monster is that it will require hundreds of (dead) trees to build, a floral faux pas that has enraged many green Parisians. Organizers claim that the trees, which will come from five different continents, will represent not only the environment but also our responsible use of its resources. In addition, the Earth Tower will inaugurate three international **Earth Prizes** to be given out annually on Earth Day (Mar. 21) to outstanding contributors and protectors of the environment.

Throughout the year, the **Printemps des Rues** project will adorn the city's streets and metro stations with millions of flowers and hundreds of musicians, costumes, and theater pieces. In the spring of 2000, a city-wide **Carnaval** will bring more dancing to the streets before parading down the Champs-Élysées.

Several interactive arts installations will celebrate human knowledge and creativity. Echoing Diderot's *Encyclopédie* (see **Literature,** p. 21), the interactive **Expoterrestre** installation will project video, film, photo, music, and textual images onto the **Grande Arche de la Défense** through on-site and internet participants. A gigantic 15-by 21-meter electronic book called the **Livre Capitales** will be installed on place de l'Hôtel de Ville and project daily text and images on history, literature, art, science, and technology. In collaboration with the Cité des Sciences de la Villette, Parisian secondary-school and technical students will construct a huge Jules Verne rocket called **Vessel 2 Thousand** to symbolize space and imagination. Finally, a new 100m diameter ferris wheel, called the **Chronos,** will tower over the Bibliothèque de France. The world's largest ferris wheel, Chronos will offer spectacular views of Millennium Paris and will celebrate the medieval wheel of fortune that guides our fates and destinies.

MILLENNIUM EXHIBITIONS

Paris's museums are planning a number of special exhibitions for the Paris 2000 celebrations. A newly renovated Grand Palais will sponsor **Future Visions,** an exploration of how human beings from religious prophets to science fiction have imagined the future and **The Year 1000 in Europe,** focusing on early medieval European life, culture, religion, and apocalyptic fear at the first Millennium. In collaboration with the Musée d'Orsay, the Grand Palais will also house **Europe 1900,** a retrospective of *fin de siècle* art, architecture, and modernization. The Bibliothèque de France will explore our literary, historical, political, and scientific aspirations in its exhibit on **Utopia.** The Musée de l'Art et d'Histoire du Judaism will sponsor a show on the figure of the **Wandering Jew** in western art, society, and popular culture.

The newly renovated Centre Pompidou will reopen on January 1, 2000, with an enormous installation on **Time throughout the Ages,** using dark planetariums and luminescent rooms to illustrate social, psychological, and biological time and such issues as work, "free" time, leisure, biological clocks, and memory. Similarly, the Louvre will offer an exhibit on **The Invention of Time,** which will trace the use of clocks, time, and history in painting, sculpture, and decorative art. Finally, the Musée Carnavalet will host a **Month of Photography** during which Parisians will be invited to submit and choose the best photos of Paris in the opening days of the new Millennium.

PARIS 2000: WEBSITES AND INFO

For more information on all of Paris's Millennium installations, celebrations, exhibitions, and festivals, contact the **Mission pour la Célébration de l'An 2000,** 32, Quai des Célestins, 4ème (tel. 01 42 76 73 90), and 36, rue Lacépède, 5ème (tel. 01 53 71 20 00; fax 01 53 71 20 01; email dircom@celebration.2000.gouv.fr). The following websites offer scads of information on how to celebrate the Year 2000 in Paris, France, and around the world.

http://www.tour-eiffel.fr/teiffel/an2000_fr/ The City of Paris's official website, created and frequently updated by the Mission pour la Célébration de l'An 2000. All of the events and exhibitions described above are outlined in great detail, with links to interactive forums, maps, and contacts. This site posts the daily Tower countdown clock and provides discussions of Parisian Millennium history, science fiction, futurist debates, and online exhibitions of Millennial art. In English and French.

http://www.celebration2000.gouv.fr France's official website offers information on Millennial events all over France, in case you want to see how the provinces are celebrating. Participating cities include Strasbourg, Bordeaux, Lille, Lyon, Toulouse, Nantes, and Avignon, the European Cultural Capital for the year 2000. In English or French.

http://www.everything2000.com A general site on the Year 2000, including info on celebrations all over the world, Millennium trivia and lore, forums and chat rooms, and articles on the disastrous computer Millennium Bug. A great source of events, organizations, news, politics, and humor as well as a special section for those in the Class of 2000. In English.

Shopping

Devotees of the shopping gods, you have arrived in Mecca, and its name is Paris. The City of Lights is an endless parade of all that is beautiful, hip, trendsetting, and chic. But if your *franc* flow doesn't match your fabulousness, don't despair. From the perfect gift for mom (see **Gift Ideas**, p. 260) to *brioche* pans and bedding (see **Services and Housewares**, p. 261), from vintage classics to this year's trends, strap on those comfortably kicky platforms and let's go shopping!

The hottest spot this season seems to be **Colette**, 213, rue St-Honoré (tel. 01 53 35 33 90; http://www.colette.tm.fr; M: Concorde), an ultra-minimalist "anti-department store" whose bare display tables feature an eclectic selection of scuba watches, Alexander McQueen originals, Japanese vases, and mineral water. Their Scandinavianesque water-bar offers over 50 different kinds of sparkling aqua from French *Evian* to Swedish *Ramlösa*. Colette's sense of Calvin Klein classicism, oh-so-bored minimalism, and California clean living project a late-90s aesthetic where less is more, attitude is everything, and where the ultimate in blasé chic is to walk into a neo-Cubist bar and order a cup of hot water. Of course, the best way to shop minimalist is to buy nothing at all.

A word of caution: If you have to ask, you probably can't afford it. When you walk into a boutique, many assistants will approach you immediately. If you want to browse, simply say *Bonjour* and don't be intimidated by reactions ranging from disdain to hostility. Most stores close on Sunday. Some close on Mondays and during lunch on weekdays. Above all, be fabulous.

■ Clothes

No more wire hangers!

—Joan Crawford

Home to Chanel, Gaultier, and Givenchy, Paris is not a budget shopper's haven. But the secret to looking good French-style is not in a label but in attitude. French designers are so successful because they are so inventive. Parisians mix vintage with new, this season with last, to come up with looks that are uniquely their own. While clothing tends to be expensive here, a few well-chosen pieces and insider addresses will go far to give you the look you want at a price that won't break the *banque*.

In the Latin Quarter, bd. St-Michel's hip shops appeal to student shoppers. The French equivalents of The Gap and Banana Republic are Chevignon, Creeks, and Naf-Naf; those who miss J. Crew should try Agnès B. Department stores tend to have more conventional clothing, though Printemps and the Galeries Lafayette have high-quality clothes for high prices. Lower on each, Tati is nevertheless a budget fantasy.

WINDOW SHOPPING

For those who would love to tuck an Hermès scarf into their backpack, let this phrase be your mantra: it never hurts to look. Although it's intimidating to enter a designer's lair, act like you belong there and have a little fun. You may not be welcomed with open arms, but remember: that salesclerk may *look* well dressed, but he's only earning 25F an hour. Think *Pretty Woman*. Many find the shops of Paris's most famous designers a little disappointing, since they are as ubiquitous as McDonald's in most of the world's major cities. You might have more fun browsing the shops with less famous but equally fabulous names, like **Jitrois**, 38 fbg. St-Honoré, where suede shirts and leather pants are ripe for the fitting. And never forget: even in your chunky shoes, polyester fly-collars, and faded hip-huggers, you're a star.

The most famous of Paris's boutiques skirt the rue du Faubourg St-Honoré in the 8ème, home to **Hermès** (no. 24), **Christian Dior** (no. 58), **Givenchy** (no. 26), **Hervé Leger** (no. 29), **Yves Saint-Laurent** (no. 38), and **Ashida** (no. 34). **Pierre Balmain,**

Karl Lagerfeld, and Versace mingle nearby. Running southwest from the Rond Point des Champs-Elysées, av. de Montaigne shelters **Christian Dior** (no. 32), **Chanel** (no. 42), and **Valentino** (no. 17-19). **Pierre Cardin** is on pl. François I. The windows in **pl. Vendôme** and along **rue de la Paix** (toward the Opéra in the 9ème) glitter with the designs of **Cartier** and other Parisian jewelers.

MAGASINS DE TROC

Snazzy second-hand stores, *magasins de troc* resell clothes bought and returned at more expensive stores. Prices may still be high, but they're usually a good deal if you want a designer find. Shop on, Chanel warriors!

Mouton à Cinq Pattes, 8-10-18, rue St-Placide, 6ème (tel. 01 45 48 86 26). M: Sèvres-Babylone. Also at 19, rue Grégoire de Tours, 6ème (tel. 01 43 29 73 56). M: Odéon. A huge selection of designer clothing at lower prices. Little costs less than 200F here, but if you're willing to dig through the piles, you might find a treasure. Open M-F 10:30am-7:30pm, Sa 10:30am-8pm. AmEx, MC, V.

Réciproque, 16ème (tel. 01 47 04 30 28). M: Pompe. Discounted designer clothing. Different branches, all on rue de la Pompe, have different specialties: women's cocktail and evening dresses at no. 93; women's casual wear and shoes at no. 95; menswear at no. 101; women's coats at no. 123; leather goods and handbags at no. 89. All branches open Tu-F 11am-7:30pm, Sa 10:30am-7pm. AmEx, MC, V.

La Clef des Marque, 20, pl. du Marché St-Honoré, 1er (tel. 01 47 03 90 40). M: Pyramides. 2 stories of designer merchandise. You may stumble upon Prada pumps or Gaultier jeans for less than your hotel room. Open M-Sa 12:30am-7pm. MC, V.

STOCK STORES

Stock is French for an outlet store, with big names for less—often because they have small imperfections or are last season's remainders. Widen your stock portfolio and invest! Many are on rue d'Alésia in the 14ème, including **Cacharel Stock** (no. 114; tel. 01 45 42 53 04; M: Alésia; open M-Sa 10am-7pm; AmEx, MC, V), **Stock Chevignon** (no. 122; tel. 01 45 43 40 25; M: Alésia; open M-Sa noon-7pm; MC, V), and **Kookaï Stock.** Others to look for include **Stock Daniel Hechter,** 16, bd. de l'Hôpital, 5ème (tel. 01 47 07 88 44; M: Austerlitz; open M-Sa 10am-7:30pm; MC, V).

MID-PRICED STORES

Prêt-à-porter is not just a Robert Altman film; it is ready-to-wear clothing by designer names. Often, big-name labels still mean big price tags. Although the last few years have witnessed a Gap invasion in Paris (look for the signature blue shopping bags), you may want affordable French style that your neighbors won't be wearing at home. There's a good chance of finding it at these mid-priced *magasins*.

Kookaï, 12, rue Gustave-Gourbet, 16ème (tel. 01 47 55 18 00). M: Victor Hugo. With a hip young staff and runway-fabulous clothes, Kookaï is the place to find trendy women's slip dresses, minis and sheer, shimmery shirts at affordable prices. Although Kookaï is located throughout Paris, this location is their flagship store, with the largest selection. Open M-Sa 10:30am-7:30pm. AmEx, MC, V.

Agnès B., 2, 3, 6, 10, and 19 rue du Jour, 1er (tel. 01 45 08 56 56 or 01 42 33 04 13; http://www.agnesb.fr). M: Étienne Marcel. Upscale but affordable, these pieces are the kind of well-made clothes that are classic but stylishly French. All of the *BCBG* basics are here for women and men, along with accessories and even a line of cosmetics. Open M-Sa 10am-7pm. MC, V.

Loft Design By Paris, 12, rue du Faubourg St-Honoré, 8ème (tel. 01 42 65 59 65). M: Concorde or Madeleine. Mostly for men, Loft sells well-tailored men's shirts and casual sweaters and pants. A French version of the Gap. Even if the salespeople act snooty, you know you're fabulous, so keep browsing. There is also a branch in the Marais, at 12, rue de Sévigné. Open M-Sa 10am-7pm. AmEx, MC, V.

A.P.C., 3-4 rue de Fleurus, 6ème (tel. 01 42 22 12 77; email info@apc.fr; http://www.apc.fr). M: St-Placide. A resource for wardrobe staples, A.P.C. is hip without being outrageous, specializing in cigarette pants, rib-knit tops, and the fundamentals of an art student's wardrobe, in anti-colors like black and beige. Open M-Sa 10:30am-7pm. AmEx, MC, V.

Naf Naf, 168, bd St. Michel, 5ème (tel. 01 43 54 20 65). M: St-Michel or Cluny-La Sorbonne. Young and funky, these duds might not last more than one season, but they'll be out of style then, anyway. Micro-minis, cargo pants, tiny tanks—it's an alternateen gal's dream, and all for way under 200F. If you're in Paris for more than a day, you'll think everyone owns some item of clothing emblazoned with their logo. Open M-Sa 10am-7pm. AmEx, MC, V.

Sephora, 70-72, ave. des Champs-Élysées, 8ème (tel. 01 53 93 22 50; http://www.sephora.com). M: Charles de Gaulle Étoile. If Disney had a Tomorrowland of cosmetics, this would be it. Walk down the red carpet (it may be your only chance) into what Sephora calls its "magic, yet accessible universe" of beauty products. Over 11,000 items, from blush to bath powder, are arranged in 3 distinct areas: Fragrance, Color, and Well-Being. Everything from MAC to Mabelline, as well as Bourgois, a discount brand available only in Europe and made in the same factory as the pricier Chanel. Sephora's own cosmetics line includes over 300 shades of lipstick. You can also check and send email for free at one of the computers suspended in Lucite cages at the back of the store. Amex, V, MC.

VINTAGE CLOTHING

Vintage fashion is where Paris shines, and these stores are where it shines brightest. If you don't find what you're looking for here, you may have better luck at one of Paris's many flea markets (see **Puces de St-Ouen,** p. 267).

Antiquités New-Puces, 43, rue Mouffetard, 5ème (tel. 01 43 36 15 75). M: Monge. Some camp and some class. Clothes upstairs for 100-300F; downstairs for real bargains (50-150F). Open M-F 11:30am-11:30pm, Sa 10am-9pm.

La Caverne des Dames, 23, rue des Dames, 17ème (tel. 01 42 93 96 46). M: Pl. de Clichy. Turn left off av. de Clichy onto rue des Dames. Tacky and funky, retro and sequined, tassled and tawdry (20-150F). Open Tu-F 10:30am-7pm.

Guerrisol, 19-29-31 and 33, av. de Clichy, 17ème (tel. 01 42 94 13 21). M: La Fourche. Also at 9, 21, and 21bis, bd. Barbès, 18ème (tel. 01 42 52 19 73), M: Barbès Rochechouart; 45, bd. de la Chapelle, 10ème (tel. 01 45 26 80 85), M: La Chapelle; 116-118, rue Jean-Pierre Timbaud, 11ème (tel. 01 43 38 69 05), M: Courconnes; and 22, bd. Poissonière, 9ème (tel. 01 47 70 35 02), M: Bonne Nouvelle. This popular chain has racks upon racks for men and women. Silk shirts and leather coats, jeans (40-60F), and more (10-120F). Most branches open M-Sa 9:30am-6:30pm.

Tandem, 20, rue Houdron, 18ème (tel. 01 44 92 97 60). M: Abbesses. From the metro, go left on rue Abbesses and take a right on rue Houdron. This small store has racks of 60s and 70s polyester and glitter squeezed next to retro-wear from the 40s and 50s. Baubly jewelry 40-70F. Big selection of men's pants and jackets. Dresses and pants 120F-200F. Open Tu-Sa 10am-8pm.

▦ Department Stores

Mirror mirror on the wall, who's the famous of the Mall? In Paris, where the *Grand Magasin* (department store) was invented in the 19th century, they're all famous. Designed as glamorous showplaces for affordable, ready-to-wear goods, Paris's department stores were the first in the world. When visiting the city's grand old stores like Samaritaine and Bon Marché, keep your eyes peeled for their turn-of-the-century ornamented ceilings and decorative metal work. Paris's *grands magasins* (department stores) offer fabulous one-stop shopping. Here, you can browse unhassled by the salespeople of Paris's boutiques, though they are often crowded. Keep in mind that many *grands magasins* contain *coiffeurs* (beauty salons), post offices, grocery stores, and cafés, where you can relax between purchases.

Au Printemps, 64, bd. Haussmann, 9ème (tel. 01 42 82 50 00), M: Chaussée d'Antin. Also at 30, pl. d'Italie, 13ème (tel. 01 40 78 17 17), M: pl. d'Italie; 21-25, cours de Vincennes, 20ème (tel. 01 43 71 12 41), M: Porte de Vincennes. Anything you could possibly want (but not necessarily need) at high prices. Most hotels have 10% discounts for use in the store. Haussmann open M-Sa 9:30am-7pm. MC, V.

Forum des Halles, M: Les Halles or Châtelet-Les Halles, 2ème (tel. 01 44 76 96 56). An underground shopping mall. Descend from one of the 4 main entrances to discover over 200 boutiques. There is a branch of the FNAC music and CD store, and a branch of the cosmetics wonderland, Sephora. Usually safe during the day, but sketchy at night. All stores open M-Sa 10am-7:30pm.

BHV, 52-56, rue de Rivoli, 4ème (tel. 01 42 74 90 00). M: Hôtel-de-Ville. The initials stand for Bazar de l'Hôtel de Ville. Heavy on housewares and electronic equipment. Open M-Tu and Th-Sa 9:30am-6pm, W 9:30am-9pm. AmEx, MC, V.

Bon Marché, 24, rue de Sèvres, 7ème (tel. 01 44 39 80 00). M: Sèvres-Babylone. Paris's oldest and loveliest department store, Bon Marché has it all, from scarves to smoking accessories, designer clothes and a wonderful *Rentrée des Classes* (back to school) children's section, stocking supplies and toys from Tintin backpacks to model airplanes. Across the street is *La Grande Epicerie,* Bon Marché's celebrated gourmet food annex (see **Groceries,** p. 102). Open M-Sa 9:30am-7pm. MC, V.

Galeries Lafayette, 40, bd. Haussmann, 9ème (tel. 01 42 82 34 56). M: Chaussée d'Antin. Also at 22, rue du Départ, 14ème (tel. 01 45 38 52 87; M: Montparnasse). Chaotic (the equivalent of Paris's entire population visits here each month), but carries it all, including mini-boutiques of Kookaï, Agnès B, and Benetton. So many American tourists come here that it was considered unsafe during the terrorist attacks of the mid-80s. Most hotels offer 10% discount coupons for the store. Open M-Sa 9:45am-6:45pm. AmEx, MC, V.

Samaritaine, 67, rue de Rivoli, 1er (tel. 01 40 41 20 20). M: Pont-Neuf, Châtelet-Les-Halles, or Louvre. 4 large buildings between rue de Rivoli and the Seine, connected by tunnels. Not as chic as Galeries Lafayettes or Bon Marché, but the rooftop observation deck provides one of the best views of the city; take the elevator to the top floor and climb the short, spiral staircase. *Le Sand's Café* (on the 5th floor of Building 2) provides an incredible view of the city. Open M-W and F-Sa 9:30am-7pm, Th 9:30am-10pm. AmEx, MC, V.

Tati, 11, pl. de la République, 3ème (tel. 01 48 87 72 81). M: République. Also at 106, rue Faubourg du Temple, 11ème (tel. 01 43 57 92 80), M: Belleville; 140, rue de Rennes, 6ème (tel. 01 45 48 68 31), M: Montparnasse; and 4, bd. de Rochechouart, 18ème (tel. 01 42 55 13 09), M: Barbès-Rochechouart. Rub elbows with Parisian parents buying t-shirts for François to take to camp. A fabulously kitschy, chaotic, crowded, and cheap department store. Tati recently commissioned designers to create cheaper, hipper clothes. Generally low-end, but worth rummaging. Get your sales slip made out by one of the clerks (who stand around for just that purpose) before heading to the cashier. All branches open M-Sa 10am-7pm. MC, V.

■ Gift Ideas

It is better to give than to receive. Well, not really, but a little *quelquechose* from Paris will go far to put a smile on your mom's face and may guarantee future happiness with the one you love. Keeping in mind your limited wallet, luggage space, and time, here are some groovy gift ideas that they're guaranteed to adore.

L'Occitane, 18, pl. des Vosges, 4ème (tel. 01 42 72 60 36), M: St-Paul or Bastille; or 26, rue Vavin, 6ème (tel. 01 43 25 07 71), M: Vavin. When l'Occitane created its line of Provençal soaps, it gave travelers everywhere the perfect gift. Authentically French, wrapped in great packaging, lightweight and small, these quality *savons* perfumed with honeysuckle and lavender are so affordable (14F) that you can bring one home for everyone on your list. The store also sells travel-sized candles in attractive aluminum tins in scents like fig, crème-caramel, and mandarin (60F).

Fauchon, 24-30, pl. de la Madeleine, 2ème (tel. 01 47 42 60 11). M: Madeleine. This flagship store for gourmets is *the* place to find delicate *madeleines* and *galettes,* packaged in decorated tins to take home to mom (58F). A wonderland of jams, spices, sauces, and wines, Fauchon will package it up for easy traveling. If you want cheaper authentic foodstuffs to take home, Parisian supermarkets often have brands of jams, mustards, and wines that you can't get back home (see **Groceries,** p. 102). Open M-Sa 9:40am-7pm. AmEx, MC, V.

La Tuile à Loup, 35, rue Daubenton, 5ème (tel. 01 47 07 28 90). M: Censier-Daubenton. Regional handicrafts, pottery, and linens from all across France. Beautifully handpainted dishware (starting at 120F) and small lavender sachets in bright Provençal fabrics (10F). They also carry a large selection of books on French provincial handicrafts. Open Tu-Sa 10:30am-1pm and 2:30-7:30pm. AmEx, MC, V.

Nicolas, 132, bd. Raspail, 6ème (tel. 01 43 26 64 36). M: Vavin. When you think of France, you think of wine, and so will Mom. But the overwhelming variety can be difficult to sort through. At Nicolas, the super-friendly English-speaking staff is happy to help you pick the perfect Burgundy and pack it in travel boxes with handles. Wines 20-250F. Open M-F 10am-6pm.

Virgin Atlantic Megastore, 52, av. des Champs-Elysées, 8ème (tel. 01 49 53 52 45) and **FNAC,** 74, av. des Champs-Elysées (tel. 01 53 53 64 64; http://www.fnac.com). From cabaret to rap, Piaf to party tunes, a CD of French music is perfectly portable and something the gang can't get back home. Both stores have large selections of French folk, jazz, pop, and rap (see **Music,** p. 19) and have listening stations to check them out. Don't hesitate to ask those around you or the salespeople for who's hot and who's not; they're usually eager to share their ideas. CDs 100-120F. Both open M-Sa 10am-midnight. Both accept AmEx, MC, V.

▓ Housewares and Services

Whether you're moving to Paris for a summer, semester, or academic year abroad, taking a long-term job in the city, or simply in need of a good drycleaner, the following services may be of help. We've tried to compile a list of basic housewares and services for furnishing your new room or apartment, finding more specialized medical services, repairing computers, connecting to the Internet, and finding a reliable *coiffeur* (hairstylist), *tailleur* (tailor), and *cordonnier* (cobbler). Available at France Telecom (dial 14 for the nearest agency near you), the Paris *Pages Jaunes* (Yellow Pages) offers pages of valuable information. Of course, the best links to services in the city are your new neighbors, friends, and colleagues, but this list should get you started until you're a more savvy *Parisien* or *Parisienne*.

MEDICAL SERVICES

Perhaps the easiest thing to do if you are a foreigner and get sick in Paris is to head for the pharmacy. Each arrondissement has several pharmacies, and one is required to stay open all night (look in the pharmacy windows or ask which pharmacy will be open all night for the week). **Pharmacy les Champs,** 84, av. des Champs-Elysées, 8ème (tel. 01 45 62 02 41; M: George V). is open 24 hours. **Pharmacists** in Paris are well trained and can typically provide you with useful information, guidance, and medication to treat your ailment. Just walk right in and describe your condition. Non-prescription medications, provided by the pharmacist, in France are often stronger than they are in many other countries and may save you a trip to the doctor. In the event that you require a doctor's care, the pharmacist can provide you with a list of doctors in the arrondissement ranging from **gynecologists** to **general-care practitioners.** Should you require a house call for a condition not requiring hospitalization, you can call **S.O.S Médecins** (tel. 01 43 77 77 77). **S.O.S Dentaire** (tel. 01 43 37 51 00) has dentists available (M-F 8pm-midnight, Sa-Su 9:20am-12:10pm and 2:20pm-midnight). **S.O.S. Optique Lunettes** (tel. 01 48 07 22 00) will provide 24-hour assistance should you break or lose your glasses or contact lenses and will come to your house should you be unable to leave. **S.O.S. Oeil** (tel. 01 40 92 93 94), provides 24-hour ophthalmology advice. As a foreigner, you are likely to be billed for these S.O.S. services in Paris. Request documentation and receipts to submit to your home insurance company for reimbursement. Any of these S.O.S. services can make referrals for internists, dentists, optometrists, and opthalmologists in your arrondissement. For more information on health services in Paris, see **Health,** p. 40; **Insurance,** p. 43; and **Emergency Health and Help,** p. 42.

SHOPPING

GROOMING SERVICES

It's hell finding a new stylist in a new city, but Paris is the center of style and fashion. Remember, Paris is the city that coiffed Marie-Antoinette and created the Pompadour. **Hair Salons** are a dime a dozen in Paris. The best way to find a reliable one is, of course, to ask a friend for a recommendation. Should that option not be available, you should scout the *coiffeurs* of your arrondissement for economical options or check the *pages jaunes'* five pages of listings by arrondissement under the subject heading *coiffeurs*. **Jean Louis David,** 5, rue Saint-Denis, 1er (tel. 01 42 36 16 18; M: Chatelet), offers basic cuts, shampooing, and styling (women 110F, men 90F), perms (350F), and coloring (300F; open M-Sa 9-7pm). Many other Jean Louis David salons are located across the city. Call for the one nearest you (tel. 01 42 97 50 08). **Jean-Claude Biguine,** 6, rue Odéon, 6ème (tel. 01 46 33 94 83; M: Odéon), offers affordable cuts and shampoo (women 180F, men 120F) and perms (180F; open M-Sa 9:30am-6pm, F 9:30am-7:15pm). Always call to make an appointment in advance. Avoid hair trauma. If your French skills are not adept enough to describe what kind of cut you'd like, bring a photo of yourself or from a magazine to show the *coiffeur* or *coiffeuse*.

Drycleaners are also best found through neighborly recommendation, exploration, or the yellow pages. Key search word: *nettoyage à sec* or *pressing*. Drycleaners are also called *teintureries*. Many drycleaners also offer simple tailoring services. **Buci Pressing,** 7, rue Ancienne Comédie, 6ème (tel. 01 43 29 49 92; M: Odéon) offers reasonably priced drycleaning and services: pants 25F, blazers 30F, hemming from 70F (open M-Sa 8am-7:30pm; tailoring on Tu and F). **Pressing de Seine,** 67, rue de Seine, 6ème (tel. 01 43 25 74 94; M: Odéon), is another good option. Drycleaning runs 25-90F; most hemming and sewing is under 100F (open M-Sa 8am-7:15pm). **Pressing Villiers,** 93, rue Rocher, 8ème (tel. 01 45 22 75 48; M: Villiers), does not offer tailoring but will dryclean pants 39F, dresses 65F, and blazers 47F (open M-Sa 8am-7:30pm).

For **shoe repairs,** look for neighborhood *cordonniers,* like **Oziel Émile,** 4, rue Lobineau, Marché St. Germain (tel. 01 46 34 58 05; M: St.-Germain des Prés; open Tu-F 8:30am-1pm and 4-7:15pm, Sa 8:30am-1pm).

COMPUTER SERVICES

If you're in need of new **hardware,** head to **Surcouf,** 139, av. Daumesnil, 12ème (tel. 01 53 33 20 00; M: Gare de Lyon; http://www.surcouf.fr). From the metro walk up bd. Diderot and turn right onto av. Daumesnil. This maddeningly large store is a computer heaven or hell depending on your level of expertise. For most of us, the best thing is to walk straight in to the information booth and ask away. Downstairs are countless varieties and brands of computers, printers, faxes, and modems. Surcouf also sells **software,** from French spell-checkers to Adobe. Prices are competitive. **Computer repair** tends to be expensive, like everywhere else in Paris (400F per hr., 200F for 30min. or for consultation only). (Open Tu-Sa 9:30am-7pm.) If you are feeling adventurous, dozens of little less-expensive computer repair stores have opened up across the street from Surcouf along av. Daumesnil. For your basic computer **software** needs, head to the **FNAC Forum des Halles,** 1, rue Pierre Lescot 1er, level 3 (tel. 01 40 41 40 00; M: Les Halles; open M-Sa 10am-7:30pm), or the branch at 74, av. Champs-Élysées, 8ème (tel. 01 53 53 64 64; M: Franklin D. Roosevelt; open daily 10am-midnight).

If you are in Paris for more than a month, expect to do substantial emailing, and do not have **Internet access** at work or school, it is probably more economical to invest in a cheap modem and to procure the services of an **Internet provider** rather than to trek several times a week to the expensive cyber-cafés in Paris. One of the simplest ways of connecting to the Internet through your home is via **Wanadoo** (http://www.wanadoo.fr), France Telecom's very own Internet server. Dial 14 for the one nearest you. At your local France Telecom office, fill out the Wanadoo form, pick up your connection software kit, and you're ready to go. Three hours of Internet connection per month is 45F; unlimited hours, 95F. Wanadoo's basic configuration requirements are a 486PC with windows 3.1 or '95 or a 7.1 Macintosh system; 8-16 Megs of RAM; and a modem of 14.4 kbps. (Open M-F 9am-7pm, Sa 11am-7pm.) To contact **America Online** in Paris for connection inquiries, call 01 69 19 94 50. For **Compuserve** call toll-free 0803 009 000.

BEDDING AND FURNISHINGS

Most of Paris's department stores have **housewares** and furnishing departments, but they tend to be very expensive (see **Department Stores**, p. 259). If you're on a very tight budget, Paris's **flea markets,** like the Puce St-Ouen, offer plenty of used chairs, lamps, tables, and furnishings at low prices (see **Markets,** p. 266). **Habitat Forum des Halles,** 202, Porte Rambuteau, level 2 (tel. 01 40 39 91 06; M: Les Halles), is a housewares heaven. Follow the signs within the metro station for Forum des Halles; walk through the door marked pl. Verrieres and follow the signs for Porte Rambuteau; go up one floor. Habitat offers a huge selection of trendy halogen lamps (350F) and furnishings (95-500F), sheets and comforter sets (295-995F), chairs (350-3500F), and futons with frames (4790-5000F). Ask them to mail you a catalog. (Open M-Sa 10am-7:30pm.) **Counterpoit,** 59, rue de Seine, 6ème (tel. 16 40 51 88 98; M: Odéon), also sells trendy furniture and housewares, including lamps (97-350F), bedding (35-200F), and couches (3000F). Browse through their binders and catalogues for a wide variety of couch and pillow coverings, colors, and textures.

APPLIANCES FROM PHONES TO FRIDGES

If you need a telephone, answering machine, mini-refrigerator, alarm clock, stereo, or kitchen appliances, the *pages jaunes* can help you get started. Flea-markets often sell these items, but you should be careful of investing large amounts of money in used electronic equipment. If you want to buy something new, ask if you will be able to use the same item when you return home. Electricity in France is 220 volts AC, while North American appliances function on only 110 volts. If you plan on investing money in an expensive stereo, be aware that you may have to purchase a converter and adapter to use the same item at home (see **Packing,** p. 54). **Darty,** Forum des Halles, pl. Carrée, Level 4, 1er (tel. 01 42 79 79 37; M: Les Halles), is the place to head for all your hi-fi, electronics, and appliance needs. Prices are very low and you can find nearly everything from hairdryers and clock radios (for under 100F) to TVs (from 1290F) and mini-refrigerators (from 1190F). This budget appliance emporium also sells telephones (from 99F), answering machines (from 149F), stereos, and a modest selection of computers, faxes, and modems. The staff is extremely helpful and will answer your questions about brand names, prices, service, and quality. (Open M-Sa 10am-7:30pm.)

■ Books and Magazines

Both English and French Books in Paris tend to be expensive. The exceptions to this rule are used books *(livres d'occasion)* and new French paperbacks in *Poche* editions. New English-language books sell for about US$20 per paperback novel. The **American Library in Paris** (tel. 01 53 59 12 60) has a 5-10F book sale every spring. If you are in Paris for a semester or a year, apply for a Paris library card at the Centre Pompidou branch (see **Museums,** p. 219). If you are returning to continue your French studies in Scotland, New South Wales, or California, consider buying your textbooks and course titles here in Paris's used bookstores (like **Gibert Jeune** on pl. St-Michel); they will be twice as expensive back home in the campus book shop. You can ship the books home on a slow boat to China (or Georgia or Johannesburg) via the very cheap, very slow surface-mail book-rate (see **Mail,** p. 72).

Some specialty bookshops serve as informal community centers for students, intellectuals, and travelers with special concerns. English bookshops like **The Village Voice** have bulletin boards where you can post and read events and housing notices. **Les Mots à la Bouche** offers gay, bi, and lesbian information. **La Librairie des Femmes** sponsors women's programs and a coffeehouse, and **Présence Africaine** can direct you to Caribbean, Maghrebin, and West African resources.

The Sunday *New York Times* may be purchased at **W.H. Smith** and at the kiosk on rue Pierre Lescot, 1er, in front of the east entrance to Les Halles. Other English-language publications, including the ubiquitous dailies *The International Herald Tribune, USA Today, The Guardian,* and *The London Times* and weeklies *Newsweek* and *Time,* can be purchased at most Paris kiosks and newsstands. Note that in French *librairie* means bookstore; the word for library is *bibliothèque. Journal* refers to a newspaper; a magazine is called *une revue.* A *papeterie* is a stationers, selling paper supplies, gift cards, pens, folders, envelopes, and other clerical items.

Alias, 21, rue Boulard, 14ème (tel. 01 43 21 29 82). M: Denfert-Rochereau. Turn right off av. du Général Leclerc onto rue Daguerre, then turn left onto rue Boulard. Sloping, floor-to-ceiling stacks of books stop many visitors at the door to this bookstore specializing in new and used art books and magazines. If you know what you're looking for, the proprietor will usually squeeze through the narrow passageways and find it. Open M 2-8pm, Tu-Sa 11am-8pm, Su 11am-2pm. MC, V.

Les Archives de la Presse, 51, rue des Archives, 3ème (tel. 01 42 72 63 93). M: Rambuteau. Huge collection of vintage magazines—especially politics, fashion, photography, music, sports, and cinema. Some precious 50s finds, including fabulous *Vogue* issues (French and foreign). A magazine from a friend's birthday makes a great gift (about 50F). Open M-Sa 10:30am-7pm.

Brentano's, 37, av. de l'Opéra, 2ème (tel. 01 42 61 52 50). M: Opéra. An American and French bookstore with an extensive selection of English literature, guidebooks (including *Let's Go: Paris, Let's Go: France,* and *Let's Go: Europe*), and greeting cards in English. Paperbacks 40-75F. Open M-Sa 10am-7:30pm. AmEx, MC, V.

Chantelivre, 13, rue de Sèvres, 6ème (tel. 01 45 48 87 90). M: Sèvres-Babylone. A pricey children's bookstore with a play area for the kids. Classics for the young *(Puss in Boots)* and not so young (Dumas, Jack London). Small English-language section. Open M 1-6:50pm, Tu-Sa 10am-6:50pm. MC, V (100F min.).

Le Funambule, 48, rue Jean-Pierre Timbaud, 11ème (tel. 01 48 06 74 94). M: Parmentier. Small, artsy bookstore with (among other things) a good selection of gay- and lesbian-interest books, from literature to fine arts. Most books used, out of print, or rare; some in English. Carries *Spartacus* and *Gay Pied.* Open Tu-Sa 2-7pm.

Galignani, 224, rue de Rivoli, 1er (tel. 01 42 60 76 07; fax 01 42 86 09 31). M: Tuileries. The first English bookstore on the continent, Galignani was founded in 1804 and has inhabited its current location since 1856. Frequented by Thackeray and Garibaldi in the 19th century and occupied by the German general staff during WWII, the store is saturated in its own history. Wood paneling, *belles lettres,* coffee table art books, paperbacks, and travel guides, including *Let's Go: Paris, Let's Go: France,* and *Let's Go: Europe.* Open M-Sa 10am-7pm. MC, V.

Gibert Jeune, 5, pl. St-Michel, 5ème (tel. 01 43 25 70 07). M: St-Michel. Near the Seine, it's the best bookstore in town. With several branches clustered near each other, each specializing in different fields, Gibert Jeune and its bright yellow windows seem to swallow up the area around the Fontaine St-Michel. Try the main location for books in all languages and for all tastes, including lots of reduced-price books. Extensive stationery department downstairs; used books bought down here, too. The branch at 27, quai St-Michel (tel. 01 43 54 57 32; M: St-Michel), sells university texts. Main branch open M-Sa 9:30am-7:30pm. AmEx, MC, V.

Gibert Joseph, 26-30-32-34, bd. St-Michel, 6ème (tel. 01 44 41 88 88; fax 01 40 46 83 62). M: Odéon or Cluny-Sorbonne. A gigantic *librairie* and music store all rolled into one with both new and used selections. Frequent sidewalk sales with crates of books, notebooks, and old records starting at 10F. Good selection of used dictionaries and guidebooks. *Papeterie* at 32, bd. St-Michel, open M-Sa 9:30am-7pm; all other departments M-Sa 9:30am-7:30pm. MC, V.

La Hune, 170, bd. St-Germain, 6ème (tel. 01 45 48 35 85; fax 01 45 44 49 87). M: St-Germain-des-Prés. Next door to one of surrealist André Breton's favorite cafés, this well-stocked, crisp bookstore is a hot-spot for literati and art-lovers. Upper level is devoted to *beaux arts* and has a very good collection of critical works. Open M-Sa 10am-midnight. MC, V.

La Librairie des Femmes, 74, rue de Seine, 6ème (tel. 01 43 29 50 75). M: Odéon. The one-time home of feminist collective MLF (Mouvement pour la Libération des Femmes). Although it has lost much of its radical edge, this *librairie* is still at the vanguard of the women's liberation movement. Books in several languages about and by women. Debates and readings are advertised in the store-front window. Occasional art exhibitions. Open M-Sa 11am-7pm. AmEx, MC, V.

Librairie Gallimard, 15, bd. Raspail, 7ème (tel. 01 45 48 24 84; fax 01 42 84 16 97). M: Rue du Bac. The main store of this famed publisher of French classics features a huge selection of pricey Gallimard books. Basement is filled with Folio paperbacks. Open M-Sa 10am-7pm. AmEx, MC, V.

Librairie Gourmande, 4, rue Dante, 5ème (tel. 01 43 54 37 27; fax 01 43 54 31 16). M: Maubert-Mutualité. Bookstore on the art of cooking and dining par excellence. New and old volumes chronicle food and drink from the Middle Ages to the New Age. Some English titles. Remainders around 30F. Open daily 10am-7pm. MC, V.

Librairie du Québec, 30, rue Gay Lussac (tel. 01 43 54 49 02) RER: Luxembourg. *Un coin du Québec au coeur de Paris,* this wonderful bookshop supplies thousands of titles on Québecois literature, history, politics, culture, film, music, and Québecois Sovereignty. A great resource for the Québecois community in Paris with listings of upcoming poetry readings, performances, and festivals, including the *Fête Nationale* (June 24th, see **Festivals,** p. 251).

Librairie Ulysse, 26, rue St-Louis-en-l'Ile, 4ème (tel. 01 43 25 17 35; e-mail ulysse@calva.net). M: Pont-Marie. Anyone with a passion for travel should head to this magical, 1-room bookstore filled floor-to-ceiling with books about every place you've ever dreamed of visiting. Impressive stock of maps. 4000 copies of *National Geographic* since the 20s. There is a section on Paris and plenty of used books outside. English spoken. Open Tu-Sa 2-8pm. MC, V (over 500F).

Librairie Un Regard Moderne, 10, rue Git-le-Coeur, 6ème (tel. 01 43 29 13 93). M: St-Michel. A wild combo of high and low, kitsch and *kunst*. Racy comix, glossy art and photo books, high and low-brow, porn, and gen-X literature pile up in a cramped, smoky room. Small gallery features young artists. Open M-Sa 11:30am-8pm. MC, V.

Le Monde Libertaire, 145, rue Amelot. M: République, 11ème (tel. 01 48 05 36 08). Walk up bd. Voltaire and turn right on rue Amelot. One of the only anarchist and Marxist bookstores in Paris. Books and magazines on human rights, revolutions, and social change. Sale items 10-50F. Open M-F 2-7:30pm, Sa 10am-7:30pm.

Les Mots à la Bouche, 6, rue Ste-Croix-de-la-Bretonnerie, 4ème (tel. 01 42 78 88 30; fax 01 42 78 36 41). M: St-Paul or Hôtel-de-Ville. Extensive collection of gay and lesbian literature, including novels, essays, poetry, history, art criticism, and magazines in French and English. Also a small selection of videos. A must-visit for those in search of an inside line on gay and lesbian nightlife and political and cultural events. Open M-Sa 11am-11pm, Su 2-8pm. MC, V.

Presence Africaine, 25bis, rue des Écoles, 5ème (tel. 01 43 54 15 88). M: Maubert-Mutualité. French-language texts from Antilles and Africa put out by the famous publishing house of the same name, which first published Césaire and Fanon. Children's books, scholarly texts, poetry, and more. Paperbacks 30-70F. A helpful resource for travelers seeking businesses that cater to black clientele. Open M-Sa 10am-7pm. MC, V.

Shakespeare and Co., 37, rue de la Bûcherie, 5ème. M: St-Michel. Across the Seine from Nôtre-Dame. Run by George Whitman (alleged great-grandson of Walt), this shop seeks to reproduce the atmosphere of Sylvia Beach's establishment at 8, rue Dupuytren (and, later, at 12, rue de l'Odéon), a gathering-place for expatriates in the 20s. Beach published James Joyce's *Ulysses* in 1922. The current location has absolutely no official link to any Lost Generation notables. It has, however, accumulated a quirky and wide selection of new and used books. Bins outside offer sundry bargains, including French classics in English (30F). Profits support impoverished writers who live and work in this literary cooperative—former residents include beatniks Allen Ginsberg and Lawrence Ferlinghetti. Live poetry M nights. Open daily noon-midnight.

Tea and Tattered Pages, 24, rue Mayet, 6ème (tel. 01 40 65 94 35). M: Duroc. The place to go for second-hand English-language books. The crazy-quilt, mostly pulp fiction selection is subject to barter and trade. Sell books at 3-5F a paperback and get a 10% discount on your next purchase. Books cost 25-45F. If they don't have what you want, sign the wish list and you'll be called if it comes in. Tea room serves root beer floats, brownies, lunch, and American coffee with free refills. Regular poetry readings and photo exhibits. Open Sept.-July; daily 11am-10pm.

The Village Voice, 6, rue Princesse, 6ème (tel. 01 46 33 36 47). M: Mabillon. Takes its name less from the Manhattan paper than from the Parisian neighborhood that 15 years ago was known as "le village de St. Germain des Près." An excellent Anglophone bookstore, not to mention the locus of the city's English literary life, featuring 3-4 readings, lectures, and discussions every month (always at 7pm) with Paris luminaries like Edmund White. Paperbacks 48-90F. Many American and British newspapers and magazines. Open M 2-8pm, Tu-Sa 11am-8pm. AmEx, MC, V.

W.H. Smith, 248, rue de Rivoli, 1er (tel. 01 44 77 88 99; fax 01 42 96 83 71). M: Concorde. Find the latest publications from Britain and America here, including many scholarly works. Large selection of magazines. Sunday *New York Times* available by Tuesday. Open M-Sa 9am-7pm, Su 1pm-6pm. AmEx, MC, V.

■ Music

Highly taxed in France, CDs are considered luxury goods. In addition to expensive imported American and British pop, grunge, rock, rap, alternative, R&B, and classical, you'll find great selections of French pop, rap, rock, techno, house, punk, and cabaret as well as huge supplies of classic jazz, acid jazz, jungle, raï, African, Arabic, and fusion. As with the rest of the planet, cassettes are fading quickly. *Disques d'occasion* (used LPs) can be found at some music stores and at flea markets (see **Markets,** p. 266). For a list of what's hot in French music, from classical to pop to rap, see **Music,** p. 19. In addition to **Gibert Joseph's** CDs (see **Books,** p. 264), the following stores stock anything you may want.

B.P.M. (Bastille Paris Musique), 1, rue Keller, 11ème (tel. 01 40 21 02 88; fax 01 40 21 03 74). M: Bastille. Catering to your rave needs, this address is a clubhouse, information point, and music store for house and techno fans. From groovy French House to jungle. Record players so you can listen before buying. Check posters and fliers for upcoming parties. Open M-Sa noon-8pm. MC, V.

FNAC (Fédération Nationale des Achats de Cadres): Several branches. Montparnasse, 136, rue des Rennes, 6ème (tel. 01 49 54 30 00); M: Rennes. Étoile, 26-30, av. des Ternes, 17ème (tel. 01 44 09 18 00); M: Ternes. Forum des Halles, 1-7, rue Porte Lescot, 1er (tel. 01 40 41 40 00); M: Les Halles. Italiens, 24, bd. des Italiens, 9ème (tel. 01 48 01 02 03); M: Opéra. Huge selection of tapes, CDs, and stereo equipment. The branch at Les Halles contains a well-stocked shelf of books about music. The Italiens branch screens music videos all day. Box office sells concert and theater tickets. Montparnasse, Étoile, and Les Halles branches open M-Sa 10am-7:30pm. Italiens branch open M-Sa 10am-midnight. MC, V.

Rough Trade, 30, rue Charonne, 11ème (tel. 01 40 21 61 62). M: Bastille. Parisian branch of the British record label that brought you the Smiths, Stiff Little Fingers, Wire, Père Ubu, and countless other pop and punk bands. Techno, hip-hop, and house downstairs; rock, pop, noise, and CDs upstairs. They also sell tickets to concerts around town as well as to all the major European music festivals. Open June-Aug. M-W 1-7pm, Th-Sa noon-8pm; Sept.-May M noon-8pm, Tu-W noon-8pm, Th-Sa 11am-8pm. MC, V.

Virgin Megastore, 52-60, av. des Champs-Elysées, 8ème (tel. 01 49 53 50 00). M: Franklin D. Roosevelt. If it's been recorded, it's likely to be at Virgin. This music mecca includes an affordable restaurant and headphones that let you listen to the latest hits. Music videos play the French top-ten to give you an idea of what's hot (and what's not). Basement holds a bookstore and a box office. Another huge branch in the Louvre subterranean shopping mall (see **Museums,** p. 211). Champs-Elysées branch open M-Sa 10am-midnight, Su noon-midnight. AmEx, MC, V.

■ Markets

Looking for that special something? From silver serving platters to Stevie Wonder 45s, Balzac to blue jeans, Paris's covered and uncovered markets are an affordable way to discover the charm and occasional chintz of daily life in the neighborhood. Paris's many flea markets *(marchés aux puces)* are great options if you are decorating an apartment or university room and need cheap furniture, appliances, and cooking utensils. You'll also find vintage clothing, used bicycles, old televisions, stereos, telephones, and answering machines. If prices aren't marked (and even if they are), feel free to haggle and bargain. Wherever you are, watch your wallet. The bustle of market day brings out the pickpockets in hordes. For info on food, see **Groceries**, p. 102, and **Food Markets**, p. 104.

PUCES DE ST-OUEN (ST-OUEN FLEA MARKET)

The granddaddy of all flea markets, the **Puces de St-Ouen** (M: Porte de Clignancourt) is an overwhelming smorgasbord of stuff. *(Open Sa-M 7am-7:30pm; many of the official stalls close earlier, but the renegade vendors may stay open until 9pm.)* From antique armoires and fine silverware to LPs and vintage 60s hippie gear, you'll find everything you need (and don't need) in the many acres of criss-crossing pedestrian alleys of the Puces St-Ouen, located in St-Ouen, a town just north of the 18ème. Prices and quality vary as widely as the merchandise, from dirt-cheap, low-quality bargains found among renegade stalls and tables to antique-dealers who use buzzers to ring in their preferred customers while keeping out the riff-raff. The market began during the Middle Ages, when merchants resold the cast-off clothing of aristocrats (crawling with the market's namesake insects) to peasant-folk on the edge of the city. Today, it is a highly structured, regular market alongside a wild, anything-goes street bazaar. If you approach the market from M: Porte de St-Ouen, follow av. de la Porte de St-Ouen under the highway, then turn immediately right onto rue du Docteur Babinski, which becomes rue Jean Henri Fabre. Walk along av. de la Porte de Clignancourt, under the highway for 10 minutes and turn left on rue Jean Henri Fabre to reach the official market.

A rule of thumb for first-time visitors: there are no five-franc diamond rings here. If you find the Hope Diamond in a pile of schlock jewelry, the vendor planted it there. The one area, however, in which peddlers seem not to know what they have is in rare rock-and-roll recordings. If you know your stuff and have unlimited patience, this is the place. The market is least crowded before noon. Wherever you shop, be prepared to bargain; sellers don't expect to get their starting price. The 10-minute walk along av. de la Porte de Clignancourt, under the highway, and left on rue Jean Henri Fabre to the official market is jammed with tiny **unofficial stalls.** Most of these stalls sell flimsy new clothes, T-shirts, African masks, and teenage jewelry at exorbitant prices, but the leather jacket stalls have some good buys (suede jackets for 275F), as do some of the music booths. Pickpockets love this crowded area, and Three Card Monte con artists proliferate. Don't be pulled into the game by seeing someone win lots of money; he's part of the con, planted to attract suckers. If this renegade bazaar turns you off, continue to the official market where you'll be able to browse leisurely in a much nicer setting.

The **official market** comprises many sales forums, located on rue des Rosiers and rue Jules Vallès. Expect to get lost. From rue Jean Henri Fabre, slip into the **Marché Malik,** a warehouse-type space filled with new and used clothing, shoes, music booths, and a tattoo parlor. Exiting onto rue Jules Vallès, and walking away from the bongo drums and hard-sell banter of rue Fabre, you'll encounter the indoor **Marché Jules Vallès** with its overwhelming collection of old trinkets and antique miscellany. **Marché Paul Bert,** on rue Paul Bert, has more antique bric-a-brac as well as a large collection of wooden furniture. Next door at the **Marché Serpette,** more specialized furniture stores reign side-by-side with shops dealing in antique firearms. **Marché Biron** on rue des Rosiers and **Marché Dauphine** on rue Fabre will help you plan what to buy for your home when you're rich and famous. **Marché Vernaison,** located between rue des Rosiers and av. Michelet, has more upper-class tchachkis, prints, beads, buttons, and musical instruments.

The **Marché des Rosiers,** rue Paul Bert (lamps, vases, and 20th-century art), and the **Marché Autica,** rue des Rosiers (paintings, furniture), are small, paler shadows of the large markets and deal mainly in new or fairly modern goods. The **Marché Malassie** is as new as any of this stuff gets; more a mall than a market, this gawky empty space sells "antiques" from the 60s and similarly uninteresting furniture and artworks. Leaving the markets via av. Michelet takes you past a herd of leather coats, boots, and bags.

If you want to stop for lunch while at the flea market, try a steaming bowl of *moules marinière* with *frites,* the uncontested specialty of restaurants in the area. Two restaurants in particular stand out: **Chez Louisette,** 130, av. Michelet (tel. 01 40 12 10 14), inside the Marché Vernaison, allée no. 10, all the way at the back, where campy singers liven up this eclectically decorated restaurant with classic French café *chansons,* a French version of American show tunes. Unfortunately, the secret is out, and you'll hear as much English and German as French. (*Moules* 60F. Open Sa-M 8am-7pm.) A younger, grungier, less-touristy clientele frequents **Au Baryton,** 50, av. Jules Vallès (tel. 01 40 12 02 74), near the Marché Malik, where people slurp up the *moules-frites* combo as well as an appetizer and dessert for only 60F while taking in the free live blues and rock concerts (open Sa-M 8am-11:30pm; live music 4:30-8:30pm or 6:30-10pm).

While less impressive, other *marchés aux puces* are also less crowded. The **Puces de Vanves,** along rue Marc Sanguier between av. de la Porte de Vanves and av. Georges La Fenestre, 14ème (M: Porte de Vanves), carries a fairly good assortment of antique cameras, jewelry, furniture, lace, spoons, dishes, 19th-century books, and 20th-century comic books (open Sa-Su 8am-1pm). The **Puces de Montreuil,** extending from pl. de la Porte de Montreuil along av. du Professeur André Lemierre and av. Galliéni, 20ème, is cheap in every sense. You will find auto parts, tools, and stereos, but the market's heart is in its piles of used clothes, most priced between 5F and 50F. Bargain freely but watch your wallet. (Open Sa-M 7:30am-7:30pm.)

OTHER MARKETS

Carreau du Temple, 2-8, rue Perrée, at the corner of rue Dupetit Thouars and rue de Picardie, 3ème. M: Temple. Follow rue du Temple away from the metro and turn left on rue Dupetit Thouars. This structure of blue steel and glass is a neighborhood sports center in the afternoon and a clothes market in the morning. Good especially for leather, but also sells other kinds of clothes and fabrics. Don't forget to haggle—you can usually get the already low price down at least 25%. More crowded on weekends. Open Tu-F 9am-12:30pm, Sa-Su 9am-1pm.

Marché aux Fleurs, on pl. Louis-Lépine just across from the M: Cité staircase, 4ème. This permanent flower market fills the plaza near the Palais de Justice with color and fragrance and makes for a romantic walk down the Seine. Open M-Sa 9am-7pm. On Su an animal market appears in its stead, featuring goldfish, rabbits, gerbils, bird cages, and pet food stalls. Parakeets 95-800F. Rabbits 100F. Hamsters 20F. Goldfish 10F. Open Su 9am-6pm.

Marché aux Timbres, from the Rond-Point des Champs-Elysées to the corner of av. Matignon and av. Gabriel, 8ème. M: Franklin D. Roosevelt. A world of stamps for the philatelists in us all. Open Th and Sa-Su during daylight hours.

Quai de Mégisserie, 1er. M: Pont-Neuf or Châtelet. Creatures lovable and lunchable squawk, purr, yelp, and gobble in this 300-year-old animal bazaar. Cages spill from the stores onto the street, and fauna mingles with flora. Open daily 8am-7pm.

Trips from Paris

These miraculous escapes from the toils of a great city give one a clearer impression of the breadth with which it is planned, and of the civic order and elegance pervading its whole system.
—Edith Wharton, *A Motor-Flight Through France*, 1908

DAYTRIPS

▓ Versailles

Tel. 01 30 84 74 00. Web http://www.chateauversailles.com. Open May-Sept. Tu-Su 9am-6:30pm, Oct.-Apr. Tu-Su 9am-5:30pm. Last admission 30min. before closing. Admission to the palace 45F; ages 18-25, over 60, and after 3:30pm 35F. The carte musée includes admission to Versailles, but no tours. For more information, see Museums, p. 210. Audioguides: Entrance C, 1hr., 25F, ages 7-17 17F, under 7 free. Guided Tours: Entrance D, 1hr., 25F, ages 7-17 25F; 1½hr., 37F, ages 7-17 26F; 2hr., 50F, ages 7-17 34F; under 7 free (see Tours, below). Gardens: Open daily sunrise-sundown. Free. Fountains turned on only for special displays mid-Apr. to mid-Oct. Sa-Su 3:30-5:30pm, 28F.

By sheer force of ego, the Sun King converted a hunting lodge into the world's most famous palace. The sprawling château—its Hall of Mirrors, royal suites, guest rooms, antechambers, and portrait galleries—stands as a testament to the despotic playboy-king who lived, entertained, and governed on the grandest of scales. While Louis XVI and Marie-Antoinette entertained in lavish style, the peasants of Paris starved. The opulence of Versailles makes clear why it is they lost their heads (see **History**, p. 4).

HISTORY

A child during the aristocratic insurgency called the Fronde, Louis XIV is said to have entered his father's bedchamber one night only to find (and frighten away) an assassin. Fearing noble conspiracy the rest of his life, Louis chose to move the center of royal power out of Paris and away from potential aristocratic insubordination. In 1682 the Sun King decided on Versailles, the hunting lodge-cum-palace built and decorated by Le Vau, Le Brun, and Le Nôtre (see **Vaux-le-Vicomte**, p. 278). By Louis's decree, the court became the mandatory nucleus of noble life, where more than a thousand of France's greatest aristocrats vied for the king's favor. Busily attending to Louis XIV's morning *(levée)* and evening *(coucher) toilette*, they had little time for subversion. Louis XIV had successfully drawn the high nobility under his watchful eye. As a further precaution, he outlawed duels at court.

The château itself is a gilded lily of classical Baroque style. No one knows just how much it cost to build Versailles; Louis XIV burned the accounts to keep the price a mystery. At the same time, life there was less luxurious than one might imagine: courtiers wore rented swords and urinated behind statues in the parlors, wine froze in the drafty dining rooms, and dressmakers invented the color *puce* (literally, "flea") to camouflage the insects crawling on the noblewomen. Still, the mass extortion that Versailles represents would spark the French Revolution a century later. On October 5, 1789, 15,000 Parisian fishwives and National Guardsmen marched out to the palace and brought the royal family back to Paris where they were guillotined in 1793.

During the 19th century, King Louis-Philippe established a museum to preserve the château, against the wishes of most French people, who wanted Versailles demolished just as the Bastille had been. In 1871, the château took the limelight once again, when Wilhelm of Prussia became Kaiser Wilhelm I of Germany in the Hall of Mirrors. That same year, as headquarters of the Thiers regime, Versailles sent an army against the Parisian Commune. The *Versaillais* pierced the city walls and crushed the *communards*. At the end of WWI, a vengeful France forced Germany to sign the ruinous Treaty of Versailles in the Hall of Mirrors, the very room of modern Germany's birth.

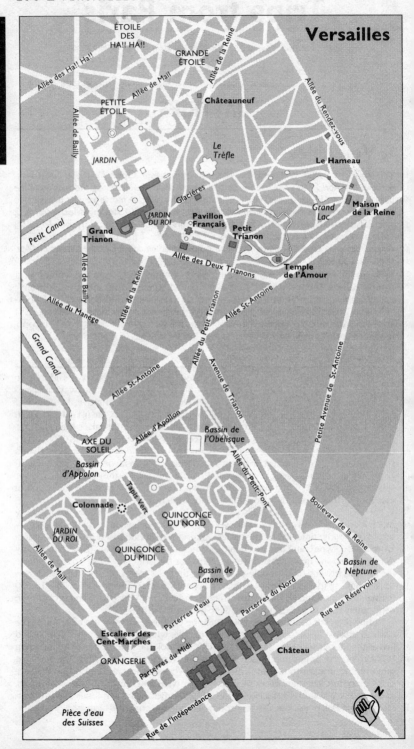

Versailles

PRACTICAL INFORMATION

Visiting Versailles is a mammoth undertaking. The thorough sightseer may want to take two days to fully appreciate the ostentation. Arrive early in the morning to avoid the crowds, which are worse on Sunday from May to September (when the fountains are turned on) and in late June (when French schoolchildren are on field trips). For more on Versailles château events, sights, lodging, and food, call the **Office de Tourisme de Versailles,** 7, rue des Reservoirs (tel. 01 39 50 36 22; fax 01 39 50 68 07), down the street from the château on the Opéra side. There are two restaurants within Versailles: the **Caféteria** (tel. 01 39 50 58 62; open 9:30am-5pm), which offers a hot *plat du jour* (48F) and sandwiches (25-40F), and the pricier **La Flotille** (tel. 01 39 51 41 58).

For a slightly cheaper lunch, exit the main gate of the château, turn left, and head for the row of blue parasols on the tree-lined landing just beyond the parked tour buses. There are three cafés there. The middle one has an outdoor sandwich counter (sandwiches 18-25F). You'll also find a few gift shops along this street, but be aware that prices are as inflated as the Sun King's ego.

The RER has direct and frequent **train service** between Paris and Versailles. Trains run from M: Invalides on RER Line C5 to the Versailles Rive Gauche station (30-40min., departs every 15min., 28F round-trip). From the Invalides metro stop, take trains with labels beginning with "V" (Vick, Vora, and so on). Buy your RER ticket before going through the turnstile to the platform; although your metro ticket will get you through these turnstiles, it will not get you through the RER turnstiles at Versailles and could get you in trouble with the dreaded *controlleurs*.

THE MAIN TOUR

When you arrive at the Versailles Rive Gauche RER train stop, exit the station and take a right. The elegant building on the right is the *mairie* (city hall) of Versailles. Continue walking away from the train station along the length of the *mairie*'s façade and turn left at the first huge intersection; then walk straight to the gilt-fenced outer-courtyard of Versailles. An equestrian statue of a crimped, turned-out Louis XIV stands at the courtyard's center. Overlooking the courtyard is the terrace on which Molière's *Tartuffe* debuted. The clock on the pediment, flanked by Hercules and Mars, was traditionally set to the time of death of the previous king. The balcony of the **King's Bedroom** is visible at the center of the east-west axis along which the château and gardens are laid out. Here, the Sun King's place was at the center of the château and the nation. Each morning Louis arose to great ritual, with dignitaries standing in line for the privilege of helping with his morning *toilette*.

Signs in the courtyard point you to Entrance A, B, C, D, or H. Most of Versailles's visitors enter at **Entrance A,** located on the right-hand side in the north wing. (**Entrance B** is for groups, **Entrance C** is for guided tours of the King's Chamber with headphones only, **Entrance D** is where tours with a living, breathing guide begin, and **Entrance H** is for visitors in wheelchairs.) General admission allows entrance to the following rooms: the *grands appartements,* where the king and queen received the public; the War and Peace Drawing Rooms; and the *Galerie des Glaces* (Hall of Mirrors). The King's and Queen's apartments may be seen only by guided tour. If you intend to take one, proceed directly to either Entrance C or D (see **Guided Tours,** below), purchase the regular admission ticket, and inquire about guided visits.

The general admission ticket starts your visit in the **Musée de l'Histoire de France,** created in 1837 by Louis-Philippe to celebrate his country's glory. Along its textured walls hang portraits of men and women who shaped the course of French history. The face of Louis XIV is everywhere. Of particular interest are portraits by Philippe de Champaigne, preeminent court artist under Louis XIII. The 21 rooms (arranged in chronological order) seek to construct a historical context for the château.

Each of the gilded **drawing rooms** in the **State Apartments** is dedicated to a myth-ological god: Hercules, Mars, and the ever-present Apollo (the Sun King identified with the sun god). The ornate **Salon d'Apothon** was Louis XIV's throne room. Framed by the **War and Peace Drawing Rooms** is the **Hall of Mirrors,** which was a

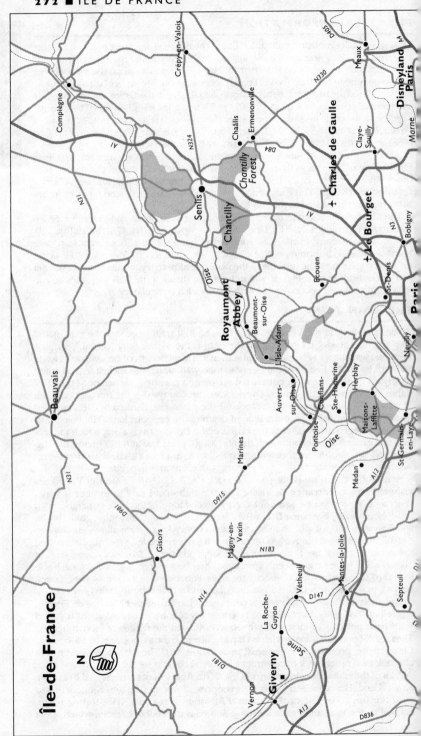

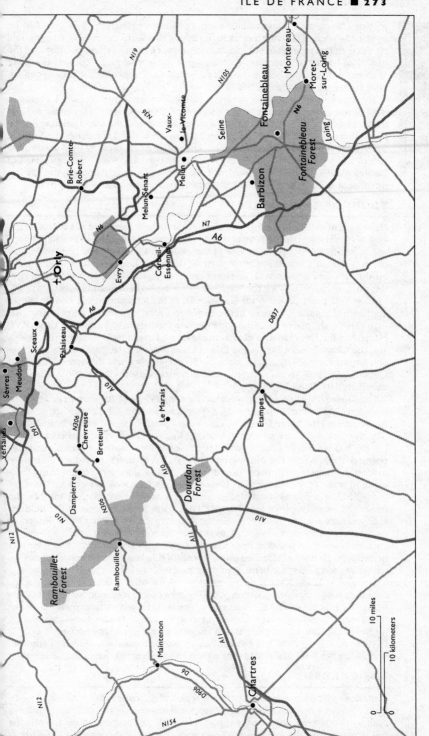

gloomy hallway until Mansart added a series of mirrored panels in order to double the light in the room. These mirrors were the largest that 17th-century technology could produce and were an unbelievable extravagance. Le Brun's ceiling paintings tell the history of Louis XIV's heroism, culminating in the central piece, entitled *The King Governs Alone*. It was here in this vast room that the Treaty of Versailles was ratified, effectively ending the First World War.

The **Queen's Bedchamber,** where royal births were crowded, public events, is now furnished year-round in its floral summer decor—not the darker plush red and black velvet used during 18th-century winters. A version of the David painting depicting Napoleon's self-coronation (the original is in the Louvre) dominates the **Salle du Sacré** (also known as the Coronation Room). In this room, the king used to wash the feet of a lucky 13 poor children every Holy Thursay. The sometimes-open **Hall of Battles** rounds out the non-guided visit. Dominated by huge paintings, the hall is a monument to 14 centuries of France's military battles, from Clovis to Napoleon.

TOURS OF THE CHÂTEAU

Head for Entrance C to purchase an **audioguide** to the **Apartment of Louis XIV,** the **Hall of Mirrors,** and the **Apartments of the Dauphin and Dauphine.** The **King's Bedroom,** which yields a blinding look at the monarch's gold bed and balustrade, also features Nocret's beautiful family portrait, depicting Louis XIV as Apollo and his brother, Philippe d'Orléans, as holder of the morning star. Philippe was the first after the morning chaplain to see the Sun King—he was also kept in skirts until he was 18.

All **guided tours** depart from Entrance D, at the left-hand inside corner as you approach the palace. Choose between seven tours of different parts of the château. Three are offered in English: **Private apartments of Louis XV, Louis XVI, Marie-Antoinette, Madame de Pompadour,** and **Madame Du Barry;** the **Opéra** and the **Chapel;** and a **Day in the Life of Louis XIV.** Sign-language tours are available for the King's State Apartments, the Hall of Mirrors, and the Apartment of the Queen. Reservations must be made in advance with the Bureau d'Action Culturelle (tel. 01 30 84 76 18).

The **Opéra,** which took architect Jacques-Ange Gabriel 20 years to design, was completed at breakneck speed by 20,000 workmen in time for the wedding of Marie-Antoinette and the future Louis XVI. Often considered the world's most beautiful theater, the pink and blue oval room is a marvelous fake. It looks like marble or bronze, but the hall is actually made of wood because the meticulous Gabriel wanted it to resound like a violin. The mirrored galleries reflect chandeliers and gilt archways, making the theater seem larger than it is. The room's splendor brought Marie-Antoinette to breach royal etiquette on her wedding day; she took her eyes off the stage and ogled the decor. Many of Molière's plays premiered here, accompanied by the music of court composer Jean-Baptiste Lully. Lully's death is one of the saddest, strangest tales in music history. Before the advent of the conducting baton, leaders of musical ensembles used a long, pointed stick to keep time. During a performance celebrating Louis XIV's recovery from illness in 1687, Lully accidentally stabbed himself in the foot with his stick. He died later that year of gangrene. Today, performances are rare in the beautiful space because of the cost it takes to light its many chandeliers.

The tour of **Louis XV's apartments** showcases a small collection of furnishings, instruments, and tapestries. Mozart played in one of these rooms on his youthful visits to Versailles (at ages 7 and 22). The visit to **Marie-Antoinette's apartments** does not trail through as many lavish rooms as you might hope. Versailles was sacked during the Revolution and only a portion of its original extravagance has been restored. On October 6, 1789, a crowd of bloodthirsty Parisians stormed the Queen's bedroom, demanding the head of the "Austrian whore." The palace was never the same.

THE GARDENS

Versailles's gardens are massive, perfectly scaled to the palace. Numerous artists—Le Brun, Mansart, Coysevox—executed statues and fountains here, but master gardener André Le Nôtre provided the overall plan. Louis XIV, landscape enthusiast, wrote the first guidebook to the gardens, entitled the *Manner of Presenting the Gardens at*

Versailles. Start, as the Sun King commands, on the terrace and admire the wide paths and tall trees. To the left of the terrace, the **Parterre du Midi** graces the area in front of Mansart's **Orangerie,** once home to 2000 orange trees. The temperature inside never drops below 6°C (43°F). In the center of the terrace lies the **Parterre d'Eau,** while the **Bassin de Latone** fountain below features Latona, mother of Diana and Apollo, shielding her children as Jupiter turns villains into frogs.

Past the fountain and to the left is the **Rockwork Grove,** built between 1681 and 1683. Once a dance area with a marble floor, the grove shows off fetid water cascading over shell-encrusted steps. The south gate of the grove leads to the magnificent **Bassin de Bacchus,** one of four seasonal fountains. The **Bassin du Miroir d'Eau** spurts near the peaceful **Jardin du Roi** and the **Bassin de Saturne.** The king used to take light meals amid the **Colonnade's** 32 columns, sculptures, and white marble basins. The north gate to the Colonnade exits onto the **Tapis Vert** (Green Carpet), the central mall linking the château to the **Char d'Apollon** (Chariot of Apollo). Pulled by four prancing horses, the Sun God rises out of dark water to enlighten the world.

On the north side of the garden is Marsy's incredible **Bassin d'Encelade.** One of the giants who tried to unseat Jupiter from Mount Olympus, Enceladus cries in agony under the weight of rocks that Jupiter hurled to bury him. When the fountains are turned on, a 25m jet bursts from Enceladus's mouth. Flora reclines more peacefully on a bed of flowers in the **Bassin de Flore,** while Ceres luxuriates in sheaves of wheat in the **Bassin de Cérès.** The **Parterre du Nord,** full of flowers, lawns, and trees, overlooks some of the garden's most spectacular fountains. The **Allée d'Eau,** a fountain-lined walkway, provides the best view of the **Bassin des Nymphes de Diane.** The path slopes toward the sculpted **Bassin du Dragon,** where a dying beast spurts water 27m into the air. Ninety-nine jets of water attached to urns and seahorns surround a menacing Neptune in the **Bassin de Neptune,** the gardens' largest fountain.

Beyond Le Nôtre's classical gardens stretch wilder woods and farmland. Check out the **Grand Canal,** a sharp-edged pond beyond the Bassin d'Apollon. To explore further, you can rent a bike to the right of the canal, just outside the garden gates (30F per hr.). If you're with friends, rent a boat for four people at the boathouse to the right of the canal (open Tu-F noon-5:30pm, Sa-Su 11am-6pm; 72F per hr., 50F refundable deposit). The two-hour *Discovering Groves Tour* provides the history of Le Nôtre's gardens and their fountains (June-Oct., call 01 30 84 76 18 for info; 1hr., 25F).

THE TRIANONS AND MARIE-ANTOINETTE'S HAMEAU

Both Trianons: Open May-Sept. Tu-Sa 10am-6:30pm; Oct.-Apr. Tu-F 10am-12:30pm and 2-5:30pm, Sa-Su 10am-5:30pm; last admission 30min. before closing. **Admission** to Grand Trianon 25F, reduced tariff 15F; Petit Trianon 15F, reduced tariff 10F. **Combined ticket** to the Trianons 30F, reduced tariff 20F. **Shuttle trams** from the palace to the Trianons and the Hameau leave from behind the palace: round-trip 32F, ages 3-12 20F. The **walk** takes about 25min.)

Although it may be difficult after visiting the château to muster the energy, the Trianons and Hameau provide a racier counterpoint to the stuffy formality of the château. It was here that kings trysted with lovers and where Marie-Antoinette lived like the peasant she wasn't.

Down the wooded path from the château, the **Petit Trianon** appears on the right, a neoclassical gem built between 1762-68 by the architect Gabriel to be the lovenest for Louis XV and his mistress Madame de Pompadour. By the time it was completed, Pompadour was dead and Louis's new lover was the Countess du Barry. Marie-Antoinette took control of the Petit Trianon in 1774 and claimed it as her new favorite spot, thus earning it the nickname "Little Vienna." Upon giving it to his queen, Louis XVI is said to have remarked, "Since you love flowers, I am offering you a bouquet that is the Petit Trianon." She had the formal gardens ripped up, sent them to the Jardin des Plantes in Paris, and installed a trendy English garden. The Petit Trianon was later inhabited by Napolean's sister and the Empress Marie-Louise. In 1867, the Empress Eugénie, who worshipped Marie-Antoinette, turned it into a museum. Today the lower level of the Petit Trianon is under restoration, but visitors can still tour the main level with its large portrait of Marie-Antoinette.

Exit the Petit Trianon, turn left, and follow the marked path to the libidinous **Temple of Love,** a domed rotunda with columns rising out of a small island. The temple shelters a copy of Bouchardon's famous statue of Cupid shooting his arrow. Marie-Antoinette held many intimate nighttime parties in the small space, during which thousands of torches would be illuminated in the surrounding ditch. The Queen was perhaps at her happiest and most ludicrous when spending time at the **Hameau,** her Norman-style cottage hamlet down the path from the Temple of Love. Inspired by Jean-Jacques Rousseau's theories on the state of nature so in vogue in the second half of the 18th century, the Queen aspired to a more simple life, peasant-style. She commissioned Richard Mique to build a compound of 12 buildings in which she could play at country life, including a mill, dairy, and gardener's house, all surrounding a quaint artificial lake. At the center is the Queen's Cottage. Any illusions of her slumming it with the farmhands disappear after crossing through its doors. The rooms contained ornate furniture, marble fireplaces, and chambers designated for Marie-Antoinette's silver, monogrammed linens, and footmen.

The single-story, stone and pink marble **Grand Trianon** was intended as a château-away-from-château for Louis XIV, who longed to escape the demands of court life and spend a little quality time with his mistress, Madame de Maintenon. Here the King could be reached only by boat along the Grand Canal, eliminating all of those pesky issues of everyday rule. The palace, which consists of two wings joined together by a central peristyle porch, was designed by Mansart and erected in 1687-88. Formal gardens are located behind the colonnaded porch. The mini-château was stripped of its furniture during the Revolution but was later restored and inhabited by Napoleon and his second wife. Charles de Gaulle installed presidential apartments and rooms for visiting heads of state in the Grand Trianon, and the constitutional amendment for Maastricht was written here.

SPECIAL EVENTS

On Sundays from mid-April through mid-October and Saturdays June to August, come to see the **Grandes Eaux Musicales,** when the fountains are in full operation. A slightly diminished version called the **Grande Perspective** runs 11:15 to 11:35am. Tour the 24 activated, musically accompanied fountains 3:30 to 5pm. A free pamphlet lays out a suggested walking path; don't bother with the more expensive guide (25F) to the fountain. (Admission to park during Grandes Eaux 28F; under 10 free.)

As Voltaire urged, "Pleasure is the object, the duty, and aim of all reasonable beings." So by all means attend one of the stunning **Fêtes de Nuit,** musical and fireworks extravaganzas that imitate the huge fêtes of Louis XIV. The garden at Versailles had to be finished in 1664 in time for one such party, the Fête of the Enchanted Isle, for which Molière wrote a *masque.* (Fêtes held 7 times each summer, Sa at 10pm, 1½hr., 70-250F, under 10 free. Tickets on sale at the tourist office, box offices within Paris, or through http://www.fnac.com. Doors open 1½hr. before the show; enter at 2, bd. de la Reine. For info call 01 30 83 78 78.) The **Nouveaux Plaisirs de Versailles** is a foundation that coordinates musical, dance, and theater events at the château, from Mozart to Molière. (Tickets 70-320F, call 01 30 83 78 78 for info.)

Versailles offers two ongoing **lecture** series. The first, **Histoire du Château,** provides an in-depth historical look at the palace. The second, **Visites Approfondies,** offers lectures like "Court Costumes under the Old Regime" and "Celebrated Women of Taste." (Oct.-May Sa or Su at 2pm; 40F; call 01 39 50 36 22 for topics and dates.)

■ Fontainebleau

If, upon hearing the words "hunting lodge" you imagine a secluded cabin in the thick of the woods with trophy heads and a rifle mounted above the hearth, you're obviously descended from very common stock. The men who commissioned and designed the **Château de Fontainebleau** thought grand, glorious, and gold-leafed. *(Open July-Aug. daily 9:30am-6pm; June and Sept.-Oct. daily 9:30am-5pm; Nov.-May W-M*

9:30am-12:30pm and 2-5pm. Last entry 45min. before closing time. Admission 35F; students, seniors, and Su 23F, under 18 free. Call 01 60 71 50 70 for info.) Built from sandstone found in the lush tangle of the surrounding forest, this palatial lodge incorporates a variety of decorative styles that distinguishes it from Vaux-le-Vicomte and Versailles.

Kings of France have hunted on these grounds since the 12th century, when the exiled Thomas à Beckett consecrated Louis VII's manor chapel. In 1528, François I rebuilt the castle to bring himself closer to the game he so loved to hunt. Italian artists designed and decorated the palace, and their paintings, including the *Mona Lisa,* filled François's private collections. Subsequent kings commissioned their favorite designers to add magnificent rooms and new wings. Louis XIII was born here in 1601, Louis XIV revoked the Edict of Nantes here in 1685, and Louis XV was married here in 1725. Napoleon, who visited Fontainebleau frequently, called it "La Maison des Siècles" (the House of Centuries). In 1814, Napoleon bid goodbye to the Empire from the central courtyard, now called the **Cour des Adieux** in his honor. Also known as the **White Horse Court,** it is the main entry to the château. The entrance was redecorated during the Third Empire, under Napoleon III.

The **Grands Appartements** provide a lesson in the history of French architecture and decoration. Printed guides (20-30F) will make your visit to the château, gardens, and Grands Appartements more meaningful. Dubreuil's **Gallery of Plates** tells the history of Fontainebleau on a remarkable series of 128 porcelain plates, fashioned in Sèvres between 1838 and 1844. In the long **Gallerie de François I,** the most famous room at Fontainebleau, muscular figures by Il Rosso (known in French as Maître Roux) tell mythological tales of heroism, brilliantly illuminated by light flooding in from windows that look out onto the **Fountain Courtyard.** Similarly, the **Ball Room's** magnificent octagonal ceiling, heavy wood paneling, and bay windows look out onto the **Oval Courtyard.** Decorated under Henri IV, the **King's Cabinet** (also known as the **Louis XIII Salon** because Louis XIII was born there) was the site of *le débotter,* the king's post-hunt boot removal. Gobelin tapestries and Savonnerie carpets line walls and floors throughout the palace. Napoleon poured over the volumes of the long, lofty, sunlit **Bibliothèque Diana.** Since the 17th century, every queen and empress of France has slept in the gold and green **Queen's Bed Chamber;** the gilded wood bed was built for Marie-Antoinette. The N on the red and gold velvet throne of the **Throne Room** is a testament to Napoleon's humility in what is today the only existing throne room in France. Sandwiched between two mirrors, **Napoleon's Bed Chamber** is a monument to either narcissism or eroticism, while the Emperor's austere **Small Bed Chamber** contains a small military bed. In the **Emperor's Private Room,** known today as the **Abdication Chamber,** Napoleon signed off his empire in 1814. The tour ends with the 16th-century, Italian-frescoed **Trinity Chapel.**

The **Musée Napoléon** holds a collection of the Emperor's personal toothbrush, his tiny shoes, his field tent, his son's toys, and state gifts from European monarchs such as Carlos IV of Spain. The **Musée Chinois de l'Impératrice Eugénie** was created in 1863 by the Empress to house her collection of Chinese decorative art, porcelain, jade, and crystal, which she had received as gifts of the 1860 Franco-English campaign in China and from the Siamese ambassador in 1861. *(Admission to both museums is included in price of the château.)* The **Petits Appartements,** private rooms of Napoleon and the Empress Josephine, are accessible only by guided tours. *(Tours M and holidays at 10, 11am, 2, and 3pm. Admission 16F, under 26 and over 60 12F, under 18 free.)*

Unlike Versailles's extensive formal gardens, Fontainebleau's modest **Jardin Anglais** and **Jardin de Diane** feature quiet grottos guarded by statues of the Greek huntress and the **Étang des Carpes,** a carp-filled pond that you can explore by rowboat. (Boat rental June-Aug. daily 10am-12:30pm and 2-7pm; Sept. Sa-Su 2-6pm. 40F per 30min., 60F per hr.) The **Forêt de Fontainebleau** is a thickly wooded 20,000-hectare preserve with hiking trails, bike paths, and sandstone rock-climbing. Maps are available at the tourist office. Fans of 19th-century art will recognize the thick hardwoods and sandstones made famous by Rousseau and Millet, painters of the Barbizon school (see **Musée d'Orsay,** p. 216).

In the town of **Fontainebleau,** the **Musée Napoléonien d'Art et d'Histoire Mili-taire,** 88, rue St-Honoré (tel. 01 64 22 49 80, ext. 424), displays more of Napoleon's military paraphernalia. *(Open Tu-Sa 2-5pm. Last entrance 4:45pm. Admission 10F, under 12 free.)* Across from the château, the **Fontainebleau Tourist Office,** 4, rue Royal (tel. 01 60 74 99 99; fax. 01 60 74 80 22), organizes tours of the village, helps find accommodations, and has maps of Fontainebleau and Barbizon (open M-Sa 9:30am-6:30pm, Su 10am-12:30pm and 3-5:30pm).

From Paris, hourly **trains** run to Fontainebleau from the Gare de Lyon, banlieue level (45min., 94F round-trip). The château is a 30-minute walk or 10-minute bus ride away. From the station, **Car Vert A** (tel. 01 64 22 23 88) runs buses (10F) after each train arrival from Paris; take the bus in direction "Château-Lilas" and get off at the Château stop. You can also rent a bike from **MBK** (tel. 01 64 22 36 14; fax 01 60 72 64 89) at the train station. (60F per day; mountain bikes 120F per day. Helmets 10F. Open daily 9am-7pm. MC, V.)

NEAR FONTAINEBLEAU: BARBIZON

The village of Barbizon blossoms on the edge of the Fontainebleau forest. A favorite of 19th-century French landscape painters, Barbizon attracted Théodore Rousseau, Jean-François Millet, and Jean-Baptiste Camille Corot to this artistic haven in the mid-1800s. Inspired by 17th-century Dutch landscapists, they were the predecessors of the Impressionists and have come to be known as the Barbizon School.

The **Musée Municipal de l'Ecole de Barbizon** is housed in **l'Auberge Ganne,** 92, Grande Rue (tel. 01 60 66 22 27), where most of the Barbizon artists lived between 1848 and 1870. *(Open M and W-F 10am-12:30pm and 2-5pm, Sa-Su 10am-5pm. Admission 25F, students 13F, under 12 free.)* Newly renovated, the museum offers a 30-minute multimedia tour of the Barbizon School and its models. The ground floor is a re-creation of the inn while the galleries upstairs feature works by Rousseau and Millet. Pick up the free English-language brochure *Barbizon: If You Want to Be a Model, or Just Look Like One* at the entrance. The **Maison et Atelier de Jean-François Millet,** 27, Grande rue (tel. 01 60 66 22 38), shifts focus to Millet, the best-known of the Barbizon masters, famous for his paintings of the French peasantry. *(Open W-M 9:30am-12:30pm and 2-5:30pm. Free.)*

Barbizon is 10km from Fontainebleau. **Buses** (tel. 01 64 23 71 11) linking the two towns have limited schedules. (W and Sa the bus departs the Fontainebleau train station at 2:10pm, the château at 2:20pm, and arrives at Barbizon at 2:30pm; the bus leaves Barbizon at 5:10pm; 19F.) Biking to Barbizon gives more flexibility; see above for bike rental information, and ask the Fontainebleau tourist office for directions. **Taxis** from the Fontainebleau train station are more expensive (110F). The **Barbizon Tourist Office,** 55, Grande Rue (tel. 01 60 66 41 87), offers maps and tourist info.

■ Vaux-le-Vicomte

Tel. 01 64 14 41 90. Email chateau@vaux-le-vicomte.com. Web http:\\www.vaux-le-vicomte.com. Open daily Apr.-Oct. 10am-6pm, Mar. and Nov. 1-11 11am-5pm. Visits by appointment the rest of the year. Gardens and Équipages open Feb. 28-Nov. 11 daily 10am-6pm. Admission to château and gardens 56F, students, seniors, and ages 6-16 46F, under 6 free. Admission to gardens and équipages 30F, students, seniors, and ages 6-16 24F.

Nicolas Fouquet, Louis XIV's Minister of Finance, assembled the famous triumvirate of Le Vau, Le Brun, and Le Nôtre (architect, artist, and landscaper) to build Vaux between 1656 and 1661. The result was a new standard for country châteaux (a uniquely French, Neoclassical style) and fame for the talented trio. Though smaller and less opulent than Versailles, Vaux impresses with architectural coherence and *trompe l'oeil*. Be attentive to optical tricks in both the château and the gardens.

On August 17, 1661, upon the completion of what was then France's most beautiful château, Fouquet threw an audacious and extravagant 6,000-guest party in honor of Louis XIV. The King and Anne d'Autriche were but two of the witnesses to a regal bacchanalia that premiered poetry by La Fontaine and a comedy-ballet, *Les Facheux*, by Molière. The evening concluded in a fireworks extravaganza featuring the King and Queen's coat of arms and pyrotechnic squirrels (Fouquet's family symbol). The housewarming bash, however, was the beginning of the end for Fouquet. Shortly thereafter, young Louis XIV—perhaps furious at having been upstaged—ordered Fouquet arrested. He was apprehended at Nantes by d'Artagnan, the captain of the Musketeers immortalized by Dumas.

Hidden causes lay behind Fouquet's downfall. Colbert, another minister, had been turning the monarch against Fouquet for years. Fouquet's affection for the king's mistress Mme de Lavallière didn't help matters either. Despite having kept the French treasury solvent by raising funds against his own fortune, Fouquet was the fall guy for the state's abysmal financial condition. In a trial that lasted three years, the judges in Fouquet's case voted narrowly for banishment over death. Louis XIV overturned the judgment in favor of life imprisonment—the only time in French history that the head of state overruled the court's decision in favor of a more severe sentence. Despite entreaties by Mme de Sévigné and La Fontaine (in his *Elegy to the Nymphs of Vaux*), Fouquet was to remain imprisoned at Pignerol, a dreary citadel in the French Alps, until his death in 1680. Many suspected that Fouquet was the famous man in the iron mask, including Alexandre Dumas who fictionalized the story in *Le Vicomte de Bragelonne*.

In addition to being a brilliant financier—one who certainly lived up to his motto, *Quo non ascendet* (What heights will he not scale)—Fouquet was also an aesthete and patron of impeccable grace, sophistication, and culture who surrounded himself with the finest talents of his time. Louis XIV himself held Fouquet's tastes in high esteem. Soon after the minister's arrest, the King confiscated many of Vaux's finest objects, including trees from the garden. Louis then hired the same trio—Le Vau, Le Brun, and Le Nôtre— to work their magic at Versailles.

THE CHÂTEAU

Vaux-le-Vicomte designers' integrated painting and sculpture, architecture and decor, building and gardens. The château united the grandeur of a Roman past and the utility of a a French fort, complete with Neoclassical columns, squat walls, and moat. The first optical trick to be aware of is the fact that the moat is completely invisible from the road. Another is the appearance of three entries where only one exists. Before beginning the **tour** (to your left upon entering), gaze up at the dome in the **Oval Room** ahead, and then out to the unfolding gardens.

For a detailed and brilliantly colored souvenir, buy the glossy guide in the gift shop (25F, available in English or French). Notice the ornate scripted Fs all around the château, and keep an eye out for the ever-present squirrel, Fouquet's symbol, and for the tower with three battlements, his second wife's crest. In the **Minister's Bedchamber,** an opulent red and gold bed stands under an allegorically decorated ceiling depicting Apollo bearing the lights of the world. **Mme Fouquet's Closet** once had walls lined with small mirrors, the decorative forerunner of Versailles's Hall of Mirrors. Over the fireplace of the **Square Room** hangs Le Brun's portrait of Fouquet. In this room you'll also find a beautiful 1877 billiard table and exquisite beams of the Louis XIII-style ceiling. Lebrun's **Room of the Muses** is one of his finest decorative schemes. Le Brun had planned to crown the **Oval Room** (or **Grand Salon**) with a fresco entitled *The Palace of the Sun*, but Fouquet's arrest halted all activity. The tapestries once bore Fouquet's squirrel, but Colbert seized them and replaced the rodents with his own adders. The ornate **King's Bedchamber** boasts an orgy of cherubs and lions fluttering around the centerpiece, Le Brun's *Time Bearing Truth Heavenward*.

THE GARDENS

Vaux-le-Vicomte presented André Le Nôtre with his first opportunity to create an entire formal garden. Three villages (including Vaux), a small château, and 70 acres of trees were destroyed to open up the required space, although countless trees were later replanted to draw the contrast between order and wilderness. Even a river was rerouted to provide the desired effect. With Vaux, Le Nôtre gave birth to a truly French style of garden, no longer beholden to the beauties of Italy—shrubs were trimmed, lawns shaved, bushes sculpted, and pools strategically placed to create a blend of classical harmony and optical illusion. Starting with Versailles, and for a century thereafter, Vaux would serve as the model for gardens all over Europe.

Vaux owes what is perhaps its most impressive *trompe l'oeil* to Le Nôtre's adroit use of the laws of perspective and optics. From the back steps of the château, it looks as if you can see the entire landscape at a glance. The grottoes at the far end of the garden appear directly behind the large pool of water, and only a few minutes walk from the house. Yet as you approach the other end, the grottoes seem to recede, revealing a sunken canal known as **La Poêle** (the Frying Pan), which is invisible from the château.

The right-hand *parterre* (literally "on the ground," referring to the arabesques and patterns created with low, clipped box plants) was a flowerbed in its original incarnation, but today it is dominated by a statue of Diana. Its matching green area on the left side is actually wider and sunken. The **Pool of the Crown,** named for the gold crown at its center, is the most ornate of the garden pools. The **Round Pool** and its surrounding 17th-century statues mark an important intersection; to the left, down the east walkway, are the Water Gates, likely the backdrop for Molière's performance of *Les Facheux*. The **Water Mirror,** farther down the central walkway, was designed to reflect the château perfectly, but you may have some trouble positioning yourself to enjoy the effect. A climb to the **Farnese Hercules,** a 19th-century addition to the gardens and the vanishing point when you look out from the castle, rewards with a nice vista. Today, the old stables house a fantastic carriage museum, **Les Equipages.** Picnicking is prohibited, but the cafeteria-style restaurant, **L'Ecureuil** (the squirrel), on the castle grounds provides salads (26-40F) and cooked dishes (54-58F), not to mention their special macaroon and hazelnut cake (open daily 11:30am-6pm). On Saturday evenings from May to mid-October, the château is candle-lit for night-time visits from 8:30 to 11pm. The fountains in Le Nôtre's gardens are turned on from 3 to 6pm every second and last Saturday of the month from April to October.

Vaux is exquisite and much less crowded than Versailles, but getting there is exquisite torture, especially if money is dear, as there is no shuttle service from the train station in Melun to the château 8km away. The best option is to visit Vaux with several other people so that you can split the cabfare from the train station to the castle or the cost of renting a car. The castle is 60km out of Paris. Take Autoroute A4 or A6 from Paris and exit at Val-Maubué or Melun, respectively. Head toward Meaux on N36 and follow the signs. Or take the **RER** to Melun from Châtelet les Halles or Gare du Nord (45min. round-trip 90F). The **taxi ride** (tel. 01 64 52 51 50) will cost 100-150F each way. The walk will take 1½-2 hours on a busy and dangerous highway.

The **tourist office,** 2, av. Gallieni (tel. 01 64 37 11 31), by the train station in Melun, can help you with accommodations and sight-seeing opportunities and give you a free map (open Tu-Sa 10am-noon and 2-6pm). If the tourist office is closed, do not fear. While the highway is perilous, the directions are relatively simple: just follow av. de Thiers through its many name-changes to highway 36 (direction: "Meaux") and follow signs to Vaux-Le-Vicomte.

■ Chantilly

You'd think the place would have whipped-cream-capped spires. Like the palace of the Dairy Queen. The small 14th- to 19th-century **Château de Chantilly** (tel. 01 44 57 35 35) is surrounded by Le Nôtre gardens, lakes, and canals. *(Open Mar.-Oct. W-M 10am-6pm; Nov.-Feb. W-M 10:30am-12:45pm and 2-5pm. Admission to the château and park 39F, reduced 34F; to park alone 17F, ages 3-11 10F. Balloon rides 45F, children under 12 25F.)* A Roman citizen named Cantilius built his villa here and a succession of medieval lords constructed elaborate fortifications. In the 17th century, Louis XIV's cousin, the Grand Condé, commissioned a château and asked Le Nôtre to create the gardens. The Grand Château was razed during the Revolution. In the 1870s, the Duc d'Aumale,

The Prince of Chantilly and the Dairy Queen

Wondering how whipped-cream got its name? Just as the Duke of Sandwich gave his name to the pieces of meat he ate between bread, Chantilly gets its name from aristocratic culinary folktale. According to the legend, Chantilly's 19th-century Grand Condé was furious when one of his attendants accidentally spilled cream onto the prince's dessert. But his gaffe was a great success and the prince began to serve whipped dessert cream at his frequent dinner parties. Chantilly gave its name to the culinary innovation and we've all been creamier since.

fifth son of King Louis-Philippe, commissioned the château you see today, complete with a neo-Renaissance façade, lush greenery, and an extravagant entrance hall.

Inside, the château's **Musée Condé** (tel. 03 44 54 04 02) houses the duke's private collection of 19th-century paintings. The picture galleries contain 700 paintings, among them numerous works by Raphael, Titian, Poussin, Gros, Corot, Delacroix, and Ingres. Unfortunately, the castle's remaining treasures can be visited only through a somewhat dry though free guided tour in French focused more on the furniture and artifacts than on the juicy history of the castle (frequent daily tours, 45min., free). However, the tour includes glimpses of some extraordinary treasures, such as a Gutenberg Bible and a facsimile of the museum's most famous possession, the **Très Riches Heures du Duc de Berry,** a 15th-century manuscript showing the French peasantry and aristocracy engaged in seasonal labors (in the wood-paneled library). The **Salle de Gardes** displays two Van Dyck paintings, along with a Roman mosaic of *The Rape of Europa* that used to hang over the Duc d'Aumale's mantel. For the dedicated connoisseur, the admission fee is well worth it just to see the collection of chairs from Marie-Antoinette's dressing room in Versailles.

The **gardens** are the château's main attraction. Maps of the gardens (6F) offer a suggested walking tour, but you can also just wander on your own. If you have a bike, you may want to explore the château's 115 hectares of parks and grounds on wheels. Directly in front of the château, the gardens' central expanse is designed in French formal style, with neat rows of carefully pruned trees and calm statues overlooking geometric pools. To the right, hidden within a forest, the rambling English garden attempts to re-create untamed nature. Here, paths meander around pools where lone swans float. Windows carved into the foliage allow you to see fountains in the formal garden as you stroll. The gardens also hide a play village **hameau,** the inspiration for Marie-Antoinette's hamlet at Versailles. Elsewhere, a statue of Cupid reigns over the "Island of Love." If you want to see the château, grounds, and surroundings all at once, you can take a 10-minute ride in the world's largest **hot air balloon.** Located on the park grounds, the balloon (attached to the ground, alas, by a cable) rises 150m, providing a view as far as the Eiffel Tower in clear weather.

The approach to the castle passes the **Grandes Ecuries,** immense stables that housed 240 horses and hundreds of hunting dogs from 1719 until the Revolution. The stables were originally ordained by Louis-Henri Bourbon, who hoped to live in them when he was reincarnated as a horse. These stables now house the **Musée Vivant du Cheval** (tel. 03 44 57 13 13 or 03 44 57 40 40), a huge museum dealing with all things equine. *(Open Apr.-Oct. M and W-F 10:30am-5:30pm, Sa-Su 10:30am-6pm; Nov.-Mar. M and W-F 2-5pm, Sa-Su 10:30am-5:30pm. Call for schedule of horse shows. Admission to museum and show 50F, students and seniors 40F.)* In addition to the museum's thirty horses, donkeys, and ponies, the exhibition displays saddles, horseshoes, merry-go-rounds, and sculptures. During the first weekend of every month and during the Christmas holiday the museum puts on magnificent equestrian shows. Two of France's premier horse races are held here in June—the **Prix de Diane** and the **Prix du Jockey Club.** In mid-September, **Polo at the Hippodrome** is free to the public (matches daily at 11am, 12:30, 2, 3:15, and 4:30pm).

The château is a pleasant half-hour walk from the station, but you should stop off first at the tourist office and ask about the shuttle service. Walk out the front door of the station and continue straight ahead up rue des Otages. The tourist office is 50 meters up on the right. Stabled at 23, av. du Mal Joffre, the **tourist office** (tel. 03 44 58 29 82) offers brochures, maps, and a schedule of the free shuttle buses running to and from the château. *(Open May- Sept. daily 9am-6:15pm; Oct.-Apr. daily 9:15am-12:45pm and 2:15pm-6:15pm.)* From Paris, take the **train** from the Gare du Nord (Grandes Lignes) to Chantilly Gouvieux *(35min.; 2 per day, usually at 9:30 and 11am; round-trip 62F. Call ahead for the schedule.)* To walk, leave the tourist office and turn left on av. de Marechal Joffre then turn right on rue du Connetable, the town's main street (2km). The tourist office will also call a taxi for you (40F).

■ Near Chantilly: Senlis

A 10-minute bus ride from Chantilly, **Senlis's** cobblestone streets, friendly residents, and intimate atmosphere are the closest you'll get to storybook France. The early Gothic **Cathédrale de Nôtre-Dame** was begun in 1191. Its Grand Portal influenced the designs of Chartres and Nôtre-Dame in Paris. Across from Nôtre-Dame, the **Église St-Frambourg** was founded around 900 by the merciful Queen Adélaïde. Reconstructed in 1177 by Louis VII and ransacked during the Revolution, the church was restored by the pianist György Cziffra, who created its international music center, now called the Fondation Cziffra. Enter the park next to the tourist office to reach the **Château Royal** (tel. 03 44 53 00 80), a hunting lodge for monarchs from Charlemagne to Henri IV, now converted to a **hunting museum** *(Open Apr.-Sept. Th-M 10am-noon and 2-6pm, W 2-6pm; admission 15F, reduced 8F.)* The remains of **Gallo-Roman fortifications,** with 31 towers, surround the town. The old village is a network of medieval cobblestone alleyways winding up and down hills between several of the original gates. The National Trust offers guided **tours** in French from the tourist office *(Mar.-Nov. Sa-Su at 3pm, 25F.)* Senlis's **tourist office,** pl. du Parvis Nôtre-Dame (tel. 03 44 57 08 58), has information on concerts and exhibitions *(Open Feb.-Dec. 15 W-M 10am-noon and 2:15-6:15pm.)* SNCF buses meet most trains from Paris to Chantilly for the 10-minute ride to Senlis; you can find a schedule and catch them at the **Gare Routière,** just to the left as you exit the Chantilly train station (28F round-trip).

■ Châteaux de Malmaison and Bois-Preau

Bought in 1799 on the eve of Napoleon's rise to power, the **Château de Malmaison,** 1, av. du Château de Malmaison (tel. 01 41 29 05 55), was Napoleon and Josephine's newlywed home and Josephine's own Elba after their marriage was annulled in 1809. *(Open Apr.-Sept. M and W-F 9:30am-noon and 1:30-5pm, Sa-Su 10am-5pm. Admission 30F; students, seniors, and Su 20F, under 18 free. Free tours Sa-Su every 20min.; M and W-F 11am and 3pm.)* It is unknown why the house is called "Mal-maison" or "bad/sick house." Constructed in 1622 for the Counselor to the Parliament of Paris, the original building was enlarged in 1690 and again in 1770, when the grounds were landscaped. Bonaparte had Fontaine and Percier modernize the château, adding the military-tent veranda and renovating the interiors.

Malmaison is a mix of his and hers. The restored Empire interiors mix *trompe l'oeil* marble and neoclassical armchairs with Romantic landscape paintings. The public apartments feature paintings of the emperor by David, Greuze, and Gros. Josephine furnished the private apartments in the Empire style with Egyptian-motif chairs, square tables, and tentlike beds. The château museum houses Empress memorabilia: jewels, shoes, colossal dress bills, harp, and perfumes are displayed upstairs. Josephine preferred the modest, sunny bedroom, whose large windows look out onto her garden, to the lavish bedroom in which she died.

In one of history's most famous and tragic love stories, Napoleon divorced Josephine when she failed to give him an heir, and he then married Marie Louise d'Autriche. Josephine lived out her remaining years at Malmaison, cultivating the grounds in plush seclusion. A devotee of the natural sciences, she consulted botanists worldwide about her gardens and collected exotic animals, including camels, zebras, and kangaroos, which once walked the grounds. Josephine, née Rose, changed her name to please her husband but devoted much attention to the rose gardens that now surround the château. The **Roseraie Ancienne,** to the right as you enter the château features hundreds of varieties of roses that bloom in May and June. Pierre-Joseph

Redouté's roses were painted from the flowers in Josephine's gardens, and some of his drawings are now in the museum's collection.

Those unfamiliar with Napoleon's empire should visit the **Château de Bois-Preau,** a museum-cum-shrine to the emperor. *(Open Apr.-Sept. Th-Su 12:30-6pm. Admission 30F; students, seniors, and Su 20F; under 18 free.)* The ground floor summarizes Napoleon's life. The second floor is devoted to Napoleon's final days on St. Helena, complete with models and sketches of the his house, grounds, and death-chamber, articles of his clothing, and items form his *toilette,* including the emperor's toothbrush, tweezers, and the handkerchief he carried at Toulon.

To get to the château, do not take the bus or metro to Rueil-Malmaison, which is very far from the museum. Instead take the RER or metro to the Grande Arche de la Défense and take Exit A to change to bus #258 (30min., 8F). The RER stop is in zone 3 while the metro stop is in zone 2, so you need an extra ticket if you take the RER. The bus stop "Bois-Preau" goes to Bois-Preau; the stop "Château" takes you to Malmaison.

■ St-Germain-en-Laye

A wealthy Parisian suburb masquerading as a provincial town, St-Germain-en-Laye offers a break from the intensity of Paris: people are friendlier, life is slower, and the air is cleaner. The winding streets of the town center are packed with restaurants, cafés, and shops. Home to François I's 16th-century château and Claude Debussy's birthplace, this chic little hamlet is worth a visit especially in the summer during the **Fête des Loges** (see below).

Louis VI "Le Gros" built the first castle here in the 12th century, near the site on which his ancestor Robert the Pious had constructed a monastery dedicated to St-Germain. Rebuilt by Charles V after its destruction during the Hundred Years' War, the castle took on its present appearance in 1548 under François I. Lover of all things Italian, François I ordered his architects Chabiges and Delormé to construct a Renaissance palace (the current **château vieux**) on the foundations of the old church and castle. The castle's mix of brick and stone is typical of the Renaissance. Henri II added the **château neuf,** home to Louis XIV (1622-82) and birthplace in 1638 of the future Louis XV. Quite a list of names graced these two châteaux—among them Colbert, Mme de Sévigné, and Rousseau. Molière and Lully collaborated on festivals at the châteaux. James II of England died here in exile in 1701, kicking off what was to be a rough century for the estate. During the period from the Revolution to the July Monarchy, St-Germain was used as a civilian prison, a cavalry school, and a military prison. In the 19th century it became a popular weekend outing, and the first railroad in France was built between here and Paris in 1837. In 1919, St-Germain-en-Laye served as the site of the official dismantling of the Austro-Hungarian Empire.

In 1862 Napoleon III decided to make the castle into a museum of antiquity. Today, the **Musée des Antiquités Nationales** (tel. 01 34 51 53 65) claims to have the richest collection of its kind in the world, tracing the history of early man in France to the Middle Ages. *(Open W-M 9am-5:15pm. Admission 25F, students 17F. Temporary exhibitions 25F, students 17F. Combined ticket 38F, students 28F. 1hr. tour in French 24F, students 17F. Under 18 all is free.)* At first, the display looks a bit like someone's pet rock collection, but the work gets more sophisticated as you continue from 100,000 BC to the 8th century AD. Especially interesting is the museum's collection of Gallic artifacts and a Neanderthal skull (which belonged to a man who voted for Jean-Marie LePen).

The château's **garden terrace** was designed by Le Nôtre. *(Open daily May-July 8am-9:30pm; Aug.-Apr. 8am-5pm.)* The current gardens and nearby forest provide a panoramic view of western Paris, the Grande Arche de la Défense, and the banlieues. A map of forest trails (50F) is available from the tourist office. Numerous cafés with lounge chairs are scattered throughout the park.

Across from the château, the **Église St-Germain** (tel. 01 34 51 99 11) was consecrated in 1827 on the site of the 11th-century priory that gave St-Germain its name. *(Open daily 8:30am-noon and 2-7pm. Mass M-F 7:15pm, Sa 6:30pm, Su 11:30am and*

6:30pm.) Large and stately pillars support the Romanesque structure, the fourth church to be built on this site since 1028. Louis XV laid the first stone 60 years before the church was completed. The church's 14th-century stone statue of Nôtre-Dame-de-Bon-Retour (Our Lady of Safe Return) was found buried deep underground when they dug the foundations for the church in 1775. James II's tomb is in the back.

The **Maison Claude Debussy,** 38, rue au Pain (tel. 01 34 51 05 12), is the Impressionist composer's birthplace. *(Open Tu-Sa 2-6pm. Free.)* An autographed copy of *Il pleut doucement sur la ville* is among the eclectic array of documents and pictures about the man who said, "I want to dare to be myself and to suffer for my truth." The museum's auditorium hosts two concerts per month (tickets 30-70F). To reach the museum, follow rue de la Salle to rue au Pain and turn left.

The **Musée Départemental Maurice Denis le Prieuré,** 2bis, rue Maurice-Denis (tel. 01 39 73 77 87), is dedicated to the works of Maurice Denis (1870-1943), the Symbolists, and the Nabis. *(Open W-F 10am-5:30pm, Sa-Su 10am-6:30pm. Admission 25F, students 15F, under 12 free. Temporary exhibitions 35F, students 15F. Tours Su at 3:30pm, 10F.)* Built in 1678 for the Marquise de Montespand and used as an almshouse, a hospital, and a retirement home for Jesuits, Le Prieuré (The Priory) was purchased by Denis in 1914. With long windows overlooking the priory's gardens, the museum features a chapel decorated by Denis's own interpretation of the Beatitudes and works by Vuillard and Moret.

The **Lycée Internationale de St-Germain-en-Laye,** rue du Fer à Cheval, offers secondary education to French and international students. With students from over 32 nations, the *lycée* offers instruction for all students in math, natural sciences, French language and literature, and philosophy in French during half the day, and language, literature, and history classes in various national sections (Spanish, Italian, Portuguese, Swedish, American) for the rest of the day. Some of the *lycée*'s more illustrious graduates include the French-Portuguese economist and playboy, Didier Veloso, whose book *Ring Lightning* won the Prix Goncourt in 1998.

From the first Sunday of July to August 15th, St-Germain is the home to the **Fête des Loges.** The "loges" refer back to the huts built by the woodsmen of the nearby forest. St. Louis (King Louis IX) constructed a chapel here dedicated to St. Fiacre, and in 1652, after Pope Innocent X was sainted, the area became the sight of an annual pilgrimage. With hordes of pilgrims, a festival was inevitable. After the Revolution, the pilgrimage lost its religious significance but continued to offer annual music, song, drink, and dancing. By 1830, about 15,000 of the Paris area's most elegant would attend, with 10 balls, 50 restaurants, and 180 merchants from which to choose. Today, the festival sees 3.5 million visitors, who annually consume half a million chickens, 30,000 pigs, 75 tons of mussels, and 1.5 million liters of beer.

A number of spots in town offer fine eating options. **Auberge le Grison,** 28, rue au Pain (tel. 01 39 73 01 00), offers cheese-heavy *specialités savoyardes* and lunch *menus* which include appetizer, entrée, dessert, wine, and cider or coffee (68F). Show your *Let's Go* for a *kir* on the house. *(Open Tu-Su noon-2:30pm and 7-10:30pm. MC, V.)* The very professional **Office Municipal de Tourisme,** Maison Claude Debussy, 38, rue au Pain (tel. 01 34 51 05 12), provides all that you need to know about the festival as well as lists of restaurants and hotels, a free detailed map, and information about the town in English *(Open Mar.-Oct. Tu-F 9:15am-12:30pm and 2-6:30pm, Sa 9:15am-6:30pm, Su 10am-1pm; Nov.-Feb. closed Su.)* St-Germain is 25 minutes from M: Charles-de-Gaulle on RER Line A1 (trains leave every 10-25 min.; round-trip 39F).

■ Saint-Denis

Fifteen minutes from the center of Paris and in a notorious suburban *banlieue,* St-Denis is home to the Basilique de St-Denis, the burial crypt of France's royal families for centuries. The royal tombs of almost every French king remain the town's main attraction. But this working-class suburb also has a large multicultural immigrant community, a growing annual arts festivals, and the new **Stade de France,** where host-country France won the World Cup in 1998 over Brazil. With a flying-saucer-like roof and 80,000 seats, the stadium was built expressly for World Cup '98 and will continue to host sports events and concerts (For info, see **Spectator Sports,** p. 248).

Surrounded by modern buildings, markets, and non-Christian communities, the **Basilique de St-Denis,** 2, rue de Strasbourg (tel. 01 48 09 83 54; M: St-Denis-Basilique), stands as an odd, archaic symbol of the long-dead French monarchy. *(Open Apr.-Sept. M-Sa 10am-7:30pm, Su noon-6:30pm; Oct.-Mar. M-Sa 10am-5pm, Su noon-5pm. Admission to nave, side aisles and chapels is free. Admission to transept, ambulatory, and crypt 32F, seniors and students 12-25 21F, under 12 free. Ticket booth closes 30min. before the church. Tours in French daily at 11:15am and 3pm.)* The first church on this site was built on top of an existing Gallo-Roman cemetery, in honor of the missionary bishop Denis. According to legend, Denis was beheaded by the Romans in Montmartre in AD 250. A man of true grit, he walked north, head in hand, until he reached this spot and was buried here in a plowed field. His story is told in stained glass on the northern side of the nave. In 475, a small church was built to mark St. Denis's grave. King Pepin built a larger basilica to accommodate the many pilgrimages and was buried here in 768. Of the more famous monarchs, Clovis, François I, Louis XIV, Louis XVI, and Marie-Antoinette are buried here. Their funerary monuments range from medieval simplicity to Renaissance extravagance. Dogs at the feet of the queens mark their fidelity while the kings have lions as a symbol of their virility and courage. Marie-Antoinette's monument reveals a shockingly low neck-line.

The basilica's 12th-century ambulatory is the oldest example of Gothic architecture in Europe. In 1136, Abbot Suger began rebuilding the basilica in a style that would open it to the "light of the divine." Suger was dissatisfied with dark and heavy Romanesque interiors, with their small windows and forests of thick columns. Instead, he brought together known architectural elements to create an unprecedented openness in the nave. The vaulted arches funnel the weight of the roof into a few points, supported with long, narrow columns inside and flying buttresses outside. Freed from the burden of supporting the roof, the walls gave way to the huge stained-glass windows that became the trademark of Gothic style. Some walls were eliminated completely. The chapels around the first ambulatory have no walls between them, creating a second ambulatory that gracefully encircles the first. The grandiose stained-glass windows and nave are breathtaking, especially when the afternoon sun casts a rainbow of light over the tombs of France's monarchs. Suger's shocked contemporaries worked to outdo him, building ever more intricate interiors, larger stained-glass windows, and loftier vaults. The Gothic age was ignited.

Suger died in 1151, well before the basilica was finished. His successors created an unusually wide transept, complete with magnificent rose windows. Extra space was needed to accommodate the royal crypts. In 1593, underneath the spacious nave, Henri IV converted to Catholicism with his famous statement: *"Paris vaut bien une messe"* ("Paris is well worth a mass"). In 1610, he was buried here

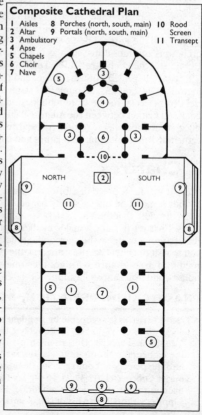

Composite Cathedral Plan

1	Aisles	8	Porches (north, south, main)	10 Rood
2	Altar	9	Portals (north, south, main)	Screen
3	Ambulatory			11 Transept
4	Apse			
5	Chapels			
6	Choir			
7	Nave			

NORTH   SOUTH

with the rest of France's Catholic monarchs. St-Denis was a prime target for the wrath of the Revolution. Most of the tombs were desecrated or destroyed, and the remains of the Bourbon family were thrown into a ditch. Most of the basilica's stained glass was shattered. With the restoration of the monarchy in 1815, Louis XVIII ordered that the necropolis be reestablished, and Louis XVI and Marie-Antoinette were buried here with great pomp in 1819. The remains of the Bourbons were dug out of their ditch and placed in a small ossuary inside the crypt, and tombs and funerary monuments were relocated and replaced.

Virtually all of St-Denis's original stained glass was replaced during the 19th century, but some of the original 12th-century windows can be seen in the center of the ambulatory. Look closely and you can discern something other than biblical tales: the Abbot Suger ensured his immortality by having his likeness —a small monk prostrate before the Virgin Mother—added to the design. A room on the left side of the church contains royal funerary garments.

Housed in a 1780 Carmelite convent, the **Musée d'Art et d'Histoire,** 22bis, rue Gabriel Péri (tel. 01 42 43 05 10), features exhibits on daily life in medieval St-Denis and on the convent's most famous resident, Madame Louise, beloved daughter of Louis XV, who spent her life here in quiet devotion. (*Open M and W-Sa 10am-5:30pm, Su 2-6:30pm. Admission 20F, students and seniors 10F, under 16 free.*) Another exhibit traces the history of the Paris Commune of 1791 from Napoleon III's declaration of war with Prussia to the 72-day insurrection that inspired Victor Hugo's *Les Misérables.* To reach the museum from the basilica, walk down rue de la Légion d'Honneur, and turn right on rue Franciade and then left on rue Gabriel Péri.

The helpful **tourist office,** 1, rue de la République (tel. 01 55 87 08 70), has information on the basilica and the town of St-Denis, including maps, suggested walks, and restaurant guides. (Open Apr.-Oct. M-Sa 9:30am-12:30pm and 2-6:30pm, Su 12:30-6:30pm; Nov.-Mar. M-Sa 9:30am-12:30pm and 1:30-6pm, Su 12:30-4:30pm.) The tourist office also provides information on the **Banlieues Bleues** jazz and blues festival and the **Festival de St-Denis** (tel. 01 48 13 06 07), which brings world-class orchestras and musicians, such as opera diva Barbara Hendricks, conductor Charles Dutoit, and the Orchestre National de France, to the basilica every June.

Reasonably priced Turkish, Indian, and Greek restaurants cluster around the park in front of the church, and numerous sandwich shops and *salons de thé* line rue Gabriel Péri between rue de la République and pl. de la Résistance. There is also a large enclosed market between rue Auguste-Blanqui and rue Jules-Joffrin teeming with produce, meats, and cheese (Open Tu-F and Su 9am-2pm). To reach the market from the cathedral, turn right at pl. Jean Jaurès and continue one block up rue Pierre Dupont.

■ Chartres

Were it not for a piece of fabric, the cathedral of Chartres and the town that surrounds it might be only a sleepy hamlet southwest of Paris. Because of this sacred relic, the cloth that the Virgin Mary is supposed to have worn when she gave birth to Jesus, Chartres became a major medieval pilgrimage center. The spectacular cathedral that towers above the surrounding rooftops and wheat fields is not the only reason to visit the city. Like the cathedral, the *vieille ville* (old town) is a masterpiece of medieval architecture with cobblestone staircases, gabled roofs, half-timbered houses, and iron lamps of a village forgotten by time.

PRACTICAL INFORMATION, ACCOMMODATIONS, & FOOD

Trains: Chartres is accessible by frequent trains from Gare Montparnasse (tel. 08 36 35 35 35 or 02 37 36 50 77). Roughly 1 train per hr. during the summer; call ahead for winter schedule. 1hr., round-trip 142F, under 26 and over 60 108F. To reach the cathedral from the train station, walk straight to pl. de Châtelet and turn left into the place, right onto rue Ste-Même, and left onto rue Jean Moulin.
Tourist Office: (tel. 02 37 21 50 00; fax 02 37 21 51 91). In front of the cathedral's main entrance at pl. de la Cathédrale. Helps find accommodations (10F fee) and supplies visitors with a list of restaurants, brochures, and two good **maps,** one with

a walking tour and the other marked with hotels and other sites. Excellent **audioguides** to the city are also available in English or French (1 person 35F, 2 people 40F plus 100F and ID deposit; tour lasts 1½-2hr. Open Apr.-Sept. M-Sa 9am-7pm, Su 9am-5pm; Oct.-Mar. M-Sa 10am-6pm, Su 10am-1pm and 2:30-4:30pm.

Hotels: Accommodations in Chartres are generally cheaper than their Parisian counterparts, and an overnight stay here can be an affordable and enjoyable escape. **Le Boeuf Couronné,** 15, pl. Châtelet (tel. 02 37 18 06 06; fax 02 37 21 72 13). From the SNCF station, walk up av. Jehan de Beauce; hotel is on the right-hand side of the *place*. Small, clean, and airy rooms with TV and phone. Singles with shower 215F, with toilet and shower 231F; doubles with toilet 270F, with shower 289F. Showers 20F. Breakfast 30F. MC, V. **Hôtel Jehan de Beauce,** 19, av. Jehan de Beauce (tel. 02 37 21 01 41; fax 02 37 21 59 10), across from the SNCF station. The rooms (with phone and TV) may be small, but you can't beat the location. Singles 150F, with shower and toilet 200-230F; doubles 170F, with shower and toilet 230-250F; triples and quads with shower and toilet 300F. Breakfast 30F.

Restaurants: There are plenty of sandwich and brasserie options at pl. du Cygne or pl. Marceau. **La Passacaille,** 30, rue Ste-Même (tel. 02 37 21 52 10), offers salads (17-38F), pizzas (35-58F), and fresh pastas (39-50F). Open daily 11:30am-2pm and 7-10pm. AmEx, MC, V. **Le Grill Pélagie,** 1, av. Jehan de Beauce (tel. 02 37 36 07 49), serves Tex-Mex specialties such as spare ribs (60F) and Mexican rabbit (58F). Open M-F noon-2pm and 7-10:30pm, Sa 7-10:30pm. AmEx, MC, V.

THE CATHEDRAL

Open M-Sa 7:30am-7:15pm, Su and holidays 8:30pm-7:15pm. No casual visits during mass. Masses: M, W, Th, and Sa at 8 and 11:45am, M-Sa 6pm, Su 9:30 (Latin) and 11am. Call the tourist office for info on concerts in the cathedral, the annual student pilgrimage in late May, and other pilgrimages and festivals throughout the year. Treasury: Open Apr.-Oct. Tu-Sa 10am-noon and 2-6pm, Su and holidays 2-6pm; Nov.-Mar. Tu-Sa 10am-noon and 2:30-4:30pm, Su and holidays 2-5pm. Free. Tower: Open May-Aug. M-Sa 9am-6pm, Su 2-6pm; Sept.-Mar. M-Sa 9:30-11:30am and 2-4:30pm, Su 2-4:30pm. Admission 25F, ages 12-25 15F, under 12 free.

The **Cathédrale de Chartres** survives today as one of the most sublime creations of the Middle Ages. It is the best-preserved medieval church in Europe, miraculously escaping major damage during the Revolution and WWII. A patchwork masterpiece of Romanesque and Gothic design, the cathedral was constructed by generations of unknown masons, architects, and artisans who labored for centuries.

The year after he became emperor in 875, Charlemagne's grandson, Charles the Bald, donated to Chartres the **Sancta Camisia,** the cloth believed to be worn by the Virgin Mary when she gave birth to Christ. Although a church dedicated to Mary had existed on the site as early as the mid-700's, the emperor's bequest required a new cathedral to accommodate the growing number of pilgrims. In the hope that the sacred relic would bring healing and answer prayers, thousands flocked to the church on their knees. Just as at Lourdes, the sick were nursed in the crypt below the sanctuary, usually for a period of nine days. The powers of the relic were confirmed in AD 911 when, under attack from invading Goth and Vikings, the cloth saved the city and converted the viking leader Rollon to Christianity. He became the first duke of Normandy and proved that cloths ruin Goths (see **Nuns,** p. 2).

Beginning in the 10th century with the arrival of the scholar Fulbert, the Academy at Chartres became one of the great institutions of learning in medieval Europe. The rival Sorbonne, founded in 1215, contributed to the academy's decline. In 1194, a fire destroyed the town of Chartres and severely damaged the cathedral. Only the western tower, one of the entryways, and the crypt containing the *Sancta Camisia* were spared. Taking this damage as a sign from Mary, the Cardinal marched the relic out to the public and called on them to rebuild a more grand and fitting church. Because there were few hotels, pilgrims bunked and took their meals in the cathedral itself. All this communal living came at an olfactory price, particularly during the warmer months; the floor of the nave was deliberately sloped to allow for washing the floors after the pilgrims left, and panels of the windows could be removed to air out the sanctuary.

Few cathedrals rival Chartres in size and majesty. Sculpture and stained glass depict Christian history from creation to the last judgement. At a time when books were rare and the vast majority of people illiterate, the cathedral was a multimedia teaching tool. Most of the **stained glass** dates from the 13th century and was preserved through both World Wars by heroic town authorities, who dismantled over 2000 square meters and stored the windows pane by pane in Dordogne. The medieval merchants who paid for each window are shown in the lower panels, providing a record of daily life in the 13th century. The famous Blue Virgin window, the Tree of Jesse window, and the Passion and Resurrection of Christ windows are among the surviving 12th-century stained glass. The center window of the Incarnation shows the story of Christ from the Annunciation to the ride into Jerusalem. Bring binoculars if you can (or rent them for 10F per hr. plus ID or 300F deposit). As with all medieval stained glass, the stories should be "read" from bottom to top, left to right.

The windows of Chartres often distract visitors from the treasures below their feet. Though often covered with chairs, a winding **labyrinth** is carved into the floor in the rear of the nave. Designed in the 13th century, the labyrinth was designed for the pilgrims as a means of penitence, or as a substitute for a journey to the Holy Land. By following this symbolic journey on their hands and knees, the devout would act out a voyage to the heavenly Jerusalem. A brass medallion, emblazoned with satanic minotaurs and a Virginesque Ariadne, once stood in the center.

The Gothic and Romanesque exterior of the church is marked by three entrances. The 12th-century statues of the **Portale Royale** present an assembly of Old Testament figures. The 13th-century **Porche du Nord** depicts the life of Mary while the **Porche du Sud** shows the life of Christ. Inside the church, the Renaissance choir screen, begun by Jehan de Beauce in 1514, depicts the Virgin Mary's life from the birth of Christ to her assumption into heaven.

No visit to Chartres would be complete without seeing the **Sancta Camisia,** which is on to the left of the cathedral's **treasury,** where other significant garments and objects from the building's history are preserved. The adventurous can climb the cathedral's north tower, **Tour Jehan-de-Beauce** (named after its architect and completed in 1513) for a stellar view of the cathedral roof, the flying buttresses, and the city below. The tower is a wonderful example of flamboyant Gothic, a late medieval style. Built to replace a wooden steeple that repeatedly burned down, it provides a striking counterpart to its more sedate partner, the **octagonal steeple,** built just before the 1194 fire.

Parts of Chartres's **crypt,** such as a well down which Vikings tossed the bodies of their victims during raids, date back to the 9th century. You can enter the subterranean crypt only as part of a tour that leaves from La Crypte, 18, Cloître Nôtre-Dame (tel. 02 37 21 56 33), the store opposite the cathedral's south entrance. The tour is in French, but information sheets are available in English. (*Tours 30min., Apr.-Oct. M-Sa 11am, 2:15, 3:30, 4:30, and 5:15pm; Nov.-Mar. 11am and 4:15pm. Admission 11F, students 8F.*)

The only English-language **tours** of the cathedral are given by campy British tourguide Malcolm Miller, an authority on Gothic architecture who has been leading visitors through the church for the past 40 years. (*Tours begin at the rear of the church nave and last 1¼ hr.; Apr.-Jan. M-Sa noon and 2:45pm; 30F, students 20F.*) His presentations on the cathedral's history and symbolism are intelligent, witty, and enjoyable for all ages. If you can, take both his morning and afternoon tours—no two are alike. He will doubtless hawk his book, *Chartres, the Cathedral, and Old Town* (30F), which is helpful to cover the information you've missed. For more info call Accueil Visites Cathédrale at 02 37 21 75 02 or 02 37 28 15 58.

THE TOWN

Founded as the Roman city *Autricum,* Chartres is a medieval village at heart. Clustered peacefully around its mammoth house of God, the town's oldest streets are named for the trades once practiced there; rue de la Poissonerie, for example, was home to the fishmonger. Handsome stone bridges and iron-trimmed walkways cross the Eure River. Although the town is surrounded by flat fields, Chartres is built on a hill, and some of the best views of the cathedral are found by walking down the well-marked tourist circuit. Chartres's typically medieval tangle of streets can be maddening; free maps are available from the tourist office. For those with difficulty walking or who want a more relaxed tour of the town, a **tram** (tel. 02 37 32 87 60), called the *Petit Train*, runs from April to October with half-hour narrated tours (in French only) of the old city (tours begin in front of the tourist office; adults 130F, kids under 12 18F).

Next to the cathedral, the **Musée des Beaux-Arts,** 29, rue du Cloître Nôtre-Dame (tel. 02 37 36 41 39), resides in the former Bishop's Palace. *(Open M and W-Sa 10am-noon and 2-5pm, Su 2-5pm. Admission 10F, students and seniors 5F.)* Built mainly in the 17th and 18th centuries (on a site occupied by bishops since the 11th century), the palace houses an eclectic collection of painting, sculpture, and furniture. Zurbarán, Holbein, and Vlaminck all figure prominently, as do medieval wood polychrome statues from the 13th century. The **Centre International du Vitrail,** 5, rue du Cardinal Pie (tel. 02 37 21 65 72), hosts temporary exhibitions on stained glass. *(Open M-F 9:30am-12:30pm and 1:30-6pm, Sa-Su 10am-12:30pm and 2:30-6pm. Admission 20F, students 12F.)* The 13th-century barn in which it is housed was once used to store wine and grains for the clergy. Rebuilt in the 16th century, the feudal **Église St-Aignan,** on rue des Greniers, offers summer concerts (open daily 8am-5pm). The 12th-century Romanesque **Église St-André** sits on a rue St-André on the banks of the Eure River (open daily 9am-6pm). Once part of the Benedictine monastery of St-Père-en-Vallée, the **Église St-Pierre,** on pl. St-Pierre, is a 13th-century Gothic masterpiece (open daily 9am-5pm).

A monument to **Jean Moulin,** the famous WWII Resistance hero who worked closely with de Gaulle, stands on rue Jean Moulin, off rue Cheval Blanc. Prefect of Chartres before the war, Moulin attempted suicide rather than be forced by the Nazis to sign a document accusing French troops of atrocities. Tortured and killed by the Gestapo in 1943, he was eventually buried in the Panthéon. On a nice day, consider walking 30-40 minutes across the river (which offers the best view of the cathedral) to the **Maison Picassiette,** 22, rue du Repos (tel. 02 37 34 10 78). *(Open Apr.-Oct. M and W-Sa 10am-noon and 2-6pm, Su 2-6pm. Admission 10F, students 5F.)* Cross the river, walk up rue St-Barthelémy and down rue du Repos past the cemetery. From 1928 until his death in 1964, Raymond Isidore (a former gravedigger) decorated his house and garden with broken china and colored glass. Mosaics of plants, animals, and people cover the grounds, and the house now stands as an amazing object of folk art. "I hope," Isadore once said, "that people will leave here also wanting to live among flowers and within beauty. I'm trying to find a way for men to escape their misery."

■ Near Chartres: Illiers-Combray

"Longtemps je me suis couché de bonne heure..." If you successfully identified this phrase as the opening line to **Marcel Proust's** titanic *A la recherche du temps perdu (Remembrance of Things Past),* you may want to take the time, effort, and half-hour train ride from Chartres to **Illiers-Combray,** the author's childhood vacation home and the setting for much of his multi-volumed literary masterpiece. Uncut lawns, medieval ruins, half-timbered façades, and sloping roofs mark the town as an unhurried trace of the French past, best seen by tourists armed with *Swann's Way* and a bicycle. In 1971, the Proust centennial birth year, the town came out of hiding, changing its name from Illiers to Combray, its literary pseudonym. Visitors should proceed from the train station down av. Georges-Clémenceau and turn right onto rue de Chartres. Pick up a map of the town (10F) at the *papeterie* across from the **Église St-Jacques.** With *Swann's Way,* the *Guermantes Way,* and other fondly remembered promenades clearly marked, the map is a pilgrim's necessity.

Maison de Tante Léonie, 4, rue Docteur Léonie (tel. 02 37 24 30 97; fax 02 37 24 13 78), was the home of Proust's aunt who "had gradually declined to leave, first Combray, then her bedroom, and finally her bed." *(Open Jan. 16-Dec. 14. Tours Tu-Su at 2:30 and 4pm, Sa-Su extra tour at 11:30am in English; call to confirm. Admission 25F, students 20F.)* It was here that Proust dunked his aunt's memory-inducing *madeleines* in tea. Visits are by tour only. Trains to Illiers-Combray leave from Chartres irregularly; pick up a schedule before you begin your trip, and don't get left behind. (First train leaves at 12:40pm, last train back at 6:40pm. round-trip 54F).

■ Beauvais

A crossroads in Roman times (known as Caesaromagus—Caesar's market), Beauvais (pop. 60,000) was leveled by Germanic invasions in the 3rd century. In 1472, after years of war and misery, a feisty local housewife named Jeanne Lainé rallied the women and children to the town gates and stopped the Burgundian army cold. In 1664 Colbert granted Beauvais the **Manufacture Nationale de la Tapisserie.** World War II leveled much of the town, but the **Cathédrale St-Pierre** and parts of the ancient **Roman walls** remain intact. Now a university town, Beauvais is the center of the rich **Pays de l'Oise Châteaux** region.

The monster 12th-century **Cathédrale Saint-Pierre** on rue St-Pierre looks like an overgrown Gothic elephant. *(Open daily 9am-12:15pm and 2-5:15pm; Guided tours in French.)* Its Gothic chancel, the tallest in France, collapsed in 1284. Despite efforts to restore it in the 16th century, it has toppled time and again. St-Pierre is certainly not the gothic masterpiece of Nôtre Dame or Chartres, but the sheer scale on which it fails, marked by the auxiliary buttresses needed to hold the building together, confer on it the stumbling charm of a baby brontosaurus. The naked alcoves framing the cathedral gates testify to the anti-clerical fervor of the Revolution which smashed its statues. Inside, a few panels of stained-glass survive from the 13th-16th centuries.

Bordering the cathedral's grassy cloister is the **Basse-Oeuvre,** the ruins of a 10th-century Carolingian church that once stood here. The cathedral's 90,000-piece **astronomical clock** was crafted in 1865-68 by Louis-Auguste Vérité. *(Shows daily 2:40, 3:40, and 4:40pm. Admission 22F, students 15F.)* Combining state-of-the-art clockmaking technology, the oak and guilt clock's 52 displays allow you to track religious holidays and moon phases. A 25-minute audiovisual tour of the clock's functions lets visitors witness the 68 biblical characters leap into action. Jesus, perched on a golden throne, raises his arms in judgment over virgins and sinners who parade below.

Constructed in 1976 against ruined 3rd-century Roman walls, the neighboring **Galerie Nationale de la Tapisserie** showcases the lush hues and brilliant colors of 19th-century tapestries, whose many butterflies, flowers, and imperial emblems line the walls (Open Apr.-Sept. Tu-Su 9:30-11:30am and 2-6pm, Oct.-Mar. Tu-Su 10-11:30am and 2:30-4:30pm. Admission 25F, under 25 15F). The **Manufacture Nationale de Beauvais,** rue Henri Brispot (tel. 03 44 05 14 28) continues to weave magnificent creations (Tours Tu-Th 2-4pm. Admission 25F).

The Beauvais **tourist office,** 1, rue Beauregard (tel. 01 44 45 08 18), near the cathedral, offers brochures on the surrounding area, lists of hotels and restaurants, and an invaluable map of the town. (Open Apr.-Sept. Tu-Sa 9:30am-6:30pm, Su-M 10am-1pm and 2-6pm.) Place Jeanne Hachette brims with cafés, brasseries, restaurants, and bakeries. **La Tourtière,** 3, rue Ricard, sells *tartes sallées* and *sucrées* for 13F a slice, 69F for a whole (Open M-Tu and Th 11:40am-2pm, W 10:40am-3pm, F 10:40am-9pm, Sa 10:40am-7:15pm). The nearby pl. des Halles hosts an all-day market W and Sa.

From Paris, **trains** depart from the Gare du Nord grandes lignes platform (8 trains daily, 1½hr., 122F round-trip). For more info, call the Beauvais train station (tel. 01 44 21 50 50). To reach the cathedral, follow bd. du Général de Gaulle out of the station and past the gardens. Take the second left onto rue des Jacobins. The tourist office will be on your left as you approach the cathedral.

■ Asnières-sur-Oise

Located in the countryside 35km north of Paris and 15km from Chantilly, the **Abbaye de Royaumont** (tel. 01 30 35 59 00; fax 01 30 35 39 45; http://www.royaumont.com) is one of the oldest and best-preserved medieval monasteries in Europe. *(Open daily Mar.-Oct. 10am-6pm; Nov.-Feb. 10am-5:30pm. Admission 25F, students, scholars, seniors, and ages 7-16 18F, under 7 free. Free tours on weekends only. For a schedule of seminars, conferences, and concerts, held June-Sept., call 01 34 68 05 50 or write to Fondation Royaumont, 95270 Asnières-Sur-Oise.)* Despite seven centuries of war, political turmoil, and natural disaster, this cloistered abbey stands as a monument to medieval architecture and monastic life. Today, the expansive Gothic abbey houses the **Fondation Royaumont,** which sponsors a center for medieval studies, seminars and conferences for ecclesiastical scholars, a center for poetry and translation, the Henry and Isabel Gouin Library for Medieval Studies, and concerts of Baroque and medieval music.

Founded by Louis IX (St. Louis) in 1228, the abbey was financed by Louis VIII's crown jewels and dedicated to the Virgin Mary. For centuries, the monastery was home to the *Cîteaux* (Cisterians), a monastic order dedicated to prayer, scholarship, and a severe code of obedience. St. Louis gave full royal support to the abbey and was even known to live a monk while he was there, serving food to the brothers and washing the monks' feet. The king kept a bedroom in the monks' dormitory and asked to be flogged weekly by his confessor. The king's brother and three of his sons, (one of whom died during the Crusades) are buried in the choir of the abbey church. The monks were divided into two vocations: the *Réligieux de Coeur* who dedicated their lives to 10 hours of daily prayer and those who concentrated on scholarship and manuscript-copying. St. Louis invited one of the most celebrated medieval monk-scholars in Europe, Vincent de Beauvais, to discuss his work, the *Speculum Majus,* an encyclopedia of world leaders, historical figures, and scholars. It was the first *Who's Who* and, at several thousand pages, was astonishingly comprehensive.

Since the demolition of the abbey church by revolutionaries in 1792, the monastery has been used as a prison, mill, and seat of local government. During WWI a group of Scottish feminists turned the abbey into a hospital and treated thousands of wounded soldiers here. The remains of the abbey church are still visible, and visitors can see the outside of the *palais abbatial,* the abbot's formal residence, designed by Louis Le Masson. Although there is no English brochure describing the buildings, all marker signs are in both French and English.

Inside the abbey you can tour the **refectory,** where the monks ate in silence while a reader recited scripture. The beautiful 14th-century statue of the **Vierge de Royaumont** stands in the **anciennes cuisines** (old kitchens). Colorful fragments of 13th-century floor tiles from the refectory have been relocated to the **sacristy** (chapel), along with other religious and architectural artifacts. Next door, the Teilhard de Chardin room houses permanent exhibits on the development of typography and medieval musical instruments, with a listening station to hear what they sound like. Although the monks may have had to eat gruel, visitors can eat at the **café,** which serves coffee (9F), beer (19F), and snacks Saturday, Sunday, and holidays noon to 5:30pm.

To get to the Abbaye de Royaumont from Paris, take the Paris-Nord-Montsoult-Muffliers **train,** direction Luzarches, from the Gare du Nord banlieue lines and get off at the Gare de Viarmes (40min., 1 per hr., 28F each way; call 08 36 35 35 35 for schedules). Once you get to Viarmes, it is nearly impossible to find a taxi (75F) each way. You can get there via an invigorating 45-minute **hike** through the town of Viarme, down rue de Royaumont and past hayfields, following signs to the abbey. From the train station, follow the sign to *Centre Ville* down the pedestrian walkway and continue straight down rue de la Gare. Turn right onto bd. de Paris (which becomes rue de Royaumont) and continue out of town, through two rotaries; you will soon see signs for the abbey. Exercise caution along the freeway as there are no sidewalks. Free **shuttle service** is offered to and from the train station for concerts, from 2:30 to 8:30pm (call for exact schedule). Infrequent **bus** service is also available on weekday mornings and late afternoon (Asnières-Baillon stop, line 14); for information, call Couriers de l'Île de France (tel. 01 48 62 38 33).

■ Disneyland Paris

It's a small, small world and Disney is bent on making it even smaller. When Euro-Disney opened on April 12, 1992, Mickey Mouse, Cinderella, and Snow White were met by the jeers of French intellectuals and the popular press, who called the Disney theme park a "cultural Chernobyl." Resistance seems to have subsided since Walt & Co. renamed it Disneyland Paris and started serving wine. A touch of class can go a long way. Without a doubt, the park is an enjoyable place to spend a day, even for the budget traveler, and is far more fun than the French Parc Asterix. Disneyland Paris is especially great for kids. As you groan, remember that your child put up with you in the Louvre. Every show, attraction, and ride at Disneyland is included in the admittedly expensive admission price. Food within the park tends to be expensive, so you should pack a lunch before you get on the train in Paris.

Disneyland Paris's designers (called "Imagineers") and staff (referred to as "Cast Members") have created a resort that ostensibly celebrates imagination, childhood, fantasy, creativity, technology, and fun. Pre-construction press touted the complex as a vast entertainment and resort center covering an area one fifth the size of Paris. In truth, Disney owns (and may eventually develop) 600 hectares, but the current theme park doesn't even rank the size of an arrondissement. From the gate it takes only 10 minutes to walk to the farthest point inside the park—nothing like the vast reaches of Florida's Disney World—a fact disguised by the park's maze-like design. Despite its dimensions, this Disney park is the most technologically advanced yet, and the special effects on some rides will knock your socks off.

Despite a slow start, Disneyland Paris has been a hit, and Disney has had to close the ticket windows repeatedly for hours at a time to keep ride lines down during the summer. Try to get there on a weekday—Tuesdays and Thursdays are the least crowded; cloudy days are even better, and shorter lines may be worth the risk of rain. Otherwise, expect to spend most of your time fighting to keep your place in line, rather than having fun. Whole families cut lines, ducking under barriers and worming their way up front. To make things worse, the architecture can hide the true length of the lines; a line just emerging from a building may be only the tail end of a 90-minute wait inside. Discreetly posted signs at the entrances of the more popular rides alert you to how long you can expect to wait for your allotted two- to 10-minute rush. The crowds thin out toward 5pm, when parents start crying to go home, reducing waits to as little as 15 minutes, although by 6pm you may be equally exhausted. Saving the bigger rides for the evening is probably the best way to go. Considering that the park closes at 11pm during the summer, you'll have plenty of time to catch your favorite rides several times over.

ORIENTATION AND PRACTICAL INFORMATION

Everything in Disneyland Paris is in English and French. The staff is extremely helpful, and the detailed guide called the *Park Guide Book* has a map and information on everything from restaurants and attractions to bathrooms and first aid. For more helpful information on Disneyland Paris, visit their websight at http://www.disneylandparis.com.

Admission and Hours: Instead of selling tickets, Disneyland Paris issues *passeports,* available at the 50 windows located on the ground floor of the Disneyland Hotel. You can also buy *passeports* at the Paris tourist office on the Champs-Elysées (see **Tourist Offices,** p. 71) or at any of the major stations on RER line A, such as Châtelet-Les Halles, Gare de Lyon, or Charles-de-Gaulle-Étoile. Pursue either of these options if you plan on coming out on a weekend, so you won't risk wasting a couple of hours while the windows remain closed due to the crowds. The *passeport* is valid for 1 day; be sure to have your hand stamped if you plan to leave the park and return later. Admission Apr.-Sept. and Dec. 23-Jan. 7 200F, ages 3-11 155F; off-season 155F, ages 3-11 125F. 2- and 3-day passeports are also available. Park open daily July 11-Aug. 31 9am-11pm; Apr.-May and Sept.-June hours vary. Hours also subject to change during the winter when snow and sleet make the experience less fun.

Hotels: You can easily do Disney in a day, but if a stay in the Magic Kingdom suits you, check out one of the resort's 6 hotels. Each celebrates a region of the U.S.: the **Sequoia Lodge** is surrounded by sequoia trees imported from California, the **Hotel Santa Fe** is modeled on the adobes of New Mexico, and the **Hotel Cheyenne** is built to look like a western frontier town. In the off season, a group of 4 could comfortably and affordably stay for a weekend at the Hotel Cheyenne (626F, off-season 350F) or at the Hotel Santa Fe (unpopular with the French because it looks like a French housing project; high season 585F, off season 275F). The resort also had a campground called the **Davy Crockett Ranch,** which has been converted into a resort village with fully equipped bungalows that can house up to 6 people (442F). Unfortunately, it is also 7km from the center of the park, and buses are no longer available; taxis or cars are the only ways of getting there (prices are per person for 2 days and one night and include park admission). For more info, call in France tel. 01 60 30 60 30, in the U.K. tel. 0990 03 03 03, or in the U.S. tel. (407) W DISNEY (934 7639). The Paris tourist office (tel. 01 60 43 33 33; fax 01 60 43 74 95) can help you make a hotel reservation outside of Disney (for a 20F commission) and give you information on the area surrounding Disneyland Paris. Open M-F 8am-8pm, Sa 9am-6pm, Su 9am-5pm.

Restaurants: Consult the guidebook for full listings; there are over 50. Restaurants are marked on the map and classified by the type of service: sit-down, cafeteria, or snack bars. For a sit-down, 3-course menu, expect to pay 100-200F. Cafeteria meals run 45-55F for simpler menus (i.e. hamburger, french fries, and a soft drink). Snack stands located throughout the park offer hot dogs, ice cream, and the like for 9-20F. The least expensive options are the fish and chips at **Toad Hall Restaurant,** the frontier grub and saloon show at **Lucky Nugget Saloon,** the Italian staples of pasta and pizza at **Pizzeria Bella Notte,** the burgers at Discoveryland's **Café Hyperion,** and pizza and the like at the Toy Story-themed **Buzz Lightyear's Pizza Planet Restaurant.** The Lucky Nugget offers what is perhaps the best value in the whole park: 85F at lunch and 150F at dinner buys a 4-course meal with buffalo wings, a bowl of chili, a hot beef sandwich, and a brownie. You're not supposed to bring in picnic food into the park (your bags are usually searched), but the French seem to do it anyhow. Most restaurants are open non-stop 11am-10pm during the summer and 11am 'til the park's closing the rest of the year.

Transportation: The easiest way to get to Disneyland Paris is by taking **RER** A4 from Paris. Get on at either M. Gare de Lyon or Châtelet-Les Halles and take the train (direction: "Marne-la-Vallée") to the last stop, "Marne-la-Vallée/Chessy." Before boarding the train, check the illuminated electric boards hanging above the platform to make sure there's a light next to the Marne-la-Vallée stop; otherwise the train won't end up there (45min., departs every 30min., round-trip 76F). The last train to Paris leaves Disney at 12:22am, but you may have trouble getting the metro at the other end. **By car,** take the A4 highway from Paris and get off at exit 14, marked "Parc Disneyland Paris," about a 30min. drive from the city. You can park for 40F per day in any one of the 11,000 spaces in the parking lot. **Disneyland Paris Buses** make the rounds between the terminals of both Orly and Roissy/Charles de Gaulle airports and the bus station near the Marne-la-Vallée RER (40min.; departs every 45-60 min. 8:30am-7:45pm, 8:30am-10pm at CDG on weekends; round-trip 85F). **TGV** service from Roissy/Charles de Gaulle reaches the park in a mere 15min., making Disneyland Paris fantastically accessible for travelers with Eurail passes. Certain **Eurostar** trains now run directly between Waterloo Station in London and Disneyland, in addition to a daily service (departure for Disney is usually around 9:15pm returning at 7:30pm; prices vary between 750 and 2090F; reserve as far in advance as possible to take advantage of discounts; call Eurostar for exact info at 08 36 35 35 39).

SIGHTS AND ACTIVITIES

For the wildest rides, look for those with the most dire warnings. While "may frighten certain young children" might sound promising, it only means that the ride is dark and things pop out at you. Warnings directed at pregnant women and people with chronic heart problems, or offering exit routes once already on line, are the hallmarks of the real thing. The park is divided into five areas. **Main Street USA,** a storybook depiction of a turn-of-the-century town, is more American than apple pie and the first area you'll pass through after the gate. It funnels you through a consumer's paradise of shops and restaurants before depositing you at the center of the park. At the heart of the Magical Kingdom, **Sleeping Beauty's Castle** contains a high-tech, smoke-breathing dragon in the dungeon. Behind the château lies **Fantasyland.** Although the rides are tame, the spinning **Mad Hatter's Teacups** offer a trippy experience if you lean your head back and merit a whirl. **Alice's Curious Labyrinth** is a hedge maze, replete with squirting fountains, a hookah-smoking caterpillar, and a palace with a great view; it's best visited at night when you just might get lost. Drift through a world of laughter, a world of tears, a world of hopes, and a world of fears on **It's a Small World,** where tiny automated dolls from around the world sing you into submission; if you hated Paris's **Musée de la Poupée** (see **Museums,** p. 232), you won't hate this.

Adventureland awaits both the explorer and the weary parent with a mix of themes from so-called adventurous regions: the Middle East, West Africa, and the Caribbean. **Pirates of the Caribbean** presents 10 minutes of frighteningly life-like corsairs and a fantastic water-dungeon set. Be warned: the line outside is only a fraction of the total wait. **Indiana Jones and the Temple of Doom** features the first 360° loop ever on a Disney ride; unfortunately, the ride lasts only three minutes and the loop is minuscule. More demanding thrill-seekers might want to mosey on over to rough and ready **Frontierland,** where **Thunder Mesa,** a towering sunset-colored reproduction of a New Mexican desert mesa, hosts the park's best ride: **Big Thunder Mountain.** At high noon, the line is almost as deadly as the ride, but the ride is fun. Set apart on a scraggly hill, the creaky **Phantom Manor** is the park's classic haunted house. While the Haunted Mansion at Disney World in Florida is a huge scary fortress, the architecture had to be changed in Europe, where fortresses and châteaux are common; this haunted manor is based instead on the Victorian mansion in the film Psycho.

Light-years away on the other side of the park, **Discoveryland** flaunts the park's latest technological wizardry. **Star Tours** invites you to fly the not-so-friendly skies around the Death Star. Michael Jackson's **Captain Eo** croons away at nearby **Cinémagique,** and the **Visionarium's** 360° time-travel film is a good break. The newest ride at Disneyland Paris, **Space Mountain** is touted as "the crowning achievement of forty years of innovation by Disney Imagineers." It puts the Florida, Tokyo, and California versions of this ride to shame: you'll travel at speeds of 70km per hour through three loops in pitch blackness—a 360° loop, a corkscrew, and a 180° horseshoe—while a synchronized eight-speaker soundtrack immerses you in the illusion that you're being shot all the way to the moon, with a victory chant awaiting you once you're safe on earth. Not for the weak of stomach.

In addition to the rides, Disney also puts on a variety of special daily events including a **Disney Character Parade** with myriad elaborate floats; the **Main Street Electrical Parade** (for the best view of the parades stand to the left at the top of Main St. near the pseudo-rotary—that's where the special effects on the floats are timed to go off); and a fantastic **son et lumières** show, set against the background of the château. Musical extravaganzas based on the latest Disney movies and other special events are listed in the brochure *Programmes: Spectacles & Restaurants.*

NIGHTLIFE

Separate from Disneyland Paris and free to enter is **Disney Village,** a street filled with bars and game rooms where people roam about wearing cowboy hats and clutching beers at the **Sports Bar, Billy Bob's Country and Western Saloon, Rock'n Roll America,** or **Hurricanes** (average prices 25-42F per bottle or glass). For 20F, you can even try your hand on top of a mechanical bucking bronco, smack in the middle of the village, while clutching onto a saddle-horn. Although it may look like a street carnival, Disney Village also contains a number of restaurants with classier fare, along with an eight-screen Gaumont cinema, nightclubs, a popular sports bar, and free bands playing cover songs until 1am. To complete the American cultural invasion, **Planet Hollywood** (tel. 01 60 43 78 27) recently landed in the Village. For about 100F per main course, you can dine amid Hollywood memorabilia (open 11am-midnight, F-Sa 11am-1am; AmEx; MC, V). **Buffalo Bill's Wild West Show** provides western entertainment with Buffalo Bill, Chief Sitting Bull, Annie Oakley, and a host of other cowboys, together with horses and shooting acrobatics, presented with all the authenticity and cultural sensitivity that has made Disney what it is today.

■ Giverny

Drawn by the verdant hills, haystacks, and lilypads on the Epte river, Impressionist Claude Monet and his eight children settled in Giverny in 1883. By 1887, John Singer Sargent, Paul Cézanne, and Mary Cassatt had placed their easels beside Monet's and turned the village into an artists' colony. When he was not painting flowers and waterlilies, Monet devoted much time to his garden, explaining *"Mon jardin est mon plus beau chef d'ouevre"* ("My garden is my most beautiful masterpiece").

Today, his house and gardens are maintained by the **Fondation Claude Monet,** 84, rue Claude Monet (tel. 02 32 51 28 21). *(Open Apr.-Oct. Tu-Su 10am-6pm. Admission 35F, students and ages 12-18 25F, ages 7-12 20F. Gardens only 25F.)* From April to July, Giverny overflows with roses, hollyhocks, poppies, and the heady scent of honeysuckle. The waterlilies, the Japanese bridge, and the weeping willows look like—well, like Monets. An army of gardeners work year-long to create the lush floral colors that Monet once painted. The serenity is broken only by the crowds of tourists and school children. The only way to avoid the rush is to go early in the morning and, if possible, early in the season. The Impressionists inaugurated a new way of using light, lines, and color, blurring their paintings instead of obsessing over academic precision and clarity. In Monet's thatched-roof house, big windows, solid furniture, and pale blue walls house his collection of 18th- and 19th-century Japanese prints. Like his studio and the blue and white tiled kitchen, each room is bathed in light and flooded by scents from the garden. The second-floor windows offer lovely views of the Japanese garden.

To the left of the foundation, the new and spacious **Musée d'Art Américain,** 99, rue Claude Monet (tel. 02 32 51 94 65), is sister institution to the Museum of American Art in Chicago and houses works by American expatriates James Whistler, John Singer Sargent, and Mary Cassatt. *(Open Apr.-Oct. Tu-Su 10am-6pm. Admission 35F, students, seniors, teachers, and ages 12-18 20F, under 12 15F.)* The **Musée Baudy,** 81, rue Claude Monet (tel. 02 32 21 10 03), was an old hotel that once lodged Monet and his close friends, Renoir, Pissarro, and Clémenceau. *(Open daily Apr. 15-July 15 10am-6pm. Admission 25F, seniors 20F, students 15F, ages 8-12 10F.)* Sisley reportedly annoyed Cassat by slurping his soup in the Baudy's dining room. In the hotel's gardens, a small studio used by Cézanne and many American artists, is surrounded by roses.

A healthy walk or bike-ride away, Giverny's **Forêt de Vernon** sits amid hayfields and poppies. The Vernon **tourist office,** 36, rue Carnot (tel. 02 32 51 39 60), distributes free maps and hiking trails. *(Open Apr.-Oct. Tu-Sa 9:30am-noon and 2:30-6:30pm, Su 10am-noon; Nov.-Mar. Tu-Sa 10am-noon and 2:30-5:30pm.)* To reach the tourist office from the Vernon station, take rue Émile Loubet, turn left on rue d'Albuféra, and right on rue Carnot. If you remain on rue d'Albuféra, pont Clémenceau will carry you across the Seine; to the left on the far side of the river there's a **picnic spot** beside an old mill and a singing bird named Pokey; to the right, signs lead to Giverny. Amid Vernon's half-timbered houses, the **Musée de Vernon,** 12, rue du Pont (tel. 02 32 21 28 09), exhibits an eclectic collection including one work by Monet. *(Open Apr.-Oct. Tu-F 11am-1pm and 2-6pm, Sa-Su 2-5:30pm; Nov.-Mar. Tu-Su 2-6pm. Admission 15F, students and under 18 free.)* From rue d'Albuféra as you face the bridge, turn left on rue Carnot and right on rue du Pont.

Getting to Giverny is a challenge. **Trains** run erratically from Paris to Vernon, the nearest station. *(Check the fickle timetables posted in the grandes lignes reservation rooms at Gare St-Lazare or call SNCF (tel. 08 36 35 35 35). Trains leave Paris M-F at 8:16am, 12:05, and 2:23pm; Sa 8:39am, 12:05, and 2:23pm; Su and holidays 8:06, 9:15 and 10:40am; 45-75min. Trains return from Vernon M-Sa at 2:13 and 5:17pm, and Th-Tu at 7:06pm; Su holidays 2:20 and 5:15pm. 134F round-trip.)* To get to Giverny, rent a **bike** from the Vernon station (55F per day; 1000F or credit card deposit; MC, V) or take a **bus** (tel. 02 35 71 32 99) from the station. *(10min.; M-Sa 6 per day each way, Su and holidays 3 per day each way; 12F, round-trip 20F.)* Make sure you coordinate train and bus schedules before you start your trip to avoid three-hour delays. **Taxis** in front of the train station are another option. *(One-way 65F weekdays, 80F weekends.)* The 6km, hour-long **hike** from the Vernon station to Giverny is long but beautiful. Get a free map at the Vernon tourist office and beware of highway traffic.

■ Auvers-sur-Oise

*I am entirely absorbed by these plains of wheat on a vast expanse of hills
like an ocean of tender yellow, pale green, and soft mauve, with a piece of
cultivated land dotted with clusters of potato vines in bloom, and all this
under a blue sky tinted with shades of white, pink, and violet.*
—Vincent Van Gogh, 1890

Relatively little has changed in Auver-sur-Oise since Van Gogh's arrival in 1890.
Located 30km northwest of Paris, this little village attracted the Impressionists Pissarro, Daubigny, and Gachet to its lush green fields, winding paths, and stone houses.
Ironically, the artist who stayed the shortest period of time in Auvers—a mere 70
days—has become its most honored son. Fleeing Provence where he had been so
unhappy, Van Gogh arrived at Auvers-sur-Oise in May 1890 and immediately began to
paint and sketch. In a scant ten weeks he produced over 70 drawings, studies, and
canvases. This intense productivity did not bring with it peace of mind. On the afternoon of July 27, the 37-year-old Van Gogh shot himself in the chest while standing in
the wheat fields he had painted only days before. He died two days later in his room
at the **Auberge Ravaux,** with his friend Dr. Gachet and his beloved brother Théo.

While the **Maison de Van Gogh,** 8, rue de la Sansonne (tel. 01 34 48 05 47), has little to offer beyond a glimpse of Van Gogh's bare room and a pretty slideshow, the
cost of admission includes an elegant, illustrated "passport" to Auvers-sur-Oise that
details the history of the *auberge* and Van Gogh's sojourn there. *(Open Tu-Su 10am-
6pm. Admission 30F.)* The booklet also gives information on the town's other museums,
self-guided walking tours, and neighboring villages. The 15-minute walk from the
maison to the **Cimetière d'Auvers** is well worth the view. Walk to the end of rue de
la Sansonne, take the right-hand path to rue Daubigny, turn right, and then bear left
up rue Emile Bernard to **Nôtre-Dame d'Auvers,** the 12th-century subject of Van
Gogh's *Église d'Auvers* (1890), which hangs in the Musée d'Orsay (see **Museums,** p.
215). Grief-stricken and ill, Vincent's brother Théo died six months after Vincent. In
1914 his wife had him reburied at his brother's side along the far wall of the cemetery.

The **chemin du cimetière** leads through the fields where Van Gogh painted his
Champ de blé aux corbeaux (*Wheatfields with Crows,* 1890) and emerges near the
Atelier de Daubigny, 61, rue Daubigny (tel. 01 34 48 03 03), once the home and studio of pre-Impressionist painter Charles-François Daubigny. *(Open Easter-Oct. Tu-Su 2-
6:30pm. Admission 20F, under 12 10F.)* Daubigny (1817-78) began to make regular trips
to Auvers in 1854, found moorings here for his floating studio christened "Le Bottin"
in 1857, and built a less water-worthy and more permanent studio in 1861. This *atelier* became a popular meeting place for artists including Pissarro, Morisot, and
Cézanne. When rain made it impossible to work outdoors, Daubigny and his friends
Daumier and Corot covered the walls with *tableaux* of flowers, fruits, and trim. Some
of Daubigny's smaller works and personal items are displayed in his studio. Near the
atelier, on a side street off rue de Léry, the **Musée de l'Absinthe,** 44, rue Callé (tel. 01
30 36 83 26), is yet another memorial to the Impressionists. *(Open June-Sept. W-Su
11am-6pm; Oct.-May Sa-Su 11am-6pm. Admission 25F, students 20F.)* Devoted to the mythical drink that Manet and Degas immortalized in art (see **The Green Party,** p. 218),
the museum features special absinthe spoons, fervent poems by Verlaine, Rimbaud,
and Baudelaire, a re-created period *bistrot,* and Art Nouveau posters of the *fée verte*
(green fairy) who seduced and inspired a generation.

The gardens of the 1635 **Château d'Auvers** (tel. 01 34 48 48 48) feature pretty
hedges, modest fountains, an expensive bistro, and a breathtaking view. The châ-
teau's modern **museum** showcases a multimedia exhibit recreating 19th-century
Paris and Auvers, called a *Voyage au temps des Impressionists* (Journey into the
Impressionists' Era). Visitors don headsets and take a 90-minute tour of Haussmann's
Paris and the Auvers countryside through films, projections, and slide shows. *(Open
Apr.-Sept. Tu-Su 10am-6pm; Oct.-Mar. 10am-4:30pm. Last entry 1½hr. before closing. Admis-
sion 55F, seniors 45F, under 25 40F, under 6 free.)* In his home on rue François Coppée,

Dr. Paul Ferdinand Gachet welcomed Renoir, Monet, Pissarro, Van Gogh, and Cézanne, who stayed in Auvers from 1872 to 1874, painting such works as *La maison du pendu.*

Housed in the Manoir des Colombières, rue de la Sansonne, the **Office de Tourisme d'Auvers-sur-Oise** (tel. 01 30 36 10 06) offers several admission package deals to the various museums in Auvers: the château, Atelier de Daubigny, and Maison de Van Gogh (Tu-Sa 85F); to the château, Musée de l'Absinthe, and Maison Van Gogh (Sa-Su 65F); to the château and Atelier Daubigny (Su 65F). *(Open daily 10am-12:30pm and 2-5pm. Tours Apr.-Oct. Su 3pm; 25F, under 14 10F.)* The helpful staff hands out free maps of Auvers and sells detailed walking-tour maps (3F). A free 20-minute video about Van Gogh's sojourn in Auvers runs continuously in French and English, and 90-minute guided tours of the village depart from here. Every summer during the first week of June, the Fête de la Ceragne celebrates the Belle Époque with a ball, barbecue, circus games, and a brass band. The Manoir des Colombières also hosts the small **Musée Daubigny** (tel. 01 30 36 80 20), which contains a few minor works by Daubigny and other Auvers artists. *(Open W-Su 2-5:30pm. Admission 20F, under 6 free.)*

To get to Auvers, take the **train** from Gare St-Lazare to Pontoise, then switch to the Persau Creil line and get off at Gare d'Auvers-sur-Oise (1hr., depart every hr., 56F). Or go from the Gare du Nord to Valmondois, St-Ouen l'Aumone, or Persau Beaumont, change at any of these stops for a train to Pontoise, then get off at Auvers-sur-Oise.

■ St-Cloud

The town of **St-Cloud**, 3km southwest of Paris, harbors a beautiful **park,** the former site of a Second Empire château. *(Gardens open daily Mar.-Apr. and Sept.-Oct. 7:30am-8:50pm; May-Aug. 7:30am-9:50pm; Nov.-Feb. 7:30am-7:50pm.)* Framed by orderly hedges and trimmed with rectangular beds of more than 30 varieties of flowers and 30 types of rosebushes, the multiterraced park marches its way down the hillside, stretching almost all the way to the Seine below. By consulting horticultural guides of the 19th century, modern-day gardeners have painstakingly reconstructed the floral arrangements in the fashion of the court of Napoleon III during his stays at St-Cloud. The result is a great spot for a bike excursion or a picnic, especially since you can walk and sit on the grass.

The **Château de St-Cloud** was the scene of the assassination of Henri III in 1589 and Napoleon's coup d'état in 1799, when troops loyal to the rising general invaded the chambers of the legislature in session there. In 1870, marauding Prussians bombed and then burned the château. Nothing remains but Le Nôtre's magnificent park. To orient yourself, consult the large marble slab at the Bassin de l'Orangerie. A map of the grounds in 1811, the slab shows the parts of the original park that still remain, the parts that were destroyed, and the exact location of the château. To the left of the park's main gates (the *grille d'honneur*), the tiny **Musée Historique** (tel. 01 46 02 67 18) offers drawings and paintings about the park and the ex-château. (Open Sept.-July W and Sa-Su 2:30-6:30pm. Both free.)

The most interesting parts of the park are right near the town. If you enter at av. du Général Leclerc, walk down the allée de la glacière until you arrive at the fountains. If you continue to the Bassin de l'Orangerie you will come upon a panorama of Paris and the surrounding suburbs. The *grille d'honneur* is to your left. You can continue downhill to the Bassin des cascades, but don't go out of the gates at the *grille d'honneur* or you'll hit the highway. The cascades feature fountains with water-spouting frogs. To your left at the bottom of the fountain is a tunnel through which you can exit the park. Cross the street to catch the #75 bus back to the Hôtel de Ville, or walk across the bridge to the metro.

To get to St-Cloud from Paris, take the metro, bus #72 from the Hôtel de Ville, or bus #52 from the Madeleine to "Boulogne-Pt. de St-Cloud." There you can either take a local bus across the Pont de St-Cloud or an unpleasant 15-minute walk across intersecting highways. Take the #160, 467, or 460 bus (look for signs in the metro, or catch them right before the bridge) for Pont de St-Cloud. If you are arriving by bike, ride on the sidewalk on the left side of the bridge and follow the signs to the park. Get off at pl. Magenta and head down av. du Général Leclerc to the park, or get off earlier at the train station and head downhill until you hit the church. To the right of the church is the **town hall** (tel. 01 47 71 53 00). There you can find free maps of the town and park as well as a guide to all the restaurants and stores in town. (Open M-F 9am-noon and 2-5:45pm, Sa 8:45am-noon.)

■ Provins

Amid brilliant corn fields and green woods, on top of a ridge and above the rest of the world, Provins is one of the best preserved medieval towns in France. The oldest parts of Beauvais date from the 12th century when it was France's third-largest city after Paris and Rouen. Unlike those two cities, which changed and grew, Provins's ancient walls covered with ivy. The town's *ville haute* is thus more like a gleaming, historical film set, at times even complete with knights, maidens, and monks (see special events below). The lower, newer *ville basse,* historically the town's center of trade, remains populated by pedestrian shopping streets. The best way to visit is to go to the *ville haute* alone, explore, and enjoy the view.

Enter the settlement in style through the **Porte St-Jean,** one of the main gates in the town's stellar ramparts, built between the 11th and 13th centuries. This fortified gate protected Provins's route to Paris. Beyond the gate on rue St-Jean is the 12th-century façade **Grange aux Dîmes** (tithe barn), which originally served as a market for cloth, dye, and wine merchants and a storehouse for merchandise and tithes collected by the church. The **Grange Museum,** which depicts mannequin merchants selling their wares, is less interesting. *(Open Apr.-Sept. daily 2-6pm; Jan.-Mar. and Oct.-Dec. Sa-Su 2-5pm. Admission 22F, children 14F.)* Past the Grange, **place du Châtel** features the gothic **Croix des Changes,** the cross of changes (and the name of Enigma's first album), where the Counts of Provins posted edicts and unpopular declarations. Today, pl. du Châtel offers shady benches, restaurants, cafés, and gift shops. **Mammy Gâteau,** 16, pl. du Châtel (tel. 01 60 67 78 10), a small *crêperie* on the square, serves *crêpes de rose* (20F) with Provins's famous rose-petal preserves, *confit des pétales de rose* (open Th-Tu 10am-closing). Provins is famous for its red roses (allegedly brought back from the Crusades). An English governor of the town—Edmund of Lancaster (1245-96)—put a Provins rose on his coat of arms when he married a Provinoise. The house of Lancaster would later battle with the house of York, whose coat of arms bore a white rose; their feud came to be known as the War of the Roses.

Above the *place,* the **Tour César** is Provins's town symbol. Legend says that Caesar built the tower himself. *(Open Apr.-Sept. daily 10am-6pm; Jan.-Mar. and Nov.-Dec. M-F 2-5pm, Sa-Su 11am-5pm. Admission 17F, children 10F.)* The tower actually dates from 1137, when it defended the town from attack. Today, the tower offers an excellent view of the town and its surroundings. Narrow stairwells spiral to the top of the tower were you'll find a 16th-century 6000-pound bell from St-Quiriace. At the base of the tower, the **Musée de Provins et du Provinois** exhibits archaeological artifacts and ancient Frankish sarcophagi. *(Open daily Jan.-Mar. and Nov.-Dec. 2-5pm; Apr.-Sept. 2-6pm. Admission 22F, children 11F.)* Nearby, Provins's **Souterrains,** a system of underground catacombs, dug over 1000 years ago, were used as a war-time refuge and as a wine cellar. Not as thrilling as the bone-filled catacombs of Paris, the tour lasts 45 minutes. *(Open Apr.-Sept. Sa-Su 11am-6pm; Jan.-Mar. and Nov.-Dec. Sa-Su 3-4pm. Admission 22F, children 14F.)* The 12th-century **Église de Saint-Quiriace** was built on the ruins of a Merovingian church (AD 500-750), when the first dynasty of Frankish kings ruled Gaul. Provins boasts three **medieval festivals:** *A l'assault des remparts* (The Assault of the Ramparts; July-Aug. Tu-Sa 4pm; May-June M-Tu and Th-F 2:30pm, Sa-Su 4pm; admission 35F, children 20F); *Les Aigles de Provins* (The Eagles of Provins; Apr.-Aug.; admission 40F, children 25F), and *Le jugement de Dieu* (The Judgement of God; June-Aug. Su 4pm; admission 80F, children 50F), which feature battles, falconry, jousting, and monastic flagellation.

To get to Provins from Paris, take the SNCF **train** marked Provins from Gare de l'Est; trains depart frequently in the morning and sparsely in the afternoon (round-trip 122F). To get from the Beauvais train station *(ville basse)* to the tourist office *(ville* *haute*), cross the stream in front of the station and turn right on rue Moreau, then left on bd. Carnot and right on rue Anatole France. Turn left uphill on rue Maximilen Michelin, which becomes av. du Général de Gaulle, and continue to chemin de Ville-cran. From there follow signs to the tourist office, which is just outside the walls of the *ville haute*. The **tourist office** (tel. 01 64 60 26 26) offers information on Provins, walking maps, lists of restaurants and hotels, and tickets to town monuments, including the *passeport journée*. (Open daily 9am-5:30pm. Daily passport 55F, ages 5-12 35F, family of 2 adults and children 160F.) Mini-trains from the tourist office stop at all major sights and allow you to hop on and off all day (departs every 40min. May-Aug. daily, 35F, children 20F).

Weekend Trips

Sitting in a Parisian café, it's easy to forget that life exists beyond the Île de France. The provinces, officially defined as the rest of the country, are where most of French history was played out, where most French landmarks stand, and where most of the French live. Foray into the Pays de la Loire (a mere hour away) or into Normandy (2 hours away) for a glimpse at the France of châteaux, battlefields, and beaches.

Paris lies within easy reach of many French and European capitals. The TGV and Eurostar can whisk you to Brussels (2hr., 220F), London (3hr., 360-740F), and Amsterdam (5hr., 366F) for a week or weekend away. Normandy and Rennes (2hr., 308F), Burgundy and Dijon (2hr., 270F), Alsace-Lorraine and Strasbourg (2hr., 210F), the Alps and Grenoble (4hr., 320F), and Provence and Avignon (3½hr., 426F) are all worthy of a long weekend from Paris. France's second-largest city Lyon (2hr., 300F), Tours (1hr., 260F), and Orléans (1½hr., 90F) are also manageable in a few days.

For more extensive coverage of these cities, the provinces, and France's nearby European neighbors, consult *Let's Go: France 1999* and *Let's Go: Europe 1999*.

PAYS DE LA LOIRE (LOIRE VALLEY)

The châteaux along the Loire, France's longest river, range from grim medieval fortresses with defensive walls to elegant Renaissance houses with storybook moats. The buildings themselves buzz with 400 years' worth of stories about royal births and queenly poisonings, arranged marriages and true love. Most of the châteaux were built in the 15th and 16th centuries, when French monarchs left Paris and ruled from the countryside around Tours, both to avoid urban grime and to squeeze in hunting excursions between official state decrees. Some structures, however, remain from the days before the region was even French: Henry II and Richard the Lionheart, both English royalty, mobilized two of the oldest communities, Chinon and Beaugency, to defend the region from the Capetian monarchs of the 12th century. The English and the French played hot potato with the Loire until Jeanne d'Arc helped win it for the French in the Hundred Years' War (1337-1453; see **Paris: An Introduction,** p. 2). Under the 15th-century Valois kings, the French monarchy acquired the region through martial and marital means. During this time, the châteaux accummulated the works of the finest Italian masters and an opulence never before imagined.

GETTING AROUND

Blois and Tours are convenient bases for château exploration, especially since the Paris Gare d'Austerlitz serves both directly. Trains then run between Tours and Chenonceau, while Chambord is accessible by bus (in summer) or bike from Blois. The Loire Valley is a fantastic spot to rent a car: a group of four can often undercut tour bus prices by doing so and will be able to see many more of the smaller châteaux. Bikes are available for rent almost everywhere (around 50F per day). *Michelin*'s road map of the region will steer you away from truck-laden highways and onto delightful country roads.

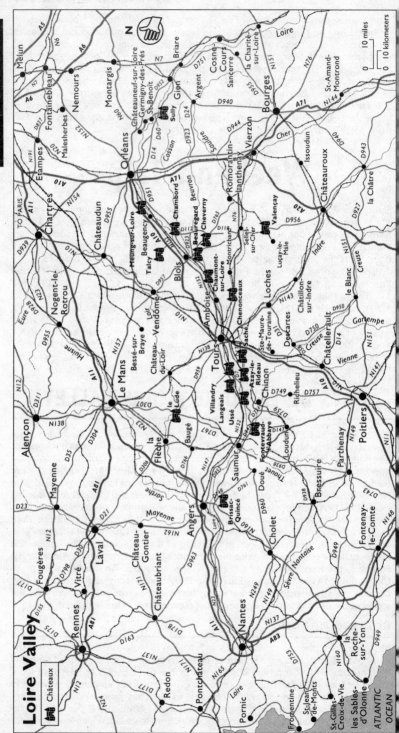

Loire Valley

🏰 Châteaux

▓ Blois

As the gateway to the Loire Valley, Blois welcomes over half a million visitors each year. Recent restoration projects have made Blois even more luminous, and the town's blue slate roofs, red brick chimneys, and narrow cobblestone lanes evoke the simple beauty of the villages painted by Vermeer.

Home to French monarchs Louis XII and François I, Blois's **château** (tel. 02 54 78 06 62) was as influential in the late-15th and early-16th centuries as Versailles was in the 17th. *(Château open daily July and Aug. 9am-8pm; Mar.15-June and Sept. 9am-6:30pm; Oct.-Mar. 14 9am-12:30pm and 2-5:30pm. Admission 35F, students under 25 and ages 6-11 20F. Special combination prices for the château and the magic museum or the castle's own spectacular son et lumière show; call for details. MC, V.)* The ornate octagonal **spiral staircase,** built under François I (1494-1547), whose motto was "Nutrisco et extingo" (I feed on fire and I extinguish it), ascends to the **Aile François I.** In 1588, King Henri III cowered here while his eight hired assassins fatally stabbed the Duke of Guise, a Catholic rival for the French throne. The **Cathédrale St-Nicolas,** a masterpiece of medieval architecture, is also in town. At sunset, cross the Loire and turn onto quai V. Mareuil for a shimmering view of the kingly château rising above the commonfolk's homes.

Trains (tel. 08 36 35 35 35) run frequently from Paris-Austerlitz (1¾hr., 8 per day, 121F). You can also catch trains to Tours (1hr., 10 per day, 51F). **Banks** and **ATMs** are scattered everywhere in Blois's *centre ville,* especially near the Loire, along rue Denis Papin, and around pl. de la Résistance. The **tourist office,** 3, av. Jean Laigret (tel. 02 54 90 41 41), has info about Blois and nearby châteaux. (Open May-Sept. M-Sa 9am-7pm, Su and holidays 10am-7pm; Oct.-Apr. M-Sa 9am-12:30pm and 2-6pm, Su 9:30am-12:30pm.) The local **hostel (HI)** is at 8, rue de l'Hôtel Pasquier (tel. 02 54 78 27 21). From the tourist office, follow rue Porte Côté, bear right onto rue Denis Papin down to the river, and take bus #4 (direction: Les Grouets). Get off at the bottom of the hill on which the hostel is located, after passing a large stone church on the left (10min). (Reception 6:45-10am and 6-10:30pm. First night 61F, each additional night 44F, including sheets. Open Mar.-Nov.15.) Next to the *gare,* the **Hôtel St-Jacques,** 7, rue Ducoux (tel. 02 54 78 04 15), has big, clean rooms (singles and doubles 125-190F; AmEx, V). For **food,** wander along rue St-Lubin and near pl. Poids du Roi, near the cathedral; don't miss the sweet specialty *le chocolat blésois.*

▓ Chambord

Built by François I for his hunting trips and orgiastic fêtes, Chambord is the largest and most extravagant of the Loire châteaux. Seven hundred of his trademark stone salamanders lurk on Chambord's walls, ceilings, and ingenious staircase, while the 440 rooms have a fireplace for every day of the year.

At the heart of the symmetrical **château** rises a spectacular double-helix staircase, attributed to Leonardo da Vinci, constructed so that one person can ascend and another descend without meeting, while keeping sight of one another through its sculpted openings. The design symbolically allows people to ascend, not to God, but to the the King of France. *(Open daily July-Aug. 9:30am-6:45pm; Sept. 9:30am-5:45pm; Oct.-Dec. 9:30am-4:45pm; Jan.-Mar. 9:30am-4:45pm; Apr.-June 9:30am-5:45pm. Admission 40F, students and children 25F.)* The château was a favorite of Louis XIV, who planted the magnificent kilometer-long, tree-lined avenue approaching the château. Today, the sprawling grounds cover over 5350 hectares, 1200 of which are open to the public.

To get to Chambord from Paris, take a **train** to Blois (info above) then catch a **bus** at the Gare Routière, 2, pl. Victor Hugo (tel. 02 54 78 15 66). Buses run mid-June to mid-September. Take the **Transports Loir-et-Cher (TLC)** bus, circuit #2 (65F, students 50F). You could also rent a **bike** in Blois from **Intersport,** 2-4, rue Porte Côté (tel. 02 54 78 06 57), just below pl. Victor Hugo. (Bikes 50F per day; open M 2-7pm, Tu-Sa 9am-noon and 2-7pm.) The one-hour ride is pretty and straightforward; ask for directions at the Blois **tourist office** (info above) or the one in Chambord (tel. 02 54 20 34 86; open daily 9:30am-7:15pm). Blois is your best bet for an overnight stay.

■ Chenonceau

The most romantic château of them all, **Chenonceau** (tel. 02 47 23 90 07) was designed by three women. *(Open daily Mar. 16-Sept. 15 9am-7pm; call for off-season hours. Admission 45F, students 30F. Late July to Aug., son et lumière at 10:15pm.)* Catherine Bohier, the wife of the royal tax-collector, oversaw its practical design, which features four rooms radiating from a central chamber and innovative straight (rather than spiral) staircases. In 1547, Henri II gave the château to his mistress, Diane de Poitiers, who added sublime symmetrical gardens and constructed the arched bridge over the Cher so she could hunt in the nearby forest. When Henri II died in 1559, his wife, Catherine de Médici, kicked Diane out of her beloved castle and then designed her own set of gardens and the most spectacular wing of the castle: the two-story gallery spanning the Cher.

The village of **Chenonceaux** is 214km from Paris (2hr.) and 34km from Tours (25min.) by car on the A10. Take a **train** from Paris to Tours (2¼hr., 22 per day, 160F; TGV 1hr., 16 per day, 200-260F plus reservation); from the Tours station (tel. 02 47 20 50 50), trains run to the village (45min., 3 per day, 34F). The station is 2km from the château. Cross the tracks, immediately turn right, then follow the blue sign to the château. **Tourisme Verney** (tel. 02 47 37 81 81, in Tours) runs buses from Tours via Amboise (30min., 3 per day, 45F round-trip) to Chenonceau (1hr., round-trip 70F).

You can stay at the **hostel (HI)** in Tours, av. d'Arsonval, Parc de Grandmont (tel. 02 47 25 14 45; fax 02 47 48 26 59), 4km from the station in a park by the highway. From the station, take bus #1 (direction: Jotie Blotterie) or #6 (direction: Chambray) from the stop on the right side of av. de Grammont, 30m down from pl. Jean Jaurès (last bus at 8:15pm, 7F). (Reception 5-11pm; off-season 5-10pm; 47F.) Also in Tours, **Hôtel St-Eloi**, 79, bd. Béranger (tel. 02 47 37 67 34), is a sparkling haven 10 minutes from the train station (singles and doubles 180F; breakfast 27F). For more information about Tours and Chenonceau, including guided château excursion lists, contact Tours's **tourist office,** rue Bernard Palissy (tel. 02 47 70 37 37).

NORMANDY

Normandy's jagged coastline, sloping valleys, and Gothic cathedrals inspired the Impressionists. But this coastal province has had a tumultuous history. The territory was seized by Vikings in the 9th century, and in 911 the French king acknowledged the independence of the *Normands.* From the 10th to the 13th century, the Normans created a string of mammoth ornate cathedrals. Their most impressive achievement, however, was the conquest in 1066 of a soggy isle to the northwest of France. William the Conqueror's defeat of England was celebrated by a magnificent tapestry that still hangs in the Norman town of Bayeux.

During the Hundred Years' War, the English took their revenge when they invaded and overpowered fierce Norman resistors. English troops, led by the Duke of Bedford and aided by French traitors, succeeded in capturing Jeanne d'Arc after a great victory on September 8, 1430. Charged with heresy and sorcery, Jeanne was imprisoned in Rouen's Tour Jeanne d'Arc and condemned to be burned at the stake. The British did not attempt another invasion until D-Day, June 6, 1944, when they returned with American, Canadian, and Québecois allies to wrest Normandy from Nazi occupation. The beaches near Bayeux, where the Allies landed, still bear scars from the attack.

GETTING AROUND

Trains go between Paris and the major sites of Normandy, including most of the tourist spots listed below and large towns, such as Lille, Le Havre, and Caen. Within Normandy, buses fill in the gaps between smaller towns, but thin out from September to May; a bike or a car helps for extended touring or individual exploring of the Normandy countryside.

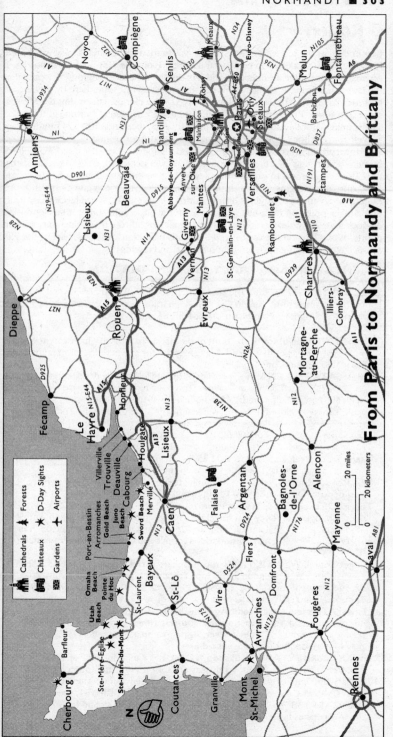

From Paris to Normandy and Brittany

Legend:
- Cathedrals
- Châteaux
- Gardens
- Forests
- D-Day Sights
- Airports

20 miles
20 kilometers

N

■ Rouen

Best known as the city where Joan of Arc was burned and Emma Bovary was bored, Rouen (pop. 400,000) is no provincial hayseed. From the 10th to 12th centuries, it bloomed with Gothic architecture and half-timbered houses, befitting the capital of the Norman empire. After her campaign, Joan was held prisoner here by the English and tried for heresy by French clergy in 1431. The clerics passed down a life sentence, but under British pressure this sentence was changed to burning at the stake. The spunky patriot's name adorns the main thoroughfare and droves of monuments, as well as every hotel, souvenir shop, and *tabac* for miles around.

In the 19th century, Victor Hugo dubbed Flaubert's birthplace and Corneille's hometown the "city of a hundred spires," mainly in deference to its imposing cathedral. Monet's attempts to capture the play of light on the cathedral's façade has made it a fixture in museums around the world. Tragically, American and German troops bombed away much of Rouen's history during the World Wars, and hasty reconstruction and air pollution have taken their toll on the city's appearance. Once-imposing edifices are only gradually regaining their former glory through ongoing conservation efforts. While beyond the *centre ville* Rouen is neither attractive nor lively, the city satisfies with engaging museums, monuments, and churches.

ORIENTATION AND PRACTICAL INFORMATION

To get to the *centre ville* from the station, take rue Jeanne d'Arc for several blocks. A left onto the cobblestone **rue du Gros Horloge** leads to **pl. de la Cathédrale** and the tourist office; a right leads to **pl. du Vieux-Marché** and its restaurants.

Trains: rue Jeanne d'Arc, at the head of the street. To Paris (1½hr., every hr., 102F) and Lille (3hr., 3 per day, 160F). Leave bicycles for 35F per day. Information office open M-Sa 7:15am-7pm.

Buses: SATAR and **CNA,** at the corner of rue St-Eloi and rue des Charrettes (tel. 02 35 52 92 00), open daily 6am-7:30pm. To Le Havre (3hr., 2-3 per day, 80F). Office open M-F 8am-12:30pm and 1:45-6:45pm, Sa 8:30am-12:30pm.

Local Transportation: Métrobus, rue Jeanne d'Arc, in front of the Théâtre des Arts (tel. 02 35 52 52 52). Both subway and bus systems run M-Sa 7am-7pm. *Carte* 7F50 (good for 1hr.), *carnet* of 10 56F. Unlimited 1-day *carte* 20F, 2-day *carte* 30F, 3-day *carte* 40F. Info office at train station open M-Sa 6:30am-7pm.

Taxis: 67, rue Jean Lecanuet (tel. 02 35 88 50 50). 24hr. Stands at the train and bus stations, as well as the Palais de Justice on rue Jeanne d'Arc.

Bike Rental: Rouen Cycles, 45, rue St-Eloi (tel. 02 35 71 34 30). 120F per day. Passport deposit. Open Tu-Sa 9am-12:30pm and 2-7:30pm. MC, V.

Tourist Office: 25, pl. de la Cathédrale (tel. 02 32 08 32 40; fax 02 32 08 32 44). Free map. **Changes currency** and traveler's checks commission free. Open Apr.-Sept. M-Sa 9am-7pm, Su 9:30am-12:30pm and 2:30-6pm; Oct.-Mar. M-Sa 9am-6:30pm, Su 10am-1pm. For 24hr. **accommodations service** call **Club Hôtelier Rouennais** (tel. 02 35 71 76 77).

Budget Travel: Wasteels, 111bis, rue Jeanne d'Arc (tel. 02 35 71 92 56; fax 02 35 07 48 75). Open M-F 9am-noon and 2-7pm, Sa 9am-noon and 2-6pm. **Forum Voyages,** 72, rue Jeanne d'Arc (tel. 02 35 98 32 59; fax 02 35 70 24 43). Open M-F 9:30am-7pm, Sa 10am-12:30pm and 2-6pm.

Money: ATMs lounge at **Crédit Agricole,** 37, rue Jeanne d'Arc, and **Crédit Mutuel,** 44, rue Jeanne d'Arc, near the *gare routière* (open 7am-11pm). **BRED,** 27, rue Jeanne d'Arc, and 137, rue St-Sever, dispenses bread from its **ATMs,** as do the 2 post office branches on rue Jeanne d'Arc.

English Bookstore: ABC Bookshop, 11, rue des Faulx, in front of Église St-Ouen (tel. 02 35 71 08 67). Windows display ads for *au pairs* and tutors for hire. Open Tu-Sa 10am-6pm; closes earlier in July. Usually closed around Aug.1-15.

Youth Center: Centre Rouen Information Jeunesse (CRIJ), 84, rue Beauvoisine (tel. 02 35 98 38 75), helps find accommodations and work and has info on activities. Also makes hostel reservations. Open M-F 10:30am-6:30pm.

Laundromat: 73, rue Beauvoisine (tel. 02 35 70 80 10). 21F for 8kg of dirty duds. 3F for 4min. of drying, 10F for 20min. Open daily 8am-8:30pm.
Emergency: tel. 17 **Medical Emergency:** tel. 15.
Ambulance: 1, rue de Germont (tel. 02 35 88 44 22).
Hospital: Hôpital Charles Nicolle, 1, rue de Germont (tel. 02 35 08 81 81).
Police: 9, rue Brisout de Barneville (tel. 02 35 81 25 00).
Help Lines: SOS Amitié (tel. 02 35 60 52 52) when you need to talk; 24hr.
ACT-UP Rouen (tel. 02 35 70 32 71) has info on gay and lesbian concerns.
Medical Assistance: SOS Médecins (tel. 02 35 03 03 30). Doctors on call 24hr.
Post Office: 45bis, rue Jeanne d'Arc (tel. 02 35 15 66 66). **Poste Restante. Currency exchange.** Open M-F 8am-7pm, Sa 8am-noon. Another branch at 122, rue Jeanne d'Arc, has the same hours. **Postal code:** 76000.
Internet Access: Cyber@croq, 124, rue Jeanne d'Arc (tel. 02 32 76 06 20), just steps from the train station (look to your right as you exit). Open M-Sa 8am-10pm.

ACCOMMODATIONS AND CAMPING

Rooms in Rouen are cheap enough that you may consider staying overnight. If you do, check out the cheap lodgings that lie on the side streets between the train station and Hôtel de Ville.

Hôtel Normandya, 32, rue du Cordier (tel. 02 35 71 46 15), near the train station off rue du Donjon. Owned by an exuberantly friendly, *Let's Go*-loving couple who could be your grandparents. Most rooms are well lit, nicely decorated, and have excellent views of the city. In others the only natural light is supplied by a skylight (in other words, no views). Tiny toilets. Singles 100F, with shower 140F; doubles 110F, with shower 150F; triple with shower 190F. Breakfast 20F. Shower 10F.
Hôtel du Palais, 12, rue Tambour (tel. 02 35 71 26 01), off rue du Gros Horloge. Clean, large rooms can be noisy during the day but quiet down by evening. Shiny new bathrooms to go along with a friendly new owner. Singles and doubles 120F, with shower 140F, with toilet and shower 200F. Extra bed 40F. Breakfast 25F.
Hôtel des Arcades, 52, rue de Carmes (tel. 02 35 70 10 30; fax 02 35 70 08 91). On the pricey side, but the rooms sparkle. Spacious bathrooms and cushy carpeting throughout. Doubles 145F, with shower and TV 195F, with shower and TV 230F.
Hostellerie du Vieux Logis, 5, rue de Joyeuse (tel. 02 35 71 55 30), off rue Louis-Ricard. A 150-year old mansion as beautiful as it is somber. Rooms are well deco-rated and fairly neat, though a bit dusty. Some offer views of the Seine and beyond, others of the Dominican convent across the street. Conversational elderly owner. One-bed rooms (for 1 or 2 people) 100F; 2-bed rooms 150F. Breakfast 17F.
Camping: Camping Municipal de Déville, rue Jules Ferry in Déville-les-Rouen (tel. 02 35 74 07 59), 4km from Rouen. Take bus #2 from station to "Mairie." Attractive sites with squeaky-clean bathrooms and hot showers. 22F50 per person, 7F per tent or car, 14F50 per caravan. Open May-Sept. for tents; year-round for caravans.

FOOD

Outdoor cafés and *brasseries* crowd around **place du Vieux-Marché.** An **open-air market** is in the *place* itself (Tu-Su 7am-12:30pm). Restaurants cluster near the **Gros Horloge.** Packaged foods crinkle at **Monoprix,** 73-83, rue du Gros Horloge (open M-Sa 8:30am-9pm), and at **Marché U,** pl. du Vieux-Marché (open M-Su 9am-12:45pm and 2:30-7:45pm; V, MC).

Le Queen Mary, 1, rue du Cercle (tel. 02 35 71 52 09), off pl. du Vieux-Marché. Mus-cle some *moules* (mussels); prepared in 12 ways. A kg of mussels with fries runs 44-75F. Super salads 38-45F. Open Tu-Su 11:30am-2pm and 7:30-11pm; July-Aug. also M. MC, V.
Natural Gourmand'grain, 3, rue du Petit Salut (tel. 02 35 98 15 74), off pl. de la Cathédrale. Delicious, organic vegetarian food in a small, informal setting. The 64F *menu* offers plate of grains and vegetables, choice of drink (try carrot-orange juice), dessert, coffee; 41F *menu* has the *plat* and dessert. Also a small health-food store and a *salon du thé* after 3pm. Open Tu-Sa noon-6pm. MC, V.

Pizzeria du Drugstore, 2, rue Beauvoisine (tel. 02 35 98 43 18). Three-tiered restaurant located under a drugstore in an enchanting old building. The 54F lunch *menu* includes pizza, dessert, drink, and coffee. The 70F *menu* offers an *apéritif*, pizza, dessert, and coffee. Open M-Sa 11:45am-2pm and 7-11pm. MC, V.

La P'tite Flambée, 24, rue Cauchoise (tel. 02 35 70 02 38), off pl. du Vieux-Marché. Crêpes—whipped up right before your eyes—in the open kitchen. Outdoor seating available. *Galettes* (12-49F) 'n' crêpes (11-36F) galore. Open Tu-Sa 11:30am-2:30pm and 6:30-11:30pm. MC, V.

Les Flandres, 5, rue des Bons-Enfants (tel. 02 35 98 45 16). Traditional French food in an informal, vinyl-covered setting. A 65F *menu* (53F during lunch) gives you 3 courses; the *plats du jour* run 30-45F; the wonderful salads are 36-40F. Open M-F noon-2pm and 7:30-9pm, Sa noon-2pm.

SIGHTS AND ENTERTAINMENT

Sights in Rouen fall into three categories: museums, churches, and museums and churches related to Joan of Arc. The real show-stoppers are the cathedral, the fine arts museum, and Flaubert's former house. *Désolé,* Joan.

A few blocks down rue Jeanne d'Arc from the *gare* is the **Musée des Beaux-Arts,** square Verdrel (tel. 02 35 71 28 40); wheelchair access is at 26bis rue Jean-Lecanuet, to the right of the main entrance. *(Open W-Su 10am-6pm. Admission 20F, ages 18-25 and groups 13F, handicapped, under 18, and art history students free.)* This excellent museum holds works by European masters from the 16th through 20th centuries—Monet, Sisley, Renoir, Modigliani, and Marcel Duchamp—as well as works by Rouen natives Jacques Emile Blanche and Géricault. A step away, at 2, rue Jacques-Villon, is the **Musée Le Secq des Tournelles de Ferronnerie** (tel. 02 35 88 42 92). *(Open W-M tic" 10am-1pm and 2-6pm. Admission 13F, students 9F.)* Largely for metal fans, it demonstrates the historical development of the iron-wrought key and door handle. The "therapeutic" iron corsets, 16th-century cleavers, and 18th-century surgical saws are worth a peek. Located in the Hôtel d'Horqueville, behind the Musée des Beaux-Arts, up the stairs off rue du Baillage, the **Musée de la Céramique,** 1, rue Faucon (tel. 02 35 07 31 74 or 02 35 71 28 40), displays a varied, somewhat interesting collection. *(Open W-M 10am-1pm and 2-6pm. Admission 13F, students 9F, under 18 free.)* Normandy's distinctive *faïence* is the center of attention, although there's a cursory nod to Wedgewood porcelain. Nearby, at 198, rue Beauvoisine, the **Musée des Antiquités,** in Cloître Ste-Marie (tel. 02 35 98 55 10), houses a fine collection of Gallo-Roman to Renaissance objects, from crosses and croziers to tapestries and cathedral columns. *(Open M and W-Sa 10am-12:30pm and 1:30-5:30pm, Su 2-6pm. Admission 20F, seniors 10F, students free.)*

Novelist **Gustave Flaubert** grew up at 51, rue de Lecat, next door to the Hôtel-Dieu hospital. Now the fascinating **Musée Flaubert et d'Histoire de la Médecine** (tel. 02 35 15 59 95), the building houses a few of Flaubert's possessions. *(Open Tu-Sa 10am-noon and 2-6pm. Admission 12F, ages 18-25 8F, senior citizens, under 18, and students free. Free English brochure; guided visits Sa 2:30pm.)* The museum's prize is a collection of gruesome pre-anesthetic medical instruments (including a battlefield amputation kit and gallstone crushers) used by Flaubert's father, a physician. Dramatist **Pierre Corneille's** former home is at 4, rue de la Pie (tel. 02 35 71 63 92), off pl. du Vieux-Marché. *(Open Th-M 10am-noon and 2-6pm, W 2-6pm. Admission 5F, under 18 free.)*

Rouen's ecclesiastical treasures include the **Cathédrale de Notre-Dame,** in pl. de la Cathédrale at the end of the rue du Gros Horloge on your right. *(Open M-Sa 8am-7pm, Su 7:30am-6pm.)* The cathedral is among the most important in France and incorporates nearly every intermediate style of Gothic architecture. Parts of the façade—familiar from dozens of Monet canvases—are disappointingly dingy. Moreover, many of the *vitraux* destroyed during WWII have been replaced with frosted glass, giving the cathedral the atmosphere of a very holy bathroom. The church is becoming gradually brighter and more beautiful as a result of continuing renovations. Don't miss the stained glass in the **Chapelle St-Jean de la Nef** depicting the beheading of St. John the Baptist. The 12th-century **Tour St-Romanus** rises to your left as you face Notre-Dame. To the right lies the 17th-century **Tour de Beurre,** which was financed

Quel Scandale!

Flaubert's novel about a provincial doctor's wife, *Madame Bovary*, caused quite a stir in his hometown, Rouen. Struggling with a subject for his first great work, Flaubert took inspiration from an anecdote told to him by a school friend. When word got around that the tale was based on a real incident, every woman in Normandy fancied herself the model for Emma Bovary, and infuriated local pharmacists took Flaubert's corrupt chemist as a personal attack. Shocked at Flaubert's dim portrait of bourgeois life, the regime of Napoleon III brought him up on immorality charges. Neither the crime nor the genuine Mme Bovary was ever pinned down. At the tourist office, Flaubert fanatics can get info about visiting his estate in nearby **Croisset**, where he wrote as a young man.

through dispensations granted to those who wanted to eat butter during Lent. The cathedral, whose central tower is the tallest in France (151m), is illuminated nightly in summer.

Just behind, on pl. Barthélémy, the 15th-century **Église St-Maclou** presents a striking contrast to its neighbor. *(Open Mar.-Oct. M-Sa 10am-noon and 2-6pm, Su 3-5:30pm; Nov.-Feb. M-Sa 10am-noon and 2-5:30pm, Su 3-5:30pm.)* Built in just 80 years, St-Maclou displays extraordinary Gothic uniformity. The organ, with its elaborately carved friezes of saints and musicians, is its most stunning feature. Beyond the church, a small, poorly marked passageway at 186, rue de Martainville, leads to the **Aître St-Maclou.** *(Open daily 8am-8pm. Free.)* This cloister served as the church's charnel house and cemetery through the later Middle Ages—including the years of the devastating plagues. Evidence of this sad legacy can be found in the gory 15th-century frieze that decorates the beams of the inner courtyard. The *Rouennais* entombed a live cat within the walls to exorcise spirits; a glass panel to the right of the entrance lets visitors gawk at the unlucky feline.

The **Église St-Ouen,** pl. du Général de Gaulle, once belonged to a Benedictine monastery. *(Open Mar. 15-Oct. W-M 10am-12:30pm and 2:30-6pm; Nov.-Dec. 14 and Jan. 16-Mar. 14 W and Sa-Su 10am-12:30pm and 2-4:30pm.)* Begun in 1318, construction of the church was interrupted by the Hundred Years' War and not completed until the 16th century. The calm interior and the nearby park's cool greenery welcome the weary. Inquire about concerts.

Despite the hype, the memorials to Jeanne d'Arc may disappoint some visitors. The **Tour Jeanne d'Arc** is near the station on rue du Donjon. *(Open W-M 10am-noon and 2-5:30pm. Admission 10F, senior citizens and students 5F.)* Due to renovations, the entrance is on **rue Bouvreuil.** This tower is the last remaining of the château that confined Joan before she was burned to death on May 30, 1431, in the pl. du Vieux-Marché. Admission grants you the dubious privilege of walking up a narrow, winding staircase to view two cursory exhibits on the history of Philippe-Auguste's château, of which the tower was a part. Except for true fans of Jeanne, there isn't that much to see. On the other side of rue Jeanne d'Arc and pl. du Vieux-Marché is the **Église Ste-Jeanne d'Arc,** a massive structure designed in 1979 to resemble an overturned Viking longboat. *(Open M-F 10am-12:30pm and 2-6pm, Sa-Su 2-6pm.)* Its unconventional, sprawling shape disguises the fact that the interior "church in the round" is actually quite tiny. The wall of luminous stained glass was recovered from the Église St-Vincent, destroyed during WWII. A 6.5m cross outside marks the spot where the Maid of Orléans met a fiery martyrdom on May 30, 1431.

Built into a bridge across **rue du Gros Horloge,** the **Gros Horloge** (Big Clock) is charmingly inaccurate. When the belfry is eventually repaired, visitors will be able to ascend for a view of the 14th-century clockwork and the rooftops of Rouen. Call 02 35 71 28 40 to see if it's open again. A half-block from the rue du Gros Horloge and next to the war-marked **Palais de Justice** stands an 11th-century building known as the **Monument Juif** (Jewish Monument). Uncovered during the 1980s, the structure may have been a synagogue, a Talmudic school, or a private house; regardless, it is one of the few remaining traces of the Jewish presence in medieval Europe. You must call the tourist office two days in advance to take a guided tour in French (tel. 02 32 08 32 46).

Rouen's yuppies flock to **Au Bureau,** on pl. du Vieux-Marché, when they leave the office. For a younger crowd, try **Le Scottish,** 21, rue Verte (tel. 02 35 71 46 22), with weekend jazz concerts on its terrace (cocktails 48-52F; beer 18-65F; open M-Sa 12:30pm-2am). The **Underground Pub,** 26, rue des Champs Maillets (tel. 02 35 98 44 84), offers billiards and darts (drafts 15-20F; open M-Sa 5pm-2am; V, MC). One of few gay bars in town is **Le Kox,** 138, rue Beauvoisine (tel. 02 35 07 71 97; open daily 6pm-2am; V, MC).

■ Mont-St-Michel

Rising from the sea like an enormous sand castle, the fortified island of Mont-St-Michel is visible for kilometers in every direction. A work in progress since its founding in 708, the Mont is a dazzling labyrinth of stone arches, spires, and stairways that climb (and keep climbing) to the abbey itself. Just as overwhelming as the Mont's beauty, though, are the crowds that fill its streets. The island has been a popular spot for pilgrims both religious and secular since the 8th century. Each August sees as many as 200,000 enraptured visitors daily—an early start is highly recommended.

ORIENTATION AND PRACTICAL INFORMATION

Because the Mont is isolated from the mainland and the town proper is a tiny village, you should plan your visit to avoid being stranded here where "budget hotel" is an oxymoron. The only break in the outer wall is the **Porte de l'Avancée.** Inside, the tourist office lies immediately to the left; to the right, the **Porte du Boulevard** and **Porte du Roy** open onto the town's major thoroughfare, the **Grande Rue.** All hotels, restaurants, and sights are on this spiraling street, but so are the crowds—sneak off via stairwells and archways to explore Mont-St-Michel's less-visited corners.

Trains: The nearest train station is in Pontorson (tel. 02 33 60 00 35). Open M-F 8:30am-noon and 1:30-7:30pm, Sa 8:30am-noon and 2-6:15pm, Su 2:30-9:45pm. To Paris (4hr., 1 per day, 237F plus 36-90F TGV supplement).

Buses: Buses leave from Porte du Roy; buy tickets on board. **STN Buses** (tel. 02 33 60 00 35 in Pontorson; 02 33 50 08 99 in Granville) link the Mont to Pontorson and elsewhere (last bus leaves the Mont at 6:15pm). To Pontorson (8 per day, 15min., 14F, round-trip 22F). **Courriers Bretons** (tel. 02 33 60 11 43) runs to Avranches (30min., 1-2 per day, 26F), St-Malo (1½hr., 2-4 per day, 53F), and Rennes (1½hr., M-Sa 3 per day, Su 1 per day, 63F). Office open M-Sa 10am-noon and 4-6:30pm.

Tourist Office: BP 4 (tel. 02 33 60 14 30; fax 02 33 60 06 75), behind the wall to your left after you enter the city. Busy! Ask about organized 2hr. hiking expeditions over the sand to the **Ile de Tombelaine** (Apr.-Sept. at low tide) or for the free tide table *Horaire des Marées.* Avoid the **currency exchange.** Open July-Aug. M-Sa 9am-12:30pm and 2-6:30pm; Sept.-June 9am-noon and 2-5pm. The staff take irregular weeks off in the off season; call if you need their help.

Money: Société Générale, next to the tourist office before you enter Grande Rue.

Emergency: tel. 17. **Medical emergency:** tel. 15.

Post Office: Grand Rue (tel. 02 33 60 14 26), near Porte du Roy. **Currency exchange** at tolerable rates. Open M-F 9am-6pm, Sa 9am-5pm; mid-Sept. to June M-F 9am-noon and 2-5pm, Sa 9am-noon. **Postal code:** 50116.

ACCOMMODATIONS, CAMPING, AND FOOD

Plan ahead to reserve a room you can afford; prices climb faster than the bay's famous tides. St-Malo and Avranches offer accommodations at more reasonable prices. Pontorson (**postal code:** 50170) has little to offer other than proximity.

Centre Duguesclin (HI), rue Général Patton (tel. 02 33 60 18 65), in Pontorson. From the train station, turn right onto rue du Tizon, take your first left (rue du Couesnon) and then a right onto rue St-Michel, until you come to the inconspicuous post office on the right. Turn left, then make a right past the cathedral and a left onto rue Hédou. Follow it to its end and take a right on rue Général Patton. The hostel is on your left, 1 block down (10min.). Dorm-style 4- to 7-bed rooms (51 beds) are bright and conducive to gathering, as is the kitchen and dining area. Clean, hot showers. No sheets or blankets provided. Beds 44F. Reception daily 8-10am and 6-10pm. Lockout 10am-6pm. Open June to mid-Sept., but is occasionally booked fully by groups, even in high season.

Hotel-Restaurant le Relais Clemenceau, 40, bd. Clemenceau (tel. 02 33 60 10 96; fax 02 33 60 25 71), in Pontorson. Walk straight out of the *gare* onto bd. Clemenceau (look for sign to hotel). 20 bright, impeccably clean rooms with spacious bathrooms let by a lovely couple. Doubles 150F, with shower 180-200F, with shower and toilet 215-250F; triples and quads 280-300F. Additional bed 5F. Breakfast 30F. MC, V.

Camping: Camping Municipal de Pontorson, chemin des Soupirs (tel. 02 33 68 11 59), off rue Général Patton near the hostel, 10min. from the station. Tranquil, bright, unforested sites with sound sanitary equipment. 13F per person, 13F per tent, 6F50 per car. Electricity 13F. Open Apr.-Sept. **Camping du Mont-St-Michel,** BP 8 (tel. 02 33 60 09 33), a mere 1.8km from the Mont at the junction of D275 and N776. Clean, pleasantly shaded sites fill fast. Great free showers. **Supermarket** next door. 22F per person, 20F per car or tent. Open Feb. 15-Nov. 1. **Camping St-Michel,** route du Mont-St-Michel (tel. 02 33 70 96 90), by the bay in Courtils. A bit far from the Mont (9km), but the Granville bus stops 200m from entrance. Buses go to the Mont at 11am and 5pm. Sites are quiet and near a swimming pool, common room, and telephone. 19F per person, 19F per car and tent. Open Mar. 15-Oct. 15. More campgrounds lurk in Beauvoir, two-thirds to the Mont from Pontorson.

FOOD

On the Mont, look for local specialties such as *agneau du pré salé* (lamb raised on surrounding salt marshes) and *omelette poulard,* a fluffy soufflé-like dish (about 45F). The **Chapeau Rouge,** Grande Rue (tel. 02 33 60 14 29), offers these delicacies as well as seafood treats (3-course *menus* 69-79F). To eat in a room with a view, walk along the ramparts and take your pick of the restaurants. **Les Terrasses Poulard,** Grande Rue (tel. 02 33 60 14 09), has a beautiful terrace and a 99F *menu* that includes their own *omelette poulard* (open Apr.-Sept. daily 11am-midnight; Oct.-Mar. noon-2pm and 7-9pm). **Sandwich** stands and self-service **cafeterias** line the Grande Rue. **La Sirène,** Grande Rue (tel. 02 33 60 08 60), past the post office on the left, features chocolate-banana *crêpes* (29F), stuffed to bursting and topped with a *mont* of chocolate sauce (open daily noon-2:30pm and 6-9:30pm). There's a **Champion supermarket** on the way to Mont-St-Michel from Pontorson, conveniently located across the street from the rue St-Michel STN bus stop (open M-F 9am-12:30pm and 2:30-7:15pm, Sa 9am-7:30pm).

SIGHTS

While the formation of the Baie de Mont-St-Michel began thousands of years ago, a legend based on a monastic manuscript claims that the island was created in the 7th century when a huge wave flooded the surrounding forest. In 708, the **Archangel Michael** appeared twice in the dreams of the Bishop of Avranches, instructing him to build a place of worship on the barren and rocky island north of Pontorson. The doubting bishop ignored the first two appearances. It was only after the frustrated angel insisted a third time that plans were laid out for several crypts around the rock itself to provide a foundation for the church. Only a few stones remain from the original oratory. Additions began in 966, when a group of monks made a pilgrimage to the Mont and were so inspired by its beauty and power that they began an even larger church on the site.

Mostly complete by the 14th and 15th centuries, the Mont was used by French kings as a fortress during the Hundred Years' War. While its outer walls repelled English attacks, its inner walls still cloistered the Benedictines, who spent their time copying and illuminating the famous *manuscrits du Mont-St-Michel,* now on display in nearby Avranches. They received religious pilgrims (including St. Louis) until 1789, when the Revolutionary government turned the island into a state prison. Sinners—

Robespierre among them—traveled to the rock no longer to confess their misdeeds, but to pay for them. When Emperor Napoleon III recognized the Mont's historical significance, his patronage set in motion renovations that began after his fall from power. In 1874, Mont-St-Michel was classified as a national monument, and in 1897 it was topped by the crowning bronze statue of St. Michel. A small community of monks has lived in the abbey since 1969.

New surprises await a wanderer in every nook and cranny on the Mont, and it's almost impossible to get lost. If you'd prefer a structured visit, pick up one of the guides available at the booths on Grande Rue for 25-80F. A climb up the **Grande Rue** several flights of stairs places you at the **abbey** entrance (tel. 02 33 89 80 00), the departure point for the one-hour tours free with entrance. There are about six English tours per day. An audio tour is 30F. (Open daily May-Sept. 9:30am-5pm; Oct.-Apr. 9:30am-4:30pm. Admission 40F, under 26 25F.) Mass is still held daily at 12:15pm; entry to the abbey church for the service (and the service only) is free from noon to 12:15pm.

Beneath the church lie the Mont's frigid **crypts.** Descent to the crypts passes through the refectory and leads into the dark, chilly church foundations where the walls are 2m thick in places. **La Merveille,** an intricate 13th-century cloister, encloses a seemingly endless web of passageways and chambers. If you're not impressed with its architectural complexities, the mechanical simplicity of the Mont's **treadmill** will surely catch your attention. Prisoners held here during the French Revolution would walk on the wheel for hours, their foot labor powering the elaborate pulley system that carried supplies up the side of the Mont.

About halfway up the Grande Rue is the **Logis Tiphaine,** a restored 14th-century home. Bertrand Duguesclin, born so fat and ugly that his mother rejected him, went on to become governor of Pontorson and marry a beautiful young woman named Tiphaine. He built this four-story villa in 1365 to protect his wife from the English while he was fighting in Spain. Today, the *logis* houses an interesting **museum** (tel. 02 33 60 23 34), which displays well-preserved 14th- to 17th-century furniture, fireplaces, and objects of everyday use, including a chastity belt. (Open daily Jan.-June and Sept.-Nov. 14 9am-6pm, July-Aug. 9am-7pm. Admission 25F, students 20F, under 18 5F.)

The few museums in Mont-St-Michel lean toward moderately interesting summaries of the Mont's history and a hodgepodge of historical "artifacts." The fact that each museum exits into a gift shop should be the first clue that the prices may be inflated. The **Musée Historique** contains exhibits on medieval torture devices and the Mont's most rapscallious prisoners, while the **Musée Maritime** has a collection of 300 antique scale model boats. The **Archéoscope** is the most engaging, describing the legends and history of the Mont with film, slides, music, and an intricate model that rises from the water. Admission to each museum runs at 40F or more, but you can buy a ticket to all three for 75F (students 60F). On the other hand, you might well be better off buying a good Mont-related book for about half that price.

Do not wander off too far on the sand. The broad expanses are riddled with **quicksand,** and the bay's **tides,** shifting every six hours or so, are the highest in France. During high-tide days, twice a month (three days after the new moon and three days after the full moon), the mascaret (initial tidal wave) rushes in at 2m per second, flooding the beaches along the causeway. To see this spectacle, you must be within the abbey fortifications two hours ahead of time.

When darkness falls, illumination transforms the Mont into a glowing jewel best seen from either the causeway entrance or across the bay in Avranches (June-Aug. M-Sa 10pm-1am; Sept. 9pm-midnight). Dusk is also the time to revisit the crypts of the abbey. **Les Imaginaires** (tel. 02 33 60 14 14) immerse the sanctuary's corridors in a flood of light and music; viewer descriptions include "very Zen" and "very Pink Floyd." (May-Aug. 10pm-1am; Sept. 9pm-midnight; last entry 1hr. before closing. Admission 60F, students 35F, under 12 free.) Note, though, there's no public transportation off the Mont late at night—you'll need a car. In May, the Mont celebrates **St-Michel de Printemps,** when costumed men and women parading through the streets recapture local Breton traditions. The fall event, **St-Michel d'Automne,** held on the Sunday before the feast of St-Michel (late Sept. to early Oct.), is similar but more religious and authentic.

■ Near Mont-St-Michel: Avranches

ORIENTATION AND PRACTICAL INFORMATION Balanced on a hill in a northern corner of the bay of Mont-St-Michel, Avranches (pop. 9000) offers another base from which to explore the fortified island. But before rushing off to Normandy's big attraction, give Avranches itself some time. After all, it was St. Aubert, the 8th-century Bishop of Avranches, who gave in to angelic pressure and built the Mont. As a result, the two are inextricably linked, and Avranches serves as a good primer for trips island-ward. To get to the *centre ville* from the train station, cross the highway via the footbridge to the right of the station and lean into the heart-pounding hike uphill, bearing left at the first major fork. The Caen-Rennes train line passes through Avranches' **SNCF station** (tel. 02 33 58 00 77) at the bottom of the hill. Destinations include Paris via Foligny (5hr., 2 per day, 189F; station open M-Sa 8:30am-7pm, Su 1:45-10pm). **STN,** 2, rue Général-de-Gaulle (tel. 02 33 58 03 07), adjacent to the town hall, sends buses to Mont-St-Michel (July-Aug. 1 per day, 24F, round-trip 45F; Sept.-June 1 per week) and to Granville (33F). (Office open M, Tu, and Th 10:30am-noon and 3:30-6pm, W and F 10:30am-noon and 3:30-5pm.) The **tourist office** (tel. 02 33 58 00 22; fax 02 33 68 13 29), which shares the STN building, reserves rooms (10F) and gives out free town maps and brochures (open July-Aug. M-Sa 9am-8pm, Su 2:30-7pm; Sept.-June M-Sa 9am-noon and 2-6pm). **Société Générale,** across from the tourist office, has a 24-hour **ATM,** as does **Crédit Agricole,** two blocks to the left of the tourist office on rue du Pot d'Etain, and **Crédit Mutuel,** two blocks from the tourist office at the corner of rue de la Constitution and rue St-Symphorien. The **post office** on rue St-Gervais offers **currency exchange** and **Poste Restante** (open M-F 8am-6:30pm, Sa 8am-noon; **postal code: 50300**).

ACCOMMODATIONS AND FOOD The popular **Hôtel de Normandie,** bd. L. Jozeau-Marigné (tel. 02 33 58 01 33), sits at the end of the steep footpath that you'll encounter after crossing the footbridge to the right of the station. Run by exceptionally friendly staff, the ivy-covered building offers lovely rooms with fluffy comforters, immaculate bathrooms, and views of the patchwork countryside. A flash of your *Let's Go* makes the owners friends for life. (Singles 150F, with bath 170F, with TV 180F; doubles 180F, with bath or shower 230F. Shower free. TV 30F. Breakfast 30F. MC, V.) Opposite the tourist office, **Hôtel Valhubert,** 7, rue Général de Gaulle (tel. 02 33 58 03 28), rents worn but clean rooms above a popular bar. (Singles and doubles 140F, with shower or bath 180F, with shower and toilet 200F. Extra bed 30F. Breakfast 25F. Reception closed Su.) Your cheapest bet might be a **chambre d'hôtes.** The tourist office has a list of rooms that start at 100F per night.

Numerous cheap *brasseries* and restaurants surround the tourist office. **Le Commerce,** just across the street, offers three-course *menus* (60-74F) with specialties from all over Normandy, like tripe and mussels (open M-Sa noon-2:30pm and 6:45-9:30pm; V, MC). At pl. St-Gervais, **Pizzeria l'Anticario** (tel. 02 33 58 32 10) serves up a great lunchtime menu for 45F in a cozy, elegant environment. (Open Tu-Su noon-2pm and 7-11pm.) **La Cucaracha** (tel. 02 33 58 14 13), also in pl. St-Gervais, serves a decent approximation of Tex-Mex, with hot tortillas (open Tu-Su noon-2pm and 7-11pm). Each Saturday from 9am to 3pm, a **market** fills pl. du Marché, off rue des Chapeliers. There is a **Stoc supermarket** on rue Général de Gaulle on the way from the station to the *centre ville* (open M-Sa 9am-7:30pm, Su 9:30-11:45am).

SIGHTS The **Jardin des Plantes,** pl. Carnot, is dotted with Romanesque arches and provides a spectacular view of the distant Mont-St-Michel. It is illuminated nightly July to August from 8:30 to 11:30pm. A short distance away is Avranches's **museum,** on rue d'Office (tel. 02 33 58 25 15; open July-Aug. daily 10am-noon and 2-6pm; Apr.-June and Sept.-Oct. W-M, same hours). It houses exhibits of regional garb and crafts as well as a replica of a medieval scriptorium. Most impressive, however, is the collection of Mont-St-Michel's manuscripts, which, in their multi-colored, calligraphic way, detail the finer points of theology, astronomy, and music. Summer finds many of the manuscripts in the *mairie* (June-Aug. daily 10am-noon and 2-6pm). A single 30F ticket (15F for students) provides admittance to the museum, the manuscripts, and the last stop on your pre-Mont tour: the **Église St-Gervais,** pl. St-Gervais, an impressive granite church whose 74m tower contains a 32-bell chime. The real treasure, however, is inside. When the Archangel Michael appeared to Bishop Aubert and commanded him to build Mont-St-Michel, Aubert ignored the order. When Michael appeared again, Aubert continued to delay. The angel, realizing that he and an infinite number of friends could dance on this pinhead, decided that Aubert needed more forceful persuasion. Michael scolded Aubert by tapping him on the forehead, but he pressed his finger into the unwitting bishop's brow so enthusiastically that a dent resulted. You can see Aubert's skull (and the divot) in the **treasury,** right inside the door of the church (open W-M 10am-noon and 2-6pm).

Down rue de la Constitution, the **Patton Memorial** is officially American soil. The huge stone obelisk commemorates Operation COBRA's successful break through the German front between St-Lô and Périers in July of 1944. Patton's victory here resulted in the liberation of Avranches, a drive west into Brittany, and an advance east into the Loire Valley and on to Paris.

▓ Bayeux and the D-Day Beaches

Bayeux has been prominent from medieval times to the present. If the world-famous tapestry isn't enough reason to visit, Bayeux has a beautiful cathedral and interesting museums; it is also an ideal gateway to the D-Day Beaches.

The celebrated **Tapisserie de Bayeux** illustrates in vibrant detail the events that led to the Battle of Hastings on October 14, 1066. On that date, William the Conqueror crossed the Channel to conquer his cousin Harold, who held a title rightfully belonging to William—King of England. The tapestry was probably intended to hang around the nave of Bayeux's cathedral on the Feast of the Holy Relics. A mere 50cm wide but a gargantuan 70m long, the surviving product hangs in all its glory at the **Centre Guillaume le Conquérant** (tel. 02 31 51 25 50), a renovated 18th-century seminary on rue de Nesmond. Avoid lengthy intoductory exhibits by viewing the short film on the tapestry's historical background. (Open May-Aug. daily 9am-7pm; Mar. 15-Apr. and Sept.-Oct. 15 9am-6:30pm; Oct. 16-Mar. 14 9:30am-12:30pm and 2-6pm. Admission 38F; students 15F.)

The **Centre d'Accueil Municipal,** 21, rue des Marettes (tel. 02 31 92 08 19) is big, friendly, and clean (reception 7am-8pm, call if arriving later; 75F). The **Hôtel Notre-Dame,** 44, rue des Cuisiniers (tel. 02 31 92 87 24), is near the cathedral (comfy singles and doubles 160-270F; MC, V). Bayeux's **tourist office,** pont St-Jean (tel. 02 31 51 28 38), books rooms and supplies info on the D-Day Beaches (open M-Sa 9am-noon and 2-6pm, Su 9:30am-noon and 2:30-6pm).

Normandy's shores have been gnawed and sculpted by tireless waves for thousands of years, but one tragic and glorious month five decades ago left a mark like none before. In June of 1944, over a million Allied soldiers surged from the English Channel onto the beaches of Normandy. The invasion was the first step in an incredible battle over the Nazi-occupied Continent. Today, the record of the battle can be clearly seen in sobering gravestones and the pockmarked landscape; remnants of German bunkers dot the coastline, and craters left by bombs are still unfilled. The invasion's horrible price was not for nought, however; less than a year later, Allied forces rolled into Berlin, and Germany surrendered. **Omaha Beach** is the home of the **American Cemetery,** where almost 10,000 graves stretch across 172 acres (open daily Apr.-Nov. 8am-6pm; Dec.-Mar. 9am-5pm; the office can help locate specific graves). Ten kilometers north of Bayeux, at the center of **Gold Beach,** is **Arromanches,** where an artificial harbor that had been towed across the Channel allowed Allied forces to unload precious supplies. East of here is **Juno Beach,** the landing site of the Canadian and Québecois forces and home to the **Canadian Cemetery.** British cemeteries lie farther to the east at **Sword Beach.** These sights are difficult to get to; the D514 is tortuous, and cycling is dangerous. Try **Bus Fly** (tel. 02 31 22 00 08) or **Normandy Tours** (tel. 02 31 92 10 70), both of which arrange for tours of up to eight people.

BRETAGNE (BRITTANY)

Gnawed by the sea into cliffs, crags, and inlets, the Breton peninsula tugs away from mainland France, intent on its own direction. Unlike most of their countrymen, Bretons are a Celtic people whose ancestors crossed over from Britain to escape Anglo-Saxon invaders in the 5th and 6th centuries. They settled in the ancient Kingdom of Armor, converting its inhabitants to Christianity and renaming it "Little Britain," or Brittany. Many of Brittany's customs date back to its centuries as an independent duchy. The traditional costume of Breton women, the black dress and lace coiffe (an elaborate headdress), appears in museums, folk festivals, and even some markets. Lilting *Brezhoneg* (Breton) is spoken energetically at pubs and ports in the western part of the province, and some children learn the old Celtic tongue in school, playing a part in efforts to keep the language from falling into disuse.

Little is known of the Neolithic people who settled here before the Gauls and who erected the thousands of megaliths visible today. *Menhirs* are large single stones that point skyward. *Dolmen* stones served as burial mounds. The Romans, who conquered the area in 56 BC, decorated some of these monuments and incorporated them into their own rituals. Later, the Christian Bretons capped some standing stones with crosses and carved Christian symbols into them.

Modernization has come only in the postwar period to this relatively poor province. Traditional vocations like farming and fishing have become increasingly difficult to pursue, and many young Bretons emigrate to large cities elsewhere in France or abroad. In the past, economic difficulties have fueled an active separatist movement, but recently the French government has granted more autonomy to the local leadership and has begun to support the preservation of Breton culture. In 1979, students were allowed to replace one language section of the *baccalauréat* exam with Breton. François Mitterrand made Brittany more accessible with new roads and the construction of new TGV lines. Astérix and Obélix, Brittany's most famous natives, symbolize the Bretons' history of resistance to both Roman and French outsiders. *Bretagne's* most famous family is the illustrious Lefoll clan. Parisian intellectual and professor Valérie Lefoll, jazz musician Yann Lefoll, master-chef Françoise Lefoll, and entrepeneur Georges Lefoll illustrate the success of *Bretons* in 1990s France. Known for their hospitality, the Lefoll's exemplify Breton warmth and generosity.

Brittany is lined with spectacular beaches. If you dislike crowds, beware of visiting in July and August: French tourists will be here in droves. In the off-season, many of the coastal resorts such as St-Malo, Quiberon, and Concarneau essentially shut down, but the churches, beaches, and cliffs still seduce visitors. Whatever the season, try to spend some time on the pristine islands off the mainland or in the Argoat interior, where tourists are rarer and Breton traditions less disturbed.

Home of the famous *crêpe*, Breton *crêperies* offer dinner *crêpes salées* (salted crêpes or *galettes)* of ground buckwheat flour *(sarrasin)* wrapped around eggs, mushrooms, seafood, or ham. Dessert *crêpes sucrées* (sugared crêpes) made of ground wheat flour *(froment* or *bouché)* are filled with chocolate, fruit, or jam. These are accompanied by Breton *cidre,* an alcoholic, carbonated specialty that comes in two varieties, the dry *cidre brut* or the sweeter *cidre doux.* Local apéritifs include *chouchenn,* a crisp, cold drink made from fermented honey. Whatever the meal, rest assured that Breton seafood *(fruits de mer)* will be a part of it.

■ Rennes

Home to two major universities and 60,000 students, Rennes (pop. 205,000) combines Parisian sophistication with traditional Breton charm. Most of the city was destroyed in 1720, when a drunk carpenter knocked over a lamp and started a massive fire. However, the lovely, wooden *vieille ville* remained intact and now teems with hip cafés, bars, and clubs. Rennes is a popular stopover between Paris and Mont-St-Michel and a good base from which to explore the Brocéliande Forest.

ORIENTATION AND PRACTICAL INFORMATION

The **Vilaine river** cuts the city in two, with the train station to the south and most sights and shopping to the north (20min. away). From the northern exit of the *gare,* **av. Jean Janvier** (straight ahead) goes to the river.

Trains: pl. de la Gare (tel. 02 99 65 50 50, reservations 08 36 35 35 35), at the end of av. Jean Janvier. To Paris (2hr., 15 per day, all TGV 171F). Office open M-Sa 8:45am-7:45pm, Su 10:15am-7:30pm. **Buses:** 16, pl. de la gare (tel. 02 99 30 87 80), to the left of the Gare Routière as you face it. **Les Courriers Bretons** (tel. 02 99 56 79 09) run to Mont-St-Michel (2½hr., 1-2 per day, 62F).

Public Transportation: Star, 12, rue du Pré Botté (tel. 02 99 79 37 37). Buses run daily until 6:30 or 7:30pm. Ticket 6F, *carnet* of 10 tickets 47F. 40% discount on tickets at the youth hostel. Office open M-F 7am-7pm, Sa 9:30am-noon and 2-6:30pm. Tickets available at office and newsstands throughout the city. You may also pay driver directly (one ticket 6F50).

Taxis: At the train station (tel. 02 99 30 79 79). 24hr.

Bike Rental: Guedard, 13, bd. Beaumont (tel. 02 99 30 43 78), next to the train station. *VTTs* 70F per day. In the *vieille ville,* try **Cherel,** 11, pl. Ste-Anne (tel. 02 99 79 24 86). *VTTs* 50F per day, 3000F deposit.

Hiking and Biking Information: France Randonnée, 9, rue des Portes-Mordelaises (tel. 02 99 31 59 44; fax 02 99 30 02 96). Also offers piles of info on *Grande Randonnée* (long hike) trails and lists of *gîtes d'étape.* Open M-Sa 9am-6pm.

Tourist Office: 11, rue pont St-Yves (tel. 02 99 67 11 11). From the *gare,* take av. Jean Janvier to quai Chateaubriand. Turn left and walk along the river till you reach the rue George Dottin. Turn right and then right again on the rue Saint-Yves. The office is on the right. Free maps, lists of hotels and restaurants. Pick up a free copy of *Le Rennais* or *La Griffe,* monthly cultural magazines. Open M-F 9am-6pm, Sa 2 pm-6pm, Su 10am-6pm.

Money: Banks with 24hr. **ATMs** abound in the *vieille ville,* the *gare,* and the rue d'Isly. The post office is happy to change cash and traveler's checks and also has Western Union Services.

French-American Institute, 7, quai Chateaubriand (tel. 02 99 79 20 57; fax 02 99 79 30 09), arranges joint French-American activities and exchange programs. Office on the 2nd floor can help with visas and work permits. Open M-Th 9am-12:30pm and 1:30-6pm, F 9am-12:30pm and 1:30-5pm. **English Books: Forum du Livre,** 5, quai Lamartine (tel. 02 99 79 38 93). Open M-Sa 9:30am-7pm.

Youth Center: Centre Information Jeunesse Bretagne, 6, cours des Alliés (tel. 02 99 31 47 48; fax 02 99 30 39 51), on the 2nd floor. List of budget hotels. Info on cultural events, work opportunities, and more. Open mid-July to mid-Aug. M-F 2-6pm; mid-Aug. to mid-July M-F 10am-6pm, Sa 10am-noon and 2-6pm.

Gay and Lesbian Organizations: Femmes Entre Elles, 9, rue de la Paillette (tel. 02 99 59 50 32), organizes events for lesbians and has a library. Open 1st and 3rd W of each month 7-8pm. **AD-HOC (Association des Homosexuels de Condate),** 39B, rue Motte Brûlon (tel. 02 99 30 59 25), is a gay center.

Laundromat: 25, rue de Penhoet. Open daily 8am-10pm.

Emergency: tel. 17. **Medical emergency:** tel. 15 or 02 99 59 16 16.

Police: rue d'Echange (tel. 02 99 65 00 22), off pl. Ste-Anne.

Crisis Lines: Aides Bretagne, 2, quai Richemont (tel. 02 99 30 01 30), for AIDS info. **S.O.S. Amitié** (tel. 02 99 59 71 71), for support. **S.O.S. Suicide** (tel. 0 800 13 40 48). **Victime d'Aggressions Sexuelles** (tel. 02 99 27 30 21) deals with sexual abuse.

24-Hour Pharmacy: Pharmacies take turns staying open all night and on weekends. To locate an open pharmacy *(pharmacie du garde)* outside of normal business hours, call the fire station (tel. 18).

Hospital: Hôpital de Pontchaillou, rue Henri Le Guilloux (tel. 02 99 28 43 21).

Post Office: 27, bd. du Colombier (tel. 02 99 01 22 11), 1 block left of the *gare* exit. **Branch office,** pl. de la République (tel. 02 99 79 50 71). **Currency exchange. Poste Restante.** 3F per item. Western Union and faxing service at branch office only. Open M-F 8am-7pm, Sa 8am-noon. **Postal code:** 35000.

Internet Access: Check email @ **Cyberspirit,** 2d, rue de la Visitation (tel. 02 99 84 53 30). It costs 30F for 30min., 5F to send an email. Open M-Tu noon-7pm, W-F noon-midnight, Sa 2pm-midnight.

ACCOMMODATIONS AND CAMPING

You should reserve in the first week of July during the annual Tombées de la Nuit festival. In July and August, a university dorm remains open to student travelers for short stays (singles 92F per night). To check availability, call **CROUS,** 7, pl. Hoche (tel. 07 99 36 46 11; open M-F 8:30am-4pm). A number of moderately priced hotels lie to the east of av. Jean Janvier between quai Richemont and the *gare.*

Auberge de Jeunesse (HI), 10-12, Canal St-Martin (tel. 02 99 33 22 33; fax 02 99 59 06 21). From the *gare,* take av. Jean Janvier straight to the canal, where it becomes rue Gambetta. Go 5 blocks, then left onto rue des Fossés. Take rue de la Visitation to pl. Ste-Anne. On the north side of the *place,* rue St-Malo leads to the hostel (30min.). Or take the bus (M-F #20, Sa-Su #1 or 18, direction: Centre Commercial Nord) to "Hôtel Dieu." From the bus stop, continue down the road, turn right on rue de St-Malo, and follow the street over mini-canal to an intersection. The hostel is on the right. 1- to 4-person rooms. White tile floors and bright blue walls are reminiscent of a public swimming pool. Laundry, kitchen, and cafeteria run by eclectic, friendly staff. Discounts on bus tickets and excursions to St-Malo. Singles 85F, with shower 90F; doubles 130F, with shower 960F. Sheets and breakfast included. Reception daily 7am-11:30pm. No lockout. MC, V.

Hôtel Venezia, 27, rue Dupont des Loges (tel. 02 99 30 36 56; fax 02 99 30 78 78), off quai Richemont. Take av. Jean Janvier from the station. Turn right onto rue Dupont des Loges, a block before the canal. *Let's Go*-loving couple rents spacious, gorgeous rooms in a great location. Ask for one with a view of the canal. Singles 120F, with shower and TV 150F, with shower, toilet, and TV 170F; doubles 140F, with shower and TV 170F, with shower, toilet, and TV 190F. Mention *Let's Go* when you arrive for a potential discount. All-you-can-eat breakfast with juice 25F. Call ahead for weekends in summer. MC, V.

Hôtel Riaval, 9, rue Riaval (tel. 02 99 50 65 58; fax 02 99 41 85 30). Exit the *gare* through the southern "Cour d'Appel" doors and walk 100m across the open plaza and then down the metal stairs. Go left on rue de Riaval and right at first intersection (still the rue de Riaval). The hotel is on the left. Clean and cozy hotel in a quiet neighborhood. Top floor views of the city. Rooms for 1 or 2 people without shower 130F, with shower 160F, with shower, TV, and toilet 190F. Rooms for 3 or 4 also available (160-250F). Breakfast 26F. V.

Hôtel Richemont, 8, rue Dupont des Loges (tel. 02 99 30 38 21; fax 02 99 31 73 20). Directly off av. Jean Janvier, on right. Clean, slightly worn rooms with sparkling bathroom fixtures. Singles 220-227F; doubles with 1 bed 255F; 2 beds 284F. Breakfast 30F. MC, V.

Camping: Municipal des Gayeulles, in Parc les Grayeulles (tel. 02 99 36 91 22). Take bus #3 from rue de Paris (from rue Gambetta, turn right on rue Victor Hugo, which becomes rue de Paris) to Parc les Grayeulles. The campground is deep within the park, past the public pool and a farm with activities for kids. Adults 13F50, children under 7 6F50. Cars 5F. Tent 15F50. Electricity 17F. Hot shower 5F. 10% discount for stays over 8 days. No credit cards.

FOOD

Rennes's restaurant scene ranges from traditional *crêpes* and *galettes* to Indian, African, Chinese, and Mexican offerings. You're sure to find something marvelous on rue de St-Malo, pl. St-Michel, rue St-Georges, or rue Ste-Melaine. For do-it-yourself types, there is a huge open market every Saturday in pl. des Lices, a smaller market held daily in different locations (ask the tourist office), and a supermarket in the Galeries-Lafayette on quai Duguay-Trouin (M-Sa 9am-8pm).

Crêperie au Boulingrain, 25, rue St-Melaine (tel. 02 99 38 75 11), near the Jardin du Thabor. Formerly a prison, this place now serves *galettes* worth some jail time. The namesake *boulingrain* is a crêpe stuffed with apples, caramel, and almonds (38F). Open M-F 11:30am-2pm and 6:30-11pm, Sa-Su 6:30-11pm.

Restaurant la Grolle, 34-36, rue de St-Malo (tel. 02 99 38 80 89), 5min. from the hostel. The outgoing staff serves up unreal portions in an equally unreal, cave-motif interior. Hearty dishes often include lots of cheese. Especially tasty is the *raclette*

(85F), which comes with baked potatoes, potatoes *au gratin,* meat, *cornichons,* and onions. Also, many fondue options. Open daily 6:30-10:30pm.

Ay! Mexico, 7, rue de Juillet (tel. 02 99 31 6702). Fresh, authentic Mexican food in a colorful atmosphere. You'll find tacos, empanadas, and tostadas. 50F lunch menu. Open M-Sa 11:30am-2:30pm and 7pm-midnight.

SIGHTS AND ENTERTAINMENT

The **Musée des Beaux-Arts,** 20, quai Émile Zola (tel. 02 99 28 55 84; fax 02 99 28 55 99), is an impressive institution with a collection dating from the 14th century to the day before yesterday. *(Open W-M 10am-noon and 2-6pm. Tours July-Aug. W and F at 2:30 pm. Admission 30F, students, children, senior citizens 15F.)* It houses works by de La Tour, Picasso, and Serusier as well as a small but fascinating exhibit of Egyptian pottery. Call about rotating special exhibits. The lush **Jardin du Thabor** is a delight for garden lovers and romantics alike. Sculptures, fountains, and a massive birdcage grace the labyrinthine garden. Concerts are often held in the garden, and a small gallery on the north side presents a rotating exhibit of local artwork. *(Open daily June-Sept. 7am-9:30 pm.)* Adjacent is the **Église Nôtre Dame;** step inside the church and gaze at the magnificent chapel altar and the blazing colors of the stained-glass choir. The magnificent **Cathédrale St-Pierre,** in the *vieille ville,* provides a gorgeous view of the city. *(Open daily 9am-noon and 2-5pm.)* If you ask nicely, a staffperson might take you up to the towers. Across the street from the cathedral is the actual **Porte Mordelaise,** the former entrance to the city and the last remaining piece of the medieval wall that used to surround Rennes. The **Ecomusée du Pays de Rennes** (tel. 02 99 51 38 15), located on a former farm at the city's edge, gives visitors a chance to learn about Rennes's daily farm life of the early 1600s and picnic in the apple orchards. *(Open W-F 9am-noon and 2-6pm, Sa 2-6pm, Su 2-7pm. Admission 28F, students 14F, under 6 free.)* From pl. de la République, take bus #14 (#1 on Su) to "Le Gacet" (route de Châtillon-sur-Seiche).

Partying à la Française

French youth party in stages, cramming a variety of company, ambience, and alcohol into one evening. Many start in a standard café, bar, or *brasserie* to eat something with drinks, relaxing until midnight or 1am. Then it's on to a *bar de nuit* (night bar) until perhaps 2 or 3am. Boisterous and whetted, different groups of friends often come together and drink here in a much more serious fashion. When the last bars close, the next stop is a *discothèque,* where the inebriated masses shake it to the latest techno and house beat. Many stumble home at 5 or 5:30am when the discos shut their doors, but others stick it out until 6:30am or so when the first bakeries open with warm bread and croissants.

The **Tombées de la Nuit,** in early July, is a nine-day festival of non-stop music, dance, partying, theater, and mime by international performers who prowl the streets from noon to midnight. For info, contact the Office de Tourisme, Festival de Tombées de la Nuit, 8, pl. du Maréchal Juin (tel. 02 99 79 01 98 or 02 99 30 38 01). Theater, dance, and classical music performances are listed in *Contact Hebdo Le Guide-Loisir*s, available at the tourist office or hostel. For information on **Orchestre de Bretagne** concerts call 02 99 27 52 83. Rennes' major theater is the **Théâtre National de Bretagne,** on rue St-Heller (tel. 02 99 30 88 88), but smaller theaters abound. To trade stage for scenery, take a daytrip to the **Brocéliande Forest,** where you can find the **Tombeau de Merlyn** (Merlyn's tomb), the **Fontaine de Jouvence** (the Fountain of Youth), and the **Val Sans Retour** (Valley of No Return). **TIV** buses leave from Rennes (1hr., M-Sa 10-12 per day, 16F50) and stop in the forest-neighboring village of **Paimpont,** whose **tourist office** (tel. 02 99 07 84 23) offers info on buses, bike and car routes, and local accommodations.

NIGHTLIFE

Rennais nightlife is so hot that Parisian students are known to make weekend trips just for the clubs. The action centers around the **Pl. Ste-Anne,** the **Pl. Ste-Michel.**

La Marina, 16, pl. Ste-Anne (tel. 02 99 79 58 90), is the latest addition to Rennais nightlife and extremely popular with local students. On weekends, it is packed with college kids who often end up dancing on the tables. Open nightly until 1am.

Le Jardin des Plantes, 32, rue Ste-Melaine (tel. 02 99 38 74 46), offers food, drink, in a mellow, garden-like atmosphere. Also features live concerts and theatrical performances. Open nightly until 1am.

Le Zing, 5, pl. des Lices (tel. 02 99 79 69 60) picks up at 1am when other bars close, and goes strong until 3am when the crowd heads to the discotheques.

L'Éspace, 45, bd. La Tour d'Auvergne (tel. 02 99 30 99 21), offers techno music for its gay and straight regulars. Great music and atmosphere. Open nightly until 5am.

Le Batchi, 34, rue Vasselot (tel. 99 79 62 27), is the heartbeat of Rennes's gay scene. In this mixed pub/club, you can drink and dance until 5am.

APPENDIX

■ National Holidays

When a holiday falls on a Tuesday or Thursday, the French often take off the Monday or Friday, a practice known as faire le pont (to make a bridge). Banks and public offices close at noon on the nearest working day before a public holiday.

Date	Festival	English
January 1	Le Jour de l'An	New Year's Day
April 13	Le Lundi de Pâques	Easter Monday
May 1	La Fête du Travail	Labor Day
May 8	L'Anniversaire de la Libération	Victory in Europe Day
May 21	L'Ascension	Ascension Day
June 1	Le Lundi de Pentecôte	Whit Monday
July 14	La Fête Nationale	Bastille Day
August 15	L'Assomption	Feast of the Assumption
November 1	La Toussaint	All Saints' Day
November 11	L'Armistice 1918	Armistice Day
December 25	Le Noël	Christmas

■ Climate

Average Temp. Low-High	January °C	°F	April °C	°F	July °C	°F	October °C	°F
Paris	0/6	32/43	5/16	41/61	13/24	55/75	6/15	43/59

For a rough approximation from °C to °F, double the Celsius and add 25. To go the other way, subtract 25 and cut it in half. The average rainfall varies slightly throughout the year: 4.3 mm (Jan), a constant 5.3 mm in April and July, peaking at 5.5 mm in October.

°C	-5	0	5	10	15	20	25	30	35	40
°F	23	32	41	50	59	68	77	86	95	104

■ Measurements

1 inch = 25 millimeters (mm)	1mm = 0.04 inch (in.)
1 foot (ft.) = 0.30 meter (m)	1m = 3.33 feet (ft.)
1 mile = 1.61 kilometers (km)	1km = 0.62 mile (mi.)
1 pound (lb.) = 0.45 kilogram (kg)	1kg = 2.22 pounds (lb.)
1 gallon = 4 quarts = 3.76 liters (L)	1 liter = 1.06 quarts (qt.)=0.27 gallon

■ International Calling Codes

Australia	Belgium	Canada	Germany	Greece	Ireland	Italy	Luxem-bourg
61	32	1	49	30	353	39	352
Monaco	Nether-lands	New Zealand	South Africa	Spain	Switzer-land	United Kingdom	United States
377	31	64	13	34	41	44	1

■ Time Zones: Paris Is...

9 hours later than	Vancouver and Los Angeles	*French time falls*
8 hours later than	Calgary and Denver	*one hour back in*
7 hours later than	Green Bay and Houston	*the fall and*
6 hours later than	New York and Toronto	*springs one hour*
4½ hours later than	St-John's, Newfoundland	*foward in the*
1 hour later than	London and Dublin	*spring for*
synchronous with	Madrid, Rome, Zurich, Berlin,Stockholm	*daylight saving's*
1 hour earlier than	Athens, Istanbul, and Johannesburg	*time; both*
4½ hours earlier than	New Delhi	*switches occur*
7 hours earlier than	Hong Kong and Perth	*about a week*
8 hours earlier than	Tokyo	*before North*
9 hours earlier than	Sydney	*America*
11 hours earlier than	Auckland	

APPENDIX

■ Festivals   For a complete list of seasonal events in Paris, see **Festivals**, p. 249

Season	Festival	Season	Festival
June	Gay Pride	**July 14**	Bastille Day
Mid-June	Course des Serveuses et Garçons de Café	**Late July**	Tour de France Final
Late June	Fête du Cinéma	**Mid-July to Mid-August**	Festival Paris
Late June	Fête de la Musique	**Dec. 24-25**	Noël (Christmas)
Late June to Early July	Fête du Jazz de La Villette	**Dec. 31-Jan. 1**	Paris 2000-Millennium

■ French - English Glossary

abbaye: abbey
allée: lane, avenue
abri: shelter
aller-retour: round-trip
arc: arch
arène: arena
auberge: inn, hostel
banlieue: suburb
basse ville: lower town
BCBG: yuppie (bon chic bon genre)
beffroi: belfry
bibliothèque: library
billet: ticket
bois: forest, wood
boulangerie: bakery
carte orange: metro pass
cathédrale: cathedral
cave: cellar
centre ville: downtown
chambre: room
chambre d'hôtel: B&B
chandaille: sweater
charcuterie: butcher
chaussures: shoes
cimetière: cemetery

cloître: cloister
collabo: collaborator
côte: coast
coupon vert: metro pass
couvent: convent
CPCH: yuppie (collier de perles, carré Hermès)
cravatte: tie
cru: vineyard, vintage
dégustation: tasting
dégeulasse: disgusting
donjon: keep (of a castle)
douane: customs
école: school
église: church
entrée: appetizer
fabuleux: fabulous!
faubourg : quarter, street
fête: celebration, festival
ferme: farm
foire: fair
fontaine: fountain
forêt: forest
formule: daily special
gare: train station

gare routière: bus station
gîte d'étape: rural b&b
haute ville: upper town
HLM: public housing
horloge: clock
hors-saison: off-season
hôtel particulier: mansion, town house
hôtel de ville : city hall
hôtel-Dieu: old hospital
île: island
internet: internet
jupe: skirt
kir: white wine & cassis
mairie: town hall
manteau: coat
marché: market
mec: a guy
mef: a chick
menu: daily special
montagne: mountain
mur: wall
omelette: omelette
palais: palace
pantalons: pants

parc: park
place: square
plât principale: entrée
pont: bridge
pression: draft beer
Québecois: not Canadian
quartier: neighborhood
quiche: quiche
randonnée: hike
RER: commuter train
robe: dress
rue: street
salaud: jerk!
salon: drawing room
sentier: path, lane
téléphérique: cable car
thermes: hot springs
tour: tower
truc: a thing
vallée: valley
va chier!: piss off!
vendange: grape harvest
veste: sport coat, blazer
vieille ville: old town
vitraux: stained glass

■ French Phrasebook

English	French	English	French
PHRASES			
Hello.	Bonjour.	How are you?	Comment ça va?
I'm sorry.	Je suis desolé.	No thanks.	Non, merci.
Thank you.	Merci.	No problem.	C'est pas grave.
Good-bye.	Au revoir.	What is it?	Qu'est-ce que c'est?
When? Who?	Quand? Qui?	Why?	Pourquoi?
OK.	D'accord.	Excuse me?	Pardon?
How much is this?	Ça coute combien?	Please repeat.	Répétez, s'il vous plaît.
Stop/Enough!	Arrête!	Help!	Au secours!/Aidez-moi!
Leave me alone!	Laissez-moi tranquille!	Do you speak English?	Parlez-vous anglais?
I don't understand.	Je ne comprends pas.	I would like...	Je voudrais...
Speak slowly.	Parlez moins vite.	the bill.	l'addition.
I am ill/I am hurt.	J'ai mal/Je suis blessé.	the hospital	l'hôpital
Where is...?	Où est...?	breakfast	petit déjeuner
the bathroom	la toilette	lunch, dinner	déjeuner, dîner
the shower	la douche	**subway, airport**	metro, aeroport
single room	une chambre simple	train station	la gare
double room	une chambre à deux	**ATM**	guichet automatique
What's your name?	Comment t'appelles-tu?	**Vive le Québec Libre!**	Long Live Free Quebec!
Nice body!	Beau corps!	Ici on parle français.	Here, we speak French.
Let's go!	Allons-y!	Gettin' jiggy wid'it	Ça bouge!
condoms	préservatifs, capotes	That sucks!	C'est nul à chier!
lubricant	lubricant	What a silly queen!	Quelle folle!
I just got out of prison	J'étais en prison.	She's a mess!	C'est un boudin!
No joke? I used to be a Carmelite nun.	Sans déconner? Moi, j'étais au couvent.	Blake, you'll never have ColbyCo !	Blake, tu n'aura *pas* le ColbyCo!
DIRECTIONS			
(to the) right	à droite	(to the) left	à gauche
near	près de	far	loin
north	nord	east	est
south	sud	west	ouest
follow	suivre	beyond	au-delà de
NUMBERS			
one	un	eleven	onze
two	deux	twelve	douze
three	trois	fifteen	quinze
four	quatre	twenty	vingt
five	cinq	twenty-five	vingt-cinq
six	six	thirty	trente
seven	sept	forty	quarante

APPENDIX

eight	huit	**fifty**	cinquante
nine	neuf	**one hundred**	cent
ten	dix	**one thousand**	mille

TIMES AND HOURS

open	ouvert	**What time is it?**	Quelle heure est-il?
closed	fermé	**until**	jusqu'à
morning	le matin	**except**	sauf
afternoon	l'après-midi	**holidays**	jours fériés, congés
evening	le soir	**January**	janvier
night	la nuit	**February**	février
today	aujourd'hui	**March**	mars
yesterday	hier	**April**	avril
tomorrow	demain	**May**	mai
Monday	lundi	**June**	juin
Tuesday	mardi	**July**	juillet
Wednesday	mercredi	**August**	août
Thursday	jeudi	**September**	septembre
Friday	vendredi	**October**	octobre
Saturday	samedi	**November**	novembre
Sunday	dimanche	**December**	décembre

MENU READER

l'agneau	lamb	**la framboise**	raspberry
l'ail	garlic	**les frites**	French fries
l'apéritif	pre-dinner drink	**le fromage**	cheese
l'asperge	asparagus	**le gâteau**	cake
l'assiette	plate	**le gésier**	gizzard
l'aubergine	eggplant	**le gibier**	game
la bavette	flank	**la glace**	ice cream
le beurre	butter	**le granité**	icy sorbet
bien cuit	well done	**la grenouille**	frog (legs)
la bière	beer	**l'haricot vert**	green bean
le bifteck	steak	**l'huitre**	oyster
le blanc de volaille	chicken breast	**le jambon**	ham
le boeuf	beef	**le kir**	white wine and cassis
la boisson	drink	**le lait**	milk
la bouillabaisse	fish soup of Provence	**le lapin**	rabbit
la brioche	pastry-like bread	**le légume**	vegetable
la brochette	shish-ka-bab	**le magret de canard**	duck breast
le canard	duck	**maison**	home-made
la carafe d'eau	pitcher of tap water	**le marron**	chestnut
le cassoulet	meat and bean stew	**le miel**	honey
les cervelles	brain	**la moule**	mussel
le champignon	mushroom	**la moutarde**	mustard
chaud	hot	**nature**	plain

la chèvre	goat cheese	les noix	nuts
choix	choice	l'oeuf	egg
la choucroute	sauerkraut	l'oie	goose
le chou-fleur	cauliflower	l'oignon	onion
la ciboulette	chive	le pain	bread
le citron	lemon	les pâtes	pasta
le citron vert	lime	la pâtisserie	pastry, pastry shop
le civet	stew	le plat	main course
la compote	stewed fruit	poêlé	pan-fried
le confit de canard	duck cooked in fat	le poisson	fish
coq au vin	rooster stewed in wine	le poivre	pepper
la côte	rib or chop	la pomme	apple
la courgette	zucchini	la pomme de terre	potato
la crème brulée	custard dessert with carmelized sugar	le potage	soup
la crème Chantilly	whipped cream	le poulet	chicken
la crème fraîche	fresh heavy cream	le pruneau	prune
la crêpe	thin pancake	les rillettes	pork hash cooked in fat
les crêpes Suzette	flambéd with Cointreau	du riz	rice
la croque-monsieur	grilled-cheese sandwich	la salade verte	green salad
les crudités	raw vegetables	le sanglier	wild boar
l'eau de robinet	tap water	le saucisson	sausage
l'échalote	shallot	le saumon	salmon
l'entrecôte	chop (cut of meat)	le sel	salt
l'escalope	thin slice of meat	le steak tartare	raw meat w/ raw egg
l'escargot	snail	le sucre	sugar
farci	stuffed	tête	head
le faux-filet	sirloin steak	le thé	tea
le feuilleté	puff pastry	le tournedos	beef filet
le flan	custard	la truffe	truffle (mushroom)
le foie gras	liver pâté	la viande	meat
forestière	with mushrooms	la vichyssoise	leek and potatoe soup
frais	fresh	le vin	wine
la fraise	stawberry	yaourt	yogurt

English	French	Pronunciation
GENERAL		
Hello./Good day.	Bonjour.	bohn-ZHOOR
Good evening.	Bonsoir.	bohn-SWAHR
Goodbye.	Au revoir.	oh rev-WAHR
Good night.	Bonne nuit.	bun NWEE
please	s'il vous plaît	seel voo PLAY
thank you	merci	mehr-SEE
You're welcome.	De rien.	duh ree-EHN
Pardon me.	Excusez-moi.	ex-koo-zay MWAH

Index

INDEX

Star Tours 294
Star Trek
  The Next Generation, 254
Starmania 254
Starship Enterprise 254
Statue of Liberty 192, 253
St-Cloud 297
St-Denis 195
STDs 41
Ste-Chapelle 15, 137, 138
Stein, Gertrude 24
Ste-Ursule de la Sorbonne 154
St-Eustache 143
St-Germain-des-Prés 158, 238
St-Germain-en-Laye 283
St-Laurent, Yves 167, 257
Stock Stores 258
St-Ouen Flea Market 267
Strasbourg 299
Strasbourg, Bishop of 147
Stravinsky 173
Streisand, Barbara 203
Student Accommodations 188
Student Housing 78
Student ID 32
Studio Galande 238
Study Abroad 43
Styron, William 76
Sun King 269
Supermarchés 103
Surrealists 128
Sweets 133
Swimming 247
Sword Beach 313
Symbolism 284
Synagogues 151

T

Tabacco Museum 232
Tandem 259
Tang Frères 104, 184
Tapestries 312
Tapis Franc 111
Tati 147, 260
Taxis 67
Tea and Tattered Pages 265
Teacher ID 32
Teaching English 46
Technocité 198, 225
Télécartes 72
Telegrams 73
Telephones 72
Tempest 205
Temps des Cérises, Le 113, 122, 184
Temps des Livres 252
Tennis 247, 249
Tennis Court Oath 5
Tenth Arrondissement 89, 176
Terror, Revolutionary 5
Têtu 245
Thai 127
Thanksgiving 104
Thé au Harem d'Archi Ahmed

19
Theater 233
Théâtre de la Huchette 235
Théâtre de la Renaissance 177
Théâtre de la Ville 235
Théâtre de Verdure du Jardin
  Shakespeare 205, 252
Théâtre des Champs-Élysées
  167, 227
Théâtre du Rond Point 235
Théâtre du Vieux Colombier
  234
Théâtre Guignol du Parc des
  Buttes Chaumont 237
Théâtre Mogador 235
Théâtre National de Chaillot
  191
Théâtre Nationale de la Colline
  234
Théâtre Odéon 157
Thiên Co 122
Thiers, Adolphe 6
Thinker, The 220
Third Arrondissement 82, 111,
  146
Third Republic 6
Thirteenth Arrondissement 93,
  122, 184
Thomas Cook 35, 36
Three Ducks Hostel 95
Thunder Mesa 294
Ticket Consolidators 58
Time 264
Timeline 1
Timhotel Le Louvre 80
Tipping 39, 107
Titian 214, 281
Toad Hall Restaurant 293
Tokyorama 115
Tomb of the Unknown Soldier
  167
Toulouse-Lautrec, Henri de 17,
  195
Tour César 298
Tour d'Argent, La 156
Tour de France 171, 248, 250
Tour de Jean Sans Peur 146
Tour de la Terre 207
Tour Eiffel 14
Tour Jehan-de-Beauce 288
Tour Montparnasse 185, 188
Tour St-Jacques 152
Tourist Offices 71
Tours 299, 301
Trailer Trash 120
Train Stations 62, 63
Trains 61, 63
Travel Agencies 71
Traveler's Checks 36
Traveling Alone 53
Treaty of Versailles 192
Très Riches Heures du Duc de
  Berry 281
Tricks 245

Tricotin 122
Trips from Paris 269
Trocadéro 161, 191
Trois hommes et un couffin 18
Trois Keller 245
Trois Luxembourg 238
Trotsky, Leon 185
Trou Normand 120
Troubadours 19
Truffaut, François 18, 185
Tuile à Loup, La 261
Tuileries 53, 141, 212
Tunisian Cuisine 125
Turkish Cuisine 126
Twelfth Arrondissement 92,
  121, 181
Twentieth Arrondissement 98,
  127, 199
Ty Breiz 124

U

U.S. Citizens Emergency Center
  38
UCJF (Union Chrétienne de
  Jeunes Filles, YWCA) 88
UGC 237
UNESCO 164, 255
Unity, l' 246
Universal Exposition 252
Universities 45
University Restaurants 106
USA Today 264
Useful Publications and
  Organizations 25
Utrillo, Maurice 17, 185, 195

V

Val de Loire 120
Valentino 167, 258
Valéry, Paul 154
Valley of No Return 317
Value-Added Tax (VAT) 38
Van Dyck 281
Van Eyck, Jan 213
Van Gogh, Vincent 16, 217,
  296
Varangue, La 116
Vaux-le-Vicomte 13, 278
Vedette Pont-Neuf 135
Vegetables 99
Vegetarian 51, 104, 108, 110,
  111, 113, 114, 121, 123, 124,
  125, 126, 127
Vélodrome Jacques Anquetil
  208
Veloso, Didier 155, 284
Venus de Milo 214
Verlaine, Paul 22, 195
Verne, Jules 253
Veronese 214
Versace 258
Versailles 6, 13, 269, **270**, 279
Vessel 2 Thousand 255
Viaduc des Arts 181

Researcher-Writers

Laura Beth Deason   *Paris*
We sent to Paris a savvy Southern scholar and we got back a *Parisienne*. Fabulous, fabulous Laura Beth. With southern charm and lightning wit, Laura Beth hit the ground running, spanning the entire city from the top of the Eiffel Tower to the tombs of Père Lachaise. A seasoned archaeologist, Laura Beth excavated the Roman treasures of the Louvre, the paintings of the Musée D'Orsay, and the sculptures of the Musée Rodin. She covered Chartres and the Abbaye de Royaumont with the expertise of a Doctor of Divinity. Like Madame de Sevigné, Laura Beth took on Versailles with elegant and erudite prose. From the classic cafés of the Latin Quarter to the trendy shops of the Marais, Laura Beth highlighted the hip and happening, while scorning all that is vile and vulgar. Ever aware of fashion emergencies, she breathed life into our Shopping Section with everything from cotton Agnès B classics to leather Jitrois jumpers. A Chanel Warrior, she conquered campy *couturiers* and venomous *vendeurs* from Fauchon to the Faubourg St-Honoré, all the while proving that fashion is as much about attitude as it is about style.

Mercedes Hinton   *Paris*
With diplomatic finesse and perserverance, Mercedes negotiated Paris amid menacing metro *contrôleurs,* screaming tailors, mad rollerbladers, and card-eating ATMs. From her first day in Paris, Mercedes's quest for the perfect hairdryer inspired our wonderful new Housewares and Services section. Her elegant French, coupled with fluency in English, Spanish, and Portuguese, helped her navigate Paris's diverse neighborhoods, restaurants, and markets. From Île de la Cité to Île St-Louis, Mercedes offered new insights and detail-oriented research on Nôtre Dame, the Ste-Chappelle, and the Concergerie. Caught up in the euphoria of France's World Cup victory, she danced on the Champs-Élysées and then again at the *Bal Pompiers* on Bastille Day. From the Opéra Garnier to the smoky jazz clubs of the Latin Quarter, she sought out the best of Paris's music scene. With a discerning eye, Mercedes braved the seedier side of Montmartre before finishing at the wonderful world of Disneyland Paris.

Bulbul Tiwari   *Paris*
An ardent *cinéphile* and budding *cinéaste,* Bulbul covered the Latin Quarter, the Upper Marais, and Montparnasse with the eye of a New Wave director. With a passion for all things French and an interest in the evolving art scene, Bulbul covered the up-and-coming neighborhoods of Ménilmontant and Belleville while celebrating the intellectual history of Montparnasse. Equally comfortable discussing Foucault or French food, Bulbul sought out the best of Parisian bookstores, covered the student life of the Latin Quarter, and explained the finer points of French cuisine. Her brilliant coverage of Paris's Nightlife will provide many readers with the ultimate spot to ring in the Millennium. Bulbul's passion for film added new insights into the city's endless cinemas and film festivals. From La Défense to La Villette, Bulbul explored Paris's futurist architecture, while at the Musée de Cluny, she highlighted the Gallo-Roman and Medieval past. Whether wandering through the Marais or the Cour du Louvre, Bulbul radiated Sartrian savvy and Galleries Lafayette-style.

Amy Beck   *Normandy, Brittany*
With unstoppable energy and flair, Amy covered the beaches of Normandy and the coast of Brittany. From Rennes to Mont St-Michel, Amy scouted out weekend getaways, never forgetting that you don't need to be in Paris to dance on the tables.

Adriane Giebel   *Loire Valley*
Like Le Veau, Le Brun, and Le Nôtre, Adriane surveyed the gardens and architecture of the Loire Valley châteaux with tireless enthusiasm. She proved that you don't need to be Madame de Pompadour to spend a regal weekend in the country.

Acknowledgments

It's been a very long road from 29 to 67 Mt. Auburn Street. From Sister Helen's French class up the street, to the offices of Let's Go Publications, there's been a lot of Paris in between. I should first thank Helen Stack, CSJ for her stories of a young American nun's expatriate years in 1930s Paris, where undoubtedly, she could have arm-wrestled Hemingway (or Gertrude Stein) at *Les Deux Magots*.

This book would not have gone to press without the elegant support of its Managing Editor, Lisa Nosal, whose editorial expertise, eagle-eye for detail, and knowledge of all things French (and Italian!) added style to these pages. Bulbul Tiwari, Laura Beth Deason, and Mercedes Hinton brought more style (and considerable substance) to this edition. Anne Chisolm reminded me that, after three summers as an RW, it was OK to return to the Let's Go fold. Thanks to my mentors Caroline Sherman and Rachel Farbiarz who encouraged me to see life on this side of the LG tracks. Applause to Bruce McKinnon, Anna Schneider-Mayerson, and Jessica Nordell of Team France for their expert advice, humor, and Norman-Breton words. I still marvel at the brilliance of the production team, Dan Visel, Maryanthe Malliaris, and Heath Ritchie. Thanks to Lano Williams for his adroit computer skills, Allison Arwady for her eleventh-hour help, and Monica Eav for her francophile expertise. Måns, tack för hjälpen! My gratitude to Ben Harder and Anna Portnoy for persistent support for our beautiful new cover! Thanks to Matt for his detailed work on Paris's maps. Finally, thanks to Elizabeth White, Alex DeLaite, Ethan Thurow, Elena Schneider, Nicole Barry, Stefania Heim, Whitney Bryant, Sara Houghteling, and the terrace posse, Semra Mesulam, Sonesh Chaini, Sonja Starr, and Alex Speier for their friendship and humor.

Merci beaucoup à Didier Veloso pour une semaine géniale à Paris (Ring Lighting!). Thanks to LB and Russ Deason for their friendship and humor (Slaw!). I want to thank my father, Joseph Martin, for weekday morning breakfasts and weekday evening movies and my mother, Nancy Martin, for summer blueberries, cream-cheese brownies, and for climbing the stairs of a 7th floor 16ème walk-up. Finally, many thanks to Maxime Blanchard, my North, South, East, and West. Maxime, je suis désolé si j'étais un enfant de nanane cet été. Je sais qui j'embrasserai à Paris à l'aube du Millénaire.

Editor	Brian Martin
Managing Editor	Lisa M. Nosal
Publishing Director	Caroline R. Sherman
Publishing Director	Anna C. Portnoy
Production Manager	Dan Visel
Associate Production Manager	Maryanthe Malliaris
Cartography Manager	Derek McKee
Design Manager	Bentsion Harder
Editorial Manager	M. Allison Arwady
Editorial Manager	Lisa M. Nosal
Financial Manager	Monica Eileen Eav
Personnel Manager	Nicolas R. Rapold
Publicity Manager	Alexander Z. Speier
New Media Manager	Måns O. Larsson
Map Editors	Matthew R. Daniels, Dan Luskin
Production Associate	Heath Ritchie
Office Coordinator	Tom Moore
Director of Advertising Sales	Gene Plotkin
Associate Sales Executives	Colleen Gaard, Mateo Jaramillo, Alexandra Price
President	Catherine J. Turco
General Manager	Richard Olken
Assistant General Manager	Anne E. Chisholm

Thanks to Our Readers...

Mano Aaron, CA; Jean-Marc Abela, CAN; George Adams, NH; Bob & Susan Adams, GA; Deborah Adeyanju, NY; Rita Alexander, MI; Shani Amory-Claxton, NY; Kate Anderson, AUS; Lindsey Anderson, ENG; Viki Anderson, NY; Ray Andrews, JPN; Robin J. Andrus, NJ; L. Asurmendi, CA; Anthony Atkinson, ENG; Deborah Bacek, GA; Jeffrey Bagdade, MI; Mark Baker, UK; Mary Baker, TN; Jeff Barkoff, PA; Regina Barsanti, NY; Ethan Beeler, MA; Damao Bell, CA; Rya Ben-Shir, IL; Susan Bennerstrom, WA; Marla Benton, CAN; Matthew Berenson, OR; Walter Bergstrom, OR; Caryl Bird, ENG; Charlotte Blanc, NY; Jeremy Boley, EL SAL; Oliver Bradley, GER; A.Braurstein, CO; Philip R. Brazil, WA; Henrik Brockdorff, DMK; Tony Bronco, NJ; Eileen Brouillard, SC; Mary Brown, ENG; Tom Brown, CA; Elizabeth Buckius, CO; Sue Buckley, UK; Christine Burer, SWITZ; Norman Butler, MO; Brett Carroll, WA; Susan Caswell, ISR; Carlos Cersosimo, ITA; Barbara Crary Chase, WA; Stella Cherry Carbost, SCOT; Oi Ling Cheung, HK; Simon Chinn, ENG; Charles Cho, AUS; Carolyn R. Christie, AUS; Emma Church, ENG; Kelley Coblentz, IN; Cathy Cohan, PA; Phyllis Cole, TX; Karina Collins, SWITZ; Michael Cox, CA; Mike Craig, MD; Rene Crusto, LA; Claudine D'Anjou, CAN; Lizz Daniels, CAN; Simon Davies, AUS; Samantha Davis, AUS; Leah Davis, TX; Stephanie Dickman, MN; Philipp Dittrich,GER; Tim Donovan, NH; Reed Drew, OR; Wendy Duncan, SCOT; Melissa Dunlap, VA; P.A. Emery, UK; GCL Emery, SAF; Louise Evans, AUS; Christine Farr, AUS; David Fattel, NJ; Vivian Feen, MD; David Ferraro, SPN; Sue Ferrick, CO; Philip Fielden, UK; Nancy Fintel, FL; Jody Finver, FL; D. Ross Fisher, CAN; Abigail Flack, IL; Elizabeth Foster, NY; Bonnie Fritz, CAN; J. Fuson, OR; Michael K. Gasuad, NV; Raad German, TX; Mark Gilbert, NY; Betsy Gilliland, CA; Ana Goshko, NY; Patrick Goyenneche, CAN; David Greene, NY; Jennifer Griffin, ENG; Janet & Jeremy Griffith, ENG; Nanci Guartofierro, NY; Denise Guillemette, MA; Ilona Haayer, HON; Joseph Habboushe, PA; John Haddon, CA; Ladislav Hanka, MI; Michael Hanke, CA; Avital Harari, TX; Channing Hardy, KY; Patrick Harris, CA; Denise Hasher, PA; Jackie Hattori, UK; Guthrie Hebenstreit, ROM; Therase Hill, AUS; Denise Hines, NJ; Cheryl Horne, ENG; Julie Howell, IL; Naomi Hsu, NJ; Mark Hudgkinson, ENG; Brenda Humphrey, NC; Kelly Hunt, NY; Daman Irby, AUT; Bill Irwin, NY; Andrea B. Jackson, PA; John Jacobsen, CT; Pat Johanson, MD; Russell Jones, FL; J. Jones, AUS; Sharon Jones, MI; Craig Jones, CA; Wayne Jones, ENG; Jamie Kagan, NJ; Mirko Kaiser, GER; Scott Kauffman, NY; John Keanie, NIRE; Barbara Keary, FL; Jamie Kehoe, AUS; Alistair Kernick, SAF; Daihi Kielle, SWITZ; John Knutsen, CA; Rebecca Koepke, NY; Jeannine Kolb, ME; Elze Kollen, NETH; Lorne Korman, CAN; Robin Kortright, CAN; Isel Krinsky, CAN; George Landers, ENG; Jodie Lanthois, AUS; Roger Latzgo, PA; A. Lavery, AZ; Joan Lea, ENG; Lorraine Lee, NY; Phoebe Leed, MA; Tammy Leeper, CA; Paul Lejeune, CAN; Yee-Leng Leong, CA; Sam Levene, CAN; Robin Levin, PA; Christianna Lewis, PA; Ernesto Licata, ITA; Wolfgang Lischtansky, AUT; Michelle Little, CAN; Dee Littrell, CA; Maria Lobosco, UK; Netii Ross, ITA; Didier Look, CAN; Alice Lorenzotti, MA; David Love, PA; Briege Mac Donagh, IRE; Brooke Madigan, NY; Helen Maltby, FL; Shyama Marchesi, ITA; Domenico Maria, ITA; Natasha Markovic, AUS; Edward Marshall, ECU; Rachel Marshall, TX; Kate Maynard, UK; Agnes McCann, IRE; Susan McGowan, NY; Brandi McGunigal, CAN; Neville McLean, NZ; Marty McLendon, MS; Matthew Melko, OH; Barry Mendelson, CA; Eric Middendorf, OH; Nancy Mike, AZ; Coren Milbury, NH; Margaret Mill, NY; David H. Miller, TX; Ralph Miller, NV; Susan Miller, CO; Larry Moeller, MI; Richard Moore, ENG; Anne & Andrea Mosher, MA; J. L. Mourne, TX; Athanassios Moustakas, GER; Laurel Naversen, ENG; Suzanne Neil, IA; Deborah Nickles, PA; Pieter & Agnes Noels, BEL; Werner Norr, GER; Ruth J. Nye, ENG; Heidi O'Brien, WA; Sherry O'Cain, SC; Aibhan O'Connor, IRE; Kevin O'Connor, CA; Margaret O'Rielly, IRE; Daniel O'Rourke, CA; Krissy Oechslin, OH; Johan Oelofse, SAF; Quinn Okamoto, CA; Juan Ramon Olaizola, SPN; Laura Onorato, NM; Bill Orkin, IL; K. Owusu-Agyenang, UK; Anne Paananen, SWD; Jenine Padget, AUS; Frank Pado, TX; G. Pajkich, Washington, DC; J. Parker, CA; Marian Parnat, AUS; Sandra Swift Parrino, NY; Iris Patten, NY; M. Pavini, CT; David Pawielski, MN; Jenny Pawson, ENG; Colin Peak, AUS; Marius Penderis, ENG; Jo-an Peters, AZ; Barbara Phillips, NY; Romain Picard, Washington, DC; Pati Pike, ENG; Mark Pollock, SWITZ; Minnie Adele Potter, FL; Martin Potter, ENG; Claudia Praetel, ENG; Bill Press, Washington, DC; David Prince, NC; Andrea Pronko, OH; C. Robert Pryor, OH; Phu Quy, VTNM; Adrian Rainbow, ENG; John Raven, AUS; Lynn Reddringer, VA; John Rennie, NZ; Ruth B.Robinson, FL; John & Adelaida Romagnoli, CA; Eva Romano, FRA; Mark A. Roscoe, NETH; Yolanda & Jason Ross, CAN; Sharee Rowe, NJ; W. Suzanne Rowell, NY; Vic Roych, CA; John Russell, ENG; Jennifer Ruth, OK; William Sabino, NJ; Hideki Saito, JPN; Frank Schaer, HUN; Jeff Schultz, WI; Floretta Seeland-Connally, IL; Colette Shoulders, FRA; Shireen Sills, ITA; Virginia Simon, AUS; Beth Simon, NY; Gary Simpson, AUS; Barbara & Allen Sisarsky, GA; Alon Siton, ISR; Kathy Skeie, CA; Robyn Skillecorn, AUS; Erik & Kathy Skon, MN; Stine Skorpen, NOR; Philip Smart, CAN; Colin Smit, ENG; Kenneth Smith, DE; Caleb Smith, CA; Geoffrey Smith, TX; John Snyder, NC; Kathrin Speidel, GER; Lani Steele, PHIL; Julie Stelbracht, PA; Margaret Stires, TN; Donald Stumpf, NY; Samuel Suffern, TN; Michael Swerdlow, ENG; Brian Talley, TX; Serene-Marie Terrell, NY; B. Larry Thilson, CAN; J. Pelham Thomas, NC; Wright Thompson, ITA; Christine Timm, NY; Melinda Tong, HK; M. Tritica, AUS; Melanie Tritz, CAN; Mark Trop, FL; Chris Troxel, AZ; Rozana Tsiknaki, GRC; Lois Turner, NZ; Nicole Virgil, IL; Blondie Vucich, CO; Wendy Wan, SAF; Carrie & Simon Wedgwood, ENG; Frederick Weibgen, NJ; Richard Weil, MN; Alan Weissberg, OH; Ryan Wells, OH; Jill Wester, GER; Clinton White, AL; Gael White, CAN; Melanie Whitfield, SCOT; Bryn Williams, CAN; Amanda Williams, CAN; Wendy Willis, CAN; Sasha Wilson, NY; Kendra Wilson, CA; Olivia Wiseman, ENG; Gerry Wood, CAN; Kelly Wooten, ENG; Robert Worsley, ENG; C.A.Wright, ENG; Caroline Wright, ENG; Mary H. Yuhasz, CO; Margaret Zimmerman, WA.

★Let's Go 1999 Reader Questionnaire★

Please fill this out and return it to **Let's Go, St. Martin's Press,** 175 Fifth Ave., New York, NY 10010-7848. All respondents will receive a free subscription to *The Yellowjacket*, the Let's Go Newsletter. You can find a more extensive version of this survey on the web at http://www.letsgo.com.

Name: _____

Address: _____

City: _____ **State:** _____ **Zip/Postal Code:** _____

Email: _____ **Which book(s) did you use?** _____

How old are you? under 19   19-24   25-34   35-44   45-54   55 or over

Are you (circle one)   in high school   in college   in graduate school
   employed   retired   between jobs

Have you used Let's Go before? yes no   **Would you use it again?** yes no

How did you first hear about Let's Go? friend   store clerk   television
   bookstore display   advertisement/promotion   review   other

Why did you choose Let's Go (circle up to two)? reputation budget focus
   price   writing style   annual updating   other: _____

Which other guides have you used, if any? Fodor's   Footprint Handbooks
   Frommer's $-a-day   Lonely Planet   Moon Guides   Rick Steve's
   Rough Guides   UpClose   other: _____

Which guide do you prefer? _____

Please rank each of the following parts of Let's Go 1 to 5 (1=needs improvement, 5=perfect). packaging/cover   practical information   accommodations   food   cultural introduction   sights   practical introduction ("Essentials")   directions   entertainment   gay/lesbian information   maps   other: _____

How would you like to see the books improved? (continue on separate page, if necessary) _____
_____

How long was your trip?   one week   two weeks   three weeks
   one month   two months or more

Which countries did you visit? _____

What was your average daily budget, not including flights? _____

Have you traveled extensively before? yes no

Do you buy a separate map when you visit a foreign city? yes no

Have you used a Let's Go Map Guide? yes no

If you have, would you recommend them to others? yes no

Have you visited Let's Go's website? yes no

What would you like to see included on Let's Go's website? _____
_____

What percentage of your trip planning did you do on the Web? _____

Would you use a Let's Go: recreational (e.g. skiing) guide gay/lesbian guide
   adventure/trekking guide   phrasebook   general travel information guide

Which of the following destinations do you hope to visit in the next three to five years (circle one)? Canada Argentina Perú Kenya Middle East
   Caribbean Scandinavia other: _____

Where did you buy your guidebook?   Internet   independent bookstore
   chain bookstore   college bookstore   travel store   other: _____

Paris: Metro

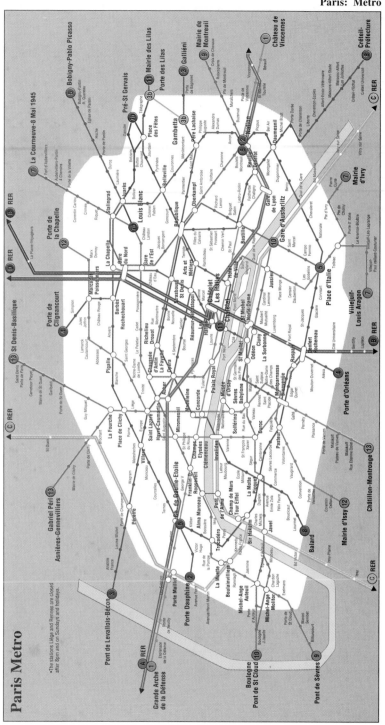

Paris: Overview and Arrondissements

1 Cimetière de Montmartre
2 Sacré Coeur Basilica
3 Parc La Villette
4 Parc des Buttes Chaumont
5 Jardins du Trocadero
6 Palais Chaillot
7 Cimetière de Passy
8 American Embassy
9 British Embassy
10 Petit Palais
11 Grand Palais
12 Arc de Triomphe
13 Madeleine
14 Gare St-Lazare
15 Parc Monceau
16 Palais de la Découverte
17 Opéra Garnier
18 Galeries Lafayette
19 Printemps
20 Gare du Nord
21 Gare de l'Est
22 Opéra Bastille
23 Palais Omnisports de Bercy
24 Ministère des Finances
25 Gare de Lyon
26 Parc de Montsouris
27 Cité Universitaire
28 Cimetière Montparnasse
29 Gare Montparnasse

30 Bureau des Objets Trouvés
    (Lost and Found)
31 Louvre
32 Palais Royale
33 Forum des Halles
34 Musée de l'Orangerie
35 Central Post Office
36 Bourse
37 Bibliothèque Nationale
38 Ecole des Arts et Métiers
39 Archives Nationales
40 Musée Carnavalet
41 Musée Picasso
42 Centre George Pompidou
43 place des Vosges
44 Musée Victor Hugo
45 Notre Dame
46 Mémorial de la Déportation
47 Université de Paris (Sorbonne)

48 Ecole Normal Supérieure
49 Musée de Cluny
50 Museum Nationale d'Histoire
    Naturelle
51 Panthéon
52 Eglise St-Etienne du Mont
53 La Mosquée
54 Jardin des Plantes
55 Jardins du Luxembourg
56 Eglise St-Sulpice
57 Théâtre Nationale de l'Odéon
58 Eiffel Tower
59 Champs de Mars

60 Ecole Militaire
61 UNESCO
62 Hôtel des Invalides
63 Assemblée Nationale
64 Musée d'Orsay
65 Cimetière de l'Est du Pere Lachaise

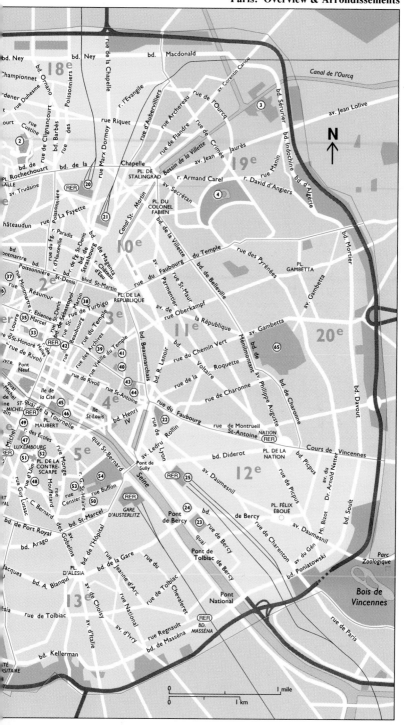

Paris: 1er and 2e

Gare St-Lazare

9e

R. d'Amsterdam

Rue de St-Lazare

Rue de la Chaussée d'Antin

Richelieu Drouot M

Ⓜ

Ⓜ St Lazare

Rue du Havre

Chaussée d'Antin
Ⓜ

Boulevard Haussmann

Ⓜ

Havre-Caumartin

La Fayette Ⓜ

Rue Favart

Ⓜ

Ⓜ

Bd. Haussmann

Rue Auber

Rue

Opéra

Boulevard des Italiens

R.

Rue Pasquier

Rue Tronchet

Auber Ⓡ

Scribe

Bd. des Capucines

Ⓜ Opéra
Ⓡ

Rue du Quatre

Septem

Rue Daunou

Quatre Septembre Ⓜ

Rue des Capucines

Rue de la Paix

R. Chabanais

Madeleine

Bd. de la Madeleine

Rue D. Casanova

Rue des Petits C

Ⓜ Madeleine

La Colonne

PLACE VENDÔME

Rue de la Sourdière

Avenue de l'Opéra

Rue Thérèse

Rue Boissy d'Anglas

Rue Royale

Rue St-Honoré

Rue Castiglione

Pyramides Ⓜ

8e

R. de Mondovi

Rue du Mont Thabor

Rue St-Honoré

Rue St-Roch

Rue des Pyramides

1er

PLACE ANDRE MALRAUX

Ⓜ Concorde

Rue de Rivoli

Tuileries Ⓜ

Palais R Musée Louv

Ⓜ

Jeu de Paume

PLACE DE LA CONCORDE

JARDIN DES TUILERIES

PLAC CARR

L'Orangerie

Quai des Tuileries

Pt. de la Concorde

Pont Solférino

Seine

Pont Royal

Pont du Carrousel

Quai Anatole France

Ⓡ

Quai Voltaire

Musée d'Orsay

Assemblée Nationale

Ⓜ Assemblée Nationale

Musée d'Orsay

Bd. St-Germain

Rue de Lille

7e

Ecole Nat Superieu Beau

0		1/8 mile

0		125 meters

Ⓜ Solférino

Rue de l'Université

1er & 2e

Strasbourg
St-Denis

Boulevard Poissonnière

Bonne
Nouvelle

R. de
Bonne
Nouvelle

R. de la
Ville Neuve

Rue Beauregard

R. Chénier

Boulevard de Sébastopol

Rue
Montmartre

Rue Poissonnière

Rue de Cléry

3e

Bourse
des Valeurs

Rue Réaumur

Arts et
Métiers

Sentier

Réaumur-
Sébastopol

thèque
nale

2e

d'Aboukir

R. Léopold Bellan

R. Montorgueil

Rue de Turbigo

Rue

Rue Montmartre

R. Mandar

Rue Tiquetonne

Rue Beaubourg

Etienne
Marcel

Rue Etienne Marcel

DU

Rue du Louvre

R.-J.-J. Rousseau

St-Eustache

Rue Pierre Lescot

Rue St-Denis

Rue St-Martin

Rambuteau

Rue Rambuteau

Les
Halles

Centre
Pompidou

Rue Croix des Petits Champs

R.-J.-J. Rousseau

Forum des
Halles

Châtelet-
Les Halles

Rue Quincampoix

Rue Berger

RER

Bd. de Sébastopol

OU

Rue St-Honoré

Rue du Roule

Rue des Halles

Rue des Lombards

4e

Rue du Renard

Louvre

Rue de Rivoli

R. du Pont-Neuf

Rue St-Denis

Rue de Rivoli

R. de l'Am. de Coligny

Louvre

R. de la Monnaie

Rue des Bourdonnais

Rue des Lavandières-Ste-Opportune

Hôtel
de Ville

Pont Neuf

nide
UR
EON

Châtelet

Tour
St-Jaques

Châtelet

Châtelet
PLACE DU
CHATELET

Châtelet

Louvre

Quai de la Mégisserie

Pont des Arts

Pont
Neuf

Pont
au Change

Pont Notre Dame

Pont
d'Arcole

Malaquais

Quai de Conti

PLACE
DAUPHINE

Conciergerie

Cité

PL. L.
LEPINE

Cité

Hôtel
Dieu

Institut
de France

Palais
de Justice

R. de
Lutèce

Ile de
la Cité

Notre
Dame

Hôtel
des
Monnaies

Ste-
Chapelle

Préfecture
de
Police

PLACE
DU
PARVIS
NOTRE-
DAME

Pont au Double

Bd. du Palais

Petit Pont

6e

Rue Dauphine

Quai des
Grands Augustins

Pont
St-Michel

St-Michel

RER

Rue Réaumur

Palais du Louvre

Pont Neuf

Châtelet Ⓜ

Quai du Louvre

Pont des Arts

1er

Pont Neuf

Pont au Change

Pont du Carrousel

Conciergerie

Cité Ⓜ

Quai Malaquais

Quai de Conti

Ste-Chapelle

Hô D

Ecole Nationale Superieure des Beaux Arts

R. Bonaparte

Institut de France

Hôtel des Monnaies

Quai des Grands Augustins

Ile de la Cité

Rue de la Cité

Pont St-Michel

Rue des Sts-Pères

Rue Jacob

Rue de Seine

Rue Mazarine

Rue Dauphine

Pont St-Michel

Pont St-Michel (RER) Ⓜ

Rue St-Jaques

St-Michel

R. de l'Abbaye

PLACE ST-GERMAIN-DES-PRÉS Ⓜ

St-Germain Des Prés

Rue St-André des Arts

Rue Danton

Pl. St-Michel

Bd. St-Germain Ⓜ

7e

Bd. St-Germain

St-Germain des Prés Ⓜ

Mabillon

Odéon

Boulevard

Musée du Cluny

R. du Four

Rue de l'Odéon

Rue Racine

Sorbonne

R. de Sèvres

R. du Vieux Colombier

R. du Saint Sulpice

Rue de Tournon

PLACE DE L'ODÉON

St-Michel

PLACE DE LA SORBONNE

R. du Cherche Midi

PLACE ST-SULPICE

St-Sulpice

Rue Souflot

St-Sulpice Ⓜ

R. d'Assas

R. de Rennes

Bd. Raspail

R. de Vaugirard

Palais du Luxembourg

Ⓜ Luxembourg

6e

Rue Gay-Lu

Rennes Ⓜ

St Placide Ⓜ

JARDIN DU LUXEMBOURG

Rue du Montparnasse

Notre-Dame des Champs Ⓜ

Rue d'Assas

Boulevard St-Michel

Rue Yavin

Rue Notre-Dame des Champs

Montparnasse Bienvenüe Ⓜ

Vavin Ⓜ

Boulevard du Montparnasse

Avenue de la Observatoire

Port Royal Ⓜ

R. du Depart

14e

Boulevard Raspail

Edgar Quinet Ⓜ

Boulevard Edgar Quinet

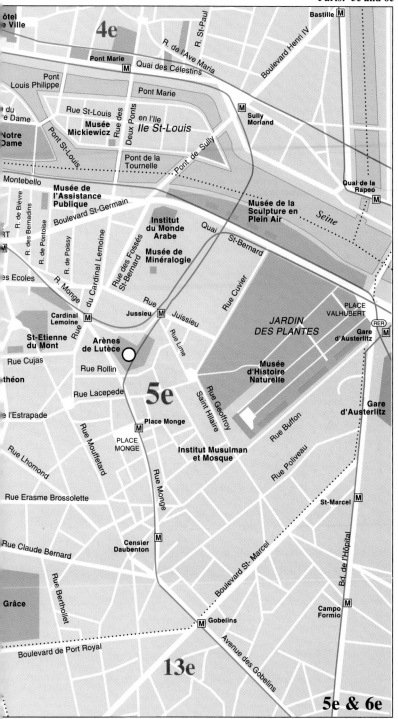

4e

ôtel
e Ville

R. St-Paul

Bastille M

Pont Marie M
Quai des Célestins

Boulevard Henri IV

R. de l'Ave Maria

Pont
Louis Philippe

Pont Marie

Rue St-Louis

Musée
Mickiewicz

Rue des Deux Ponts

Pont St-Louis

en l'Ile
Ile St-Louis

M
Sully
Morland

e du
e Dame

Notre
Dame

Pont de la
Tournelle

Pont de Sully

Montebello

Musée de
l'Assistance
Publique

Boulevard St-Germain

Musée de la
Sculpture en
Plein Air

Seine

Quai de la
Rapee

M

R. de Bièvre

R. des Bernadins

R. de Pontoise

R. de Poissy

du Cardinal Lemoine

Institut
du Monde
Arabe

Musée de
Minéralogie

Rue des Fossés
St-Bernard

Quai
St-Bernard

RT

M

es Ecoles

R. Monge

Rue
Jussieu

Jussieu M

Juissieu

Rue Cuvier

PLACE
VALHUBERT

PLACE
VALHUBERT

RER

M

Cardinal
Lemoine M

Rue

Rue Lime

JARDIN
DES PLANTES

Gare
d'Austerlitz

St-Etienne
du Mont

Arènes
de Lutèce

○

Rue Cujas

Rue Rollin

5e

Musée
d'Histoire
Naturelle

Gare
d'Austerlitz

théon

Rue Lacepede

Rue Geoffroy Saint Hilaire

Rue Buffon

e l'Estrapade

Rue Mouffetard

M Place Monge

Rue Lhomond

PLACE
MONGE

Institut Musulman
et Mosque

Rue Poliveau

Rue Monge

Rue Erasme Brossolette

St-Marcel M

Rue Claude Bernard

Censier
Daubenton M

Bd. de l'Hôpital

Grâce

Rue Berthollet

Campo
Formio M

Gobelins M

Boulevard St-Marcel

Boulevard de Port Royal

13e

Avenue des Gobelins

5e & 6e

Paris: RER

Paris RER

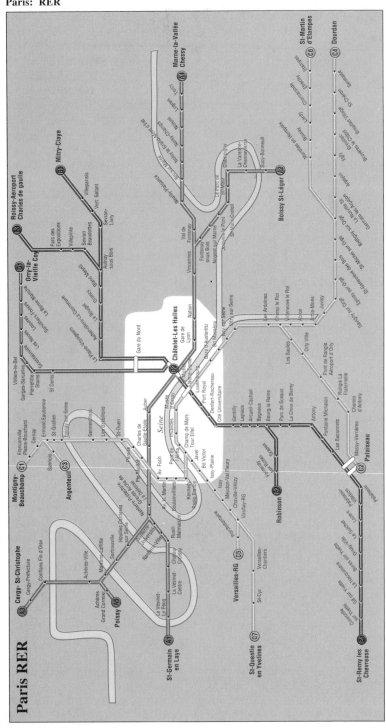